*This biography of Harry Goodhew shows the genuine fusion of the public and private lives of a man with a deep Christian piety ... an engaging narrative that skilfully weaves together the personal pastoral and political dimensions of a life lived in the service of Jesus Christ.*

**Rod Irvine, former Rector of Figtree Anglican Church,
and Helen Irvine, Professor of Accounting, PUT (retired)**

*Reading like a thriller ... the story of an outstanding Christian and Anglican archbishop set in the midst of a diocese known for its rumbustious politics ... in a role that showed what it means to be a Christian wherever you are.*

**Bruce Kay, General Secretary,
Anglican Church of Australia, 1994–2004**

*Heroes. They are in all too short supply these days ... Well, God used a man named Harry to deliver hundreds of millions from slavery to sin ... what a privilege to walk with this godly man. I am forever grateful!*

**John B. Sorensen, President and CEO,
Evangelism Explosion International**

# HARRY GOODHEW

Archbishop, Godly Radical, Dynamic Anglican

## STUART PIGGIN

Published by Acorn Press
An imprint of Bible Society AustraliaACN 148 058 306 | Charity licence 19 000 528
GPO Box 4161
Sydney NSW 2001
Australia
www.acornpress.net.au | www.biblesociety.org.au

© Stuart Piggin, 2024. All rights reserved.

ISBN 978-0-647-53046-7

First published by Morning Star Publishing in 2021, ISBN 978-0-647-53038-2 (hardcover); 978-0-647-53045-0 (ebook).

Stuart Piggin asserts his right under section 193 of the *Copyright Act 1968* (Cth) to be identified as the author of this work.

Apart from any fair dealing for the purposes of private study, research, criticism or review, no part of this work may be reproduced by electronic or other means without the permission of the publisher.

Unless otherwise indicated, Scripture quotations are taken from the New Revised Standard Version Bible, copyright © 1989 the Division of Christian Education of the National Council of the Churches of Christ in the United States of America. Used by permission.
Scripture quotations marked 'ESV' are from the ESV® Bible (The Holy Bible, English Standard Version®), copyright © 2001 Crossway, a publishing ministry of Good New Publishers. Used by permission. All rights reserved.
Quotations marked 'NIV' are taken from the Holy Bible, NEW INTERNATIONAL VERSION®, NIV® copyright © 1973, 1978, 1984, 2011 by Biblica, Inc® Used by permission. All rights reserved worldwide.

 A catalogue record for this work is available from the National Library of Australia

Editor: Sheelagh Wegman.
Cover design: John Healy.
Cover image from the *Illawarra Mercury*. Used with permission.
Text design and layout: Graeme Cogdell.

For Pam,
and in memory of
Baden and Christina Goodhew, Harry's parents.

# Contents

| | |
|---|---|
| Abbreviations | v |
| Foreword | vi |
| Prologue: 'God's Man for Sydney': Harry Goodhew's Election as Archbishop | 1 |
| 1. Parentage: All Families Have Mysteries | 20 |
| 2. Early Days: 'Faith, Hope, Love and Cricket' | 27 |
| 3. Man of Promise and Pamela: 'A Balanced, Spiritually Minded Young Man' | 42 |
| 4. Moore and Matrimony: One Ordination, Two Callings | 52 |
| 5. Early Parish Experience: A Lot of Visiting | 60 |
| 6. Parish Builder: 'Sunday at 7' | 73 |
| 7. Rector and Archdeacon of Wollongong: 'For the Ministry that Lies Ahead' | 86 |
| 8. Bishop of Wollongong: Episcopal Revival | 101 |
| 9. Bishop beyond Wollongong: 'Responding Obediently to God's Urgency' | 120 |
| 10. Twin Crises: The Fraught Backdrop to Harry's Election | 134 |
| 11. A New Archbishop for Sydney: 'A Blessing for the Whole Church' | 141 |
| 12. Bishopscourt: Spectral Visions | 155 |
| 13. Laying the Foundation: 'Dynamic Anglicanism' | 163 |
| 14. First Year (1993): 'Evangelistically Enterprising' | 178 |
| 15. Second Year (1994): 'Wild, Uncharted Waters' | 197 |
| 16. Third Year (1995): 'Loyalty to Both Christ and the Church' | 216 |
| 17. Fourth Year (1996): 'I Smile No Longer' | 229 |
| 18. Fifth Year (1997): The Coin of Transcendence | 250 |
| 19. Sixth Year (1998): Wimp, Women and Spong | 270 |
| 20. Sixth Year (1998 continued): 'The Winsome Face of Sydney' | 281 |
| 21. Seventh Year (1999–2000): 'Faith is Trusting God in Every Situation' | 301 |
| 22. Eighth Year (2000–2001): 'A Small Victory' | 317 |
| 23. Eighth Year (2000–2001 continued): 'No Other Name' | 331 |
| 24. Stepping Down (19 March 2001): 'God's Man in God's Time' | 341 |
| 25. The Ministry of a Former Archbishop: 'The Inexhaustible Vision' | 353 |
| Conclusion: Legacy of Graciousness and Generosity | 369 |
| Notes | 378 |
| Bibliography | 405 |
| Sources | 414 |
| Index | 415 |

# Abbreviations

| | |
|---|---|
| *AAPB* | *An Australian Prayer Book* |
| ABC | Australian Broadcasting Commission |
| ACC | Anglican Counselling Centre |
| ACL | Anglican Church League |
| *ACR* | *Australian Church Record* |
| AEF | Anglican Evangelical Fellowship |
| *APBA* | *A Prayer Book for Australia* |
| BBJ | Bruce Ballantine-Jones |
| BCA | Bush Church Aid Society |
| BGEA | Billy Graham Evangelistic Association |
| CBT | Cognitive Behavioural Therapy |
| CEFM | Continuing Education for Ministers |
| CESA | Church of England in South Africa |
| CMS | Church Missionary Society |
| CPSA | Church of the Province of South Africa |
| CSOM | Christian Social Order Movement |
| DEB | Diocesan Executive Board |
| ECUSA | Episcopal Church in the United States of America |
| EE | Evangelism Explosion |
| EEI | Evangelism Explosion International |
| EFAC | Evangelical Fellowship in the Anglican Communion |
| EOS | Endowment of the See |
| EU | Evangelical Union |
| GAFCON | Global Anglican Futures Conference |
| HMS | Home Mission Society (Anglicare from 1997) |
| *JRH* | *Journal of Religious History* |
| MOW | Movement for the Ordination of Women |
| NCLS | National Church Life Survey |
| NESB | Non-English Speaking Background |
| REPA | Reformed Evangelical Protestant Association |
| SC | Standing Committee |
| *SC* | *Southern Cross* (magazine of the Diocese of Sydney) |
| SDA | Sydney Diocesan Archives |
| *SMH* | *The Sydney Morning Herald* |
| SPG | Society for the Propagation of the Gospel |
| TIGS | The Illawarra Grammar School |

# Foreword

> Lord, have mercy on me – help me to be faithful to you, to the gospel and gracious to all. Help me not to allow the latter to compromise the former. Help me not to limit the former by failure in the latter.
> (Harry Goodhew, Day Book, 9 September 1994)

What's it like to be an archbishop? No doubt the best way to find out is to become one; not an option for most of us. We have to rely on evidence other than personal experience. In Harry Goodhew's case, that is in plentiful supply. There are the abundant records in the Sydney Diocesan Archives, well-managed by the vigilant Louise Trott. But, outstandingly in this case, Harry has kept copious records in his own possession. He believes that 'the poorest ink is the best memory.' Precision and accuracy, which Harry esteems, are attainable in this exercise, jeopardised only by the carelessness of the historian.

Since the very last person to dwell on what it is like to be an archbishop is Harry himself, it is providential that his records include his own personal diaries and sermons. In the former we find his deepest thoughts; in the latter the thoughts he considers most important to share with the people of God. Then, since he has such a gift for friendship, there is the testimony of those who know him well. I am very grateful to all who have consented to be interviewed for this book and apologise to the scores of others I should have interviewed. Harry and Pam Goodhew have themselves been totally forthcoming, giving me access to everything I have asked for and steadfastly refraining from correcting anything other than factual errors in what I have written. I am grateful to Richard Donnelly, Congregational pastor and school chaplain, who did not refrain from correcting my text and did so with diligence and skill.

The exceptionally rich store of source material has made possible the writing of one of the fullest biographies of an Australian bishop yet published. There is ample justification for the length of the book. The long ministry of Harry and Pam has been full of drama. That he rose from humble origins to its highest office means that there is much to learn about the church in which he has struggled as well as rejoiced. The chief justification for writing it at all, however, is surely spiritual – it is to be found in the character of Harry himself. He is at once unaffectedly humble and consistently confident. Probably no Sydney archbishop has faced such unrelenting criticism, and yet he was neither stressed by, nor resentful of, his critics. His chief concern has been that on the last day he will have to give an account. The Lord's judgement means everything; human judgement very little. He is apparently untroubled by personal hurt, and yet no-one has gone to more trouble to avoid hurting others.

Many have commented on the combination of humility and confidence in Harry. He is non-assertive, but determined; gentle, but strong-willed. In his surprising strength of will, Harry is not a stand-out in the Diocese of Sydney: it is full of very determined people. His strong will is only surprising when combined with his humility and his refusal to ride rough-shod over anyone. A key seems to be that, early in his Christian life, Harry came to see that true spirituality must issue in holiness of life. Harry is a holy man who has retained his holiness in the face, not only of unholy rows and white-knuckle politics, but also of the subtler wiles of worldliness. He believes it is required of a Christian not only to resist temptation, but also, consistent with the Lord's prayer, anything which leads to temptation. Since sin is a violation of God's honour and glory, loving God means avoiding things that dishonour him. Harry is a great reader, but he has been careful about what he reads. Once offered a Susan Howatch novel on wayward Anglican clergy, he declined on the grounds that he did not trust himself not to be led into thoughts that dishonour the Lord. His standards have been higher than those of most Christians today, even his own clergy. It meant that, when he had responsibility for the discipline of clergy, his inclination was to set the highest standards. It probably never crossed his mind not to. Zero tolerance was a bit of a shock coming from one so gentle and empathetic. It was to stand the diocese in good stead, however, when the wider church was inundated during his time in office with a tsunami of sexual abuse allegations.

This, then, was the character of the man chosen to lead the Diocese of Sydney in its most turbulent decade. He encouraged its members to look outward to its mission and not inward to its troubles. He sought to express his firm evangelical faith dynamically through the Anglican tradition. He gave many and good reasons for doing so, and his hard-defended policies have proved over time to be the path of wisdom and to win for evangelical Christianity greater acceptance on the international stage.

Harry brought to the role of archbishop an incomparable record for building thriving parishes. His determination as archbishop to focus diocesan resources and passion on ministry in the parishes meant that church growth insights were imported from all over the world, marking him out as a radical in a diocese deeply suspicious of outside influences. Harry was the most radical of Sydney's archbishops in four other respects: he worked consistently to dissolve the 'hard culture' of Sydney Anglicanism; he unfailingly practised servant, rather than authoritarian, leadership; he sought to restructure the administration of the diocese to make it more efficient; and, in a highly clericalised diocese, he maintained that the laity were 'those who mattered most.' For all these reasons, he met with staunch political resistance. Harry's policies as archbishop were consistent with the direction and values of his entire ministry, which must therefore be the subject matter of this biography. The valuable story of Harry's ministry in all his parishes, as Archdeacon and then Bishop of Wollongong, and in the years since retirement, is full of instruction on how to commend the faith in this secular age. It is a story with excitement enough, quite apart from the pyrotechnics of his years as archbishop.

From 1993 to 2001 Harry was Archbishop of the Diocese of Sydney, Metropolitan of the Anglican Province of New South Wales, and in 2000 narrowly defeated in the election for Primate of Australia. So, a word on what all that means with special reference to governance: the Anglican Church of Australia consists of 23 dioceses, each with its diocesan bishop and synod, which enacts legislation on parliamentary lines. The synod of the Diocese of Sydney is made up of about 800 members, including the archbishop as president, and the rectors and two lay representatives from each of Sydney's over 250 parishes. In the case of Sydney, the synod meets for five days annually, and it also meets to elect a new archbishop following a vacancy. Between its annual meetings, synod business is carried on by a Standing Committee (SC), elected by the synod every three years, and it therefore acts as a powerful executive. Dioceses in each state of Australia are grouped together in a province, and its provincial synod is presided over by a metropolitan who is the archbishop in each capital city. The representatives of all Australian dioceses are required to meet at least once every four years in the General Synod. Its president is the primate, elected from Australian bishops by an electoral college of 20 bishops, 10 clergy and 10 laity.

Episcopography, the genre of biographies of bishops, has its own challenges. Howard Mowll, Archbishop of Sydney from 1933 to 1958, died in office. Within two years, Marcus Loane's biography of his hero was published. It was reviewed by the leading historian of Sydney Anglicanism, Ken Cable:

> A biography of this kind is not easy to write – or to review. The subject of the study is still too close to the author and to his time for an accurate summary to be made. There are too many people yet alive whose activities must be discussed.[1]

Some would think the problems of writing Harry Goodhew's biography are even greater. He is still alive, and, for some, it is just axiomatic that biographies should not be written of the living. Marcus Loane was one who felt that way. He did not want John Reid's biography[2] of him published until after his death. But that was such a long time coming that he must have conceded it was only reasonable to relent, and he even attended the launch, though with conspicuous diffidence.

The problems associated with Harry's biography, however, may not be as great as those faced by Loane when he wrote about Mowll. Harry's episcopate ended almost two decades ago now – enough time to gain a greater perspective on it. That he is still alive has many advantages. It has been good to consult him and Pam, his wife, for, after all, only their Lord knows his life better than they do. Pam's recollections were invaluable: her memory is powerful, and she was at one with Harry throughout his entire ministry. Harry rarely used the word 'I'; he used the word 'we'. But it was not the royal plural as used by popes. By 'we' he meant 'Pam and I'. Their remarkable relationship is central to this story.

While the biographer is entirely grateful that Harry and Pam are still alive, it is undoubtedly a problem that there are still too many 'yet alive whose activities must be discussed.'[3] I would gladly have overlooked them if I could have done so with integrity. But there has been a recent providential development that brings a new perspective on this apparently intractable problem. One who knows far more than most about church politics – Canon Bruce Ballantine-Jones (BBJ) – was, at the time of writing, working on a thesis under my supervision on his own engagement in diocesan politics.[4] He was in conflict with Harry, and especially with me, for much of Harry's episcopate. We had been inveterate opponents in the struggles of the 1990s, but we have since been reminded that the diocese is one family, and that those who are for Jesus cannot continue to be against each other. Friendship and mutual respect came easily to us. We were now able to approach past difficulties with candour – with deep interest, actually, in learning what the other had been thinking and plotting! And we both feel that it is in the interests of the church we both love to be far more open about our struggles than is normally found in ecclesiastical biographies. It is the task of the historian to 'seek to understand both parties to the struggle' and to strive 'to understand them better than they understood themselves', and to take them and their quarrels 'into a world where everything is understood and all sins are forgiven.'[5]

Many who know Harry and me will suspect that I am far too close to him to write about him impartially. It is true that I find his personality captivating and his spirituality heartwarming. I usually share his approach to the momentous issues in church affairs, and I greatly admire the effectiveness of his leadership style. But I am far from being alone in that respect. Many people feel that they know Harry well and that they are very close to him. It is his genius to make people feel that.

The strange sensation I have experienced repeatedly, however, as the research into Harry's life and work proceeded, is that I have not known him nearly well enough. I now believe that it was not only his opponents who did not know him well enough. His friends did not either. We did not know what the Lord had given us when he gave us Harry as our archbishop. I hope that I will persuade my readers of that, so that we will be strengthened in our faith in the One who gives good gifts to his children.

\*\*\*

Throughout this book, Harry Goodhew is referred to as 'Harry', and Christian names are used as commonly as surnames to refer to those who appear often in the narrative. Unconventional – yes – but these are the names by which they are known to God and to each other. The Apostle Paul set the precedent, referring in his letters to the many associated with him in his mission by their personal names only. I have also departed from convention in not capitalising 'evangelical', whether referring to Anglican or non-Anglican evangelicals. The photographic record of Harry's life is extensive. It reveals that he likes his family, meeting people, sport, preaching, and overseas adventures. It also reveals that he was happy in ministry: smiling came easily to him. I acknowledge with gratitude the generosity and skill of Ramon Williams who supplied many of the photographs without charge. Special thanks to Kristin Argall, Commissioning Editor for Bible Society Australia, for her encouragement and wise guidance throughout the publication process.

# Prologue

# 'God's Man for Sydney': Harry Goodhew's Election as Archbishop

High drama invariably attends the making of Sydney's Anglican archbishops. They are elected to office by the diocesan synod. This blow-by-blow account of Harry Goodhew's election is based on a chronicle written at the time. It has both the advantage of immediacy and the disadvantage of lack of perspective, characteristic of contemporary accounts by self-absorbed participants!

\*\*\*

In October 1992, one who well understood the workings of election synods, namely ecclesiastical politician BBJ, rang me to give me some advice. Because each candidate for election as archbishop needs someone to organise his campaign, he suggested that I might head up the campaign for Harry. It was not that BBJ was supporting Harry – he was hoping that Phillip Jensen, Anglican Chaplain of the University of New South Wales, might take the prize – but he wanted all the candidates to have well-run campaigns so that the election synod would be well informed. Realising that he was speaking with a novice, he carefully and methodically outlined a six-step procedure that should be followed.[1] It all sounded like good advice to me, so I contacted Stephen Gabbott, who had been Rector of Kiama in Harry's episcopal region and was then Rector of Maroubra. He gave the idea short shrift, saying that he was 'reluctant to follow any advice advanced by BBJ.' Stephen always had a robust distaste for synod operators, of whom Ballantine-Jones was recognised as without peer. I rang Harry, who dismissed the proposal with equal expedition. 'You are far too busy to worry about that', he said, adding that he would prefer not to be elected by 'a big machine.' Never much good with big machinery, I was happy to let the matter rest.

Towards the end of January 1993, a document written by John Woodhouse, Rector of St Ives, began to circulate among those known to favour the election of Phillip Jensen. It contained some rather pointed observations on the age of the main contenders, hinting broadly that Harry, who would be 62, was too old for the job.[2] This document really precipitated the campaign for Harry. One who had seen it was Dudley Foord who rang me to express his view that it was likely to be powerfully persuasive. He believed that, in 'the sovereign plan of God', Harry was the man,³ but his understanding of God's sovereignty was an encouragement to human initiative rather than to passivity. So, on Sunday 31 January, I rang Lindsay Stoddart, Rector of Gymea, and one known to be rock solid for Harry. He was adamant that we should start organising and not waste another moment.

## The campaign for Harry: 'The cut of his jib'

The first person I attempted to lobby was Lindsay's neighbour, Paul Perini, Rector of Miranda, in Sydney's southern Bible belt. This experience taught me that I should not lobby anyone, but just give people the opportunity to talk. Paul said he had not resolved on the issue – not that he was in any doubt; it was just that he had not prayed it all through and come to a clear resolution on the matter.

About this time, Stephen Judd, co-author of the diocesan history, *Sydney Anglicans,* rang me to tell me that he intended to give Harry's campaign his support. He told me that he did not know Harry well. 'Why, then, are you supporting him?' I asked. He replied, 'I like the cut of his jib.' But he wanted to be convinced that this humble, unpretentious man had enough steel to tackle the hard parts of the job, and that he was not so sensitive that the role would be, in the words of another, 'a prolonged form of torture.'⁴ Archbishops are not meant to want to be archbishops, but it was important to Stephen to know that Harry did want it. So he took him out to dinner, quizzed him about his goals, and came away convinced. 'He wants the job,' he concluded.

A sign that Harry wanted the job, and wanted to know what to do if he got it, was that he made an appointment to meet with Sydney University church historian, Ken Cable, who knew more about the history of the diocese than anyone else. Not all the clergy are great listeners, but Harry certainly was, and Cable later confided to me that he hoped Harry would get the job. Harry was always one who sought and valued good advice. Towards the end of his episcopate, for example, Stuart Barton Babbage would offer his resignation from the position of honorary Canon of St Andrew's Cathedral. But Harry felt he could not afford to dispense with Babbage's advice. 'I greatly appreciate having you on board,' he wrote in refusing to accept the resignation, 'and value your erudite wisdom and carefully considered experience which mark your contribution'.⁵

Stephen Judd had (with Ken Cable) not only written the history of the diocese, but had also worked on the Archbishop's Commission of Inquiry and had a clear idea of what was required to make the diocesan administration work more effectively. With Stephen on board, the campaign entered a new phase. In Stephen Judd, a decisive strategist, BBJ met his match. Stephen's main strategy was to go for the lay vote. Phillip Jensen, it was commonly believed, left little room for the ministry of the laity, except in full-time church work. 'This leaves me with nowhere to go,' responded Stephen, who had a high valuation of the laity in secular roles. He also wished to try something that he believed had not been done before: each of the three stages of the synod debate was to be distinct in its emphasis:

    Night 1. Harry, the man, his qualities and his achievements
    Night 2. Harry's agenda – his policies
    Night 3. Why Harry is the man

The first support meeting for Harry was held at Robert Menzies College, Macquarie University, on 4 February 1993. It was actually quite difficult to get people to it. Phillip Jensen's zealous supporters had raided the clergy, and many of the most vocal synod clergy had been recruited to his cause. Among those present at the first meeting were some who were more anti-Phillip than pro-Harry. Their view was that many of Phillip's supporters had become paranoid about safety, which they understood as the need to guard the Bible and the gospel against 'liberal' forces. This understanding, Phillip's opponents feared, was productive of a clericalised mediocrity. Also present were clergy such as Wayne Gott and Max Boys who were clear that they wanted Harry and were determined to support him in a manner that they believed was most consistent with Harry's own character. It was a small, inexperienced and rather gentle group.

I went to see John Woodhouse at St Ives, who was good enough to explain why he supported Phillip. He was clearly strained by the whole proceedings. I told him if he was going to do this work he might as well enjoy it! He was gracious and did not hit me for this gratuitous advice. Maybe it was naïve politics on my part, but it seemed healthy to stay in communication with representatives of the other candidates. It just seemed to be what Harry would want, the consideration of which was a major concern for all who supported him.

About a week after the first support meeting, Paul Perini left a message asking me to ring him at about 11 pm, which I took to be the hour when Anglican ministers typically finish work. He told me that he had firmly decided for Harry. He particularly valued Harry's understanding of God's generosity heard in his words and seen in his life, his ability to relate to people, and his genuine concern for church growth and the spiritual health of congregations.[6]

The Revd Trevor Edwards, then Rector of Camden, was another who, like Paul and Lindsay, was totally committed to Harry. All three were to serve as archdeacons under him. Lindsay believed that an archbishop had to be a theologian, and was impressed by Harry's theological reflections on church growth: 'he was different from the McGavran school.'[7]

Between the first and second strategy meetings, Peter Kell and Dr Ron James, both laypersons associated with St Michael's, Wollongong, entered the fray. They encouraged me to get on with the job of writing a brochure for Harry and they organised for the funding of its production and posting.

The writing of the brochure was one of the most moving parts of my involvement in Harry's campaign. I contacted people in each of his six previous appointments and asked them for their views of Harry. The exciting conclusion was that, everywhere they went, Harry and Pam had been stunningly successful bringing congregations together, releasing the laity for ministry and generally presiding over the happiest and usually fastest-growing period in their histories. The important, if not necessarily scientific, inference I drew from this research was that Harry could do the same for the diocese and do it quickly.

Those present at the second support meeting on 18 February studied my eight-page document with a view to halving its length. I had a number of pages devoted to answering questions about Harry that suggested he had a range of perceived weaknesses: that he was too gentle, not a strong enough leader, was too old, and was not academic enough! Stuart Abrahams, then Director of the Archbishop's Vision for Growth campaign, who knew how to promote a cause, asked incredulously if I really intended such material to be published. I replied that it had never crossed my mind! The brochure was then taken over by Stuart. He rewrote parts of it, sharpened the argument and presentation, and found and doctored appropriate photographs. One photograph had Harry talking to two teenagers with dazzling smiles as wide as watermelons. It clearly implied that Harry was 'cool' with the younger generation, on whom the future of the diocese rested. Stuart worked on the brochure with Lindsay Stoddart and Laurie Davies, Director of the diocesan Board of Education, who also rewrote part of it and then had it produced and posted. It was sent forth on 15 March, two days after the federal election, and two weeks before the archbishop's election. It included an endorsement from Bill Hybels, whose worldwide profile as a church builder did Harry no harm.

By February, the whole of the Australian Anglican Church was absorbed by the run-up to Sydney's election synod. A letter from Melbourne, written by Susan Rogers, wife of Revd Ken Rogers, who had served for eight years at Ceduna, a decade after Harry had left, was typical. A deeply prayerful person, she had found herself praying a lot for Harry, and now she confided in him:

> Recently I've met a few Sydney people and casually asked 'Who's going to be the next Ab?' The reply is usually something like 'I dunno, but I hope it's Harry Goodhew.' Harry you have a lot of supporters and I'm sure that's because you are a 'real,' unaffected and a godly and caring person ... There are plenty of administrators around, there are academics and theologians all over the place, but there are too few holy people ... I believe in you and know that the job won't dampen your passion for Christ, your thirst for God.[8]

Another who commended Harry from afar was Tom Frame, whom Harry had helped so much as a young pupil at Wollongong High School and who was then a young priest in Wagga Wagga:

> When he was a candidate to be Archbishop, I told anyone who would listen how good he was. He wasn't an ideologue; he was a pastor with a good mind who could communicate efficiently. He remained humble and was unchanged by the possession of authority and power. I appreciated the way he pointed Sydney to the wider church to avoid the kind of siege mentality that later gained a hold.[9]

At SC on Monday 22 February, Peter O'Brien, Lecturer in New Testament at Moore Theological College (Moore College), informed me that his colleague, David Peterson, on leave in Cambridge, was keen to support Harry's candidature. I expressed some surprise as I had heard that the entire Moore College staff was behind Phillip. Peter assured me that this was not so; staff members were very divided over the issue. The next day I faxed David who gladly nominated Harry.

At the third meeting on 2 March we were joined by John Hibberd. Then working for the board of Anglican Super, he had known Harry for a long time. It was Dudley who said to John, 'We'll have to get Harry elected.' John brought a breath of fresh air to our campaign. He was always cheerful and generous with his time and his sentiments. It was important not to get too serious about all this – and John helped!

On 4 March, just four days before the last day for nominations, Harry had not received any nominations, not even from Wollongong, which did not look good as Harry was Bishop of Wollongong. I rang a member of the clergy in Wollongong who had told me some months earlier that he was a Harry man. Yes, he still intended to vote for Harry, but he had been persuaded to nominate Phillip! At this point I did what I always do when disaster strikes. I rang Stephen Gabbott, took a Panadol and went to bed, consumed with despair. Stephen was not fazed. He rang the diocesan secretary and asked him if anyone had nominated Harry. 'No-one,' confirmed Warren Gotley. This was really serious. There were only a couple more days to go before the time for nominations expired. 'Can I nominate Harry over the phone?' asked Stephen. 'Yes,' said Gotley, and the list of nominators below suggests that Stephen's was the first nomination Harry received. Then Stephen got on the phone and brought the Wollongong clergy to do their duty. Over and over again he was told that they had been bullied by Phillip's supporters and told 'if you do not support Phillip, you will have no future in the diocese.' 'I was absolutely astounded and appalled,' reported Stephen. 'Surely,' I retorted, 'they could not have been that crass.' But they were, Stephen insisted, one after another reported the same experience. Not Phillip – but some of his acolytes – who said to those they rang that if they did not support Phillip 'they were finished.' Stephen did not tell any of them that they had to nominate Harry. He just let them vent on him. They had been so badly abused by the more zealous of Phillip's devotees that Stephen likes to think that it was his phone call that gave them permission to resist the pressure of the Phillip campaign party. In the end Harry received a very respectable 25 nominations from clergy and 23 from the laity.

Harry's nominators (clergy in bold):

| | | | |
|---|---|---|---|
| **Gabbott, S.L.** | **Abrahams, S.N.** | Young, A. | Mostyn, F. |
| **Perini, P.F.** | Patrick, L. | **Harris, T.J.** | Harvey, R. |
| **Edwards, T.W.** | **Marsh, B.G.** | **Davis S.J.** | Symonds, N. |
| Smith, T.R. | Llewellyn, K. | **Defty, G.J.** | **Lincoln, G.R.J.** |
| Webb, R. | Winnall, G.A. | **Barrie, R.C.** | Caldwell, S.J. |
| **Peterson D.** | Piggin, S. | Newman, T.C. | Muir, T. |
| **Brain, J.N.** | Adam, D. | **Stoddart, L.** | Hatton, N. |
| **Woodbridge, D.C.** | **Robinson, P.K.B.** | Luke, K.W. | Bennett, E.J. |
| **Gott, W.T.** | **Vitnell, L.G.** | **Poulton, R.** | Webb, I.J. |
| **Luscombe, R.K.** | **Harvey, R.K.** | **Heslehurst, R.E.** | Kell, P.G. |
| **Frith, P.A.** | Bobin, W. | Judd, S.E. | McCarthy, A.D. |
| **Anderson, D.G.** | Shearer, R. | **Miller, R.A.** | Graham, M.J. |

There were, no doubt, some who decided for Phillip without any help from his friends. Riley Warren, Headmaster of Macarthur Anglican School, and who had admired greatly Harry's handling of the board of his school, had wished Harry well for the archbishop's election. After first welcoming the advent of the pressure group known as REPA (Reformed Evangelical Protestant Association, on which see more in chapter 10), Riley began to have doubts as it was proving so divisive. But when he learned that Phillip would stand for election, he thought he would make a 'startling' leader and that it would be wonderful for the diocese to have an archbishop with Phillip's vision for the future. Phillip stood out as a change agent where change was needed. He rang Harry to report his change of allegiance and detected that Harry was disappointed. Riley later came to realise that it was just as well Phillip had not been elected as 'we probably would not have been Anglican anymore.'[10]

On 10 March, Stephen Judd and I had lunch with Harry, and Stephen explained his strategy for getting him elected, which meant we had to have some indication from Harry of his strategy since we wanted to make this the main thrust of speeches on the second night of synod. I have never known Harry to talk so much. I guessed that it was a bit hard for all the candidates to sit at home while everybody else prepared their case and put words into their mouths.

That discussion formed the basis of an agenda paper for Harry, which we discussed at the fourth planning meeting at Miranda on 13 March, the day of the federal election. Paul Keating, Leader of the Labor Party, won the unwinnable election against John Hewson, Leader of the Liberal Party and declared it to be 'the sweetest victory of all.' A portent, perhaps, but of what? Stephen Gabbott, Peter Kell and Paul Perini all attended their first meeting on that occasion and brought a weight to the proceedings, which encouraged us. We there decided on movers and seconders for the first two days of the debate.

That day, *The Sydney Morning Herald* (*SMH*) published an article, 'War in the Cloister', by Graham Williams and Judy Robinson. It focused on Phillip Jensen and had Harry as 'Short Odds.' This was typical of the media. They always dwelt on Phillip, which did nothing for the other candidates, but it did not do a lot for Phillip either as his alleged Bolshevism was the usual substance of their reports. Phillip's problem was that it was not only the general public who learned about him mainly from the media, but possibly the majority in the synod did, too. It was not as appreciated as it might have been that at St Matthias', Centennial Park, Phillip had built up the largest Anglican Church in Australia, that his Ministry Training Scheme was providing Moore College with a third of its students, and that his preaching was a powerful antidote to the ravages of secularism. If the extent of his influence were known, it was too often construed by his critics as a baleful influence through their citing of an outrageous sentiment in one of his sermons or an anti-Anglican, iconoclastic outburst from one of his followers.

At a meeting of the Australian College of Theology on 19 March (Harry's 62nd birthday), Moore College Lecturer in Ethics, Michael Hill, took me aside to persuade me to emphasise more the uniqueness and godliness of Harry's leadership style. For decades, he contended, the diocese had been run by external constraint, whereas the way of the kingdom of God is that it grows by internal appeal and love, which Harry uniquely seemed to understand and exemplify.

*Church Scene* was published in Melbourne also on 19 March and reached Sydney the following Monday. Most of the coverage was about Phillip, but in a hostile vein. There was a short section on Harry, dictated by me, where I expressed dissatisfaction that the true candidate of change was being ignored. Then I said Harry is the exceptional one; all the rest are just typical Sydney Anglicans. For this bit of ungracious stupidity I received a very sharp letter of condemnation from Mark Thompson, who was one Moore College lecturer who did support Phillip. So, I rang him up to apologise. He asked me to apologise, not to him, but to Phillip. I replied that I would have to apologise to all the candidates, not just Phillip. He declared that Harry's campaign had been 'irreparably damaged.' I felt consumed with guilt. This was the very thing I had been so anxious to avoid. Harry would never have said such a stupid thing. Nor would most people, for that matter! After all, candidates apart from Phillip included Paul Barnett, by then esteemed as one of the world's leading scholars on the Jesus of history, and John Reid, who was extremely able and well experienced in the gospel's engagement with the meek of the earth, and was courageous and open with his convictions. One might surmise that Paul would have rocked the boat less than Harry, and John would have rocked it more, but both were eminently worthy contenders.

With just a week to go, on 23 and 24 March, Harry held his long-scheduled regional retreat at Gilbulla Conference Centre. Many were very concerned that it would be a time of great strain. But Harry carried it off with extraordinary dignity, calm and repose. He was the only one in the whole side show who seemed to be relaxed. What few could then have realised was what good shape he was in spiritually. That only became evident to me when I read through his sermon summaries for 1993, most of which he seems to have preserved methodically like everything else that he did. There are 48 such sermon summaries for 1993 and 47 for 1994. Given his other responsibilities, this is a heavy load. His addresses are alive with challenges to deeper personal spirituality and with apologetic defences of the truth of the Christian faith, drawing upon his wide reading in science, history and philosophy as well as theology. He is not obsessed with a narrow range of subjects. Even when speaking on church growth, his principal purpose is not to build the local church, but to draw all people to God. It is God in Christ who is his real passion, not the church or leadership, those matters on which he has a reputation for expertise. In preparation for a lecture for the Department of Evangelism on a pattern of ministry suitable for seniors, for example, under the heading 'what means most to me', he lists 'living by Kingdom realities', 'a steward of life, time and resources', 'a servant heart and mind – we must all appear in Christ's court.' Awareness that he must one day give an account is a constant in his thinking. In the light of that solemn reality, he has only two recommendations to make to seniors: 'Living with purpose: planning and a diary' and 'staying open to new things and ideas'. It is significant that the latter always seemed as important as the former to Harry. For one so sure he had found the truth, he was remarkably eager to discover what he did not know.

But I digress! John Woodhouse and BBJ were both on the retreat, and I invited them to accompany me on a walk so that we could have a chat about things. I suggested that it would be a very statesmanlike act if Phillip were to withdraw, even at this late stage. If he lost, I argued, the emotional attachment that he had attracted might not be able to be transferred to the new man and would make life difficult for him, and, if Phillip won, his appointment would cause major division. John Woodhouse assured me that the moment the new man was appointed, all Phillip's supporters would be behind him 120 per cent.

The fifth support meeting was held at Gymea Anglican Church on 25 March 1993. Among those who encouraged us by their presence on that occasion were author, Lesley Hicks, who, without much encouragement from any quarter, discerned that Harry was the man, Dr Ron James, who had much to contribute out of his experience of Liberal Party politics, Kevin Luke, from Oakhurst parish, Tom Muir from Beverly Hills, Charlie Newman from Figtree, and Peter Robinson, all the way from Bomaderry. After spending half an hour in prayer, we each gave our impressions of our candidate. It was a moving and incredibly exciting time as we each rehearsed the speeches we would give if called on at the synod. At this meeting for the first time was Tim Harris, then minister at Helensburgh. Tim argued that Harry was a very effective catalyst of change; that he wins countless battles without making them seem like battles at all. Tim's contribution was a highly valued one. On this night, we finalised our movers and seconders and organised for about 28 people to have speeches in their pockets for Harry.

On the evening of 26 March, I received a phone call from Gerald Davis, editor of *Church Scene*, alleging that the 'Jensenites' had done their homework and had worked out that Phillip could not win. The fallout was bitter. One of the original 18 REPA ministers had defected and confessed to Gerald in great distress. He alleged that they were working up negative things to say about all the other candidates and their main supporters, too.[11] Depressed, I rang Stephen Gabbott. He was not home, so I tried to tell Marion, but I was overwrought and incoherent. Marion assured me that this was very unlikely to have any substance as finding anything negative to say about Harry would be nigh on impossible. Nevertheless, I rang Peter Kell for his legal advice, and he wisely said, 'Ring Robert Forsyth [Rector of St Barnabas, Broadway] – he is respected by all sides.' So, I did, and he said the whole thing was baloney. It probably was, but, whatever lay behind it, it was symptomatic that the whole process was getting out of hand and it was just as well that it would all be over soon.

On Sunday evening, 28 March, Stephen Judd appeared on the Australian Broadcasting Commission (ABC) *Compass* program. He calmly told the whole world that, in Phillip Jensen's scheme of things, there was no room for the laity except as unordained clergy. Bruce Ballantine-Jones said he did not think much of this performance, which, at the time, I considered a high endorsement.

## The election synod [12]

The first day of the election synod was on Monday 29 March. It opened with a service at 3 pm in St Andrew's Cathedral. I looked down on the assembled throng from the gallery, and I thought that, given all the hoary heads below who made up the members of synod, there was no way this gathering of respectable Anglican veterans would elect a radical: Phillip did not have a chance.

The synod began at 4.30 pm in the Wesley Centre. Professor Bruce Harris, who had not attended an election synod before, found it 'an awesome occasion, but there was throughout a sincere desire on people's part to find the man of God's choice.'[13] Bp Cameron, registrar of the diocese, was in the presidential chair, and he had invited the administrator, Bp Reid, even though he was a candidate, to give the presidential address. It was inevitable, given the heightened state of emotion, that there would be those who would grumble that Bp Reid would use the occasion to increase his chances of election. The practice, however, of allowing the presidential address to be given by one who was also a nominee for election was a common feature of earlier elections. Reid's Address certainly did his cause no harm! It remains one of the finest analyses of Sydney Anglicanism on record.

On this first night, Harry's mover, Peter Kell, and seconder, Stephen Gabbott, looked at Harry's qualities and track record. They demonstrated that Harry was the most experienced of the candidates in a variety of parishes in a variety of dioceses. Peter Kell showed that his parishes were invariably characterised by growth and love and pastoral care and a remarkable motivation of the laity to minister in church, in their vocations, their communities and their homes. Stephen Gabbott argued that Harry was the least incomplete of the candidates. He conceded that

Harry was the one with the risky leadership style, in that he would not tell anyone what to do. He would let you say 'no' and you would maintain your integrity and his friendship. He was, Stephen concluded, a very capable parish and regional leader who was personable, charming, and spent a lot of time with his God.

They were two brilliant speeches, and Harry was voted on to the select list to be considered the next evening, with scarcely a dissenter. Bp Paul Barnett made it through with equal ease. Bp John Reid and Phillip Jensen also made it through, but with more difficulty. Synod rules allow nominees with a majority in either the House of Clergy or the House of Laity to go to the next stage. Goodhew and Barnett won a majority in both houses, but Jensen did not receive a majority in the House of Laity and Reid was not supported by a majority in the House of Clergy. Their elimination the next evening looked inevitable.

The second day, 30 March, Stuart Abrahams arranged for us to hold our sixth support meeting in St Andrew's House. Someone suggested that, of the four candidates, we pray that Harry would be dealt with first, and, at the synod, Harry's name was drawn first; Phillip's last. Paul Perini and Stephen Judd set Harry's broad vision and double agenda before us. He would build confidence and promote desirable change, they said. With great persistence, he would promote a new leadership culture in the diocese. Part of the reason for the crisis in confidence in the diocese, Paul argued, was that lay people were unsure about how their lay vocations could help establish the kingdom of God. This was directed at the increasingly promulgated view of the most extreme of the REPA-ites that only gospel ministry was kingdom building. Perini claimed:

> Harry yearns for lay people to see themselves as partners, not only in implementing church goals but in setting those goals. He wants lay people to grow in their confidence that what they do from 9 to 5 is of great importance. Their work is not an appendix to their Christian lives but a principal way of expressing their commitment to God's kingship – along with family life and congregational life.[14]

Peter Kemp, Rector of Parramatta, spoke with great effect on Harry's administrative achievements in the diocese. Tony McCarthy, retired General Secretary of the InterVarsity Fellowship, spoke of Harry's achievement outside of the diocese. Provoked by all the talk of the need for a 'strong leader', Chris Forbes, lecturer at Macquarie University, injected a necessary modicum of mirth when he reminded synod that they were not there to elect a Schwarzenegger. Again, Harry went through, this time to the final list, with no voiced opposition.

Being inexperienced, I did not appreciate that this was the lull before the storm. What struck me was that Harry's supporters were the ones sounding youthful and passionate. Those who spoke for Phillip sounded defeated already: they were severely handicapped by having to present their man last to a tired synod. Neither Phillip nor John Reid got through: the majority of clergy and laity voted against Phillip; whereas the majority of laity voted to let John Reid's name go forward. On the failure to elect Phillip, John Chapman later reflected:

> I think I am too close to them [Peter and Phillip Jensen]. I think Phillip is the great visionary. He wasn't always right and I am not sure he could have pulled off what he wanted to do if he had become Archbishop. I think we did well not to elect him as Archbishop. I am not sure he could have persuaded the Sydney Synod to follow him. He was too far out.[15]

The choice was now between Harry and Paul Barnett, and the mover that Paul should be archbishop was John Chapman ('Chappo') himself, one of the most effective and respected debaters in the synod. Chappo not only respected Paul's scholarship, but he also knew Harry very well; however, there was one respect in which he and Harry were so different that it seemed to him Harry was departing from the essential culture of Sydney Anglicanism. Chappo had been instrumental in moving the Diocese of Armidale to go over to evangelical tradition, and he had done so by forthrightness of speech. Since this was Australia and not Russia, he once explained, he believed that he could and should speak his mind.[16] Such assertiveness was just not Harry's way, and Chappo was frankly puzzled by it. Harry, he considered, was maddeningly consensual, infuriatingly reluctant to tell you what to do, worryingly averse to be black and white over complex issues, with a complete absence of indignation when most Sydney evangelicals would consider it is amply justified. He had a point.

Robert Forsyth rang me on the morning of 31 March to ask who was going to move and second Harry. He thought it was a big mistake to have Ann Young, a lecturer at Wollongong University, as seconder because she was a woman in a still-patriarchal diocese. He also had doubts about me as mover as I had a reputation for being not quite safe. Foolishly, I retained the role of mover, but we eventually opted for Trevor Edwards to second. Robert was right about me, but wrong about Ann. In the event, Ann got the nod immediately after Trevor seconded my motion, and she spoke with great effect. Someone behind me muttered, 'I would not be game to patronise her.'

According to our strategy, this final night of speeches was to address the subject of why Harry was the man. So, in moving that Harry Goodhew be the next Archbishop of Sydney, I began by asking the question:

*Prologue*

> Tonight we have to decide if God wants Harry for this job. Only one person can be Archbishop. The anointing for this task is on only one of them. We must determine on whom God's finger rests.
>
> How do we do that?
>
> A clue was given in Phillip Jensen's campaign. Gary Nicholson said Phillip is the exciting candidate. Did Phillip's supporters find Phillip exciting for the sorts of reasons that the media wanted to hear? Did they support him because of his personal magnetism which made some adore him and others fear him?
>
> I don't know – but I doubt it – I'll tell you why I could not speak against him. Because I thought he just might be the Lord's anointed, and I thought he just might be because he is so stunningly gifted of God as a preacher/ teacher.
>
> When you hear Phillip preach, you often hear God thrilling the heart and correcting the conscience. Synod decided that there were other considerations and resolved to look elsewhere. But the point I want to make is that Harry is stunningly gifted in a particular area, which is the area in which the Diocese most needs a gifted leader.
>
> This area is in **Christian love and practical holiness**. The fruit of the Spirit has ripened closer to perfection in this man than in any man or woman I know.[17]

I then worked through the seven-fold fruit of the Spirit, demonstrating how wonderfully Harry exemplified all seven, ending with:

> his gentleness – how self-controlled he is – I have seen him angry only once in 16 years – it was with the Property Trust (nervous laughter).[18]

My commendation of Phillip Jensen earned me the thanks of one of Phillip's mentors, Revd Maxwell Bonner, who wrote to me the next day, saying how healing that was. But I had spent far too much time on Phillip and ran out of time for giving my reasons for commending Harry. All that had to be truncated to get to my peroration:

> All the candidates believe in God, but Harry believes also in you. He believes in all of you. That is why lots of people who have never spoken in Synod before have been itching to speak for Harry.

> He believes in all of you. That is why all of you feel so unthreatened by Harry.
>
> He believes in you – in a shrewd, realistic, unique sort of way. He is a great manager of people. Brothers and sisters, I think if Harry were to be given the opportunity he would not so much ask you to put your trust in him as your leader, but rather to put your trust in yourselves as his co-workers. Do you trust yourselves enough to take him as your leader? Because if you do, with your vote for Harry will go with it your own determination to make up whatever is lacking in Harry, and in partnership with him, you will give it all you can.[19]

In seconding the motion that Harry be elected as our next archbishop, Trevor Edwards said in part:

> In the first place … he is a real team man, a peacemaker uniting people in love and a common gospel purpose. He would like to eliminate that debilitating sense of fear and competition between parishes and use our deaneries as strategic units to do together what it is impossible to do alone. He will get the best out of the Diocesan ministry team… He has the track record, experience and style to implement his vision …
>
> In the second place … you will definitely feel heard, be consulted and loved. Harry is about shared vision and working with all no matter what our background or faith expression. Harry can be like this because of the way God has made him and the way the Spirit of God has moulded him … He is warm, engaging and likeable to church people and non-church people alike. He is quick to see the positive rather than being defensively negative. He is calm, unflappable and not given to great mood swings. If you disagree he does not take it personally. He is not threatened, is extraordinarily patient and absolutely impartial …
>
> There are thus two areas where Harry has a distinctive edge. His ministry style can draw us together to build effective healthy churches. His God given personality and temperament will bring honour to Christ in the community and be for the ultimate good of all members of this church.[20]

Debating was not my forte and, too late, I realised that I should have followed Forsyth's advice and allowed another to put the motion for Harry's election. For, now I had to make a speech in reply. Throughout the evening, I was bombarded with suggestions from anxious Harry supporters about what I had to say. I rose with a great pile of incoherent and unreadable notes. I had no idea what to do with them. Furthermore, I was flustered by the fact that serious misgivings had been expressed about Harry by Paul's supporters, while there had been only one speech questioning Paul's fitness. The gist of their argument was that, in this critical hour, Paul, being a gifted and learned Bible scholar, would be better able to stand up against liberalism and defend the Bible against attack. I believed that the Bible, like God, did not need defending. But I put it more indiscreetly than that. A few weeks earlier, a returned missionary had spoken at Trinity Chapel, Robert Menzies College, where I was then Master. Over coffee afterwards, as we surveyed the sea of young people milling around, I had asked her, 'What should I do with all these young people to advance the kingdom?' She replied, 'Tell them to stop taking it all in and not giving anything out. Tell them to get out and DO something. They are constipated with the Bible.' I was very impressed with this response with its echo of James 1:22: 'Be ye doers of the word, and not hearers only' (KJV). But, when in my closing remarks for Harry, I intimated that those who wanted to defend the Bible were constipated with it, there were gasps and people covered their ears so as not to hear more. Too late. I had said it. Wonderful politics – to insult the people whose vote you want! Mark Thompson's words came back to haunt me: I had irreparably damaged Harry's campaign – twice! Forsyth later had some advice for me: 'Next time pass your speech by me before you give it!'

Not surprisingly, I thought we were murdered on the night, and not many of our humble crew got the nod to speak for Harry. But Peter Kell fought a brave rear-guard action, and Chris Forbes and Narelle Gatenby were brilliant, and Canon Ray Heslehurst batted safely on a sticky wicket. The surprise of the evening was Chappo, who could not bring himself to drive home any advantage for Paul from the debate. He concluded the evening by saying that Paul and Harry were equally eligible, which was plainly true, but not the sort of truth often found in election synods. It was the last synod speech he ever gave and one of the best, the mature verdict of an ecclesiastical statesman, aware that the whole process had become excessively personalised. It was a brilliant way to end the debate, leaving many with a pleasant taste in their mouths. Maybe there was hope for the diocese after all! Asked later for his impression of the 1993 election synod, Trevor Edwards wrote:

> It was a remarkable experience … our group covered the whole Synod in prayer and the people from our group consistently got the right tone in their speeches. Once the list had been reduced to Barnett and

> Goodhew there seemed to be a genuine attempt by the Synod to choose between two good options. In fact, the final speech was given by John Chapman in favour of Paul Barnett and yet at the end I heard him say we would be well served by either man! There was an irenic spirit …[21]

We were then required to return the next afternoon, 1 April, and cast our vote. During the morning, Charlie Newman, synod representative from Figtree parish, who was staying with me, and I prayed a lot and talked a lot and had many a telephone conversation designed to prop up our failing spirits. We suspected that Paul could not overcome Harry's lead among the laity, but he could well get the clergy vote. This fear was reinforced when we heard that some of the clergy who had supported John Reid were going over to Paul, and we suspected that some of Phillip's supporters were more interested in safeguarding the Bible than in promoting the change that they had earlier said we so needed.

As the day wore on I grew calmer. Two themes had emerged clearly in the process of promoting Harry and they seemed to be sticking: he was the only one who would promote change and he was the bishop for the laity.

It is a very good idea to allow a day between the last speeches and the final vote. It helps synod members to reflect less on the campaign and more on the candidates. My two indiscretions apart, we had conducted a good campaign, and, as with another great campaign in the secular world, we had 'worked *con amore*' for Harry, 'chiefly from love of the man.'[22] But the candidate should not be chosen on the basis of who was supported by the best campaign. It should be decided on the basis of who is the best person for the job. I comforted myself with the thought that, as synod members reflected on the candidates, Harry would get himself elected.

Our chief numbers man, Stephen Judd, who had never wavered in his conviction that Harry would be elected, hesitated just one hour before the vote. He thought it just possible that we could have a hung synod with a small majority of the clergy voting for Paul. But his best calculation was that in the House of Laity, where 237 votes were required, Harry would win with 269 votes, and in the House of Clergy, where 132 votes were required, Harry would win with 139 votes. In the event his calculation of the vote for Harry was optimistic, by two in the House of Laity and two in the House of Clergy. Harry won with 267 votes in the House of Laity (against 203 for Paul) and 137 (against 122) in the House of Clergy. Ballantine-Jones was suitably awestruck that Stephen had tipped the outcome so accurately. It was later rumoured that those who had supported Phillip met after Phillip was eliminated to decide who their vote should go to, and it was argued that Harry should be supported because he was 'an easier pushover' than Paul.

They thought they had elected 'Mr Nice Guy.'

Meanwhile, back in Keiraville, Harry and Pam had a nervous day. Marion Gabbott spent the day with them and recalls that Harry was obviously tense. He would walk into the room and then walk off again to pray or read. She asked him if he would be very disappointed if he were not elected. He admitted that he would, but he said that he would just get on with things. Driving up from Wollongong on 1 April, the day the vote was counted, Pam said to Harry, 'They won't elect you. You are not really one of the inner circle.' As usual, she had a point. Harry had not been a Moore College lecturer. He was not a North Shore Anglican from Sydney's Bible belt. Harry was the first non-Anglophile Archbishop of Sydney. He had not fought in the war; his heart was not in Oxford or Cambridge. Robert Forsyth always thought of Harry as Sydney's Jimmy Carter: he was an outsider who came to Washington.

Dear reader, you might just permit a further comparison with another American President. Admittedly, comparing Harry's election with Lincoln's election in 1861 must strike you as more than faintly ridiculous. But the parallels are really interesting. Both were four horse races; both victors were the least known of the candidates; in both, the losing contenders lost because they had made enemies or at least strong opponents, whereas both Lincoln and Harry had avoided criticising others, and their lower profiles meant that they had not only fewer powerful friends, but also fewer powerful opponents; both Lincoln and Harry were the first choice of the minority and the second choice of the majority; in both it was easy to think of the outcome as a defeat for the most aggressively supported candidate – William Seward in the US and Phillip Jensen in Sydney – rather than a victory for Lincoln or Goodhew. There are differences of course: Seward went on to become Lincoln's greatest supporter; Harry was unsuccessful in winning Phillip's support, though Paul Barnett served Harry with loyalty and warmth, just as, following the 2001 election, Robert Forsyth, who was defeated in a more bitter election, served Peter Jensen with unswerving loyalty. Then, as Lincoln's and Harry's time in office unfolded, both, though the least vindictive of men, endured the bitterest opposition. Political reality is the same in church and state.[23]

## Response to Harry's election

The official report on the election synod concludes with the words: 'The President declared Bishop R.H. Goodhew elected. After a short adjournment Bishop Goodhew entered the synod and made a speech of acceptance.' But to be present was a less clinical experience.

With the announcement of the result, post-election euphoria broke out as the feeling swept over emotionally drained synod members that the decision reached was the will of the Holy Spirit of God who had guided them in answer to their prayers. When Harry and Pam were presented to the synod, Harry was relaxed and radiant, unlike those who had been through the mill of the previous few days. His experience as an open-air preacher standing him in good stead, he had words for the occasion. He told synod members that he and Pam would be:

> the servant of each and every one of you … with whatever strength and time God gives us.

> We are sent to glorify his name. That is the deepest conviction of our hearts. To empower men and women in their daily work to be what God has called them to be, to reveal the face and hands of God … to have compassion on the just and the unjust, and be the instruments of his love for all.[24]

He spoke with such facility and grace as to immediately impress those who did not know him well.[25] The Rector of Carlingford, Les Vitnell (who did know him well), was among the many whose eyes filled with tears at the sight: 'tears of delight … gratitude … memory.'[26]

The synod broke into spontaneous song, 'A new commandment I give unto you that you love one another as I have loved you.' Harry took that to be 'the expression of a desire for all of us to find a deeper experience of Christian love, generosity and kindness in our shared life across the Diocese.'[27] Possibly, it was also the expression of a desire to put the intense and not always healthy emotions of past months behind them.

Revd Ross Poulton, from the Parish of Huskisson in Harry's Region, probably spoke on behalf of the majority when he wrote:

> I was very moved and overcome with emotion when you both entered the auditorium last Thursday night, to a standing ovation. It was the culmination of months of prayer. It was also the culmination of nights of speeches and voting … I considered it to be a real privilege to be associated with this Synod. We were looking for the man that God had chosen as our leader. I felt ready to receive whoever won that last vote. However, I felt delighted that it was you, and proud to have been associated with you both.[28]

Riley Warren, Principal of Macarthur Anglican School, wrote, for you to be elected in the first ballot, and to receive such a genuinely warm welcome and ovation, I believe is a true indication of Synod's recognition of you as God's man for Sydney at this time. I praise Him for it.[29]

From 1 April 1993 to 19 March 2001, Archbishop Harry Goodhew was to be 'God's man for Sydney.'

# 1
# Parentage: All Families Have Mysteries

Harry Goodhew was born on 19 March 1931 to Baden Powell Richard and Christina Dalgarno Goodhew (nee Fraser). On 14 June that year, at St Stephen's Newtown, Revd Albert Rook baptised him Richard Henry, but his mother, disliking his first name being shortened to Richie, very early started calling him Harry, and Harry he has been all his life.

There were to be three more children: Joyce, Peter, and Sue. Sadly, when Harry was six, Joyce died of pneumonia in circumstances that did not reflect well on the medical practitioner involved. Sixty years later, Harry was to reflect on that experience at a service 'of remembrance for families whose children have died, or are missing': 'There can be few more cruel pains than the loss of a child. We stand quietly with you this evening.'[1] Peter, 10 years younger than Harry, would go on to University and then become a pilot. He flew in Papua New Guinea and once landed on the Western highway with his mother on board. Sue, born 20 years after Harry, would become an artist. Harry was to conduct her wedding to Ian Gregory at St Paul's, Carlingford. They now live in Tasmania.

Harry was a fourth generation Australian. His great-grandfather, Henry Goodhew (1830–1916) hailed from Chislehurst, Kent, close to London. When he was two, Henry's mother died in one of England's devastating cholera epidemics. Henry and his wife, Jane, to whom Harry bears a striking physical resemblance, arrived by assisted passage in Sydney in July 1853. Henry gave gardening as his occupation. They lived first at Circular Quay, and Henry worked in the Botanical Gardens. The family then moved to a property near Goulburn where Henry helped found the cricket club: cricket appears to be in the Goodhew genes. There was a Goodhew (Christian name and dates unknown, but 'mainly associated with Kent') who is described 'as an English professional *cricketer* who made 4 known appearances in *major cricket* matches from 1789 to 1795.'[2] He made his debut in first-class cricket at Lord's playing for Kent against Marylebone in a four-day match, 15–18 August 1791, and scored one run in his first innings and 15 in his second. In his only two other first-class matches, he went backwards. Harry was destined to be a more prolific run scorer than his namesake.

Harry's grandfather, Robert, was born in 1862 and baptised in St Saviour's Church, Goulburn, New South Wales. Just the year before, Goulburn was made a separate diocese and the evangelical Mesac Thomas was appointed its first bishop.

The family moved back to Sydney in 1869 when Henry was appointed head gardener at Sydney University. The family lived on campus in a small weatherboard house known as University Cottage near the Great Hall. They afterwards moved to the stone cottage still standing near the junction of City and Parramatta Roads. Across Parramatta Road, the Grace Bros department store was opened, and Henry once rescued one of the Grace daughters from drowning in Lake Northam. The lake, which less than a century earlier had been a swamp on the kangaroo grounds of the Gadigal people, was now part of the extensive garden entrance to the University, which was beautified by the long-serving and respected Botanical Gardens director, Charles Moore, under whom Henry had worked when he first arrived in Sydney. The relationship that Henry established with Charles Moore was probably the reason why he had returned to Sydney to work in the gardens of Sydney University.

On retirement, Henry lived in Mortdale in a house that he also called University Cottage, signifying his affection for the University. But it did not rub off on his immediate descendants. His son, Robert, was by turns a plasterer, policeman, labourer, woolsorter, travelling salesman, and owner of an aerated water factory. In 1889, he filed for bankruptcy.[3] His wife, Lena Land (Harry's grandmother), was the daughter of a publican. She is remembered as a hard and difficult woman, possibly disappointed that her husband failed to provide for her in the manner, not to which she was accustomed, but to which she aspired. They had six children, of whom the youngest was Harry's father, Baden Powell Richard Goodhew (1900–1968),[4] normally called 'Otto'. A popular German name, it was a nickname used by his work mates because he had a crew cut, then fashionable in Germany.

In 1990, just a few years before he became archbishop, Harry learned that his father, Baden, had been married before. His parents did not talk about these things, but Harry recalls his father telling him quietly and without elaboration, 'The church is very hard on divorced people.' In 1924, Baden had married Marjorie Matthews,[5] had children with her, and divorced her in 1929 after, it is now believed, she had an affair. Baden is identified as the divorce petitioner on the certificate of his marriage to Harry's mother.[6]

After her divorce, Marjorie married a man named Sindell. She told her children and grandchildren that her first husband was not a good man, so the children she'd had by Harry's father changed their surname to Sindell. One of the granddaughters, living in Western Australia, discovered that her paternal grandfather was a Goodhew. Then, on reading the entry on Harry in *Who's Who*, she discovered that Harry's father was called Baden, the name of her grandfather. She contacted an astonished Harry, after which the Sindell grandchildren changed their name to Goodhew. One of Harry's older half-brothers he never met, but when Harry and his wife, Pam met the other, Roger, they immediately recognised the family resemblance. Roger had four children, three sons and one daughter, the discoverer of Harry, and they all became friendly with Harry and Pam. Even Harry's mother, who had never mentioned any of this to Harry, became part of the lives of her late husband's descendants, and Roger and his three sons were to attend her funeral.

The shock discovery was just one of a number of mysteries about Harry's background.

Christina Dalgarno Fraser, Harry's mother, was born on 4 April 1907 and baptised at Fraserburgh on the north-east coast of Scotland. She was raised on the island of Lewis, off the West coast. Lewis had experienced a number of remarkable religious awakenings, but the revival fires did not incinerate the spirit of judgmentalism in the gospel's messengers. The minister said to the girls in Christina's confirmation class, 'There you are in your white dresses – you are like whited sepulchres, clean on the outside and filthy on the inside.' This had a profound effect on her which she carried throughout her life: she was never worthy, never good enough. Harry would have a talk to her about it in her later years. On confessing that she was not sure that she was going to heaven, Harry helped her to arrive at a deeper assurance.

When Christina was 11 her parents and four sisters left Scotland for the United States. But – another mystery – Christina stayed behind in Scotland and was raised by her grandparents. She often wondered why they left her, but she came to believe that she was better off as a result. Her sisters all predeceased her, and she thought none had any Christian faith, whereas by going to Australia instead of America she became a Christian. Her grandfather worked in the Black and White whisky distillery, and she told Harry stories of how the workmen siphoned off the coveted fluid into flasks hidden on their person. Christina had considerable athletic ability. She once ran away from a boy and slammed the gate on him, knocking the wind out of him. She did not like her bike and threw it down a quarry and dropped rocks on it. Her grandfather found out and she was in all sorts of hot water. She could be aggressively high-spirited as a young woman, but she later became notably gentle, like her son.

She had been friendly with the young Countess of Seafield near Portsoy, north-west of Aberdeen. Her father had been the gatekeeper there for a time; she had become friendly with the young countess and they had played together. One of the nurses connected with them was later tried as a spy for signalling to German submarines. When she was in Australia, the countess wanted to see her on a visit, but for some reason – mystery number three! – Christina did not want to see her.

Christina had wanted to be a schoolteacher, but she overheard her grandmother, with whom she was then living, say that it would cost them a lot to have her trained as a teacher. Not wishing to be financially obligated to them, she resolved to train as a nurse instead. She went to the Glasgow Infirmary where she was housed and paid during her training.

Baden first met Christina in Scotland. At the time of his divorce, he had been apprenticed as a fitter and turner with the engineering firm, Babcock and Wilcox before becoming an ERA (Engine Room Artificer – that is, an engineer) in the Royal Australian Navy. He joined a marching band in Newtown, an inner-Western suburb of Sydney, and played the trombone. When his marriage failed, his captain, perceiving that Baden was doing it hard, persuaded him to go with a group to Scotland to attend the sea trials and commissioning of the newly built *HMAS Canberra*, a cruiser that would eventually be sunk in World War II. So, he sailed over to the Clyde where arrangements were made for the sailors to meet nurses. Baden met Christina, and wanted to continue to write to her. But she demurred: she had lots of Scottish suitors; why trouble with an Australian? It was on his second visit to Glasgow, that their paths crossed again, this time in Kelvingrove Park in Glasgow. It was not the first such tryst in this setting![7]

Shortly after meeting up with Harry's father for the second time, Christina, now pregnant with Harry, emigrated to Australia so that she could marry him. On arrival, she was met, not by Otto, but by his mother, Lena, who was displeased and remained so for the rest of her life. Otto and Christina were married in the registry office in Newtown. She gave his address as her own when she signed their marriage certificate:[8] 26 Juliett Street, Enmore, the suburb next to Newtown. Life was not easy for Christina at first in Australia. Lena was unkind: maybe she was down on Christina for conceiving Harry out of wedlock. Yet they all had to live together in the same house. Years later, when he was archbishop, a cousin spoke to Harry about the way his grandmother 'terrorised the family and what a hard time she gave my mother.'[9]

Reflecting on this apparently inauspicious start to Harry's life, his daughter Wendy, who works in pregnancy resource ministry for women with unplanned pregnancies, observes that in her line of work, this is 'everybody's story.' She has to convince women every day that the child she is carrying might turn out to be unique. Wendy knows that in most such cases it is an issue as to whether there comes a point when it is OK for such information to be shared. With reference to her father, Wendy wonders what the impact of reading a story like his would have on those in a similar situation: the teenage girl whose near relatives want her to have an abortion so that her life will not be ruined.

Given the circumstances of Christina's life, Wendy realises, she could so easily have decided not to have her child. She was single, with no family support and pregnant to a man from another country. It would have been simpler for her to have gone back to the hospital where she worked and had an abortion. Instead she chose the harder way: she sailed to a foreign country to have her baby. Her choice fills her granddaughter with admiration and wonder, and the consequence of her choice must fill all who learn of it with wonder at the way God honoured it. For God used this child to do so much to build his kingdom and to be the instrument through whom so many would come to saving faith, including his own parents. Here is ample demonstration of the truth of the Apostle Paul's words 'that all things work together for good for those who love God' (Rom 8:28) and therefore it is God's will for us to 'give thanks in all circumstances' (1 Thess 5:18).

Harry recalls the night his grandmother died (13 April 1947) at the age of 83, and his mother, dutiful to the end, sitting in with her. In retrospect, Harry wonders if the experience of witnessing his mother being bullied at the hands of his grandmother shaped his sympathy for women's suffering, which was to play an important part in his later ministry. Harry was sensitive to bullying from any quarter, and it felt to him in the 1990s that the women in Sydney diocese who longed to be ordained were treated harshly by those who opposed their ordination.

Harry remembers his father as a kind, working-class man. For much of Harry's youth, his father worked at the Australian Woollen Mills Pty Ltd in Marrickville. Two apprentices at the Mills in 1936, Ted Swift and Harry Beaumont, recalled, almost 70 years later, how considerate Harry's father was in training them. They also recalled how Harry's 'lovely Scotch [sic] mother' always made them welcome in the family home. Harry's dad was over-protective of his children: even when Harry was 21 his father would wait up until he came home. But Harry considered him a caring, loving dad, and he used to watch Harry play tennis and cricket. Harry's children recall him sitting on a stool, cleaning every one's shoes with spit and polish, ever the elegant naval man, a habit that Harry would acquire. Neither Harry's father nor mother was a strict disciplinarian, but they taught him good manners, and he always walked on the outside of the footpath and allowed women to go through doors first.

Like many a Sydney child, Harry was taken by his father to Manly on the ferry. They would catch the tram from Marrickville to Circular Quay and on the way Baden would point out the famous sign at St Barnabas's church at Broadway and then that gothic gem, Christ Church St Laurence. Harry's earliest recollection of city churches was of these two. 'An interesting combination', he observes, in acknowledgement of the fact that they represent the two ends of the Anglican spectrum, from low-church evangelical to high-church Anglo-Catholic. Acceptance of the normality of this combination within the diocese was consistent with his later experience of worshipping in both of them during his time as archbishop.[10] Neither parent was a regular churchgoer, but Harry's father occasionally took Harry to St Clement's Church of England in Marrickville. On one such occasion there was a worshipper there who made the sign of the cross on his chest. Harry asked his dad in a whisper what he was doing. 'He is a very religious man', was the reply. At the 1959 Billy Graham crusade, which made such an impact on the Australian churches, Harry spoke to his parents about Christian faith and they both prayed to receive Christ.

1.1 Harry in his father's naval uniform. Harry seemed to like uniforms and getting dressed up!

Harry's parents later moved to Parramatta. Baden Goodhew died in 1968 at the age of 68. Harry's younger son, Philip, remembers that his father was very sad. Harry's mother was to be befriended in the mid-1980s by Lindsay and Jan Stoddart. Lindsay, ordained deacon in 1985, was then the curate at St John's, Parramatta and he introduced her to a circle of Bible-believing women who welcomed her into their fellowship. As a result, Harry's mother became a stalwart of Christian faith.

Harry's mother was 61 when her husband died and she remained a widow to the end of her very long life, much loved by her children and grandchildren. Her grandson, Philip, quite an athlete, once challenged her to a footrace and lost! Her granddaughter, Wendy, on seeing her in hospital in receipt of a blood transfusion, was devastated because she thought her Gran was losing all her 'Scottish blood.' When visiting her grandmother, Wendy made a point of sitting next to the door in the back seat of the car so that she could be first out of the car and ring the doorbell before her brother, David. 'When I have grandchildren,' says Wendy, 'I want to be Gran.' As she grew older, Christina became ever more interested in her Scottish heritage, and would talk about it at length to her grandchildren, who at times thought she was at Culloden. Philip asked her the most remarkable thing she had witnessed in her life. When she answered 'electricity', he understood that she had been long on the earth.

Christina asked Pam to have her power of attorney. She probably thought Harry was too busy, and neither Peter nor Sue lived in Sydney. Harry suspects that Pam represented the daughter she lost (Joyce) because she would have been about the same age. Christina died on 13 March 2006, just short of her 99th birthday. Harry was in America with Wendy, and Pam had to sign the legal documents and organise the funeral. Wendy reports that her father was sad, not so much at losing her, but that hers had been such a hard life. In 2007 Harry and Pam, accompanied by their daughter, Robyn, sprinkled her ashes in a stream near Stornoway, on the island of Lewis.

Of those who now identified themselves as Harry's relatives, one of them had retired to Taralga, a small town near Goulburn. So, following an ordination service in Goulburn Cathedral, Pam told Harry that she would like to visit this little town where his new-found relatives had lived. At Taralga they found Goodhew Lane, Goodhew Café, and Goodhew Park. They had a late lunch in the pub, the only place open. The staff went to some trouble, feeding them on home-made pizza. Pam went into the bar afterwards to thank the staff, and a patron, sitting at a table near the bar, asked, 'Is that Harry Goodhew?' When Pam said 'yes', he introduced her to one present who was Harry's second cousin.

All families have mysteries, and Harry's family was not lacking in that department.

# 2
# Early Days: Faith, Hope, Love and Cricket

From the age of three until he went to Moore College, Harry lived in Marrickville, a suburb of Sydney then considered lower middle class and Protestant working class, and separated by a few suburbs from the dirt and drink, the fatalism and fecklessness of Irish Catholic working-class Surry Hills, memorably depicted in Ruth Park's haunting novel, *The Harp in the South*.[1]

Harry grew up, then, amidst moderate poverty and unpretentious respectability. It was not the classic middle-class puritanism of Sydney's North Shore, where the Anglican Church still thrives. But there were working-class Protestant Bible belts in Sydney, such as that which stretched from Newtown to Dulwich Hill, and another further west, which included Riverwood, Revesby and Padstow. Immediately to the west of Marrickville and south of Dulwich Hill is the suburb of Earlwood, where the father of Prime Minister John Howard, Harry's near contemporary, ran a service station and where Howard was raised in the Methodist Church. Nominal Church of England, however, was the default religion of much of Sydney in Harry's youth, and his upbringing was as genuinely 'Sydney' as any that Sydney could then provide. Maybe this helps to explain the readiness with which Sydney accepted him when he was archbishop.

Harry lived in 96 Livingstone Road, Marrickville, which his parents rented. After Harry left home, his parents lived in a Housing Commission flat in Herbert Street near the Dulwich Hill Church, and then in Housing Commission accommodation further west in Parramatta. His parents never owned their own home. The house in Livingstone Road had four bedrooms, two either side of the hallway. His parents occupied one; Harry and his brother, Peter, another; his uncle (Harry's father's brother) another (until he flew off the handle literally with an axe and Harry's mother insisted that he leave); and his father's mother – the fearsome Lena – another. It was the Depression and his father took them all in.

## Matters mental and physical

Harry had chest problems as a boy. His father carried him piggy-back all the way to Petersham to see Dr Petherbridge, a children's doctor. Otto, who was then working for Tooth's Brewery in Broadway, brought yeast and stout home to build up his ailing son. Throughout his life, Harry had difficulty with a condition related to asthma. When in Wollongong, he went to a specialist who said it was a residual smoker's cough, which was remarkable as Harry had only ever taken one puff of a cigarette. Harry also suffered chronic problems with his skin and later in life would be treated for skin cancers with peelings that were very painful. 'My skin I have inherited from my Scottish mother', he once told a congregation. 'I keep skin specialists in business and pass the same legacy on to some of my children.'[2]

On leaving the brewery, Harry's father worked in the Australian Woollen Mills just around the corner in Sydenham Road. It is now a primary school, but in Harry's day, Crusader Cloth and Stamina suits, worn by every Australian schoolboy, were made there. Terry Fearnley, who coached Parramatta in Rugby League, lived further down Sydenham Road. Nearby was Henson Park, then the home ground for the famous Newtown Rugby League Club for whom the also famous Michael 'Bumper' Farrell played. Just back from the Australian Woollen Mills and on the other side of the road where Sydenham Road met Livingstone Road, were four small businesses: a garage operated by 'Hop Harry' Stone, a pugilist of some note, which boasted a painted clock displaying the credit warning, 'This Clock Don't Tick'; a fish and chip shop; a small all-purpose store, called Bodie's; and a grocery shop where Harry used to work cutting butter and bagging biscuits. Harry's dad regularly bought a sponge cake there on his way home from work, and the Salvation Army officers in training nearby were glad to stop off at 96 Livingstone Road to sell the *War Cry* and partake of the cake. Sixty years later, the daughter of one of the Salvation Army officers told Pam that, in her family, the name of Goodhew was always remembered with thanks because of their kindness.

Harry first attended a preschool attached to St Clement's, Marrickville. There he was taught how to write on slates. He then went to the Dulwich Hill Infants, Primary and Central (High) schools which were all on the same block adjacent to Holy Trinity Church. Harry recalls that he did not 'do anything' at school until fifth class when he had a teacher called Miss Doughty. She inspired him to get interested in school and he recalls that he 'worked from then on.'

2.1 Member of the Australian Air League. In spite of this father's first name (Baden), neither he nor Harry was attracted to the Scouting movement.

From 1944 to 1946 Harry was educated at the Central School, sometimes known as a 'Commercial' school.[3] He thought highly of the principal and the deputy, but he suspected that some of his teachers were there because they were not well enough to be recruited into the armed forces. He was dux of each year. In June 1944, he was placed first out of 136 pupils. In December 1944, he slumped to second out of 138. A clue to this lapse may be found in the school report on his conduct which reads: 'Good. A little talkative.' On 12 December 1944, the Director of Education wrote to 'Master H. Goodhew' informing him that the Trustees of the National Art Gallery had awarded him second prize in Group III, Boys 12–14, of the 'Conducted Guide-Lectures Essay Competition,' and enclosing a cheque for a guinea. In the June 1945 examination, he was placed first out of 151. In December 1945, he was first out of 152. In May 1946, his last internal examination before the Intermediate Certificate, he was first out of 126. He topped English, History, Geography, Science and Shorthand.

In the Intermediate Certificate, he satisfied the Board of Secondary School Studies in English, History, General Mathematics, Combined Physics and Chemistry, Business Principles, Commercial Geography and Shorthand (Theory). In his final year, Harry was vice-captain, represented the school in both cricket and football, and was awarded the Weir Cup, named after George Weir, member for Dulwich Hill in the state parliament, and at the time Minister for Conservation in the Labor government. The cup was for the boy most successful in all branches of the school's activities. Humble Harry concedes that school did give him a sense of worth because he did well there, and because he was captain of the cricket team.

Dulwich Hill Central School was then known as Dulwich Hill Junior Technical and Commercial School. Harry was already being groomed for a future in the technical trades or, given his aptitude, in commerce, as an accountant. He was not well placed, then, either by parental example or by education, to thrive in the professions of law, medicine, or the church. This may help to explain his ability to communicate with people of all backgrounds, his lack of pretension, and his practical turn of mind. Does it also explain an apparently excessive humility about his intellectual and academic powers? Harry remained at Dulwich Hill Central School because his father wanted him to do Commerce and go out and get a job. Nearby, at Petersham, was the prestigious Fort Street Boys' High, the oldest state school in Australia, and the parish's own private school, Trinity Grammar. Harry aspired to neither of those. However, as time progressed and he did so well at school, it did cross his mind that he might transfer to Canterbury High or Sydney Tech, both selective schools. But again, his parents said it would be more sensible to stay where he was. Unaware of the full family story and not as impacted as they had been by the Great Depression, he was slightly mystified by his parents' caution. It meant that he would never matriculate at the Leaving Certificate nor accumulate a multitude of university degrees as did many of his colleagues in the ministry. But those who underestimated his intellectual power did so at their peril. After all, no matter what school one attends, one cannot be better than dux! Much later, Bp Paul Barnett, who served as one of Harry's regional bishops, would observe, 'He was no lightweight. He was very humble, and I think he may have felt that he lacked something in scholarship. But in my opinion, he was shrewd theologically. He was no dope.'[4]

Other Dulwich Hill Old Boys included John Heaps, Catholic Auxiliary Bishop of Sydney, who wrote to Harry on his election as archbishop in 1993;[5] Ray Smith, who worked in Harry's episcopal team as bishop for the Georges River region of the Sydney diocese from 1993; Graham Butchard, Commissioner of the Compensation Court of New South Wales; and Maurice Sandilands, who worked for the Salvation Army.

In spite of his chest condition, Harry was always a keen sportsperson. He played tennis, soccer and rugby, and was good at cross-country running, which he was to maintain even when he was archbishop. He also played baseball, then made popular by American servicemen who passed through the Leave and Transport

2.2 Harry (right), goalie for the Leichhardt–Annandale 18-years grade undefeated premiers, 1949.

Depot on nearby Addison Road. He acted as a 'bat boy' for the Americans, who played on Marrickville Oval, and was paid for his services in chewing gum. As with other boys of his age, the silhouettes of war planes published in newspapers became part of his memory: 'Spitfires, Hurricanes, Messerschmitts, Lancasters, Dorniers, Mosquitoes, Beauforts, Lightnings, Zeroes, Sunderlands, Wirraways and Wackets.'[6] Some American airmen, to get a closer view of their compatriots during a baseball game, once flew three Kittyhawks low over the oval, barely clearing the trees. Harry's brother, Peter, saw a Mosquito bomber disintegrate in the sky overhead, bits of it landing in Petersham. He was affected by it for years, but still became a pilot.

Of all sports, Harry's first love was cricket. He was good at it, an all-rounder. He not only played for Holy Trinity, Dulwich Hill and for Banksia Free Church in the church competition,[7] but was a grade cricketer. He played in the Green Shield cricket competition, characterised as 'the toughest and most competitive under 16 competition in the world.'[8] After he turned 16, he played for the Poidevan-Gray Shield in the under 21 competition. At the end of 1944, he received advice from the Secretary of the NSW Cricket Association that he had been nominated by his district cricket club for coaching at the Sydney Cricket Ground. He was to report to his coach, Mr G.L. Garnsey, at 10.30 am on 2 January, 1945, and he was asked to take his own bat if possible, in view of 'extreme difficulty in obtaining material.'[9] It was to be the last year of the war.

In 2006, Brian King, who had played international rugby union for Australia in the 1960s and who had worked as assistant bishop to Harry when he was archbishop, sent Harry an undated newspaper cutting. It is headed by a rhapsodic account of the cricketing achievement of the captain of Parramatta High School who took 13 wickets for 40 in Cumberland's thrashing of Western Suburbs. His name was Richie Benaud, later captain of the Australian cricket team, and Australia's best-known commentator on the game.[10] The same page reports Marrickville's routing of Waverley. Harry took a wicket and was the top scorer with the bat. 'H. Goodhew's stroke play was attractive. Six fours helped to make up his score of 48 scored in fast time.'[11]

Marrickville Park, where Harry played a lot of his cricket and from which he hit a prodigious number of balls through windows of neighbouring houses, is immediately across the road from 96 Livingstone Road. He was quite a spin bowler and once took 9 wickets for 10 runs. He was also accomplished with the bat, once scoring a century at Petersham oval. In the first game he played in fourth grade at Belmore Oval, he was bowled second ball on a wet wicket. In the second innings, he hit two sixes and a range of fours and scored 'about 60.' Richie Benaud,

6 months older than Harry, was among those he played against at Marrickville. Harry recalls that his first-grade team won the Pennant after a fairly ordinary tail end batsman on their side hit Bill O'Reilly for a winning six on the last ball of the day.

Harry went to a lot of cricket tests because the Marrickville cricket club gave tickets to their young aspiring players and they could get into 'the hill' at the Sydney Cricket Ground for nothing. So, he regularly watched cricket all day long. He was selected to play for the Australian schoolboys' squad. He left school at the end of his fifteenth year, and the secretary of the local cricket club came to his house to invite him to participate in the selection trials. Harry's grandmother, Lena, told him that Harry was not interested as he had just started work. He remained ignorant of the invitation until it was far too late. But his love of cricket survived. When Harry became archbishop, Bruce Smith, Moore College lecturer, and later teacher and cricket coach at Sydney Grammar, told his son, Rob, that their new archbishop had been 'a great fast bowler' when a student at Moore College.[12] Harry had by then left spin for the fast lane!

Harry saw Bradman play. He saw him get his 234 with Sid Barnes in the December 1946 second test against England. In a partnership that is still an Australian fifth wicket stand record, Barnes also scored 234, having thrown his wicket away on the grounds that 'it wouldn't be right for someone to make more runs than Sir Donald Bradman.'[13] But Bradman was not Harry's hero. That was Stan McCabe, and Harry was given a Stan McCabe cricket bat. McCabe had made his name in the famous Bodyline tests of 1932 when, with high courage, he withstood the fury of Larwood and scored an unbeaten 187. McCabe was a beautiful stroke maker. There was an innings (1938) where he made 232 runs in four hours, and, said Harry, Bradman called his men out and said 'Watch this. You will never see batting like this again.' The entry on McCabe in the *Australian Dictionary of Biography* was written by historian, Ken Cable, who was to support Harry's election as archbishop. 'He seemed to lack the inclination to score unnecessary runs,' wrote Cable of McCabe. 'He played with superb grace … [with] "a certain courtliness" in spirit and approach.'[14] Harry shared his hero's philosophy and style: he was not about making every shot a winner, but he was elegant in all he did, facing the Larwoods of the Diocese of Sydney when he was archbishop, with grace, courtliness and, it must be said, unbeaten courage.

## Spiritual formation

Harry's spiritual life was forged in a vibrant, too little recognised, part of the Sydney diocese: the inner-western Bible belt. By the beginning of the 20th century, the

Church of England in Sydney was being served increasingly by Australian-born men from such working-class suburbs as Newtown, Summer Hill and Marrickville. The Anglican churches in each of those suburbs were imposing Gothic structures, of cathedral dimensions, with magnificent spires that dominated the landscape. They were built between 1880 and World War I, at one of the peaks of church building and church attendance in Australian history. Robert Taylor, rector from 1866 to 1907 of St Stephen's, Newtown, where Harry was baptised, was a staunch evangelical who sent a stream of ministers and laypeople into Christian service. At Summer Hill, John Vaughan, rector from 1881 to 1918, at the age of 65 climbed a string of ladders and, with his own hands, put the top piece on the lofty, landmark spire of St Andrew's church. Muscular Christians, indeed, they put a different construction on things than clergy born and trained in Britain.

St Clement's, Marrickville, is a grand church where half-a-dozen weddings were held every Saturday; if you were late for your wedding you had to go to the end of the queue. It had benefited from a succession of outstanding ministers. Arthur Bellingham,[15] responsible for the building of St Clement's and its first rector, is remembered in a memorial tablet in St Andrew's Cathedral: 'Called, chosen, and faithful.' Like Harry after him, he was pre-eminently a pastor of souls. He was followed by William Martin, who at a men's service at 4 pm on the first Sunday of every month preached to a thousand men.[16] Then came Canon Stephen Denman (1882–1960), the well-known rector in Harry's time. He was also a boxer, and he once used his pugilistic skills on a man who dared to speak disparagingly of clergy as 'bludgers.'

Harry recalls that his earliest spiritual experience was lying on his back on the hill around Marrickville Oval asking the deep questions: What is life all about? What will I do? What will it be like when I get to the end of it? He was about 12 or 13 at the time. Of these reflections, he later wrote: 'Growing into teen years I thought a lot about life and death; what they meant, and what the former meant in the light of the latter. These considerations were part of the process that led me to Christ.'[17] Invited by a couple of the local lads, the Rodgers, he attended a Brethren Sunday School in Petersham for a short time and irregularly attended Sunday School at Holy Trinity, Dulwich Hill.

Here he was influenced by a number of single women of great character whose commitment to Christ indelibly affected Harry: Merle Wright, Kath Richardson, Monica Farrell, Gladys Moir and Marj Aspinall. Merle Wright was to meet up with Harry's mother at the Anglican Mowll Retirement Village and they became friends. Gladys Moir was awarded the MBE in 1950, and a tablet in the church commemorates her service to the Sunday School and the girl guides. Harry recalls sitting in the front pew of the church and being instructed in the prayer book by Miss Aspinall, much revered and slightly feared. 'We don't really like the prayer book,' grumbled Harry and his mates. 'That's not the point,' she responded categorically, 'we just learn to use it.' Harry would have liked to have used that substitute for argument when, as archbishop in the 1990s, he had to confront the anti-prayer book brigade within his own clergy. Marj Aspinall followed Harry's career, and when he became Archdeacon of Wollongong in 1979, attended his commissioning service. She ran a Bible class for boys and always thought of Harry as one of her boys.

One afternoon, when Harry, aged 14, bowled out of school, he came upon a green truck with the tail board down, and a speaker with a sketch board. He was telling the story of the Good Samaritan. His application was that the boys standing around were like the man beaten up who needed a Good Samaritan to come and save them. They needed Jesus. He then handed out little cards with a prayer on it, and Harry took one of them and went home and prayed the prayer. Harry was the first member of the family known to have had 'a conversion experience' as the evangelicals understood it, an assent of the heart, mind and will, to accept Christ as Saviour and Lord. The missioner was Wallace Guilford, widely esteemed as Australia's foremost children's evangelist. Years later when he was a bishop, Harry met Wally Guilford on Town Hall railway station and told him that he was the human instrument through whom he came to Christ. It is not surprising that Harry, converted in this way, himself developed a commitment to open-air preaching, a life-long passion for evangelism, and a remarkable ability to communicate with children and teenagers.

Harry's conversion was followed by regular attendance at Holy Trinity, Dulwich Hill. It occupies the highest land between the Harbour Bridge and the Blue Mountains, but it has never been 'high church.' Staunchly evangelical and missionary-minded, it became for Harry a real spiritual home. Like all the churches in that remarkable 'Bible belt', it stressed three priorities that remained central to Harry's entire ministry: the authority of the Bible for faith and life; the priority of evangelism or local outreach; and the responsibility for missions to the whole world.[18]

Holy Trinity, Dulwich Hill, is a large, well-proportioned Gothic structure, built in brick, with a high and handsome timber ceiling. But, unlike its near neighbours, the projected spire was never added to its sturdy tower. Its extensive seating was comfortably full in Harry's day, and he sometimes sang in the choir, seated in the sanctuary. Harry sang 'tenor'; 'just higher than some of the others', says Pam. On the communion table are the words 'Holy, Holy, Holy' and above it, a stained-glass window of Christ feeding the five thousand, quite beautiful, Harry recalls, particularly with the morning sun behind it at the 8 o'clock communion service.

The rather grand church building, opened in 1915, is the product of the confident vision of the then rector, George Chambers. He had founded in 1913 the nearby Trinity Grammar School (named after the church). Vice-Principal of Moore College before his appointment to Dulwich Hill, Chambers went on to become the first Bishop of Tanganyika (1927–1947). His vision was for young people and for mission, and all who attended church at Dulwich Hill caught that vision, including Harry, who would have become a missionary were it not for Pam's health. Chambers was to recruit many of the first Australian Church Missionary Society (CMS) missionaries for Tanganyika from his own parish. 'Keep back the missionary contributions in the future,' wrote Chambers, 'and you can write doom for the church upon its door.'[19] On the back wall of Holy Trinity church was a notice that read, 'The light that shines the furthest shines the brightest nearer home.' This was a missionary challenge based on the view then popular among supporters of missions that those most zealous for the gospel abroad are most likely to be zealous for it at home.

Apart from Chambers, missionaries from the parish included Hazel Dicker, Amy Gelding, a pioneer missionary who served in Tanganyika and who died in 1947, Max and Val Corbett, who also served in Tanganyika, Kevin and Dorothy Geerkans, who served at the CMS Roper River (Ngukurr) mission, N.T., Ron Ash who served on Groote Eylandt, while his sister, Joan, led the Girls' Friendly Society in the Sydney diocese, and William Wynn Jones, who succeeded Chambers as Bishop of Tanganyika, and who was founder and patron of the scout group at Dulwich Hill, known as Wynn Jones' Own.

Harry joined the church just before the end of World War II. He remembers that the church bell 'rang all afternoon' on the cessation of hostilities, and the children from Dulwich Hill School next door filed into the church for a service to mark the occasion. By that time, the rector was Ernie Millard, who came from the Church of Ireland. He was portly, like Friar Tuck, and there was a lot in his sermons about Ireland, where he had preached in the open air. On 22 April 1945, he presented Harry to Archbishop Howard Mowll for Confirmation in Holy Trinity Church. One of his daughters married prominent Sydney layman, Ernie Newman, with whom Harry engaged in open-air preaching.

Millard was a friend of the fiery female Irish evangelist, Monica Farrell, famous for her anti-Catholic invective.[20] She was a frequent visitor to the parish where Harry was impressed by her passion, but not by her anti-Catholicism. Harry's father, whose first marriage had been to a Catholic, sometimes made comments about Catholics, so that Harry grew up thinking they were different. He was a member of the persistently anti-Catholic Young Evangelical Churchmen's League. But disparaging Catholics in the spirit of that sectarian age was not in Harry's make-up. Not 'a natural hater', he was later to find it easy to befriend and pray with Catholics in the hierarchy: Bill Murray and Peter Ingham, Bishops of Wollongong, and Cardinal Ted Clancy in Sydney. 'We differed in our convictions,' wrote Harry, 'but found common bonds in friendship and shared beliefs. Praying with people takes some of the hard edges off doctrinal differences while the differences remain real.'

Another tablet in the church was 'in memory of our brother scout, John Eric Fowler, who set for us a good trail, and has now gone home, 19 October 1963. Ever with the Lord.' John Fowler lived on the opposite side of Marrickville Park from Harry. When they first met, they fired stones at each other from catapults, but in time became great friends. John was the model son and Christian. His father had died, and John took every responsibility seriously. After training at Moore College, he married a deaconess, worked at Lalor Park and died suddenly, aged 32, of a congenital weakness in a heart valve, leaving two young children. Harry was then at Ceduna in South Australia with the Bush Church Aid Society (BCA) and did not have the resources to get back for the funeral and always felt sad about that. Fellow student at Moore College, Bill Lawton, formed the view that John's death had 'a massive impact' on Harry: 'he was a lot more internal after that.'[21]

John Fowler had a sister who was Pam's special friend and who died at the age of 21 of a brain tumour. Some months after John's funeral, his mother, Dottie, wrote to Harry and Pam to tell them that she had been very proud of her son and what he had done with his life. She was a strong woman: Harry seemed to be surrounded by them. 'Goodhew, what are you doing here again?' she used to say. She lived on into her 90s. She gradually became a Christian of strong evangelical conviction. She went to Harry's ordination and also to his consecration as bishop. At the latter, she slipped on the steps of the chapter house and gashed her head. Harry's son, David, a trained nurse, staunched the bleeding. Dottie asked Harry 'to put her away' at her funeral, but he was in Tasmania at the time.

Another woman very influential in Harry's spiritual development was Adelaide, wife of the rector, Ernie Millard. She and her sister were noted for their piety: surrendering all to Jesus was the expectation. They were the product of 'Keswick' spirituality, a convention movement originating in the Lake District in England in 1875 which emphasised personal holiness. One afternoon Adelaide invited Harry to call at the rectory on his way home after school. She sat him down and gave him an apple and then asked him: 'Who is going to be first in your life?' Harry knew why she asked him that: he had shocked her the day before by joking in her hearing, 'Faith, hope and charity, but the greatest of these is cricket.' Harry knew the joke had to cease and replied, 'The Lord Jesus.' Adelaide was not always well. She used to get terrible migraines. So, all the young folk went up to her bedroom and sat around her bed while she took Bible Studies. John Fowler and Harry were members of this group, as was Gwen Hawtrey, Harry's first girlfriend.[22]

Harry's spirituality, then, could be characterised as 'Keswick'. He still reads books by the most popular of Keswick devotional writers, Andrew Murray. He also read other Keswick classics: *Life on the Highest Plane*, by Ruth Paxson; *My Utmost for His Highest*, by Oswald Chambers; and *The Normal Christian Life* by Watchman Nee. Harry later came to believe that one of the shortcomings in the Sydney diocese is the intellectualisation of the gospel. The cultivation of the heart, as practised by John Wesley and Jonathan Edwards, the twin founders of the modern evangelical movement, was perhaps a dimension too lacking in some evangelicalism. The heart, understood as 'a metaphor for the spiritual centre of the human heart',[23] was to be not only 'warm', a matter of the emotions, but 'pure', a matter of the will.

While Harry was to become an avid reader, he was not so in his youth. Reading was not part of his culture, and books were expensive. After his conversion, he read the Jungle Doctor books written by Paul White, and a book which had a lasting effect on him was the biography of the cricketer and missionary, C.T. Studd.[24] In Harry's Bible was Studd's challenging life motto: 'If Jesus Christ be God and he died for me, there is no sacrifice too great for me to make for him.'

Not long after he was converted, Mrs Carter, the BCA Auxiliary representative in the parish, accosted Harry: 'You are working now, aren't you Harry?' 'Yes.' 'Then here,' she said, handing him a BCA

2.3 Harry, aged 16, in 1947. Early on, he displayed a taste for good clothing.

collection box, 'You have to learn to tithe now, and you can put something in this every week now that you are working.' He was also strongly encouraged to be a member of Scripture Union, and he wore the little teapot badge that you weren't supposed to wear unless you read your Bible every day. He was friendly with people like Ernie Newman, who worked with the Open Air Campaigners, and they would go off some time into the bush to pray. When they worked in the city, Ernie, Harry and Graham Wade, later of Pilgrim Press, used to meet at St James' King Street to pray. So, the disciplines of tithing, Bible reading and prayer came fairly early in his life. He found them helpful and they have been with him ever since. Harry's children testify that they never had an absent father; theirs was a praying father.

In his late adolescent involvement in open-air work, associated with Jim Duffecy of Open Air Campaigners, Harry saw some amazing conversions. Snowy Royal, a bitter and cruel baiter of open-air preachers, was among the most celebrated. 'This is no joke,' he said when he gave his life to Christ. Harry and Ernie Newman preached at Sutherland railway station and at the tram terminus at Dulwich Hill. Joyce Fraser used to sing, reducing her hearers to tears. Harry also preached on the beaches with Open Air Campaigners. He did not learn public speaking, like John Howard, in the cut and thrust of school debating. He cannot recall that his school had such opportunities. But there was no better training for public speaking than open-air preaching. Harry never preached from a full script. You had to think on your feet and respond to skilled interjectors. Ernie Newman said that there were two essential requirements for open-air preaching – the capacity to attract an audience and the ability to keep it – and Harry was good at both.[25]

Open-air preaching was also the place to learn how to project the voice, and Harry had a booming voice when needed. On one occasion in synod, the chairperson, Archbishop Robinson, told him not to speak so loudly as he was deafening everybody. One historian of preaching observed: 'Pulpit preaching is a big-voiced literary genre, and evangelical rhetoric, often intended for an audience of thousands, is architectonic and not always subtle.'[26] Harry's preaching was often big-voiced, always evangelical, often literary and rhetorical, typically architectonic, that is well-structured in spite of the extempore presentation, and usually with a deeper meaning for the subtle-minded. Like the greatest of 'big-voiced' preachers, George Whitefield, whose sermons fed the Evangelical Revival, Harry's public preaching was personal and intimate. There was no doubting the faithfulness to Scripture, but its exposition was never abstract; he genuinely loved scholarship, but he never paraded it; he was eager to change minds, but more eager to woo hearts. Better than any, he had a gift for maximising inclusiveness and minimising offence.

## Spiritual crisis

The evangelical Christianity in which Harry's early faith was nurtured was intense and pietistic with a spirituality which mandated the cultivation of holiness and personal awareness of life lived in the presence of God. He therefore eagerly devoured a book, the title of which he cannot now recall, which encouraged him to pray, and to pray fervently, for God to manifest himself to him personally. The author focused particularly on John 14:18–24, especially verse 21 which, in the King James Version, reads, 'He that hath my commandments, and keepeth them, he it is that loveth me: and he that loveth me shall be loved of my Father, and I will love him, and will manifest myself to him.' Alone in his room, on how many occasions he cannot now recall, Harry prayed for hours that somehow he might know God in this intimately personal way. One evening 'something seemed to click' and a wonderful sense of being absorbed in God's love and peace came over him. It was quite transforming. He was working in the nearby suburb of Leichhardt at the time and he would walk there from his home in Dulwich Hill instead of taking public transport. The walk took him about 50 minutes, during which he enjoyed matchless intimacy with the Lord. He talked about it with a friend who later served with Summer Institute of Linguistics who would say, 'the priority is to evangelise' and Harry, not so sure now, responded, 'well, yes, but to know God, that is the ultimate.' He also talked about it with his close friend John Fowler and his then spiritual mentor, Adelaide Millard. Harry was aware that in time these two also became somewhat concerned. They saw him, he now believes, withdrawing from his association with other fellowship members in order to enjoy a personal engagement with the Lord, which had taken over his life. This spiritual high lasted perhaps a year.

Then, suddenly, it all fell away and a terrible blackness descended on him and he was shattered. It came into his mind that he may have committed the so-called 'unpardonable sin' (Mt 12:31–2; Lk 12:10). At that time he was reading Charles Finney's *Lectures on Revival* (1835) and a story there took hold of his vivid imagination. It was about a farmer weeping in a field, wanting and trying to repent, but he could not, and this filled him with a terrible lostness, and a great fear that there was no way back. Gripped himself by this fear, Harry sought the help of prominent clergy at the time. He spoke first with Revd R.M. Leghorn at Belvoir Street Baptist Church, but this problem can become a psychological state of mind not easily changed, and he could not relieve Harry's anxiety. Then there was a mission at Stanmore Baptist Church taken by the prominent evangelist, W.P. Nicholson. He issued an invitation for people to talk with him, and Harry, anxious for relief, sought his counsel. But he was himself in despair: the anointing seemed to have departed from his evangelism, he confided in Harry – his preaching was not having the same effect on people's lives. So, these interviews only entrenched Harry in his anguish.

The torment threatened to unhinge him. A terrible compulsion came upon him to speak to the people next door about Christ. He wrestled with it and became so intense that he knocked on their door in the early hours of the morning: 'they rightly thought I was nuts.' Then, his father had brought home from where he worked some parts of a weight-lifting set, and Harry, fearing that his father might not have paid for it, felt terribly afflicted in his conscience and sent some money to his father's employer to 'square off' what he thought might not have been appropriate. Catholic Moral Theology might diagnose Harry's dysfunctional behaviour as 'scrupulosity', a condition not uncommon among the devout – especially the adolescent devout. Furthermore, he was then friendly with a girl in the Dulwich Hill fellowship and he thought he had not treated her well and that relationship broke up.

Was he going through an experience commonly labelled 'the dark night of the soul' in Christian spirituality? Harry was reluctant to credit himself with having an experience that he shared with 'the great ones of God.' But, in that strange, black place, he told himself that even if he were forsaken and without any way back, still the best way to live was to live for Christ. This response to the problem is actually found in Finney's lectures,[27] and Harry may have first thought of it when reading Finney. But it seems that it was Bunyan who, over time, extricated him from the mire. Harry read *Pilgrim's Progress*, *Grace Abounding to the Chief of Sinners* and *The Holy War*: 'Bunyan was about the only one who kept me balanced and sane.' The verse of Scripture, John 6:37 'him that cometh to me I will in no wise cast out' (KJV), that meant so much to Bunyan, Harry clung to as well. Bunyan also helped him to realise how determined were the forces of doubt ranged against the Christian. 'Unbelief has as many lives as a cat,' wrote Bunyan, 'you may kill it over and over again, but still it lives. It is one of those weeds that sleep in the soil even after it has been burned, and it only needs a little encouragement to grow again.'[28] Harry identifies with this insight to this day – he has had to make an effort throughout his life to believe that Christ owns him. It had been a bitter, unsettling experience, but the great struggle he went through to recover peace with God must help to explain why he has been able to comfort many who have struggled for assurance. Would that not have been a ministry difficult if not impossible had he not experienced a weighty measure of it himself?

Gradually, the crisis passed, and Harry turned his mind to the ministry. The curate of Dulwich Hill in 1949 and locum tenens there in 1950 and 1951 was Harry Edwards. At Harry's consecration as bishop in 1982, Edwards found himself reflecting on all those called into full-time service through the ministry of the Millards.[29] In fact, Ernie Millard did not push Harry. At the time, Harry thought that his rector could well see John Fowler in the ministry, but that it was not for Harry – probably another manifestation of Harry's own moderate self-esteem. But, it must have been a remarkable fellowship at Holy Trinity. John Fowler, as scout master, Bible class leader, fellowship leader, choir master and parochial lay reader,[30] was just the most outstanding of an outstanding bunch. Another from the parish who went into the ministry at this time was Ronald Ash, later CMS missionary to the Northern Territory and then rector of a number of Sydney parishes. The parish fellowship group gave Ash a copy of the recently published *New Bible Handbook* on the occasion of his ordination, 7 December 1947. The flyleaf of the book is signed by 16 members, including Harry, the first to sign, John Fowler and Gwen Hawtrey. Charley Marrett, another on the list, was then a schoolteacher who was ordained later in the Diocese of Adelaide.[31]

Harry told Mr R.B. Emanuel, his esteemed headmaster, that perhaps he might become a minister. Emanuel had lost a son in the air force in the war, and Harry remembers being affected by his grief. He counselled Harry to have a career first, get some experience and then think about it. From the time of his conversion, however, the only real possibilities Harry considered were parochial ministry or missionary work. To do this he had to get the Leaving Certificate, because matriculation was required for entry to Moore College. But Harry was given to understand by his parents that for financial reasons – perhaps associated, he now wonders, with the need to provide support for the two boys of his father's earlier marriage – he was expected to leave school after the Intermediate Certificate and go to work. So, at the end of 1946, Harry left school to study accounting. He did several jobs, but he was restless, a condition that did not abate until he went to work for the Church of England Youth Department.

# 3

# Man of Promise and Pamela: 'A Balanced, Spiritually Minded Young Man'

They say if you want to know what a person is to become, look at what the world was like when he was 20. Harry was 20 at the beginning of the 1950s, Australia's decade of equipoise, when strong and agreed values, the fruit of the Christian heritage, ensured a nation-enhancing balance of rights and responsibilities. The number of Australians in church every Sunday rose steadily in that decade, peaking in the early 1960s in the wake of the 1959 Billy Graham Crusade when Australia came close to a national awakening. If the imposing churches Harry grew up in were built as the result of one peak in religious commitment in Australian history (late 19th Century), then his early ministry was served in another. It meant that for him the exceptional peak, with churches and Sunday schools full, and with churchgoers well engaged in addressing the needs of the nation, was the desired norm. The year 1950 is significant in the Goodhew story for another reason: he then first met Pamela Coughlan who, eight years later, was to become his life partner.

## Work experience

There is a photograph of Harry in a popular magazine in April 1946, his last year at school, studying Chinese. Underneath the photograph are the words: 'Student of Chinese, Harry Goodhew intends to go to China some day as an industrial chemist. He is determined to speak Chinese.'[1] But this was more the determination of his father than of Harry himself, who, as we have seen, following his conversion, never wanted to be anything other than a minister. Baden, however, was 'slightly to the Left' in his political inclination. He was a shop steward and he was convinced that China was going to be a great force. So, he found a minister of religion, Pastor Lo Shui Kwong, who gave lessons in Mandarin, and Harry joined the class. As he wanted to be a missionary, Harry may have thought that learning Mandarin might prove useful.

When Harry left school to study accounting, his rector, Ernie Millard, wrote him a reference. He had noticed in Harry 'the indications of sound character' and observed that he was 'a young man of much promise', of 'manly bearing', and 'neat in his appearance.'[2] Harry was aware that Millard may not have been as certain that Harry should train for the ministry as he was of other young men in his flock. Reflecting as archbishop on the possibility that local parishes and their ministers might have a greater say in the selection of those to be trained as clergy, he conceded that the idea had difficulties: 'I do not know that my own parish clergyman would have supported me when I began.'[3]

His school principal, Mr R.B. Emanuel, was more effusive in his reference for Harry. He found him to be

> a courteous, gentlemanly, reliable and thoroughly trustworthy young man, possessed of a very pleasing personality and keenly interested in all branches of the school's activities … his happy nature, his keen sense of duty and fairness, together with his moderation of judgment, have won the esteem of pupils and teachers alike.[4]

The qualities that all admired in the future archbishop were already so in evidence that it prompts the obvious question: was Harry's exceptionally pleasant personality the product of nature or grace? Peter Ingham, auxiliary bishop in the Catholic Archdiocese of Sydney, perhaps captured the truth when he wrote to Harry on his retirement: 'Harry, you are a living example of what we Catholics call "grace building on nature!"'[5]

In 1947 Harry worked for the Frederick Stearns and Company Division of Sterling Drug Inc., first as a junior clerk and then as a cost clerk. His employer testified that he was 'an excellent type of young man and worthy of every trust.'[6] This overlooked the fact that Harry broke yet another window there, playing cricket at lunch time. He and his friend, John Fowler, started together with this pharmaceutical company, which was in Glebe. On the tram to and from work, prompted by the example of Frank Hulme-Moir, then General Secretary of CMS and from 1954 Bishop of Nelson in New Zealand, they talked to people about Christ.

Meanwhile, Harry's father had enrolled Harry in the Hemingway Robertson Institute. Founded by the influential businessperson, Charles Victor Robertson, it offered training in accountancy by correspondence. The Managing Director wrote to Harry to congratulate him on completing his certificate in Practical Mercantile Bookkeeping and achieving 95 per cent in the examination.[7] He received the Hemingway Robertson Institute's Certificate of Proficiency in Practical Bookkeeping in July 1948 and the Bookkeeping Diploma of The Association of Accountants of Australia a year later.

Then in 1948 Harry worked for the soft-drink manufacturer, Cottee's Passiona Limited, in Leichhardt. The firm's secretary wrote that Harry had an aptitude for work and 'an intelligent approach.' He was 'a lad of more than average intelligence and ability.'⁸ He resigned to take up a position with P.L. de Monchaux and Willcock, Chartered Accountants, for whom he worked until 12 May 1950, and was described as 'painstaking and conscientious.'⁹

From May 1950 to June 1952, Harry worked for Griffith, Grill and Love, doing endless tax returns. He was bored and restless. Among the firm's clients was Austral Rock Milling Pty Ltd, the offices and works of which were in Gladstone Street, Newtown. From June 1952 to 15 October 1953, he was the firm's accountant, keeping a complete set of books and production and costing statistics. His manager wrote of him on his departure that he was 'particularly neat and accurate in his work' and that his 'honesty was unquestionable.'¹⁰

## Youthful ministry

Towards the end of 1953, Harry accepted the position of staff worker with the diocesan Youth Department. His father was disappointed. He had wanted more from life for Harry than a trade had given him, which was why he had enrolled him with Hemingway Robertson to study accountancy, but he had not bargained on Harry entering the ministry. He thought his son was throwing away his life prospects.

3.1 Harry on appointment to the Youth Department in 1953, with dapper tie and suit, Scripture Union badge and not a hair out of place.

Through Campaigners for Christ, Harry had become associated with its director, Alex Gilchrist, a national broadcaster. He connected Harry with many of the leading evangelical organisations of the day: the Katoomba Christian Convention, Asia Pacific Christian Mission, Language Recordings Incorporated, Capernwray Missionary Fellowship, and the Far East Broadcasting Company. Harry was beginning to develop his capacity for association with scores of evangelical societies. While most young evangelicals were content to put their efforts into one or two such societies, Harry connected with many Anglican and interdenominational bodies, thus developing a rare overview of the total evangelical Christian scene.

His chief interest was evangelism. Of great significance for the future prosperity of the evangelical movement, new energy and increased resources were then being put into winning young people to Christ. Howard Mowll, Archbishop of Sydney from 1933 to 1958, was the leading evangelical strategist of his day, and he made youth work a top priority. In 1942, the most dangerous year of World War II, Graham Delbridge asked Mowll if he could become a chaplain to the forces. Instead, Mowll made him chaplain to youth, and asked him to form the Church of England Youth Department, even though there were no funds for the purpose.[11] It was a decision which attracted a lot of criticism at the time. Yet, it laid the foundation for the spiritual lives of thousands. It is one of the reasons why the diocese today is as strong as it is, with support from youth the envy of all other Australian dioceses.

The new stress on youth work, promoted by Arcbishop Mowll, coincided with Harry's own youthful years.

> Evangelism was the key to progress, with the under-25s as the main target group. A mission by youth to youth, organised for 1951, aimed at contacting all those confirmed in the diocese in the previous ten years. This focus on youth was to produce the enormous young people's fellowships that filled the churches in the fifties. The Youth Department … became one of the most significant organisations in the diocese.[12]

Graham Delbridge, gregarious and fun, was a great success. Then, in 1952, going against Mowll's wishes – not many were prepared to do that – he accepted appointment to Adelaide as Rector of Holy Trinity.[13] In succession to Delbridge, Mowll appointed Arthur Deane as Chaplain of the Youth Department. Deane was more scholarly than Delbridge, but his spirituality was vintage Keswick, like Harry's, and he was destined to become the respected Principal of the Sydney Missionary and Bible College at Croydon. It was he who spotted Harry at a fellowship tea at Dulwich Hill: 'He was a balanced, spiritually minded young man, and as soon as a vacancy occurred for a lay worker, I put his name forward.'[14] So Harry was appointed staff worker with the Youth Department, a position he held in 1953/4.

His first area of paid ministry was destined under God to become one of the major emphases of his time as archbishop. Ray Smith, who later would serve as a bishop under Harry, recalls that the churches of Sydney's inner west all had vibrant youth ministries: Newtown, Petersham, Marrickville, Summer Hill, Dulwich Hill, Earlwood, Kingsgrove, Belmore and Campsie – further evidence of a Bible belt. Harry recalls that the Methodist minister at Dulwich Hill often spoke of revival. Ray Smith wonders if the vitality resulted from the work of the Youth Department itself.

Harry's role in the Youth Department included looking after properties as accountant, speaking at house parties, and visiting churches. The Youth Department magazine for December 1954 bade Godspeed to their 'popular staffworker' and added that 'Harry's list of house parties, fellowship teas, youth meetings, and children's afternoon teas reads like a cricket score board.' Among the churches he then visited was St Barnabas, Littleton, a branch of St Paul's, Lithgow on the western boundary of the diocese. The rapture on the children's faces as Harry related to them the story of the Potter's wheel was recalled 40 years later by the Sunday School Superintendent, who used the story many times after that.[15] Harry's story-telling ability was matched by his sensitivity, both great assets for a youth worker. At one of the many house parties at Chaldercot, a Youth Department camp site, a young man lit a cigarette in the kitchen and was sent outside quite rightly, but rather peremptorily, by the cook. Harry was uneasy with anything peremptory and went outside to comfort the offender.[16] For Harry, upsetting sinners was usually too high a price to pay for moralising!

## Pamela

Even by traditional standards, the Goodhew marriage requires some understanding. It not only worked, but it worked brilliantly for both parties. Neither Harry nor Pam is particularly mystical, but they did forge a mystical union. Not only did Pam not seek a life independent of Harry, she felt called to live with and for him. He reciprocated and rarely spoke of 'me' and 'my' thoughts: it was always 'us' and 'our' thoughts. One who was a mystic, Revd Geoff Bingham, in writing of what he thought was the Christian ideal for marriage, accurately described the real secret of the Goodhew marriage:

> If then we view man and woman merely in regard to a romantic alliance or in procreation and the rearing of children, we will miss the fact that the point of their being and living was the vocation God gave them ... marriage is for vocation, and vocation with a goal.[17]

For Harry and Pam, marriage was a vocation – a vocation with a goal.

Born on 7 March 1935, Pamela Coughlan is four years younger than Harry, and she was only 15 when they first met. She had always been serious about faith. She cannot remember a time when she did not love God. Her father used to say, 'Pamela is a very serious child.' At Hurlstone Park her Sunday School teacher, Miss Samways, was physically disabled, and Pam was impressed and always enjoyed her teaching, which was carefully prepared. Nevertheless, there came a time when, of her own volition, she left the church at Hurlstone Park to join St Aidan's, the little branch church of Dulwich Hill parish. There a fellowship leader gave a memorable address, 'In the year the king died, I saw the Lord', based on Isaiah 6:1. It was an important time for her spiritually: she thought she knew the Lord, but she did not know Jesus in the way that the fellowship leader explained it. Coming to know Jesus in this new way was, in her understanding, a 'natural addition' to her faith. That is when she became a Christian, she believes, even though she thought she already was a Christian. Conversion, the arrival at a personal faith that Christ has died for them, is an important experience for evangelicals. It is a matter of decisive significance, no matter how 'religious' they are beforehand.

Pam went to a variety of schools. At Canterbury primary school she did a test, on the basis of which she was sent to an Opportunity Class at Summer Hill. She found it an 'interesting, exciting, inspiring' school. She then attended St George's Girls High School, at Kogarah. It was a selective high school, and she did Maths I and II in the Leaving Certificate. This was unusual for a girl then, but she was a Coughlan! This meant she was smart and very able. She was to keep the family's books through their married life, even though Harry was the trained accountant.

Pamela Coughlan grew up (left) in Sydney. She attended St George Girls High School (right)

3.2 Pam Coughlan.

Strangely, Pam was not without experience in the same field. One night, she was praying about her future when she came to the decided conviction that she should become a nurse. She was only 16, however, when she finished the Leaving Certificate, and nurse training could not begin until she turned 18. So, she took a job for 18 months with a firm of accountants and enjoyed the experience enormously, largely because of the people with whom she worked. They called her 'Lofty' because she was so short. She was an accounts clerk, working a comptometor, an adding machine used, for example, to compute wages. 'In the end,' observed Pam, 'it was easier to do it in your head.'

On turning 18, Pam began her nursing training at Marrickville Hospital in time for the 19 December 1953 Sydenham Rail disaster, which killed five people and injured 748. Marrickville Hospital was the first port of call for hundreds of the injured. There it was determined whether they were to be admitted or sent on to another hospital. The system then devised to identify and diagnose victims was later employed by the NSW government in the development of disaster management plans. Pam had a lot of experience in surgery at Marrickville. When she applied for a position in the operating theatre at nearby Camperdown Children's Hospital, the matron appointed her immediately on hearing she had been at Marrickville Hospital. She was in the theatre when the first heart lung machine was used, in this case on a tiny 'blue baby.' The theatre was full of people and there were cameras everywhere – a momentous occasion she never forgot.

Pam's father, Kevin Lloyd Coughlan, could be something of 'a control freak', gruff, opinionated and rather critical of any who disagreed with his way of thinking. He liked to hold court and was forever talking about Mensa, an organisation whose membership is open only to those with an IQ in the top 2 per cent of the population, and he enjoyed intellectual jousting. Kevin believed in God, but was less enthusiastic about church. He had reason for his reserve about religion: in the depths of the Depression, he had asked a church member for a loan. He was happy to oblige, provided Pam's father paid 50 per cent interest! He never asked anyone for anything after that, and he never lost his bitterness over it.

Kevin was, however, intensely appreciative of his brother, Revd William George Coughlan, and his work in the church. George, as he was known to the family, was a Master of Trinity Grammar School, teaching Latin, and a curate at Holy Trinity, Dulwich Hill.[18] He was awarded first-class honours in the Licentiate of Theology (ThL), which was then considered the major academic qualification for Anglican ministers. Always interested in young people, at Corrimal on the South Coast he formed the first youth fellowship in any church in the Sydney diocese. During the Depression years, he reduced his stipend to the level of the dole to match the circumstances of the families around him.

George Coughlan, always 'Cog' to those who knew him but 'Uncle George' to Pam, was not a narrow evangelical. He spoke at Student Christian Movement meetings at Sydney University rather than the more conservative Evangelical Union (EU). An enthusiastic ecumenist, he organised the Christian Social Order Movement (CSOM) conferences during World War II, offering Christian perspectives on national postwar reconstruction. The General Synod of the Anglican Church in 1943 appointed George, by then Director of the CSOM, to develop a nationwide program for the promotion of Christian values in all aspects of society. He was tireless and had a flair for publicity, promoting the CSOM through radio, public meetings and a journal, *New Day*. He envisaged an extensive network of local branches, in every parish in every diocese throughout the land, and indeed in churches of other denominations as well. Coughlan's CSOM is said to have made a significant contribution to the debate on 'the future shape' of Australian Society.[19]

Pam did not embrace Uncle George's Christian socialism, but she was aware of and felt unhappy about 'the rude treatment' accorded him 'by outriders of the evangelical Sydney Anglican diocese.'[20] Pam and Harry remained lifelong evangelicals, but vigilantism was not in their nature, and their respect for the inquiring mind allowed them to appeal to the same young inquirers who found Uncle George's views so appealing.

Pam's mother, Marjorie Edna Grace (nee Arnold), died in 1977 of a massive heart attack in her 60s. She was a smoker. Pam's father died at age 90. He lived on in the same apartment with his son, Rowley, who had suffered oxygen deprivation at birth. It was always felt that he could not live on his own, and therefore it fell to Kevin to look after him. Actually, Rowley was fine and, when Kevin died, he lived on his own and looked after himself. Kevin had what granddaughter Wendy described as an Australian relationship with God: 'the man upstairs, him and I are mates,' he had it all worked out. When Wendy tried to talk to him about his faith shortly before his death, he told her that he knew she was worried about him, but all is fine.

Pam first met Harry in 1950 at the big youth fellowship at Holy Trinity, Dulwich Hill. Pam was then attending the branch church, St Aidan's, down near Dulwich Hill railway station. Shirley Wilkinson was the main organist there, but when she was not available, Pam played the organ along with two other teenagers, Lorraine Burge and Pat Larkins, who maintained a lifelong friendship and followed the career of Pam and Harry with interest.[21] Pam was given one lesson on how to play the organ by the curate, Harry Edwards. He was very musical, and one night he played the first hymn in the service and then he announced that Pam would play the last, 'Through all the changing scenes of life.' Her career as a church organist was launched. Her complex father cannot have been too displeased because he consented to be choirmaster there at the same time as Pam played the organ. For his part, Harry was to be often grateful throughout his ministry to have an organist with him when he preached.

Harry taught Sunday School for a time at St Aidan's. The Revd John Reimer later recalled: 'you are the first teacher, some of whose words in teaching I still recall, and those words were very significant in my early growth as a Christian.'[22] In the tiny hall behind St Aidan's church, Harry and Pam first met John Chapman (Chappo), who was to become the diocese's most valued evangelist, and who was to train at Moore College with Harry. At that first meeting, Chappo made a big impression by announcing, 'I stand up to preach and sit down to teach and tonight I am going to teach,' and he sat down.

To impress Pamela, Harry took her to watch him play cricket in a game played over two days in the church cricket competition. Harry played for the Banksia Free Church, which was attended by a number of members of the Open Air Campaigners with whom Harry was then a volunteer. Harry scored two centuries, and it was suggested that, as a grade player, he should not play in such a lowly competition. But Pam was impressed as intended. She was not his first girlfriend: she was aware that all the girls loved him because he treated them nicely. But Harry was Pam's only boyfriend. They were engaged in the last year of her nursing training at Marrickville. Pam's father was not pleased: when Harry asked him for Pam's hand in marriage, Kevin did not hide he was disappointed that his daughter was marrying a a member of the clergy. He thought there was no future in that. Pamela thought differently. When Harry proposed, she is reported to have responded, 'I thought you'd never ask.'

Harry had found a very special life partner. Pam proved, in the estimation of friend and counsellor, Margaret Fuller, to be 'amazingly adaptable.' She was a great fighter for Harry and an affirmer of him. She was very present, but not too present. Margaret found her quite a humble person, at times tentative, deferring to those whose advice she sought. Marion Gabbott considers Pam a very competent, warm and thoughtful person. She was not trained as a theologian, and, while she has given Harry plenty of advice over the years, Stephen Gabbott doubts if she ever substantially shaped his thinking. This remarkable observation is probably true: Harry was always very open to advice, but he was not easily influenced even by those closest to him.

A near disaster then threatened to cut short their engagement and everything else. Shortly after Pam became a theatre sister at the Children's Hospital in Camperdown, she and Harry drove down to St Michael's, Wollongong to speak at an evening meeting of their Fellowship Group. By now in Moore College, Harry was driving a vehicle loaned to them by fellow student, Peter Chiswell. On the return journey, late in the evening, Harry turned the car over on a corner of the old road back from Wollongong near Helensburgh. It just happened that the vehicle behind them was an ambulance! Because Pam had trained at Marrickville Hospital, she had great confidence in the medical team there, so the ambulance transported them there. After Pam had her nose packed and stitched, Harry returned her to the Children's Hospital. Then the full force of what might have been struck him.

> I can remember walking back to College from the Children's Hospital, past the King George Hospital in Missenden Road to Carillon Avenue. I was struck by the contrast between the new lives coming to birth at King George and the fact we had almost ended ours a few hours before. I guess I may have been experiencing some measure of shock, but I can vividly remember vowing that I would henceforth take the tenuous character of human life seriously in seeking to draw people to Christ.

Harry later wrote that this near-death experience 'helped me focus my life and work.'[23] It was a life and work from which neither Jesus nor Pam would ever be absent.

# 4

# Moore and Matrimony: One Ordination, Two Callings

Harry studied for three years at Moore College, the diocesan theological training seminary. 'A very unpromising bunch of would-be ordinands entered Moore College in 1955,' Harry later recalled. 'However, as we interspersed water throwing with some study, we as a group of almost all single men grew close together.'[1]

## Moore matters

A year off its centenary, Moore College was not in robust health, or at least that is what its principal, Marcus Loane, thought. The college had a mortgage, and Loane hated being in debt. The previous year, the much-loved Classics tutor, Herbert Minn, had resigned to take up a University post in Auckland, and the four remaining lecturers were inadequately housed. Loane was dissatisfied with the low standard of theological knowledge of the students who had been to Moore in T.C. Hammond's time and was quite determined not to admit anyone without matriculation or its equivalent.[2] Harry was one of three in his student cohort who had not matriculated, as he had not done the Leaving Certificate. He was only admitted to Moore on the condition that, while there, he would complete the remaining examinations for membership in the Australian Society of Accountants, which Loane took to be the equivalent of matriculation. Harry completed all of it apart from taxation, which meant that technically he never satisfied Loane's expectation.

On 4 February 1955, Archbishop Howard Mowll licensed Harry as a catechist in the parish of St Peter at Cook's River, where he was known as 'Handsome Harry'.[3] In April of the same year he took his accountancy exams. He was placed equal third in Australia in Bookkeeping and Accounts with a mark of 85 per cent. It was not training irrelevant to high office in the Anglican Church of Australia. Indeed, the gift was put to immediate use: Harry was the business and sales manager of the college magazine, *Societas*, in his first year.

Marcus Loane had become Moore College principal at the beginning of the previous year. The significance of this both for Harry and the diocese is twofold. First, Marcus was an evangelical whose Anglicanism was important to him: it was to remain so for Harry, too, for the rest of his life. Second, Harry was 'pre-

Broughton.' That is, he did not train (like most of the clergy who elected him and were to work under him) under Broughton Knox when he was principal. The extremely influential Knox cared less than Loane for Anglicanism. True, Knox was vice-principal when Harry studied at Moore, and in 1982, after Loane declined, Harry invited Knox to preach at his consecration as a bishop. In truth, Knox did not, in Harry's time at college, exercise the same dominance as he did after he became principal. Harry was more shaped by Loane's piety than Knox's rationality. 'Marcus was a spellbinding lecturer,' observes Bill Lawton, who entered Moore the year before Harry. 'He became caught up in his subject, transported, his whole being captivated. He spoke poetically, carefully, passionately. He brooked no questions.'[4] Broughton Knox was more interested in propositions than poetry and precision rather than passion. Once in control, he imbued those he trained with a fear of the slippery slope, the conviction that doctrinal error or theological weakness would plunge the diocese into disaster. Harry was no liberal, but he never became obsessed by the slippery slope. A number of Knox-trained clergy thought Harry's Anglicanism and his disinterest in the slippery slope were weaknesses.

The college staff also consisted of two senior resident lecturers: Donald Robinson and Harry Bates. Robinson's esteem for Harry was to be demonstrated when in 1982 he chose Harry to be Bishop of Wollongong and was pleased when, a decade later, Harry was elected archbishop. Harry Bates was among the many clergy who wrote to Harry on his elevation to the episcopate in 1982. He had, he recalled, the 'happiest of recollections of fellowship' with Harry at college and, referring to Harry's years at Coorparoo in Queensland, had been delighted some 16 years later to witness 'the finished product' as Harry 'presided over the work of one of the leading churches in Brisbane.'[5] Bates taught Church History, Hebrew and voice production at Moore College. Perhaps from him may be traced the English inflection that so many Moore graduates employed when preaching. Harry, for example, spoke, not of the Holy Spirit, but the Hurley Spirit.

At college, the book that most impressed Harry was Luther's *Bondage of the Will* and he also read, as required, Calvin's *Institutes*. He bought the old Beveridge edition of *The Institutes* and read it in the bus before he entered college. A strong dose of Calvin was good for him. It made his faith more objective, less given to self-indulgent introspection. Harry had a fairly tender conscience and he suspected that at times it was not always particularly healthy.

If Harry was then something of a pietist in his spirituality and remained so, he was comfortable with the Sydney evangelicalism of his day. It was then becoming more intellectual even if it had not become as rationalistic as it was to become under Broughton Knox. English evangelicalism was then attempting to defend itself against the charge that it was fundamentalist, obscurantist and anti-intellectual. It was also while he was at Moore College that Harry was treated to the sublime scholarship of Edwin Judge, resident tutor in 1957 appointed to teach Ancient History to ordinands. Then a young lecturer at Sydney University and subsequently Professor of History at Macquarie University, Judge contributed massively to the intellectual defence of Christianity, not by aggressive polemical apologetics, but by unassailable scholarship. Harry did not aspire himself to be an intellectual, but he respected the vocation of the Christian academic, enjoyed learning about and debating their findings, and never found it necessary, as did some in the Pietist tradition, to put down the mind in order to promote the heart.

At college, there were lively debates on Keswick spirituality, a movement that fostered personal intimacy with Jesus in the power of the Spirit. There was keen debate over whether being 'crucified with Christ' (Gal 2:20) meant conquering the power of sin as well as its penalty. The argument of such books as L.E. Maxwell, *Born Crucified* (1945), then closely read at Moore College, was that sin results in death, but Christ has conquered death and therefore sin, and to be identified with Christ was to be put beyond 'the touch and the reach of sin.'[6] There was some awareness of the dangers of 'sinless perfection',[7] but this did not dampen the hunger for personal holiness. Marcus Loane brought out ardent souls such as Larry Love to inspire the students with their spiritual duty. The author of *Called to be Saints* and *Called to be Servants*, he was all for encouraging people to rise early to pray and meditate on the Scriptures. Harry has never given up on the disciplines.

The archbishop, Howard Mowll, was not then to Harry the great hero that he was to become in Sydney legend. He has since cast his shadow over all his successors, largely because of his reputation as 'an initiating Father-in-God.' By Harry's time as a Moore College student, the wind had almost gone out of his sails, although he was still an imposing figure. Harry went to see him early in 1958 to be interviewed before he was priested, and he asked Harry what he would do in a new housing area. Harry was 'burbling on' when he realised that the archbishop had fallen asleep.

Marcus Loane, more than Mowll, was a hero to Harry. Loane used to refer to Harry's cohort at college as 'the last of my boys.' He saw them in a special light. In his final year at college (1957), Harry was Deputy Senior Student. The Senior Student was Dudley Foord, who was to be consecrated bishop two years after Harry. He was eight years older than Harry and had been a tutor in Physics in the University of Sydney and then worked for the Ford Motor Company. He

4.1 The Moore College Class of 1957: (Rear) Don Allen, John Holle, Hugh Voss, Cecil Kelley, Duncan Pierce, John Collins, Graham Goldsworthy, Henry Radcliffe, Barry Slamon; (Centre) Les Vitnell, Ward Powers, John Emery, Bill Lawton, Allan Lang, Fred Edwards, John Jones, Owen Weaver, Trevor Thorburn, Ron Herbert; (Front) Michael Eagle, Richard Hosking, Barry Marsh, Dudley Foord, Marcus Loane, Harry Goodhew, Jim Taylor, Robert Dowthwaite, Ken Baker, John Imisides (Ray Wheeler was away at a funeral).

was President of Sydney EU in 1950 and the InterVarsity Fellowship organising secretary for the 1951 Sydney University mission which has gone down in history as arguably the best organised and the most fruitful: Dudley never departed from the conviction that the Holy Spirit has no objection to good organisation! Harry would agree with him. Dudley and Harry became arguably the most effective leaders of the local church of their generation.

Those familiar with the history of the diocese will recognise many of Harry's fellow students as much respected ministers of the gospel. They remained in many cases important to each other through the years of service ahead. They included: Ken Baker, who was to succeed Harry as Rector of Coorparoo in Brisbane diocese; Rob Beal, a medical student who was allowed to stay in college as he was the chapel organist; he later became Director of the South Australian blood bank and a widely recognised haematologist and Harry was to become Godfather of one of his children; Don Cameron, assistant bishop in the Sydney diocese; John Chapman, in college for a year, one of Australia's most effective evangelists; Geoff Clarke, who received first-class honours in the ThL, a hospital chaplain for much of his ministry; Robbie Douthwaite from South Africa; John Emery, an outstanding preacher; Graeme Goldsworthy, later lecturer in Old Testament at Moore College; Ronald Herbert, who served in the Diocese of Brisbane; John Holle and Michael Eagle, both with high-church inclinations, the former of marked pastoral gifts, the latter served in Tasmania; John Imisides, later Rector of Shellharbour, who left the Anglican Church under the influence of the Charismatic movement; Frank Johnson and Cecil Kelley, both Anglo-Catholics, the former becoming a Roman Catholic; John Jones, naval chaplain; Tony Lamb, respected for his staunch evangelicalism; Bill Lawton, revered lecturer in theology at Moore College; Barry Marsh, always alert to the heritage of the diocese; Ward Powers, who lectured in numerous theological colleges; Jim Taylor, missionary to Indigenous Australians; Ray Wheeler, archetypal evangelical minister; and Les Vitnell, who succeeded Harry as Rector of Carlingford and did good work directing ministries to new housing areas.

Peter O'Brien, three years behind Harry, recalls that Harry, more than anyone, pastored younger students. On the eve of Harry's election as archbishop, Peter, now lecturing in New Testament at the college, described Harry as 'the finest minister Moore College has ever produced.' It helped that he was part of one of the finest cohorts of students to train at the college. The Class of '57 continued to meet annually on the anniversary of their ordination (2 March).

In the intimacy of Moore College it was hard to keep a secret, and Bill Lawton even knew what was under Harry's bed: a carton full of many volumes of the works of John Owen, the Puritan divine, which he had picked up second hand. Donald Robinson, then vice-principal, told Harry that he would never read them. Harry confesses that he did not read them all, but what he did read he found strengthening. Already Harry had a heart and head for the most robust of spiritual writers, as well as the devotional works popular with the Keswick movement. And he was strong in body as in spirit. 'Harry was muscular,' Bill Lawton recalls,

> he was extraordinarily well built. He took me in hand because I was very puny. He did body building with me. He had me weight-lifting. He ran regularly around St Paul's oval and he had a group of people who used to run with him.

Bill also considered that Harry had strong convictions, which was common enough at Moore, coupled with a liberality of mind, which was a rarer quality. He was open to influences from others. He would not necessarily change his mind, but he allowed such influences to stimulate his thinking and his responses.[8] The combination of unwavering conviction and unfailing openness to new ideas was to be a lifelong characteristic.

In his second year, Harry passed in Old Testament, New Testament (English), Doctrine, Church History, and New Testament (Greek), but the college registrar, Frank Cash, sent Harry a copy of the result on which was written, 'Pass in all subjects ... EXCEPT, alas, Prayer Book.' It was not the last time Harry would be adjudged to have let the diocese down when it came to the prayer book! In 1995 at synod he failed to persuade his brethren to give a fair trial to the proposed *A Prayer Book for Australia*.

Harry was awarded the Licentiate in Theology (Th.L.) through the Australian College of Theology with second-class honours in 1957. In his first year out in 1958, he was awarded the Moore College diploma with second-class honours. T.C. Hammond instructed him on Cranmer and the Lord's Supper. This time Harry made up for his lack of performance two years earlier, coming first in that class. Donald Robinson was surprised with Harry's high mark, as 'T.C.' had a reputation as a hard marker. Cranmer's thought continued to influence Harry after he became archbishop. 'He spoilt me for all these other things,' says Harry, with reference to novel departures like lay presidency.

Though a catechist at Cook's River in his first and third year at Moore, he spent the middle year attached to St Mark's Revesby. Jim Keith, later science lecturer and lay reader, had just become a Christian the year before and he recalls that Harry's series of sermons on Romans made great sense of his new-found faith. He thought Harry amazingly erudite because he spoke of 'eons' instead of ages. He was so impressed by Harry's preaching that he persuaded his mother to come to church with him. She was completely unchurched, and Harry performed up to expectations. He preached what Jim considered a quite magnificent sermon. When Jim asked his mother what she thought of it, she replied coolly that Harry would probably make quite a good preacher 'in a few years.' Jim had just started at University, and Harry kept hinting that he really should join the EU. When he eventually did so, he was not disappointed. Jim also recalls that there was a young woman in the congregation who was quite desirous that Harry would marry her, so Jim used to tease her with a ditty rhyming 'Harry' with 'marry'. She was devastated when Harry turned up at St Mark's with Pam, his fiancé.[9]

## Marriage and ordination

Harry was made a deacon on the second Sunday in Lent, 2 March 1958, by Archbishop Howard Mowll. The pre-ordination retreat was taken by the archbishop, together with evangelical hero, C.H. Nash. The Principal of the Melbourne Bible Institute, Nash was highly esteemed by Mowll.[10] He was then in the 92nd and final year of his life.

The ordination service had originally been set for 28 February, and Harry, as was the custom, arranged to be married on the Saturday following his ordination. But the Queen Mother came to town, and the ordination date was changed to accommodate the Royal Visit. Archbishop Mowll asked Harry if he could change the date of his wedding. 'If I did, Sir,' said Harry, 'I fear you will have one less ordinand, as my father-in-law will kill me.' Not wishing to be responsible for a homicide, Mowll gave permission for Harry to be married on the day before his ordination. The Church survived this unprecedented break with tradition.

Indeed, it may have been providential. When Pam reflects on the remarkable closeness between her and Harry throughout the decades of their team ministry, she wonders if it may have had something to do with the fact that they were married before Harry was ordained. Right from the start of their married life, she thought of their ministry that 'we are in this together.' True, she concedes, at the ordination no-one laid hands on her, but she thought that possibly God had done just that. Not that this was a mystical experience exactly; Pam believes that it was largely cultural. When a woman married in the 1950s, it normally spelled the end of her own career, replacing it with involvement in her husband's career. It was also partly spiritual: they had both been brought up on stories of deeply committed Christian couples, such as Hudson and Maria Taylor, who together endured great hardship for the sake of the gospel in China.

Pam was very clear right from the beginning that her role as Harry's wife was to facilitate him in ministry. But, ever the realist, she did not believe she was all that significantly involved in Harry's career for many years, and that she was content to occupy a behind-the-scenes role. She would look after the children and let him get on with ministry. Yet, while she did not seek a prominent role for herself, Harry sought to promote her right from the start. From the very beginning of their marriage, Harry talked over everything with her. He was the one, she recognised, who had the training and the exposure to new ideas and speakers, and she was grateful that he shared all this with her. She felt Harry was 'training' her.

Not all wives would rejoice at the thought that their husbands were 'training' them, but they both appreciated that he had received training and that it was good to share it. Pam always felt that Harry's 'training' meant she was able to keep up, not only with his plans for ministry, but also with 'the world of theology', of which Harry always kept abreast. Pam only became conscious that there was anything unusual in this when they were ministering to a member of the clergy and his teary wife, whose complaint was that she never knew what he was thinking or what was going on.

Harry never manifested the type of sexism that seeks to keep women out of the male domain. Quite the reverse. Harry always urged Pam to do more, to go beyond her comfort zone, and to attempt those things she felt nervous about. She felt that her upbringing had left her without confidence in many areas of social interaction. She acquired a reputation for being forthright, but, in that, she was something of a surprise to herself as she felt in her early life that she never had an opinion about anything that she was confident enough to express. It was Harry who gave her that confidence, and while he sometimes laughed nervously or pressed her hand at a forthright pronouncement from her, he had only himself to blame. He was not himself habitually forthright, and sometimes he needed her to be that on his behalf. It was between the two of them that the truth was spoken in love, with Pam emphasising the first half of the equation and Harry the second!

Harry was married to Pamela Coughlan on 1 March 1958 by Revd Ken Leask at St Peter's, Cook's River. Marcus Loane preached at the wedding on Matthew 6:33: 'seek ye first the kingdom of God, and his righteousness; and all these things shall be added unto you' (KJV). Loane had been consecrated as a bishop in the week prior to their wedding and he always remarked to Pam afterwards that their wedding was the first occasion on which he 'got dressed up.'

Harry and Pam are so different in personality that it seemed reasonable to ask their daughters, 'given that your parents are just so different from each other, why do you think they chose to marry each other?' But both Robyn and Wendy were astonished by the question and both said, quite independently of each other, that they had never thought of it. Pressed now to think of it for the first time, Robyn wondered if Harry had been attracted to Pam's dedication. Wendy suggested that in the early years of marriage people grow together in order to make it work, and maybe Pam and Harry were not all that different at first, but that over the years the differences between them are accentuated as each trusts the other to be true to himself or herself. An interesting and perceptive insight! Preaching at a marriage renewal service when he was archbishop and 38 years into his own marriage, he observed that it was necessary marriage should be a lifelong bond: 'God has created everyone as unique. That means there will be some incompatibility in every marriage. It takes time and indissolubility to enable this to work.'[11]

# 5

# Early Parish Experience: A Lot of Visiting

Harry's career in the church made him a widely experienced parish man, in city and country, in the Diocese of Sydney and elsewhere. He was a highly effective motivator of lay people and left a legacy of strong and loving congregations. Before his appointment as archdeacon in 1979, he was to serve in six parishes.

## Bondi, 1958

Harry's first curacy was at St Matthew's, Bondi. He was licensed as curate to the rector, James Noble, on 2 March 1958. While the Rector worked St Matthew's, Bondi, Harry ministered principally at St Andrew's, Bondi Beach. He was to be paid in monthly installments, the first of which was not due until April Fool's Day, so Harry was in no danger of losing his trim figure, and nothing was done to dispel the rumour that clerical families are in some danger of malnutrition. It did not help that Harry and Pam were broke at the beginning of their marriage. John Chapman came to the rescue. He gave Harry and Pam £25, a large sum in those days, enabling them to put down a deposit on a bedroom suite.[1] Jim Noble left soon after Harry arrived, and Harry spent part of his year working there on his own before David Crawford, who conducted most of his ministry in beach-side suburbs, arrived.

For the work at Bondi Beach, the church had purchased a two-storey set of flats. The lower floor became the church, church vestry, Sunday school rooms, and bathroom; the upper floor was the residence. The downstairs bathroom boasted an old bath of ample proportions. The chief challenge was choosing a time when there was no call by someone from the church wanting to use the bathroom.

It was in this salubrious environment that Harry and Pam spent their first night together following their wedding. As they sat having supper in their

5.1 Harry with Pam, Bondi, 1958.

small dining room with a window overlooking the next-door unit, Harry noticed a smile of embarrassment on Pam's face. She whispered, 'There is a man undressing for bed next door.' The man in question obviously realised that he was being observed. He dashed out of view. He then reached gingerly with one arm for the cord to lower the blind. In the process, he somehow twisted the cord so that the blind would not come down. He then pulled at it to get it to come down, and in so doing tore the blind. From that time on the blind remained down and torn, a permanent reminder of their first night together.

There were other firsts. Clothing was dried on a clothesline held up by the traditional prop. Pam's first wash finished up in a muddy heap when the prop broke, depositing the contents of the line on the sparsely grassed backyard.

Another first came at the end of the year when Harry was thoroughly taken in by a professional con man. While Pam was in hospital expecting Robyn, their first child, a vagrant came to the front door armed with a doctor's letter indicating that he had been hospitalised and for the time being had nowhere to stay. Harry took him in, fed him, and gave him a bed for a couple of nights only to discover that it was he who had been taken in.

It was also at Bondi, after taking a funeral for someone he did not really know, that for the first and only time he was asked directly whether the deceased had gone to heaven or hell. He had just climbed into the funeral director's car with the wife and daughter of the deceased. Harry was a little startled by the daughter's direct and challenging question, but he knew that she had asked it seriously. He said, 'To go to heaven people need to turn to Christ, and one never knows what anyone does in their dying moments.'

A claim to fame from their time at North Bondi was their association with comic actor, Garry McDonald. His parents, Reuben and Moyra, worshipped at North Bondi, and Garry and his brother were members of the Sunday school. Reuben was in the rag trade and was a warden and synodsman. Moyra was 'the classiest lady in the church' and very kind, lending Harry her car when he needed it during the whole year they were in North Bondi. She fell pregnant and said, 'This is Harry Goodhew's fault.' She had confided to Harry that she wanted another child. Harry prayed that she would, and she had a little girl. Although Harry was only at Bondi for 12 months, Moyra declared 'Mark my words. Harry will be an Archbishop one day.'

The children from the Bondi Beach Sunday school were instrumental in a remarkable conversion. It is a very Jewish area, and living next door was a Jewish woman who heard the children singing choruses during Sunday school. One day she met Harry when shopping and she asked him for the words of the songs. Harry discovered that she was laboriously reading through an English Bible seeking to know God, patiently listing the words that she did not understand and needed to look up in a dictionary. She was somewhere in Kings or Chronicles when Harry called on her. She had to do her seeking quietly as she did not wish to raise the opposition of her Jewish husband. Harry showed her pictures, then produced by the Lutherans, of biblical themes such as the crossing of the Red Sea and of events in the life of Christ. She was mesmerised by them because they were based on the Old and New Testaments and she had not realised that they were both one. She was converted and became involved with the Jewish Christian Mission.

Right from the start, Harry's winsomeness and leadership qualities were strongly in evidence. So too was his appetite for pastoral work. He did a lot of visiting. It was during his time at Bondi that for the first time he sat up all night with someone who was dying. On another visit, he could hardly squeeze into a hoarder's home, which was full of newspapers. Beach suburbs are notoriously difficult areas in which to reach teenagers, having to compete with an alternative religion: surfing. Fifty-six years later, after a church service in Brisbane, Pam met Roslyn Fewtrall, who had been 16-year-old girl in the church at Bondi in 1958, and recognised her. Pam was thrilled that she was going on with the Lord.

Towards the end of their first year, on the Festival of St Thomas the Apostle, 21 December 1958, Harry was ordained to the priesthood. Bp W.G. Hilliard officiated. He was then administrator of the diocese, Archbishop Mowll having died on 24 October. Leon Morris, who had returned from his labours with BCA to lecture at Ridley College in Melbourne, took the pre-ordination retreat.

Archbishop of Canterbury, Michael Ramsey, was to declare Holy Orders a vocation of 'unique difficulty and unique happiness.'[2] Harry was now set to make this dual discovery for himself. But the first difficulty he faced was due to his common humanity, not his special vocation. While Harry was at his ordination retreat, Pam gave birth to Robyn at St Luke's Hospital, Potts Point. Robyn had an uncertain start in life, and, on the day of Harry's ordination, was transferred to King George V Hospital, without Pam, where she remained for a number of weeks. Having gone into hospital from North Bondi, Pam was to come home to their next church, St Bede's at Beverly Hills, still without her new baby. How hard was that for her? Life had to go on. There was no time then to dwell on how hard it was. But over 50 years later, in Figtree Church, the minister spoke of his own first baby and how amazing it was to bring it home. And Pam found herself sobbing. She could not contain herself and she thought 'what is wrong with me?'

All those years later, Pam accepted that it had been hard – very hard. She was away from Harry for months. She had toxaemia and, from about 6 months on in her pregnancy, struggled with blood pressure and fluid in her legs. She was hospitalised and then sent home to her parents for a week and then back to hospital and then home for a week. She was a month in hospital before the birth, while others came and went home with their babies. The staff made a bit of a joke of it, saying that she had been there since the hospital was built, a slight exaggeration as the hospital was built in 1919. In the first weeks, Pam would express milk and Harry drive it into the hospital and it was just tipped into a big vat with everybody else's breast milk. Robyn did not even get her own mother's milk. For two weeks Pam did not see Robyn at all. On the day Harry was ordained, Robyn cried all day. She was in hospital for six weeks after her birth. She continued to suffer appallingly with constipation, and Harry and Pam had to take her to Royal Prince Alfred Hospital and sit with her all day while she screamed. She went into an operation screaming at being separated from her mother, and she came out screaming and they just gave her to Pam and said, 'take her.' She had a pyloric spasm and a hiatus hernia causing her to bring up all her milk. Pam recalls that so many people said, 'we cannot understand why this is happening to you; you are such good people.' Even a minister said that to her, but Pam thought this was not great theology. Instead, she discovered that she had to rely on God and not on herself. In spite of all, they did not think of Robyn primarily as someone who was sick, though she was in fact very sick. Instead they thought of her as 'a cute little thing.'

## Beverly Hills, 1959–63

Bp Hilliard inducted Harry as curate-in-charge of the new provisional district of St Bede's, Beverly Hills, on 16 January 1959. It had been a branch of St John's, Penshurst. Here the next two of their four children were born: David (1961) and Wendy (1962). Robyn did not flourish and was so short that she could walk under a table without hitting her head. But she was not without character. During a visit from Archbishop Gough, Mowll's successor, she was sitting in her high chair at tea time, and she said to their guest who was drinking a cup of tea, 'Watch out you don't spill it.'

The work at Beverly Hills grew quickly and strongly under Harry, becoming a provisional parish in 1961. Part of the reason for its growth at this time was that the 1959 Billy Graham Crusade resulted in many being added to the church. At the Crusade, Harry was adviser to counsellors.[3] Another reason for the growth was that Chappo, then working in the Diocese of Armidale, would regularly visit them for the evening service. In the rectory at Beverly Hills afterwards, he would talk, and the young would listen for hours, so that parents would call to see where their children were. The males left their Brylcream stains on the wallpaper in the lounge room where they sat on the floor. Chappo was a speaker of astonishing power, but he himself would say even then that the best preacher in Sydney is Harry Goodhew. Harry's children loved Chappo. They called him Uncle John.

Harry also welcomed the brilliant and riotously funny Dr Alan Cole, Moore College lecturer, as a missioner at Beverly Hills. Alan always remembered that an irreverent member of the team referred to it as the mission at 'B-Hills'.[4] What he never knew was that, when he stayed with the Goodhews for the mission, he was put into a room behind a frosted glass window, which he thought made him invisible. He was in the habit of coming to the door in his underpants and sticking his head around the door to regale Harry and Pam with some typically wry observation on the world, unaware that they were observing more of the missioner than he knew. Alan always refused to take money for his services. If any were pressed upon him, he would give it away. So, when Harry found out that Alan would really love to have a rice-paper concordance, Harry bought it for him. Much thumbed by this greatest of Bible teachers, it was on Alan's desk when, 45 years later, he died.[5] After Harry became archbishop, no-one would give him more advice than Alan Cole.

Though so recently ordained, Harry was soon in the business of training clergy. He was guest lecturer in New Testament for the Church Army training college in 1962 and 1963. He also spoke at missions in other parishes during this period. For example, he and Ken Short took a mission in the nearby suburb of Punchbowl, Ken speaking to the adults and Harry taking the children's meetings. Ken was to play a major role in Harry's life, preceding him as Bishop of Wollongong. Further afield, fellow Moore College student, Ray Smith, invited Harry to conduct a 'Friendship Evangelism Campaign' in his Parish of Ashford in the Armidale diocese. Ray recalls that many were converted who became very involved in the life of the parish, which became then 'really alive.'[6] Ray 'thought the world of Harry' and, when in 1976 Clive Kerle retired at Bishop of Armidale, Ray was eager to nominate Harry as his successor.

5.2 Parish cricket team, Beverly Hills, 1960. Harry at front, second on the left.

They enjoyed a long friendship of mutual respect in the cause of the gospel, and Ray would serve under Harry as an assistant bishop.

Harry's legacy at Beverly Hills lived long. Twenty years after he left, on his consecration as Bishop of Wollongong, his 'friends in Christ' at St Bede's gave him a 'superb' robes case to hold his new episcopal vesture. Many a prophetic word is spoken in jest. Almost 20 years after Harry left Beverly Hills, and five days before he even knew that he would be made a bishop, Beverly Hills parishioner, Eric Marchoni, wrote to Harry.

> I was elevated to the holy office of Warden this year so that may be some divine direction that Richard Henry may be, one day, elevated to the office of Bishop of the Anglican Church in Australia???!!! Be extremely hard for me to call you "Your Grace", being steeped in low church, authorised version, 1662 Prayer Book background, voting Labour [sic] – following South Sydney![7]

Another parishioner, Tom Muir, who worked in the public service, prayed for Harry daily from his Beverly Hills' days, believing that God had something particular for him to do. His wife, Val, gave Harry a small travelling communion set, which he used throughout his ministry. Tom was to be in the synod in which Harry was elected.

## Ceduna Mission 1963–6

A deputation to the church at Beverly Hills by Bill Rich of BCA spoke of the vacancy in the remote outback at the old Mission at Ceduna in South Australia, and the need to have it filled. Harry felt constrained. He prayed about it and talked with Marcus Loane, then assistant bishop, and with Jack Dain, CMS federal secretary and later Assistant Bishop of Sydney. Dain recalled this interview as a 'fragrant' memory.[8] The Goodhew family then spent three years with BCA in Ceduna. The Archbishop of Sydney wrote,

> I shall be very sorry to lose you from this Diocese but I am glad that you are willing to accept this challenge to special service and I hope that we shall have the pleasure of having you back again in due course.[9]

The Ceduna Mission District, then in the Diocese of Adelaide, was the size of Victoria, stretching from Smoky Bay in the east to the WA border and north to the transcontinental railway line. It was then said to be the largest parish in Australia, with about 80,000 square miles of territory. Harry's job involved ministry to far-flung communities on farms, sheep stations, and railway outposts or 'sidings', of which there were 25 in Harry's day.[10] These mission trips took him away from home for up to six weeks at a time. There were regular Sunday services at five of the district centres and weekday services at a further three or four.[11] At Ceduna itself, Harry was the minister in a large team of BCA workers, and he took two services on Sundays in the local church, St Michael and All Angels. He was also the Mission to Seamen Chaplain at Thevenard, the deep-sea port just south of Ceduna, a role he described as interesting.

Since 1925 the BCA had staffed Ceduna's community hospitals with nurses, and the Flying Medical Service operated from there. They were a great gift to the town, enabling its development through the provision of medical security.[12] BCA was also essential to the financial viability of the church, as the region was often afflicted with drought and depressed wheat and wool prices.[13] Dust storms were endemic: one minister (Ken Rogers) announced that any farmers in the district missing their top soil should call at the rectory to collect it.[14]

The BCA nurses were devout Christians, eager to evangelise as well as to heal. Matron Florence Dowling, who had already been at Ceduna for decades, was of the old school, 'a Dohnavur-mission type', Harry recalls. She idolised Amy Carmichael, the Keswick missionary, who worked for half a century at Dohnavur in India, rescuing girls from temple prostitution and establishing the Sisters of the Common Life, an evangelical religious order for single women. Matron Dowling stood no nonsense: 'If you were in hospital and very sick and you heard Sister Dowling coming down the corridor, you suddenly became much better.'[15] Another nursing sister, Betty Tierney, was to keep track of Harry's subsequent career. Yet another sister who was there in Harry's time was Vera Holle. She frequently housed Harry in the mortuary at the BCA hospital in Penong, 70 km west of Ceduna. Among those who visited Harry and Pam while they were at Ceduna and enjoyed their hospitality was Dianne Sidebottom from Beverly Hills parish. She was accompanied by Joy O'Neill who ended up working for BCA for 24 years.[16]

One of the single nurses in Harry's time was Mavis Bell. She came up to the communion rail after a night on duty and when everyone else left she was still there, fast asleep. She encouraged a farmer, Robert Skinner, who left the Navy in the same year as Harry arrived in Ceduna, to attend church, which he did occasionally. Mavis fell in love with Bob's father, Ernest, a widower. Their wedding was in Melbourne on Saturday, 11 June 1966. Harry, Bob and Ern drove to Melbourne in Ern's Holden ute, leaving just the day before the wedding. On the way, Ern spotted a galah, high in the sky, and said 'I wonder what that is a sign of.' Bob replied that it was a sign of a high-flying galah, a response which all on the bench seat of the ute considered very funny. In Melbourne, Harry took the wedding service, and Bob, who was his dad's best man, made a speech about as long as his observation on the galah. After the reception, Harry and Bob climbed into Mavis's yellow Mini Minor and drove all night back to Ceduna. Bob drove too fast and the Mini's motor was never the same again. The round trip was 2,500 kilometres, all in three days. Harry gave Bob a New Testament in memory of the trip which he read 'cover to cover and it changed my life for the better.'[17]

5.3 Reunion of BCA workers in Adelaide, November 1994.

'They were good women, great women,' Harry says of the BCA nurses. 'They were indeed,' Pam agrees.[18] In October of their first year at Ceduna, Pam gave birth to their fourth child, Philip. Her waters broke a month before he was due. Pam was rushed into hospital, which was just down the road. Matron Dowling came into the Goodhew home, packed bags for each of the three children, and dispatched them to other homes to be looked after for the duration of the emergency. If there was not a lot happening at the hospital, she would send one of the staff to the rectory to help with the ironing. No rest for the saints! Matron Dowling regularly had the Goodhews to the hospital for Sunday lunch. She would direct Pam to one of the bedrooms to lie down and rest, and she arranged for children, frequently Aboriginal children, to play with the Goodhew children. 'She had me under her thumb,' recalls Pam, 'but she was a mother figure, and she was very kind.'

The family was now complete, and it was a happy one. Robyn, who was five when they moved to Ceduna, remembers being content there. They had pets: Pompom, a lamb, and Pal, a dog, who was 'some sort of animal we could all sit on.' Her fondness for these pets sowed the seed of her desire to become a vet. Wendy remembers that they had another dog, which was far from nice; this may explain why she did not become a vet. Robyn started school there, walking two miles along the railway track to catch the school bus. She recalls that Belita, an Indigenous woman, could make such an impressive bird call that her father recorded it, and she remembers going to the BCA hospital to have her ears 'syringed out' by Sister Holle and Sister Hope. David's first memories are of Ceduna: he remembers his

5.4 Family (now completed by the birth of Philip) at the Ceduna Mission, 1964. Left to right: David, Harry, Wendy, Philip, Pam, Robyn.

father chopped the head off a chook and it ran around the yard, and he remembers the squeal of crabs as they were dropped into boiling water. He remembers his mother washed his mouth out with soap because he told someone to shut up. Wendy recalls a holiday the family had in a shack in Smoky Bay, 45 km south-east of Ceduna. Eleven mouse traps were set on the first night and 22 mice met their end. Wendy also recalls that a green snake came into the kitchen, probably in search of mice. Pam ordered the children up on to a table and waved a stick at the intruder until it disappeared through an opening in the corrugated iron wall. Harry was absent from this drama, but Pam rang him, and he came and removed his family from danger.

A parishioner who became a lifelong friend of the Goodhews at Ceduna was Dulcie Wright. Her experience is evidence of Harry's trademark use of lay people to build the church. Born and bred locally, Dulcie was married to Ken, co-owner of the grocery store in Ceduna when Harry was there, and something of a legend in the town: footballer, firefighter, a 'do anything for anyone sort of person.' He was also a church warden, synod representative and lay reader. Dulcie was always involved with the church, but she came to believe that before Harry came she was a seeker, who sought to please God out of duty. Harry put out a questionnaire to find out what his parishioners wanted him to preach on or what they thought they needed. He also distributed books to church members, including *The Reason Why*, and he listed books that they might read. She remembers Calvin was on the list. Then Harry asked her and a friend, Val Puckeridge (a nurse), to take Religious Instruction in the local school. Dulcie did not have a job at the time, so she thought she'd 'give it a go.' They gave it half an hour and could not get home quickly enough and had a strong coffee to recover.

> The kids were not feral like they are now, but it was such a drama. Anyway, we did it for a while, and the main thing is that I learned a lot. I learned how to teach and I got involved with the Sunday School. Val became the most faithful and spiritual of Christians.[19]

In fact, Val's pilgrimage, like Dulcie's was one from nominal to assured faith, and Harry was instrumental in that, too. Ever the keen evangelist, he once stopped Val in the street and asked her if she knew that she was going to heaven. She thought about that a lot afterwards and years later, when she heard that Harry was preaching in Broome, Western Australia, to which she had relocated, she sought him out and confessed that she had not then had that assurance, even though she had taught Religious Instruction at Harry's invitation at Ceduna. She added that she hoped he would not mind, but since then she had become a Charismatic. Harry did not mind.

Dulcie's recollections paint a vivid picture of what life must have been like, especially for Pam, during their ministry at Ceduna.

> I can still see Harry's little tribe all sitting up the front in church. I remember him saying that it was a pity he was stuck out the front when he really should be down there helping Pam sort out the children. On the World Day of Prayer, Pam was invited to speak, and I drove her up to Penong. The poor girl by the time she had dealt with everything at home, when she got in the car, she was still working on her message. She said, 'That's it – I can't think any more'. But we had a lovely time anyway. Her social outing was to walk up the street and visit the BCA sisters in the hospital just for an hour or so while Harry looked after the children.[20]

'City-slickers', such as Harry, were bound to get into trouble in the Australian outback, and Tom Mayne, who worked on the radio base at Ceduna, tells the following stories about two such incidents.

> Harry and I decided to go across country to Tarcoola, on the trans line to visit BCA nurses who were stationed there. We travelled west down the highway from Ceduna and then turned off and headed north through the scrub (as we were told by one of the locals) until we came to a windmill. 'All you do then is follow the track,' he said. We then discovered there were numerous tracks! ... After driving around (probably in circles for half an hour or so), Harry decided that he would have to suffer the embarrassment and call Tarcoola on the car HF radio

and tell them we were lost. They thought this was a great joke, having to 'talk us in'.[21]

Harry was having mosquito problems and the most likely source was larvae in the tank water, so on one of his preaching trips to places like Mudamuckla and Nunjikompita (where I usually accompanied him to teach Sunday School) he was yarning to an old hand about his mosquito problems. 'Oh ya just put a bit o' kero inta the tank, mate.' So on returning home, Harry emptied half a bucket of kerosene into his water tank: Disaster! The tank had to be drained and water tanked in to replace the lost water. In the meantime, buckets were carted from the Maynes to the Goodhews. Another day in the life of a Bush Padre.[22]

One day Harry dropped in on the Maynes because he wanted to see Tom, but he was out fixing a radio receiver for a local farmer. Pattie, as Harry called her, was in the kitchen cleaning fish. She was crying and deeply distressed. She had two young children and was not managing. She was, she explained to Harry, near to having a nervous breakdown. One of the children had suffered an accident, and she felt an overwhelming failure as a mother. She was distraught and just wanted to go back home to Sydney, but felt guilty about leaving Tom. To her surprise, Harry without hesitation told her to go back to Sydney with the children. 'We'll look after Tom', he assured her. So, she did, 'I took the little girls, aged 2 & 3, and travelled back to Sydney, knowing that Harry had given me permission to leave and I was not deserting "the Lord's work".' Some weeks later she returned to Ceduna to pack and to leave 'properly' with Tom. It was then that she told Harry that he would one day be a bishop.[23]

The deep-seated reason for Patricia's distress emerged much later. She had been abused as a child and then later as a young woman by her minister. It was at Ceduna that memories of the abuse 'were beginning to surface almost constantly.' Harry knew none of this then and indeed only learned of it 30 years later when he and Pam were at Bishopscourt. Then, reports Patricia, 'Harry came to the rescue and organised counselling for me with the Anglican Counselling Centre – the best gift I could have ever wished to receive.' Over 50 years later, at the age of 83, she was awarded a doctorate by the Australian Catholic University for a thesis on sexual abuse in the Anglican Church.

Tom Mayne also observed Harry's pastoral gifts at close range at Ceduna and admired them.

He was a person of strong convictions and there was never any doubt about where he stood. But he had a likable, approachable, warm personality and he was always welcome at the outstations and hospitals on the Trans-Australian [railway] lines. Even then he displayed qualities of leadership, mediating decisively in crises or difficult times with Christian grace. He would always get down on his knees before he became involved in a fight.[24]

Another of Harry's co-workers was Stan Hummerston, who was director of the medical service at Ceduna. He observed that Harry's strength was his humility and his dependence on God.

In the pastoral area, there is none better. I witnessed his firmness in dealing with an alcoholic. He is firm when he needs to be. But he really listens to people and he gives them responsibility. He was always working to get the Parish to stand on its own two feet. It did, and it's been a strong evangelical parish ever since.

A pattern seemed to be emerging in Harry's character: firm when he had to be, 'but never aggressive.'[25] The reason why the iron in Harry's relationship with transgressors was rarely observed was not because it was absent, but because it was private. He was careful not to embarrass people, so the rare rebuking that did come from his lips was never in front of others.

Harry's three years at Ceduna were to become looked on as the stuff of legends. It helped that he took 9 wickets for 11 runs in a cricket final. The following day (Sunday), the Smoky Bay team thought they should honour him. They all went to church and sat in the back row. Harry said, 'What's this? Is this a church parade?' They replied, 'We suppose it is in a way.' 'Well,' said Harry, 'if it's a church parade you will have to sit up the front,' and he moved them all up the front. A legacy of Harry's ministry was that subsequent clergy were always asked 'Can you bowl?'[26]

5.5 Harry and Pam catch up with double amputee, Bob Ryan, in a visit to Ceduna in 1980.

Later in 1980, Harry, by then Archdeacon of Wollongong, addressed a church growth conference at Port Lincoln, South Australia. He was received very warmly and was invited, while there, to pay a visit to Ceduna. He recalls that the women welcomed Pam back with open arms. She had not felt at the time that she was particularly involved in the work of ministry there because of her responsibility to raise their young family of four children, and was secretary of the kindergarten. On one occasion she won a prize for being the friendliest person in town, and, when she expressed her astonishment, she was told that 'when you go down the street, you smile at everyone.' She said, 'that is because I don't know anybody by name and therefore feel that I should say good day to everyone.'

Among those who met with Harry at that reunion was diabetic, stroke victim and double amputee, Bob Ryan. He had been a parish councillor during Harry's time. He was now so incapacitated by ill health that all he could mutter was 'bloody hell', much to the embarrassment of his good Christian mother, although Bryant Salmon, a farmer of substantial frame, said 'he just says that because he is so glad to see you.' He was certainly glad to see Harry at the reunion to which his son drove him in a utility to meet up with Harry and Pam at the Ceduna rectory, and he sat in the ute while they yarned with him.[27]

With people such as Bob Ryan in mind, Harry later wrote

> I will always be grateful to the people of the Ceduna Mission. They taught me a lot about life with its great joys and deep sorrows. It was a great privilege to serve there. We have great admiration for those who served before us and did so much, and appreciation for those who followed.[28]

# 6
# Parish Builder: 'Sunday at 7'

Returning from remote Ceduna to the Diocese of Sydney, Harry was inducted into the Parish of St Paul's Carlingford on 6 September 1966. He was offered the position in May at the same time as he became aware that Marryatville, an Adelaide parish, was also interested in appointing him. Harry and Pam 'covenanted with God' to accept the Carlingford offer by 30 May unless the Lord made it plain that he had an alternative purpose for them. He was attracted to Marryatville 'in its future as a scene of evangelical witness',[1] but since nothing definite was offered he concluded that the Lord was not in the possibility. Archbishop Loane was very glad to have Harry back in the Sydney diocese.[2]

## Carlingford, 1966–71

Carlingford was a growing area when Harry arrived. It had a beautiful, but small, stone church on a very busy road, quite unsuited to a growing congregation. But that was not the biggest challenge faced by the Goodhews at this time. Pam's health, always a concern, worsened and was hard to hide at Carlingford. She spent three months in bed with acute polyarthritis, from which it took a year to recover. The problem was so serious that Harry thought he would have to give up ministry. For months he had to get Pam out of bed and help her to walk. One who especially helped was Effie Begbie, wife of the archdeacon and Chaplain General of the Australian Military Forces, Alan Begbie. She and her children attended Carlingford church during Harry's time there. Pam felt badly about all the help she received from Mrs Begbie because 'she was a famous lady', an esteemed speaker at Christian conventions. But Effie chided her: 'You know the Scripture, "it is more blessed to give than to receive", well then, when you won't allow people to give, you deny them the blessing.'

The children have little recollection that there was any problem. Somehow the clothes were washed, the ironing done, and the children fed. Neither was their proper upbringing neglected. Robyn, the eldest, observes that being in the receipt of discipline was an experience chiefly of the Carlingford days, when she and her siblings were of an age to be 'more naughty.' She recalls being smacked by her father on a couple of occasions, which was all she needed to come to the settled conviction that the parental authority was to be respected. 'Mum was worse,' she chuckles, 'she had the wooden spoon, the ruler, and the feather duster.' Robyn can boast that she is one of few children who has walked under the busy Carlingford Road which was a construction site. She, Wendy and her friends managed to penetrate the fenced perimeter and walk through the large pipes under the road. Robyn did not tell her parents, as she knew 'they would be horrified.' Reflecting on her childhood, Robyn's verdict is that it was happy: she felt safe and secure.

Wendy, too, was happy with her lot. She said to Pam, 'I actually do think that Dad is like Jesus, because he does not sin, he does not do anything wrong. He never says an unkind word. He is not rude.' One night during the Carlingford period, after some conflict between them, Harry was going out to a meeting and he entered her room and said, 'I just want to say that I apologise. I'm sorry,' and he kissed her and went off to his meeting. Wendy knew that she was the one at fault and she went howling to her mother to say that 'He didn't do anything wrong. I did, but he apologised.'

David was not quite so certain that his father was perfect. 'I was emotionally scarred forever when he stood on the sidelines while I, aged 6, played soccer for the Roselea Soccer Club, yelling at me, "What did you do that for, David?"' Jokes aside, the experience left David in awe of his father's sporting prowess and with some doubts about his own.

Philip, the youngest son, was three when the family came to Carlingford. He recalls that the small church there was full and always lively. Philip remembers his father as a good storyteller who could keep the attention of the young as well as the old. Philip particularly recalls the story of Will's garden, with Harry acting all the parts. It must have been part of his repertoire, because, when prompted, Harry recalls it in minute detail.

Not all good storytellers make good preachers, but Harry was certainly both. At the 1970 synod, in the second last year of Harry's time at Carlingford, a committee, with Harry as a member, was appointed to investigate establishing a college of preachers.[3] Other members included Dudley Foord, then Dean of Students at Moore College; John Chapman, by this time Director of the Department of Evangelism; David Hewetson, then CMS Education Secretary for New South Wales; Bruce Smith, Moore College lecturer; and Peter Watson, then the minister of Lalor Park, and later one of Harry's bishops. They were all good communicators, with Chappo and Bruce Smith already highly esteemed for their florid oratory. Chappo knew when to stop, although his ebullient humour meant his hearers never wanted him to. Smith looked like a rugby player and perspired like one when he preached, but his words were liquid poetry.

The college of preachers was dedicated to the transformation of the preaching of all Sydney clergy by selling them on the idea of 'expository preaching'. Understood as preaching through whole sections and chapters of the Bible, it was not all gain for the Diocese of Sydney. In unimaginative hands it could be mechanical and boring with ministers persevering with their series on the temple in Leviticus when all around them the world was going up in flames. Harry's own exegetical preaching was exemplary. He brought to the task his own powers of reasoning, wide reading, an ear for poetry, a gospel-grounded passion to win souls and deepen commitment, and the common sense (or is it uncommon sensitivity?) to keep it at a length not to tax the concentration span of the average person in the pew. Harry was a practitioner of the view that preaching is as much about the hearer as the speaker. He managed to communicate that he cared about people, that he loved them. 'To love to preach is one thing,' said Richard Cecil, 'to love those to whom we preach is quite another.'[4] And Harry was quite capable of suspending the exegetical series whenever the world went up in flames.

The congregations at Carlingford grew in leaps and bounds in Harry's time and the little stone church at Carlingford was quite unsuited. It was too small, and the chairs placed in the narrow aisle made it a fire hazard. It was also deficient in oxygen and it was not unknown for people to faint: Harry actually caught one young woman as she collapsed.[5] Harry had to begin the task of getting parishioners used to the need to move elsewhere. Inevitably he received flak, but he was adept at such negotiations and laid a good foundation for his successor. The challenges of growth had always interested him, and in 1971, his last year at St Paul's, he was made a member of the diocesan Structures Committee, which researched and proposed major diocesan and parochial reorganisation. He found reflecting on such challenges congenial, and two decades later he was to write the Report on the Committee for the Development of Parish Property and Ministry which contributed to his election as archbishop.

The rector's warden at St Paul's in Harry's day was Arthur Goswell, who later recalled that the parish was then 'very active and very alive.' 'His deep conviction and love for Christ gave him a deep concern for people as individuals. Carlingford was a very strong, caring parish in his day.' Another Carlingford couple, Fay and John Gibson, remembered Harry's ability to communicate, his warm friendliness and his regard for the youth of the parish.[6] Malcolm Babbage, son of Stuart Barton Babbage, attended St Paul's in 1971 and 1972. He was the student catechist at the nearby Church of England Boys and Girls Homes and they lived in a house provided by them in Carlingford. His recollections of Harry's ministry are 'extremely warm'; he always felt very positively towards both Harry and Pam, and he had the sense that they were well loved in the parish.[7]

Harry was always close to Marcus Loane and respectful of him. Only once did he let his guard down. He was driving the family up to Springwood in the Blue Mountains for the opening of Blue Gum Lodge by the archbishop. Pam said to Harry, who was wearing a tie, that he should have put on his clerical collar, as the archbishop requested it. To this Harry retorted, 'Yuck – archbishops.' When the archbishop subsequently knocked on the door of the rectory, Philip answered it with the greeting, 'I know who you are. My father said something rude about you.'

In 1970 a renewed attempt was made to appoint Harry to Marryatville (actually, to the Parish of Kensington) in East Adelaide. Harry was aware of its strategic importance and, though he doubted that the timing was right because he had much to do at Carlingford, he went to Adelaide to discuss the matter with the wardens. Marcus Loane was displeased because he believed that Sydney was 'so very short of clergy of evangelical character and conviction who are thoroughly competent parish men' that he 'would deplore any attempt to nominate someone from this Diocese.'[8] Harry replied that he and Pam had declined the offer and were at peace, which they took as signifying the Lord's approval of their decision. He hoped the archbishop did not suspect that they were tiring of Carlingford, but Marryatville offered some 'special features' and they believed they ought to be open to any leading from the Lord.[9] Loane replied, not surprisingly, that he agreed with Harry's decision, adding 'I also feel that your sense of the peace of God in your heart is the witness of His Spirit with your spirit that this is the right decision.'[10] Then, on 27 May 1971, Harry was offered the Parish of St Alban's, Lindfield, by Marcus Loane. Harry replied that he had given the matter a week's prayerful consideration and 'as best as I am able to discern God has not indicated in any decisive way that I should leave Carlingford.'[11]

## Coorparoo, Queensland, 1971–6

In August of the same year, however, Harry informed his archbishop that the Archbishop of Brisbane had offered him the Parish of Coorparoo.[12] He had discussed the matter with Donald Cameron, CMS General Secretary, and Donald Robinson, Vice-Principal of Moore College, who both felt that, because it offered genuine opportunities for evangelical ministry, it was an offer that could not be ignored. Marcus Loane agreed that it was an exceptional opportunity which, since it had come to him unsought and unexpected, would be difficult to decline. But he added, 'I am extremely sorry to think that we are to lose you for the time being from the Diocese of Sydney. This is a very real loss to me personally, and I want you to know how much I look forward to your eventual return.'[13]

St Stephen's Coorparoo was one of the largest Anglican churches in the

Diocese of Brisbane. In 1962, when he was at Beverly Hills, Harry had spoken at a house party for the young people there. A parish councillor and one-time street preacher with the Open Air Campaigners in Brisbane, Vic Smith,[14] thought Harry would make an excellent rector and, when, almost a decade later, a vacancy occurred, nominated him. After the family arrived in Coorparoo, Vic and Nola Smith invited them over, took a pawpaw off a tree and gave it to them (the children had never seen one before). Their daughter, Bronwyn, quickly became friends with Robyn.

Coorparoo was big and used to doing things in a big way. The upper crust of Brisbane society worshipped there. The local branch of the Liberal Party used to meet in the church hall. The rector from 1957 to 1963, Jim Payne, was one of those people who knew everybody and invited all to church. Members of the Australian cricket team and of the English cricket team used to worship at St Stephen's when they were playing in Brisbane. It was the first church in Australia to adopt the Wells Scheme of freewill offering, which was so successful in increasing the income of churches. For the purpose, Payne filled the Brisbane Town Hall with a thousand people and brought out pianist Winifred Atwell from the United States to entertain them. It was also believed to be the first fully air-conditioned church in Australia. Attendances had continued to grow under John Greenwood, who preceded Harry as rector. On Christmas Day 1964, 1,400 attended the church. Evangelism and youth work flourished. Harry's challenge was to keep a thriving church growing at a time when churchgoing began to ebb all over Australia.

On learning of Harry's nomination, the Archbishop of Brisbane, Felix Arnott, was reported to have been aghast at the prospect of a Sydney man as rector in one of his parishes, but the staff of Moore College assured him that Harry would not be stupid. Arnott had lectured Harry in Church History at Moore as he was then the Warden of St Paul's College, located next to Moore. Passing through Sydney, he invited Harry and Pam to have lunch with him at the airport and was so impressed that he strongly endorsed the offer. 'I liked them both very much,' he reported to Marcus Loane.[15] So did Marcus, who, in his response to Arnott, wrote 'He is one of the most able and attractive men of his age group in Sydney and will certainly make his mark in any parish where he may serve.'[16] Arnott formally offered the parish to Harry on 23 August 1971, explaining that it was one of the most important and active in the diocese, that the parishioners ranged from those who favoured a move towards Sydney evangelicalism to those content with the more normal Brisbane use of vestments, and that the previous minister had achieved a balanced, happy regime. Arnott inducted Harry into the parish on 15 November 1971.

## Family matters

Now that the children were older, Pam felt able to be more involved in Harry's ministry. Her peers, she understood, would have thought that there was a 'role' for women and another for men. Pam did not exactly buck that attitude, but she did not endorse it without thinking. She was aware that there were some ministers' wives who were very involved: they had a reputation for being the unofficial rector and they ran everything. Pam knew she wasn't that. On the other hand, she could not accept for herself the view, which was to become prominent later on, that a minister's wife should have a role that was entirely apart from that of her husband.

Pam always thought it important that she should let women in the church know she supported them, but she did not feel that she needed to run everything. She endeavoured to attend all the women's events, and then she would organise other events in the rectory. Directly opposite the church, the rectory became the base for Pam's ministry of extraordinary hospitality to the parish. Sunday night suppers were always in the rectory and so she felt responsible for them. Many women would gravitate to the kitchen and talk to her while she prepared food, and this actually gave her an extensive ministry appreciated by many women. The men were not so sure. Always eager to participate in whatever it was that came out of the oven, they noticed that Pam would not continue working in the kitchen while she talked to people. Multitasking was not her forte. When addressed she would interrupt her food preparation and give the visitor her undivided attention, thus delaying the advent of the food. Wise visitors sought to engage her in conversation after, rather than before, the meal! The children also had to devise a way of coping with Pam's many guests. She would say, 'FHB' (Family Hold Back) until the guests were served. The children did not feel neglected, but they understood that their parents' ministry was outward focused, and they were shaped by it in many ways, accepting the value of putting other people before themselves.

Harry was busy, but available to his children emotionally. Even the youngest, Philip, sensed that his father was now involved in a big operation. It was more high-church Anglican than Carlingford, with processions at services preceded by the cross bearer. There 'were robes and more robes' and altar boys. Philip, looking on, felt small. But all was well in this strange, new world because he also felt that his Dad was big and in control.

For Robyn, however, the move to Brisbane was more difficult. At Carlingford, she had completed her first year of secondary education at a local comprehensive school and she wanted to go to the local school in Coorparoo. But Harry and Pam wanted her to go to 'a good school', so she successfully sat an exam for entry to

Brisbane State High. A selective school, one had to be either brainy or sporty to get in. Robyn was very shy and for months said nothing at school.

Part of the family routine was to have a Bible reading and prayer at each evening meal. Many sons and daughters of the rectory, once they reach the age of self-consciousness, have found such routines a problem. But Robyn did not. She was aware that her father was prayerful, because she and the other children would often find him at prayer both in the morning and in the evening. They located him often on his knees. Wendy never found living in a rectory a problem either, primarily, she says, because her father was never embarrassing. Much of what she learned about the Christian faith she absorbed from the family discussions around the meal table.

Robyn and Wendy both thought their father was perfect. He knew everything and he was always there, remarked Robyn. She felt that his only fault was that he was too nice, and this actually annoyed her at times. Wendy, when asked to identify her father's weaknesses, could only say, 'He likes chocolate.' Her assessment of her father, though partly the product of filial affection, would be shared by many. 'He has been given a gracious, kind, generous personality that looks for the best and desires to encourage and that is his nature.' According to Philip, Harry's only fault is that 'he can be too kind – he speaks to nutters for hours about some crazy theory.'

David was fascinated by his father's study. It was meticulously organised, with information catalogued in an elaborate system of notebooks, cards and folders. David understood this to be a manifestation of self-discipline, which he knew was a quality he did not share in equal measure. He observed that his father inclined to the latest technologies when it came to his office – he has always kept up with developments in computers. There was one matter where David did keep up with his father's preferences: his taste for good clothing and shoes. Harry once drove to Goulburn, David recalls approvingly, to pick up a pair of Baxter boots. Harry did not always approve of his own expensive tastes, once recording, 'Was lured by my own stupidity into spending too much money on an overcoat. Lord help me.'[17] Like his own father, Harry could not bear to have dirty shoes, and later despaired over the slackness of his clergy in this matter. Harry and Pam both had a liking for quality furniture and crockery, for Parker and Chiswell furniture and Wedgwood crockery, which they liked to use when entertaining. They were classy by instinct, but also by upbringing. Pam's mother, Mrs Coughlan, had been 'a very proper entertainer.'[18]

It was at Coorparoo that Robyn began to notice that her father's sermons were rather more impressive than those of some others, which she dismissed as lectures.

Of all the preachers she has heard, she puts him at the top. She did compare her father's preaching with others and was aware that there were very good preachers – such as Chappo – but for a regular diet she favoured her father. She admired the fact that his preaching did not go on for too long, that it was always to the point, and there were numerous quotations from luminaries along the way to illustrate the point. Her father was widely read, she observed, and she was glad of it. Wendy, though younger, was aware that she was being affected spiritually by her father's sermons.

## The dynamics of a 'big church'

Harry's ministry at St Stephen's Coorparoo started in its jubilee year. He began by leading the parish in a review of its ministry direction. He was good at the process of involving church members and, without imposing his own views upon them, helped them to be aware of the changes that were taking place in Australian society and the responses demanded by those changes. It was at Coorparoo that Harry pioneered the concept of the 'big church'. The multi-staff parish was then quite rare within the Anglican system, where the rector was often the only paid member of staff who did anything volunteers would or could not do. He developed a new church staff team, including dynamic youth worker, Rod Story, whose appointment almost caused one parish councillor to have apoplexy, but he was destined to become the Australian Director of Evangelism Explosion (EE). Evangelism was always top priority. Vic Smith said,

> Harry took Coorparoo from a low church to a worshipping Christian family. It was absolutely wonderful. He brought EE to the parish and we saw people converted every week. He had almost the whole Diocese eating out of his hand and asking about evangelism.

Harry's sensitivity meant he was always careful about managing change. One parishioner, Keith Thompson, was very impressed one Sunday evening when a youth service was about to begin and Harry noticed an elderly woman from the morning congregation arrive and resolved, out of respect for her, to change his mind not to robe.[19] Yet he was quite capable of dramatic change when he concluded that it was necessary. He made the decision to stop sung evensong at the church and replace it with a youth service. It involved a lot of heated discussion, with Pam insisting that the choir members should not be pushed out of the church. So 'Sunday at 7' was launched, often conducted by Rod Story. The choir moved to the 10 am service. 'So it wasn't a problem?' Rod was asked. 'It was a problem,' he conceded, 'but we got there. Harry was always a visionary: he could always

6.1 Harry and morning congregation, St Stephen's Coorparoo, 1972.

see where there was a need for change.' Sunday at 7 was contemporary with a lot of interaction with the audience. There was Rod with his roving green mike and people would share their stories and Harry encouraged it. Rod makes three observations on Harry's ministry at Coorparoo. It was characterised by clarity ('the clearest preaching I have ever heard'), vision and innovation, and all this in the context of total commitment to personal evangelism. In the first couple of years of Harry's ministry at Coorparoo, over 200 people came to Christ.

Once Sunday at 7 was under way, Harry invited Archbishop Arnott out to give it his blessing. At that time the archbishop presided over a diocese with hardly any evening services and with so little youth work that it would prove lethal to the future of the Anglican Church in Brisbane. He was happy to see young people in an Anglican Church on a Sunday evening. On the night, with the archbishop present, Rod Story took the service and asked members of the congregation if there were matters they wanted prayer for. Felix Arnott asked him to pray for someone who had just died. Praying for the dead was just not done in evangelical circles, but Rod got around that somehow. Harry and his team resolved not to get upset over matters like that – they felt that more was at stake.

Rod and Helen Irvine found Sunday at 7 'electric.' They had been attending a Methodist church and on one occasion Harry was invited to speak there at a fellowship tea. Harry took a flower from a vase and said Australians are a cut-flower generation, cut off from God, looking beautiful, but dying. Helen never forgot it, and Rod recalls sitting next to him afterwards and 'earbashing him for hours.' Their next-door neighbour was on the Scripture Union council, and he said to Rod and Helen, 'Harry will not stay long in Coorparoo. He'll be a bishop soon.' Harry had such an influence on Rod that in 1976 he entered Moore College to train for the ministry. Appointed catechist at Panania, the rector, Les Monaghan, informed that Rod came from Brisbane, said, 'So, you are one of Harry's boys.' 'He is certainly the reason why I am an Anglican,' Rod testifies, and one of 'the plethora of people who Harry touched, encouraged and mentored.'[20]

## Extra-parochial ministry

The parishioners at St Stephen's were not a little proud that their new minister was so quickly accepted across the diocese, which normally had no time for evangelicals. His approach was irresistible: he understood that the exclusive gospel is best served by being inclusive. The critical importance of civility, combined with the primacy of evangelism, was Harry's formula, so simple that it is astonishing that it was so rare. Vic Smith's wife, Nola, testified

> Harry is the most humble, gracious man I've ever met. He spoke at rural deanery conferences for clergy and laity on parish outreach and served on the Council of the Home Mission Department. He built a great rapport with senior clergy in the Diocese. They invited him to lecture on evangelism at Church House. He remained firm in his own convictions, but in a very, very nice way.

Harry's diocesan seminars on evangelism in Brisbane were well attended. When, at the request of Archbishop Arnott, he trained people in dialogue evangelism in St Ann's House in Brisbane, Harry and Rod Story had put out about 50 chairs, but 250 turned up to receive the training. He actively promoted the Evangelical Fellowship in the Anglican Communion (EFAC) in the diocese and invited prominent evangelicals to visit, including John Stott, who spoke to the clergy at Bishopthorpe and preached in the cathedral. Stott, a bachelor, stayed with the Goodhews and spoke afterwards of the pleasant experience that was. The children loved him. He gave the impression of eating a china plate by putting a coin on it which made a cracking sound when the plate was put in his mouth. David asked him how he came to write all those books while his father had not written any.

'Your father,' replied Stott, 'has a wife and four children. He gives his time to you. I don't have a wife or children, so I have time to write books.' Alan Cole and Chappo also stayed, also much to the delight of the children. Alan made funny vibrating noises by plucking the vocal cords in his throat. Chappo allowed Harry's children to 'drown him' in a friend's swimming pool. The children realised that living in a rectory was, in many ways, very privileged.

6.2 Harry and Isabel Reilly with presenter, Digby Wolfe, *This is Your Life*, 3 October 1976.

In 1975 Harry was guest lecturer in Christian Doctrine at the Queensland Bible Institute, and in 1975–6 was a member of the Theological Reading Group, made up of principals of Anglican and Roman Catholic theological seminaries in Brisbane and members of the faculty of the Religious Studies department of Queensland University. To this point, Harry's academic achievements had not been numerous, largely because he had devoted his time and energy to pastoral ministry. At last he felt able to find time to try his hand at university studies. He enrolled as a part-time student at the University of Queensland in semester one in 1976, which was to be his last year at Coorparoo. He studied Hebrew and achieved the highest possible grade point average of seven.

## An international student of church growth

Much of the outstanding success of Harry's ministry at Coorparoo was due to the new perspectives he gained from overseas pastors. Harry was unusually open to learning from any source and his knowledge of the factors involved in growing churches increased exponentially through international travel. It was in 1974 Harry that first went overseas on a fact-finding mission to research church development. He attended the Lausanne Congress on World Evangelisation and visited leading churchmen in America and England. At the Congress, he roomed with Alan Cole, in Morges, a village just outside of Lausanne. Apparently, their landlady was not friendly, and Alan later reminisced with Harry about 'that time at Morges with the stingy landlady.'[21] But Harry found Alan's behaviour more remarkable. 'He would wake up early in the morning, sit straight up in bed, and begin to address the Lord about the affairs of the day.' Harry also saw a bidet there for the first time. 'I had no idea what it was, so I washed my shirt in it to Alan's great amusement and humorous comments about my great humility.'

It was on this trip that Harry forged links with American church leaders that were to remain strong, proving of lasting blessing to the Australian church. He enjoyed an enduring friendship with church growth guru, Bill Yaeger of Modesto. It was on the basis of his experience of Ray Stedman's church in Palo Alto that Harry introduced something of the 'body life' insights and programs to Coorparoo and hatched the name 'Sunday at 7', youth-friendly, largely liturgy-free services of worship, which have since made such a dramatic change in evening worship in Sydney churches. Harry also admired the seeker-sensitive services that were building huge congregations under Bill Hybels, at Willow Creek just out of Chicago, and later invited him to visit Australia. This led to the creation of 'Willow Creek Australia', a ministry to equip, resource and develop Australian churches. Harry visited Robert Schuller in Orange County (the Crystal Cathedral had not yet been built), and there he was impressed by the Bethel Bible reading program, which he was to introduce first at Coorparoo and later in Wollongong. He invited to Brisbane Dr Win Arn, who, with Donald McGavran, was one of the early exponents of church growth theory. Based on all these American models, Harry saw an opportunity for more aggressive and effective ministry than he had previously seen in Australia.

They also 'probably laid the foundation for much that I don't like now,' he has since confessed, referring to the widespread throwing out in the 1980s and 90s of the true worship baby with the Anglican bathwater. But in the mid-70s, he was reaching out to the young people of Brisbane, where hardly anything was being done for them. He had to do something. He rather hoped that, once people were won, they could be initiated into the Anglican tradition.

## Evangelism Explosion

Perhaps the most significant of his visits in America was to Dr Jim Kennedy, founder of EE, at Coral Ridge Presbyterian Church, Fort Lauderdale in Florida. With him Harry developed a connection that bore dramatic fruit in Australia and beyond. Dr Kennedy's church had grown from 246 when EE was started in 1962 to 3,134 in 1974, the year of Harry's visit (precise statistics were always treasured by church growth aficionados). The church was filled with those who had been shown the way of salvation, who were confident of going to heaven, and who had the confidence to share their faith with others. If the substance of the ministry was the everlasting gospel, the process by which it was conducted was the multiplication model. 'The key word is multiply,' explained Dr Kennedy.

> The Book of Acts reads that 'there were added 3,000 to the church', and later, '5,000 more were added'. Then we read that 'the disciples multiplied', and then 'they multiplied exceedingly'. It is this shift from addition to spiritual multiplication that offers the one real hope of sharing the gospel with a world population that is, itself, continually multiplying.[22]

Concerning process, Dr Kennedy had made a series of discoveries, critical to the success of this remarkable ministry. First, that he personally had to learn how to evangelise one on one; second, that he needed to train other members of his congregation in how to evangelise – on-the-job training was the key to this; then that he needed to train trainers; then that those so trained needed to train pastors of other churches all over America; then that pastors and lay people needed to be trained from all over the world. Simply put, EE had two elements: training people to memorise a simple outline of the gospel and then how to share it with people through on-the-job training.

On his return to Australia, Harry arranged for his youth worker, Rod Story to attend an EE Clinic at Fort Lauderdale in 1975. For Rod, it was a life-changing experience. 'I returned to Australia strongly convinced of two realities. One, I could now lead people to the Lord. Two, I could equip others to do so, too.'[23] On the very first night Rod returned from America, he spoke at a youth meeting and three young girls gave their lives to Christ. Harry asked Rod to train others. But, he said to Rod, 'I want you every Tuesday to go out and knock on doors, invite people to church and see if you can tell them about Jesus, before you start to train anyone here at the church.' It was a good thing, Rod later recalled, 'I've never had a fear of knocking on doors.'[24]

Coorparoo was the exemplary evangelical parish in a non-evangelical diocese. Vital yet sensible, experimental yet orthodox, welcoming yet clear in proclamation, it was a high point in Harry's career in the ministry.

# 7

# Rector and Archdeacon of Wollongong: 'For The Ministry That Lies Ahead'

Just when Coorparoo was proceeding famously, Harry received an offer, dated 4 June 1976, to become Rector and Senior Canon of St Michael's Provisional Cathedral in Wollongong.

## A gigantic struggle for guidance

This precipitated probably the most agonising decision of his career. He later recalled, 'God knows the struggle that was and he alone is the final arbiter over our decision.'[1] At the same time as the offer came from Wollongong, the Vicar of West Tamworth, Ray Smith, advised Harry that he would like to put his name forward for election as Bishop of Armidale, following the retirement of the popular Clive Kerle. Armidale had become an evangelical diocese under Kerle, thanks largely to the efforts of Harry's old Moore College mates, John Chapman, Peter Chiswell and Ray Smith himself, all of whom had been working in the Diocese of Armidale, and the evangelicals wanted to keep it that way.[2] Harry's first thought was that he would have no choice but to accept it should it be offered to him. But the firm offer to go to Wollongong preceded any offer from Armidale, putting Harry in a quandary. His human instinct was to remain in Coorparoo because the parish was experiencing dramatic growth and influence; his sense of duty made him suspect that he would have to go to Armidale if offered that; Wollongong was at first a distant, third preference.

If, however, Marcus Loane, who made the offer, and Ken Short, Bishop of Wollongong, who keenly wanted Harry to accept, had learned anything from their apprenticeship under the august Howard Mowll, it was how to lean. Harry said 'no' to Ken Short a number of times, but Ken would not take 'no' for an answer. He invited Harry to come and stay for a week in Wollongong so that he could get a feel for its potential. Harry said that he would need to bring the whole family. Bp Short readily agreed. Harry was advised that the Chapter of the Provisional Cathedral unanimously wanted him, that St Michael's was a very important parish from a civic as well as spiritual perspective, that it was in excellent shape following the successful incumbency of its retiring rector, Canon Basil Williams, that the rural deanery was 'one of the most united and harmonious in the whole Diocese', and that Harry would be made rural dean, thus expanding his opportunity to serve. Furthermore, it was not unreasonable to ask Harry to leave Coorparoo, contended Marcus Loane, because he had been there for the acceptable minimum of five years and his successor would be an evangelical.

Following lengthy discussions with Marcus Loane and Ken Short, Harry thought that he should consider the Wollongong offer on its own merits without reference to Armidale. The election synod would not be held until the end of July and it would be unfair to hold off a decision on Wollongong until August. Harry was also moved by Ken Short's enthusiasm for the work in that region and he felt that he and Pam could easily allow their 'hearts to beat along with his.' On the other hand, Harry had come to the conclusion, mainly through what he had learned from his overseas visits, that ministry of the type he was developing at Coorparoo required him to remain for longer than he had in his previous positions. He had only been at Coorparoo for five years, but he had come to suspect that it might be wisdom to stay for 20. He promised to give the archbishop a firm answer by 25 June.[3]

Marcus Loane responded that he agreed with Harry that normally one should not leave such a parish as Coorparoo except for a work that was equally or more strategic.[4] He said he would be happy with whatever decision Harry reached.

Harry's promised answer was anything but firm, however, and Marcus was anything but happy with it. The correspondence witnesses to the agony Harry felt in seeking guidance and finding the will of God. Harry left advising Marcus to the very last minute, and his letter to Marcus is dated 24 June, the day before the deadline. He confessed that he and Pam had found it impossible to weigh the relative merits of the two parishes, that they found their present work 'immediate, absorbing and for us, challenging and encouraging' whereas Wollongong was 'in a sense someone else's vision', and that the few with whom they had shared the problem felt strongly they should not leave, with one, Ron Herbert, insisting that it would be quite wrong to leave. Harry continued

> All this has made us feel that we could not make a decision by simply weighing pros and cons. We have therefore asked God to enable us to make a decision based on the issue of whether or not your letter came at His instigation and therefore represented a clear call from Him or whether it was a human word which we should not heed. Hesitatingly we have resolved to see it as a word from God. I cannot now describe to you the empty feeling that such a choice produces within my heart. We can only look to that Father who has saved us and undertaken to be

> our shepherd. We trust that in His great mercy He will not suffer us to make a step that is contrary to His will.

Harry then moved on to consider the question of Armidale. Ray Smith had asked him if he could leave the matter open until after 28 July, when the election synod should have been able to resolve whether or not to send an invitation to Harry. Harry confessed that Pam felt they should not think any more about Armidale, but Harry thought that 'any evangelical to whom that position was offered would be almost obliged to accept.' He concluded that he would take Marcus's advice on whether or not to hold off until after 28 July.[5]

This letter is intriguing at a number of levels, and not only on the issue of guidance. It had long been suspected by many who knew Harry that he was destined for the purple. But now for the first time, the real possibility of an episcopal future may have been planted in Harry's mind, and his hesitancy in putting the Armidale possibility to rest suggests that he was attracted to the prospect. The letter also reveals what an interesting team Harry and Pam were. Harry always included Pam in any decisions he made. It was never 'my feeling' or 'my decision'; it was always 'our decision.' But here Harry and Pam were not on the same wavelength, and the difference underlines the strength of their relationship. Harry spoke of the emptiness of his own heart at the decision to go to Wollongong; Pam did not. If she felt empty-hearted, she would not put that burden on Harry. And she was much clearer than Harry in working through the Armidale situation. Harry would always be stronger for Pam's stoutheartedness and decisive clarity. Once a decision was made there was no point in regretting it.

Marcus Loane agreed with Pam on both the matters that Harry felt. 'My own view,' he wrote to Harry, 'is the same as Pam's; i.e. having reached a decision with regard to Wollongong you ought not to think further about Armidale.' On guidance, he resorted to the Keswick spirituality to which both he and Harry subscribed.

> I do not feel at all happy that this should be a decision which leaves you such an 'empty feeling' in your own heart. I feel that you need the testimony of His Spirit with your spirit that this is the right choice. If you have this assurance then His grace will sustain you, both in leaving a parish you love and in starting anew ... I will write by the same mail to inform Archbishop Arnott that the Parish of Wollongong has been offered to you and I hope it will have his goodwill. I will take no step to make your decision known until I hear from you again and I earnestly trust that when you write it will be with a clear mind and the full

assurance of faith.[6]

Loane's language is a classic statement of the view of guidance that then prevailed in Sydney. Perhaps today, while Sydney Anglicans might still use such terms as the 'testimony of the Spirit' and 'full assurance', they do so in connection with one's faith, rarely one's sense of guidance.

Harry had copied to Ken Short his letter of 24 June to Archbishop Loane. Bp Short had been praying for Harry and Pam more earnestly than for any other matter since his arrival as bishop the previous year. He was clearly very eager to appoint Harry and relieved to learn that Harry had all but accepted the offer. But he could see that Harry needed encouragement and his long letter to Harry, dated 29 June, was well calculated to do that. He said that he had felt exactly the same as Harry when he had been appointed to Wollongong and had to leave the Parish of Vaucluse where the work was thriving. He said he had 'dried up inside – for a while!!'

> Yet now, with hindsight, because that call was a Word of God for me, I can say fully that He has not forsaken me, and the joy of serving and the different opportunities have all had their glorious compensations. So, my brother, I appreciate your feeling – and I know, as you do, that God graciously and tenderly leads us on. You know, it is the branch that bears fruit, that he prunes, so that it may bear more fruit.

> I will now pray that God will remove the hesitancy and will start to give you a sense of anticipation and expectation so that there will be a real desire to begin His work here in Wollongong with drive, faith and a deep sense that He has been equipping you by experience and training for this very hour and job.

Having thus treated with Harry's heart tenderly, he proceeded to treat his mind robustly, arguing with reference to Harry's nuanced position on Armidale, that it 'defies reason'.[7]

Thus, outnumbered by the Archbishop of Sydney, the Bishop of Wollongong, and by his wife, Harry submitted to the invitation to Wollongong as God's call and he wrote his supposedly unequivocal acceptance to the archbishop on 6 July 1976.

> I am sorry about my 'empty feeling'. We are both now 'settled' about our decision and move forward with confidence in God. We do not look forward to terminating our work at Coorparoo, it has been one of the richest periods in our life, the break will hurt.[8]

To his credit, surely, what concerned Harry more than the emptiness in his own heart was the emptiness in the heart of members of his congregation. But he had come to believe that God would more than compensate them for what they believed was not a good move. That had been the considered reaction of at least some of his dearest friends there, leading Harry to the belief that God had something far 'more encouraging for them in the future.'

Harry did not receive the 'full assurance of faith' immediately. After he had made the decision, he met up with Bp John Reid and poured out his heart on the subject. 'I think I have made the biggest mistake of my life,' he told Reid. 'Even so,' counselled the bishop, 'you must push on.'

The congregations of Coorparoo were devastated. Rod Story was heartbroken. Harry was just a 'fantastic bloke to work with.' 'He met with me regularly,' recalls Rod, 'he prayed with me, he built up the team.' He remembers thinking, 'why on earth would anyone want to go to Wollongong?' and he asked Harry, 'Are you sure you want to do this?' Even today part of Rod wonders if it was the right thing, as Coorparoo, although it continued for a time with the culture which Harry had created, was never the same again.

When the family left Coorparoo for Wollongong, they believed it important to leave on a cheery rather than a sad note. For the farewell on 28 November 1976, they wrote a four-stanza song set to a tune from the musical *Oliver*.

> *Consider yourselves our friends*
> *Consider yourselves part of our family*
> *We've taken to you so strong*
> *It's hard to be leaving for Wollongong.*

All four of their children sang it along with them. But Harry had to work at the cheerfulness. Robyn would be left behind to go to University. Wendy did not want to leave. She had a boyfriend. They had been very happy years for her. She had graduated to Youth Group. She no longer had to stay at home on Friday nights and eat crumpets.

At the farewell a layperson (was it Vic Smith?) spoke of Harry's qualities shown more by his example than by words. The obvious qualities were mentioned: **Commitment** to the work and **Concern** for people. But Harry's distinctive genius lay in a third 'C', namely **Confidence**. 'Perhaps what many of us saw in you most was this unbounded confidence matched to a deep humility.' It was a remarkable combination. An equally perceptive letter was written to Harry by another layperson, P.C. Vickery. Harry was the seventh rector of Coorparoo, and Vickery identified each with a stage in the growth of a person from birth. Strikingly, he identified Harry with marriage. No wonder Harry's departure from Coorparoo was so agonising both for him and his parishioners: it felt like marital separation. This deeply personal letter to Harry ended with this perceptive testimony to the universality of Harry's appeal.

> Harry, you came to us with all the strengths of honest, open-hearted humility. You were different and appealing. We openly asked 'is he strong enough?' and 'can he last?' – you were and you did.
>
> Before long, Ladies were saying 'He's every Mother's Son' – Men said 'He's a Man's man.' Youth came whilst the aged and afflicted simply loved you. Above all you were the catalyst of the 'great in-between' (the neither too good nor too tough). You are a lot of things to a lot of people. If you have a fault it is of being too generous with yourself and your time. Yet, you did have time to be a husband to Pam and a father to your family.[9]

A confidential letter from Archbishop Arnott reveals how much he had come to trust Harry and to share with him some of the burdens of his office. He began his letter with the lament that he would miss Harry and Pam greatly and ended it with the words, 'Thank you for all that you and Pam have done for me and the Diocese.'[10] He wrote to Marcus Loane in Sydney in a similar vein.

> I must say I received it with lamentation but I suppose I never hoped to keep Harry Goodhew here permanently. He has done a remarkable job at Coorparoo and has fitted in most loyally and happily into the Diocese and I believe he and Pam have both been extremely happy here.[11]

Harry's departure from Brisbane made front page news in the *Courier Mail*, Brisbane's premier newspaper. Its headline read, 'Father Goodhew says his last Mass.' Nobody was happy to see him go: not the members of his congregation, not the archbishop or the clergy, nor the press, nor the people of Brisbane. Bereavement and anger are close emotions. There were those who believed that powerful Sydney had deprived poor Brisbane of its best opportunity of strengthening the feeble evangelical cause in the diocese. They were reminded of the incident recorded in 2 Samuel 12 where King David had taken the poor man's only little ewe lamb instead of selecting a sheep from his own extensive flock. They had a point. The Diocese of Sydney did not need another strong rector nearly as much as Brisbane did.

Was a deeper providence at work? Harry would never have become a bishop in the diocese of Brisbane, and it may be that Sydney needed a bishop of Harry's graciousness more than Brisbane needed a rector of Harry's ability. On Harry's becoming a bishop just six years later, Dorothy Robinson, a parishioner of Coorparoo who had done much to assist him in his ministry there, recalled his reluctance and confusion on leaving. Well, she suggested, 'surely this is the answer – He wanted you in Wollongong for this purpose – for the ministry that lies ahead.'[12]

## Rector of St Michael's, Wollongong

In making the offer to Harry, the bishop in Wollongong, Ken Short, assured his archbishop that the Cathedral Chapter at St Michael's had followed the constitutionally correct procedure 'as far as the ordinance is concerned.' They had spent a lot of time thinking about the sort of man they needed: one strong in pastoral gifts; able to communicate well from the pulpit; a teacher and evangelist; an evangelical of conviction; one involved in missionary enterprise; 'a married man whose wife would support him in the work'; one who could take his place with the civic authorities of the city, with the university, and also be a 'man's man' since this was the city of steelworkers; one who would be in his mid to late 40s and a team player rather than a 'loner'.[13] Such a catalogue of virtues is duplicated every time a church reflects on who they want in a minister: one who combines the gifts of St Paul and Billy Graham. In this case, however, and even though Ken Short assured Marcus Loane that the members of the Chapter worked on this list before introducing any names for consideration, it is impossible to ignore the impression that they had Harry in mind all along, for the list fitted him like a glove. Even his age – 45 – was just right!

Though their hearts were still 'a little tender' at leaving Coorparoo, Harry and Pam were greatly encouraged by the warmth of the welcome they received on 10 December 1976, when Harry was inducted as Rector of St Michael's, Wollongong, Senior Canon of St Michael's Provisional Cathedral, and Rural Dean of Wollongong.[14] Solicitor, Peter Kell, a member of the Cathedral Chapter, later reported, 'Harry came into the place like

7.1 Archdeacon Goodhew at the induction of prefects, Wollongong High School, 1980.

a sky rocket lighting the place up.' He arrived with quite a reputation and much was expected of him. He was at pains immediately to quash the 'success' image. 'I'm not a miracle worker. The church contains people of all gifts. I don't have the lot – very few. So I expect each one of you to put the gifts of God into good use for him.'[15]

On relocating to Wollongong, the family moved into the rectory in Church Hill, adjacent to St Michael's. Wendy quickly overcame her disappointment at having to leave Brisbane. It helped that she had such an athletic, normal, father. She never felt shame in being in a rectory family; in fact, she admits to feeling proud. She was a prefect at Wollongong High School and once a week there was an assembly and a local pastor would come to give the devotions for that week. As a prefect, she was able to introduce the minister, and so she would say, 'Devotions for this week: my Dad!' always with perfect confidence because he was 'a good guy; people liked him.'

In those school assemblies were some who were doing it tough, in whom, though so young, hope was already all but extinguished. Tom Frame, relinquished for adoption at birth and then living with a violent and alcoholic foster father,[16] heard Harry gladly.

> I was much influenced by Harry's school assembly addresses in 1977–78 when I could have drifted away from Christian faith. He was easily the most engaging speaker at the morning assembly which was from about 8:40am to 9am. It involved the whole student population ... I recall him speaking about the dark night of the soul, and the need to answer the questions Christ was asking. To be honest, I can't remember much more other than thinking I was obliged to take his invitations to thought and reflection seriously. He spoke in moderated tones. Harry was not a ranter nor an emotional manipulator. His was an appeal to the mind without making faith seem like a cognitive exercise ... So, Harry was my favourite cleric until I joined the Navy in 1979.[17]

Tom became a lay reader at St Michael's in 1985 by which time Harry was Bishop of Wollongong, and again he found Harry 'a great encourager.' Tom went on, with Harry's support, to become Bishop to the Defence Force, a public intellectual and major historian both of the navy and of the church. He recalls not so much what Harry said in those school assemblies, but how he said it.

> Harry always wore a clerical collar and looked the part. His ten-minute talks were well constructed as I remember it ... they were sequential and re-started where they ended. I recall he was a careful crafter of

words because I was interested in words myself as a would-be writer. Many of the other clergy who gave these talks either didn't know how to speak with teenagers or read a dreary script or tried to be too 'cool' ... Harry realised he didn't need to speak down to us ... As I recall it although now through older eyes, Harry was probably bishop material back then.[18]

For Philip, the youngest member of the family, the move to Wollongong was welcome. He looks on his time there as good years. There was a youth group at St Michael's and under youth worker, David Short, and curate, Simon Manchester, both destined for remarkable ministries of their own, lots of good things happened. Philip was popular at school because he was so good at sport, thanks to the genes of his father and grandmother, 'Gran', who used to be a sprinter. Basher Downes was his coach and, while most were scared of him – he used the cane a lot – Philip was a fan and appreciated his emphasis on excellence and doing your best. Harry would minister to Basher when he was dying of cancer.

Later at university, Philip would listen to his father's sermons. He recalls a series on 'Celebration of Certainty': we can be confident of God's love for us because He assures us of it, and we should celebrate the fact and live confidently in His presence. He listened to these tapes over and over again. He thought his father had a good way of expressing the faith and linking truths together. He felt that either his Dad had got better with age or else he had become better at listening. Harry had the power to communicate without props and videos in 15 minutes and he did it by drawing on a rich variety of sources, literary and sociological as well as biblical.

Philip became a major supporter of Rod Story in his ministry as Australian Director of EE. Rod relocated from Brisbane to Wollongong to be near Harry and to operate the ministry from there. He joined the Parish of Figtree and organised mission trips overseas with EE. 'Successive youth groups have gone on these mission trips,' observes Philip. 'It's very empowering for people to talk about the gospel, to start a conversation, share one's faith and know what to say if they say "yes".'

It was not long after arriving in Wollongong that the Goodhew children made many friends and brought them home to the rectory. They liked being there because, they said, 'Your family is so nice and your Dad is so nice to us,' and they started going to church and youth group and were converted. Andrew Glover, Phil Howes, Stuart Brooking, Richard James, and Matthew Pickering were among those who were encouraged to go into the ministry through the ministry of Harry and his family. 'You don't realise,' Matthew Pickering told Wendy with reference to her family life, 'how good your life is and how many people do not have what you have.'

Yet Robyn and David were not entirely happy with what they had. They were a little bit alternative, whereas the two younger ones were more conformist. When the family had relocated to Wollongong, Robyn had stayed in Brisbane to complete a university course in veterinary science. Harry was distressed at having to leave her there. He had always been close to her and wanted it to stay that way, but Pam insisted that it was the making of Robyn as it freed her to stand on her own feet. She began to get used to her freedom and staying out late, and found her holidays in Wollongong something of a trial. She used to go walking on the beach with a boy from the fellowship. Harry disapproved and, on one occasion, went looking for her. She understood why he did it, but she was embarrassed, nevertheless. She told him not to do it again, but he took no notice! He was clear about his role as protective parent.

David's difficulties were more protracted. He found it hard to discover his identity. He had a motorbike, grew his hair long and had a discreet tattoo. He was challenged by a number of scientific questions. After school, David went into nursing, on the example, advice and urging of Pam. He liked it, deriving satisfaction from the opportunity to reduce suffering and make people more comfortable. His aptitude for the caring professions came most obviously from his mother who had been a nurse, but David had long been impressed by his father's unfailing care for the needy in his parish, his courtesy and practical assistance to all who knocked on the door. David later went into nursing administration and then into geriatric care. He profited from discussing the managerial side of these roles with Harry, who became well read in management theory over the years.

David had been aware when living at home that there were many people who 'owned' his father, and the ministry was such an absorbing matter for both his parents that, after he married, he at first resolved not to work for the Home Mission Society (HMS, now Anglicare) while his father was in the diocese. He recalls going to a church where it was assumed because of his surname that he would become a member of the parish council. Harry was so well known that David felt the need to withdraw from that scene in order to find himself. He learned, over time to handle the attention his surname attracted: when anyone would ask, 'are you …?', he would answer, 'yes, he has the privilege of being my father.'[19]

David became interested in photography and in exploring the spirituality of the surf and the bush. He continued to attend church on a Sunday, though not with any enthusiasm. Sandra, his wife, stuck by him, praying for him. His parents responded in a way consistent with their personalities. Pam would have moments when she would 'escalate and dogmatically express her ideas irrespective of the prevailing winds'[20] whereas Harry would be loving and gentle and say all the right things, and feed him articles to help him keep thinking about things. David did not find any of this unpalatable: he took it rather as evidence of his parents' concern for him. Nevertheless, he did not read many of the books Harry sent to him. Rather, he handed them over to Sandra who read them and reported on their content to him. But Harry scored a direct hit on David's questing soul with C.S. Lewis audio books. To the persuasive reasoning of C.S. Lewis, David put into the balance the language of the prayer book, great slabs of which he knows off by heart, and returned to the fold stronger and more settled.

## Five steps on how to grow a church

Harry was only at St Michael's from 1976 to 1979. Yet in those few years, he wrought the same radical transformation that he had achieved in his previous parishes. His ministry brought the whole body to life. How?

First, he ensured that there was plenty of love in the air. In the evangelical tradition, generally bishops are not considered to be successors of the Apostles. But if they were, of all the Apostles, Harry was most like the Apostle John who modelled and taught the followers of Jesus to 'love one another.' Dorothy Lee, who had attended St Michael's for 40 years and was grateful for the succession of committed rectors who had taught God's word, wrote to thank Harry for teaching the members of the family at St Michael's to love one another.

> It became a more friendly, caring, loving congregation and so a happier one. I know it was your example of gentleness and love – your taking time to listen, and care which helped us all so much to grow in love, concern, and fellowship for each other.[21]

When he first arrived, Harry did feel the difference in temperature between the sunny disposition of the much-blessed congregation at Coorparoo and the rather conservative, even perhaps a little cold, atmosphere that he found at St Michael's. He addressed the need head on. He held a 'Warm-Up' weekend, where the congregation came to the parish hall and participated in games and activities to 'break the ice.' He opened the northern door of the church – previously it was closed and used for storage – and closed the southern door (except for weddings) to encourage people to stay and chat over an alfresco morning tea or lunch on the lawn.[22]

Second, like all good leaders he defined a better reality. He did this chiefly through his preaching, which was always thought-provoking and sometimes magnificent. His children were becoming interested in trying to understand how he did it. His sermon notes were sparse. He never seemed to write them out in full. He would say, 'I'm just going to close my eyes for a bit,' and while he was doing that, he would collect his thoughts. But they were thoughts unusual for their clarity and relevance to strengthening the local church community. He gave all parishioners a simple workable definition of ministry: it is 'the service which Christians offer to one another and to the world for Christ's sake.' 'We have woken up to the gospel and to our responsibility,' said one parishioner. Harry had a remarkable 'ability to explore deep and difficult truths in language that was simple and easily understood by all levels of the congregation,' observed another.

Third, he encouraged lay members to exercise their gifts in ministry and increase their confidence through training. He and Pam nurtured and coaxed rather than bludgeoned traditional pew-warmers into new areas of ministry they never dreamed they could attempt. For example, he encouraged Phyllis Younger, who was the wife of the verger, to start a Wednesday afternoon leisure club as an outreach to the older Wollongong community. To increase the Bible knowledge and therefore confidence of parishioners, he introduced the Bethel Bible course. To increase confidence in evangelism, he introduced EE.

Fourth, he added staff, and to increase lay involvement and the smooth running of the church, he established a range of subcommittees including education, aged care, prayer, visitation evangelism, church services, music, literature, property and finance, and a range of youth ministries. It worked because it all made sense.

There was, fifth, a more fundamental reason why Harry was so effective. He was authentic. He did not take a purely or even primarily instrumental view of people in the pews. They were not there just to build up the church. Rather, the church was there to build them up. As he looked on them each Sunday from the pulpit, he came to realise that they faced worlds of concerns, worries and challenges that he could not ignore.

Harry's empathy, however, was not only for those who were struggling: he also empathised with people in their dreams and aspirations. He was genuinely interested in what motivated the members of his congregations and he invested in their self-actualisation through the achievement of their own goals. His openness to all sorts and conditions of men and women, and his willingness to spend any amount of time encouraging them to realise their dreams, was supplemented by Pamela's willingness to extend hospitality to all. What together they discovered by experience was actually a remarkable secret for growing churches: focusing on helping people to fulfil their own dreams as well as achieving the goals of the church is a powerful means of building up the body of Christ, as is recognised in the most recent literature on church growth.[23]

## Archdeacon of Wollongong and Camden

Harry was appointed Archdeacon of Wollongong and Camden on 1 November 1979. Peter Kell, rector's warden at St Michael's, was disappointed. It had been absolutely amazing what Harry achieved in a few years as Rector of Wollongong: Bethel and EE; the music; the expansion in the ministry team and in lay ministry; the rise in spiritual temperature and in morale; the Good Friday rallies in Wollongong for the region, which attracted attendances of 900–1,000. The St Michael's parish council, which had been tight with money, when Harry wanted to do all these things, gladly invested in a better future. Peter Kell saw Harry go on to be a great encourager of the clergy as archdeacon, and later, Peter recognised, 'as regional Bishop he was magical.'[24] Those so grateful for the ministry he had given them, on his departure for another field of labour, over time would also give thanks for the fruitfulness of 'the ministry which lay ahead.'

Harry had come to the position at St Michael's as a parish minister and only ever thought, at least at a conscious level, that such was what he would be. He had to bury the prospect of being a bishop and get on with the work at hand. But as he spoke to Bp Ken Short, it became apparent that, if there were to be real advance, it would have to be across the parishes rather than in just one or two. Harry had already arrived at the settled conviction, which he so strongly advocated as archbishop, that the real work of the diocese takes place in the local churches, and that bishops and archdeacons should primarily see their roles as that of helping clergy to make their parishes as effective as possible. His new position allowed him the opportunity to further develop his fertile thinking on how to grow churches.[25] There can have been few in the diocese by experience and imagination better equipped for that role. Philip recalls going on walks with his father and Bp Ken Short, where they would discuss their ideas and plans and what would go into the regional magazine, *In Touch*. Philip was struck by the torrent of ideas that poured out of Harry and how readily Ken Short agreed with him. Ken's wife, Gloria, was so impressed by Harry's work in Wollongong that, on his appointment as archdeacon, she put into verse her feeling that he might one day be archbishop:

> He came from Joe's city an ordinary Revy
> To the Surf and the Smoke of the Gong

> And the Church very soon made Harry a heavy
> Unable to wait very long
>
> They made him a Canon with Chapter and Stall
> He 'shot' into fame very quick
> And Harry our Canon was right on the 'ball'
> Even Ken couldn't teach him a trick
>
> With Harry comes Pam: with small Tim[26] and the brood
> To charm us and keep us in trim
> With wide open door and excellent food
> We find it so hard to keep slim
>
> With the dog and the kids they make quite a team
> Not forgetting the singing canary
> To the boys in Church house – it would obviously seem
> They like Harry, not long hairs and hairy
>
> So now he is one of the Venerable crew
> But minus the gas and the gaiters
> But listen to me, the years will be few
> Bishopscourt will be sooner than later.

In the event, Bishopscourt was still 15 years in the future (three as an archdeacon and 12 as a bishop), but they were years of training in the essentials of what the diocese needed to get its parishes moving ahead.

In this twin role of archdeacon and parish consultant, Harry assisted Ken Short and did whatever was required of an archdeacon, but his passion and main focus was in the parishes. He and Pam visited parishes getting to know the clergy, their families, and some of the local leaders. He spent time with individual clergy talking about their work and offering advice when he thought it would be helpful. He ran courses for clergy and laity on such matters as preaching, evangelism, and church management.

Harry and Pam initially feared that they would miss the intimacy of having responsibility for a parish family, but they thrived in this new role and quickly came to love it. They were to look back on these days as a halcyon time in their ministry. Harry later reflected:

> One of the downsides of being Archbishop was that when we visited parishes across the Diocese it was not like visiting in the Region. Previously, we nearly always stayed in rectories for lunch and spent time

with the parents and their kids. Some of those we knew as youngsters are now in ministry with families of their own. As the Archbishop we [surely a very revealing pronoun!] would generally make our way home after participating in a morning service somewhere in the Diocese and quietly lament together about how different it was in Wollongong.[27]

It was while he was archdeacon that Harry was appointed to the International Board of EE. When the organisation, based in Fort Lauderdale in Florida and headed by Dr Jim Kennedy, resolved to go international, its directors did not do things by halves. They established an International Board of Directors and a well-staffed International Center [sic]. They wanted to establish a national board in Australia, and to oversee that process had appointed an advisory council, with Bp Jack Dain as its chairperson. They appointed Harry as chairperson of the National Strategy Group. It was indeed a good choice, allowing Harry over time to work successfully for a major change in the organisation. He could see what changes needed to be made, but he was not impatient and was respectful of cultures that differed from Australian norms. EE's new international Board now had equal numbers of North Americans and others from other parts of the world. But it met only annually, and Dr Kennedy retained his pivotal position as chairperson. The serious ongoing management was exercised by him and by a small executive committee made up of people associated mainly with Coral Ridge. An organisation fully open to international values was still two decades away, but a start had been made. Archie Parrish, Senior Vice-President of EE, and Jack Dain valued Harry's advice about those who might exercise leadership in EE in Australia. Impressed with Harry's wisdom and maturity, Dain could see that he was dealing with future bishop material.[28]

# 8
# Bishop of Wollongong: Episcopal Revival

The election of Donald Robinson as Archbishop of Sydney on 1 April 1982 had a domino effect in the episcopate. Robinson had been a bishop in Parramatta from 1973. He appointed Ken Short, then a bishop in Wollongong, to replace him in Parramatta. The announcement that Harry was to be appointed Bishop of Wollongong in succession to Ken Short was made by Archbishop Robinson to the SC on 27 April 1982. 'We are all very pleased' by this 'welcome' news declared Broughton Knox.[1] Like most matters announced at SC, the news became public knowledge the next day. What stands out in Harry's elevation to the episcopate is that it was greeted with near euphoria, quite astonishing by Sydney standards.

## Response to Harry's appointment

Evangelical Anglicans, we are told, do not get as excited by the appointment of bishops as do those of a different tradition. But, as evidenced by the surviving letters, it is difficult to conceive how the excitement occasioned by the announcement of Harry's appointment could have been any greater. The historian's impression that these letters were exceptional in their number and enthusiasm was confirmed by an observation made by Professor Edwin Judge, historian and synodsperson. He recalls that, when in 1965 he wrote to Jack Dain, congratulating him on his appointment as a bishop by Archbishop Hugh Gough, he received a reply thanking him and saying that it was the only letter of congratulation he received. Judge surmises that Dain's appointment had been unpopular, possibly because he was an English person appointed by an English person. If true, Dain's experience must have been as exceptional in one direction as Harry's was in the other. Harry was buried under an avalanche of congratulatory correspondence.

Most bishops would have expected more recognition than Dain received. After all, such occasions are at least a valuable opportunity for representatives of church organisations and parishes to get a hearing from the incoming bishop. Further, the consecration of a bishop is always an opportunity to reflect on the nature of leadership in the church, and these letters reveal what qualities clergy and laity want to see in their bishops.

The letters are also evidence of the nature of relations with other dioceses and church parties. So, as Harry was welcomed by his fellow bishops, he was also instructed by them on what it means to be a bishop in the church of God.

One more qualified than most to instruct him was David Hand, who had been a bishop in Papua New Guinea from 1950 and archbishop from 1963, and was in the second last year of his long episcopate. The day of Harry's consecration, St Peter's Day, 1982, would be the 32nd anniversary of his own consecration. A celibate Anglo-Catholic, Hand was once mistaken by the Duke of Edinburgh for a Roman Catholic. When Hand pointed out that he was Church of England, the Duke replied, 'Are you sure?' Hand was sure from personal experience of one thing: that the life of a bishop was not meant to be easy. He had witnessed in 1951 the destruction wrought by the Mount Lamington volcano explosion, which incinerated 3,466 people and was described by Colonel J.K. Murray, Administrator of the Territory, as a scene of desolation more terrible than he had witnessed in either of the two world wars.[2] Hand mentioned to Harry that, at a consecration of two bishops 18 years earlier, he had been 'moved by the Holy Spirit' to take as his text, 'they clothed Him with purple, and platted a crown of thorns, and put it about his head' (Mk 15:17, King James Version). 'We share with Him in the royal purple at our peril,' exegeted Hand, 'if we do not also share with Him in the fellowship of His sufferings.'[3]

Harry received congratulations from many of the Australian bishops who were not evangelicals: Ralph Wicks of Brisbane, Owen Dowling of Canberra and Goulburn, Hamish Jamieson of Carpentaria, John Lewis of North Queensland, Bruce Rosier (Willochra), Alfred Holland (Newcastle) and the urbane Oliver Heyward, Bendigo, who welcomed Harry 'to the episcopal bench.' The primate, John Grindrod, who had replaced Felix Arnott as Archbishop of Brisbane, wrote that 'Brisbane was delighted' at the news, evidence of Harry's wide acceptance within that high-church diocese in which he had served so faithfully. Grindrod added that 'Queensland sunshine seems to be having its good effect on the episcopate; yourself, Peter Carnley and Phillip Newell!'[4] Newell was appointed Bishop of Tasmania in that same year. Carnley, Archbishop of Perth from 1981, was to defeat Harry in the election for primate in 2000. Among the bishops outside of Sydney, the Bishop of Grafton, Donald Shearman, had heard of the happiness Harry's appointment had produced:

> I gather from a number of people whom I know in the Sydney area that your appointment as Bishop of Wollongong has met with a great deal of enthusiasm and this must be enormously helpful for you to know.[5]

Among the evangelical bishops, Jack Dain, who had worked closely with Harry in the ministry of EE, and now on the eve of retirement, wrote to Harry: 'I do not believe any appointment has been more widely and warmly acclaimed.'[6]

Clive Kerle, who had been the Bishop of Armidale and was then Rector of St Swithun's, Pymble, the parish that was destined to perturb Harry's early years as archbishop, wrote: 'If Donald Sydney's appointments are all as wise as this I will retire at peace with God and full of confidence. Helen and I think the new Bishop in Wollongong and his wife will be the right people in the right job.'[7]

John Reid, assistant bishop in Sydney, wrote:

> I want to say that I am very pleased indeed that you are to be consecrated bishop. It seems to me wholly right and it gives me very real satisfaction … I have no doubt that this news will be very well received in the Wollongong area. Everything I've heard is that you have a wonderful acceptance in that area already.[8]

From Fuller Theological Seminary in California, Marcus Loane, following retirement as archbishop, on a lecture tour of North American seminaries arranged by Billy Graham,[9] passed on to Harry his meditation on 1 Peter 2:25. It speaks of Jesus as the shepherd and bishop of our souls, and Marcus had seen it translated as 'shepherd and watchman.' He observed, 'I like that very much; it seems very suggestive of what a Bishop should be.'[10] Harry must have written in response, asking Marcus to preach at his consecration. As Marcus had been his college principal and then his archbishop, he was an obvious choice. But he would not return from overseas before the consecration and had to decline. So, Harry asked Broughton Knox instead. Broughton was touched. 'I want to express to you my deep appreciation of this honour and I am moved by your kindness in thinking of me.'[11] For Broughton it was more than an honour, and he wrote to Archbishop Robinson beseeching his prayers 'as I prepare.'[12]

The senior clergy could not conceive of a better appointment. Alan Cole, then Federal Secretary of CMS, and destined to be a copious letter writer to Harry when he became archbishop, wrote, 'I could jump for joy to think of you as Bishop in Wollongong. May the Lord bless you and your "elect lady".'[13] Stuart Barton Babbage, then Master of New College, and surely the most episcopal material never to become a bishop, wrote, 'We are all delighted about your appointment. God has given you a great gift of friendship, and I am sure you will be much loved.'[14] Dudley Foord, Rector of St Ives, wrote, 'We are glad and receive this news with great pleasure.'[15] Canon John Chapman, Director of the Department of Evangelism, wrote, 'I cannot fully explain to you the delight that it was to have the Archbishop nominate you for the new work. I didn't really mind if it was going to be Wollongong or Parramatta so long as it was going to be you.'[16] Old Archdeacon Fillingham advised Harry to let the words of Isaiah 41:10 be writ large in his heart and mind, and to check out the Authorized Version rendering of 2 Corinthians 9:8, 'although a bit out of context' – very Sydney![17] At the time of his appointment, Harry was chairperson of the Church Army, and its federal director, Gilbert Page, wrote that the news of Harry's appointment was 'very thrilling.'[18] David Cohen, Rector of Manly, said 'There is no-one I know whom I believe could handle it better.'[19] Neville Malone, CEO of the diocese, gave the news his usual measured consideration: 'I am particularly gratified by this appointment as I know that God has granted to you all the spiritual gifts so necessary for this office in the Church.'[20]

As for lay people, so loved and respected were Harry and Pam in their previous churches, in the Wollongong Region where he had served as archdeacon, and among the members of the central administration in Sydney, that they were inundated with the warmest of congratulations. Many well-wishers reported being 'thrilled' or 'overjoyed' by the news, while the more reserved settled for 'delighted'.[21] Canon David Peterson, who had taken over from Harry as Rector of Wollongong and was later to support Harry in the campaign to make him archbishop, wrote, 'I am sure you are aware of the great enthusiasm of the people of St Michael's about your consecration to be our next Bishop. People keep on telling me how much they rejoice at this appointment.'[22] Canon Len Harris, who was retired but serving as a locum in a number of parishes in the Wollongong Region, reported on the joy Harry's appointment had generated in all those parishes. He hoped that Wollongong would yet be made a diocese separate from Sydney and he believed Harry's leadership would be received with the 'same joy' in all the parishes of the 'proposed Diocese.'[23] In a similar vein, Basil Williams, who had been Harry's predecessor as Rector of Wollongong, 1960–76, wrote:

> your whole area is perhaps the best in the diocese and has great potentiality, and you know it well. We still trust that one day it will become a diocese in its own right and that part of your commission will be to work to that end.[24]

As we shall see, a different way forward was to be found when Harry became archbishop.

Alan Patrick wrote that his parishioners at Camden were 'very thrilled and pleased' with the news.[25] From Chatswood, Kevin and Anne Jacups wrote: 'We are both thrilled about it for your sake and for Wollongong's ... it was a bit disappointing for us that you will not be "Bishop of Chatswood".'[26] From Coorparoo, Sylvia Marshall enthused about Harry's appointment: 'Everybody in Coorparoo is talking about it with beaming faces. Me too.' From Keiraville parish, Margaret Lamb wrote: 'We want you to know how much respect, love and support you have from a wide cross section of lay people.'[27] Already Harry was the layperson's bishop. 'I have never known, personally, a man to rise to such a position,' wrote another, 'but having known and admired you both over the years, and as I look at the Scriptures, I can see no one more suitable to gain such recognition.'[28]

Typically, letters of congratulations to Harry also recalled moments when Harry had touched the lives of his grateful correspondents. From the church of his childhood, Holy Trinity, Dulwich Hill, Dorothy Fowler, mother of John and Margaret, wrote: 'I don't mind telling you that ... I had a weep for joy and then back came all the memories ... and I thank God I have been spared to see this day.'[29] From Carlingford Peppi and Peter Whiteman said that they always knew that Harry would be appointed a bishop eventually, but it was 'great' that his abilities had been recognised while he was 'still young.'[30] From Brisbane, Rod Irvine, the future Rector of Figtree, which was to become one of the largest churches in the diocese, with no little help from Harry, wrote, 'Please be assured of our prayers and great joy at this new appointment ... It was your leading that encouraged us into Moore College and the ministry for which we will always be grateful.'[31] Ray Lindsay, from Carlingford church, wrote, 'My mother thinks so much of you, she calls you her pin up boy. She feels so proud to have a pin up boy for a Bishop.'[32] 'Praying' George Piper wrote formally:

> I would be failing in my responsibility as Secretary of the [Wollongong] Readers Association, if I failed to tell you that your appointment has caused a response from members of deep appreciation and loyalty, and expectancy of continued encouraging and good leadership.[33]

So many were pleased by this appointment that Archbishop Robinson was praised for his 'good judgment', for his 'superb choice'. To those aware of Harry's effectiveness in every previous appointment, it seemed a logical choice. Reminded of Paul's words in 2 Corinthians 8:18, Greg Hammond wrote: 'With him we are sending one of our company whose reputation is high among our congregations everywhere for his services to the Gospel.' Joy, wife of Eric Marchoni, warden of Beverly Hills, who had written to Harry five days before the announcement jesting that 'Richard Henry' would be made a bishop, wrote,

> Can't say we were surprised! Eric said years ago that this would happen. It wasn't said in a prophetic sense (I don't think) but just because he has such a high regard for you. Betty French said this morning that you would finish up archbishop! How about that! Move over Donald Robinson.[34]

Among those who knew Harry well was a concern that the role of bishop would remove him from 'the people'; 'you are a "people" person.'[35] Those who lived in Harry's region were glad to count him as 'our bishop.' There was considerable appreciation of 'Bishopess' Pam in these letters. One who dwelt on this dimension to Harry's appointment was Jim Holbeck, who had worked with Harry at Coorparoo, was then Dean of Armidale, and was to become the Director of the Healing Ministry in Sydney:

> I must say it was not unexpected that you would finish up wearing the purple. Our time with you was a real eye-opener to us of how someone could lead, without appearing to be aggressive and domineering. Indeed the whole family was so close and showed such love that it was a model for clergy families, and this obviously was a factor in your appointment. So Pam – our congratulations to you and to the children.[36]

Many of the letters mentioned the impact the appointment must have made on his family. From Carlingford, Rene Gregory wrote of the response of Harry's normally quiet, serene mother to her son's appointment: 'Chrissie was quite overcome by the news and it was a privilege to share her obvious joy.'[37]

Reporting on this tsunami of delight at Harry's appointment runs the risk of turning this biography into hagiography, the most dreaded form of writing on ecclesiastical matters. But, if so, it is the bishops, clergy and laity who have made it so. This biographer did not write those letters! Evidently, Harry's appointment was an opportunity for Anglicans and other evangelicals to express what the Faith endorsed but the culture then found difficult to express; namely, love for one another, and especially for one who had become a genuine friend in Christian fellowship.

## Consecration and installation

Harry and Pam faced bankruptcy owing to the necessity of purchasing episcopal robes! They also faced anxiety getting them to the cathedral on time, for they did not have long to procure them. To Ted and Judy Brennan from Coorparoo, who were among the many who contributed to the purchase of his robes, Harry wrote,

> The cost of Episcopal robes is a strong incentive to do away with them altogether! I remember reading once in Pascal that robes of office were necessary to cover the foolishness of those who wore them and to give them some sense of grandeur which they didn't possess in themselves. The price of them makes me feel that I can put up with my own public foolishness![38]

8.1 Vince O'Farrell, *Illawarra Mercury* cartoonist, lampoons Harry's elevation to the episcopate for his opposition to female ordination. *Illawarra Mercury*, April 1982.

Bp John Reid took up a collection to cover the cost of the robes, which were purchased from J. Wippell and Company in Exeter, England. They cost £528.40.

On 28 June, Harry went into retreat at Gilbulla Conference Centre. He was joined by three clergy (Barry Marsh, Reg Hanlon, and David Peterson) and two laypersons (Peter Kell and Stuart Piggin). There was some reflection on the assessment of a previous Archbishop of Sydney, William Saumarez Smith, that 'he gave encouragement rather than leadership.' Harry was so good at the former that his considerable gift for the latter could easily be overlooked. There was no doubt among all present that whatever leadership Harry gave would be servant leadership.

In St Andrew's Cathedral, Sydney, on Tuesday, 29 June 1982, St Peter's Day, the traditional day for such events, Archbishop Robinson consecrated Harry Bishop of Wollongong in the Diocese of Sydney. To allow those from Wollongong to get up to Sydney after work, the service started at 7 pm. From the opening hymn, it was an unforgettable demonstration of Christian love, unleashed through the emotional fervour of Charles Wesley's prayer.

> *My gracious Master and my God,*
> *Assist me to proclaim,*
> *To spread through all the earth abroad*
> *The honours of your name.*

It had long been the custom in the Church for the bishop-elect to choose the preacher.[39] The choice of preacher therefore gave some indication of how the new bishop understood his role and what he hoped might be achieved through it. In asking Marcus Loane, and then, on Marcus's inability to preach, Broughton Knox, Harry was identifying closely with the fundamental thrust of Moore College, namely, to preach the gospel and teach the Bible. The majority of consecration sermons are preached on 1 Timothy 3:1–7, which speaks of the qualifications of a bishop or overseer. Instead Broughton chose as his text 2 Timothy 4:17, 'the Lord stood by me and gave me strength, so that through me the message might be fully proclaimed and all the Gentiles might hear it. So I was rescued from the lion's mouth.' David Crawford, Rector of Malabar, considered Broughton's text 'an intriguing choice … but inspired.'[40] Like all sermons preached in Sydney, Broughton's was heard by glad hearts and analytical minds. Canon Tony Lamb considered it 'tops', but not all were as enthusiastic. Accustomed to the warmth and encouragement of a Goodhew sermon, Broughton's lay hearers found his clinical style and cool reasoning more challenging than they had anticipated.

With the words, 'Most Reverend Father in God, we present to you this godly and learned man to be ordained and consecrated bishop,' Ken Short, who had been so instrumental in getting Harry to come to Wollongong in the first place, and Peter Chiswell, an old friend and from 1976 Bishop of Armidale, presented Harry to the archbishop. Harry stood between them, dressed in a cassock. He was there interrogated or examined by the archbishop in a series of eight questions 'so that the congregation present may hear how you are determined to act in the church of God.'

Harry then withdrew and put on the rest of his episcopal vesture as provided in the rubrics of the 1662 Consecration of Bishops. One who looked on at this point in the service with peculiar satisfaction was Captain Gilbert Page, Federal Director of the Church Army. It was he who had collected Harry's robes from Wippell's in England and escorted them safely to Sydney just in time for the consecration.

Harry then kneeled before the archbishop while the congregation sang the ancient hymn 'Come Holy Ghost, our souls inspire'. In the most solemn moment in the service, Archbishop Robinson, together with the then primate, Archbishop Grindrod, and the Bishops of Armidale, Bathurst, Canberra/Goulburn, Grafton, Newcastle[41] and Riverina – that is, all the Bishops of the Province of New South Wales – and by Sydney's Assistant Bishops Reid, Short and Cameron,[42] laid hands on Harry, and the archbishop said, 'Receive the Holy Spirit for the office and work of a bishop in the church of God, now committed to you by the laying on of our hands.' The archbishop then gave Harry a Bible with the words, 'Think upon the things contained in this book. Practise them that what you learn may be evident to all.'

It was then common practice for an archbishop to present the newly consecrated bishop with a staff and a ring, symbols of his role as both a shepherd and as married to his diocese. But Donald Robinson did not present any of his assistant bishops with staffs and rings, since he was always precise about such practices and he believed that a diocese could have only one 'bishop'. So, while he was happy to have Harry addressed as the Bishop of Wollongong, rather than the bishop in Wollongong, Donald Robinson made it plain that Harry was responsible to him.

The women of St Paul's, Carlingford, one of Harry's previous parishes, provided supper at the reception in the chapter house after the service, and Gerald Christmas, the diocesan registrar, spoke on behalf of the laity and Dudley Foord on behalf of the clergy. Donald Shearman, Bishop of Grafton, who had already heard of the widespread esteem for Harry was nevertheless surprised by the joy of the happy throng who attended the service.

> Your Consecration was a great event for the whole Church. I was especially delighted to see such an enormous crowd. It was almost impossible to move in the supper room afterwards and I introduced myself to a number of folk who had come at obvious inconvenience to themselves especially to be with you on that occasion. The buses and carloads that came up from the south is a fair indication of the very great affection and regard with which you're held in the Wollongong region.[43]

Harry later confessed that he was profoundly moved by the service. 'The sense of being prayed for by so many people at the same time was quite overwhelming.'[44] Harry longed to be faithful in his calling, and with the unprecedented consciousness that so many were praying for him, he was able to trust that God would grant him that grace in this new role.[45] As the church in her wisdom no doubt intended, Harry meditated on the significance of being consecrated on St Peter's Day. He felt considerable empathy with Peter in his weakness and lack of courage. Yet Christ prayed for him and committed a ministry to him, though his human hands were weak. Harry took heart from that, and from the 'sustaining reality' that Christ endows his people with gifts for service.[46]

The next evening Harry and Pam, never known to waste an opportunity to bless others, attended the induction of Jack Knapp as Presbyterian minister at Wollongong. Then the following day, 1 July, Harry was installed as Bishop of Wollongong in St Michael's Provisional Cathedral, Wollongong. The archbishop began the service with prayer.

> Stir up the zeal and love of many ... and grant that all, both clergy and laity, may labour with a single eye to your glory ... Grant us so to be joined together in unity of spirit by their doctrine, that we may be made a holy temple acceptable to you.

In answer, the anointing of the Spirit was palpable: the holy flame was bestowed and freely burned. The goodwill of the congregation overflowed, and all present resolved to serve with fresh courage. Harry had good reason to believe that the formality of Anglican worship was entirely compatible with spiritual blessing and empowerment for service. From many such experiences, he increasingly questioned the wisdom of dispensing with the heartfelt beauty of liturgical worship in the empty pursuit of relevance. If, a decade later, this stance was to cause strife with those eager to dispense with prayer book worship, Harry would face that strife with a gift that he prayed to be confirmed at that service of Installation.

> *Let holy charity*
> *Mine outward vesture be,*
> *And lowliness become mine inner clothing.*

Another of Harry's gifts was also evident in this service: his gift for evangelism. The Bible reading at the installation was read by lay reader, Chris Dixon, whom Harry had helped in her journey from Marxism to faith. She remained a lifelong friend and a stalwart of faith. Harry arranged for her to be employed as the Scripture Teacher at a local high school, to be paid by the combined churches. At the 20th anniversary of Harry's consecration as bishop, she sent him a quotation from John Donne, which spoke of heaven and incidentally how all of Chris's aspirations that had attracted her to Marxism were fulfilled in Christ.

> And into that gate they shall enter, and in that house they shall dwell, where there shall be no cloud nor sun, no darkness nor dazzling, but one equal light, no noise nor silence, but one equal music, no fears nor hopes, but one equal possession, no foes nor friends, but one equal communion and identity, no ends nor beginnings, but one equal eternity.

Harry was to preach at her funeral in 2008.

It seems hard to credit, but so great was the love and joy generated by Harry's appointment as bishop that it felt like a religious revival. On the one hand, it was so obviously right; on the other, it was 'a surprising work of God.' He had dramatically increased the appetite for ministry in every parish he had been. Now it was hoped all the churches in his episcopal region would experience the same blessing.

## Harry's care of the Wollongong Region

Archbishop Robinson knew precisely what he wanted Harry to be and to do. He appointed Harry to be 'Assistant Bishop in the Diocese of Sydney ... resident in Wollongong with the title "Bishop of Wollongong".[47] He spelled out Harry's priorities in a letter dated 24 June 1982, a week before his consecration.

> While I shall do all I can to keep you within the fellowship of our 'corporate episcopate' and of the Diocese in general, it is of the first importance that you give yourself to the pastoral care of the clergy and parishes of the area. The chief value of our regional system has been in the increased pastoral oversight it has made possible.

Harry would have said 'amen' to that. He was to give his own associate bishops similar direction when he became archbishop. Harry's 'territory' included the area deaneries of Berrima, Macarthur, Shoalhaven, Sutherland and Wollongong. He worked regularly with his area deans to foster the work of the region, an approach, when archbishop, he asked his regional bishops to implement diligently because he had seen its effectiveness in Wollongong.

His was a very happy region in the diocese. His pastoral care for those for whom he had responsibility was exceptional. Many good clergy were pleased to move into his region. Allen Quee, for example, Rector of Beverly Hills when Harry was appointed bishop, became Rector of Dapto in 1984, and, in a move boldly supported by Harry, Rod Irvine, who had been drawn into the ministry by Harry, moved from Brisbane to become Rector of Figtree in 1987. Harry was responsible for 75 active clergy, both male and female, 17 parish-based full-time workers, 10 Careforce workers, and about 50 retired clergy and their wives. He was also involved with the Lay Readers' Association in Wollongong, planning their conferences and training lay readers. At the Bishop's House in Oleander Ave, Figtree, Philip had to pass through his father's study to access his bedroom. He often saw his father praying, with a folder open with the names and photos of all his clergy and their families, and he would pray for them all.

As chair of the regional council, Harry encouraged it to work through a number of interest-based working parties. He held well-attended clergy conferences and ministry training seminars. He and Pam followed the lead given by Ken and Gloria Short and met with parish nominators (whose job was to find ministers to replace departing ministers) to tutor them in their role. In all the programs aimed at developing the quality of leadership among the clergy and lay leaders, Harry was ably assisted by his archdeacon, Vic Roberts, and his wife, Delle. In particular, Vic conducted training sessions for clergy and laity in the labyrinthine mysteries of the Sydney Church Ordinance. Between them, Harry and Vic really mounted an in-service, post-ordination, on-the-ground training program for regional churches, dealing with leadership issues, preaching, developing strategies for church growth and offering encouragement in practical ministry. Both Harry and Vic grounded their programs in solid research conducted through tertiary institutions; Harry on church growth and Vic on the use of the lectionary in services of worship.[48]

## Harry's research on church leadership

In 1985, Harry enrolled in a Master of Arts degree at the University of Wollongong and wrote a thesis on church growth to help him think systematically and strategically about the leadership factor in the growth of local churches.[49] He was awarded the degree with honours on 12 October 1990.[50] He found it a congenial as well as a useful exercise; he enjoyed the research and writing, read copiously in the burgeoning literature on church growth, grasped issues quickly, processed data with speed and accuracy without oversimplifying, devised interesting and important hypotheses, and wrote, as he preaches, with clarity and grace.

In his thesis Harry established that, overriding all other factors, the senior minister's leadership is the critical factor in the growth of the local church. He defended the very academic-sounding proposition that the leadership of the local church will be effective the more successfully it:
   a. matches internal strategies with external reality
   b. addresses the criteria of accessibility (proximity), cultural fit (congruity), and usefulness in meeting needs (utility)
   c. identifies the stage in the growth cycle the church is in, so that it can develop appropriate managerial policies.

For two important reasons, however, Harry's research was much more than an academic exercise. It was very practical, based on a survey of six local churches in the Illawarra Region, five of which were Anglican. Though the one that was not Anglican grew the fastest, Harry was able to demonstrate that it was not Anglicanism which slowed growth – an important conclusion that made him reluctant to depart too far from Anglican traditions when he became archbishop. It enabled him to give practical advice to ministers who needed a clear sense of their own identity and who longed to see their churches grow. As to identity, he said a church leader is best understood as a servant, an overseer, a shepherd, and a steward. A shepherd, he maintained, is one who communicates the meaning of faith by evangelism, pastoring and teaching and who maintains the character of the functioning church community. Ideally the ministerial leader should be relaxed and confident in God and in the gifts that God has given him. As to the key to church growth, that is relatively simple. 'Churches grow when they give themselves to God's purpose, give priority to effective evangelism, and involve laymen and train them.'[51]

In spite of the fact that he was writing this thesis to satisfy a secular university, Harry rightly insisted that there is a divine, spiritual factor in effective church leadership. Harry put it like this:

> The continued growth of a local church depends upon the capacity of the leader to fashion an environment in which people come alive to the reality of God, are enabled and empowered to develop, confirm, and express their relationship with God, and in which they find a fulfilment of their spiritual hopes, ambitions, and desires.[52]

Harry's distinctive thrust appears to have been that the supernatural and the pragmatic should be synthesised. He wrote in his thesis approvingly of the approach of the Rector of Figtree, Rod Irvine. A Queenslander, Rod had not been a rector before, and he had not yet settled on a leadership style. But he was apparently working with two models. One was the supernatural model, born of his interest in the history of revival and his respect for Jonathan Edwards, the church's leading theologian of revival, and for John Wesley, the founder of Methodism. This model relies on God to call people into fellowship with himself through Spirit-anointed preaching. The other model, favoured by pragmatic church-growth theorists, was to emphasise the 'how to do it' technology of making churches grow. Rod Irvine, Harry suspected, had the wit and the will to synthesise the two (as indeed had Wesley, who was a pragmatist with a burning heart). It was good to manage things well, better to 'let God arise,' and best to do both. People come to church, Harry knew, primarily to find and experience God. If they believe that God is present, they will not be absent.

## Church schools

As bishop, Harry was associated with three councils of church schools in the region: Macarthur Anglican School, The Illawarra Grammar School (TIGS), and St Peter's Campbelltown School. He was involved in the establishment of Macarthur Anglican School in 1984, thus gaining the valuable experience he exercised when he presided over the creation of a number of new low-fee Anglican Schools when he was archbishop.

As for TIGS, Harry worked hard to have the very successful headmaster, Peter Smart, appointed there. Peter later became diocesan Registrar assisting Harry as archbishop. Peter first met Harry when the latter was at Coorparoo and Peter would travel up to Brisbane from Tamworth for the CMS General Committee. Harry was also involved from time to time with the Diocese of Armidale in Bp Peter Chiswell's time. Peter Smart felt he got to know Harry well first at St Peter's Anglican Church, South Tamworth, and then at Calrossy Anglican School in Tamworth, where Peter was the Headmaster from 1976 to 1988. Harry rang him one day to say that he was coming through and wanted to call on him. He told Peter that he wanted him to apply for the position of Headmaster at TIGS, then in need of some help. Peter had already rescued a needy Calrossy, but it was not clear that Harry would get his own way either with Peter or with the TIGS council. In the event, the council voted narrowly to appoint Peter, an outcome only achieved by requiring council member, Joan Loane, who had a bad back, to be in attendance to vote for Peter; and she had to lie on the floor to do so. But still Peter was not sure that he wanted the job. While he was with a school group in New Zealand, Harry rang him every couple of days to tell him that they needed an answer. When they came back from New Zealand, Harry and Pam met the group at Sydney airport and then rang again when Peter returned to Tamworth. Harry was quietly determined, and he said to Peter 'we need an answer by Monday.' Peter said, 'All right then, I'll come.' Elizabeth, his wife, was in the kitchen; she overheard this conversation and said, 'What did you say?'

Harry's determined pursuit of Peter is evidence of a surprising aspect of his personality. How could one so gentle be so resolute? Reflecting decades later on 'the Servant of the Lord' in Isaiah 42 and Matthew 12, Harry observed that both Isaiah and Matthew focus on *style* and *effectiveness*.

> The style of the Servant's ministry would not be bruising and crushing, like that of a triumphant Cyrus. Rather it would be (and Matthew says it was in fact) quiet, gentle and restorative. However, for all its gentle demeanour, the Servant's ministry would be effective, persistently pursuing his appointed task until he established God's purpose in the world.[53]

Harry was chairperson of the TIGS council and was far from prescriptive, but Peter heard the unstated expectation that he should make the school 'more Christian' and he knew it had to be a good school, well run and economically sound. Harry continued as chairperson of council and came to more activities than one would expect of a bishop. When he became archbishop, Peter invited him to speech night. It was a breach of archbishop's protocol, in that he had always gone to the King's School speech night, but the TIGS speech night was on the same evening,

8.3 Opening of Richard Johnson Anglican College at the University of Wollongong, 11 March 1993. Left to right: Canon Raymond Heslehurst, Noriko Dethlefs, Mr Justice Hope, Harry, Peter Kell and Pam. Between Justice Hope and Harry is a photograph of Sir Vincent and Lady Fairfax, who purchased the property.

and Harry went to TIGS. He had a heart for what was being done there.

At the beginning of 1985, Harry spoke at the Prefect Induction at TIGS. His address featured a catalogue of words beginning with 'F', and the last 'F' was a 'Frenchman', the Sociologist Jacques Ellul. Richard Donnelly, a teacher at the school, was an Ellul fan and was struck by Harry's breadth of reading and his capacity to communicate in such a 'meaty, challenging and completely non-patronising way' to the students. Richard joined a reading group with Harry, which morphed into the senior common room of the Richard Johnson College, the Anglican residential college of the University of Wollongong.[54] Then, at the opening of the Illawarra Grammar Centre, the school's new hall, Harry said that TIGS is a school that teaches young people not only how to live, but how to die. 'It took my breath away,' said Donnelly.[55]

Peter and Elizabeth Smart were invited by two Wollongong couples, Peter and Faye Kell and Jeff and Marg Fuller, to join a support group for Harry. It was highly significant for the Smarts because it enabled them to get to know Harry even better. They continued to meet when Harry was archbishop. Harry had been advised to appoint a spiritual director when he became archbishop, but it was to this group that he would look for spiritual direction. They would pray together and discuss issues of a type that one would bring before a spiritual director. Over three decades later, they were still meeting, especially on the anniversaries of his consecration as bishop and his election as archbishop.

## The H and P Team

Harry's elevation meant that Pam, too, had to step up. And she did. Never for a moment had Harry given her the impression that she was just an ancillary; neither would he accept any self-doubts that she had. Not only did he reassure her, but, consistent with his instincts as a trainer, he helped her practically to perform tasks that she doubted she could do. When they had first come to Wollongong, the leaders of the Mothers' Union had asked Harry to speak at their festival and Pam to speak at the lunch afterwards, an event to which 250 had accepted the invitation to be present. She had never spoken at such a public event, and when she expressed some reserve about accepting the invitation, Harry said, 'I'll help you.' So, between them, they put together an address. And then the chief organiser asked Pam if she would be funny, since, unless she were, some of those present, being elderly, might have difficulty staying awake after lunch. Again, Pam was tinged with anxiety, and Harry again came to the rescue. He sat up at midnight and wrote some doggerel verse for her about dinosaurs. It was at the time when the Mothers' Union, along with the rest of Australia, was thinking about what it would be like to cut the apron strings with Britain. What would it mean for the Mothers' Union to become autonomous? The moral of Harry's poem was that extinction is the certain fate of those who fail to change. It took some 10 verses for the dinosaurs to become extinct, by which time all the ladies were wide awake, and many asked afterwards, not for a copy of the talk, but for a copy of the poem!

So, having survived that ordeal, Pam kept accepting the invitations to speak, which she kept receiving. She realised that, now that Harry was a bishop, people would expect her to be able to make a habit of giving such speeches. She believed that taking advantage of such opportunities would allow her to be with people and get to know them. It was an extension of Harry's ministry in another sense. Many of her talks were fashioned on his: she would take one of his addresses and together they would work on it until they had a talk they felt suitable for the occasion.

Pam could see that this approach was not for everyone, and it would be hard for bishops' wives who could not bear the weight of such expectation. She was now a more confident person thanks to Harry's support. But she was not unreflective about her role. She had always tried very hard not to be judgemental of the women who thought differently from her and from each other about the role of the minister's wife. This became an increasingly emotive issue in the diocese, not only because feminism was on the rise, but also because its antithesis was also on the rise and became the butt of humour that was not always generous: there were clergy wives with a reputation for being stronger than their husbands, it was observed, but who, out of loyalty to what they believed was biblical doctrine and diocesan culture, insisted on being submissive to their husbands. Pam was strong, but she did not insist on being submissive, and thought the submission thing was being overdone by the zealous traditionalists. She preferred the view of John Stott, who always had the last word as far as Harry and Pam were concerned that, in the New Testament, the word submission meant to put yourself under someone in order to hold them up.

Pam was ready to give Harry advice, but she readily withdrew if he did not take it. When Harry had difficulty with a co-worker, Pam would say to him, 'why don't you speak to him? Just tell him!' Harry would say, 'No. If I moved in on that situation, he would read it like this, and then that would cause this to happen.' He always seemed to understand how people would react in a given situation. Then he would decide if that is what he needed to have happen, or if it were better in the end not to do anything. Perhaps most act on the belief that everyone thinks the same way as they do, and therefore they are free with advice and, if leaders, with directives. Harry did not make this presumption and thus avoided provoking adverse reactions, but some read the decision not to act as indecision. It meant that Harry was a superb manager of people – of most of them anyway. But not even he could win them all!

## Harry and the social dimension of the gospel

For over a century, Wollongong has been home to working-class culture. There the union movement and the Labor Party have both thrived. The Anglican Church, though elsewhere traditionally conservative in its political sympathies, was more inclined to the left in Illawarra. There the clergy instinctively, if not always in a calculated way, sympathised with working-class aspirations. Harry, the son of working-class parents, was no exception. He easily felt people's pain. In his first year as bishop he was distressed by the unemployment level during the Wollongong recession. He gathered a group of committed laypeople around him (a typical stratagem) and appointed a social worker to establish programs to foster employment. The appointee established Employment Resources, which soon proved so successful in providing employment opportunities that it moved to a large factory. It won such sizeable grants from federal and state governments that it provoked a spot of industrial sabotage from the local Communists who had hitherto enjoyed a lien on such funding.

8.4 The Illawarra Steelers, formed in the same year as Harry became Bishop of Wollongong, were glad of the support of one so close to the highest power.

8.5 Harry and Catholic bishop of Wollongong, William Murray, upset the state government by expressing concern over unemployment created by the closure of the Tallawarra Power Station, 1988.

Harry was also instrumental in the establishment of Evelyn House (a Girls' Friendly Society home for homeless girls). He advanced cross-cultural initiatives and promoted good community relations with the civic authorities and with the police. He was involved in the appointment of Revd Neil Brain to a chaplaincy at the Lysaghts steel works, which led to clergy participation in management training programs there.

When a local power station was closed down in 1988, putting many out of work, Harry sought the support of the Catholic bishop, Bill Murray, and they made an effective protest that won the ringing endorsement of the local press. It has been said that 'History knows a cynical law: that in all lands politicians dislike ecclesiastics who interfere.'[56] So Harry and Murray evoked a hurt response from the NSW Premier and responsible Minister. In the Gulf crisis of 1990/1991, when a UN force opposed Iraq's invasion of Kuwait, Harry, who had good relations with the redoubtable union leaders, Merv Nixon and Paul Matters, cooperated with the South Coast Labour Council in a statement enjoining greater efforts on behalf of peace. Like his predecessor, Ken Short, Harry had a good working relationship with Wollongong's Lord Mayor, Frank Arkell, and both sought to share Christ with him. But Arkell was adept at changing the subject. While under investigation for paedophilia in 1998, he was savagely murdered.

Although a churchperson first and a citizen second, Harry was remarkably successful in winning the interest and support of civic authorities. He addressed social issues in the print media, on radio and TV. He wrote a weekly column

8.6 Rod Wishart, winger for the Steelers and destined to become the greatest pointscorer in the club's history, joins with Harry to promote the 'Can the Recession' food appeal for HMS, 1991.

for the *Illawarra Mercury*. Concerned about the impact of economic recession on families, including the disillusionment of youth, he spent his final days in Wollongong on his Can the Recession food drive. He was assisted by Rugby League test winger, Rob Wishart, who played for the Illawarra Steelers. He and Harry had an instant rapport, and Wishart worked hard to get the food drive going, ensuring its success. Harry understood the role of a football team in lifting morale during a recession and commended the Steelers for it.[57]

Of his multifarious responsibilities, the one that engaged Harry most, of course, was the growth of the local church. Harry and Pam met with rectors and their wives to encourage them in every initiative, and Harry and his archdeacon, Vic Roberts, met with church councils and held parish consultations to review their strategies for growth. Bruce Ballantine-Jones has argued consistently that Harry Goodhew was the most effective regional bishop the diocese had ever had, working 'assiduously to encourage ministers to be innovative and enterprising' and blessed with an 'engaging personality' that endeared him to 'clergy and people alike.'[58] None could do more than he to give himself 'to the pastoral care of the clergy and parishes of the area' as Donald Robinson directed him. But the Bishop of Wollongong's assiduous encouragement was to reach well beyond his region.

# 9

# Bishop Beyond Wollongong: Responding Obediently to God's Urgency

Harry Goodhew's vision was not confined to his region, and, in his years as Bishop of Wollongong, he developed areas of expertise that, one sees clearly in retrospect, were preparing him for a higher role. Three may be identified as critical: he became an expert in the 'science' (or is it the 'art'?) of church growth; he travelled overseas and developed a deep desire to strengthen the worldwide church; and he participated in an astonishing array of diocesan committees in which he developed the administrative skills essential to the management of a large diocese.

## Church growth and evangelism

Harry was to be quite exceptional among Australian archbishops in his enthusiasm for the application of church growth theory to the development of local parishes. His predecessor, Donald Robinson, opted for an English way of church revitalisation and imported his brother-in-law, Bruce Reed of the Grubb Institute, to give advice on how to make parishes in general, and worship in particular, work. It was not Robinson's consuming interest, whereas the growth of vital parish communities was undoubtedly Harry's first love. He was the leading authority on the growth of parishes among his generation of Australian bishops.

On 11–13 October 1992, less than six months before he became archbishop, Harry sponsored, at Darling Harbour in Sydney, a well-attended Bill Hybels conference, 'Building a Church for the Unchurched'. It was a bold move on Harry's part because not all favoured such an approach. But it was one of the initiatives that helped him to win the election, because it gave to the clergy and lay leaders evidence that Harry would be a change agent in the parishes, the instrumentalities that mattered most in the diocese.

Harry's interest in learning from the best overseas experiences reinforced his commitment to EE as an international ministry. In 1982 he attended the international board meeting of EE in Fort Lauderdale, an exercise he repeated in May 1983, and in February of most the years he was bishop. It was also in 1983 that Rod Story, who had been appointed Coordinator for EE ministry in Australia while he was still at Coorparoo, became the National Director of Australia for EE and moved to Wollongong, principally because Harry was there. In 1987 Rod was appointed EE's continental vice-chair for Oceania, which comprised 25 nations, including Indonesia as well as Australia and New Zealand. Meanwhile, Harry had been appointed chair of Australian EE. He was selected for this post ahead of a number of other dynamic Australians who were highly committed to EE, Rod Story suspects, because he was astute and had worked out how to get along with Americans. Harry is a genuine team player, something Americans appreciate and with which they can identify. Archie Parrish, the first international director and executive vice-president of EE, in particular identified with Harry and put him forward as the one best calculated to serve EE at the international as well as the national level and one who would bring consensus rather than conflict.

9.1 Dr D. James Kennedy, founder of Evangelism Explosion, and Harry, 25 August 1991.

At Wollongong, Harry mentored Rod Story and kept him going when Rod thought everything was falling apart. Rod recalls turning up at Harry's door on occasions and bursting into tears because he felt so defeated. Harry was always ready with what Rod came to call 'Goodhewspeak'. 'He never said, "you need to wake up to yourself", but what he said instead was "it would be good to think about such and such," which is really the same thing, but it was always more constructive somehow.'[1] Rod tried to learn from Harry what he thought needed to be reproduced in himself.

## Ministry overseas

Harry continued to develop an international reputation, and the church in Australia benefited from his overseas contacts. He was involved in bringing English evangelist, J. John, to Australia on his initial visits. He supported bringing to Australia, Larry Crabb, noted American psychologist, sensing that many clergy and laity were feeling the need to develop their pastoral skills. He wrote a report for Moore College on its projected Department of Mission after visiting similar centres in the United States.[2] He was a visitor and lecturer at Trinity Episcopal Seminary in Pittsburgh, the foundation principal of which was retired Australian CMS missionary, Alf Stanway.

Harry and Pam especially developed an interest in ministry to the churches in less affluent parts of the world. In July 1984 they visited Sri Lanka for World Vision. Sri Lanka's religious complexion is different from India's; it is predominantly Buddhist, with some Hindus, but few Muslims. The west coast of Sri Lanka had, since the 17th century, been deeply influenced by Christianity, first by Portuguese Catholics, then by Reformed Dutch missionaries, and then by English CMS and Society for the Propagation of the Gospel (SPG) missionaries.

Harry was advised in advance that his hosts were very liturgical, and that he would have to wear robes and that they could be bought cheaply in Singapore on the way over. He corresponded with the robe maker and was asked what colour he would like, and he chose cardinal red. It turned out to be lolly pink, and so the historical record contains photographs of processions with a giant in lolly pink vestments. Over a three-week period, Harry visited a number of places to encourage pastors. He gave about 70 addresses and drank gallons of Fanta supplied to him by his hosts.

9.2  Sri Lanka, 1984. Harry is dressed in a lolly pink cassock.

Harry and Pam made a second trip to Sri Lanka in 1985/6. This time the purpose was to attend the 125th anniversary celebrations of Holy Emmanuel Church, Moratuwa and to take a mission at nearby Dehiwila. Holy Emmanuel Church is a substantial cathedral-like structure, with an imposing tower, the gift of Jeronis deSoysa who had been converted from Buddhism through the ministry of William Oakley, a CMS missionary. Harry represented Robert Runcie, the Archbishop of Canterbury at the celebration on 27 December. Present for the occasion was Prime Minister of Sri Lanka, Ranasinghe Premadasa, who only ate bananas as he feared being poisoned. His fears were justified: he was assassinated in 1993 by a Tamil Tiger suicide bomber in Colombo. The civil war in Sri Lanka, the preliminary tremors of which were being felt during Harry's visit, did not end until May 2009.

Holy Emmanuel Church had developed ministries to meet a wide range of needs (educational, social and spiritual) in the surrounding community. Unlike India, where the church was strongest among the lowest and outcaste peoples, in Sri Lanka Christianity had long attracted the allegiance of national leaders, and those in the professions were strongly represented in the congregation. Harry, for example, accompanied Dr Vinodh Ramachandra, a nuclear physicist and student worker, to Colombo to meet Christian University Students in FOCUS, an evangelical student body.

From 24 December 1985 until 1 January 1986, Harry preached usually more than once a day at Moratuwa. He preached first to 600 people on Christmas Eve. His sermon was translated into Sinhala by the assistant minister, who had trained at the Union Bible Seminary in Maharashtra, India, under Graham Simpson, a CMS missionary from Sydney. Then, on Christmas Day, Harry preached to an English-speaking congregation of about 400 at 5.30 am, and then to a further 1000 at two following services, where his sermons were again translated. He preached on New Year's Eve at a watchnight service when, at midnight, the service was suspended to allow for the ringing of bells and the exploding of firecrackers. Then he preached again on 1 January at 5.30 am and 7.30 am at services at which there were more than 700 communicants.

From 2 to 5 January 1986 Harry took a mission at Dehiwila at St Mark's, known as the 'Church of the Open Door'. Situated on a busy main road, it had been opened for 24 hours every day for 20 years. Nearby is St Thomas' College, Mount Lavinia, perhaps Sri Lanka's finest secondary school. Founded by the first Bishop of Colombo, James Chapman (1845–61), it boasts a cricketing competition older than 'the Ashes'. Harry was warmly commissioned by the diocesan bishop, and then the mornings were occupied with Bible studies and the evenings with mission meetings. Meanwhile, Pam was as busy as Harry, taking women's meetings, Bible studies, and counselling. The 'team' of two was at its fully functioning best. Harry was gratified with the response and by the heartwarming farewell from the parish at the end of the mission. One present at the Dehiwila mission was the mother-in-law of Roger Herft, then Bishop of Newcastle and later Archbishop of Perth. She later recalled that Harry exhorted them all to pray daily and read their Bibles, and she had ever since.

Over the 18 months since his previous visit, Harry detected a strengthening of the evangelical presence in the Church. He saw evidence of this, for example, at St Luke's Borella (a southern suburb of Colombo, just north of Dehiwila). This was a CMS church and had no candles on the holy table. Here, Harry addressed about 150 delegates of the Anglican Evangelical Fellowship (AEF), whereas only about 20 had been present when he addressed the AEF on his previous visit. A substantial contribution to evangelical health was being made by the vicar of Holy Emmanuel, Revd Lakshman Peiris. The decisive sealing of his understanding that salvation is by grace was made by Australian CMS missionary, Geoffrey Bingham, when he preached a series of sermons on 'The Grace of God' at Dehiwila. Lakshman was assisted by a WEC missionary, Betty Rode, who had studied at the Bible College of Victoria under another near contemporary of Harry, Ken Churchward. Through Betty Rode's adult Bible study class, they met one of the selectors of the Sri Lankan cricket team who had played against Australia when it was under the captaincy of Richie Benaud.

In his visits to Sri Lanka, Harry grew in his appreciation of the faithful work done by CMS since its first missionaries arrived there in 1817 and the many contributions made by Australian missionaries to the church in Sri Lanka. He commented also on the contribution of John Stott who, through his own presence, his preaching, his books, his church back in London and arrangements made to allow Sri Lankans to have periods of study or experience in England, had benefited many church workers. But the chief conclusion he drew from their Sri Lanka experience was theological.

> It was brought home to us again that Christ rules in his Church by His Word and by His Spirit. Where the Word is not known and reflected upon, and made the basis for living, then Christian experience is vague, weak and sometimes misdirected. Where there is a concentration purely on the Word without the vivifying effect of the Spirit there can be a dry intellectual approach to the faith which risks nothing, dares nothing, and does not know the experience, or courage that is born of a living faith.[3]

## Diocesan administration

Before his election as archbishop, Harry had served on an astonishingly wide range of diocesan committees. It was a lot of hard work. It is an unglamorous side of church life and would be a labour for the historian to chronicle in detail and wearisome for the reader. There is, however, much drama here, because in effect, in these committees that involved Harry in many tiring journeys by road to Sydney, he was gaining an overview of the workings of the diocese. Unbeknown to him, he was being groomed for his future role as archbishop and getting to work with those who would within a few years become his chief advisers and co-workers.

To those who knew the reality behind the scenes, such as BBJ, by now very experienced in diocesan affairs, Harry's stewardship in this area was impressive. He wrote good reports, observed Ballantine-Jones, and chaired harmonious, productive diocesan committees. He did not run into frustration in those activities. He was committed to careful research on the church scene and on Australian culture. He did not assume he knew it all. His theological contribution to these committees and commissions was not that of a technical theologian, but of a very competent practical theologian. He probed gently, asked questions and always seemed to be able to get a body to focus on its chief tasks. Many would doubt that such a temperate soul could give dynamic leadership. In fact, he was extraordinarily successful in getting things done. In a number of the major initiatives of the Diocese of Sydney in the years immediately prior to his election as archbishop, he was a principal agent.

Harry:
- served on the Doctrine Commission and helped write reports on ordination and baptism
- contributed to the National Youth Synod
- contributed to *Looking into the Parish* (1973), which sowed seeds that came to fruition a decade later. Bruce Ballantine-Jones sees this report as 'signalling the arrival of *change* as a major diocesan preoccupation.' It was part of a strong push for reform.[4]
- participated from the start in 1984 of 'Vision for Growth', formed by Archbishop Robinson to raise $6 million to plant churches in 17 new areas of expanding Sydney, and Vision 2001, which replaced Vision for Growth in 1990
- chaired the Archbishop's Committee on ministerial formation (reported 1984), which resulted in the formation of a unit called Continuing

Education for Ministers (CEFM). Harry probably did most to organise post-ordination training in Sydney.
- served on the General Synod SC and was a member of the General Synod's Committee on Ministry and Training established in 1981 to report on Ministry Training in Australia and to recommend common guidelines for the all the dioceses of Australia
- served as Chairperson of the Church Army, Vice-President of CMS and SAMS, and Chairperson of BCA
- was a member of the Board of Evangelism and chairperson of the committee for the Decade of Evangelism, moving at the 1990 Sydney synod to receive the call from the Lambeth Conference to make the years 1991 to 2000 a Decade for Evangelism
- chaired a synod committee on the remarriage of divorced persons
- chaired a committee on lay presidency
- was involved in the development and execution of the National Church Life Survey (NCLS). Harry assisted in the development of the questions on leadership in the Survey, which he developed for a doctorate at Macquarie University on which he was about to embark when it was overtaken by his election as archbishop.

In all the major concerns then occupying the diocese, Harry was a central player. He chaired committees tasked with finding the most efficient way of developing parish property and ministry, with resolving whether to regionalise the diocesan structure or divide it into new dioceses, and with the possibility of lay presidency at Holy Communion. With less enthusiasm, he wrestled with the increasingly difficult issue of the remarriage of divorced persons and he tampered with the powder keg of female ordination.

## The development of parish property and ministry

The diocesan bureaucracy consisted of a wearying plethora of committees. It was not easy to see which, if any, made any difference. Those with sufficient stamina to wade through these murky waters concluded that the leading diocesan organisations in terms of the future of the diocese were the Archbishop's Commission of Inquiry, the Financial Priorities committee, the Development of Parish Property and Ministry committee, and the Committee on Regionalisation.

Bruce Ballantine-Jones was on all four of the above. Harry was on the last three, and through his chairing of the Development committee, exercised a formative influence on the first, even though he was not a member. Harry's Report on the Committee for the Development of Parish Property and Ministry

(June 1990) was a document ahead of its time, Ballantine-Jones believes, calling for administrative structures to supplement the parish and advocating the trial of selected area deaneries as ministry units. Part of the reason why Harry's region was so progressive and content was that he encouraged area deans to take responsibility for the development of ministry in their areas.

The appointment of the Commission of Inquiry was announced by Donald Robinson in his presidential address to the 1990 synod. Many initiatives taken by zealous individuals over time made claims on the limited resources of the diocese, and the archbishop strongly felt the need for a mechanism to assess and distribute funds in such a way as to maximise the effectiveness of gospel ministry. His Commission of Inquiry was tasked to report to him on such a mechanism. Its terms of reference were 'To examine the ministry organisations of the Diocese with a view to their inter-relation so as to assist the archbishop in determining needs and priorities within the general purposes and aims of the Diocese.'[5]

Guided principally by Geoff Kells, Managing Director of CSR, the members of the Archbishop's commission made far more radical recommendations than anyone anticipated. In that, however, they were not uninfluenced by Harry who, as Chairperson of the Committee on the Development of Parish Property and Ministry, had reported, 'The work of this Committee is predicated upon the conviction that the time is right for the Diocese to restate its basic mission and to develop fresh strategies to pursue that mission effectively.'[6] The commission quoted those words with approval and sought to do both – to restate the diocesan mission and to develop new strategies. It suggested, therefore, a new clearer mission statement for the diocese, namely,

> To be the Church of the believers in Jesus Christ within its boundaries manifest in parish congregations and to:
> - faithfully gather for worshipping, teaching and fellowship
> - vigorously proclaim the Christian faith
> - courageously affirm scriptural truths
> - actively nurture its members
> - lovingly care for the needy
>
> Hence: 'Worshipping and Witnessing through Parishes.'[7]

The commission recommended streamlining the bureaucracy to facilitate decision-making and policy-formation, replacing large elected bodies with smaller CEO-chosen task forces, reducing the executive role of the SC, and replacing that role with a Diocesan Executive Board (DEB).

Merchant banker, David Fairfull ('Fearless'), the newly appointed CEO of diocesan administration, believes that Kells' report for the commission was the best presentation he had ever seen. Never before had the problem been analysed so deeply. Yet the report was cut from 180 pages to about 30, in double-spaced typing! From a strategic point of view, it was incomparable, and if 50 per cent of it had been implemented 'it would have been brilliant.' But it was doomed from day one, and while a DEB was appointed 'it never went to where Geoff Kells wanted it to go.'[8] Bruce Ballantine-Jones argues that the Archbishop's Commission failed because it violated the diocesan culture. 'To try and superimpose a business model on a body that was passionate about its rights and suspicious about centralism was naïve.'[9] Of course, it might be suggested that Kells and company understood the diocesan culture all too well, and their concern to change the culture arose not from naiveté, but from desperation to save the ship they loved from sinking.

The whole experience was to put Harry in an ambiguous position when he became archbishop. He would not diverge from the recommendations of the Development committee and he tried, but was not so successful in implementing the radical restructuring commended by the commission. In this matter, as in others, he was committed to changing the diocesan culture and, in hindsight, it would have been better, financially and managerially, had he succeeded. But his proposed changes were too radical for those who alone had the power to implement them.

## The regionalisation or subdivision of the diocese?

Harry's two predecessors as archbishop, Loane and Robinson, had both keenly advocated the division of the huge Diocese of Sydney. They believed that new dioceses of Wollongong and Parramatta should be carved out of the existing diocese. Both archbishops had come to the conclusion that it was impossible to give effective episcopal oversight to so many parishes. Both areas were growing strongly and, in particular, the people of Wollongong, where the Roman Catholics had created a separate diocese, were keen to see the Anglican Church in Wollongong come out from under the control of Sydney. For Loane, the creation of new dioceses was something of a crusade, and his first synod in 1966 voted to support an investigation into the possibility. In 1968, synod gave in-principle support to the creation of Wollongong as a separate diocese. The next year, St Michael's Wollongong was made a provisional cathedral, and Graham Delbridge was appointed as the first bishop in Wollongong. Things were moving fast, and the creation of a separate diocese in Wollongong looked inevitable. Similarly, in Parramatta, St John's was designated as a provisional cathedral, and Gordon

Begbie was appointed bishop.

There was, however, apparently a fatal flaw in the plan. Nine parishes in the district of Sutherland, the southernmost part of the city of Sydney, would have to be part of the Wollongong diocese or it could not be viable; however, the people of the Shire of Sutherland thought of themselves as Sydney people, not Wollongong. Tony Lamb, Rector of Caringbah, published in 1970 a strongly reasoned rebuttal of the proposal to create new dioceses. He argued that such dioceses always lost their evangelical heritage, and he proposed keeping the Diocese of Sydney intact, while allowing greater decentralisation of the regions of the diocese under regional bishops. This proposal was exactly what the Diocese of Melbourne opted for in the same year. Melbourne, whose archbishop, Frank Woods, was at the height of his powers, and backed by the findings of a thorough investigation into diocesan organisation in Britain,[10] moved dramatically, an unusual experience for any Anglican diocese. Melbourne was divided into three regions – Southern, Central and Western – and an assistant bishop was appointed over each region, while the archbishop retained responsibility for clergy training and appointments of clergy to parishes.[11]

Sydney would take another quarter century to implement the same arrangement. In 1986 Harry himself moved for the appointment of a committee to canvass all the options. It was chaired by Sir Harold Knight, Governor of the Reserve Bank, and Harry, along with Bp Ken Short and Bp Don Cameron, served on it. It recommended devolution, but not separation. Archbishop Robinson, in 1989, again expressed frustration that full separation was not being entertained. Harry again moved that a further report be made to the synod in 1991. By that time the Parramatta regional council had decided it wanted to be separate, while Wollongong had concluded the proposal was not viable. Harry was made chairperson of a group charged with the responsibility of working out further steps towards regionalisation within the *one* diocese and reporting to the 1992 synod. He did report in 1992, but synod postponed consideration of the report until 1993, by which time Harry was archbishop. He departed from his predecessors in his lack of support for the creation of new dioceses, but presided over a form of regionalisation in 1995 that allowed the real devolution of powers to regional councils.[12] It worked so well that it would actually be one of Harry's most important achievements as archbishop.

## Remarriage of divorced persons

Archbishop Donald Robinson's strongly conservative stand on the remarriage of divorced persons was a source of frustration to those of his clergy who, on pastoral grounds, desired a more flexible approach. Robinson believed his sole responsibility was to maintain the law of the diocese, which was that a clergyperson could only officiate at a marriage of a divorced person when that person's former partner had committed adultery.[13] He had particular difficulty in allowing the remarriage of one whose previous spouse was still alive and who had not been unfaithful.

In 1984, following the report on divorce of a committee appointed by synod, Harry moved that remarriage of divorced persons be permitted 'without necessarily requiring the assent of the diocesan bishop' and that the final decision was to be made by the officiating clergyperson.[14] Synod, in the following year, passed an ordinance consistent with the Goodhew proposal, but the archbishop refused to consent to it. A stalemate ensued for the remainder of Robinson's episcopate, with clergy increasingly taking matters into their own hands, deciding without reference to the archbishop who they would agree to remarry. Indeed, increasingly the clergy were ignoring the archbishop's will in a number of matters in which he was considered too restrictive, ranging from divorce to experimental church services to the requirement that all changes to parish buildings, including rearrangements of furniture and even painting, be approved by an archdeacon. It could be argued that it was an improvement to have rectors deciding such matters, since they were closer to them than centralised bureaucrats. But it was better still to have a system whereby the rector's decision was referred for consideration by central authorities, who could thus bring a second layer of accountability and achieve a measure of uniformity across the diocese. Such an arrangement was beginning to be the practice by the end of Robinson's episcopate. In the matter of divorce cases, that was the practice that would be adopted when Harry became archbishop. The rector referred any contentious applications for remarriage to his regional bishop, who took it to a bishops' meeting for review. The issue of the remarriage of divorced persons, which so encumbered Robinson's episcopate, evaporated overnight in Harry's time and was no longer a problem. It reflected Harry's instinct to recognise and accept reality while maintaining standards, and to achieve a balance between them.

## The ordination of women

On the most divisive of current issues – female ordination – Harry was vulnerable. He was not in favour of it, but he found it more difficult than most conservatives to upset those who did favour it. On 12 February 1989, Harry had assisted Archbishop Robinson, together with Bps John Reid and Donald Cameron, in ordaining 14 Sydney women as deacons. Among those ordained was Narelle

Jarrett, Principal of Deaconess House, who expressed the hope that this would smooth the way for the ordination of women to the priesthood.[15]

On 23 December 1991 the Bishop of the Diocese of Canberra and Goulburn, Owen Dowling, announced that he intended to ordain 11 women to the priesthood. Archbishop Donald Robinson asked him to withdraw and desist, but Dowling declared that he could not. A Sydney layperson, Laurie Scandrett, and two clergy on 16 January 1992 commenced court proceedings to block the ordination. On 28 January Mr Justice Rogers dismissed the application. The plaintiffs appealed. Fascination with this stoush went way beyond the Church, as the role of women was the most contested social issue in Australia in the 1990s. Press interest was at fever pitch. The day after Judge Rogers' decision, the *Illawarra Mercury* reported on the battle on its front page, with a large picture of Harry, and followed this up with a cartoon depicting Harry dressed in full clerical dress, saying that he wore the trousers. He declared that women priests would not be recognised in Wollongong, implying that, if Wollongong became a separate diocese, it would continue to support the Diocese of Sydney in its opposition to female ordination. In retrospect, his position then was not as hardline as some would have liked. He said he agreed with the judge's decision that a civil court should not decide a church matter, and he added:

> We will have to wait to see how things develop. These are unchartered waters for us. At the present time, I am not a supporter of women in the priesthood. That is not to say that I couldn't live and work with it some time in the future if [women priests] were universally accepted in the Anglican church. But for the present, the answer is no, not while I'm the bishop.[16]

Three judges then upheld the appeal, blocking the ordination at the last minute, and asked for the matter to be determined at a future date. With the highly charged matter still awaiting determination, Harry accepted the politically risky role of chairing a diocesan conference on the ordination of women. The motion by Revd Tim Harris at the October 1991 Sydney synod to hold the conference the following year had passed without debate. On 27 June 1992 the conference, with speakers 'generally recognised as being within the evangelical tradition of the Anglican Church of Australia',[17] was held at St John's Parramatta.[18] With Harry in the chair, speakers included Chris Forbes, Ancient History lecturer from Macquarie University, and Kevin Giles, pastor and theologian, who gave the case for female ordination, and two Moore College lecturers, David Peterson and Glenn Davies, who presented the traditionalist case. The conference caused much excitement.

The anti-ordination camp was judged by the majority of the 370 attendees to have been defeated on the day, but they were probably pro-ordination anyway. The report of the synod committee who organised the conference claimed to be written 'firmly and unashamedly from an evangelical perspective.'[19] The issue was not whether the authority of Scripture should be accepted — it was accepted by all parties. The issue was the interpretation and application of Scripture in this complex area.

The pro-ordination forces were heartened and were further encouraged a week later when the judges in the Scandrett v. Dowling case ruled that the courts were not empowered to deliberate, since female ordination was not a matter of property in which alone they had jurisdiction. The conservatives were seriously displeased. While the majority at the Parramatta Conference were pleased with Harry for his impartial chairmanship, the conservatives were made aware that Harry's gracious impartiality could leave the diocese in a place they did not want to be.

At the General Synod, which in 1992 endorsed the canon for the ordination of women, BBJ tried to lock in all the Sydney representatives in opposition by the incendiary if legal demand for an open vote rather than a secret ballot. Over afternoon tea he changed his mind. Bruce maintains he worked this out for himself. In the folklore, Harry Goodhew and others told him to 'pull his head in.'[20] On the plane going back to Melbourne, a priest sitting next to Muriel Porter told her that he had intended to vote against the ordination of women, but he was so appalled by the Sydney people that he voted for it. In the event it was passed by one vote. There is much speculation on who that one vote was! It was not Harry, although there were here a couple of straws in the wind. He was not nearly as adamant on the issue as other conservative evangelicals and he was clearly respected, even on this issue, by those from other dioceses who supported the ordination of women.

## Continuity between Donald Robinson and Harry Goodhew

When Harry became archbishop, there would be more continuity with the progress that had been made under Archbishop Donald Robinson than discontinuity, in spite of all the talk of a fresh start. A popular perception was that Harry inherited a diocese that had become hostage to law. Donald Robinson insisted on the application of the law. He was not heartless in its application, just insistent. Harry was more flexible, more pastoral, more relaxed. But, perhaps contrary to expectations, he too came to the conclusion that observing the law was essential to retaining the role and effectiveness of the archbishop, and he lost friends over it because they believed that they were getting an archbishop whose instinct was for liberty rather than law.

Harry was very loyal to his archbishop, another of his admirable characteristics, although he regretted having to persevere with policies which he considered might not have been the best calculated for the growth of the church. But Donald was grateful. On Sunday, 7 February 1993, after retiring as archbishop, he wrote to Harry to thank him for his support and for his work in Wollongong. 'You have been an exemplary assistant Bishop, and it was a great comfort to know that you were caring for that part of the diocese.'

Others outside the Diocese of Sydney were aware that a star had arisen in the episcopal firmament, and there was an attempt in 1990 by South Australian evangelical Anglicans to nominate Harry for election as Archbishop of Adelaide. He did not hold his breath. Famously, David Knox, father of Broughton, had declared that in Adelaide they would elect a kangaroo in preference to an evangelical.[21] Nothing more was heard of the proposal, either by Harry himself or any kangaroo.

Towards the end of 1992, when Harry learned that he might be nominated to the Sydney synod as a candidate for election as archbishop, he wrote in his journal,

> O God, have mercy on me: please do not let me get into that situation if it is not your will. But on the other hand, if I do finish up there, I want to know that I have recourse to your Holy Spirit, for whatever may come.

Reflecting on Acts 1, he took comfort from the thought that God's Holy Spirit would guide the synod members in their choice. To fill a gap in the ranks of the Apostles, they searched for the men they considered had the necessary qualifications, and then they prayed, 'Lord you are *kardia gonestes*. You are the heart-knower. Show us who your choice is.'[22] The Lord would do it again in the Sydney election synod.

# 10

# Twin Crises:
# The Fraught Backdrop to Harry's Election

The election of every one of Sydney's archbishops has been a great drama. In recent decades, the major challenge confronting the church, the Western world over, is secularisation. Ultimately, the struggles in election synods have been over the best way to respond to that challenge. Evangelicals have been divided over how to respond, and that division accounts for the heat in election debates. So, some account needs to be given first of that division within the evangelical movement in Sydney.

By the early 1990s, around the time of Harry's election, in Australia, as in Britain and America, the evangelical movement had become so divided that many wondered if the honoured label was of any further value. There were conservative, exclusivist evangelicals and progressive, inclusive evangelicals. This division is too easily identified as an outgrowth of the rift, by now a century old, between fundamentalists and liberals. The division is better understood, perhaps, as reflecting that in the wider world between neoconservatives, who stood for traditional values, and inclusivists, who sought a new civic order based on tolerance and liberty. In the dispute about how best to position the evangelical movement to maintain its influence in a secular world, the conservatives had little doubt that they had the correct solution. A leader in the exclusive camp, Bruce Ballantine-Jones, then Rector of the Parish of Jannali, and Vice-President of the Anglican Church League (ACL), said in 1992, the year before Harry became archbishop:

> The Anglican Church will either grow or decline according to the clarity of biblical preaching and commitment to biblical truth. If the Anglican Church becomes a pale reflection of modern sociological attitudes we will sink into irrelevance.[1]

In practice this meant denying to inclusivists the power to be inclusive. It meant making purity of doctrine everything and unity nothing. The exclusives believed that what was needed was 'a revival of the spirit of the Reformation which put truth above institutionalism and salvation of people above internal coherence.'[2]

At Easter 1992 Ballantine-Jones made front page news in the secular media when he said that Sydney Anglicans might have to leave the national church. The reaction to his provocative declaration at such a holy time was so fierce that, in a rare display of self-doubt, he asked Robert Forsyth, then Rector of St Barnabas', Broadway, 'Have I done the wrong thing?' He had not only scandalised the anti-Sydney forces in the national church, but the instinct of inclusive evangelicals in Sydney was to deplore such a defection. His supporters came from the exclusivist camp. 'Fundamentalists' is not the right label for them; 'radical conservatives' is better. They numbered among them the most vocal, the most articulate in the diocesan synod.

## Crisis in the diocese: REPA

If Harry was an inclusivist, and the most vocal, articulate members of synod were exclusivist, how did he get elected? The simple fact is that the majority of synod members were not exclusivist, and they were not so because the exclusivists had, in anticipation of the election, overplayed their hand. In the year before the election, they had started a spotfire that had threatened to burn down the whole edifice, and so the majority in the synod reached for the extinguisher. The threatening conflagration was REPA, and the incendiary was Phillip Jensen, University of New South Wales chaplain.

Phillip Jensen believed that the constitutional crisis in the Anglican Church of Australia, precipitated by the fight over the ordination of women, was a good opportunity to make a concerted stand for conservative evangelicalism within the Anglican Church of Australia. The 1992 Scandrett vs Dowling judgment on the ordination of women allowed dioceses to go their own way without hindrance from the national church. Phillip saw this as a great opportunity for the Diocese of Sydney to separate itself from what he called 'the liberal Catholicism' of the rest of the Anglican Church of Australia.[3]

REPA was born following a visit which Phillip paid to the Anglican primate, Keith Rayner, in Melbourne. Phillip offered the primate his assistance in dealing with the crisis in the Anglican Church. Archbishop Rayner rejected the offer. Rayner calculated that one-third of the clergy of the Sydney diocese was conservative evangelical, one-third was 'Anglican', and there was a middle third that would be happy to go either way. Since the Diocese of Sydney was actually more Anglican than Sydney's conservative evangelicals would allow, argued the primate, once women were ordained, the diocese would settle down.

Ballantine-Jones maintains that Jensen was made the more determined to counter the national church as the result of this rejection. Phillip shared with

Bruce that he wanted to start a revolution. Bruce's late wife, Raema, who was privy to this conversation, was impressed, observing to Bruce afterwards that Phillip would make an excellent archbishop. This may have been the beginning of the push to make Phillip archbishop, a push with which REPA became inextricably bound, in spite of the protestations of some of its members to the contrary.

REPA was formed in February 1992 by 18 members of the clergy, rectors of large Anglican churches. They became known as the 'colonels', thus distinguishing themselves from the bishops, the 'generals'. Among the colonels, perhaps a minority were revolutionaries in the Phillip Jensen/Ballantine-Jones camp. Robert Forsyth was a REPA colonel in the moderate division! The name REPA was devised by Jim Ramsay, Rector of Liverpool, on the spur of the moment as the founders needed a name under which to open a bank account. The name 'Reformed Evangelical Protestant Association' was unashamedly theological, and the determination of its founders was to explore and implement changes flowing from that stance. Its opponents branded it as 'fundamentalist' and 'the Opus Dei of the evangelical World.' Going public in March 1992, REPA claimed, by April, to have had 170 of Sydney's 271 clergy as members. As each had paid $50 to join, this was a tribute to the organisers, although some paid up fearing they would be 'left behind' if they did not join.

Phillip Jensen was no shallow strategist. He was not motivated by the desire either to outflank Rayner or to defeat the more inclusive of the evangelicals. He believed that the role of the Anglican Church in secular Australia was diminishing to the point of extinction, and that the best way to reverse this trend was to have 'more and more people out and about preaching the gospel of Jesus Christ and gathering up those converted into evangelistically minded congregations.'[4] Phillip insisted that the Anglican Church was in crisis, demanding drastic action. As he explained to a REPA meeting,

> The baby boomers have given away Anglicanism. Do we slide the deckchairs further and further back as the water rises? ... If we leave it too late our resources will run down. I think it is our last fling.[5]

The reason the REPA colonels gave for the diminishing role of the Anglican Church spelled trouble for the inclusivists; namely, that the strategy of the Anglican Church had been theologically compromised in the preceding generation.[6] The principal problem, they believed, was an internal one, a diagnosis that divides, rather than an external one, the threat of which unites. 'We face a lack of confidence in the gospel,' it was claimed, 'expressed by a futile clinging to institutionalism and authoritarianism matched with a great willingness to open ourselves up to every fad and fashion of human philosophy and heresy.'[7] It followed that the compromise had to be rooted out, and a good way of doing that was to conduct an audit of diocesan organisations to assess if they made a positive contribution to gospel ministry. The 'Diocesan Audit' which REPA members were invited to fill in covered 120 diocesan organisations, excluding parishes, but ranging from church schools to retirement villages, from regional bishops to the synod. For each of these, respondents were invited to put a tick in one or more of six columns. Of the six options, five were unnervingly negative.

Within a month of REPA's launch, the colonels acknowledged that there was any number of reasons why the movement disconcerted people: that it looked like a conspiracy arising from the friendship of its founders; that it was not open about its agenda; that it was clerical, leaving no room for the laity; that it was pro-large church and unsympathetic towards small churches; that, since it was established a year out from the election of a new archbishop, and was working on issues which would have to be considered by synods from 1993 to 1998,[8] it was a lobbying group.[9]

A REPA think tank that met in July 1992 addressed the question, 'Why the incredible reaction to REPA. The fear, the suspicion, the accusation of hidden agenda's [sic], the DISTRUST?' The response? 'REPA has hit a real nerve. If we can only understand and analyse why, we have a lot to learn.'[10] What they learned, however, did not help them. Opposition to REPA was excessively emotional and, for that reason, could not be contained or refuted. It was argued that REPA was symptomatic of the problem in the diocese rather than a solution; that it dignified the disloyalty of the rebels in the diocese; that it was a blatant move to snatch political power in the diocese by a group that was narrower, it was claimed, than the ACL,[11] formed in 1909 to defend the Reformed, Protestant and evangelical nature of the Anglican Church.

One who provoked an energetic response from the colonels was Bp John Reid. In a courageous move, which damaged his chances of election as archbishop, Reid chided his 'dear friends' in REPA in the *Southern Cross*. He suggested that it would have liberated people from 'fear of the hidden agenda' if REPA had worked for change in a partnership of clergy and laity through synod.[12] The REPA apologists rightly protested that, through their think tanks, they had developed many motions to be put to the next synod, and they intended 'to work in all the legitimate avenues of Christian fellowship – including Synod.'[13]

Bp Reid, however, had made an important point. Phillip Jensen had not, until then, been at all interested in synod. He had sought to achieve largely outside of the synod process what many in the synod were working for anyway.

Ballantine-Jones acknowledges that, up to 1992, Phillip had played hardly any part in diocesan affairs, only rarely attended synod, and, when in 1993, he was nominated for election as archbishop, many members of synod 'had never laid eyes on him.' Phillip was very interested in strategies for the diocese, but not in the political processes of synod. For him, REPA was really an opportunity to promote among significant diocesan leaders his convictions about the way forward. These included his view that the diocese was compromised, that it lacked freedom because it was too bound up in legal considerations, and that 'American Church Growth stuff" was not the answer. We needed to find our own answers.[14]

Not all Sydney Anglicans shared Phillip's frustrations. Professor Bruce Harris, then serving on the SC, believed that the structures and programs for renewal and growth that REPA wanted were already in place in the diocese.[15] Some, including Archbishop Robinson, professed bafflement about REPA's real purpose. Others were just cross. Shortly before the election for archbishop, Dr Russell Clark, then a consultant physician, and before and after a medical missionary with CMS, wrote an 'Open Letter' to the founding 18.

> It is our church – yours and mine.
>
> Why are you harming it? ... REPA has within one year caused fear, dismay, and disharmony, and already has damaged friendships – I fear permanently ... My problem is I do not understand why you have done this? What is so wrong with our existing structures in Sydney? We have no heretics in high places in Sydney. Clearly I am now dismissed by some of you as a liberal, as I see no Biblical problems with the ordination of women, am tolerant and encouraging of charismatic activities and am committed to social action. But none of our leaders in Sydney have any other desire than to be true servants of our Lord with an authority based upon the Scriptures ...
>
> I ask you to withdraw Phillip's nomination for Archbishop.
>
> Phillip is a divisive force now, and I can see no other outcome than a fragmented and divided church in Sydney for a generation, should Phillip be appointed.[16]

Russell Clark's insinuation that REPA was designed to get Phillip elected archbishop was widely suspected in the diocese.[17] Stephen Gabbott, for example, on the foundation of REPA immediately came to the conclusion that it was a front for the election of Phillip, and that those who denied it were being less than transparent. Even John Chapman, who was to Phillip Jensen what Jack Lang was to Paul Keating, criticised those who thought it an 'insane' failure not to use political muscle to get the right man elected archbishop. Chappo would say to any who thought that way, 'Brother, just say your prayers.' It was not that he was exceptionally pious. He had been at the election of Clive Kerle as Bishop of Armidale 30 years earlier and always thought it was a miracle that no human could have contrived that a Sydney evangelical could win in such a diocese. Thanks to that experience, he was happy to trust God in such matters!

A front to get Phillip elected was not how the founding 18 of REPA understood it. Phillip had said to them that he would not stand if they asked him not to. Forsyth and Terry Dein, then Rector of St Andrew's, Wahroonga, persuaded Phillip not to run, saying it would be a disaster. In October 1992, the majority of them did ask him not to stand, and he agreed to their request.

Among the REPA 18, however, one absent when this decision was made was John Woodhouse, Rector of Christ Church, St Ives. He was a champion of the conservative cause, but this did not mean that he was committed to the heartless reiteration of tired dogmas. He was the most radical of conservatives, with a vision of a new formulation of Reformed theology as socially relevant as it was biblically literate. He despaired of the church's retreat from engagement in the marketplace of ideas and its loss of spiritual cut-through. In Phillip Jensen, he saw one who was both more alert than any to the crisis in the church and more able than most theologically, a Bible teacher without peer. In response to Woodhouse's urging and that of Robert Tong, Phillip was asked by the REPA SC, now augmented to 36 by the addition of 18 laity, to reconsider his decision not to stand. Phillip consented. It fell to Forsyth to inform John Reid of this development. Reid warned Forsyth of two concerns: unrealistic expectations and demagoguery. Chappo, who had let it be known from the outset that he was opposed to Phillip's election, was waited on by a delegation that pressed him to change his mind. But he did not. He considered Phillip unelectable and not good for the diocese, for he would want to do things synod would never countenance and there would be 'terrible turmoil.' So he told them that Phillip was 'too hot to handle' and 'far too violent in the way he speaks.'[18]

The storm of emotion already unleashed by REPA was fatal to Phillip's prospects. If REPA had been, in the minds of some, an instrument for getting Phillip elected as archbishop, then it was an inept instrument. Politically, Phillip's supporters had overplayed their hand, alienating not only those in the diocese who put Anglicanism ahead of evangelicalism and those who favoured inclusive evangelicalism, but also the moderate exclusives such as Chappo. So, in the synod election for archbishop in 1993, while Phillip was the choice of the minority who wanted a strong leader, he was considered too radical by the majority. The disappointment of the minority would continue to be a problem for Harry after his election.

On the eve of the archbishop's election, the diocese was hopelessly riven. By overplaying its hand, REPA had ensured that Phillip could not be elected, but it was sufficiently powerful to ensure that any who criticised it also jeopardised their electoral hopes. Such were John Reid and Paul Barnett. Harry did not pay his $50 or join REPA, but he never criticised it publicly, a restraint that paid dividends in the election.

Shortly after the election, Harry met with the REPA SC for a discussion that was reported as 'warm, constructive and open.'[19] Harry was candid with them. He made the point that reform begins with the heart, and he recalled a statement of Broughton Knox that to reform church life we must 'let the Word do it', implying that the primary purpose of the word was to change hearts. Harry said he wanted to see the clergy lead by example as much as by teaching. 'I want to see godliness in your lives.' He added that he wanted to see women affirmed and valued in their ministries, and that it was essential for evangelistic effectiveness that churches be places where people are encouraged and happy. In the event, REPA went underground, its more uncompromising founders refocusing on revamping the ACL as defender of conservative evangelicalism.[20]

# 11

# A New Archbishop for Sydney: 'A Blessing for the Whole Church'

Late on the night of the election result, Harry rang his daughter, Wendy, to tell her the news. Her first thought, 'Poor Dad, he's got to go through all this, he's like food to the lions.' She asked her father, 'So, how are you going to approach this?' He replied, 'God knows who I am. He knows exactly who Richard Henry Goodhew is, and I so much trust his sovereignty that if it is his wish that I should be in this role, he knows what I have to offer; he knows that I will do this job from the essence of who I am, and that's what I will do.' It was, of course, an intimate revelation from a father to a trusted daughter, but it was evidence of his real priority, which was spiritual. For Harry, easily the most important qualification for the work of ministry was the state of the heart. The God of the Bible was one who tested the hearts of his servants. He tested Abraham, Israel, Job, Hezekiah, Peter, and Paul – even Jesus himself. Harry later wrote

> Success can give rise to pride in any of us, just as apparent failure can tempt us to doubt and despair. We need to pray for a heart that holds success or failure, and everything in-between, before God … God … will do whatever it takes to make us true sons and daughters: not simply in status, but in living truth. He will, in mighty grace, conform us to the likeness of his Son.[1]

The most important thing for Harry was not that he had a heart for the job, but that he had God's heart for the job.

Wendy asked her father what he wanted people to pray for, and he asked her (and most people who asked the same question) to pray for strength – for physical strength – for he knew well enough that the job is exhausting. It was a prayer that was answered, and the

11.1 Philip, Wendy and Robyn at their father's installation as archbishop, 29 April 1993.

astonishing thing was that Pam, too, was given sufficient health to keep pace with Harry; amazing considering that she had suffered from high blood pressure since she was a teenager and was on tablets for it from the age of 19. Wendy admits that she also felt great pride at the election result, 'not pride for myself, but he's a great man, and he's going to do a great job. People will love him.'

Son Philip's first thoughts were, 'Oh no, that will be a lot of work,' and when he saw him at the York Apartments, where the new archbishop and his wife were first accommodated as Bishopscourt was not ready to receive them, 'he was already signing letters … clearly putting in the hours, but I could see he was excited with the challenge and he had ideas, but I thought, he doesn't need that.'

On the day following the election, Frank Mostyn, Rector of Austinmer, an idyllic Illawarra beach-side suburb, took himself for a swim, no doubt to wash away the feverish emotions of previous days. He was astonished to learn from his fellow swimmers how many people had been following the election with great interest. 'I think he is a very popular choice,' he said, 'not just among the people in the parishes but also among people in the community as a whole. He is loved by everyone.'[2]

## Letters of congratulation

Perhaps the very first to pen his congratulations to Harry was Bp Ken Short. His letter is dated 1 April, 9 pm.

> The Lord has graciously answered prayer and Synod has been obedient! Congrats my brother – we are thrilled! … May you have the discernment to love the REPA bods back into the fold, and for the whole healing process which must go on after an election Synod.

Sir Marcus Loane was among the first to 'prayerfully' congratulate Harry on becoming 'the tenth Bishop, and seventh archbishop, of Sydney.' The morning after the result was announced, he wrote:

> You will be the last of Archbishop Mowll's men to hold this office, and I am glad to think that you were one of my men in College days … My ideal for an Archbishop of Sydney is that he should be a man who will uphold the historic character and time-honoured traditions of evangelical Churchmanship, derived from the New Testament, confirmed at the Reformation, and exemplified through the great episcopates of Bishop Barker and Archbishop Mowll.[3]

The primate, Keith Rayner, Archbishop of Melbourne, was also quick to send his congratulations. In his letter, dated 2 April 1993, he alluded to the REPA faction.

> It was a great pleasure to hear the news of your election as Archbishop of Sydney ... I am sure that your well-deserved reputation as a pastoral bishop, a healer and a centre of unity has been a major factor in your election, and represents the desire of the great majority of Anglicans for the Church to move forward with determination, vigour, and a strong sense of common purpose in fulfilling the mission which our Lord has committed to us ... There has certainly been a reaction in the rest of the Church to what has been perceived ... as a faction within your Diocese who were consciously seeking to loosen the fellowship and links with the rest of the Australian Church ... My hope is that your election may in itself be a sign of a positive spirit of reconciliation, healing and unity.[4]

Old Archdeacon Fillingham, now even more venerable than he was when, 11 years before, he congratulated Harry on becoming a bishop, repeated his advice from the earlier letter to take to heart 2 Corinthians 9:8 in the Authorized Version rendering.[5] From Carlingford, Roy Guthrie sent Harry a detailed computation to establish that the Lord would return in 1993.[6] In his reply, Harry did not comment that he would thus be preserved from the heavy load of his episcopate, but he thanked Roy and his wife, Rita, for keeping a watchful eye on his mother.[7]

The letters received by Harry in response to his election as archbishop were even more numerous than those he received when he was appointed bishop. Perhaps, however, they were not as effusive. True, Ron Gregory on holiday at Port Macquarie, picked up *SMH* the day after the result was reached, and finding Harry on the front page, shed tears: his prayers and those of his wife Rene and many others were answered.[8] And Susan Rogers wrote from Melbourne, 'When I heard the election results I burst into tears and at the same time had a big grin on my face. It is very happy news and a blessing for the whole church (not only Sydney).'[9] But the election campaign had been so draining. It felt a bit like the eerie silence at the cessation of hostilities.

Many expressed relief that Harry had been chosen, thus putting off the division in the Anglican Church that many feared was inevitable. Many expressed the feeling that the Holy Spirit, in answer to earnest prayer, had led the synod to choose Harry, and that the synod had thus found the Lord's will. 'The Holy Spirit won out after all'[10] or 'It transpires ... that the Holy Spirit can work even through synod. The Church is to be congratulated on its choice of Archbishop,'[11] or 'even with prayer for the guidance of the Holy Spirit, being human, there was a certain apprehension. I believe your election was truly the working of the Holy Spirit.'[12]

It had been a battle to discover the mind of God, a battle that had reinforced the awareness that the church was not in a healthy state of brotherly love. There was a longing for reconciliation, healing and unity, and the belief that Harry was the most likely to be instrumental in their promotion, but there was also little doubt that Harry would have his work cut out.

Others, who were not so closely involved with the politics of the election, had other reservations about the result. They feared that Harry would no longer be as accessible as he had once been. So many felt that they had a special friendship with Harry, and they suspected that they would not be able to enjoy it as much in the future. Wollongong supporters, in particular, were in two minds. They were pleased, but the man they loved was moving, they feared, out of reach. Even if they did not know the maxim, 'a friend in power is a friend lost', they feared the truth of which it speaks.

A further feature of these letters was the advice that so many of them offered. Apparently, people were content to let Harry find his way as a bishop, but not as an archbishop. The vintage advice-giver was Alan Cole. He wrote from Singapore two days after the election result was announced, beginning with 'I will not presume to give any advice', and then proceeded to give Harry four major pieces of advice. First, in this anti-authoritarian age, the only authority Harry could count on having was that willingly accorded to him by those whom he led, and that would only be forthcoming if they recognised his prayerfulness, Christlikeness and his loving concern for them. 'Few people can resist love.' Second, Harry would need to give full, careful explanations of the decisions he made, coupled with careful listening to those with whom he disagreed. Third, Harry should not be afraid to make and accept change, while still finding a place for those who could not accept change. He recognised that Harry might have trouble with the 'Reformation without tarrying for any' men, but while they were extreme and over-simplistic, many of the things they suggest 'seem good and right.' Fourth, he hoped that Harry would simply be 'Archbishop Harry', not 'Most Rev.', that he would live in a 'sensible house', though he dearly loved 'the old place', and that clerical collars and all 'the false mystique that surrounds "the Clergy"' would go.[13]

Broughton Knox, recently returned from his term as foundation Principal of George Whitefield College in South Africa, gave clear directions on the path Harry must follow.

> I know that an Archbishop of Sydney only has a limited initiative in appointments to parishes, but none can be made without your concurrence so I pray that only those ministers who know and are able to and will teach the <u>whole</u> counsel of God and will preach faithfully

and regularly the cross will be appointed ministers of parishes in the diocese, for the eternal destiny of parishioners and their neighbours depends on this.[14]

There were some letters from clergy who had not supported Harry, but not as many as would be required to assure him that all was well. A weakness in the system for election in the diocese is that the names of a candidate's movers and seconders are made known to all synod representatives. This is designed to demonstrate a candidate's capacity to garner support, but the downside is that, once the election is held, those who did not support the successful candidate are well known. They might not then feel at ease in immediately and warmly congratulating the successful candidate. For whatever reason, there were few letters from those who had not supported Harry. The few who did, argued along the lines that much prayer had gone into the synod; the Lord had spoken; they were happy with the outcome. Those who had not at first supported Harry, but who best understood synod processes, were also content. Peter Jensen, for example, who was then Principal of Moore College, and destined to follow Harry as archbishop, wrote:

> I think that we are all feeling rather excited that the Lord has answered our prayers with yourselves. If you had been at the Synod you would have sensed I think that the group as a whole moved fairly deliberately in your direction – but not unthinkingly. This is what we had been praying for ... and I think that we are all giving much thanks![15]

Bruce Ballantine-Jones wrote

> Raema and I want to express our joy and happiness at the outcome of the Synod vote. The process was difficult, especially for you both, but I feel that the result was right and you come into office not only with the goodwill and support of the diocese but with a program for change already developed and ready to go. There has never been such a happy coincidence as this.[16]

There was nothing either hypocritical or self-serving in these sentiments. Bruce had supported Phillip Jensen initially and would have been excited if Phillip had been elected, but he was realistic enough to know that Phillip was a long shot. When Phillip was eliminated, Bruce turned his support readily to Harry. But he wanted to see change, and it was change away from traditional Anglicanism. His support for Harry was not unconditional.

The problem with letters like Peter Jensen's and BBJ's was that they were in the minority. From the parishes that did not have a reputation for conservative

Reformed faith, support was forthcoming. For example, from the relatively small parish of St Luke's, Mosman, 99 parishioners signed a letter of support for their new archbishop. Son of Bruce Smith, Father Dave, now Rector of Dulwich Hill, the parish where Harry grew up, sent Harry a congratulatory card signed by more than 50 parishioners. From the 'highest' church in the diocese, Father Austin Day wrote to assure Harry of his prayers and those of his other 'kindly supporters' from among the high-church Anglicans such as Dr Ron James.[17] Austin Day, eight years later, was to write to Harry on the latter's retirement. Judging by the crabbed handwriting, it cost him dearly to write that note, in which he simply said to Harry, 'Many thanks for all your kindness to me.'[18] The Sunday following the election was Palm Sunday and at St Alban's, Epping the congregation broke into spontaneous applause at the announcement that Harry was to be their new archbishop. But from some of the largest, conservatively evangelical churches, there was silence.

Perhaps another ominous sign for Harry was that he received so many letters of congratulation from clergy, especially bishops, from outside the diocese, relieved that Sydney had chosen the man most likely to avert schism. Ged Muston, the recently retired Bishop of North West Australia, for example, wrote:

> I am quite sure that, despite the present difficulties, the seeds of greater unity in our Church are present, waiting to be watered and fed. Your appointment will bring great encouragement to those who hope for that unity, and who want to see us take the opportunity *together* to bring the Gospel to this country.[19]

Bruce Wilson, Bishop of Bathurst, wrote that he was relieved and delighted by Harry's appointment. He was relieved because he felt that Harry would make the tension between Sydney and the other dioceses creative rather than destructive. He had feared the appointment of one who might even sever the relationship. He was delighted because he felt Harry would build links and have the high regard of bishops both of the Province of New South Wales and of the national Church.[20] Bp Brian Kyme, Administrator of the Diocese of Perth, wrote: 'We have been praying ... that a man with a pastoral heart who avoids controversy for its own sake might be selected to the See and we are delighted that you are to take the helm.'[21] David Murray, Assistant Bishop of Perth, reported having followed the election with his prayers and heard of Harry's election 'with thanksgiving.'[22] The Bishop of Gippsland, David Sheumack, greeted Harry's selection 'with a great deal of joy.'[23] Bp John Lewis wrote that his Diocese of North Queensland applauded this very congenial and popular appointment 'which we all receive with goodwill and great expectations.'[24]

Perhaps a third ominous sign was that women who desired to be ordained chose to be heartened by Harry's election. Colleen O'Reilly, the deputy chair of Anglicans Together, wrote to Patricia Hayward, Convenor of the Sydney Movement for the Ordination of Women (MOW), counselling patience and moderation.

> I would hope that the next few years see trust replace suspicion and that we can learn to live with mutual regard of one another even as we hold differing views and practices in our common life in Christ Jesus … The morning after the Election Synod I feel quietly confident that we have a new Archbishop for a new day in the Church in Sydney and I pray that we can all learn new and mature ways to work together for the mission of the Church.[25]

Patricia agreed and shared at the MOW AGM on 18 April 1993 the view that the way to change the mind of synod voters is not through confrontation and emphasising the justice of their case, but by showing the gospel of Jesus, evangelical scholarship, the weight of biblical evidence, and people's experience.[26] Meanwhile, supporters of the ordination of women knew that they would have at least a willing ear from Harry and so gave him plenty of appropriate advice. Heather Pulsford from Wollongong, for example, advised Harry, 'Don't forget that, at Pentecost, the women weren't sent into the kitchen to wait until all the gifts had been handed out.'[27]

There were also letters from those who accepted that the Archbishop of Sydney was a pre-eminent position in civic life. The twice-knighted Member of the NSW Legislative Council, Sir Asher Joel, wrote, 'Your distinguished career and sense of dedication undoubtedly weighed heavily in your favour when the synod met to elect a successor to my very good friend Archbishop Robinson.'[28] From Burwood in Melbourne, Graeme Gair wrote, thanking God that the Anglican Church had found a leader and enclosing a biography of Joseph Booth, 'a Great Leader of the Anglican Church in Victoria.'[29] The NSW premier congratulated Harry on his election to this position of 'great honour and responsibility' and hoped for close dialogue between his ministerial colleagues and the church.[30]

Sydney had appointed the archbishop it needed at the time. The majority wanted peace and unity rather than the prevailing of one philosophy or brand of tradition over others.[31] Many felt more 'secure' as a result of Harry's appointment.[32] Few were under any illusion that the future would be easy for Harry or the diocese, but the Lord, in his mercy, had given his Anglican flock in Sydney an opportunity to behave itself. The laity were happy, many citing the Scripture in recognition of Harry's godliness, 'Those who honour me I will honour' (1 Sam 2:30; Jn 12:26). And the clergy, wondering if Harry had all the requisite gifts for such an impossible task, took comfort in the Scripture: 'The one who calls you is faithful, and he will do this (1 Thess 5:24).

Robert Forsyth reported on the synod in his monthly column, 'Bah Humbug', in *Southern Cross*. This column continued throughout most of Harry's archiepiscopate, ending only in 2000 when Robert was appointed by Harry as Bishop of South Sydney. His column gives one man's impartial assessment of diocesan issues while Harry was archbishop. He had been one of the REPA 'colonels' and never wavered in his opposition to the ordination of women; he was therefore trusted by the 'hardliners'. But he was also committed to the Anglican heritage and constantly challenged those impatient to depart from that heritage.

> April 1993
>
> What a week!
>
> We praise God for the election of Harry Goodhew as our next archbishop. But what did the election synod tell us about ourselves?
>
> At times it was exciting, at times it was entertaining, at times it was funny, at times it was tense, but it worked. And today we have a new archbishop and a new era is dawning for our great diocese.
>
> Here are some of my reflections after the exhausting week of the election synod.
>
> 1. The panic merchants were wrong. The 1993 Election Session showed the maturity and Christian grace of our Synod as few meetings in recent years have done. I cannot remember a happier synod. All the angst and fear of the last months that there would be blood on the floor, division in the diocese and "war in the cloisters" has been proved to be unnecessary. This Synod has revealed (what most of us always knew anyway) that our church can deal with strongly held differences without disaster.
>
> Not that it was without effort. The President of the Synod, Donald Cameron, was outstanding at his genial best, leading us with a rare combination of firmness and humour. (The one thing I can't understand is how Bishop Cameron keeps on getting away with his well-worn,

motherless child "I'm just a poor amateur" act, while showing such consummate mastery of his responsibilities. Why do we keep falling for it?)

2. Everyone is for change. The one thing on which every speaker agreed and which every candidate (we were told) offered was that Sydney Diocese must chart new directions. There is less consensus on what the change must be. Is it to be, (as one speaker offered) "a change along the road we already know" or is it rather something much more radical and revolutionary? Although it was the slogan of the supporters of one particular candidate, I felt that the whole synod was yearning for what was called "a change in leadership culture" in our diocese and churches. I hope we are not putting too high an expectation on the archbishop.

3. There is a felt need for healing and a new peace in our diocesan relationships. I am convinced that the events of 1992 (the Anglican Church of Australia's *annus horribilus*?) were still having their effect, let alone the sense that Christian life and mission are getting much harder in the increasingly secular Sydney. I suspect that this synod itself may prove to be the first step in such healing ...

7. We were confused about God's guidance. We were told that one man was the choice of divine providence because he was the older and more experienced man, and also that another man was probably God's choice because there was so much opposition to him, and yet another because he was so well loved by all. One speaker told us to look for the one on whom God's finger rested, and another that whomever we chose would be God's choice, no matter what. Many people appreciated the information sheets sent out before the Synod, others thought they were pre-empting the synod and even the Holy Spirit. Despite all this, I think we got it right.

## The response of the press

In the days immediately following his appointment, Harry received some attention in the media. He was interviewed by Quentin Dempster on the ABC's *Stateline* program on Friday 2 April, the day after his election, and faced unfriendly fire 'graciously and wisely'.[33] Peter Jensen, who eight years later was to handle the press with similar grace, was perhaps a little surprised by how well Harry handled the media and his skills in communication, and commended him for it.[34] He was not the only one impressed. One of his Moore College classmates heard Harry on 2GB while driving and was in some danger of running off the road, as tears filled his eyes as Harry so easily brought the Lord into the conversation. So, he wrote a limerick in honour of the interview.

> There was a young bishop called Harry,
> Who media questions would parry,
> 'I'll just preach the Word,
> About Jesus the Lord,
> While 'er I've got breath – should He tarry!'[35]

Revd Philip Kitchin wrote from Moss Vale that he was pleased that at least one election went right in New South Wales, and that an obvious seal upon Harry as the future leader of the diocese was the pleasant, friendly yet authoritative way that he had handled the several TV interviews he had seen.[36]

Generally, the media responded favourably to Harry's election; the Illawarra media very favourably. Kara Martin, reporter for WIN-TV, the local station, wrote to Harry, 'I shall miss our interviews (I never asked tough questions like Quentin Dempster!) and your interest in me which made me feel very special.'[37] The *Illawarra Mercury* had front page photos of Harry for two days in succession and much adulatory reporting, under such headlines as 'we're all proud of you,' and 'the man of the people.' One reporter enthused about Harry's preaching at a confirmation service he had attended.

> He spoke with such authority ... He made people listen ... It was excellent oratory. And so, it doesn't surprise me at all that our own Bishop Harry Goodhew has gone to the very top of the Anglican tree. The church could not get a finer man for the job.[38]

Harry was described in *SMH* as 'an exemplary Christian to the fingertips.'[39] It was considered a wonder that the *Australian* even managed to understand that it was possible to combine gentleness with strength![40] The *Telegraph* focused on the problems the church had with modern society – female ordination, multiculturalism and unemployment – but reported Harry's words fully on those issues.[41]

Two months after his election, Harry was featured by *SMH* in an article headed 'Daddy's girl' as one of five fathers with their daughters. He is pictured hugging Wendy, who spoke of her father's 'totally transparent' Christian life and the fact that she never felt she could not talk to him. 'He would always sit and listen.'[42] She was soon to face a great personal problem and took it to her father who, she believed, could always sort things out. She said to him, 'I don't know if I can walk through this,' and he said, 'Let my faith be enough for you today.' Wendy commented,

> Dad didn't have the answers either, but he had the faith. His first response to really major difficulties was to go down on his knees and pray. That is what I know he is at the core. God is his first refuge.

## Grace in the vanquished

While the human focus was on the man at the centre of the drama, one of the most encouraging manifestations of God's grace was at work at the periphery. Elections are brutal experiences for the vanquished, especially for one defeated as narrowly as Paul Barnett. It had been hard for him and Anita, his wife, to have to stand before the election synod while all its attention and applause were fixed on Harry and Pam. At the conclusion of the election synod, Bp Peter Watson and his wife, Margo, gathered up Paul and Anita, taking them to a nearby hotel for coffee and consolation. The next morning, Boak Jobbins took flowers to Paul and Anita to express his solidarity with them in their disappointment. Surprisingly, Paul and Anita did not quite see it that way, and any disappointment was short-lived. When they arrived home after the event, Anita's mother asked how it went, and when told the outcome, she said, 'Thank goodness for that.'

Both Paul and Anita are clear that by the very next morning they were over it. Paul was aware even then that Harry had 'a calling for it'; that he knew what he wanted to do with the role. Paul admits that he had little idea what he would have done. He only stood because he was prevailed upon to do so by those who wanted to block the forces gathering momentum behind REPA. He is quite sure that the better candidate was chosen and that his own role as regional bishop more suited his gifts and inclinations. He worked well with Harry, who gave him a free hand. The outcome as it developed under Harry, Paul believes, especially after regionalisation was achieved in 1996, made the diocese function far more effectively than it had at any time since Archbishop Mowll. 'I've never regretted it actually,' insists Paul, 'never, not for a moment.'[43] That this was his genuine conviction is confirmed by Revd Jeremy Tonks. In 1993 he was in his second year at Moore College and he recalls speaking to Paul in the college dining room the morning after the election. 'He spoke very confidently of the fact that he believed that synod had, under God, elected the right man for the job at that time. Looking back over eight years I can only agree with him.'[44] In retrospect, one can also only agree that, in Paul Barnett, God had also anointed the right man to give Harry the support he needed in the difficult years ahead.

## Installation

On 29 April 1993 Harry Goodhew was inducted as archbishop at St Andrew's Cathedral in a thrilling service.

> I Harry, by the providence of God elected Archbishop of Sydney, come to take my place in this cathedral church of St Andrew. I ask for your prayers that I may be a shepherd who will walk in God's way and watch over his people with loving care for the honour and glory of Christ our Lord who has purchased us with his blood.

11.2 Pam at Harry's installation as archbishop.

He preached gloriously, paraphrasing the KJV of Solomon's words in 1 Kings 3:7–9, 'I am but a little child. I do not know how ... therefore give your servant a listening heart.' This is more than a response to Solomon's personal need, said Harry. It proclaims that the life of the people is lived *coram Deo* – in the presence of God, the magnificent other. 'That magnificent other is the one who loves us.' As C.S. Lewis said, he is not a senile benevolence who wishes for us to be happy in our own way, but he is a consuming fire. He requires three things of us, a triad that makes up true spirituality, and those three are 'orthodoxy, orthopraxis and orthokardia' (and as he said those three words, the camera recording the service panned on his daughter, Wendy, who raised an eyebrow in filial bemusement): 'right believing, right doing and right heartedness.' Harry insisted that the first is not sufficient – we have to go beyond arrant intellectualism, and we must have desire for this lover who loves us – we must be passionate for Christ. The tests of the validity of a life lived *coram Deo* are prayer, personal godliness and holiness of life, and a love for the church.

Retiring archbishop, Donald Robinson, was very encouraged by the service and by Harry's sermon 'in particular.' 'You struck exactly the right note and I am sure many would have thanked God and taken courage.'[45] Bruce Kaye, later Secretary of General Synod, said in response to Harry's emphasis on spirituality and evangelism that true evangelicalism had been restored to the diocese in place of the harsh brand of Christianity. Ted Doncaster of the Parish of Willunga in the Diocese of the Murray wrote to thank him for his comments on *coram Deo*,[46] but Chappo wrote to reprimand him for using Latinisms. Chappo's point was that the Bible in English was sufficient to communicate the mind of God and that preachers should not have to resort to vocabulary from other languages. After all, had not the Reformation paid with blood for the transmission of the gospel in the language of the people? But Canon Raymond Heslehurst, then Rector of Keiraville in the Wollongong region, thought differently. He believed Harry to

11.3 At his installation at St Andrew's Cathedral, the door is opened to Harry, flanked by supporters of the ordination of women.

be among the finest of preachers because of his effectiveness in connecting with people's feelings. He thought of John Keating, the teacher in *Dead Poet's Society*, the recently released popular film. Keating had inspired his pupils with the term *carpe diem*, which had a far more transformative impact on them than its English translation 'seize the day' would have had. Similarly, observed Raymond, no-one would ever forget Harry's installation sermon because of its Latinism.[47]

Standing outside the Cathedral in the rain were four men who supported the ordination of women, among them Rob Brennan, husband of Patricia, the MOW activist. They held up a banner inscribed with the words, 'Harry: It's time we gave women a fair go!! Their exclusion is our loss.' 'We feel as strongly as the women,' Rob Brennan explained, pointing out that every recent survey by church and secular organisations had shown that a clear majority of Anglicans favoured the ordination of women, which was being blocked by a minority of 'reactivist men.' It was a demonstration the effectiveness of which was in inverse proportion to its size: every paper the next day reported on Brennan's words outside the Cathedral at greater length than on Harry's inside the Cathedral.

Following Harry's installation, Revd Jim Holbeck, who was well known to Harry, having served as his Senior Curate in Coorparoo and who had been the leader of the Healing Ministry in Sydney following the retirement in 1988 of Canon Glennon, wrote to him.

> Two things came to my mind as significant last Thursday evening during the service. One was that we have in you both, a servant-hood role of leadership being modelled before the whole diocese, which will be humbling to us all, and so necessary at this time. The second was the tremendously heart-felt applause as you were presented as Archbishop. It seemed to me to express a deep sense of gratitude to God for your election, and a sense of joy mixed with great relief. Relief that the apprehension as to the future of the diocese was over, and that the Lord had over-ruled to His glory, and we were glad![48]

The relief that Holbeck reported in his letter is further evidence of the high state of anxiety within the diocese. It seems that the diocesan family had a considerable aptitude for such anxiety. It was just as well then that it had in its archbishop one who was remarkably serene in the face of conflict and the pressure of an unrelentingly heavy workload. He trusted that over time, as people got to know him, they would learn to trust him. Commonly, people who did not know him well, and thought him at first too gentle to be a strong leader, came, often to their own surprise, first to respect him and then to trust him. This would have occurred more readily perhaps, if not for the so-called 'Pymble matter', which was to be so destructive of trust, and which, unfortunately, happened so early in his archiepiscopate.

# 12

# Bishopscourt: Spectral Visions

When Harry was elected archbishop, it was unclear where he would live. He and Pam were initially accommodated in a high-rise apartment in York Street in the city, pending a decision on the suitability of Bishopscourt, the traditional home of Sydney's Anglican archbishops.

It was the role of the Property Trust and the Endowment of the See (EOS) to determine where the archbishop would live. At the time of Harry's election the property market was flat, and it was calculated that the diocese would only make about $2 million on the sale of Bishopscourt. The conclusion was reached that it would be better to continue to accommodate the archbishop there.[1] One member of SC was so opposed to the archbishop continuing to be housed in such 'luxury' that he refused to visit Bishopscourt again. It was, in fact, anything but luxurious, as not a lot had been done to it during the episcopates of Marcus Loane (1966–82) and Donald Robinson (1982–93). When asked what was done to the house in his time, Loane said, 'I got rid of the bar'. Bishopscourt was in need of complete refurbishment. It was freezing in winter and the whole place smelled of kerosene from the ancient heaters then in use.

A 1991 report on Bishopscourt, recommending its sale and the building of another residence elsewhere, had been dismissed by Archbishop Robinson on the grounds that it failed to understand 'the place it occupies in connection with the role of the Archbishop', that synod should not be 'beguiled merely by the prospect of freeing capital funds for other purposes' and that 'the role of the Archbishop would probably change significantly if Bishopscourt were dispensed with.'[2] He then wrote firmly to the EOS Committee, 'my experience has led me to believe that the advantages of the present residence for the Archbishop's task are very great, and could not, if at all, be had in any alternative arrangement.'[3]

Six days after his election, Harry expressed his views to David Fairfull, CEO of diocesan administration.

> To express myself adequately on the subject, I need initially to address the ideology which I espouse with regard to the role of the Archbishop of Sydney. This bears directly on the way he is accommodated. In my view the Archbishop is the Bishop of Sydney. As such he must represent the Church in the life of the city which bears that name. He must have the capacity to relate in an appropriate fashion to the Crown, to the

> Government, to the business community and to the general population of Sydney. I do not wish to abandon the role of being the public face of the Church in the city. Indeed, I wish to expand it as far as possible. Therefore I wish that the accommodation and facilities will enhance rather than detract from that role.

While that reads like a bid to stay at Bishopscourt, Harry's preference then was that the diocese would build a new residence, 'functional but not opulent… designed to serve the needs of successive Archbishops for the next 50 years.' Part of the reason for his lack of enthusiasm for Bishopscourt was that an inspection had horrified him and Pam. He went on:

> I find it difficult to understand how a responsible church could allow that residence to get into its present condition. How we have not been sued by our neighbours over the condition of the vacant block I do not know. The house itself has been poorly cared for and the 'out-of-sight' conditions of the building are lamentable.

Such grumpiness did not sound like Harry, but he hadn't finished yet. If it could be made habitable in quick time, he and Pam were prepared to live there for two years while a solution was found, but, he concluded, he was not prepared to 'wait around forever while committees argue backwards and forwards as has been the case for the last decade.'[4]

## Pam refurbishes Bishopscourt

When the decision was eventually made to house Harry and Pam in Bishopscourt, Pam presided over the demanding refurbishment process. It was repainted and recarpeted throughout, and extensively refurnished. Glyn Evans, from the firm Allen Jack & Cottier, heritage architects, visited Bishopscourt occasionally to consult with Pam. She met more regularly with a team of three: a builder, John Buchanan; Sheila Cook, an interior decorator, mother of David Cook, Principal of the Sydney Missionary and Bible College; and Mark Francis, who worked in diocesan administration as Secretary of the Property Trust and of the EOS. They could have spent a lot more on the refurbishment than they did, but they were creative in getting the same result with less money. 'We have saved them a motza,' David Fairfull was in the habit of saying as the refurbishment progressed.

Before the Goodhews arrived, and without any involvement from them, the EOS and the Property Trust, through Lawson's, auctioned off some of the furnishings that had been in the house since Mowll's time. This included furniture and other items, such as statues, that had been left in the house by Thomas Sutcliffe Mort, the second owner of the house. It also included Mowll's cutlery, which was good quality sterling silver and was used throughout the Loanes' and Robinsons' times, but no longer matched.

A descendant of Mort, Charles Mort, was unhappy with the sale, especially of statues of Florence Nightingale and of the Good Samaritan. The latter was by the noted English sculptor, Charles Bell Birch (1832–1893), which sold for $2,600.[5] Since the sculptor was paid 1,000 guineas in 1858, it was a steal. 'Why didn't you buy it?' asked Charles's son, David, of his father who attended the auction. 'I didn't have $2,000 and neither did you,' replied his father.[6] He was distressed by the wanton disposal of the family patrimony. 'I am very upset and bewildered by the action,' he wrote to Harry,[7] and he rang Pamela to tell her so. She understood his feelings, but she was also clear in her own mind that Bishopscourt was not primarily a museum. In any case, before the sale of Greenoaks to the Church in 1912, most of the contents of the house had been sold in a monster sale,[8] and much of the treasure that Mort had brought out from England had found its way back to the homeland 80 years before Harry's election. Canon Stuart Barton Babbage's observation on Harry, that 'he made sweeping changes at Bishopscourt, summarily disposing of some of its historic treasures'[9] owes much to the flair of the observer. Harry never summarily disposed of anything! But he was in control now, responsible for all actions taken during his administration.

It was not until six months after the election that the Goodhews were able to move into Bishopscourt. It was a mammoth effort to complete the refurbishment so quickly, as it was a vast project. It required not only a utilitarian outcome that Bishopscourt would make a contribution to paying its way through putting it to greater use for the promotion of the Church's ministry, but it also had to be done tastefully and with full compliance with heritage requirements. Pam was well equipped for the task, with good colour sense and the ability to get things done without sacrificing quality. To heat the house and eliminate the kerosene fumes, a ducted gas heating system was installed. The contractor appointed to install the new system had 30 years' experience and he said that he needed every one of those years to do the job, adding that the building probably heard some words it was not in the habit of hearing.

The Goodhews replaced the sterling silverware with good quality nickel-plated cutlery, and augmented the dinner sets and glassware so that it all matched. They replaced the Queen Anne sideboard in the dining room with one that had been in the basement and that Pam thought more suitable. Pam took some silver out of the safe and installed it on the new sideboard. She also arranged for Linda

Davies, the wife of John, the caretaker, to take an advanced cooking course so that she would be better equipped to cater for distinguished guests. Among such were Mrs Jenny Macarthur-Onslow and members of the National Trust who visited Bishopscourt on 3 September 1994. Pam was assured in advance that 'every care' would be taken, each room 'manned by a member' of the Committee, no-one would touch anything, and shoes and umbrellas were to be removed in the event of rain.[10]

## A brief history of Bishopscourt

A rambling Gothic mansion in Greenoaks Avenue, Edgecliff, Bishopscourt is perhaps 'the best Gothic picturesque house in New South Wales.'[11] Compared with Swifts, the home of Catholic archbishops from 1923 until 1984, it is modest. 'This is a shack,' said Christine Jensen of Bishopscourt after a visit to Swifts, 'But Greenoaks is a more genteel house, a more classic house in a way.'[12]

It began its life as a small three-room cottage in 1835. A second floor was added in 1840 by Thomas Woolley, a prosperous ironmonger. In 1846 the house was purchased by the most entrepreneurial of all the Colony's settlers, Thomas Sutcliffe Mort, a founder of the Australian Mutual Provident Society, who made his fortune in the frozen meat and wool trades. He changed the name of the house to 'Greenoaks', acquired surrounding land to make the estate an extensive 13 acres, and augmented the house first with additions by architect, J. F. Hilly (1851–5), and then by additions, commenced in 1860, designed by his personal friend, Edmund Blacket.

In 1878 Mort died. Greenoaks was rented out, but Mort was survived by his second wife, Marianne, and it is her ghost, it is said, that (or is it who?) still haunts the house. Others contend that the ghost is not that of Marianne. It must be that of Mort's first wife Theresa (nee Laidley) whom he had married at Christ Church St Laurence in 1841. The story goes that the ghost was chiefly to be found on the north-facing deck, looking out over the harbour, in a vain bid to see her deceased son return to Sydney from England. In 1858 Charles Sutcliffe, aged 10, died at Eton College. He had been thrown into a stream during a schoolboy 'ragging' and died of pneumonia.[13] The organ at nearby St Mark's Darling Point, the church built on land donated by Mort, is dedicated to his son's memory. Marianne married Thomas in 1874 and had two sons (Max and Guy) by him before his death in 1878, but neither of them died while Marianne was at Greenoaks, which she left a decade after her husband's death and settled in England. The ghost is more likely, then, to be that of Theresa. Harry delighted in telling his grandchildren about the ghost and then taking them down to the basement and pointing out broken

12.1 Pam, Harry and the grandchildren at Bishopscourt. This photo was taken for a Christmas card.

crockery and what he claimed were bones. David's two eldest loved visiting Bishopscourt for this reason, but Jackson, Wendy's son, was not yet five when he heard this story for the first time and was so freaked out by it that he would never go into the basement again.

Greenoaks was acquired from the trustees of Mort's estate by Campbell Langtree in 1910. He subdivided the property and sold the house and two acres surrounding it to the Anglican Church. Renamed 'Bishopscourt', it was the residence for John Charles Wright, Archbishop of Sydney from 1909 to 1933, and it remained the residence for the archbishop until 2013, the end of the episcopate of Harry's successor, Peter Jensen.

## The White House of Sydney Anglicanism

The refurbishment over which Pam presided in 1993 transformed Bishopscourt into a working house, a functioning conference and meeting centre for diocesan agencies. Like the White House, Bishopscourt has a west wing and a south wing. The White House has an east wing, which Bishopscourt does not, but Bishopscourt has a north wing, which the White House does not. In Harry's and Pam's time, the south and west wings were converted into guest accommodation.

The chapel was added by Archbishop Mowll. Harry remembers the late Bp Brian King singing with great enthusiasm in the chapel, where the staff team met weekly for worship. Harry brought into the chapel a Moore College group and made them sing 'St Patrick's Breastplate'. 'Now this is a hymn,' Harry exhorted them, 'it says it all.' Pam, as she played the harmonium in the chapel, thought it took a long time to say it. The vast study near the chapel was lined with bookcases that Pam found in Salamanca Place in Hobart. She negotiated to acquire them over the phone, thus saving a fortune on built-in bookcases.

The first floor of the northern wing was where the Goodhews set up their living quarters. It was relatively humble, inferior to many a diocesan rectory. It has a main bedroom with dressing room (which Pam used as a study) and bathroom. There is a lounge room and deck. The deck is 'where the ghost was supposed to be.' It has views across Double Bay towards Manly and views across East Sydney, a carpet of purple when the jacarandas flower. From here the Goodhews used to watch the start of the Sydney to Hobart yacht race, though growing trees now seriously restrict the view. Above the main staircase is a capacious landing, which the Goodhews made into a family room with bookshelves. In the kitchen Harry would make bread, pounding the dough to release the tension engendered by his chief tormentors, he jokes (well, I think he was joking).

With Pam presiding, the refurbishment was finished with commendable speed and it was to stand the test of time. After a decade in Bishopscourt, Harry's and Pam's successors, Peter and Christine Jensen, made very few changes, tweaking a couple of the kitchens. The roof, which had been patched up after the 14 April 1999 Sydney hailstorm, was re-slated because it was leaking badly; the tops of the chimneys were replaced because they threatened to tumble down; and the stained-glass windows, the earliest domestic stained glass in Australia, were cleaned.

## Goodhew hospitality at Bishopscourt

Such a facility of course only gave the Goodhews greater scope to exercise their famous hospitality. Harry and Pam found it a great ministry centre. Harry loved the 'bubble and vibrancy' of living in that part of Sydney. His team of bishops met there each week, and once a month they were joined by the archdeacons, the dean, and their wives. Potential ministers were interviewed there; in-service training was given; dinners were held for clergy and other guests. Each Ascension Day, the school chaplains visited; and there were dinners for academics and for politicians, to encourage them to take Christ into their professions. Fundraisers were held there for Anglicare, and promotional evenings for the Billy Graham Evangelistic Association and for EE. There, Bp Brian King, chaplain to the armed forces, held dinners for members of the armed forces, and clergy elected as bishops there went into retreat in preparation for their consecration. Stuart Barton Babbage held a dinner for Keith Mason when he was appointed President of the Court of Appeal. It was in admiration for his support for the ordination of women, explained Dr Babbage, and Harry and Pam 'readily agreed.'[14] Bishopscourt also served as a venue for bishops' wives conferences, for dinners for Moore College and Mary Andrews College staff and students, for retiring clergy, and for the chairs of Anglican schools and colleges. Barney's (St Barnabas, Broadway) regularly held staff retreats there. St Matthias', Centennial Park, came for its staff conference every year. Pam assumed responsibility for running the conferences at Bishopscourt. All went well until the government introduced fringe benefits taxation on conferences, and Pam had to start accounting for every meal taken – 'a bit of a nightmare.'

Interviews of potential headmasters of church schools were held there. Among headmasters selected there was Phillip Heath, appointed head of St Andrew's Cathedral School in 1994. Harry always looked on him as one of his most successful appointments. After his interview, Phillip confided in Pam with great seriousness that he thought he had let Harry down. Harry, he said, had always wanted him to be a minister. 'I'm sure Harry will absolve you of that sin,' she responded, 'Just be a good headmaster.' He obeyed her.

At the end of his episcopate, Harry spoke warmly of Bishopscourt's usefulness to the diocese.[15] Many Anglicans, no doubt, agreed with Alan Cole that the archbishop should be accommodated 'in a sensible house', one that is not so conspicuously inconsistent with the church's need to identify with the poor. But Harry and Pam believed that people did not realise how sensible it was. They were able to do things there that they would not be able to do anywhere else; that they might not have had the inspiration to do anywhere else.

Following the 2008 Global Financial Crisis, when the diocese lost $180 million, the SC brought a recommendation to synod for the sale of Bishopscourt to raise much-needed cash. Opposing the motion, Stephen Judd, Donald Robinson's son-in-law, observed correctly that, when VIPs and heads of state are invited to Bishopscourt, they come. The proposal to sell Bishopscourt was soundly rejected. Peter Jensen, then incumbent at Bishopscourt, abstained from the debate on the proposed sale, but on its conclusion, observed perceptively that in its decision to keep Bishopscourt, synod was declaring that it is 'in the city for the long haul.'[16] In 2012, however, synod, under sustained pressure from the forces of iconoclasm and economic rationalism, resolved to sell Bishopscourt, which had been given the reputation of 'a lazy asset.' It was sold for $18 million, well below the price that opponents of the sale considered reasonable. 'We toss out so many good things,' complained David Goodhew. He compared the disposal of Bishopscourt to dispensing with the prayer book.[17]

Moves to sell Bishopscourt, however, can be traced back to 1962 when Archbishop Gough suggested that the house might have outlived its usefulness. The same suggestion was made to SC in 1982. On both those occasions Bishopscourt was saved, just as it was at the beginning of Harry's time in office, by a depressed real estate market, a cyclical occurrence in Sydney. As the years passed, maintenance costs became increasingly prohibitive and the facilities decreasingly fit for purpose. It was considered past time to bite the bullet and let it go. It just took a passionate speech in synod in 2012 from Revd Peter Lin, then rector of multicultural Fairfield and from 2015, Bishop of the Georges River region, to make it happen. He professed to be profoundly embarrassed that any minister of the gospel was housed in such opulence. The majority in synod held this truth to be self-evident.[18] Since self-evident truths are not grist for the historian's mill, I refrain from further commentary.

# 13

# Laying the Foundation: 'Dynamic Anglicanism'

It might have been expected that Harry would hit the ground running. Keeping the office running smoothly were highly competent personal assistants, first Dorothy Steel whom Harry inherited from his predecessor and then Ruth Sefton who had previously worked for the Vice-Chancellor of Sydney University. Both Dorothy and Ruth were members of the Brethren. To them, when they drew his attention to some apparently insurmountable cataclysm, he would say 'But, we are having fun aren't we!'[1] For his own part, Harry was fully conversant with diocesan institutions and procedures. As a bishop, he had always sought advice. Now he willingly consulted the veteran, Bp Cameron, on such matters as subjects for discussion at a forthcoming bishops' conference. Diocesan secretary, David Fairfull, suggested Harry might chair meetings of HMS, the Youth Department, Anglican Retirement Villages, Glebe Board and Property Trust, with 'minimum involvement but keep control.'[2] These were all diocesan bodies, but Harry agreed also to serve as president of three extra-diocesan organisations of vital importance to the health of the Anglican Church: BCA, CMS, and EFAC. A man of prayer, Harry also consulted God, writing early in his Day Book,

> Lord, there are with you answers for every problem I seek you for ways of dealing with:
> 
> - The personalities which make up Standing Cttee
> - The Anglican Media Council
> - Our investment policy.[3]

He already had a clear view of what he wanted to do and how to do it. He wanted first to use the resources of the archbishop and his team (bishops, archdeacons and area deans) to strengthen parishes and to deepen the spiritual commitment of church members. Asked 'What is meant by the term, "the Diocese"?' Harry replied, 'I think the Diocese has meant for me primarily, the parishes—the people and those who minister to them.'[4] He directed his team to take as their first task the encouragement of the clergy and congregations in the local churches in their area, and to achieve a greater measure of regional and deanery planning in order to advance ministry capabilities across the diocese. He wanted, second, to expand the team of bishops from four to five so that his bishops could give more concentrated pastoral support to the clergy in their areas, particularly in those parts of the diocese where the Anglican Church was languishing. Third, he wanted to restructure the central administration by having many of the roles and responsibilities of the SC transferred to a smaller body, nominated by him, called the DEB. All three proposed changes proved much harder to achieve than he had hoped, reflecting the ongoing tensions and lack of trust within the diocesan family.

## Harry's mission statement

Reluctant to impose his own will on those working most closely with him, Harry hoped to be able to develop a set of priorities through workshopping with his colleagues. So, shortly after his appointment, there was a meeting to decide on a mission statement. It was, said Harry a 'most frustrating process.' Present, among others, were skilled and experienced managers, including David Fairfull, Geoff Kells and Warwick Olson (director of the media company Pilgrim International). But, there was just no agreement (too many leaders?) and Harry, who was keen to move forward, said to his staff uncharacteristically, 'we will never get agreement like this. We are just wasting time.'

It was Paul Barnett who provided the key to progress in the development of the mission statement. Given his disappointment in the election synod, Paul's unfailing helpfulness to Harry from the very start was an encouraging sign of God's grace at work. When Harry became frustrated with disagreement over the mission statement, Paul suggested to Harry that he devise it himself. So, Harry came up with four of his renowned five points. Then Paul observed that there was nothing about Anglicanism in any of the four points. So, the most famous of the points ('dynamic Anglicanism') was added. Bps Barnett and Watson then said to Harry, 'why don't you go with that?'

Harry's mission statement[5] read

> To enable God's people in this Diocese to be
> - Observably God's People
> - Pastorally Effective
> - Evangelistically Enterprising
> - Genuinely Caring
> - Dynamically Anglican

The five points are certainly not the product of committee think; they have distinctive 'Goodhew' written all over them. Even in the last of the five – while it was Paul who suggested adding Anglicanism, it was Harry who added 'dynamic'.

In wanting Sydney Anglicans to be 'observably God's people', Harry hoped that they would have 'a passion' for God and his word and display 'an impressive life of brotherly love and care.' His call for 'a more observable life of walking by the Spirit rather than by the flesh'[6] looks unexceptional, especially as it is biblical. There were those, however, who said that they did not know what Harry meant by this. Pam was unimpressed. 'What was there not to understand about "observably God's people"?' she asked. 'Why couldn't they understand what he meant? It was ridiculous.'

Harry's second aim, pastoral effectiveness, involved believers being 'sustained in their discipleship at every stage of their life.' The third, to be 'evangelistically enterprising' was the most characteristic of Sydney Anglican aspirations. To 'communicate Christ' was the responsibility of every member of the church and of every church. Fourth, to be 'genuinely caring' required the church to address the issues that 'debilitate' society and 'damage' individuals.

It was the last that drew the most comment. It was a theme Harry was to refer to often in his episcopate. 'Dynamic Anglicanism' he understood as 'fitting the strengths of our tradition to the needs of the present and future amongst all Australians and giving a lead to Anglicans in this country and elsewhere as to the best shape for Anglicanism in the next century.' Harry thus indicated that his vision for evangelical Anglicanism stretched beyond the Diocese of Sydney to the wider church both in Australia and internationally. In response to the question, 'what should Harry do to achieve this aim?' his bishops recommended that he should protect Anglican order, lead his episcopal team, be the face of the Church to the community and give support and encouragement to the laity of the Church.

Harry's talk of 'dynamic Anglicanism' was received with some mirth. Some dismissed it as an oxymoron: Anglicanism could no more be dynamic than a 'maybe' could be a 'definite'. Harry, they said, was 'clearly confused' – yet another oxymoron that Sydney Anglicans love to use of those with whom they disagree. Harry was not confused. He thought it was not a complicated matter, but it was nuanced. He suspected that a reason why so many laughed at the term was because they had lost confidence in the essence of Anglicanism.

Harry did want change. He wanted it as much as any, and more than most. But he wanted to promote it within Anglican parishes, through consultation and experimentation. Instead of grafting on to Anglican forms the practices of North American evangelicals, as Harry himself had done at Coorparoo, there were those who wanted to see those, together with home-grown practices, displace all

Anglican forms. Harry insisted that it was essential to maintain good worship traditions, but to do it in a way that is not stuffy, so that young people can access it and will not feel it is beyond them, and so that it does not eliminate the depth and mystery of an encounter with God. If you had a heart for what Anglicanism is, Harry believed, you could draw people into a form of it.

In itself, Anglicanism is not hostile to new ways of doing things – those new ways can be fully incorporated, thus enriching Anglicanism. By 'dynamic Anglicanism', Harry did not want people to be sticklers in their use of forms. He wanted worship leaders to relax and to lead people in a warm, uplifting service. Such worship stems from the recognition that this is God's community and he is present in it. People should go away from church services feeling that they have met with God and with his people. Harry was himself the most successful practitioner of this enriched, dynamic Anglicanism. But too many could see only his Anglicanism and not the experimentation, and accused him of opposition to change.

Ray Smith, destined to be appointed as Harry's fifth bishop, thought Harry's fivefold mantra was 'fantastic' but added, 'It was mocked, which I found objectionable. We are supposed to be Prayer Book and 39 Articles people.' Robert Forsyth observed of the whole fivefold mission statement, 'It did not get traction, but in terms of what he wanted to do, it was excellent. Dynamic Anglicanism got traction, but for the wrong reason.' Forsyth thought Harry was ahead of his time here – by the end of the episcopate of Harry's successor, Peter Jensen, it was considered, even by those who had been REPA iconoclasts, that it was a good thing to be an Anglican. Immediately after Donald Robinson, however, many people were of the view that Anglicanism was what was wrong with the church and they wanted to get rid of it.

While expecting his bishops to embrace the five points, Harry trusted them to do so 'according to their own style', drawing on the 'particular gifts of each.'[7] He believed that, in this matter, he had developed 'clear objectives with a basic strategy that allowed for flexible application.' He invited his assistant bishops, together with their archdeacons, to compile strategy documents for their regions, to give exemplary leadership to their regions, and to develop personal ministry development plans for themselves and their spouses. Feminism had not yet reached the point where wives were encouraged to do their own thing!

Harry developed his own personal strategy document. It well illustrates the proposition that effectiveness in ministry is dependent on spiritual integrity in private and on doing oneself what one expects others to do. Harry's first personal aim was 'To seek to walk humbly with God, grow in my life and ministry and offer nurture and support to my immediate family.' To achieve the last, he set himself to phone his mother every second day, his children every week, and his brother and sister every month. He also aimed at encouraging Pam in her own growth and ministry. In the essential spiritual disciplines, Bible reading and intercessions, he resolved to evaluate his practice, both with Pam and with a spiritual adviser, with whom he was to meet every three months. In the event, he did not appoint one spiritual adviser, but six! As mentioned earlier, his spiritual advisory group was made up of some close Wollongong friends, all of whom were mature in the faith and fruitful in their own ministries: Jeff and Margaret Fuller, Peter and Faye Kell, and Peter and Elizabeth Smart. Over time, as he was beset by the trials of office, Harry added another spiritual aspiration: not to let the vision be dimmed or clouded by disappointment with people or with ventures.

## Diocesan Executive Board

At the beginning of Harry's episcopate it was felt that diocesan administration had become too bureaucratic. Harry was eager to see the streamlining of decision-making and policy-formation and the development of a more effective executive structure. The appointment of an Executive Board to take over many of the powers of SC, however, was a change that the SC was not prepared to accept. It was a decidedly unromantic body, disinclined to allow Harry any sort of a honeymoon. It flatly refused to hand over its powers to a largely appointed, non-elected executive.

Harry did establish the DEB, but he was not able to appoint to it the people of his own choice. David Fairfull told Harry and his bishops that they would control difficult people in the diocese if he put them on the DEB, giving them a sense of ownership. Harry, accordingly, invited Phillip Jensen to be on the DEB. Paul Barnett said, 'Phillip has had a great ministry and is used to being in charge. I don't think it will work.'[8] Ray Smith agreed, 'Phillip just had his own ideas and his own agenda.'[9] Part of the problem was that Phillip's own ideas and agenda were so powerful and consistent that it is understandable he was reluctant to give up on them just because he failed to be elected as archbishop. He wanted to plant churches in other dioceses and across denominational boundaries.[10] He believed that Bible-believing Christians in all denominations had far more in common with each other than they had with 'Sociological Anglicans', those who belonged without believing. There was no point in 'Confessing Anglicans' trying to collaborate with 'Sociological Anglicans'.[11] Phillip's agenda began to be implemented without Harry's unequivocal blessing and flowered in his successor's episcopate. It was an agenda that grew churches. Harry, as we shall see, did want to support the energy and initiative of this church-planting strategy, but he wanted to cooperate with other Anglicans rather than ignore them, and he wanted to preserve Anglicanism in the process.

Ultimately, Phillip's ideas and agenda were incompatible with Harry's, and this probably best explains why they never did find a way of working harmoniously. The problem may not have been just or even primarily a matter of personality. Paul Barnett believes it goes to the nature of the episcopate in the Diocese of Sydney; namely, that the archbishop really is very limited in his powers. The one real power he has is the right to choose who he will ordain to the ministry. But bishops come and go. It is the clergy who stay on. Rectors know they will outlast the archbishop. Sydney is a very clerical diocese, more clerical than Melbourne. It's a rector's diocese. If a rector has his own supporters, he can stymie the will of the archbishop. It is not self-evident that this situation is bad. It is more democratic than the episcopal dictatorship that has bedevilled many an Anglican diocese. Church historian, Owen Chadwick, observed that 'the real leaders of English religious thought and revival were never archbishops, but were always the simple priests, like a Wesley or a Keble or a Maurice.'[12] True enough, but the 'always' is not true, and it is a view that makes it very hard to be an archbishop!

The DEB was supposed to be the means of steering Harry's vision for the diocese. It met at least once a month but never worked well, and Harry in practice relied more on his episcopal team to promote the ministry policies recommended by the Committee on the Development of Property and Ministry. It was a lost opportunity. Robert Forsyth was not alone in dismissing the DEB as 'a joke.' In his final synod in 2000, Harry admitted that the DEB had struggled. It had not been able to fulfil the role envisaged by the writers of the Report of the Archbishop's Commission and was reduced to a subcommittee of SC and subject to its oversight.[13]

## Harry's episcopal team

Because Harry was shaped as a facilitator of parish health and growth in Wollongong in his time there as archdeacon (1979–82) and as bishop (1982–93), he was convinced of the value of episcopal oversight both in the pastoral care of clergy and in the encouragement of laity. It has been argued that it was a 'moot point' for Harry to focus on the strengthening of parishes.[14] Perhaps those accustomed to debating in the higher courts of the church thought an archbishop should focus on more exciting issues such as defending the Bible or theological orthodoxy or moral issues or social justice or Sydney's position in the General Synod.

Harry saw the issues dealt with in SC as significant, but he never considered that they were as important as the life of the parishes, which often went on completely oblivious to SC. So, when he became archbishop, he was strongly motivated to advance parish ministry wherever he could. He therefore deliberately chose bishops with a strong record of pastoral care; he increased the number of regions, and therefore bishops, from four to five and he ensured that the extra episcopal oversight could be paid for without a further financial impost on the parishes. Happily, the diocese was not short of money. The secretariat, of whom David Fairfull was CEO, had invested wisely, making an extra $2.3 million available for the synod to distribute in October 1993. This enabled parish assessments to be eliminated altogether in Harry's time, so as to leave more funds at the local level for increased ministry. Harry remained ever grateful to David Fairfull for keeping the financial ship of the diocese afloat and making it possible for him to have a bishop, archdeacon and secretarial staff for each of the five regions of the diocese.

In the end, those chosen as assistant bishops did not have a reputation as successful diocesan operators. Harry did not have a John Reid or a Don Cameron or a Jack Dain, all of whom 'rode shotgun' for the archbishop. For this, he paid a price, as progressively his opponents wrested control from him, and his bishops did not defend him in a way bishops more practised in diocesan politics would have done. In any case, in Harry's opinion, competence on the episcopal bench prior to his time had not been all gain; he confessed that he had been irritated to get to diocesan meetings during Donald Robinson's episcopate to find that the outcomes had already been stitched up by John Reid and Jack Dain. And if they were not stitched up in episcopal team meetings, they were in SC. This was part of the culture he desired to change.

Most members of SC, however, appeared more comfortable with politics than with piety and had an excessive admiration for tight control. Donald Robinson had steered SC superbly and he had an even more adroit assistant in Bp Cameron. According to 'Fearless' Fairfull, Cameron typically rose when it was almost time to go home and members were wearying with an intractable debate, and he would say, 'What a magnificent debate. I have listened to both sides of the argument, and I must say I agree with everyone. So I move that we form a committee to progress this matter.' 'Moved,' the archbishop would say. 'Is there a seconder?' A compliant bishop would raise his hand. 'Moved, seconded – all those in favour say 'aye', the ayes have it – now Bishop Cameron do you have anyone in mind to serve on this committee?' 'Myself as chairman and the CEO.' 'All those in favour? Carried.' Later that night, the CEO would drag himself, exhausted by the debate, into Cameron's office, and Cameron would say, 'Well, David, how did I manage this evening?' And Fearless would reply, 'Bish, you were magnificent.' And Cameron would say, 'well, I think we put that matter to bed for 7 years,' and it was never heard of again.[15]

If Harry deliberately chose bishops who were pastors rather than politicians, would it have been better if they had been both? Was it possible to be a successful bishop in Sydney by concentrating on the pastoral and allowing the diocesan politicians to have their way? In such a politicised environment, such 'purity' was probably not workable. Professor Michael Horsburgh, who, though an opponent of evangelical hardliners, was consistently elected to SC, put the situation like this.

> Within the Diocese the Archbishop is valiantly trying to create a leadership team that can concentrate on pastoral matters. Commendable as this is, the effects of such pastoral activity are yet to be seen in the political life of the Diocese.
>
> The fact is that the apparent achievements of the Archbishop's pastoral initiatives are negated by the evident and continuing exclusiveness of the political structure. The two must go together.[16]

Bp Cameron worked part-time for Harry for five months after the election. His like was not seen again in Harry's time, with the result that too little was put to bed. Harry later recollected that, in the early days of his episcopate, he did not anticipate any unwillingness from the SC in pursuing the goals of church growth and development. He accepts that, among his bishops, he did not have a Donald Cameron or a John Reid to press the 'Archbishop's Matters.' At that stage he did not think he would need such. Perhaps naively, he devoted no attention to building a strong political power base in the SC. Perhaps shrewdly, he believed others might do that if necessary. In retrospect, Harry concedes he might have forfeited some political fire power in his appointments. It was not only that his appointees were not primarily interested in ecclesiastical politics. They were also given freedom by Harry to express their own views. Sometimes, they would even 'indicate uncertainty' with Harry's policies at SC, a practice that Margaret Rodgers, the consummate politician, regretted.[17]

In April 1993, when Harry was elected archbishop, the Diocese of Sydney was already divided into four regions (North Sydney, South Sydney, Parramatta and Wollongong) and 27 area deaneries. Paul Barnett was already Bishop of North Sydney. Peter Watson was Bishop of Western Sydney (Parramatta) and now agreed to become Bishop of South Sydney. Peter was a close friend of Paul and supported him in the election for archbishop. In an ideal world, Harry might have preferred to have chosen his entire episcopal bench from scratch. But Harry was actually grateful that two such experienced men were already in place, and he had considerable difficulty in finding another three bishops. It would have been very hard for him to find all five.

Harry caused some astonishment when he did not appoint his own archdeacon in Wollongong, Vic Roberts, as a bishop. Riley Warren, in a letter of advice to Harry shortly after the election, wrote commending Vic. 'I have … benefited personally by his, and Delle's ministry, and know how highly he is thought of. I urge you therefore to consider him as you make your future appointments.'[18]

Vic was experienced, efficient and energetic. Donald Robinson, the previous year, had offered him the position of Dean of Sydney, but Vic had declined it.[19] He and his wife, Delle, like Harry and Pam, were a good team. But the chemistry between Harry and Vic, making for deep friendship and trust, was not there. Peter Kell observed that at least this non-appointment meant that 'Harry might make an archbishop' because it showed he had the capacity to make hard decisions. Vic moved on, accepting the position of Rector of St Mark's, Darling Point, which is adjacent to Bishopscourt. They were neighbours, but the tension between them remained. Pam was anxious about it, but returned missionaries, who ran a counselling service, expressed the view that there are 'some things you can never mend. You just have to leave them where they are and move on.'

In his search for three assistant bishops, Harry approached Peter Corney, then Melbourne's best-known evangelical, and Glenn Davies and Peter O'Brien, both lecturers at Moore College, all of whom declined. Peter Corney had recently declined the invitation to become Bishop of Willochra, on the grounds that he believed he could be of more use in Melbourne. He declined Harry's invitation for the same reason. Glenn Davies laughed self-deprecatingly at the thought of becoming a bishop and indicated that he had just returned from overseas study leave and had an obligation to the college. He would later become Rector of Miranda and then bishop and archbishop. Peter O'Brien, New Testament lecturer at Moore, felt that his gifts best suited the academic world.

Shortly after his election, Harry, and the bishops he inherited, Paul Barnett and Peter Watson, met at Paul's beach house at Avoca. They reviewed a long list of names of possible new bishops, and Harry, on the warm recommendation of Bp Ken Short, decided to nominate Peter Kemp, Rector of Parramatta. He was academically well qualified, and a much-experienced parish clergyperson, whom Ken Short considered to be one of the best clergy in the Western region. He had a nine-year ministry in Mt Druitt and oversight of Tregear for a time, two of the most challenging areas of Sydney. He had done some very hard yards. He had been appointed to St John's, Parramatta, as the rector and senior canon and was highly regarded locally. He was due to retire shortly before Harry, giving Harry the opportunity to appoint one who might make a suitable successor as archbishop. The endorsement by SC of the archbishop's episcopal nominees was required, but it was understood that this was a formality. Such understandings are misunderstandings waiting to happen in an environment such as Harry now faced.

On 26 July 1993, the SC departed from convention and rejected Harry's nominee, embarrassing the archbishop and hurting Peter Kemp. Apparently, about six members did not vote, creating a situation where there were not enough votes to be two-thirds of those present and voting. This rejection was not totally without precedent; if not in Sydney, then in the wider church. Archbishop Frank Woods in Melbourne in 1970 invited Howard Hollis, his former Domestic Chaplain, to be an assistant bishop. But his diocesan council vetoed this appointment, having received just the year before the powers to do so. That power was Canon No. 6 of *The Constitution, Canons and Rules of General Synod*. It was a power that applied in Sydney as well, but it had rarely been exercised there, and the convention among the less legally minded was that the archbishop's appointees would be accepted. The SC's refusal to approve this appointment was an action with long-term consequences.

Harry was successful, however, in his nomination of Brian King, Rector of Manly, and Reg Piper from Holy Trinity Adelaide. Apparently, Reg was unusually indecisive over his appointment. Before Harry's election, one of Reg's assistant ministers, Paul Harrington, who was to succeed Reg as Rector of Holy Trinity, was invited to consider moving to Shenton Park in Perth. He was very happy working under Reg and wanted to stay if Reg did. So, he said to Reg, 'Let's just say Harry is elected Archbishop and he invites you to succeed him as Bishop of Wollongong, would you accept?' Reg hesitated before answering in the negative; and so Harrington decided to stay in Adelaide. When this scenario became a reality, Reg was thrown into a tailspin. A man of prayer, after time with the Lord, he said to his wife, Dorothy, 'I have definitely decided not to accept.' 'I see,' replied Dorothy, 'and what might your reasons be for that decision?' By the time he had finished explaining them to her, he had changed his mind. His daughter, Elizabeth, unaccustomed to her father's uncharacteristic vacillation, would ask, 'And which way are we leaning today?'[20]

Harry consecrated King and Piper on St Matthew's Day (21 September) 1993 as Bishops of Parramatta and Wollongong respectively. But a further bishop had still to be found for the new fifth region he wished to create. This was to prove a fraught process, but the reasons for it were simple and cogent. He particularly wanted to address the needs of the south-west area of the diocese where parishes, struggling with adverse sociological and demographic developments, were in need of 'a major task of reconstruction.'[21] Harry suspected that his SC might not be sufficiently representative to be aware of this need. His proposed fifth region, consisting of Bankstown, Liverpool, Marrickville, Petersham and Strathfield area deaneries, would be a difficult one, in need of 'a great deal of ploughing before a gospel harvest can be reaped.' With 41 parishes and 51 churches, most poorly attended, its population was substantially from a lower socioeconomic and working-class background. It was the most multicultural of the regions with the least number of Anglicans.

Harry's nominee for his fifth bishop, Ray Smith, previously Rector at Wanniassa in Canberra, was Harry's sort of minister. By grace, a servant leader with strong pastoral gifts; by temperament, a reconciler, Ray had served in America for four years on the staff of Trinity Anglican Seminary, Pittsburgh. He there developed courses for the laity and attended numerous church growth conferences, so that he knew how to do what Harry chiefly wanted: to grow parishes. Ray Smith had written after Harry's election, 'There is nobody's leadership I would more gladly work under.'[22] Yet he found the decision a difficult one to make. He had felt called to Wanniassa, had been there for only a few years, and had even hoped that Harry would retire to Canberra and become part of his team there. When Harry, shortly after his election, had approached him to be Bishop of Parramatta in succession to Peter Watson who moved to South Sydney, Ray declined the invitation. Harry was very disappointed, recording in his Day Book, 'Ray Smith decided to stay in Canberra – but if this is God's will I must be content.'[23] Then, when embarked on a busy program to visit all the area deaneries, he confessed, 'Feel greatly the inability to have Ray Smith as an Assistant Bishop but God knows.'[24]

On 2 July, Harry confided in his diary 'not a good day for me.' After three months in the job, he was beginning to feel frustrated that his plans were not crystallising, and he was not the only one exasperated by the slow progress. Geoff Kells, who had worked hard to streamline diocesan management, asked what was Harry doing, levelling the leadership team with the charge that they 'do not value time.'[25] Sinking to what appears to have been the nadir of self-confidence, Harry spoke some good sense to himself.

> My test now is not only godliness but ability – do I have the resources to do what the office requires. I earnestly sought God to be excluded if it was not right to be elected. I judged that on all round abilities I was not that far behind the other candidates. But now is the test. I must recognise my weaknesses and compensate for them by drawing on

others. My ability is to draw on other people. I must not be ashamed of it but make it a strength.[26]

On 27 July 1993, Ray Smith attended a meeting of EFAC. When he saw Harry at the meeting, he was shocked by his appearance.

> He looked ashen and terrible. 'Harry,' I said, 'are you all right?' 'No,' he replied, 'I had a bad Standing Committee last night. They've rejected my nomination to be the bishop of the new region." He added, "Would you take it on?"'

Ray felt as if he had been hit by an arrow. He could not sleep. He consulted with Paul Barnett and Peter Watson. He knew he would have to accept. In spite of his previous rejection of Harry's offer, he could think of nothing more wonderful than working with Harry in his team.[27] Ray knew that he was no Don Cameron or Jack Dain. 'They were great Bible teachers, great administrators, great legislators, great debaters.' But he understood that Harry wanted pastoral men for the Parramatta and Georges River regions, 'because they were the most difficult regions.'[28] He wanted bishops who worked with the clergy to grow congregations.

In August 1993 Harry announced the new fifth region to SC. Concerned that his nomination for the region's bishop would meet with the same resistance as had met his nominee the previous month, Harry went to great lengths to explain his reasons for putting forward this name. The challenging nature of the new region would require 'sympathetic leadership from a skilful pastor.' With reference to the previous rejection of his nominee, he said that he 'would like to feel that the SC might have sufficient confidence in me and sufficient sympathy with the ends that I am seeking to achieve to allow me the liberty of choosing staff who, in my judgment, will best enable me to fulfil the strategies which I seek to pursue.' He ended his nomination with the gladiatorial challenge, 'I trust that I will have the strong support of SC members for this name.'[29]

Ray Smith, accepted by a subdued SC, was consecrated on All Saints Day (1 November) 1993. He implemented Harry's philosophy and strategy fully in his region, later reporting:

> The region has been operating on the understanding that mission and ministry is conducted at the local church and parish level. If ministry is not happening there it is not happening … The regional staff, including the bishop and the archdeacon, are encouraged to spend the bulk of their energies in the Region.[30]

Harry's episcopal team met every Monday morning. Paul Barnett considered that the meetings were well run. He did not feel that time was wasted. The contributions of the regional bishops were listened to and almost always acted on. 'They were fruitful, good meetings.' For Ray Smith, they were the highlight of his week.

Harry's encouragement to his bishops to be active in their regions in support of the clergy and their parishes seems to have worked. In one year, the greatest percentage increase in attendance in the diocese was in Ray Smith's region. Although it was off a small base, it was significant because the region was so difficult. The drive to make parishes as strong and effective as possible was no 'moot point' to Harry. It may be that this strategy meant the extent of clergy stress and breakdown was lower than it has been in other periods of the diocese, when the same episcopal resources were not devoted to their care. Harry would later discover more sophisticated justification for his emphasis.

> By way of vindication of the philosophy of offering personalised support at the point where ministry is being exercised, I can now draw on my experience with Evangelism Explosion across the globe. We previously had an implementation rate of about 20%. That is, for every 100 persons/churches attending an initial EE Training Clinic, 20 of those would implement the ministry when they returned to their church. Feeling this was less than acceptable, we developed a program of training and deploying Implementation Field Workers: people who went back with those who attended a clinic to assist them in getting started and who would return from time to time to encourage and advise them. The upshot of this process operating now over some years has been to see the implementation rate rise from 20% to somewhere above 70%. I am convinced that 'Point of Operation' support is crucial in ministry and I believe we fail our clergy in this regard ... The limited contact that I have with clergy these days leads me to believe that they feel this lack of support. Times are tough spiritually and ministry is harder than it was. My conviction is that it will get harder in the foreseeable future and the need for the sort of support I was aiming to provide will be even greater.[31]

All of his bishops were to serve Harry with unswerving loyalty and with growing respect and affection. Towards the end of Harry's episcopate Brian King, famous for his mantra, 'West is Best', was to write to Harry on behalf of himself and his wife, Pamela.

> Pamela and I are very conscious of the closing of a chapter that has been very special. Your choosing us for the role way back in 1993 must have

been a bold, even adventurous step for you, because we were untried and inexperienced in such a wide Diocesan ministry. We thank you for your faith in us.

We have tried to do our best, for the sake of the Lord's work, and for the Western Region, but especially for the support and extension of your own hopes and dreams, both yours and Pam's. Forgive us for our weaknesses.

We pay tribute to your admirable term, your marvellous and moving spirituality, your attitude, work and witness 'Coram Deo.'[32]

## Jesus loves me

The early months of Harry's episcopate were exceptionally stressful. The pressure mounted, too much apparently even for his incomparable serenity. There was indecision about whether he would live at Bishopscourt, criticism of his strategic focus on parishes and his defence of Anglicanism, the difficulty of appointing new bishops, and the criticism of those he did appoint as too pastoral and insufficiently political. The disappointments multiplied and the stress told, while his engagements continued unabated. Harry was invited to preach to the Sunday evening university congregation at St Barnabas, Broadway. He knew it was 'used to high grade and intelligent preaching.' His sermon, based on Ephesians 4:1–16, addressed the question 'What is church for?' He spoke of churches as colonies of heaven, where self-interest gives way to true family relationships, as centres where effective pastoral care is exercised, and as fountains of enterprising evangelism.[33] When the service was over, he went out to the car to drive home. He had never had any heart problems, but that night as he sat in his car, he had intense pain down both arms. His symptoms, he realised, were not inconsistent with a heart attack. He lifted his heart to God and sang at the top of his voice.

*Jesus loves me this I know*
*For the Bible tells me so*
*Little ones to him belong*
*They are weak, but he is strong.*

*Yes, Jesus loves me!*
*Yes, Jesus loves me!*
*Yes, Jesus loves me!*
*The Bible tells me so.*

He sang it over to himself all the way to Bishopscourt. By the time he reached home, the pain had subsided and did not return. He learned again the lesson that God was his God and that he could trust him. At his farewell service as archbishop he told this story, and Nicky Chiswell, composer and musician, who was then presiding at the piano, played the tune at the end of the service. 'Harry has sometimes said that he would like that hymn to be sung at his funeral,' Pam observes. There is no better summary of Harry's Christianity than 'Yes, Jesus loves me! The Bible tells me so.'

The next day, Monday 16 August, Harry had seven meetings, beginning at 9 am. All he wrote in his Day Book about the incident was, 'Interesting service at Broadway – God blessed me.'

# 14

# First Year (1993): 'Evangelistically Enterprising'

A matter to which Harry gave early attention (though it took three years to develop) was a new procedure for the recruitment and training of ordinands. He was always conscientious to fulfil the undertakings he had made when installed as archbishop, among them to 'be faithful in ordaining, commissioning, and laying hands upon others.'[1] Advised that the right to choose whom he would ordain to the ministry was his only real power, Harry and his episcopal team determined that they should be involved significantly in the selection of students to enter Moore College as candidates for the diocese.

## Ministry training

What this entailed in practice was challenging the right of the college to exercise that power on his behalf. That practice had developed only under the principalship of Broughton Knox. When T.C. Hammond and Marcus Loane were principals, the college was subservient to the archbishop and was committed to furthering his aims. When Harry was a student at Moore College, neither he nor anyone else was in any doubt that the principal was there to serve the archbishop. But under Broughton Knox, the college took to itself the task of selecting men for the ministry and offering them to the archbishop. Harry wanted to be a lot more involved in that, and he took the process of selecting clergy into his own hands.

Harry understood that this was a risky strategy to adopt so early in his episcopate. He was in some danger of damaging his relations with the college and thus causing disaffection among the most powerful clergy in the diocese. He did not take this step only because he had the authority and the power to do so. He had far more compelling and radical reasons than that. Basically – his real motive – he wanted to change the diocesan culture. Warm hearts were what Harry wanted to see in his clergy, as well as cool heads. The diocesan culture he wanted to change was generated by what he saw as too many clergy with hot heads and cool hearts.

Criticism of Moore College and much anxiety over the type of minister it was producing were prominent aspects of the anti-REPA hysteria. Moore College graduates, it was alleged, preferred ruling to serving. In attempting to address these problems, Harry was prepared to allow that the criticism had some legitimacy. He also believed that current debates in synod, which uncritically favoured lay presidency, showed 'confusion' in the understanding of the clergyperson's role, and that the development of 'a coherent doctrine of the ministry' was needed. Further, he felt that the training of the clergy was deficient in critical areas. They were too little trained in how to grow a church community and 'after college training' was inadequate. It was a long-held belief of his. He had devoted a lot of energy while serving as Bishop of Wollongong to persuading Archbishop Robinson to devote more money and resources to CEFM. Harry wanted to see spiritual and emotional support for all clergy, spouses, their children and church workers.

Harry wanted rectors to be gospel men, but he also wanted them to be able pastors. His leadership team specified the characteristics considered essential to candidates for ministry in the Diocese of Sydney. They should be committed to promoting 'dynamic Anglicanism' and have pronounced spiritual qualities as well as theological convictions. Since most of the churches in Sydney were small, Harry set as a benchmark that rectors should at least have the skills to lead congregations of 100 parishioners. They were to be trained with that in mind. Those married were to have a family life that commended the gospel. Psychological fitness was to be assessed.

Perhaps even more controversially, Harry desired to relax the expectation that every clergyperson in the diocese had to be Moore College trained. He accepted the force of the argument that the Moore College strait jacket was a fundamental cause of the diocese's proverbial narrowness. He wanted fresh perspectives. He perceived that there were graduates of the Sydney Missionary and Bible College and even of the School of Christian Studies, which Bp Barnett had established at Robert Menzies College when he was Master there, who were well trained theologically and highly motivated for ministry. But this could not but be a bone of contention: no college happily approves of competition!

The implementation of Harry's policy for clergy selection and training required a new team of ordination chaplains. Between 1996 and 1999, Revd Paul Perini served as Harry's ordination chaplain and archdeacon for ordination and ninistry development. His task was 'to develop an integrated process covering the experience of ministers from selection to retirement.'[2] A panel was appointed to assist him, made up of those with a variety of skills and different backgrounds, including Margaret Fuller, a Social Work graduate of the Univeristy of Sydney and qualified counsellor, and Elizabeth Smart, who completed the training in counselling provided by the Anglican Counselling Service in Tamworth. Candidates (and, if married, their wives) spent a day at Bishopscourt, where they met and were considered by the members of the panel. Many, including their wives, recall those occasions with delight.

The senior staff of Moore College were not keen to surrender the power to which they were accustomed. They continued to interview prospective candidates, as did Harry's appointees. Archdeacon Perini had been given one of the toughest tasks in Harry's leadership team. On his appointment, he told Harry he would like to give it two years, and Harry concluded, 'He wants an 'out' I think if it all gets too much.'[3] Paul Perini coordinated candidate selection, brought the process under the archbishop, and developed better focused selection criteria and a psychological assessment process. He created a clergy assessment centre modelled on what the Presbyterian Church of America, a conservative evangelical denomination, was doing in the United States with church planters. He became vicar of St Hilary's, Kew, in Melbourne in late 1999, but the other members of the selection committee remained in place until after Harry retired in 2001. The tension also remained in place, with the college principal and archbishop sticking to their guns. Commendably, there was never a failure of civility between them.

## Growth strategies – general and regional

By early 1994 each of the regional bishops had developed regional strategy papers. They all sought to come to grips with the five defining features of Harry's vision, but there was no mechanical uniformity of approach: each bishop was happy to express the liberty Harry had given him to develop strategies compatible with his own gifts and interests.

Paul Barnett, Bishop of North Sydney, admired for his prodigious output of scholarly books, resolved on a personal level to 'unlearn being a workaholic.' His objectives included helping to 'shape a zealous expression of Anglican evangelicalism, but with biblical dimensions of liberality which are rapidly disappearing at this time, and with deep concern that the insights of true and reformed Anglicanism are at the point of extinction.' His region incorporated most of the diocese's 'Bible belts', with 12,687 in the region's churches on a census Sunday. Paul noted that he should avoid an 'over-directive approach' as rectors are not bishop's curates. He resolved to 'learn how to cope with and understand the spectrum of theologies and churchmanship within the Region.' There followed a list of those parishes in the Northern Region, written in Harry's hand, which might especially require of its long-suffering bishop to 'learn how to cope.' The list comprises 24 of the region's 64 parishes, indicative that the Diocese of Sydney is far from monochrome in its tradition. The large number of churches then in the 'Charismatic' camp is especially interesting, while the question marks indicate there was some uncertainty about their categorisation.

| REPA | Charismatic | Central church |
|---|---|---|
| Gladesville | Avalon | Dee Why |
| St Ives | Balgowlah | Mosman – St Luke |
| Chatswood | Beacon Hill | Cremorne – St Peter |
| North Sydney | Allambie Hts? | Greenwich – St Giles |
| | Belrose | Artarmon |
| | Northbridge | Gordon |
| | Longueville | Hornsby? |
| | Ryde | Epping |
| | Nth Epping | Hunter's Hill |
| | Wahroonga (St Paul's) | |
| | Berowra? | |

In the South Sydney region, where Sunday attendances totalled 6,233, different styles of tradition were considered to create major barriers between parishes, resulting in mutual disinterest. The bishop, Peter Watson, would have preferred to have stayed in Parramatta, and Harry was grateful to him for agreeing to serve in South Sydney. He and his archdeacon, first Paul Perini and then Trevor Edwards when Perini took on the ministry development role, were to foster the integration of ministries between parishes. They identified the need to work to lessen the perceived sense of threat to other parishes from the largest of the region's 54 parishes, St Matthias', Centennial Park. They were to encourage the leaders of that parish to consider the implications of the eventual change of leadership. This was indicative, of course, that Harry and his team were as nervous of Phillip Jensen, Rector of St Matthias', as the rectors of other parishes in the region. As a strategy for the restructuring of that parish, it had 'we can't really do much about this' written all over it!

For the Western Sydney region, Bp Brian King prepared an elaborate colour-coded strategy document based on wide consultation and considerable research, both demographic and managerial. With 55 parochial units, with a Sunday attendance of 10,208, this was the region of greatest growth potential: its population was expected to reach that of the third largest Anglican diocese in Australia by the end of Harry's episcopate. There were six area deaneries, in two of which (Prospect, and especially, Parramatta) the percentage of people born overseas was higher than the Australian average, as was the percentage of the population unemployed. Ministry to seven groups of non-English speakers was either in operation or planned by Mersina Soulos, a very dynamic Anglican, appointed to head up cross-cultural ministries for HMS. Almost a million dollars was available to supplement the stipends of workers or for land acquisition, not a lot for such a needy region. Since Parramatta region had been contemplating becoming a separate diocese for some time, its regional council, known as Parramatta Area Regional Council, was an active and experienced body, and the chief strategy envisaged was to make greater use of the council in the identification of need and the deployment of resources, especially in new and fast-growing areas where church plants were required. Brian King and his wife, Pamela, worked very hard in their large region. From 1994, Brian was also Bishop to the Defence Force and chaired the Olympic Games Task Force.

Bp Reg Piper inherited the Wollongong region, where 10,139 attended church in 47 parochial units. Fresh from an effective ministry at Adelaide's evangelical powerhouse, Holy Trinity, and with a doctorate on church growth and relatives in Wollongong, Reg relished the challenge of developing an effective strategy. For the sake of the wider diocese, he set himself to study new prayer books and to study the constituents of 'Dynamic Anglicanism'. His strategies for 'widespread growth' included 'fresh and culturally appropriate ministry approaches [and] restructuring ... for more flexible ... ministry.' Reg insisted that it was untrue that he had tattooed on the back of five fingers the terms, 'observably God's people, pastorally effective, evangelistically enterprising, genuinely caring and dynamically Anglican,' but he kept them constantly in mind, and found real-life manifestations of each in local Illawarra parishes, on which he reported for the regional newsletter, *In Touch*.

Georges River region, as we have seen, Harry added to the four he inherited. Sometimes labelled 'the dead heart', it was created by transferring 12 parishes from the North Sydney region, 29 from South Sydney, and 10 from Parramatta. Its bishop, Ray Smith, was determined to plant new churches in his region and to foster cross-cultural ministry. With about 5,364 attending 120 congregations in 51 parochial units, Ray wished to double both the numbers attending and the number of congregations within the eight years of Harry's episcopate. To do this, he proposed the intentional use of evangelistic, church growth and church planting programs, to identify multicultural people groups within the region and develop programs to evangelise and integrate them into new and existing congregations. It was a stiff challenge: demographically the region was increasingly multicultural and religiously pluralistic, and a smaller proportion of church members than in other regions were tertiary-educated or employed in the professions, those traditional foundations of Anglican strength. Ray also gave considerable thought to what was involved in being dynamically Anglican. This included

> valuing and upholding the principles of the Reformation, the 18$^{th}$ Century Evangelical Revival and the 19$^{th}$ Century evangelical Missionary Movement ... giving an important place ... to the two Gospel Sacraments: Baptism and the Lord's Supper [and] accepting the historic threefold order of ministry as prescribed in the Anglican Ordinal (1662) as a valid and beneficial form of ministry.

The last was an assertion of opposition to the current promotion of lay presidency within the synod.

Harry's archdeacons were an important part of his leadership team. His decision to appoint Di Nicolios as archdeacon with responsibility for women's ministry was well received. The archdeacons did not meet often as a team, spending most of their time with their regional bishops. Trevor Edwards considered regionalisation Harry's greatest achievement, because it was accompanied by growth in many parishes. Trevor's responsibilities were greater because his bishop, Peter Watson, was expected to assist Harry with the central administration of the diocese. Perhaps because he had to work so hard, Trevor was gratified by the evidence of growth in the region of South Sydney.

Trevor suspected that Harry had an 'inner cabinet' who were more influential than his team. Asked who he thought might have been in this inner cabinet he nominated Peter Kell, Warwick Olson, Stephen Judd and Stuart Piggin. It is true that three of those four, together with Lindsay Stoddart, Rod Irvine and Graham Wade (who worked under Olson at Pilgrim International), did meet with Harry very occasionally. We did give Harry advice on what he should do, but it was not a regular or frequent gathering, and I don't think any of us ever observed that Harry acted on any advice he received on those occasions! Trevor also suspected that Pam was part of this inner cabinet which, in view of her presence, he restyled a 'kitchen cabinet', and he suspected that Pam was the first port of call when Harry wanted to sound something out. Asked, if he were in that role, would he not do the same thing, namely check out such things with Ruth, his erudite wife, he answered in the affirmative. But he thought it was an important observation anyway, 'as Pam is such a strong woman.' When Peter Smart became diocesan registrar at the beginning of 1997, he became part of the inner sanctum. 'Harry's kitchen cabinet was Peter Smart and his bishops and Pam,' said Peter Kell, adding, 'Pam was not always correct, but she is very shrewd. They have a lovely relationship. He listens patiently. He does not always follow her advice, but he always gets it, and she is often right.'[4]

## The Blue Ticket

The morning after SC rejected Harry's nomination of Peter Kemp as bishop, Justice Peter Young wrote Harry a note. 'Stick in there! Archbishops usually win in the end. Especially those who are supported by prayer.'[5] Harry's support, however, was wrought not only by prayer, but also by politics. The rejection of Peter Kemp was a step too far, provoking a reaction. The decision was made by some of Harry's supporters to organise a ticket for elections (it became known as the Blue Ticket) at Harry's first synod, promoting those more favourable to him. That was no easy task, because Harry's opponents were convinced that those most opposed to Harry were those who were best for the diocese. On Thursday, 5 August, Laurie Scandrett, managing director of Grantchester Financial Services, came by the office and took Harry out to lunch. Laurie was among those convinced that Harry was not making the best use of the natural leaders of the diocese. He presented Harry with the 'A' Team, a comprehensive list of the best leaders among his clergy, divided into four categories: $A^{++}$, $A^+$, A, and $A^-$. There were five names in $A^{++}$, five in $A^+$, four in A, and one in $A^-$.[6] Of the 15, only three of Harry's team or known supporters made it into the 'A' Team: Paul Barnett in $A^{++}$, and Reg Piper and Boak Jobbins who scored an A.

Harry's first synod (October 1993) was to be the first session of the 43rd synod. A synod covers three years, with elections to SC and other diocesan committees in the first session of each triennium. So this gave Harry an opportunity, just seven months after his election, to get a SC that was more sympathetic to his aspirations than the one he inherited. Already the SC had stymied some of his initiatives. Apart from the rejection of Peter Kemp, SC would not allow him the DEB he wanted to streamline diocesan administration, insisting on limiting its powers and controlling its membership.

Riley Warren recalled that Harry would sit in SC, head in hand, and would not see people wanting the call. Warren concluded that Harry was depressed by the situation. He coped, said Warren, but was unhappy. He gave the impression that he was in a den of vipers.[7] Peter Smart thought that he was, too. He thought the refusal of Harry's nomination of Kemp was a way of saying to Harry, 'You are not in charge here. It had nothing to do with Peter Kemp.'[8] Now, it was time to defend Harry by using the weapon of his tormentors.

'Essentially,' wrote BBJ, who suffered defeat at the hands of the Blue Ticket,

> it was made up of Goodhew friends and supporters, determined to strengthen his role as Archbishop. One member, Lindsay Stoddart, described their group to me, and separately to Laurie Scandrett, as the 'Bishop's Party', meaning a party to support Goodhew. It was a direct challenge to the ACL.[9]

The founders of the Blue Ticket included Warwick Olson, Stephen Judd and Stuart Piggin. The philosophy behind their thinking, they believed, was more consistent with Harry's inclusive leadership style. They were Sydney evangelicals, committed to Jesus, his word and his gospel. They were not, in their own thinking, liberals, but valued unity as a key to evangelistic effectiveness (Jn 17:20–23). They found it significant that in the NCLS,[10] which tells us so much about Christianity in Australia, the majority of churchgoers are moderate on issues of biblical interpretation and social involvement: they do not espouse inerrantist views of the Bible or oppose all social commitment as a dilution of the gospel. They are also more moderate on the ordination of women and the Charismatic movement, and are sceptical of strong opposition to both. Espousing liberty of conscience, Blue Ticket supporters did not make good party men or women. They simply wanted to end the club mentality that control resided only with those who belonged.

In all of this, Harry was neither advised nor consulted. It was thought that he should remain above political machinations. But the founders of the Blue Ticket did consult widely in order to get answers to a number of questions. Should a separate ticket be run, or should an attempt be made to persuade ACL to include on the ticket nominees with broader sympathies? Canon Ray Bomford, recently retired from St John's Cathedral in Parramatta where he had been succeeded by Peter Kemp, insisted that a separate ticket was essential. He was proved right by the decision of the ACL to produce a ticket for the 1993 synod that was narrower than ever, removing from nomination those known to support the ordination of women and those who had been conspicuous in campaigning for Harry at the archbishop's election. It felt like 'payback' time, and if the Blue Ticket had not been formed, Harry would have met with even more resistance in SC.

A second question was, by what name did the new group want to be known? They considered themselves moderate evangelicals, but they wanted to be known as true evangelicals. How about evangelical Anglicans or Anglican evangelicals? It was the failure to address this question that meant the new group would become known by default as 'The Blue Ticket', simply because their campaign literature was printed on blue paper.

A third question was how to get new blood onto the SC. Blue Ticket founders believed that those habituated to power in SC constituted a narrow, unrepresentative clique. The new group wanted breadth and new talent, and therefore wanted its ticket to represent the regions. It was suggested that this could be given as the chief reason for coming up with a ticket. Ironically, the Blue Ticket was never able to represent the regions as effectively as the ACL, with its superior machinery, and it was regionalism, three years further down the track, that spelled doom for the Blue Ticket. But it was some consolation that the Blue Ticket was successful in provoking ACL to be more sensitive to regional representation than it otherwise might have been.

Judd, Olson and Piggin were joined at a strategy meeting on 11 August 1993 by Archdeacon Nicolios, Revd Laurie Davies (Director of the Anglican Board of Education) and Tony McCarthy (who had been General Secretary of both the Australian Teachers' Christian Fellowship and the Australian Fellowship of Evangelical Students). They resolved that their purpose was

> To get on to Standing Committee men and women who intend to:
>
> 1. work with the Archbishop and not against him. We are not after rubber stamps, but, for the sake of the Diocese, we must have people who are prepared to reach agreement over policy;
>
> 2. promote a balanced evangelical faith stressing right-heartedness (orthokardia) and right actions (orthopraxis) as well as right thinking (orthodoxy);
>
> 3. move the focus of the decision-making bodies of the Diocese off internal contests of power and refocus them onto the wider community;
>
> 4. create an atmosphere of trust in the Diocese;
>
> 5. bring fresh, lay initiatives to the life of the Diocese;
>
> 6. promote people of independent mind, who are not party people, but who are prepared to think for themselves and not be afraid of club censure;
>
> 7. promote people to Standing Committee who are not single issue people, but who will bring new blood to the Standing Committee which has been run for years by people who are not representative of the wishes of the majority in the Synod.

The founders of the Blue Ticket compiled a list of eight REPA hardliners whom they wanted removed from SC. But, so as not to provoke the ACL into a more extreme stance, they decided to nominate some conservatives along with more progressive evangelicals to the diocesan secretary by 30 August, the deadline required for synod. Then, in September, to all members of synod a ticket was posted, on which biographies of progressive evangelicals were given. Now it was up to members of synod to decide what they thought of this new political presence in the diocese and, in particular, if they would remove from SC some of the eight targeted by the Blue Ticket and replace them with some of those not on the ACL ticket.

Harry was bemused by all the political activity in which he was not involved. On the eve of his first synod, he wrote to his self-appointed mentor, Dr Alan Cole, 'You wouldn't believe the number of tickets that are being run. We will either have all dissenting Protestants or raving Anglo-Catholics on the Standing Committee!! It's great fun!!'[11]

## Harry's first synod: a new broom

Synod normally met for five days over two consecutive weeks, three days in the first week, and two in the second. Harry decided that this synod would meet from 11 to 13 October 1993 and then 7 and 8 March 1994, to allow for greater reflection on its business. On convening in the Wesley Centre for the synod, it did feel as if a new broom was at work. Gone was the ritual singing of 'Veni Creator Spiritus', which the traditionalists loved. Instead synod members were treated to brief Bible studies by the dean, Boak Jobbins, and the singing of a different hymn each day. Harry gave a spirited presidential address. He was projected onto the enormous screen in the Wesley Centre. At least, everyone thought, our archbishop is high-tech! He had just the previous Thursday been to Wollongong University to receive a Doctor of Letters, *honoris causa*, and he was at the synod resplendent in the red and blue doctoral gown that he received on that occasion. Computer graphics and video clips enhanced the presentation. Harry majored on the big issues and did not avoid the difficult ones of women and lay presidency. Peter Kell, so instrumental in Harry's election, felt vindicated by Harry's performance in synod.

> Presidency of Synod he did brilliantly. Marcus and Don Cameron as chairman of committees ran a tight ship. If you looked sideways, you got squashed. It was a very formal, dour sort of Synod. Don Robbie was still very school masterly. Then Harry burst on the scene, fair and friendly and charming and relaxed. He introduced humour into Synod. He was very good, notwithstanding the fact that there were some pretty

bitter debates at times, but he managed that quite well ... Harry was the supreme communicator and you felt uplifted by his addresses.[12]

At the beginning of his presidential address, Harry looked back to 1 April, the day of his election. 'On that evening we stood and sang together, "A new commandment I give unto you that you love one another as I have loved you." May it be so among us.'[13] He first described his spiritual formation, for those who did not know him well. Testifying to the spirituality in which Sydney Anglicanism had shaped him, he identified himself as 'an Evangelical Christian.' But in his desire to get to know as many of the diocesan family as possible, his visits had already covered the 27 deaneries of the diocese, and he was struck by its diversity. Sydney had a reputation as the most monochrome diocese, but Harry now suspected that it was more diverse than 'a number of others in Australia.' He therefore wanted to assure all in the diocese that he would seek to act with charity and fairness towards all who expressed their Christian commitment through the doctrine and formularies of the Anglican Church.

Harry then confronted some divisive issues head on. He addressed the need for liturgical reform, partly driven by the fact that the Australian Church was developing a new prayer book, which was to be produced by 1995.[14] On the ministry of women, he called for continuation of the dialogue, though he supported the move to disallow discussion of the matter until the 43rd synod was over, amounting to a moratorium on the divisive debate until the 1996 synod. On lay presidency, he conceded that he was having difficulty with it at the level of order, not theology. He explained that the implementation of the regionalisation of the diocese had been delayed because of the need for accompanying legislation and the need to get new bishops settled into their regions, and that the development of policy on sexual misconduct by clergy was necessary.

On social issues, he manifested, as he had when Bishop of Wollongong, a concern for the unemployed, detailing a surprising number of initiatives to address the

14.1 Philip, David, Pam, Harry and Christina, Wollongong University, 7 October 1993. Harry gave the occasional address and was awarded an honorary doctorate.

problem. Next, in that, the year of Indigenous people, Harry called for strong support for the process of reconciliation. On 3 June the previous year, in the Mabo case, the High Court of Australia had dismissed as fiction the claim that Australia had been *terra nullius* (uninhabited at the time of colonisation in 1788) and established that native title existed wherever Aboriginal and Torres Strait Islander people had maintained an unbroken connection with the land since British colonisation. Christians had an obligation to respect the truth, and the truth was that only the Australian colonies had not recognised native title rights, and that the court's decision was therefore not the result of the rewriting of history by the late 20th-century peddlers of white guilt.[15]

Harry had congratulated the NSW government on its successful bid for the 2000 Olympics to be held in Sydney. He indicated that he wanted to give a strong lead in hitching a ride on the Olympics for the gospel. In response, synod supported the archbishop's strategic planning to take advantage of evangelistic opportunities provided by the Olympics.

Harry then devoted the last and largest part of his address to strategies for growth. He explained his five key aims, dwelling especially on what he understood was involved in being evangelistically enterprising and dynamically Anglican. He drew on his MA thesis in reviewing the different types of desirable growth, claiming that, in a rapidly changing society, many who did not attend church wanted the church to be more active in society, helping especially with the definition and transmission of values. He drew the attention of synod to the great resources and insights stemming from the NCLS and called for experimentation to promote growth. He explained that to promote 'dynamic Anglicanism', he had increased the amount of episcopal oversight and support, increasing the number of assistant bishops from four to five and reducing the number of parishes for which each was responsible, so that the level of pastoral support could be increased.

Harry's program for growth was impressively focused. According to BBJ, its problem was not its content, but whether the diocese could 'pull it off.' 'What Goodhew needed for his program to take hold was the willing cooperation of the diocesan heartland, the key leadership blocs and a clearly worked out organisational structure to turn good intentions into actual outcomes.'

The political tensions denied him 'those necessary elements', in Ballantine-Jones' view, adding for good measure that 'the Blue Ticket challenge didn't help either.'[16]

## Synod elections

It may not have helped the ACL, but it helped Harry. Following his presidential address, greatest interest in the synod was not in any of the debates, which were rather predictable, but in the election of SC. It was perceived, as we have seen, that SC was not as supportive of Harry as it might have been. ACL, backed by REPA, had put out a very conservative ticket – not one person on it was known to favour the ordination of women.

Two laypeople who had been on the 1990 ACL ticket for the first session of the 42nd synod and who had campaigned for Harry's election, Stuart Piggin and Warwick Olson, were removed from the 1993 ticket. Five others also prominent in their support for Harry – Stephen Judd, Rod West, Tony McCarthy, Bronwyn Hughes and Chris Forbes – were all absent from the 1993 ACL ticket. This may have been not because they supported Harry, but because they favoured the ordination of women. Bronwyn Hughes was then heading up Anglican Media and she had been approached by Laurie Scandrett with a view to the possibility of her standing for election to the General Synod. But he wanted to know if she would support their opposition to the ordination of women. When she replied that she was in favour of the ordination of women, Laurie was aghast and retreated in a huff.[17] It brought home to her how politicised the diocese had become, a situation she found repellent. 'You cannot win this,' Warwick Olson advised her. Feeling threatened, she resigned. She was replaced the following year by Margaret Rodgers, who was far more used to the political games played by her male colleagues.

A letter signed by two of the bishops, Paul Barnett and Peter Watson,[18] gave gentle support for the Blue Ticket, arguing that it was necessary to have SC members who supported the archbishop and that it was important to have representatives from across the diocese rather than concentrated in a few of the larger parishes, which tended to be the case with the ACL ticket. The group 'Anglicans Together' decided not to have its own ticket. But it urged its supporters '**not** to adopt the Anglican Church League recommendations' and, if they had difficulty supporting some of the names on the Blue Ticket, then it suggested the names of three other clergy and four other laity.[19]

The ACL ticket had hitherto swept all before it, but it was not to be this time. The ACL did manage to get five clergy and five laity elected who were not nominated on the Blue Ticket. But the Blue Ticket succeeded in getting elected three clergy (Bill Lawton, John Livingstone, Lawrie Bartlett) and five laity (Stuart Piggin, Stephen Judd, Warwick Olson, Tony McCarthy, Rod West) who were not on the ACL ticket. Among those supported by ACL who lost their positions in SC were BBJ, the most experienced of ACL powerbrokers, Vic Cole, then ACL president, and Laurie Scandrett, who had been the most visible Sydney layperson to support court proceedings against the ordination of women. So, the Blue Ticket was successful in removing three of the eight it had targeted for removal. Support for Harry thus increased in SC, especially when one added Harry's team of bishops and archdeacons, all of whom were on SC. Votes would continue to be tight, but now Harry was as likely to win a vote as lose it. This increased the opportunity for genuine debate within SC.

It was a very significant and unprecedented defeat for the ACL. It meant that the ACL could react in either of two ways. It could move back to the centre now occupied by the Blue Ticket and support the archbishop. Or, it could continue with its hardline position and be perceived as opposing the archbishop. At least one of its council members, Revd Silas Horton, believed that the ACL had been ambushed by REPA and he did not like it. He wanted it to adopt a more moderate evangelical position. So, one view of the outcome was that, as a result of being hijacked by REPA, ACL had lost the middle ground and had become an extreme group, which the synod had rejected. ACL could no longer count on its nominees being elected. It would have to move back to the centre, or its days would be numbered.

In the event, that turned out to be triumphalist Blue Ticket wishful thinking. The response of the ACL was rather to conclude that, while it had lost a political battle, the remedy was not to change policy, but to reorganise and not let itself be outmanoeuvred again. This was the position of BBJ who had lost his membership of SC, but he would not retreat from the battle. He became 'Lenin in Finland, plotting his return,' observed Robert Forsyth who twice defeated Ballantine-Jones in synod elections. Those who follow Australian politics will recognise the scenario: the factions consider it unthinkable that they should not broker power. Hardline ACL supporters believed the liberty advocated by the Blue Ticket was no way to run a strong diocese, threatened by the liberalism and secularism which had proved lethal to the work of the Church in other dioceses.

For his part, Harry would have to consider the ACL's current unpopularity and not allow the diocesan agenda to be dictated by it. In particular, he would have to take note that all those elected to SC, contrary to the wishes of ACL, were in favour of the ordination of women. The diocese was very divided over this matter and Harry would have to find a way of ameliorating the unhappiness of those distressed by the hard line of the diocese on women. Harry was still not in favour of the ordination of women, but he respected those who were, and he realised that the majority of Anglican churchgoers in Sydney supported it. Typically, within the diocese, the SC was more conservative than the synod, which in turn was more conservative than the members of congregations. But now SC was more reflective of the electoral synod that had elected Harry. He would have to seek for a better deal for women. On 14 December 1993, Di Nicolios was collated as the Archdeacon for the Promotion of Women's Ministry, the first female archdeacon to be appointed in the diocese. On appointment she remarked, 'I look forward to some exciting years!'[20]

Among the more astute of the clerical supporters of the Blue Ticket was David Crain, then Rector of Yagoona. Though unusual for a committed evangelical, he had trained at Morpeth Theological College in the Diocese of Newcastle, where he graduated with first-class honours in theology. In the evangelical family, he had been a close friend of Herbert Stoddart, Lindsay's father, and was converted chiefly through the ministry of Marion Gabbott when she led the youth group at Greenwich in Sydney. He had favoured the election of his regional bishop, Paul Barnett, in the 1993 election, as he experienced every visit of Paul to his parish as 'wonderful'. He was a shrewd observer and found it odd that Archdeacon Vic Roberts did not appear keen to support Harry, when everyone else from his region was eager to get the call to speak on Harry's behalf. He concluded rightly that there had to have been some tension between the two. Crain had worked in the Diocese of Newcastle and in the Diocese of Lichfield in England and was concerned about Sydney's relations with the wider Anglican Communion. He was convinced that Sydney's hardliners were spoiling those relations. On the outcome of the synod elections, he wrote:

> Well the blue ticket campaign worked wonderfully well – beyond my dreams. A large number of synodsmen [sic] obviously welcomed the chance for a decent evangelical alternative ...
>
> You did so well it is a pity you didn't go for a General Synod reshuffle too. We have a number there who make no positive contribution. The removal of Bruce Ballantine-Jones from General Synod is vital. In that arena his performance is a massive handicap to our causes. I was distressed to learn he had been voted back on to the Financial Priorities Committee. I would rather he was on Standing Committee and off it. Too late now. However, it shows the ACLers will be on the lookout for any chance to get him back on Standing Committee or General Synod. It would be wise for those who believe things will go better without Bruce running them to work out now their best reserve candidates (e.g. Ray Smith for General Synod) so as to be instantly ready should a vacancy occur.[21]

But a storm cloud more threatening than an unsympathetic ACL now appeared on the horizon.

## Pymble

Harry was barely six months into his episcopate when the lay leaders of the parish of St Swithun's, Pymble, on Sydney's North Shore, resolved that they could not work with their recently appointed rector and sought to have him removed. The 'Pymble matter' was reported copiously in the secular press for more than a year. It was a symptom of a Sydney pathology identified in a REPA discussion paper, dated 23 June 1992, on the subject of 'Clericalism/Anti-Clericalism'. Its author attributed the problem of chronic unhappiness in congregations to the current generation's distaste for authoritarianism and of the clergy's unhelpful insistence on their own rights. 'Clergy insist upon their rights backed by biblical texts about submission to their authority. Lay people vote with disinclination to be involved and finally with their feet. Instead of being on the same team we are pitted against each other.' These words were prophetic of the horror that overtook St Swithun's, Pymble, by the end of 1993. There, the most intransigent and determined of rectors, who, in the best Sydney clerical tradition, would submit neither to the laity nor to bishops, and who believed in the primacy of the teaching office of the Anglican rector, confronted equally determined parishioners. But this time, the final determination of the laity was not to vote with their feet.

In October 1993, the church wardens of St Swithun's asked their rector, David Gilmour, who had been appointed only earlier that year, to resign on the grounds that his style of leadership did not work for them. On 9 November, the Pymble parish council voted 7 to 2, with two abstentions, to support the wardens. This created an impasse: the rector refused to resign; the majority of parish leaders continued to ask him to resign; a minority of parishioners asked him not to resign; and the archbishop could and did recommend to the rector that he resign, but could not demand it. As too often happens in such fraught struggles, combatants do things they later regret or should regret. On 7 November, one parishioner attacked Gilmour at a prayer meeting. As Gilmour later described it, 'With [the prayer book] open at the final vow for the ordination of priests, he demanded that I explain why I had not taken the Archbishop's (until then) private advice that I should resign.'[22] Another parishioner informed Gilmour that she no longer could accept his authority. She walked out of church at the beginning of his sermons, only desisting when a parishioner begged her not to do that. Gilmour was sorely provoked and, in his extremity, allegedly declared, 'That's none of my concern if people leave. I'm only concerned with the teachable ones and I don't care if there are only a few teachable ones left and the rest go.'[23]

Harry realised from the outset that his own involvement in the Pymble matter could do him no good. He could have backed away. He could have left it to Paul Barnett, the regional bishop. But he felt he had an obligation to demonstrate concern for the lay people and to seek a remedy other than a legal one. When the lay people appealed to him for help, he felt he could not just say, 'This is no concern of mine – sort it out yourselves.' He felt he had to get on with it. Nevertheless, he was branded as Pontius Pilate for his pains, and Pymble parishioner and SC member, Neil Cameron, remonstrated forcibly down the phone to Harry, apparently on the grounds that Harry was not getting on with it quickly enough.

Ballantine-Jones criticised the archbishop for trying to deal with the matter pastorally when he also had to preside over a disciplinary process. Harry's first instinct, however, had certainly been to deal with the matter pastorally. He met with David and the churchwardens on a number of occasions. For the sake of the health of the parish, Harry thought it best if David should move. He believed a spot could be found where David would thrive and therefore he ensured an offer was made to David that another location would be found for him. But David was not prepared to accept that.

With the situation now at white heat, on 22 November, 17 parishioners charged David Gilmour, under the Tribunal Ordinance 1962, with 'breaches of ritual ceremonial and discipline' and of 'conduct disgraceful in a clergyman and productive or likely to be productive of scandal or evil report.' The parishioners were using a very blunt instrument to achieve their purpose. Gilmour was not accused of any of those heinous misdemeanours that have blackened the name of the church in recent decades. He was, Harry always insisted, 'an able and devoted servant of Christ whose orthodoxy and morality have never been in doubt.'[24] What he was really accused of was an inability to get on with the lay leaders of the parish. They found him insensitive, unwilling to take advice, and even of not fitting in with life on the upper North Shore of Sydney. They alleged a breakdown in pastoral relations. At the archbishop's request, a congregational meeting was held on 30 November. It was chaired by Justice Peter Young, who was not a member of the congregation, and at the end of the meeting an 'exit poll' was taken. Of the 270 present, 147 'supported the actions of the wardens and parish council', 67 were opposed, 33 were undecided, and four were informal. A letter to synod from 14 parishioners, dated 25 January 1994, argued that the exit poll was a violation of an undertaken given to Gilmour before the meeting that no vote would be taken. Justice Young was unaware of this undertaking, a regrettable failure in the process.

## First Year (1993): 'Evangelistically Enterprising'

On 18 December 1993, Harry convened a meeting with the rector and the churchwardens to explore the possibility of resolving the issue without resorting to ordinance procedures, but no agreement could be reached. So, Harry asked the diocesan chancellor, Justice Ken Handley, if there were anything else he might do to resolve the dispute. Handley advised him that an alternative measure, the Incapacity and Inefficiency Ordinance 1906, might be invoked. It had been used in 1972–3 to remove the rector of St Saviour's, Redfern. Like all rectors, he had life tenure and was guilty of no offence, but he just could not run a parish and numbers had diminished close to zero.

Then, between 27 December 1993 and 16 January 1994, fires raged along the NSW eastern seaboard. Walls of fire 80 metres high engulfed Sydney's bushland suburbs. Two firefighters and two civilians were killed, and 375 homes or buildings were destroyed or damaged. The worst losses were suffered in the parish of Jannali, where BBJ was rector. There over 90 homes were destroyed, many belonging to his parishioners. BBJ reported, 'I was standing in Lincoln Crescent just before the fire hit. Ten minutes later, it was all gone.'[25] On 10 January, Harry visited the fire-ravaged parishes of Helensburgh, Menai and Jannali to ensure that affected residents were offered the Anglican Church's help. Although instinctively more interested in the church's social responsibility than in internal church politics, Harry, over a cup of tea in the Jannali rectory, raised with BBJ the matter of Pymble. BBJ counselled Harry that, if he followed the chancellor's advice and used the 1906 Ordinance, he would lose the clergy.[26] BBJ's response to the disaster was so appreciated that he was awarded the Medal of the Order of Australia. Harry not only made money available for the immediate relief of victims, but he also ensured that Anglicare (as HMS came to be called) was given a government-recognised role in disaster response. Terry O'Mara, a senior public servant in the government's disaster relief program, left his position to become director of disaster relief in Anglicare.

Once the legal process began, the archbishop was obliged to do what ordinances required of him. It was perceived by many clergy as an assault on clerical security of tenure, and they supported the

14.2 Visiting bushfire-affected areas of Sydney by helicopter with Jim Longley, NSW Minister for Community Services, January 1994.

rector. Backing came from REPA supporters, some of whom, a year earlier, had proposed that a rector might be removed if two-thirds of the parish membership voted for it.[27]

The disruption continued into Harry's second year as archbishop. Harry insisted that the view that this was an attack on clergy tenure was nonsense. 'It was a very particular case, a very particular person and a very particular group of people.' But trust was evaporating fast. Alan Cole, who advised Harry on most matters, gave Harry the following advice:

> I pray nightly that <u>it may not get to the civil courts</u>. Right from the 'Red Book'[28] case onwards, that has never done any good, and only dragged the name of the Church in the dust ... It may easily upset a lot of the clergy: what if a godly man antagonises some powerful members of his congregation? Can they remove him by this method? ... Is the old way of "voting with your feet" not the best, even if slow and very painful for a parish at the time? If there are few people, and therefore limited funds, won't the problem solve itself? Any good parish will recover, <u>in time</u>.[29]

To this Harry replied,

> It was a great tragedy to find one of our leading congregations tearing itself apart after having been such a happy and spiritually productive place under the previous ministry ... At the point where I was introduced, it had become something of a 'killing field' ... It is very hard to find a middle ground when people and pastor are at each other as has been the situation here. I think it has been unfortunate that some of the lay feelings have been represented as the expressions of high-rolling business executives who like getting their own way. I don't think that really is the case. Some of the people involved are very lovely, godly people and are deeply grieved by all that has taken place.[30]

With the matter set to destabilise Harry's second year, his commitment to the laity was proving costly. It is not possible to have happy laity if the clergy are unhappy. 'When one member suffers, we all suffer,' observed Harry, adding,

> Personally, I am deeply distressed for David and his family and for the members of St Swithun's. We must find a way of resolving this dilemma that is in keeping with our claim to be the people of God. May God have mercy on us.[31]

## 15

# Second Year (1994): 'Wild, Uncharted Waters'

So numerous and diverse were the challenges Harry faced throughout his episcopate, most would consider the job quite impossible. The Sydney synod continued to push for lay presidency and against a new prayer book (*APBA*). Standing Committee continued to resist the proposal for a streamlined management structure. It also insisted on having a say on the Pymble matter instead of allowing the legal processes to run their course. Supporters of the ordination of women pushed for more ministry opportunities for women, and Harry, upset by the refusal of some rectors to allow women to preach, ordered a comprehensive survey of opportunities for women in the diocese. Critics of Anglicanism without the distinctive Sydney imprint forged plans to plant evangelical churches in other dioceses.

### The many pressing concerns of the archbishop

It would be understandable if Harry had expended all his energy reacting to the challenges he faced, but he found the strength to be proactive as well. At regional conferences within the diocese, Harry's five points were getting a good work out. He and his bishops stayed on script whenever they had the opportunity, and tried not to be too defensive when their hearers chuckled over 'dynamic Anglicanism'. Harry persevered with plans for a stronger role in the training of ministers, in spite of ongoing resistance from Moore College.

Diocesan administration received attention. Early in 1994, a new media team was appointed. Harry committed the diocese to Vision 2001, 'the tool which enables the whole diocese to act in mission with co-ordinated direction and purpose.'[1] It built churches in new housing areas on the fringes of the city and revitalised inner city churches that had witnessed demographic change. To deepen the spiritual life, the first Cursillo, a short course in Christian pilgrimage, was held in the diocese in September. Pam and Harry had attended a Cursillo in Armidale in April 1988 and were impressed, but held off introducing it to Sydney until they had people to lead it in whom they had confidence. Jeff and Margaret Fuller, Harry's trusted Wollongong prayer partners, attended one in Armidale in 1994, and Harry persuaded them to lead one in Sydney. The Armidale Cursillo leaders came to Sydney and helped with its introduction.[2]

Meanwhile the machinery of the Anglican Church of Australia continued to crank on, apparently slowly, but demandingly. For Harry, this meant bishops' meetings; provincial synod and metropolitan visits to other dioceses in the Province of New South Wales, consecrating new bishops and preaching at their synods; and meetings of General Synod committees. A new secretary of General Synod, Bruce Kaye, was appointed, and on 27 October, Harry preached at his commissioning. Bruce Kaye's office, like Harry's, was in St Andrew's House, and Harry enjoyed regularly conferring with him. It was an especially fruitful relationship, as Bruce Kaye had a strong grasp of the historic development of Anglicanism and an exciting vision of where it needed to go in Australia in the future. Bill Lawton, who served on the Liturgical Commission in the years when *APBA* was subjected to ferocious opposition from Sydney conservatives, thought highly of the competence and leadership exercised by Bruce Kaye through this period.[3]

Not all Harry's concerns were ecclesiastical. The ministry of compassion was particularly demanding in 1994, with the need for relief for drought-afflicted farmers, the Archbishop's Winter Appeal, seeking to redress poverty in the Year of the Family. Then there was an appeal in response to the horrific genocide in Rwanda.[4] At the same time, new Australian government regulations affected schools, charities and welfare bodies, which needed to develop identities as corporations, in parallel with their identities as ecclesiastical bodies. Towards the end of each year, Harry attended in Anglican schools as many speech days as possible.

Harry was aware that much stronger sexual abuse protocols needed to be developed. The homosexual lobby was becoming increasingly vocal. Together with three of his assistant bishops, Harry condemned the first telecast by the ABC of the Gay and Lesbian Mardi Gras parade,[5] an early indication of his determination to draw the line against the ordination of practising homosexuals. In the same year, the diocese established AIDSLink to deliver pastoral care for those with HIV and AIDS.

Then, as archbishop, Harry's views were sought on many issues of public interest. 1994 was the International Year of the Family, and how both to define it and to help it were hotly contested topics. Prince Charles announced in June 1994 that he wanted, when he became king, to end the 450-year-old role of the monarch as supreme governor of the Church of England and Defender of the Faith. Britain was now a multifaith society, and he wanted to be the defender of faith or faiths.[6] The Archbishop of Canterbury suggested that this seemed

Christina and Baden Goodhew, Harry's parents. Photo taken in Croydon Park, Sydney, about 1960.

At Coorparoo, the family grew! Left to right: Wendy, Philip, Pam, David, Harry, Robyn.

Harry's consecration as bishop, St Peter's Day, 29 June 1982. Peter Chiswell, Bishop of Armidale, on Harry's right; Ken Short, Bishop of Wollongong on his left. Members of Harry's family in the background, from left to right: David, Robyn, Phillip, Wendy, Pam.

Eighteen bishops lay hands on Harry at his consecration.

Harry delivering his *coram Deo* sermon at his installation as archbishop.

Harry, archbishop elect, sits in his cathedral, his presiding and teaching chair, at his installation as Archbishop of Sydney, St Andrew's Cathedral, 29 April 1993. On the right, Boak Jobbins, Dean of Sydney.

Rod Story (left), National Director of Australia Evangelism Explosion with his wife, Rhonda, with Harry at his installation. In March 2020, Harry finally stood down from the Australian Committee of Evangelism Explosion.

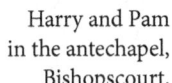

Harry and Pam in the antechapel, Bishopscourt.

Official portrait of Harry by Archibald Prize winner, Judy Cassab, June 1994. Did she capture the complexity of his personality – humility with determination?

Service, 20 April 1997, in Westminster Abbey for the sesquicentenary of the creation of the dioceses of Adelaide, Melbourne, Newcastle and Cape Town. Left to right: Bp Peter Watson; Bp Roger Herft (Newcastle); Archbishop Harry Goodhew; Archbishop Njongonkulu Ndungane (Cape Town); George Carey, Archbishop of Canterbury; Dr Wesley Carr, Dean of Westminster Abbey; Archbishop Keith Rayner (Melbourne); Canon John Peterson, Secretary-General of the Anglican Communion; Stuart Smith (representing Adelaide).

Harry with the Archbishop of Canterbury, George Carey, August 1997.

Harry's episcopal team and their wives at the Lambeth Conference, 26 July 1998. Left to right: Peter and Margot Watson, Reg and Dorothy Piper, Pam and Harry, Shirley and Ray Smith, Anita and Paul Barnett. Bp Brian and Pamela King remained in Sydney, with Brian serving as administrator of the diocese in Harry's absence.

At the 1998 synod as President, Harry, wearing his Wollongong doctoral robes, announces that he would not withhold assent if the synod approved of female ordination.

Harry preaching at St Andrew's Cathedral on the occasion of its reopening, 30 January 2000.

Forty years after his epochal Southern Cross Crusade in Australia, Billy Graham met Harry and Pam, June 1999. Harry was an adviser to counsellors at the 1959 Crusade.

Harry addressing the crowd at Easter Awakening, 23 April 2000.

Harry introduces Robert Forsyth at the latter's consecration as bishop, 13 June 2000.

Harry with Prime Minister John Howard and Howard Dillon, CEO of Anglicare, at the Wintercare Gala Luncheon, 30 June 2000.

Bp Forsyth, Harry, and Bp Barnett at Harry's last ordination of deacons, St Andrew's Cathedral, 9 December 2000.

Family and members of the Sydney Anglican Indigenous Persons Ministry Committee at the ordination of Ray Welsh and Neville Naden, 3 February 2001. 1. Julie Welsh (sister of Ray Welsh); 2. Aunty Amy Williams (dec.); 3. Malveena Welsh (Ray Welsh's daughter); 4. Revd Ray Welsh (dec.); 5. Revd John McIntyre (dec.); 6. Aunty Jean Carter (Stolen Generations); 7. Pastor Ray Minniecon; 8; Archbishop Harry Goodhew; 9. Archdeacon Geoff Huard; 10. Malveena Welsh (Ray Welsh's wife); 11. Archdeacon Allan Donohoo; 12. Jenny Shillingsworth; 13. Tom Mayne; 14. Aunty Jean Phillips; 15. Sharon Minniecon (Ray Minniecon's wife); 16. Cathy Naden (Neville Naden's wife); 17. Revd Neville Naden.

Ordination of Ray Welsh (left) and Neville Naden (right), 3 February 2001. They were the first Aboriginals ordained after synod voted $1.2 million towards support for Indigenous ministry.

Four archbishops of Sydney at the 50th anniversary of Marcus Loane's consecration as bishop, 2008: Marcus Loane (1966–82), Donald Robinson (1982–93), Harry Goodhew (1993–2001), Peter Jensen (2001–2013).

Harry and Pam in retirement in Wollongong, 2018.

to deny the uniqueness of Christ as the one way to God. Harry agreed.[7] In the same month, the Anglican primate, Archbishop Rayner, at the Melbourne Clergy Conference condemned the pope's apostolic letter rejecting female ordination. What concerned him, he explained, was not 'the rightness or wrongness' of the decision, 'but the exercise of authority to stop a theological debate which is clearly an unfinished one.'[8] The Archbishop of Canterbury opposed the pope's letter for the same reason.[9] Harry was at the head of a diocese that had put a moratorium on the matter for three years, but he knew that could not stop the debate. Ministry to Sydney's Indigenous population, the largest in Australia, commanded his attention. He visited the Crossroads Community Christian Centre in Redfern in March and ordained Bill Bird, a founder of the Aboriginal Evangelical Fellowship, as minister to the Community on 29 May.[10] In his address to the provincial synod, Gilbulla, 13–15 February 1994, Harry expressed the hope that the state government, in its legislation complementary to the federal Native Title Act 1993, would do so 'in the spirit of the Mabo case rather than its legal technicalities.'[11] In May, the General Committee of the Christian Conference of Asia met in Sydney, and Harry preached at an ecumenical celebration to mark the meeting in St Andrew's Cathedral. To Asian delegates, he said, 'You live out your discipleship in populations which include all the major world faiths. You are often small minorities in these situations. We have much to learn from you. We need your help.'[12] On all these matters, Harry's opinions and actions were forensically dissected, especially by his critics.

The diocesan family, then, was large and diverse with many passionate commitments. To lead such a tumultuous band of pilgrims would have been torture to one set on a narrow strategy of his own. But that was not a problem for Harry, whose broad-ranging strategy fostered individual initiatives, and who took as much interest in the priorities of others as he did in his own. He wanted to encourage every initiative for Christ, but that in itself took more time than he had, and it was an exhausting load. Very conscious, however, that he had only eight years in the job, he was happy to work hard.

## The family

Harry could be surprising in his views on matters of public concern. In March 1994, for example, he called Christians to be realistic in their approach to the International Year of the Family. Earthly families, he advised, were never intended to meet all our needs. In its zeal to defend the family, the church has both left couples ill-prepared for the challenges of marriage, and failed to give adequate support to those who lead a single life. We should not overlook the contribution and value of people outside the parameters of traditional families, nor deny the problems, especially violence, which many face within such traditional families. The church should be alert to give practical assistance to families adversely affected by abuse, unemployment and financial hardship. In 1994, there were 750,000 dependent children living in 400,000 Australian families, in which no parent had a job. Yet the church should not accept that nothing could be done about the soaring breakdown in marriages. It should offer the hope of reconciliation in Christ. Harry expressed his regret that in the International Year of the Family, the Mardi Gras had chosen as its theme 'We are family.'

> Like the characters of Alice in Wonderland, we can make words mean whatever we like. However, in my opinion, 'family' has a long and recognised meaning of relationships formed by blood and supported by law. To use it to denote any or all sorts of relationships empties the word of its specific meaning.[13]

In his sermon at the Mothers' Union Festival at St Andrew's Cathedral on 25 March 1994, Harry cited surveys that showed that family life is easily the commonest concern of Australians.

Harry's most extensive treatment of problems facing families was in the address he gave at the HMS Festival Dinner on 6 May. He affirmed that there is 'no more fundamental concept to the well-being and good ordering of society' than families. He suggested that churches, 'found at the coalface, caring for those in need', best understand problems facing families. Groups, comprised of father, mother and children, representing families in crisis in 1894, 1944, 1969 and 1994 came on to the stage and stood behind the archbishop while he explained how the HMS had dealt with each crisis. This demonstrated that HMS had always been at the cutting edge of caring for families in need, that it was always essential to respond to the contemporary context, and that this requires analysis and willingness to change. Among new ministries for this purpose was the National Anglican Caring Organisations Network, which offered skills training to the long-term unemployed, and Harry listed practical steps individual parishes could take to help families in need.

On Saturday, 5 November, 'Family Fun Day', a whole-of-diocese party, was held at the Bicentennial Park, Homebush. Organised by a committee chaired by Pam, more than 3,000 attended. Harry addressed his diocesan family, as did Jim Longley, Minister for Community Services in the NSW Government. On 30 April 1996, after the state Liberal party was assigned to a long period out of office by Bob Carr's Labor government, Harry was to commission Longley as the CEO of the Anglican Retirement Villages.

## The drought

Harry had been advised by the bishops of Bathurst, Riverina and Armidale that some drought-affected farmers were struggling to even buy the barest necessities. The adverse effects of the drought were further brought home to him when he made metropolitan visits to the remaining three dioceses in his province, Canberra & Goulburn, Grafton, and Newcastle, preaching the synod sermon in each diocese. Clergy were reporting higher suicide rates among rural men; not only higher than those in the city, but among the highest in the world. He made emergency grants for drought relief throughout the state. He asked the federal government to waive the assets test for farmers so that they could apply for social security benefits and Austudy for their children. He called for improvements in the Income Equalisation Deposit Scheme and for banks to be more generous in their treatment of those whose incomes were threatened by drought.[14] Speaking at the Annual Festival of Flowers at St Andrew's Cathedral, Pam observed that the drought was 'a powerful reminder of our dependence on God.'[15]

15.1 As Metropolitan of New South Wales, Harry was concerned by the effect of drought on rural dioceses, October 1994.

## Lay presidency

At the Sydney synod meeting on 7 and 8 March 1994, the chief areas of contention were two matters about which Harry had reservations: the planting of evangelical churches in other dioceses and lay presidency. One who supported lay presidency in March, Robert Forsyth, had changed his mind by June. Only those with primary pastoral care for the congregation should be licensed to preside at the Lord's Table, Forsyth now contended. He also wondered if we were free to make such a change and still claim to be members of the Anglican Church of Australia.

That mattered to him, but he also agreed with those who believed the whole thing was a 'yawn' and we should be concerned with far more important things.[16]

Forsyth's comments provoked outrage. Barry Newman, the most vocal of the lay advocates for change, accused Forsyth of ignoring 'the theological confusions and misunderstandings' that he alleged the traditional Anglican position represented.[17] Figtree diocesan lay reader, Phil McKerrow, insisted that his desires as a layperson were being 'mocked', and that if Anglican forms get in the way of this desirable change, who cares? Far better anyway to replace Anglicanism with an Australian evangelical church.[18] From Croydon parish, organist Michael Deasey found McKerrow's strident views 'depressing' and 'gently' suggested that 'many still do care about Anglicanism.'[19] On the eve of the October synod, Deaconess Margaret Rodgers, Chief Executive of Anglican Media, warned against lay presidency via the media. 'If passed, it would be very bad for ecumenical relationships within the Anglican Church.'[20] The scene was set for one of those gargantuan struggles that are a specialty of the Sydney synod.

## The Pymble matter

In 1994, 'the Pymble matter' was a play in three acts of agonisingly long duration, before, during and after synod. It was a contest between two equally determined players. David Gilmour's opponents, as we have seen, sought to have him removed through two ordinances: The Tribunal Ordinance 1962 and the Incapacity and Inefficiency Ordinance 1906. David was cleared under the Tribunal Ordinance 1962 on 30 March 1994, the complainants having failed to comply with the requirements of the ordinance. They were instead hoping to have Gilmour removed by the other ordinance. It provided first for a report from an enquiry committee, an arrangement designed to prevent frivolous charges being brought against a clergyperson. The majority report of the Enquiry Committee, dated 1 March 1994 (predating by a month the decision of the Board of Enquiry of the Tribunal Ordinance and therefore rendering it redundant), concluded that there were 'circumstances that raise the question of removing the Reverend David Gilmour from the Parish of Pymble on the ground of incapacity or inefficiency.' Three commissioners (Justice Reg Blanch, Bp Ken Short and Revd John Brook) were then appointed to conduct the inquiry.

At the SC meeting of 26 April 1994, the ever-conciliatory Bp Ray Smith pleaded movingly for a non-judicial solution. It required a careful and equally empathetic speech from the chancellor to sway most members to accept that, all things considered, the judicial route would actually prove the most merciful and effective. Paul Barnett paid Harry a warm tribute. He said that Harry had been consistently compassionate towards David, and imaginative in his attempts to solve the problem. It was a very emotional speech, and Paul was near to tears. It deeply impressed members torn by the pain of it all. Standing Committee ended the evening subdued, but apparently seeing the wisdom that it was necessary to face the issue and proceed. Afterwards, Paul Barnett stayed behind to be with Harry and give him his support. Harry was very moved and grateful.

On 12 September 1994, David Gilmour let it be known that he would contest jurisdiction on his matter. On 14 September Harry rang Paul Barnett, who confessed to feeling the strain. It was affecting his heart. 'Nothing wrong with the pump,' he reported, but he would wake at night with a rapid heartbeat. On this, Harry commented, 'I know something of this.'[21]

David refused to cooperate with the inquiry, and the three commissioners were clearly unimpressed by the stalling tactics of his solicitors.[22] They were also unconvinced by a claim, advanced by Moore College principal Peter Jensen and historian Ken Cable,[23] that the ordinance did not apply here because 'incapacity' and 'inefficiency' meant 'old and/or unstable.' The commissioners rejected this on three grounds. First, the terms were undefined in the ordinance and therefore they should be given their ordinary meaning. Second, the fact that in some early drafts of the ordinance, the phrase 'physical and mental' appeared and was then struck out, suggested that the synod that passed the ordinance intended the meaning to be unqualified. Third, the ordinance provided that a rector removed from one parish by means of the ordinance would not therefore be deemed unfit for another parish; whereas if incapacity and inefficiency meant physical or mental impairment, a rector so encumbered would not be fit to serve in any parish.[24] The commissioners did agree that, given the rarity and seriousness of removing a member of the clergy, such a step would require a high degree of evidence of 'inefficiency or incapacity in fulfilling ministerial duties.'[25] They concluded, however, that they had overwhelming evidence of David's insensitivity, authoritarianism, unwillingness to hear advice, and inability to work with staff, and that therefore he was incapable of, and inefficient in the performance of his ministerial duties to such an extent that the work of the parish could not be sustained while he remained as rector. They reported to the archbishop that it was expedient to remove the rector and that it should be done as soon as possible.

At SC on 19 September considerable time was spent on the Pymble matter. Phillip Jensen moved that SC's report to synod should include a minority report. 'This finally gained no support, Phillip was the only one who voted for it.'[26]

The report from the three commissioners was handed to Goodhew, Gilmour and his solicitors on 23 September 1994. It was based on 900 pages of evidence, which cost $150,000 to process. The cost appalled especially those who thought the whole matter should not have been dealt with legally. The 1994 synod was just two weeks away. Before the synod began the media were reporting that 'the curious business' at St Swithun's, Pymble, would erupt again. Members of the synod had been lobbied by David's supporters and opponents. It was reported that a petition in his favour, signed by 150 of the parish's 400 members, would be presented at synod. Letters in support of Gilmour dismissed the complaints about him as trivial, including the exception taken to his own observations that 'one of the problems in the parish is the North Shore values so evident in parish life' and that he would be 'very surprised if the Anglican Church survives past the year 2000.'[27] A letter signed by seven members of the Parish of Robertson reported their 'outrage' at the way the matter had been handled and the 'horrendous' waste of money incurred by the process.[28]

'A Further Supplementary Report' from 17 members of SC distanced itself from the procedures that Harry had implemented. Standing Committee had voted not to make a minority report, so the supplementary report was evidence of a determination by David's supporters not to leave the matter in the hands of the archbishop where it properly belonged, since he was responsible for clerical discipline. Standing Committee's role in the Pymble affair was unhelpful. Members complained about the time spent at each meeting in 1994 on the matter, seeking to lay the blame for this distraction, as well as its huge expense, on the archbishop as he became embroiled in the legal quagmire. Standing Committee could and should have left the legal process to take its course without constant intervention and monitoring by itself. The widespread anxiety among clergy that their tenure was unsafe was unjustified, as Harry was acting on consistently received legal opinion that the whole matter was not about clergy tenure, but pastoral capacity, and that it was not a doorway to the scrutiny of a number of parishes.[29]

Pymble was not the only issue Harry had to address. On the same day as he received the commissioner's report on the Pymble matter, he addressed the need for representative church bodies to deal with governments, he met with a concerned citizen on the spread of Islam and its implications for the Australian way of life, and he received a delegation on the problems created for the Council of Christians and Jews by aggressive evangelism on the campus of the University of New South Wales, where Phillip Jensen was chaplain. To the last Harry stressed the need for Christians to be genuinely friendly to Jewish people and for all to realise that 'evangelism lies at the very heart of the Christian faith.'[30]

## Second synod, 1994

Harry's presidential address to his second synod, 10 October 1994, dealt with wide-ranging subjects of importance to the future of the Church. Yet it was a dyke, holding the tsunami of Pymble only for as long as the address itself. The archbishop commended taking advantage of present government policies to develop low-fee Christian schools. Shortly after his election, Harry had been urged by Riley Warren, Headmaster of Macarthur Anglican School, 'to determine ... a strategy for the use of this potentially great asset' on the grounds that Anglican schools were 'an extraordinary gift from God.'[31] While maintaining the existing Special Religious Education provision in state schools, the decreasing willingness of a state system to reflect Christian values meant that it was necessary to develop an alternative educational system. It was not primarily an ideological matter. Australia had become the country with the highest incidence of youth suicide in the developed world. 'If the culture which surrounded my generation allowed people to live through world war and retain hope,' reasoned Harry, 'what have I and others like me created that makes many of our youth feel so hopeless?'[32] Harry wanted schools that not only crafted those 'who tomorrow will be confident, caring participants in the game of life', but who will also be 'secure in a personal relationship with the living God.'[33]

At a meeting of 30 principals at Bishopscourt, when asked what he expected of church schools, Harry had said that he would like to see each student given the opportunity to develop their potential, to be encouraged to be thoughtfully critical while given a place to stand, to give thoughtful consideration to the claims of Christ, and to be imbued with a spirit of service to others. He observed that more students from state schools seemed to be entering full-time Christian service, and he hoped Anglican schools would produce those who had a mission to touch our society and world for Christ and be effective apologists for the faith – that is, those who constituted a 'Protestant Opus Dei'.[34] Maybe, Harry was already of the mind that existing Anglican schools were not delivering these outcomes sufficiently and should be supplemented by schools of a different type. The Sydney Anglican Schools Corporation, Harry now reported to synod, was exploring the feasibility of developing up to 15 new schools in Sydney's growth areas, where the lowest possible fees would be charged.

It was the beginning of quite a drama. At the time of the 1994 synod, the leader of the federal opposition was Alexander Downer. John Howard replaced him as leader on 30 January of the following year and he defeated Paul Keating to become the 25th Prime Minister of Australia on 11 March 1996, a position he held until 3 December 2007. It was during this period that the Prime Minister worked resolutely for the advancement of low-fee church schools. Following his defeat in the 2007 election, Howard wrote to Harry to say that he was 'immensely proud' of many things achieved by his government, including the 'change to the "old" new schools policy, which has resulted in many low-fee Anglican and other independent schools being established over the last ten years.' He thought that was 'a huge breakthrough,' and he gave Harry some of the credit for it. 'It was your call on me, when I was Leader of the Opposition, accompanied by John Lambert which started the process going.'[35]

John Lambert had been removed as Deputy Director-General of the NSW Department of Education in 1994 by Virginia Chadwick, Minister of Education. At the same time as he received news of his removal, he also received what he believed was a call from God to develop low-fee Christian schools. He then became Director of Schools Development at the Sydney Anglican Schools Corporation, a position he held from 1994 to 2009. He was enormously energetic and committed to the cause of Christ, and had an eye for both detail and the big picture. In his autobiography, Howard credited 'the urgings from Sydney Anglicans' for originating his government's New Schools policy,[36] and he noted with satisfaction the rapid expansion of low-fee independent schools. By 2010, 34 per cent of Australian school children were in non-government schools. 'There is no country in the world which has embraced freedom of choice in education more faithfully than Australia,' observed Howard proudly.[37]

In his 1994 presidential address, Harry also commended the work of Archdeacon for Women, Dianne Nicolios. He reported that in some parishes the preaching of female deacons was not welcomed, and expressed his regret at this as it would make intelligent, gifted women doubt that they had a place in the diocesan workforce. The Movement for the Ordination of Women had maintained its objection to the three-year moratorium, passed in October 1993, on debating the issue of female ordination. The moratorium was on synod's debating female ordination, not on Harry's mentioning the subject, which he did in each of his presidential addresses throughout the moratorium. Members of synod were handed an open letter from Revd Lucille Piper. 'There are women like me who have good qualifications and Sydney is literally throwing us out,' she complained in explanation of her decision to seek ordination outside the diocese.[38] Harry was still not convinced that female ordination was right, but he felt deeply that the reception given to women within the diocese with that aspiration was very wrong. He wanted to maximise their opportunities for ministry.

Harry also encouraged the synod to take a positive attitude towards the place of the diocese in the national church. Those who believed evangelicalism to be the best expression of Anglicanism, he argued, should work with others to commend that conviction. In particular, it was important to contribute to the development of the new prayer book (*APBA*). It was to be produced imminently and Harry commended the contribution to it from prominent Sydney Anglicans, Lawrie Bartlett, David Peterson, Bill Lawton and Margaret Collison.

Paul Barnett and David Peterson, who lectured in theology and worship at Moore College, had already demonstrated the value of the involvement of Sydney representatives in the process. In June 1994 the Liturgical Commission of General Synod, meeting in Sydney, finalised a first draft of *APBA*. On 3 September it was reviewed at a prayer book conference of the Province of New South Wales, called by Harry. There Paul Barnett successfully proposed revisions of significance to evangelicals, relating to the resurrection of Jesus from the dead and his full satisfaction for our sins.[39] David Peterson, consultant to the Liturgical Commission, was critical of those who wanted to dispense altogether with prayer books.

> People regularly tell me how disappointed they are with the 'home-grown' liturgies that have appeared in many congregations. Sadly, the people who are most critical of the Prayer Book and think that they can do so much better themselves, are sometimes blind to their own inadequacies.[40]

Bill Lawton's presence on the Liturgical Commission brought another dimension entirely to the consideration of the new prayer book. Those who were cross with Harry over his support for it had only one concern: whether or not it was in alignment with conservative evangelical orthodoxy. When the other members of the commission became aware that Lawton was not interested in pushing a Sydney agenda, they opened up a conversation to develop a liturgical service that could be adapted by Indigenous people. Instead of a full service, they developed a set of headings and invited Aboriginal Anglicans to write their own prayers. One such prayer was 'God of Holy Dreaming' devised by Revd Lenore Parker, an Indigenous Anglican priest. The commission heard gladly Lawton's passionate concern to address more strongly, and within the primary liturgical structures, the themes of injustice, intolerance and racism. Harry was as committed as his conservative critics to evangelical orthodoxy, but he did not allow that commitment to exclude other considerations such as the need for liturgies that expressed the most pressing of human needs. He was delighted that Bill Lawton, a Sydney Anglican, was able to lead the Liturgical Commission into reflecting on

God's concern for the human condition. Regrettably it meant that Lawton, like Harry, was to be subjected to a 'great deal of hostility.'[41]

Harry waxed most passionate in his address when talking about the training and support of his ministers. He said that, as an archdeacon and then bishop in Wollongong, he and his wife, Pam, had given their 'best strength' to this work. He wanted to have ministers who gave leadership that was 'biblically shaped, theologically sound, pastorally competent and evangelistically oriented.' He and Pam had come to 'love and prize' all those under their care as ordained workers. But having given that assurance, he declared that his primary commitment was to the Good Shepherd and his flock.

> Therefore my responsibilities are: first the shepherd, then his people, and in that context, those who pastor them ... The laity of the diocese are its life and strength. They are the witnesses who will share Christ by word and deed with their relatives, friends, and other contacts.[42]

With Pymble weighing on his mind, Harry was signalling that he wanted to correct the clericalism in the diocese, which had caused so much grief to the laity and about which Pymble was a distressing object lesson.

## The Pymble matter at synod

Harry addressed the Pymble matter in a long addendum to his presidential address.[43] He advised members that the report of the three commissioners had been completed and he had invited a response from David Gilmour. The Pymble matter was not listed for debate, and Harry said of it that it was 'an extremely painful issue' and declared that he would have much preferred 'to say absolutely nothing at all' about it. He explained that he had taken what he described as 'a gospel directed, Ordinance sanctioned approach.'

> By using an Ordinance after serious negotiations, and as a last resort, to seek a resolution for a difficult and stalemated situation, we are not using 'law' as it occurs in 1 Corinthians 6. What we are doing is using a process by which some impartial people of stature amongst us make a determination and report it to me. That appears to me to be eminently fair and, given the circumstances of the case, 'pastoral' in its operation. It cannot be 'unpastoral' to give to all parties an opportunity to be fairly heard and have their contribution dispassionately considered.

He expressed the hope that synod would allow the commission of inquiry that he had appointed to take its course and not discuss the matter further.

This hope was in vain. When the opportunity came for synod members to ask questions of the president, he was deluged with hostile questions principally bearing on the right of the central administration to intervene in the affairs of local parishes. Unforgettably, David Gilmour made a personal statement to an electrified house.

> I have died a thousand deaths over the last twelve months, and a myriad of humiliations ... I love these people, all of them, and I am grieved that for some reason, be it shyness or the way God has wired me up, or their expectations, I don't know, but I am grieved that to some people it seems I am not credible. I have often asked myself, who can be credible to these detractors, and yet to be able to give to all people in this church the ministry they need?

David spoke of 'high-flyers ... used to getting their own way.' His congregation did include corporate heavyweights, and David had come to believe that his refusal to submit to either the culture or the powerful were matters of conscience, which he could not surrender. Speaking of all the members of his flock, he explained:

> They want a pastor who will treat them all with the same importance, who will not be a respecter of persons. They want a 'cure of souls' to all parishioners, not just a chaplain to those who want to call the tune. My greatest folly is that I believe with all my heart in the fundamental difference between these two things.[44]

It was a powerful and persuasive message, eliciting much sympathy in the synod. The chancellor, Ken Handley, sitting on the stage, leaned across to Harry and quoted Proverbs 18:17. 'He that is first in his own cause *seemeth* just. But his neighbour cometh and searcheth him' (KJV, emphasis added).

The chancellor explained to the synod that, when he advised the archbishop that the 1906 Ordinance might be invoked, he did so on the grounds that there was such a total breakdown in the pastoral relationship between the rector and a substantial majority of parishioners, that it would be impossible for the rector to minister to that group. He had not concerned himself with the allegations against David Gilmour – they were for the inquiry committee to investigate. He had just advised as to the law; he had not formed his view of what the ordinance meant on the basis of his knowledge of Pymble, and thus refuted David's allegation, made in his personal statement, that the ordinance had been 'massaged' to fit the needs of those who wanted to remove David. Handley explained how he had come to the conclusion that 'incapacity' and 'inefficiency' meant just what they said and not physical or mental infirmity. On the grounds that the ordinance had only been used twice in 88 years, it could hardly be feared that it would or could be used for a wholesale assault on clergy tenure.

He then addressed what may have been the crux of the matter.

> I ask Synod the rhetorical question: What should be the Diocese's primary concern in cases such as this? It seems some of you think it should be for the welfare of the shepherd. I think it should be for the welfare of the sheep, and I think that is biblical. In 1917 in the English case of Rice v Bishop of Oxford, the Archbishop of Canterbury, who had a judicial role under similar legislation, said this, and I quote:

> *The interest of the parishioners – that is to say the religious well-being of the parish as a whole – ought to be, in all cases, the paramount consideration, and I am glad that the law makes it possible effectively to give to that consideration its rightful place.*

The chancellor's statement was a powerful and comprehensive explanation of the process followed in the Pymble case, perhaps ensuring that in the perspective of history, the archbishop did well in an intractable situation. But it was too soon for that: Harry did not have enough firefighters to extinguish the conflagration. A motion, moved by Phillip Jensen, to appoint a select committee to review the administration of the Tribunal Ordinance was approved, and appointed six clergy and seven laity to it. It took years for its deliberations to forge a new policy to address the issues raised by the Pymble matter.

## Lay presidency

*Southern Cross*, embargoed from reporting on the Pymble matter until the procedure under the Ordinance had been completed, made out that lay presidency was the main game. 'October's Second Session of the 43rd synod was no ordinary gathering. The eyes of the world were on Sydney, expecting a vote which would make history. And they weren't disappointed.'[45]

Most in the synod supported the proposal to introduce lay presidency, or lay administration as they preferred to call it, and its proponents believed that Harry could be prevailed upon to give his consent. Before becoming archbishop, he had chaired a committee that advised there were no theological objections to it, and he was understood to support it. When, as archbishop, he let it be known that he would not consent to it, there were some – BBJ was one – who accused him of having misled the diocese, that he had previously approved of it, but changed his mind after being elected. Harry later wrote:

> Laying aside the fact that there is no sin in changing one's mind for good and proper reason on any topic, I contend that Bruce's perceptions are erroneous. I do not think that I ever gave lay and diaconal presidency my wholehearted approval, or indeed, any qualified approval as a measure to be adopted in this Diocese.
>
> I was Convenor of a Committee that submitted a Report to the Standing Committee dated June 24, 1985. That Report contained a paragraph (6) which said,
>
> A dissenting view was expressed, however, to the effect that there is insufficient need for this provision in the Diocese, and that a Reformed view of word and sacrament does not of necessity require that those licensed to preach should also preside at the Lord's Supper.
>
> I believe that those words were included at my request.

Harry's desire to see Sydney play a larger role in the life of the wider Anglican Communion led him to believe that a unilateral move to lay and diaconal presidency would militate against Sydney's influence in that forum, for it was not an issue on which the Communion had consented to any break with the existing tradition. So, in his presidential address, Harry let the synod know that he would not consent to an ordinance approving lay administration.

Sydney's clergy, however, were rarely deterred from acting by the views of bishops. John Woodhouse, then Rector of St Ives, moved that lay people be allowed to preside at the Lord's Table at Holy Communion. Though it would be a world first, it was not, he explained, an attempt to foist change on anyone; it was just to remove an absolute prohibition. His real, and perhaps only reason for opposing prohibition was that 'there is nothing supporting it in the Bible.'[46]

In fact, the proposed ordinance was a very radical one for two reasons. First, it threatened to reduce the diocese to a sect. Very few even of the Reformed churches allow lay administration, and not even the Pentecostal churches allow it in practice. Second, the proposed ordinance went far beyond the intention of most who served on the various committees, which recommended that lay administration be allowed *in exceptional circumstances*. But this proposed ordinance sought to replace the absolute prohibition with absolute permission, in the sense that if the church committee and churchwardens wanted to have lay administration and the rector concurred, that would have been possible.

*The Sydney Morning Herald*, in reporting on the debate, had a photograph of the archbishop who, it declared, would have to give his consent after the third reading of the bill at the 1995 synod. The paper's photo caption read, 'Archbishop Woodhouse.'[47] The following Saturday *SMH* made amends by publishing a photograph of the real John Woodhouse in suit and tie. Woodhouse observed:

> You would have noticed something very symbolic about that debate in the way the speakers for both sides dressed. Nearly every speaker against the move wore a clerical collar.
>
> Yet on our side, all of the people who spoke wore suits and ties, even though nearly all of us were clergymen.[48]

On Wednesday, 12 October 1994, synod voted in favour of the bill, 224 to 148 in the House of Laity and 119 to 77 in the House of Clergy. The press reported that, in voting for lay presidency, synod had 'leapt into wild, uncharted waters.'[49] Commentator and journalist, Chris McGillion, reported that many Anglicans would see the vote as a victory for REPA, and that John Woodhouse's parish of St Ives was 'in the heart of REPA territory.'[50] McGillion concluded,

> Sydney has struck out alone. In the process it has pushed aside the Anglican Church's search for a coherent Australian identity. And it has effectively dropped the wider Anglican Church's commitment to seek unity with the Roman Catholic Church.
>
> Like most leaps of faith, it is either a heroic decision or a supreme folly.[51]

The most powerful of the clergy were frustrated by Harry's opposition to lay presidency. They believed that the only thing stopping the introduction of lay presidency was that the synod was too submissive to legal constraint. Remove the fear of the legal and it would free up the synod to obey the word.[52] On the other hand, the percentage of those who voted for it was barely 65 per cent. The opposition was strong enough to make Harry feel justified in not granting consent – not that it was required of him to make such calculations. To Alan Cole, who counselled he concede the possibility of lay presidency at least in exceptional circumstances, Harry replied:

> I think your comments about trying to find some limited operation may well be the way forward, but at the moment the Synod is on a roll for an unlimited capacity for lay people to operate in this way and I would be surprised if the Archangel Gabriel could turn it in another direction.[53]

How justified was Harry's feeling that the capital of his goodwill was not unlimited and that he had now spent more of it? Gerald Davis, editor of *Church*

*Scene*, reported that there was a proposal 'at least half developed' to move a vote of no confidence in the archbishop. It was perhaps because he was aware of this intention that SC veteran, Richard Lambert, sought to counter it by giving notice of a vote of confidence. An attempt to bring on the motion immediately failed. The reporter, Gerald Davis, couldn't help himself. 'Blood in the water attracts sharks, and I suspect some REPA men are not past using this mess to maul Archbishop Goodhew, if they can, and have him diminished for their own purposes.'[54]

For this implication, Davis later apologised unreservedly.[55] But the archbishop's opponents were increasingly committed to the view that the diocese needed saving from the archbishop's administration. The simple fact remained, however, that, without his consent, the lay presidency ordinance was going nowhere, and it never did. Harry's feeling that mandating lay presidency would forfeit much of Sydney's leverage on international Anglicanism at a time in history when its opportunity was so great, was shared by his successor, Peter Jensen, who quietly let the matter drop.

## The Pymble matter after synod

On 16 October 1994, Alan Cole wrote to Harry, 'Can't say anything on Pymble – except that until <u>one</u> side (whichever!) acts in a Christian way, and withdraws, out of love, it won't heal.'[56] Just before Christmas 1994, Alan wrote again to Harry, 'I would not presume to give advice, but I think, going on what I hear, that it would be <u>most</u> unwise to use that particular Ordinance in the same way ever again.'[57]

David Gilmour did accept the archbishop's invitation to respond to the commission report, and on 23 November gave to the archbishop 'a considerable body of material' for him to study.[58] On 1 December, David, together with John Woodhouse, met with Harry. The archbishop invited David to resign, and when he refused, in accordance with the ordinance, handed him an instrument of deprivation, which removed him from his parish and gave him three months to vacate the rectory, along with his terminally ill wife and two children. No-one was happy, David and Harry least of all. Harry's own feelings are evident in his response to the proceedings.

> Lord, may some good come from this sad affair. The fact that David has not abandoned the prospect of taking further action makes these encounters very formal. It would be nice to be able to reach out to him in a more personal way.[59]

The next day, a Friday, there were reports on Pymble in *SMH* and on ABC radio. David said he intended to be at St Swithun's services on Sunday. On Ken Handley's advice, Harry sent David a letter saying he ought not to interfere with the services. He could see that it was probably necessary to send such a letter, but he regretted having to do so. 'The poor guy needs the chance to say an appropriate farewell.' Harry also concluded that he may have made a mistake in not talking to the media, as one of the TV channels had an actor, 'sounding like a pompous cleric,' reading some of his words.[60]

At the same time, a world not obsessed by Pymble continued to exist. Harry found time to watch a video of Rod Story's trip to Kalimantan, Borneo, for EE. 'God be praised for Rod,' observed Harry. And the dean of the cathedral, Boak Jobbins, met with the St Andrew's School council to confirm Phillip Heath as its new headmaster.

On the Sunday following, a member of the congregation rang Harry to report that things were 'reasonably quiet' at Pymble, while Dudley Foord rang to inform him that he had advised David not to take the matter further. But the conflagration was still to burn white hot before it would die down. It was feared that David wanted to run the whole matter in the public arena. Neil Prott, Rector of Kurrajong, convened a meeting for 'Concerned Clergy' at which he would make available the commissioners' report plus other material. In the light of this threat, Harry, again in two minds, made the report available at SC on 12 December. Some on the SC who believed the matter was the archbishop's responsibility and did not concern them handed the report back.

On 16 December, the meeting of Concerned Clergy was held in the Sydney suburb of Miranda. It was attended by 75 clergy and was addressed for an hour by Phillip Jensen and for 25 minutes by John Woodhouse. Phillip said that now the clergy had to 'massage' their flocks, and bishops could get rid of ministers as in America where liberal bishops could remove evangelical clergy. This was an acknowledgement of the fear that power had shifted from the clergy to the laity and therefore to the bishops. Previously, Sydney clergy could anticipate the support of their archbishop in quarrels with their laity. Now they no longer had that assurance. Phillip conceded that the archbishop did the best job he could with the tools he had, but the move against Gilmour had resulted in a great breakdown of trust.

The Pymble affair, however, did not undermine trust. It had already been destroyed, as the REPA 18 had discovered to their astonishment two years earlier. Sydney Anglicans, who had been driven to emotional extremity by REPA, had been kept in that same unhappy state by the Pymble matter; the long legal process had kept the matter on the agenda for much of 1994, incubating division and discontent. Powerful senior clergy, unhappy with Harry's appointment, concluded that he was unsafe, a verdict that they normally reserved for those who strayed theologically.

Although David was moved on, he did not withdraw from ministry in the Sydney diocese. Bp Ray Smith found him a place at Campsie, for when he was ready, and reports that he did a valuable work there. David had been under pressure unimaginable to most of us, which may explain his more extreme words and actions. To his warden, Robert Cartwright, who requested his resignation prior to the 1994 annual vestry meeting at Pymble, David is reported to have said, 'Harry is finished. He has lost the support of the Clergy in instituting this outrageous action and crippled his term and the office of Archbishop.'[61]

There is little doubt that Harry's term in office was impaired significantly by the Pymble matter. Yet, even in retrospect, Harry never wished that he had left Pymble to sort itself out. It was one of those tough calls that goes with the territory of leadership; he always felt he just had to get on with it. To a woman who rebuked him afterwards for his treatment of David, he could only say that he appreciated her position, but all that they both could do was to leave the matter to the last day, when we will all stand before the judgement seat of Christ.

## Reflection born of exhaustion

On Friday, 30 December 1994, Harry wrote in his Day Book:

> Lord I feel impotent and powerless. A city to be won for Christ, a diocese of churches to be led according to your will. How?
>
> And beneath it all the horrible suspicion that this is all about me and not about you.
>
> How to be a good man, like Barnabas? A devoted, passionate man like Paul?

# 16

# Third Year (1995): 'Loyalty to Both Christ and the Church'

From the perspective of self-confidence, Harry was not in a good place at the beginning of the new year. 'Why am I doing what I am doing? Am I hindering or helping?' he asked himself. From the perspective of confidence in God, he was in a better place, and he prayed, 'Lord, I am now what the years have made me. Let grace undo what sin has bound up.'[1]

Ministry opportunities provided some relief from the stress of conflict. Harry was refreshed through attending as a speaker, in the third week of January, at the Victorian CMS Summer School at Rawson Village in West Gippsland. The Anglican Church is always at its best at the CMS Summer School because there its heart and mind are focused on the 'one thing needful.'[2] Harry's message to church workers about the need to develop a well-rounded strategy for each church was challenging: is the theological objection of evangelicals to dependence on works too easily accompanied by a spiritual laziness that stunts real effort for growth? He had an equally challenging question at the opening of the Law term service in Sydney on 30 January: are lawyers in danger of becoming 'somewhat cynical' by their experience of 'the vagaries of human nature'? Typically, he had some poetry for them, which, penned by John Donne, must have tested their intelligence as well as their hearts. He had prayed earnestly for the event, that the Lord would have mercy on his hearers and save and sanctify them, and afterwards thanked the Lord for his enabling. Apparently, his hearers were not displeased: they heard him again at the May 1995 Law Week dinner on the subject of 'A Tolerant God' (later published).

Harry was also looking forward to a visit to America, where he was to preach on 19 February at Coral Ridge, Fort Lauderdale and then from 20 to 22 February attend the annual board meeting of his beloved EE. It was an organisation consistent with his desire to make evangelism a top priority in his years as archbishop. He wrote to his clergy, urging them to make a more concerted effort to reach more young people in the diocese with the gospel. Richard Harvey reported to Harry on an EE youth clinic, attended by 25 clinicians, hosted by St Matthew's, Manly, where he was rector. His own son, Darren, had attended the clinic and testified that it was the best week of his life. Subsequently, at Sutherland

Railway Station, Darren was approached by some young people who asked him to buy them some beer.

> He of course said he wouldn't, but he could give them something else and then proceeded to ask them the two questions and went on to share the Gospel and one of the boys prayed to receive Christ there and then.[3]

News of every evangelistic success was always a tonic for Harry.

Harry found it hard, however, to count as joy all the responsibilities that then pressed upon him. In the first week of February, clergy meetings were held in all five regions. They were really the first opportunity Harry had to account to all his clergy for his actions in the Pymble matter. In preparation, he prayed, 'Show us mercy which we do not deserve. Lord, I hardly know what to ask. I am not anxious to justify myself but people ought to know why I did what I did.'[4] On Wednesday, 1 February 1995, at St James', Croydon, in the South Sydney region, Harry held the first of the regional meetings. Afterwards he reported, 'Not too bad a meeting. People were reasonable.'[5] At the meeting for the North Sydney region on the morning of 2 February, Harry observed, 'It was not easy. Neil Flower objected to the meeting being taped. John Woodhouse tried to cast doubt on matters of fact in the Commissioners' Report.' In the afternoon on the same day, he met with the clergy from the Parramatta region, recording, 'Some pointed questioning from Neil Prott and Neil Macken.' The latter was rector of Northmead, the parish David Gilmour held before Pymble. There were those who said that Harry's attempt to explain himself at such meetings was a weakness, that an archbishop should confine himself to a synod statement or an *ad clerum*. 'Damned if you do; damned if you don't,' I think is the secular expression.

## When conflict becomes personal

In March, Bruce Ballentine-Jones published an article on the dangers of centralism in the Diocese of Sydney.[6] He identified the Pymble matter as evidence of this trend, along with the proposed DEB with a membership nominated by the archbishop, and the numerical dominance of the archbishop's team in the SC, and even the increasing power of SC itself.[7] Bruce's Blue Ticket opponents were sceptical. The Pymble matter did not have to be taken as evidence of increasing centralism – there were no winners there; an archbishop-appointed DEB was already seen as an impossibility; Bruce had never been fussed by the increasing power of SC until he was no longer on it; and none were more in favour of decentralising regionalism than Harry and the Blue Ticket. Harry, however, did not take Bruce's arguments with a grain of salt. Instead he graciously invited Bruce to meet with him on

18 April to discuss the matter. Both appreciated the opportunity to reconnect, and Bruce agreed to write up a summary of their discussion.

Within a week, however, the temporary ceasefire collapsed. At SC on 24 April, Bruce's nomination to General Synod was strongly opposed, and Glenn Davies was elected in his stead.[8] One of the REPA colonels, Jim Ramsay, reported to Bruce the arguments against Bruce's election expressed in SC. Stephen Judd was quoted as alleging that Bruce was 'a lightning rod for antipathy to evangelicals' and that it would be inappropriate for SC to elect one who had been rejected by the synod at the triennial elections. Stuart Piggin was quoted as saying that Bruce was a subversive influence and that what was needed instead of combativeness was the 'politics of cooperation' and 'a reputation for fairness.'[9] Understandably, Bruce was hurt. At the time, he and, he suggested, other conservatives, believed that such an attack on him could not have been made without Harry's support, or at least his acquiescence. Livid, he wrote immediately to the archbishop.

> When we had our discussion last week I indicated that I would lay out my comments in writing so that what I was wanting to say could be clearly understood. In the light of the opinions about my suitability to represent the Diocese which were allowed to be expressed on Monday night I do not think that is now appropriate.

When Harry received this letter he rang Bruce, who kept a record of the conversation. Bruce inundated Harry with the full flood of his frustration. Disappointment with the calibre of leadership emanating from Church House (the archbishop's leadership team) was widespread, he alleged. This action would be seen as a move against the ACL. What was ACL to do about that, given that he was President? Many at SC had been appalled at what had been said about him there. 'It was unprecedented.' This was a Church House line and they voted as a block against him. His record in General Synod was one of cooperation, he only ever acted on the basis of group meetings and consultation, he never attacked people personally, he always played hard and fair, he was the voice of moderation who had tried to stop the ACL from deleting Harry's supporters from its voting ticket as this would be divisive, and he was now not considered fit to represent the diocese when it was he in the past who had stood up for the it. Further, Harry was no longer considered 'one of the boys' and conservative evangelicals no longer talked to him. He thought Harry had wanted to bring people 'like me' together, but this was just driving them further apart, and it was discourteous, to say the least, that Glenn Davies had not been informed that Bruce had already been nominated.

This outburst calls for analysis at a number of different levels. What does it reveal about how much goodwill Harry still had in the bank, and what was his response at the time? Bruce's attitude at the time is only too evident in his outburst, but what does he think today? What did the Blue Ticket people think of Bruce's arguments then and what do they think of them now? Bruce's claim that the disenchantment with Church House was widespread, and that Harry was no longer considered one of the boys, were certainly matters for concern. Harry could not but help notice that he had not been invited to as many of the big churches run by the most conservative of rectors, as to the smaller and so-called 'stole'[10] churches. True, he was far from being left out in the cold. He had enough to do: he made 42 visits to parishes in 1995, 35 in 1996, 27 in 1997, and 33 in 1998. Yet, this situation certainly grieved him, as he was expert in and committed to growing big churches and he wanted to see more of them in Sydney.

In his response at the time, Harry began by telling Bruce that it did not appear to him what was said in the debate was either malicious or defamatory. He apologised if he was wrong in that assessment. He did not know if Church House voted as a block. He did not know how they voted, but he did concede that they talked about such matters among themselves. He was aware that Glenn Davies was to be nominated, but he was not behind that move. He had not thought through the full implications of a vote between Bruce and Glenn; by which he meant, presumably, that he did not anticipate the vehemence of Bruce's reaction.

Bruce now acknowledges that the matter was 'petty in itself', but it 'highlights the personal dimension of the conflicts of those times.' 'This was a painful conversation,' wrote Bruce in an early account. He added perceptively, 'It was a private one and as in any private conversation, people speak in a kind of shorthand, often with passion and with a certain freedom born of years of friendship.' In a later account, he chose to emphasise the more impersonal, political dimension to the incident. 'It was a manifestation of a power struggle that was to dog the rest of Goodhew's term and was destined to end with the disappearance of the Blue Ticket as a political force.'[11] What has not changed is Bruce's conviction that the move against him was illegitimate and that he was the natural heir to a seat in the General Synod. This is a manifestation of the view that there was a natural leadership in the diocese that Harry overlooked. Bruce believed that it was not only or even primarily a personal matter. He was the President of ACL, and this was a move against the ACL. 'Whether they realised it or not,' Bruce later wrote, 'this was an attack not only on me personally but on the ACL as well.'[12]

As to what Blue Ticket people thought then and what they think now, a couple of points need to be made. We honestly believed, ever since Easter 1992 when

Bruce's declaration that the Sydney diocese was in a mood to leave the national church went viral, that Bruce was doing the diocese more harm than good, and we held that this belief was virtually incontrovertible and also widespread. We also disliked the practice of getting all the Sydney members of General Synod to caucus so that they all vote in the same way. That might be good politics, but it doesn't seem right. Speaking personally, I certainly did not see this as a move against the ACL and I was probably not even aware that Bruce was its President. In retrospect, I can see its real, if not legitimate, importance, but I did not at the time. All that said, Bruce was probably entitled to feel aggrieved that his motives were misrepresented. Unusually among politicians, Bruce always signalled his punches. One knew where he stood. He was a straight shooter, and, while like most of us, he could take things personally as he clearly did here, he did not engage in personal attacks. The tragedy of the matter is that we were living in different worlds. Poor Harry. He had little enough to do with it, while those around him succumbed to the politicisation that renders one incapable of empathy with the other side. How different it all should have been.

When Glenn Davies became aware that the election for the member of General Synod was a contested one and that he had been elected at Bruce's expense, he immediately signalled that he would not accept the appointment. Bruce believed that this should have been the end of the matter and that, in the May SC, he should have been elected unopposed by its members, including chastened Blue Ticket supporters. He was ropable when he learned that Archdeacon Lindsay Stoddart now intended to stand against him. But this time, Bruce won the vote. Quietly observing all this from the sidelines was the astute David Crain. He gave three reasons for Bruce's victory this time round.

- Few people thought the matter was all that important, as most Sydney people do not realise that BBJ's presence 'actually loses votes' in General Synod.
- It was an opportunity to appease the ACL to ease the tension a little.
- The debate decided the matter as it was evident that Bruce was more cognisant of General Synod matters than Lindsay.[13]

In a meeting on 30 May at Bishopscourt, Bruce and Harry talked about the feelings of restlessness in the diocese, but found it hard to specify what to do about it. Generally, the meeting was friendly; not tense, fairly frank, but not as pointed as the earlier conversation.'[14] Bruce was open with Harry about the changes he was bringing about in the ACL and that he intended to play a role in the future. The uneasy truce was resumed. It lasted for just over a month.

## The 1995 General Synod and the *Prayer Book*

From 3 to 7 July 1995 the General Synod of the Anglican Church of Australia met in Melbourne and passed legislation that a new prayer book, namely *A Prayer Book for Australia* (*APBA*) be accepted as a book of 'Liturgical Resources authorised by the General Synod.'

Harry's role in the matter precipitated another crisis in his relationship with BBJ in particular, and the Sydney conservatives in general. The Sydney members were accommodated in a hotel opposite the Melbourne Grammar School where the synod was held. Harry and Pam stayed at Bishopscourt with Keith and Audrey Rayner. Harry later rejected entirely any suggestion that staying with the primate represented an attempt on his part to separate himself from his fellow Sydney representatives. The gracious invitation of the Rayners to stay with them was in line with the hospitality mutually extended between archbishops and it would have been discourteous not to accept it.

According to Bruce, Harry chaired meetings with Sydney representatives to discuss strategy, and it was at one such meeting that it was agreed to seek the postponement of consideration of the new prayer book for another three years, by which time all dioceses would have had the opportunity to consider it. Instead, Harry himself successfully moved the immediate adoption of the book as a liturgical resource, so that it could be tried in practice without according it the authority of being definitive of the doctrine of the Anglican Church of Australia. The words 'Liturgical Resources authorised by the General Synod' were to be included on the front page of the book. Harry recalls:

> This was agreed to and they appear there to this day (à la Kings and Chronicles!). I recall that Dr John Woodhouse was not happy with this measure unless the words were printed in very large type across the face of the book. The print is not large, but the words bear witness to the fact that that BCP is the authorised standard of doctrine and worship in this Church, while *APBA* is simply another source of liturgical resources authorised for use.

The Sydney conservatives professed to be shocked and the Anglo-Catholics rejoiced, with Bp David Silk of Ballarat unhelpfully crowing to the media that, like Hitler, he had 'no further territorial ambitions' and with journalist Chris McGillion reporting of Harry, 'Appeasement, some says, is his middle name.'[15] Bp Silk was to learn, however, that ecclesiastical politics is not as smooth as his name when, not only Sydney, but his own diocesan synod of Ballarat, rejected the

*APBA*,[16] while McGillion awoke to the reality that a drama deserving of book-length treatment was being enacted here.

Harry's perception differs radically from that of BBJ. The latter makes the process sound like a Labor caucus, with all delegates obeying a pledge to uphold the party line or be ostracised for ratting on their mates. Attending a synod and talking with only one group was just not Harry's style. His recollection is of a far more fluid situation, involving synod meetings, private discussions, and conferences with a range of people. As representatives horse traded over details between sessions, scenarios were formed, reformed, amended, abandoned, and replaced. Harry recalled meetings along the way with Peter Corney and some of the Melbourne evangelicals, and that at some point there was agreement, expressed by Corney, that they should, with some reluctance, support the book because it was probably the best that they could get at this point in history. Harry also recalls talking these issues through with Peter Chiswell, Bishop of Armidale, who was of the same opinion.

Sydney conservatives had no intention of taking their defeat in the 1995 General Synod lying down. A pre-Sydney synod conference on the prayer book was held at Moore College on 2 September 1995. It was organised by ACL, and the speakers were Donald Robinson, Edwin Judge, John Mason and David Peterson. The first three were known to be critics of *APBA*, and therefore the outcome was preordained. Bruce Ballantine-Jones was quite explicit about that. 'The ACL's intention was that this conference should alert synod to the flaws in *APBA* and be the beginning of a political campaign to defeat the book at the 1996 synod when it was due to come up for consideration.'[17]

Very early in the struggle, Harry concluded that the Sydney synod would never approve the *APBA*. He persevered, however, because he believed that the struggle over a new prayer book would constrain conservative Anglicans, jealous of the Reformed purity of faith and worship, to develop their own prayer books or approved services of liturgical worship and this would be a great improvement on allowing each clergyperson to be the sole determinant of what should go in to and what should be left out of services. The Archbishop's Liturgical Panel was tasked with developing a prayer book for Sydney, watched over by the Doctrine Commission. The resulting *Sunday Services: A Contemporary Liturgical Resource* was not published till 2001, just after Harry left office. In Archbishop Jensen's term, an understanding of the value of liturgical services was to be recovered to a degree, resources such as *Contemporary Services* added, and a diocesan website modelling both contemporary and traditional liturgies was to be created.[18] Just as Harry's opposition to lay presidency would prove to be prescient, so his resistance to the dismantling of liturgical worship would also prove to be the path of wisdom. But in the nadir of the dispute over the prayer book, the worst of Sydney's culture was only too evident. A visiting theology lecturer, after meeting with two of those who opposed Harry's stance on the matter, reported that he was 'shell-shocked' by the vehemence of their opposition to him: they appeared to 'hate' their archbishop. An attempt was made to reassure him that, while it was understandable that visitors might be shocked by the Sydney 'culture', there was 'nothing personal' in it. He was unconvinced: it felt like a deeply personal animus.

## The power of prayer

Harry was not consumed by this culture war within the diocese. He maintained his prayer life, his concern for the everyday problems faced by others, and his desire to reach with the balm of the gospel those who were troubled by life's challenges, whether churchgoers or not. On 13 August 1995, for example, he preached two quite outstanding sermons, both illustrating, in different ways, the power of prayer. The first was at the centenary of Anglican ministry at Berala. His text was Acts 6:4, about on giving 'attention to prayer and the ministry of the word' (ESV). He said that prayer and the word were the principal coins in an economy that stretches beyond the immediate and, therefore, powerful beyond estimation. He made this point memorably with the help of a quotation from a favourite author, Jacques Ellul, the Professor of Law and Sociology, who fought with the French Resistance, and was a man of action.

> Precisely because our technological society is given over entirely to action, the person who retires to one's room to pray is the true radical. Everything will flow from that. This act in society, which is also an action on this society, goes very much further than the concrete involvement, which it still does not shirk.[19]

The second was at a service on the same day at the Anzac Memorial in Hyde Park, Sydney, to mark the 50th anniversary of Victory in the Pacific and the end of World War II. He researched the subject matter thoroughly, but his message was simple, beginning with the words,

> Two scenes from 15th August 1945 capture the emotions of that memorable day. One is well known: the other never referred to, as far as I know.
>
> One is ... the dancing man. In the image of that blithesome capering figure the photographer captured for succeeding generations the joy

and relief experienced by those who heard the news of Victory in the Pacific.

There was another. *The Sydney Morning Herald* of August 16 reported that:

> Amid the noise and excitement in Martin Place yesterday morning, a soldier in jungle green knelt in quiet reverence in front of the Cenotaph.
>
> An elderly woman joined him immediately. It was not long before 12 women were kneeling around the soldier. They were all visibly affected and some were weeping. The scene hushed the crowd.

And he ended with the words

> If we would dance, we must first kneel. If we would make peace, then we must discover peace with God. If we would enjoy the fruits of love we must first learn what it means to be loved by God in pardon and acceptance and in that love learn to give love ourselves, freely and fully.

Harry knew how to speak to all Australians. They heard him gladly, grateful for the comfort and challenge of the words he habitually brought to occasions of community concern.

## Sydney synod, 11–13 and 18–19 October 1995

For the second year in a row, however, in his presidential address, Harry was not heard gladly by all members of synod. Regrettably, too many of the matters he covered in his presidential address were those in which he was in disagreement with his conservative critics. He reiterated his understanding of what it meant to be an Anglican; that while it was important to be innovative in helping people to hear God's word, there was value in common prayer regularly repeated, and that the clergy had a responsibility to nurture Christ's followers 'from the beginning of their Christian walk to the end of their days.' The prayer book protected the laity from idiosyncratic emphases of clergy and, without it, the vertical dimension of worship was lost, over time starving the laity of true worship. He reported that he had asked both the Doctrine Commission and the diocesan Liturgical Committee to evaluate the extent to which *APBA* 'adheres to the doctrines and principles of worship of this church', but that serious consideration of *APBA* had to be held over to the 1996 synod, since its final amended version had not yet been received. When it was, he would call a series of meetings around the diocese to consider it, and he intended to give parishes permission to trial it, otherwise proper evaluation would be difficult. Up until his retirement in 2001, Harry continued to give permission to use *APBA* to the few parishes in the diocese that requested it.

On the wider Australian church, Harry said that, while the fundamental truths of the Christian gospel could not be compromised, unnecessary division was also unacceptable to God.[20] He counselled against separation and withdrawal from the wider Australian church. Not only would they suffer, but so would Sydney.

> If we do [isolate ourselves], I think there is every chance we will turn in on ourselves and devour one another. Inevitable steps after formal breach of relationships would be, first, the isolation of those within this Diocese not thought to be really evangelical, then divisions between 'soft' and 'hard' evangelicals, between Prayer Book evangelicals and non-Prayer Book evangelicals, divisions between evangelicals who assert this and others who assert that.[21]

On lay presidency, Harry informed the synod yet again of where he stood, so that members would be helped to understand his response and also to guide them in their prayers for him.[22] He expected the prayers even of those who did not support him.

At the 1995 synod, it was decided to implement some of the recommendations of the 1992 report on regionalisation. Regional councils would be given funds to support their own initiatives. This was consistent with Harry's philosophy of always giving encouragement to grassroots initiatives. He was not only aware that the diocese was weak at the centre and strong in the parishes, but he believed that it should remain that way. The centre existed for the sake of the parishes. He believed that growth would be far more likely to result from 250 local, humble initiatives than from one centralised, grand initiative.[23]

## Blue Ticket problems

Regionalisation was not all gain. Some ministry programs, supported from the centre, were axed. Harry's power was also reduced. From the 1996 synod elections, about half the members of SC were to be elected from the regions. Supporters of the Blue Ticket were keen for regionalisation, but they were ill-equipped to win support for their candidates in the regions. With a small organising group and no formal membership, it had been hard enough to do it centrally.

'Now I don't want the Blue Ticket any more than anyone else,' wrote the politically alert David Crain. 'It is a nuisance – but so absolutely necessary.' Stephen Judd and Warwick Olson, the Blue Ticket's chief strategists, were keen promoters of regionalism in the interests of democracy and efficiency. But, complained Crain, the Blue Ticket did not appear to be doing anything to recruit suitable regional candidates. Rather it appeared determined to give to the ACL, through regionalism, the power it had lost under the current system. 'Wouldn't that be ironic?' he asked.[24]

Lovers of irony won't be surprised to learn that this is exactly what happened. It was more important, of course, that regionalism should succeed than that the Blue Ticket should prosper but, unlike the ACL, the small Blue Ticket brigade was in no position to strengthen itself in the regions. The ACL, by contrast, from November 1995 organised itself into seven regional chapters, which would hold two meetings per year, one in April or May, and the other 'in the lead up to the next meeting of Sydney synod.'[25] An aim of each regional chapter was 'To provide a means for members to discuss together, in consultation with the Council, nominations for Synod and regional committees.'[26]

Crain wrote an analysis for the Blue Ticket of the current prospects under the heading 'Responding to Regionalism' and with the rubric 'Let's get cracking.' Two of Harry's bishops, he reported, were confident that Harry would have another supportive SC after the 1996 synod. Crain could see no reason for this confidence, suspecting that Harry's supporters would be 'totally done over.' He advised that it would take time to find suitable candidates for the regions and so he began the process by canvassing possibilities in each of the regions.

It was good advice, and on 17 January 1996 the Blue Ticket organisers met to 'get cracking.' But the writing was already on the wall. An ominous number of invitees sent their apologies; and, while they asked to be given details of the ticket, they were not keen to add their signatures to endorse the Blue Ticket. The ACL was reasserting its power, which meant that identifying with any other group was risky. Parish representatives to synod were to be elected at annual vestry meetings in parishes in February and March. So in January, the ACL sent out a flyer to all its members and clergy fostering the election of synod representatives who were 'committed evangelicals.'[27] The Blue Ticket sent out no corresponding advice, with the result that the 1996 synod had fewer of its supporters from whose ranks nominations to SC could be made.

The Blue Ticket was not to be 'totally done over' in the 1996 elections, but it was greatly weakened, and therefore Harry was weakened. In the 1999 elections, the Blue Ticket was to be comprehensively 'done over'.

## Exhaustion

Harry kept himself marvellously fit. He loved running and jogged daily well into his 70s. Great stamina has been a conspicuous characteristic of a number of Sydney's archbishops: Howard Mowll and Marcus Loane come readily to mind. Of Harry's stamina, Bp Paul Barnett, himself the embodiment of the Protestant work ethic, observed:

> As one privileged to work with him and as one who has always worked hard (too hard, says Anita) I have to say that I have not met anyone who works as hard as this man. I simply don't know how he does it. It must come from God. Yet in all the hundreds of hours I have been at various meetings with him I have never spotted a drooping eyelid or caught a glimpse of even a well-disguised yawn. We easily take for granted the smooth operation of arguably the best administered diocese around. This is attributable to a number of people and factors, but to no one more than this archbishop.[28]

Harry's high energy level is evident in his diary. At the end of a fraught year, we find him brushing up on his grasp of Hebrew grammar, planning for the new year, preparing talks for a New Year's Day broadcast and a sermon for Summer School, taking his mother to the pictures and baby-sitting his grandchildren.

Physically and emotionally, however, Harry was running on empty. It did not help that, on New Year's Day, he went to see Australia play the West Indies and left early because of rain, only to learn afterwards that he missed a thrilling finish to the game with Michael Bevan (78 not out) hitting Australia to victory with a four off the last ball. On 3 January, Harry wrote in his diary, 'I am feeling mentally weary. Hope a few days quiet will overcome this fatigue.' On 15 January, he wrote, 'Rather a bleak day for me. I am feeling mentally weary. Must take steps to overcome this.' On the 16th he reported, 'I should be preparing, but I feel a deep need to restore my spiritual and mental health.' On 17 January 1996, I paid him a visit at Bishopscourt to present him with a book that I had dedicated to him. He told me that he had ended the year close to exhaustion, and that he could not pray. He was, he said, in a black hole. He just did not have the energy to form any thoughts in his mind. He said that the body made its own demands on our spirits and that we must roll with the punches that our body dishes out to us. So, he claimed, he just sat for a few days and thought of nothing.

On perusing his diary, however, it is quite impossible to find any few days when he just sat and thought of nothing. He was anxious about Pam's health, as she had been suffering severe toothache for more than a fortnight in spite of treatment. On the very first day on which he records his weariness, he also reports that he read a paper by Peter O'Brien on N.T. Wright's controversial position on

justification, which was causing the conservatives much angst. On the day before he reported his fatigue to me, he reflected on the move by Gladesville Church to plant a church in the territory covered by the Diocese of Newcastle. He formulated his own position in terms so concise, he was clearly thinking well.
- Churches with this sort of energy must be encouraged
- I want churches to be as enterprising as possible in outreach
- I want to maintain integrity in my position as a bishop in this church
- I want to preserve enough structure to preserve this institution for the future.

The day after his conversation with me, he read a report of Stephen Gabbott on the difficulties of ministry in the South Sydney region. 'We cannot afford to say this is too hard,' he wrote, adding that with a view to the needs of the marginalised, dysfunctional, or 'ethnic groupings', the parish system should not be abandoned, but should be supplemented. Then, in the evening, he met with a group whom he was to lead on a tour of Israel. 'It promises to be fun,' he said, adding that there is a good religious humour section on the internet.

For the Archbishop of Sydney, there was not much time, even for exhaustion.

# 17

# Fourth Year (1996): 'I Smile No Longer'

The weight of his responsibilities as archbishop did not dim Harry's enthusiasm for evangelism. From his teenage years, when he preached in the open air, he maintained a commitment to reaching the unsaved with the gospel. At the beginning of 1996, his enthusiasm shone as brightly as ever as he sought to involve the diocese in his vision of being 'evangelistically enterprising'. He safeguarded this commitment through his active role in the ministry of EE. It was a case of mutual reinforcement; his role in EE strengthened his zeal for evangelism which, in turn, made him a constant friend and supporter of EE itself. This interdependence of evangelistic zeal and determination to promote EE was never more evident than at the beginning of his fourth year as archbishop.

## Evangelism and Evangelism Explosion

By then, EE was able to claim that it had done what IBM, GM and the CIA had not done: it had a presence in every nation on earth. The executive vice-president of EE International, Tom Stebbins, wrote to Harry early in 1996 to inform him that EE had now been launched in 210 nations. 'Only North Korea is left and we sent two of our vice presidents to Asia yesterday to explore every crack in the wall.'[1] With a preference for depth over breadth, Harry wondered about just how effective the presence of EE was in every nation. Typically, he kept such reservations to himself and warmly commended the work of EE. He wrote to Bp Ray Smith informing him that Tom Stebbins was to visit Australia. He was to lead a training clinic for Vietnamese pastors and leaders at St John's Park, a Sydney suburb, and Harry encouraged Ray to take advantage of it as it would prove 'a real advantage to the work among Vietnamese people in your Region.'[2] Then he wrote to Tom Smith at the Anglican Youth Department, informing him of an EE youth clinic in Manly in July,[3] and to all his regional bishops to inform them that Tom Stebbins would conduct a three-day master plan training seminar.[4]

Harry eagerly supported all initiatives for evangelism and, while he loved EE, he was far from insisting that it or any other evangelistic program was the only, or even the best one. Such comparisons never crossed his mind. On 5 March, a Tuesday, he spoke after working hours on 'A word of hope in a world of hype' at 'A Business Person's Evangelistic Rally' at St Andrew's Cathedral, organised by the Department of Evangelism. 'The Great Con,' he argued, was that true and lasting happiness comes from success in business, advancement in career, fame or notoriety, the security promised by scientific and technological advance, being lucky in love, or the belief that you can ignore God and be truly happy. He quoted Leo Tolstoy's verdict that such a con was cruel and absurd, and followed with Tolstoy's fable of the predicament of a man who fell down a well and clung to a branch halfway down with a wild beast above, a dragon below, and two mice eating away at the branch. The situation was hopeless and death inevitable. That is every person's situation. Harry observed that 'Tolstoy was a singular person. He solved the issue in a way which was uniquely his, but he solved it at the feet of Jesus of Nazareth.' Harry ended with an appeal which owed much to Billy Graham.

> Are you essentially living with hype: goals, hopes, ambitions, relationships, tasks, all good enough in themselves but destined to die away and sparse fare for a creature made finally to be happy only in God? Or do you have a sure and certain hope built on the God who has shown himself in Jesus? I invite you to receive Jesus now. You will never have a better opportunity.[5]

Following the appeal, the choir of St Paul's, Castle Hill, sang, 'I Choose Jesus'.

Then on 16 March Harry spoke on 'The Priority of Men's Ministry' in a 'Winning Men '96' program that had grown out of a gospel initiative in 1994 of St Mark's, Sadlier, a Sydney church, and was supported by the best-known Sydney conservatives, Phillip Jensen and John Chapman (Sydney Anglicanism's outstanding evangelists at the time), Jim Ramsay, Ray Galea, Neil Prott and John Woodhouse, among others. Harry researched his subject deeply, drawing on the findings on gender differences documented in the NCLS. He took as his text 2 Corinthians 5:10. 'For all of us must appear before the judgement seat of Christ, so that each of us may receive recompense for what has been done in the body, whether good or evil.' He was burdened to challenge men to be accountable and to be more conscious of the presence of God in every aspect of their lives: their time, gifts, opportunities, families, friends, and character.

Clearly, Harry supported the old time evangelism as well as the evangelistic experiments of the diocesan Department of Evangelism, but he was also involved in a longer-term shaping of international evangelistic enterprise through his involvement with EE and his personal friendship with its revered founder, Dr Jim Kennedy. Harry's influence would contribute to substantial change in that ministry after Dr Kennedy's death, but it was only possible because Harry was reputedly one of the founder's most trusted friends. Because Harry was patient and made allowances for American values, he was able to nudge the organisation towards change. The EE system was always being criticised on theological grounds, and Dr Kennedy was sensitive on that score. EE had links with over 400 denominations worldwide and there was enormous scope for theological disputation. Dr Kennedy was known to have only two or three people with whom he was prepared to have an open conversation on theology, and Harry was one of them. He found Harry's demeanour such as to create trust, being 'quick to think; slow to speak.' So, when he gave Dr Kennedy the benefit of his considered advice, the advice was usually taken.[6]

In the American Spring, EE held 'CELEBRATION '96', where at least one representative from every nation gathered together to rejoice in what God had done. This was, to Dr Kennedy's knowledge, the first time this had happened in the history of humanity. He reported to Harry,

> Testimonies from around the world made the cost and commitment of this work painfully clear. More than a few were with us at the risk of their lives. Yet, their devotion to the Gospel in the face of such opposition strengthened the resolve of the whole assembly. As one put it, 'It makes any obstacles I face in sharing the Good News seem trite.'[7]

But the cost of getting into every nation was not only human. It was also financial and, a serious reduction in a large donation from $900,000 per year for three years to $500,000, put EE into a financial crisis. Rod Story was told that he would have to raise his own support from then on, and Tom Stebbins' visit to Oceania and projected clinics were cancelled. Both Rod and Harry saw this as an example of cultural insensitivity and were cross at the lack of consultation. Harry joined Rod in objecting to these decisions, the latter with characteristic bluntness, the former with uncharacteristic firmness, and both unpopular measures were overturned. Stebbins' visit was something of a triumph, and Harry wrote to Dr Kennedy, thanking him for relenting and commending Stebbins' ministry. Harry also wrote to board member Sterling Huston, expressing his gratitude for his role in reversing the decision to cancel the visit. He also made explicit the lesson learned from the experience, signalling the changes that had to happen.

> Your connections with the Billy Graham Association will have alerted you to the importance of interaction with people outside of the United States when a ministry is international, especially as international as EE. I have sometimes thought that the Board in not always as attuned to that reality as perhaps it should be and, therefore, to that degree limits the forward movement and consolidation of EE overseas.[8]

Such difficulties make or break organisations. In this case, thanks to the Christian love and humility that accompanied the required forthrightness, the EE Board, soon with Sterling Huston himself at the helm, attuned itself admirably to the reality of an international ministry. That was a development after Harry stepped down as archbishop and was to be one of the finest achievements of his retirement years.

## Ordination of female deacons

Meanwhile the movement for greater recognition of women in ministry continued, accompanied by some dramatic events. An ordination service for women deacons was held at St Andrew's Cathedral on Saturday 10 February 1996. Sue Emeleus, ordained deacon at the service, vividly recalls the experience.

> Di Nicolios, Archdeacon for Women ... organised us for the ordination service. The last thing she said to us before we processed into the Cathedral was ... 'and don't talk to the press'.
>
> After the service, someone came up to me and said 'Do you think women should be priested?' I said 'yes' and the person said 'would you mind standing here for a minute?' A few moments later the person came back with cameras and microphone! It was the ABC and I gave my reasons why women should be priested. That night on the ABC news there was a segment when they had filmed the ordination service, and afterwards asked Harry about women's ordination to the Priesthood. Harry spoke briefly saying he didn't think women should be priests ... and the cameras immediately switched to me, just ordained, and saying I thought women *should* become priests. I was very upset and rang Harry the next day and said I didn't want to appear disloyal to my Archbishop on the day of my ordination. He was just lovely, so gracious. He said it was OK with him, and he also said that he knew I would never be disloyal to him.
>
> My eldest son, Tom, ... spent one year living in Bandung, Indonesia, while he studied electrical engineering ... On the night of the ordination, Tom was with some friends watching the ABC news. Suddenly the ordination service came on and Tom exclaimed, '*There's my mother!*' ... I thought what a wonderfully compassionate sense of humour God has! My disobedience in speaking to the press was used by God to make sure all my sons saw my ordination (the other two sons had been present in the Cathedral).[9]

## Port Arthur massacre, 28 April

Harry was on leave in Israel and London from 12 March to 14 April 1996. On the second day of his leave, Thomas Hamilton, in Dunblane, Scotland, shot 16 school pupils and one teacher dead, before turning the gun on himself. It was the deadliest mass shooting in British history. That may have sowed a seed in the troubled, intellectually limited mind of one,[10] who two weeks after Harry's return from leave, shot 35 dead and wounded a further 23 in Port Arthur, Tasmania, at that time the worst such incident in world history. Australia was traumatised by this calamity, which occurred the day before the third anniversary of Harry's installation as archbishop.

On Thursday 2 May, Harry preached at the Ecumenical Service of Prayer for the Victims of the Port Arthur Massacre in St Andrew's Cathedral. He recorded in his diary that it was 'a very moving occasion' with 700–800 present. In the congregation were representatives of all the churches, governments of New South Wales and Tasmania, the police, ambulance and fire brigade. School pupils laid 35 roses on the Lord's Table in memory of those killed.

Such disasters, it is now understood, have many victims, radiating out in concentric circles: from the killed and injured; to those forever blighted by the sudden loss of those dear to them; to those who would never be able to eradicate from their minds the hideous images of terror and death; to those who wonder why they were spared when others nearby were not; to those in the police and caring professions who had to disarm the perpetrator and care for casualties; to those who knew the perpetrator and who had to continue to live in the vicinity. Harry acknowledged all of them at the beginning of his sermon, culminating in his acknowledgement that the whole nation was in mourning. The massacre, numbing in its ferocity, had left all Australians reaching for reasons and explanations. 'What happened in Port Arthur involved us all. As a people, as a nation, as human beings made in the image of God, we have been assaulted and humiliated. We have been diminished.' He had words for the many dimensions of this tragedy – and then, God's answer:

> There is a Shepherd who has himself walked the dark and lonely valley of death and rose triumphant. Today he holds out his hand to every man and woman, boy and girl who will grasp it in sincerity. ...
>
> I commend that glorious Shepherd to you my friends.
>
> And I commend you to him.[11]

The psychological impact of an event as calamitous as the Port Arthur massacre does not evaporate overnight, and Harry was not content to preach on it only on this one occasion. He continued to refer to it in his sermons as he moved around the diocese. He also supported the Prime Minister, John Howard, in his brave and successful move to introduce strict gun control, and on Sunday 28 July he attended a rally designed to promote that end. Meanwhile, in demonstration of the reality that the responsibilities of an archbishop in office are unrelenting, a trauma much closer to home had developed around him.

## Sexual abuse: the Wood Royal Commission

On 7 and 8 May 1996, Harry appeared before the royal commission into corruption in the NSW police force. The commission had begun its work in 1994, but its terms of reference had been widened to include the issue of child sexual assault, and non-government agencies were found to have harboured people who had committed criminal offences against children. The chief commissioner was J.R.T. Wood, Seventh-day Adventist of high standing in the community with a reputation as one 'more righteous than the Bible.' He gave none of the witnesses an easy time. Counsel assisting the Wood Royal Commission was Patricia Anne Bergin, destined to be made a judge of the Supreme Court (1999–2017). Appearing before them was a formidable experience, and Harry found the process uncomfortable, as he was probably meant to. He had to sit in front of a screen on which a document would appear, asked to comment and be subjected to sustained questioning.

It would be wrong to imagine, however, that Harry was a hare caught in the headlights of the legal machine. Although it is true that the churches were only recently awakened to the seriousness of the issue of sexual abuse, Harry was not unprepared for this test. On 15 March 1992, the ABC's religious affairs program *Compass* broadcast 'The Ultimate Betrayal', alleging that up to 15 per cent of Australian clergy may have committed sexual offences. Most Christian viewers seemed to be too shocked to begin to admit that there might be an epidemic of clerical sexual abuse of children. Harry's predecessor, Donald Robinson, agreed with Archbishop Hollingworth that the 'Church is well able to govern its own household in these matters and that if complaints are received they are properly dealt with.' He believed cases of clerical sexual abuse were 'extremely rare.'[12] But the program gave permission to a significant number of viewers to report their own experiences of being abused by ministers. Very quickly, it became the greatest scandal affecting the churches in anyone's memory.

Certainly, from the beginning of his episcopate, Harry was aware that here was a diabolical stain on the life and witness of the church, which should not and could not be covered up. Before his first synod he had requested SC to appoint a Sexual Abuse Task Force to develop procedures to deal with clerical sexual misconduct. At the 1993 synod he explained that the church would have to develop strong protocols to address the problem. 'This speech was an historic event,' reports the historian of the movement to redress clerical sexual abuse in the Sydney diocese. 'For the first time an Australian Anglican Archbishop was responding to the imperative need to publicly admit the reality of sexual misconduct within the Church's faith communities and the dilemma of how to deal with the matter.'[13]

In the 1994 and 1995 synods, Harry had apologised for the delay in developing the protocol. Although many still doubted the seriousness of the problem, the delay was not caused either by lack of cooperation or by an attempt to defend the institution. The main cause of the delay in developing workable policies was that it was such a multifaceted problem, involving 'counselling, legal issues, information and referral services, insurance, education, prevention, and investigation.'[14] Personally frustrated by the delay, Harry implemented interim measures and sought to be both well-advised and widely read on the issue. He had announced to the 1994 synod that he intended to appoint contact persons who could advise the abused and recommend to them reporting matters either to police or to a small advisory committee. The latter, known as 'Harry's Committee', put the relational dimension of the issue ahead of the legal and included those who had suffered from sexual abuse. This included Beth Jones, who under the nom de plume Cathy Ann Matthews, had written the confronting *Breaking Through: No Longer a Victim of Child Abuse*.[15] Harry also valued the compassion and expertise of Sue Foley, who served on the Sexual Abuse Task Force, and who was then the manager of Child and Family Services, Care Force (later Anglicare). She continued to press Harry throughout 1995 and early 1996 to finalise the abuse protocol, and he continued to reassure her that progress was being made.[16] Regrettably, it was not issued until June 1996, and the suspicion that the Wood Royal Commission may have hurried it along is reinforced by the fact that it does address the commission's concerns. In 1995 Harry had read Neil and Thea Ormerod's book, *When Ministers Sin: Sexual Abuse in the Churches*,[17] which contains a case study reputed to be of a Sydney Anglican member of the clergy. Then, as soon as he learned that he was to be called to give evidence before the royal commission, Harry was advised by David Fairfull, CEO of the diocesan secretariat, to confer with Father Brian Lucas, later the general secretary of the Australian Catholic Bishops' Conference.

Fairfull knew Lucas because every month he had invited the CEOs of the major denominations to meet with him, and they shared intelligence of mutual interest. Because he trained as a lawyer, Lucas annually did some work in the courts to keep across the law on sexual abuse.

It was with some awareness, then, of the problem of sexual abuse that Harry came before the Wood Royal Commission. He knew where his interrogators wanted him to go, but he did not respond defensively, and he wanted to be honest. He had come to the conclusion in the light of all the testimony at the commission that 'it did not appear that all that might have been done was done.' He was not able to claim that the church had protocols in place to deal with the problem, nor was he able to refute the accusation, now frequent in the press, that the church was dragging its feet on the matter. Harry was questioned about the case of a North Shore rector, referred to by the commission as AC1, who had abused a young parishioner between the years 1979, when she was 14 years old, and 1983. The victim, AC2, had reported the matter to a Presbyterian minister in 1984. The minister challenged the accused, who confessed to the charge.[18] The matter had been reported to Bp Donald Cameron by the girl's father, who declined to take the matter further, as defamation laws were then, on balance, likely to protect the accused, as public awareness was to believe the accuser. The allegedly offending rector stayed in his parish for another decade before resigning shortly before the royal commission.

Bishops are responsible for clerical discipline and are only too aware that their clergy required disciplining in many areas, but sexual abuse by clergy was a matter that some, including Harry, found frighteningly novel. Harry therefore felt that any indignation with the way Bp Cameron had handled the matter was anachronistic. With the benefit of hindsight, however, he agreed at the royal commission that 'irrespective of the truth of the matter, it was unacceptable that AC1 had been able to continue in the parish for 10 years after the complaint was made, without any investigation having been conducted.' Pressed further on the same point, he added, 'If it is true it is totally inappropriate and worse than that.'[19] His admission that the way the church had handled this case was a 'disgrace' was widely reported in the press.[20]

On 9 May, Harry was interviewed by *SMH*, *The Australian* and the *Daily Telegraph*, and by the dour journalist Quentin Dempster on ABC Channel 2. An undated letter to Harry from Alan Cole assured him, and Don Cameron, too, of his prayers. He added, 'You were great on TV – gentle and humble and not trying to whitewash. The Lord must have shut Quentin's mouth, like the bees???' That evening Harry met with his strategy group at Bishopscourt: Olson, Irvine,

Wade, Judd, Piggin, Stoddart. In an amazing demonstration of his capacity to compartmentalise the many stresses of his role, Harry did not raise with them the issue of the royal commission, remarking only on the fact that the 'majority want lay presidency.' Both lay presidency and clerical sexual abuse were issues that persisted throughout Harry's entire episcopate. He early made up his mind that the former was a non-starter in spite of the strength of support for it, and was not really troubled by it. The issue of sexual abuse, however, he realised was of much greater consequence for the church and therefore he applied himself with focused diligence to developing protocols for dealing with the matter.

On 21 May, he recorded, 'talked through Sexual Abuse Protocols with Pattie Mayne. We have more work to do on them. Esp. role of the Contact person.'[21] Harry was now aware, as he had not been in Ceduna in 1963 when he advised Patricia Mayne to return to Sydney (see chapter five), of her own experience of sexual abuse, and she had become one of his key advisers on appropriate protocols.

On Friday 24 May 1996, Harry was interviewed again by Quentin Dempster on the ABC program *Stateline*. The following day, the previous archbishop, Donald Robinson, wrote to Harry, who was due on 30 May to address the clergy and the media on issuing a protocol on sexual misconduct. Robinson congratulated Harry on his TV interview, but asked him to refrain from commenting on incidents or procedures followed during the two preceding episcopates (that of Marcus Loane and that of Robinson himself). While conceding that such a protocol could be a good thing and that public expectations had changed since their time, Robinson did not think it followed necessarily that their processes were either reprehensible or ineffective.[22] On 31 May, Bp Donald Cameron wrote to Harry advising that, in response to requests that he understood originated from Harry, he had made a statutory declaration in relation to matters arising from the proceedings of the Wood Royal Commission. He regretted the embarrassment that the publicity had brought on Harry and the diocese.

On 2 June, *Southern Cross* published an article on the matter. It was written by Margaret Rodgers and reported that at the Wood Royal Commission Harry had spoken 'strongly against the way the Anglican Church had failed to act on information of alleged sexual abuse, saying that if it were true, it was a "disgrace".'[23]

On 6 June, Bp Cameron again wrote to Harry, expressing dismay at the *Southern Cross* article and, in particular, Harry's use of the words 'failed' and 'disgrace.' He wanted to know if he still enjoyed Harry's 'unqualified support.' Harry replied in a long letter, dated 10 June, assuring Donald Cameron of his confidence and respect, and expressing the hope that he still had his friendship.

He explained that the new protocol he was issuing was based on the growing understanding of the impact of sexual abuse, especially on the young. Harry then defended the editor of *Southern Cross* on the grounds that she had been accused of not being sufficiently specific about other matters and that, as so much had been said in the press about the Wood Commission, she could not avoid reporting on it. Compared with other press treatments of the issue, he thought *Southern Cross*'s treatment was balanced. In retrospect, Margaret Rodgers, always cool in a crisis, did her best work in ensuring the strengthening of the Safe Ministry and Abuse Protocols of the Anglican Church. She had, as her successor recognised, the 'depth of intellect to see the raw issues.'[24]

Harry concluded his letter to Bp Cameron with one of the most anguished expressions of feeling of his episcopate.

> Well friend there it is. I will not be sorry to be quit of the ambiguities of this present existence. I have a course to run and I will try to do it to the best of my ability. I will certainly finish this part of my journey with fewer friends than when I began. That will, I trust, be solely due to foolishness or ineptitude and never to malice. I have a prayer I use which says in part: 'Let me do no harm to your people, your Name, or your cause. Lead me by your Spirit that I may lead your people according to your will.' May the Lord be gracious and grant me my earnest request.

Harry's friendship with Don Cameron remained intact. On 7 January 1997, the bishop wrote a long, and one might say, very Cameronian letter to Harry, giving him advice on what to read. He counselled that 'reading should have a measure of reasonable privacy and reasonable assurance of freedom from interruption. Both these are scarce commodities, especially for Archbishops.' By the end of 1999 Cameron was writing again to Harry to express how impressed he was by the 'measure' of Harry's 'magnanimity'. He had been reminded of the words of A.C. Tait when he was Bishop of London, 'Oh, that the liberals were more religious, and the religious more liberal.'[25]

Achieving justice for the abused, however, proved far tougher than maintaining his own friendships. At the 1996 synod, six months after the royal commission, Harry spoke at length about the new sexual abuse protocols, and synod passed the Church Discipline Ordinance 1996.[26] Harry was happy to see further subsequent revisions of his protocols. It was a weakness in the protocols that, while the abused now had access to five contact persons, it was still up to Harry to decide what further needed to be done in each case. That was an unsustainable model.

Harry was not always able to deliver the outcomes that the abused desired and needed. In the case of AC2, for example, she asked Harry to take more steps than he already had against her abuser, AC1, on the grounds that his resignation and quiet departure was insufficient retribution for the damage that he had done to her. She pursued the matter in a civil court, lost, and $65,000 costs were awarded against her. On legal grounds, Harry never met with her. A better way needed to be found. In April/May 2000 the Professional Standards Unit was established under the direction of Philip Gerber in response to lobbying from the TAMAR group of women concerned to transform the church's ministry to the abused. In 2001, after he became archbishop, Peter Jensen would arrange for AC2's costs to be met by the church's insurers. Concerned for her healing and restitution, he subsequently wrote her a letter of apology and arranged to meet with her to express his deep regret.[27] As with the Gilmour case, legalities had frustrated Harry's pastoral inclinations. It is counterintuitive to allow the pastoral to trump the legal, but it may in the end be the better way, especially in cases that are not themselves illegal, and neither David Gilmour nor AC2 was guilty of any illegality.

## EFAC conference

From 26 to 30 June 1996, the EFAC conference was held in Melbourne, and Harry gave the presidential address. Formed in 1961 by John Stott and Marcus Loane, EFAC never really caught on in Sydney because the ACL saw it as a possible rival. Harry, however, had seen the good work EFAC had done in other dioceses, especially Brisbane, and gave it his full support. The 1996 conference was an opportunity for him to survey the current state of evangelical Anglicanism, worldwide. In demonstration of his strong relationship with Bp Cameron, just a fortnight after their awkward exchange of letters, he cited Cameron's opinion that the Anglican Church of Australia was an anachronism, 'splendidly ready for the 1950s.' Harry analysed the influence on the state of Christianity of postmodernism, multiculturalism, religious pluralism, secularisation, the demands of Indigenous Australians for greater recognition, and feminism. He insisted on the critical importance of engagement and openness rather than withdrawal and defensiveness. He called for the reaffirmation of the authority of Scripture, of Jesus as the only way of salvation, of commitment to social justice and care for the needy and the environment, as well as to deeper spirituality and authentic Christian living. He called for careful reflection on the consequences of division and conflict among evangelicals, citing the observation of theologian Alister McGrath. 'One of the most tragic aspects of the recent evangelical experience in England is that a few of its more disaffected members seem to think that abusing other evangelicals somehow amounts to defending the gospel.'[28] On this, Harry commented, 'There have been occasions when I would have regarded this as an apt comment on our own Australian situation, or even my own diocese.' He had by now ample experience to justify his claim that 'our division is our danger!' There is pain aplenty, as well as eloquence, in his diagnosis of the danger.

> Division can consume our energies, keep us increasingly focussed inward rather than outwards, and blind us to the immediacy and hazards of the intellectual challenges which endanger biblical faith commitment in our society. Evangelical division, played out on a public stage for all to observe and ponder, will eventually leave us unheard, friendless and with emptying pews, since it denies our witness to the gospel of love.

Harry appealed to those who pressed for evangelicals to leave the national church or to establish 'Bible churches' in other dioceses to remain 'firmly' within the Anglican Church of Australia, to play their part in shaping its future, to thus avoid a legacy of schism, and also to enrich their own ministry through learning from the spirituality and wisdom of others. He rehearsed the arguments he would use in the forthcoming Sydney synod for accepting as much of the *APBA* as possible, thus keeping a commitment to common prayer and liturgy, and to take advantage of the undoubted strengths in the book, such as the Funeral Service for an Infant who has died near to the time of a birth. 'The pastoral intent behind them should be applauded,' Harry argued.

He acknowledged that attesting to the exclusivity of Christ as the only way of salvation was a challenge in a pluralist multicultural society that valued inclusivity and tolerance of all views. He prayed that evangelicals would always attest to Christ alone as Saviour, while not denying that it was imperative to seek to cooperate with all in matters of common concern and to avoid laying any foundation that could lead to the justification of racism, violence or oppression.

## The effect of regionalisation

The year continued, with commemoration and new church dedication services in churches, founders' day ceremonies and head teachers' inductions in church schools, memorial services for those who had died in the police service, speaking at the ACL annual dinner, conferences on the prayer book, addressing community organisations on ethics, explaining Anglicanism in churches with NESB congregations, 'dynamic Anglicanism' in After College Training days, and

Sydney Anglicanism at bishops' conferences and synods outside the diocese. It all required great stamina and focus to find the words to encourage all these organisations and communities, in church and state, to thrive and seek to live by heaven's values while on earth.

Meanwhile, his own team of bishops and archdeacons thrived as a result of the new policies and practices arising from the regionalisation of the diocese. Regional pastoral care and central administration was the formula. It was 'brilliant ... outstanding,' said Paul Barnett.[29] Ray Smith's regional council, for example, developed a 'Vision and Mission Plan' which covered church planting among the NESB (Non-English Speaking Background) in addition to children's and youth ministry, leadership development, and community care ministries. The plan was reviewed annually by task forces. Alan Cole lent his unequivocal support to ministry among people of NESB. The work multiplied among Mandarin, Cantonese and Hakka Han speakers in Cabramatta, Marrickville and Hurstville; Vietnamese speakers in Regent's Park and Punchbowl; Arabic speakers in Greenacre and Belmore; and, at Hammondville, Hindi speakers from North India and Tamil speakers from South India. At Campsie, where Mersina Soulos, Director of Multicultural Ministries for Careforce, had devised appropriate ministries, there were 19 different ethnic groups associated with the church, including Chinese, Pakistanis and Maori. The regional council ably assisted this development, its frequently controversial and always lively quarterly meetings benefiting from the community-minded and politically engaged layperson, Eric Jones. Ray Smith, himself, visited multicultural congregations regularly. He challenged his hearers to obey Christ's command to create a church for all nations and not just one race, but he also counselled them that they have a special responsibility to reach out to those of Chinese background.[30]

Ray also encouraged his clergy to work together as teams, fostered the work of area deaneries, visited all his clergy regularly, met with first incumbents and also with assistant ministers two or three times a year, held an annual clergy conference, convened prayer gatherings, and produced *Streamline*, a regional newsletter. He gave a fresh focus to each year's programs, beginning with the year of Bible teaching, moving on to the year of prayer, then the year of evangelism, then discipleship, worship, pastoral care, small groups, and community care and involvement.[31] In all this, he constantly sought to make his program consistent with Harry's. He was gratified by the outcomes that it was an efficient means of growing churches and meeting the demographic and secular challenges of the age. It was a challenge to find ministers to go to its struggling parishes and to keep resources up to new promising ministries. It helped that the vision was so clear 'to see an expanding fellowship of healthy, growing, culturally relevant congregations that together' were 'advancing God's kingdom through conversions and disciplemaking.'[32]

Sadly, there were ministries that were casualties of regionalisation. The HMS Department of Cross-cultural Ministries under Mersina Soulos was abolished and its work devolved to the regions. When the time came for her departure, she took her shoes off and dusted them off outside St Andrew's House. She bumped into Bp Cameron who said 'I believe that you can read Greek and pronounce it correctly. Here. Read John 1.' She did and then started to cry. Bp Cameron said, 'I will pray for you every day for the rest of my life.' She needed his prayers. She was burnt out, sick for eight years and her husband left her. It took her over a decade to begin to withdraw from the despair she felt.

Part of the problem was that HMS itself was destabilised by regionalisation. In particular, the 'parish support and development' function of HMS was devolved to the regions, and at the same time it was depleted by an enervating struggle between those who argued that its welfare role was its principal one and those who wanted it to primarily help the parishes in evangelism.

## Death of Mary Andrews

On 16 October, 12 days before the opening of the 1996 synod, Harry received a phone call from Marion Gabbott. She had just been to see Deaconess Mary Andrews, missionary to China 1938–51, and then Head Deaconess and Principal of Deaconess House. She lay dying in hospital. Gasping for breath, Mary, who was always insistent on having her own way, ordered Marion to 'push hard for female ordination.' Marion was an articulate and forceful opponent of female ordination and, in her integrity and courage, the equal of her old college principal. So she said to Mary, 'I cannot do that.' But the disagreement and Mary's condition distressed her and she shared her distress with her husband, Stephen. He said to her, 'Ring Harry.' So Harry went to Deaconess Andrews and prayed with her. He was the last person to see her alive, and he spoke at her funeral.

## Synod elections

The 1996 October synod was the first ordinary session of the 44th synod. This meant elections for three-year appointments to SC. It was the first synod in which the majority of SC members were elected by regions. By the time of the election synod the regions were so controlled by the ACL that only in the Southern region did non-ACL nominees have any chance. Nevertheless, the ACL powerbrokers were not accustomed to leaving anything to chance, and Ballantine-Jones and Robert Tong met with Stephen Judd to see if a joint ticket could be agreed on. In other words, this would mean that there would be no Blue Ticket. Judd expressed the fear that the Blue Ticket would be 'dudded' by the ACL. Ballantine-Jones replied, 'I have never welched on a deal, and if the ACL did not back me they would have to find a new President.'[33]

Agreement could not be reached, however. At the end of August the ACL reported to its followers that it regretted the decision of the initiators of the Blue Ticket to run a separate ticket and impressed upon them the need to support ACL recommendations 'wholeheartedly.'[34] Tony Lamb, ACL vice-president, in a personal letter, made a last attempt to get the Blue Ticket to desist to minimise the division which had resulted from it. He conceded that the ACL had blundered in 1993, but it was now essential to rectify the damage that was being done by this division.

It was too late. Too much time and energy had been put into nominating candidates for the two tickets. In the end, there was more overlap between the recommendations of the parties than differences, but the differences were still substantial. In its first letter to members of synod, the Blue Ticket implied that the ACL had been taken over by those determined to recommend candidates from within a very narrow range of the evangelical spectrum. Whereas 'The Blue Ticket has always been proudly evangelical and, like the Anglican Church League of a previous generation, has an inclusive spirit.'

This time round, all five regional bishops wrote to synod members, urging them to exercise their vote carefully so as to elect members of committees, especially SC, who were capable of independent and strategic thinking.[35] It did not mention the Blue Ticket or the ACL, but its thrust favoured the former.

In the event, ACL won 80 per cent of contested positions, actually low by historic standards. The Blue Ticket lost Justice Peter Young, Tony McCarthy and Carol Holley, but the ACL lost Barry Newman, and by its surprising support for Rod West, recently retired Headmaster of Trinity Grammar School, gave to the Blue Ticket another supporter in SC. Most disappointing for the ACL, BBJ did not make it back on. Laurie Scandrett, another ACL victim of the Blue Ticket in 1993, did not even make it to the election. The Blue Ticket controlled SC had chosen not to elect Scandrett to synod, which meant he could not be nominated for membership of the SC. This made BBJ and the ACL leaders 'very cross' – they thought it did not show goodwill.[36] They made up for it by ensuring that Stuart Piggin suffered the same fate at the 1999 election. Individuals were getting hurt. It was an unhealthy escalation.

The new situation was not healthy for Harry, either. Not only did he lose supporters from the regions, but regionalisation meant that the SC was now bigger than it had been, increasing from 48 to 59 members, most of whom supported the ACL. Further, the archdeacons were no longer allowed to vote in SC as it was considered that this would advantage the archbishop's team too strongly, thus reinforcing centralism, which regionalisation was designed to weaken. As the result of all these developments, Harry lost any chance of controlling the SC. In fact, he could count on fewer than 20 of the 59 votes. 'It would not have mattered then if Harry had Jack Dain and Don Cameron to make their powerful speeches,' reflected Paul Barnett. Harry's opponents had the numbers.

This whole episode, right in the middle of Harry's episcopate, raised in an acute form a dilemma that is chronically faced by the Diocese of Sydney. Is political activity in the manner practised by the ACL legitimate in the Church? Does the end – namely preserving the diocese from the ravages of liberalism – justify the means? ACL leaders are aware that these misgivings constantly trouble the faithful. So, sometimes they seek to address the issue. Just before the 1996 synod there was one such attempt. Ian Carmichael, then Honorary Secretary of the ACL, wrote an article for the *ACL News* entitled 'Is Politics a Dirty Word?'[37] It made a number of good points: ACL is not *just* a political organisation – it also educates and communicates; it has to function in a political environment – synod is a political body, based on the parliamentary model; ACL gives advice on people to be elected to an electorate, too big and too busy to be informed without help; ACL has contributed to the creation of an environment where evangelicalism can flourish, a very rare experience, worldwide.

A fifth point, however, was too much for Harry. The *ACL News* article said, 'The Synodical process is not based on truth but on numbers. Decisions in Synod are made on the basis of majority opinion. Furthermore, Synod members are not always elected on the basis of their godly discernment and wisdom.'[38] On this Harry commented with uncharacteristic acerbity in his presidential address at the 1996 synod. In his previous addresses he had expressed his conviction that members should seek the mind of God and the leading of the Spirit and should therefore be open to persuasion. The more political approach, which preferred to cut to the chase and count the numbers, distressed him. He observed that, if the majority felt that way, we should give it away. He commended instead each individual making up his or her mind before God and voting accordingly, independently of group pressure. It will be an argument that goes on as long as the ACL controls the synod!

## 1996 Sydney synod

On 18 October, Glenn Davies, Rector of Miranda, wrote assuring Harry of his prayers for the 1996 synod, due to begin 10 days later. 'May God be honoured in our deliberations and may the watching world be encouraged by the manner of our debate.' His hopes were substantially realised: at the end of the synod, John Cornford wrote to Harry that he had feared, because of the matters on the agenda, synod would descend into an ungodly fight, but instead godliness was 'demonstrated by 99%.' 'Harry, that in no small measure has been due to your preparation and leadership.'[39]

The most emotion-charged matter on the agenda was consideration, for the first time after a three-year moratorium, of the proposal to ordain women to the priesthood. The previous month, Archdeacon Di Nicolios, had released her *Report on Women's Ministry*, showing that 73.5 per cent of clergy respondents to the survey were in favour of women preaching and leading services and that women in ministry constantly expressed the desire for their ministries to be 'recognised and valued.'[40] A bill before the synod, moved by Keith Mason, then Solicitor General of NSW, and seconded by Julia Baird, later a journalist with *SMH* and the ABC, proposed that women should be admitted as presbyters (priests) while denied appointment as rectors. This was designed to concede the conservatives' insistence on male headship while allowing women to preside at the Lord's Table without the necessity for diaconal or lay presidency. Harry presented all sides of the debate, reiterating that he still stood at the conservative end of the spectrum on the issue, 'while being strongly committed to advancing ministry by women in the church.' He said that he wished that he could relieve the tension attending the matter, but he did not think he could. 'If all concerned were able to concede that the issue is about how to apply the teaching of the Bible in a changed social context,' he advised, 'and not about abandoning Apostolic authority then some heat might be taken out of the debate.'[41]

Easily the longest part of his presidential address was devoted to public worship, dealing with three interrelated issues: reception of the new prayer book (the *APBA*), the need for common prayer, and the ongoing relevance of Anglican forms. Historian Brian Fletcher was to write of the 1995 General Synod adoption of the *APBA*:

> From all sides came complaints, Sydney representatives on General Synod taking so strong a stand that the book appeared doomed. Fortunately their wise and moderate Archbishop, Harry Goodhew, saved the day by insisting that earlier prayer books remain in existence

> and proposing that within his diocese individual parishes could use the book only with the archbishop's permission.[42]

But saving the day in the wider church meant losing it in his own diocese. Harry insisted that the matter was bigger than whether or not the *APBA* should be adopted. The issue in Sydney was whether or not there would be any common prayer or liturgical worship in diocesan churches. Harry reminded synod that the matter had a legal component that was not easily set aside. 'When you elected me archbishop of this diocese you required me to promise to uphold its laws and regulations.'[43] Then Harry turned to the fundamental issue of the relevance of Anglicanism to reaching the lost for Christ.

> I have referred on numerous occasions to the idea of being Dynamically Anglican. Initially I too smiled at the mirth with which this idea was greeted … I smile no longer. I think it may point to a deep malaise. It could witness to a deep uncertainty about who we are … I do not detect the same embarrassment among Baptists, Roman Catholics or Presbyterians.[44]

There followed his fullest explanation of dynamic Anglicanism. He said that Anglicanism has four dimensions – theological, public worship, ministry, ethos – and he went on to explain that

> These four dimensions operate **dynamically** when those who hold them are infused with love for God and for others; when they walk by the Spirit and are empowered by him; when they endeavour to be contemporary without being shallow; when they are both maintenance and mission minded; when they grow where they are planted, and while functioning with common forms, display a flexibility appropriate to their commitments and situation. At the heart of an Anglicanism which is truly dynamic is anointed preaching. Such preaching is born of God's Word, prayer and the operation of the Spirit. It is loving, warm and passionate. It is the most powerful medium used by God for the edification of his people.[45]

In the event, both the motion to allow female ordination and that to allow the use of the *APBA* were rejected by similar margins. In the House of Laity, the vote was close but negative, the clergy decidedly negative. Bruce Ballantine-Jones and others thought they detected a shift in Harry's position towards the acceptance of women's ordination.[46] They were not the only ones with sensitive antennae on the subject. A reporter said to Harry after the vote, 'You seem to be divided over the issue.' 'That was very perceptive of him,' Harry thought.

Following the first SC after the synod (18 November 1996), a weary Harry invited me to have coffee with him. He confessed that he was disappointed by the synod. Robert Forsyth had lost by one vote to conservative Peter Tasker for election to the presentation board;[47] Phillip Heath, the much-respected Headmaster of St Andrew's Cathedral School, had been beaten by a conservative woman for the South Sydney regional council; and Archdeacon Diane Nicolios's report on women[48] was again given scant regard and put off entirely until February 1997 without endorsing any part of it. Harry was worried by the hardliners, whom he felt had committed themselves to 'saving the Diocese.' I told him I had met that day with Grant Maple, then director of the Anglican Education Commission, who suggested that we should attempt to undermine the confidence of the hardliners. Harry admitted that his own confidence in the case against female ordination was being undermined. He doubted if the passage in I Corinthians 11 supported opposition to female ordination and he urged my side in the political struggle to put out a steady stream of material to undermine the No case.

At the time of writing (2020), while the hardliners have not been undermined, and female ordination to the presbyterate is still not approved in the Diocese of Sydney, the value of Harry's thinking, on common prayer and liturgy, has not been so permanently resisted. Archdeacon Lindsay Stoddart was one who profoundly respected Harry's views on the prayer book. He had long concluded that Harry was 'highly intelligent', that he was in the habit of making decisions in a 'well thought out manner' and that his position on the prayer book was 'well thought through.'[49] In 2013 the diocese produced a book entitled *Common Prayer: Resources for Gospel-Shaped Gatherings*. At the back of the book are numerous acknowledgments of material from the much-feared *APBA*. The long-term effect of thinking like Harry's on the Australian church is perceptively, if optimistically, conveyed by historian Brian Fletcher.

> The Australian church ... was highly conscious of belonging to something larger than itself. It was part of a family and needed to bear this in mind when re-examining itself. This family might be growing more diversified but it also had shared beliefs and values that bound it together. No branch of the church was prepared to follow a path likely to lead it into the wilderness. National overtones had crept into the life of every province but there was still an overriding consciousness of belonging to a single Christian communion. The new nationally oriented prayer books and hymnals had much in common making worship possible for Anglicans no matter where they travelled. The

Australian church was conscious of this and took this factor into account when preparing its own revisions. Autonomy was conditional and not absolute. It freed the church in unprecedented ways but did not alter the fact that it owed allegiance to the church that had given birth to Anglicanism.[50]

## Indigenous ministry

Meanwhile, back at the 1996 synod, an event occurred that Tom Mayne, who three decades earlier had worked alongside Harry in Ceduna, took to be 'a miraculous work of the Spirit of God.'[51] Mayne moved a motion, seconded by John McIntyre, the Rector of St Saviour's, Redfern, and later Bishop of Gippsland, requesting $1.2 million, spread over four years, for the support of Indigenous ministry. They had done their homework, revealing that the Anglican Church was well behind other churches in the resources it devoted to Indigenous work. Before the synod they made presentations around the diocese, to which the response was one of 'breathtaking negativity.' 'Great idea, Tom,' was the common theme, 'but it has no hope of succeeding.'

In his presidential address, Harry had explained that the purpose of the grant was to create a trust and use the income generated to train Indigenous ministers to work among their own people, that the diocese had the largest concentration of Aboriginal people in Australia, that much needed to be done to make amends for the impact white people have had on them, and that he hoped a positive response would be made to this challenge.

Mayne and McIntyre were competent synod performers, and both made moving speeches. Then Revd David Mulready, Rector of Penrith, moved to amend the motion to 'direct' rather than merely 'request' SC to create the fund. When the vote on the amendment was taken on the voices, it appeared to be lost. But Mulready asked for a count, which resulted in the amendment being passed. When the amended motion was put, it was carried 640 to nil. All were mightily moved, none more than Tom Mayne himself.

> This was a miracle. As we later learned, before we addressed the Synod the Indigenous visitors in the public gallery sensed, 'God is here – we can feel it'. We felt overwhelmingly humbled, realising that this was not something we could boast about but rather, it was the work of the Holy Spirit.

Always eager to capitalise quickly on any propitious development, Harry rang Tom Mayne the morning after the passage of the motion to discuss the appointment of the Aboriginal Task Force. The matter was dear to Harry's heart, and he was able to hit the ground running because, two months before the synod, he had been in correspondence with Archdeacon Alan Donohoo, who had suggested the names of those who might serve on an 'Archbishop's Committee for Aboriginal Strategy'[52] (later termed the Task Force). The first meeting of the Task Force was held on 1 November 1996.

If the passage of the motion was a miracle, perhaps an equally great miracle followed. Standing Committee went beyond what had been asked of it, approving the whole $1.2 million grant in the first year. Harry may have lost control of SC, but evidently the Lord had not! The church had been awakened to its responsibility to First Australians, largely through the 1992 Mabo case (see chapter14), and the conscience of Christians on Aboriginal disadvantage had been enlightened by the publication in 1990 of John Harris's moving, monumental study of the Aboriginal experience of Christianity, *One Blood*.[53]

With Harry in a mind to do what he could to redress racism, the ever-alert Alan Cole pressed him to also strengthen the Church's commitment to multicultural ministries. Cole consistently pushed the need for ministry to the Chinese, and, shortly after synod, wrote to Harry urging him to meet with Ernest Chau, who was leading the Chinese churches in establishing the funding of evangelism among the Chinese under the new regionalism.[54]

At the same time, the retirement of Thomas Smith as Director of the Anglican Youth Department gave Harry the opportunity to reflect on another of his passions – ministry to youth. A layperson of exceptional integrity, Tom Smith embraced the challenges of a rounded ministry to youth. Living the faith as well as proclaiming it, his heart as well as his mind were engaged in bringing young people to maturity, both discipled and disciplers. Like Tom, Harry was burdened both by the current social problems facing youth, especially suicide and drugs, and by how critical youth were to the future of the church. 'They will be the future clergy, the parish leaders, and the missionaries and evangelists of tomorrow.'[55] In the following year, ministry to youth was reorganised under the banner of 'Youthworks', and in 1998 Lindsay Stoddart was appointed its first CEO, and the Youthworks College formed to give specialised training to youth ministers.

With lots of new initiatives testifying to the vitality of the Church, Harry was happy. Just before Christmas, he and Pam travelled to Wollongong for a farewell to Peter and Elizabeth Smart. Peter was leaving his role as Headmaster of TIGS (where he had been as effective as Harry knew he would be) to become diocesan registrar working with and for Harry. That was to make Harry happier still.

# 18

# Fifth Year (1997): The Coin of Transcendence

At the beginning of 1997, now midway through his episcopate, Harry reset his personal goals. He wanted to maintain the increased impetus for cross-cultural and indigenous ministry, and to continue to reform ministerial training. It was a year of frequent meetings with his own Liturgical Panel, with the Aboriginal Task Force, with Howard Dillon, CEO of Anglicare, now reconstituted as a national corporation, and of fundraising for the refurbishment of St Andrew's Cathedral. The second half of his time in office was to be more concerned with the international work and character of the church. From 17 to 27 February he was in the United States, a visit that included attendance at the EE Board Meeting; from 18 April to 13 May he was in the United Kingdom and Africa, a trip that included participation in a service in Westminster Abbey and meeting with the Archbishop of Canterbury; and from 22 September to 2 October he was again in the United States, this time to join with conservative bishops to prepare for Lambeth '98. In subsequent years he would spend even more time abroad. In Australia he invested much time and thought in three major events: a first-ever National Anglican Conference in Canberra in February; the Melbourne Clergy Conference in June; and the visit of the Archbishop of Canterbury to Australia in August.

## Peter Smart, registrar and archdeacon

At the beginning of 1997, Peter Smart took over from Stan Skillicorn as diocesan registrar with a brief to assist the archbishop. Bp Watson saw that Peter needed a parish to go along with his diocesan administrative duties; he needed to mix with people. So, on 30 January, Peter was collated as archdeacon and instituted as Curate-in-Charge of Christ Church, Lavender Bay. Harry preached. For the first couple of years, Peter's wife, Elizabeth, really ran the parish. It grew and, after a few years, became a full parish. When Harry left, Peter stayed on for a year as Registrar with Peter Jensen before becoming the full-time rector of Lavender Bay.

'Peter Smart', said Wollongong lawyer, Peter Kell, 'is a very quiet, but clever man.' A good judge of character, Peter Smart knew Harry's strengths. He thought, for example, that Harry dealt with the media in an exceptional way. 'He was always so cooperative and he did a terrific job for the diocese in the city of Sydney.' But Peter was surprised at how little power Harry seemed to have. He was not the headmaster, observed Peter, who had himself been a very successful headmaster. Harry, Peter noticed, never told anybody what to do. 'He never exerted that kind of thrust you might have expected.' He got things done without betraying himself, but, in Peter's view, he could have pulled rank more. It is an interesting observation. Few have been closer to Harry than Peter Smart, but even he had difficulty in appreciating just how comprehensively Harry practised non-assertive servant leadership. He was very aware of his responsibility as archbishop, but he was never tempted to 'play the rank.'

Elizabeth Smart was concerned that Peter would be giving up something by coming under Harry and would no longer be in charge. But Peter did not find this a problem. He became part of a four-person team alongside Harry, Ruth Sefton, Harry's personal assistant, and Sally Gail, who had been Peter's receptionist at TIGS and had agreed to come to Sydney to be his personal assistant. Each day, Ruth would deal with 300–400 emails and then sort the postal mail and take it to Peter to deal with. There were lots of meetings. Peter dealt with all the complaints and signed all the licences.

Peter was also welcomed into Harry's leadership team. He found that Harry's bishops were of one mind and he always felt accepted as an equal. Every week, Peter met with them, and with the archdeacons whenever they were there. He enjoyed it. 'All arguments were settled and to a man they supported Harry.' He understood that Harry wanted his bishops to support their men – he wanted them to be on the ground holding their men up in a pastoral sense, and 'they were all good at that.' Peter's experience reinforces the view that Harry's leadership team was united, happy and effective. They were endlessly criticised by Harry's opponents for not being more politically potent, but this was the frustrated bleating of those who believed they could do a better job – an untestable belief!

Peter wonders if Harry expected him to 'exercise oratory' in SC and synod, but he quickly detected that, whenever he spoke, people thought he was speaking for Harry and that effectively silenced him. Peter hated SC. It was so negative, so divisive. 'We went into Standing Committee knowing in advance what every vote would be. It was always 23–21. I found that horrible.' Harry survived it, but he may have put up with too much baloney. 'Marcus would have shut them up. And Peter [Jensen, Harry's successor] did not have to put up with the nonsense: with him they were like clap dogs.'[1]

## Low-fee Anglican schools

The 1997 meeting of bishops of the Province of New South Wales (6–7 February) agreed to the need for common province-wide protocols for the vetting of children's workers, another step in the slow march towards insulating the church against child abuse. The bishops also received with enthusiasm a report on the development of Anglican low-fee schools. 'Such development was seen as crucial to seize the "Window of Opportunity" recently opened. Our Anglican profile will be raised, a serious gap in our society involvement will be filled, and fulfilment of our gospel mission will be enhanced.'[2] Offering a Christian education that the less affluent could afford was not the only gap filled by the multiplication of Christian schools. They effectively replaced Sunday schools, which had been the chief instrument for the training and development of young people in Christian values, and which had been in decline since the 1960s.

## National Anglican Conference, Canberra, 8–12 February

The close proximity and ongoing friendship of Harry and Revd Dr Bruce Kaye, General Secretary of the Anglican Church of Australia, now bore fruit in a unique development for the Anglican Church. The SC of General Synod, in October 1994, approved Bruce Kaye's idea of a national conference of Anglicans. It would mark the 150th anniversary of the Australian Anglican Church as a separate province of the Anglican Communion. But it was concerned with the future, not the past. 'Exploring our Future: Anglicans in Australia in the Third Millennium' was directed to helping Anglicans engage more effectively with Australian society. A steering committee had been appointed in March 1995 under Harry's oversight. There was an awareness that religion had retreated from public engagement into private spirituality and an inward-looking preoccupation. It was time to 'listen to society with respect'; 'identify where we are as Australians'; 'understand … cultural diversity, pluralism, postmodern environment'; and 'develop our Christian public discourse.' The specific aims included fostering youth leadership, lay and indigenous participation, and it was to be a listening conference, 'learning from each other.'[3]

Such an Australia-wide conference had never been held before, and not all Anglicans were as open as Harry to the idea, as Bruce Kaye recalls.

> Harry was appointed as Chair as part of a political deal to provide some cover from Sydney and to have someone who could be relied on for keeping to the integrity of the plan … After Harry was appointed, BBJ sought me out to tell me that appointing Harry in no way implied support from Sydney.[4]

On the program committee were two Sydney evangelicals, Robert Forsyth and Ralph Bowles, then Rector of Coorparoo. Kaye reported to Harry that they were both 'very content with the program.'⁵ But Margaret Rodgers, CEO of Sydney Anglican Media, observed that 'no obvious concessions' had been made in the program to attract 'Sydney people', and that two of the speakers, Dorothy Lee and Elizabeth Templeton, had a 'liberal hermeneutic' which would not 'attract Sydney.'⁶ Professor Lee was invited to give Bible studies during the times of worship at the conference. She was chosen in preference to Desmond Tutu, who was suggested, but did not receive support.

Revd Tim Foster, Associate Minister of Gymea Anglican Church, expressed to the archbishop his grave concern that the opening of the conference would feature an Aboriginal smoking 'cleansing' ceremony. To share in such a ceremony would be to 'participate with demons,' he argued. 'This concession to political correctness is nothing less than idolatry... to "cleanse" the place from evil spirits through an idolatrous ceremony is only to invite them in.' He asked Harry to withdraw his endorsement of the conference.⁷ Harry replied that if the ceremony were as he said it was 'a serious matter.' He consulted Arthur Malcolm, Aboriginal Assistant Bishop of the Northern Territory, and was able to report back to Tim Foster that the ceremony, which was important to Aboriginal people, 'carries the connotation of repentance.' Harry added, 'Like you, I find myself in some difficulty when it comes to understanding what occasions mean to people of a totally different culture. I can only take guidance from those who understand the situation better than I do.'⁸

In the event, 38 Sydney people registered. Margaret Rodgers expected them to be 'from a small number of parishes which [were] not central to the mainline views of the Diocese.'⁹ Among them, however, was John Woodhouse, Rector of Christ Church, St Ives, and a future principal of Moore College. It was hoped that 500–750 from all around the country might attend.¹⁰ In fact, 800 attended full-time and 250 more on a daily basis. Partly because nothing had been tried like this before, more people wanted to come to this event than there were places to put them. It was held on the campus of the Australian National University. 'Clearly the Conference struck a chord' and the conference generated a profit of almost $50,000.¹¹

'Coming up to this conference was like preparing for a wedding,' said Harry afterwards, 'a great deal of thought and even nervousness – and then the day comes.'¹² Harry had invited the prime minister, John Howard, to address the conference, advising him that it would be 'the largest and most representative gathering in the history of our church.'¹³ Howard was happy to accept – as was Kim Beazley, Leader of the Opposition. Howard and Beazley, both professing Christians, spoke first. 'It was important to have our political leaders here,' said Harry, 'they set

18.1 Harry, Kim Beazley (Leader of the Opposition), John Howard (Prime Minister), and Keith Rayner (Primate) at the National Anglican Conference, 1997.

the context for us. We want to be appropriate, helpful, challenging in our own Australian context and to have them there was very meaningful.'[14] Howard said he respected and valued the voice of the churches on so many issues, and that while he could not say that his government would necessarily agree with that voice, it would always be listened to carefully. Beazley thought the church was especially equipped to address pride and self-justification and to bring a voice of justice and humility to the pressing matter of Aboriginal reconciliation. In this matter especially, there was need for the still voice of conscience and no-one was better placed to proffer this than the members of this conference and the religious community.

Harry was of the view that the best and informed minds reflecting on our national life were needed to tell us what the situation was, 'and then we can address it.' So, a number of social analysts addressed the conference.[15] Bettina Cass, Professor of Sociology at the University of Sydney, whose research had been so valued by the diocese in the Year of the Family (1994), reviewed challenges to family life and the nature of policies required to support families in a neoliberal age of economic rationalism. Social commentator, Hugh McKay, suggested that intergenerational differences were less understood than multicultural differences, but that all the generations had one thing in common: insecurity. Professor Julian Disney, Director of the Centre for International and Public Law at the Australian National University, spoke on the need for a stronger contribution on social policy from churches. They seem to be more energised, he observed, by debates on theological matters that, to the outsider, do not seem to merit the time and attention devoted to them. This observation occasioned rueful laughter from conferees who had suffered from the current obsession with lay presidency.

Large wall hangings were also unveiled. This project was co-ordinated by the General Synod's Women's Commission, assisted by the Mothers' Union, and designed by Sydney artist, Vicki Conomy. The hangings, said Harry, gathered up the feelings of a large number of people in a beautiful way. Dr Ruth Shatford, who chaired the Women's Commission, said the hangings allowed women to express their views in ways other than the written word. They were designed to convey 'the joy and pain, hope and confusion of women's current experience' celebrating the contribution that women offered society and the church of the future.[16]

Canon John Peterson, Secretary-General of the Anglican Consultative Council, reeling from witnessing the effects of the Rwanda genocide, urged Anglicans to work together as a global family, a family under fire, a family of suffering. Scottish theologian, Elizabeth Templeton, spoke of the significance of the gospel.

> It means that where anyone: child, man, woman, criminal, physically or mentally handicapped person, atheist, agnostic, Hindu, divorcee, lesbian – where anyone, however fragile, however lonely, however bitter, however dehumanised, comes in touch with us as Christian community, we are to meet them as Christ, – **them** as Christ, not us as Christ.[17]

Bill Lawton, then serving on the Liturgical Commission, challenged conferees with 'the immense task of rewriting liturgy and reinventing church in the face of injustices that scar our society and let's do it in company with those who shape our reality from below, make again the model of our community the little child, the poor, the oppressed.' Listening to the needy became, perhaps, the main emphasis of the conference.

Graham Cole, Principal of Ridley College, observed that a pluralist culture needs to see how people disagree in the bonds of peace. Presentations and worship led by Aboriginal leaders and young people filled Harry with hope. With others, Harry sat with a group of Aboriginal Christians, listening to them tell their own personal stories. One in particular rivetted him.

> A woman, maybe in her late 50's, testified to two things: her faith in Christ and a life of terrible abuse suffered by her and her children at the hands of her former husband.
>
> She told how grateful she was for the first and for those who had brought the message of Christ to her and how terrible the second had been.
>
> She recalled how, in desperation, she was driven finally to lay hands on a gun, to load it, and to wait for her drunken spouse to return. The time of waiting was filled with agonising conflict. The memories of past treatment meted out to her and her children filled her with pain and rage. Terror generated confusion and desperation.

> She heard the voice from Hell urging her to deal once and for all with the source of her pain and confusion. Yet too, she heard the voice of her Saviour. What she contemplated was not his way. The inner conflict raged. As the door opened and her husband entered it reached a terrifying crescendo.
>
> 'The Lord', she said quietly, 'prevailed'. Trembling and exhausted she unloaded the gun, and spared her husband's life.

Harry was powerfully impressed by the strength and beauty represented in her person and speech.[18]

The conference was a personal triumph for Harry. Deserving of much of the credit for its success were Bruce Kaye, the mastermind behind it, George Browning, Bishop of Canberra Goulburn, who laboured untiringly to host the conference, consistently espousing unity within the Anglican Church,[19] and Archbishop Rayner of Melbourne, whose support was unstinting. But it was Harry's leadership that gave to the event the warmth generated by the discovery of an unexpected and delightful unity. Canon Peterson wrote afterwards to Harry:

> Your presence had an enormous impact on the Conference. Everyone appreciated the kind and gentle way in which you received people. You are doing a magnificent job and we are grateful for your leadership in Sydney.... The concerns of the Church as you look forward to the Third Millennium were articulated in the Conference and your role in enabling that to happen was most significant.[20]

At the meeting of General Synod in February of the following year (1998), president and primate, Archbishop Keith Rayner would report:

> It is just a year since the National Anglican Conference took place in Canberra. I do not recall a more exciting event in the life of our national church. What began as a risky experiment in the mind of our General Secretary emerged under the chairmanship of Archbishop Goodhew as an inspiring, unifying and seminal event for our church.

Recalling the event over 20 years later, Kimberly Sawyer, an assistant minister at St Andrew's Cathedral and Chaplain of St Catherine's School, said that it was a great occasion. Harry so impressed her with his gracious chairing of the conference and his capacity to bring together Anglicans of all ages and diverse traditions, that she resolved there and then to model her own style of ministry on his.[21]

## Chappo's letter

On 4 April 1997, Harry's mum turned 90. He always called her 'Mother' and left instructions that the whole day was to be kept free for her. On the same day, John Chapman wrote to Harry about the 1996 synod and Harry's *Ad Clerum* on the prayer book (31 January 1997) where he had reminded his clergy of their promise, when ordained, to use only the prayer book when leading their congregations in worship, or an alternative, if permitted by lawful authority. Chappo had been a student with Harry at Moore College, as we have seen, always thought of Harry and Pam as close friends, and was much loved by Harry's children. He had rejoiced in Harry's appointment as the Bishop of Wollongong and, while Harry had not been his first choice as archbishop, he came a close second, in Chappo's estimation, to Paul Barnett. Now he had come to believe that Harry was the right man for the job, but his relationship with Harry had become more complicated during his time as archbishop.

In particular, Chappo disagreed with what he perceived to be Harry's growing insistence on conformity to prayer book liturgical worship. He argued that those who grew up with the youth services conducted in the evenings in Sydney parishes, from the late 1960s, could not be happy in structured, liturgical worship. They had become used to variety, experimentation and a relaxed approach to worship, and Chappo believed that it was essential to allow the experimentation and variety to continue. Most churchgoers no longer had loyalty to a denomination; they were united in the gospel and would go wherever the Bible was clearly taught.

Chappo observed that, in Sydney in a typical parish, three services had developed: a liturgical service, a family service loosely based on page 39 of *An Australian Prayer Book* (*AAPB*), and the experimental evening youth service. He thought that was working very well. It gave people variety and choice, and at least one of the three seemed to suit the needs of most. If people were forced to depart from this pattern, it would be bad news. 'Brother,' wrote a clearly passionate Chappo,

> we did not elect you to uphold the law! Nothing was further from our mind. The reason why the Synod elected you ... was because we believed you would be flexible with regard to law. Your supporters assured us that this would be the case.

Chappo reminded Harry that it was he, Harry, who had set the diocese along the road to experimentation in worship. He had introduced informal elements into the evening services at Coorparoo, which had been so well received; it was he who encouraged church leaders to hear and heed Bill Hybels and his 'user friendly' services;[22] it was he who, in his address at the ACL dinner immediately before the election synod, had insisted on 'visionary leadership.'[23]

To this letter to Harry, Chappo attached the draft of an article that he had intended to submit to *Southern Cross*, but then thought better of it as it looked too adversarial to Harry, which was not its real intention. Its real intention was to express his conviction that despair must inevitably result from any attempt to reform Anglicanism through the synod. He gave, as an example, Harry's indication that he would withhold assent to the ordinance on lay presidency. The archbishop, argued Chappo,

> gave as his reason for this that, since he was the Archbishop for the whole Diocese, and that since 40% of the representatives of the parishes did not want this, it would be pastorally irresponsible to allow something which 40% did not want. I found this very difficult reasoning to follow. Is he not the Archbishop of the 60% who want the change? … Why are Archbishops like this?

Part of the reason, Chappo contended, was that archbishops tended to be in their early 60s by the time of their appointment and were therefore conservative. This argument had some flaws – most of Sydney's archbishops had not been in their 60s when appointed; there had been very few instances where archbishops had withheld assent; and Harry was not conservative in his thinking in spite of his age. But affable Chappo was lethal in debate, and he had two more arguments to make.

First, archbishops tend to become defenders of the law, but they would never have been elected on a 'law and order' ticket. Their supporters made certain promises on their behalf to election synods; they should tell the candidates the promises they have made, and it is a great pity that candidates do not hear the synod addresses of their supporters. Those frustrated with Harry were quick to point out that those who campaigned for him in the election synod had over promised. A bit like Barack Obama, once he became president; he could only disappoint, so great had been the claims made for him in his election campaign. It is, of course, debatable whether successful candidates are obliged to fulfil the promises made on their behalf by their supporters. Harry had always been insistent that he could not be beholden to any of his supporters.

Second, Chappo suspected that bishops get infected by the 'bishops' club'. They keep meeting each other without any clergy or lay people present, and in such a setting evangelical bishops are easily 'nobbled' by the rest. Such meetings of the club should be discouraged, as they watered down the decisions of diocesan synods in ways always 'contrary to the gospel.'[24] Such an argument, with its foundation in suspicion of bishops, is very Sydney. And Harry was not doing a lot to demonstrate that it was unjustified! It is, in fact, an argument grounded in the long history of what can happen to evangelical Anglicans when they become bishops: they are tempted to move beyond evangelical boundaries and see the pluses in other parties of the Anglican communion. It was famously (if unreliably) reported of the improbably named Field Flowers Goe, third Bishop of Melbourne (1887–1901), who was an evangelical and strong CMS supporter, that on his appointment as bishop, he said, 'I've been known previously as an Evangelical — henceforth I will not be known as anything.'[25] Or George Henry Stanton, another evangelical, after his consecration by many bishops in St Paul's Cathedral, London, observed, 'In virtue of such rich and wide consecrating grace, your Bishop feels that he ought to be as large-minded and open-hearted as is the great Anglican branch of Christ's Catholic Church.'[26]

Chappo had history as well as experience to back his argument, but it did not fit Harry well. Goe and Stanton were both at Oxford together and were far more exposed to, and shaped by, other schools of tradition than Harry ever was. No, Harry remained as evangelical and as evangelistic as ever; it was just that he believed that the wording of the prayer book better preserved the gospel than the unauthorised, unvetted formulations of those who wanted to do their own thing.

## Melbourne Clergy Conference

From 16 to 18 June 1997, Harry spoke at the Melbourne Clergy Conference, on the theme 'Ministering on the Edge of a New Era.' He did a lot of preparation and gave three Bible studies and a workshop. The catalyst for the conference was the 1996 NCLS. Harry had always supported the survey over the years. His workshop on the leadership required to grow local congregations was crammed with insights based on his long experience and contained much practical advice. While insisting that leadership in the local church is the key to progress, it has little to do with the leader himself and much to do with the congregation. 'The progress of the Led is what is significant. Leadership is that which enables the Led to make progress. The Led not the Leader.'[27] Harry believed that most leaders are not born; leadership must and could be learned. He agreed that, in most congregations, leadership is best if it is shared, collaborative, rather than exercised by one person. Leadership is not a position: it is an action. It is concerned with results, not status. Of the 13 specific practical recommendations with which Harry ended his workshop, the last two are the most distinctively Harry:

- Love people.
- Never, never, never give up.

Perhaps the really surprising thing about Harry's contribution to this conference came not from the practical voice of experience in his workshop, but in his challenge to hard thinking in his three Bible studies. He there demonstrated his profound interest and skill in big-picture apologetics. On the verge of the third millennium, with the help of St Paul in 2 Corinthians, Harry argued that the gospel, when first proclaimed two millennia earlier, created a new era, and that this development should 'constitute our whole understanding of life' rather than any gospel created in response to either modernity or postmodernity.

> All Christian life and ministry ... is 'New Age' or 'New Covenant' life and ministry. As those who bear responsibility for the churches we must maintain ourselves within those parameters and assist our churches and individuals both to know and to function within the framework of that big picture. There is a new song to be sung today, a contemporary version of the original melody.[28]

It is a song that ministers of the gospel must continue to sing with enthusiasm. So, he shared with them many keys to vitality in Christian ministry. One such key – allowing one's heart to be 'affected' through meditation on God's word – he was to develop into a lecture for Moore College students in September. 'The fruits of this fruitful delight in what God has made known is a perennial "greenness", a fruitfulness in all seasons.'[29] His insights into this vitalising spiritual discipline were to mature into a book, *Green: Growing Deep in a Shallow World*, which he wrote for the EE Training Centre in Fiji.[30] Harry's teaching here recalls that of the 12th-century abbess, Hildegaard of Bingen. She said that words did not exist to communicate the power of Christ to refresh the soul, so she coined a new Latin word. She called Christ himself *viriditas*, the greening. Few better exemplified freshness, openness and vitality in ministry than Harry himself. It was quite remarkable, given his workload and the pressures brought to bear on him, that he was able to keep up his reading in the four areas that interested him most; the theology of the Scriptures, arguments for the truth of Christianity, vital spirituality, and church growth. The prayers of those who undertook to pray for strength for him in body and mind as well as in spirit were being answered conspicuously. Those prayers were much needed for, not only was his workload physically exhausting, he was not without health issues that were to resurface early in 1998.

## Visit of the Archbishop of Canterbury

The year 1997 was a significant one in the history of the Australian Anglican

Church. The Archbishop of Canterbury visited Australia for the sesquicentenary of three Australian dioceses (Adelaide, Melbourne and Newcastle) and of the reconstitution of the Diocese of Sydney.[31] On 20 April 1997, Harry had attended and participated in a service in Westminster Abbey for the sesquicentenary of the consecration of the three new bishops for Australia. He took advantage of his time in the United Kingdom to visit Scotland and, on 29 April 1997, he wrote to his mother, who revered her Scottish ancestry.

> Dear Mother,
> ... I threw a few cabers in practice for the meeting of the clans in September. I think I like Glencoe most of all. We also visited Culloden and walked the Royal Mile in 'Auld Reekie'. We saw a Scottish minister taking a service in a clergyman's kilt. He looked great. I coveted one for a service in St Andrew's Cathedral!

From 4 to 6 August 1997, the 103rd Archbishop of Canterbury, George Carey, and his wife Eileen, visited Sydney for the sesquicentenary. It was a long planned-for visit. Early in Harry's episcopate, a visit from the Archbishop of Canterbury had been suggested for Easter 1995. Harry then asked his team to sound out how positively that would be received.[32] It seemed that the response would be 'half-hearted at best'; some were ambivalent about Archbishop Carey, there had been a very poor turn out for Archbishop Runcie's visit in 1988, and few welcomed the idea of yet another conference on evangelism that the archbishop would be asked to address.[33] Carey was an evangelical, but he approved of the ordination of women, was more tolerant of homosexuals, agreeing to ordain them if they remained celibate, and was relaxed about more Charismatic worship – all red rags to the Sydney bull.

In the planning, which had begun two years before the event, Sydney was a bit of an afterthought and was allocated only one day of the archbishop's time. Harry therefore wrote to the primate, Archbishop Rayner. 'Given the length of time of his stay in Australia, and the proposed time commitments in other Dioceses, I think anything less than two days could be viewed here as a slight to the foundation Diocese of this country.'[34]

The secular press, uninterested in the fact that the Archbishop of Canterbury was coming primarily to take a mission in Newcastle, proclaimed that he was coming to 'hose Sydney down.'[35] Carey was forthright in his declaration of where he differed from Sydney. 'I believe in the ordination of women. I believe that it is biblical. I believe it is right.'[36] But he also insisted that he believed in 'the Gospel that Sydney preaches' and that he would feel at home there. He was already on good terms with Harry and looked forward to spending time with him.

The visit, though now extended to three days, was far too short to accommodate all the Anglican organisations in Sydney that asked for the benediction of his presence. Ivan Head, whom Harry had installed as Warden of St Paul's College in the University of Sydney on 5 March 1995, asked ambitiously for two visits from the archbishop. Because the archbishop's itinerary was already set in concrete, he was granted neither. But a postscript to his request did him no damage. 'PPS. A suggestion for the Olympics? The 360° counter clockwise thurible swing (when lit) with full pike to the left – Degree of Difficulty 3.6???'[37]

The detailed planning included arranging for the archbishop to arrive in Sydney from Newcastle by seaplane, to be taken on a yacht on a cruise of Sydney Harbour, and to ride in a five-seat Bell Jetranger helicopter from Sydney Grammar School, Rushcutter's Bay, to The King's School at Parramatta, and then back to Government House. The NSW police provided 'a green light corridor' to facilitate vehicle expedition on the route, and the Archbishop of Canterbury expressed the wish that such a system operated in London. The visit included a lunch with Bob Carr, Premier of New South Wales, and afternoon tea with the prime minister. On Harry's prompting, Carey encouraged the prime minister to retain the reference to 'Almighty God' in the preamble to any revised Australian constitution. The visit also included a state government reception, a citizen's dinner, and a national liturgical celebration in St Andrew's Cathedral at which Archbishop Carey preached. 'We, as Christians, must be suitably humble as we celebrate these anniversaries, for we are in the presence of and in the lands of people whose religious experience goes back thousands of years.'

The Citizens' Dinner for the archbishop on 6 August in the Wentworth Hotel, which was attended by 362 people, was compered by Geraldine Doogue. Phillip Jensen objected as she was a divorced Roman Catholic, but Dr Susan Conde from radio station 2UE adjudged the archbishop's visit to be 'a triumph.' Peter O'Brien, Deputy Principal of Moore College, considered the Citizen's Dinner a very happy occasion and an excellent means of building bridges into the community in the city. He also thought Carey's visit had been very worthwhile; the staff and students of Moore College enjoyed having him and he reciprocated.[38] At a meeting of the college staff, Carey asked what was it that set Sydney apart from the rest of the Anglican Communion – a daring question and leading with the proverbial chin. To this Robert Doyle, lecturer in Church History, responded that it was because Sydney, unlike most in the Anglican Communion, got the gospel right. Carey was far from affronted by Doyle's candour. He later wrote to Harry,

> What I believe we must do in the Anglican Communion is to affirm all

the many good things that Sydney is doing – in the field of evangelism, outreach and social care. Frankly, the rest of the Church is not getting this message at all.[39]

Among the good things Sydney had done, Carey added, was to appoint Harry as its archbishop. 'I came away very encouraged by what I saw and felt there was a huge affirmation of your leadership.'[40] Harry took advantage of the visit of George Carey to discuss with him a projected visit to Dallas, United States, to develop tactics for the forthcoming 1998 Lambeth Conference, at which Harry was to make quite a mark.

## Memorial service for Diana

On 6 September 1997, a memorial service was held at St Andrew's Cathedral for Princess Diana, killed in a car crash a week earlier. Harry had already preached at a memorial service for Diana in Canberra four days earlier. That morning he had rung his mother, who had turned 90 the previous month, and in a husky voice she told him, 'I cried all day yesterday.'[41] In his Canberra sermon, he berated, not only the press, but the voyeurism of us all. 'The intrusive activities of those who feed our lust for knowledge of the intimacies of the lives of celebrities may well have occasioned her death.'[42] The Sydney service was not the easiest of occasions. Mourners started arriving for the 11 am service at 7.30, and the doors were closed at 10 am after between 800 and 1,000 had crowded into the cathedral, where the seating is uncomfortable at the best of times. A crowd of equal size stood outside in inclement weather, watching the 80-minute service on TV monitors placed in the adjacent Town Hall Square. Harry went outside to speak to the crowd. The prefects of St Andrew's Cathedral School handed out tissues to weeping mourners. A reporter photographed a weeping woman and her child, and the woman chased her, screaming, 'Go away! You are the ones who bloody started this.' The steps leading up to the communion table and the table itself were buried with flowers; large bouquets and carnations (600 of them distributed by the cathedral staff), daffodils, gardenias and roses.

Such calamities call for preaching addressed to the tender heart. In his sermon, Harry spoke of the binding effect of tragedy.

> The occasions when the international community is at one are few. Today is one such occasion. Around the world people of all ranks and stations are grieving: rich and poor, the famous and the unknown. They are, for a brief time at least, united in sorrow by the untimely and violent death of Diana, Princess of Wales ...

Harry's words, 'The simple fact is that the world loved Diana,' were taken up by the *Sunday Telegraph* as the headline for its coverage of the service. A reason why she was loved, observed Harry, was that 'Diana gave a lead in humanitarian relief. She has left both a legacy and a model of compassion and warmth towards others.' The day before the memorial service, Mother Teresa of Calcutta had died, and Harry commented on another 'woman of universal significance' who aimed to relieve the suffering of the poorest of the poor. Determined to improve the situation practically as well as spiritually and emotionally, he issued a challenge.

> Tears will record our grief but only actions will indicate how deeply she has affected us. She ought to encourage us to be generous to those in need. The test will be whether we are more generous in the future.
>
> ... We are told that 40,000 children die daily from ... preventable diseases. As a nation we provide a lamentably small percentage of our National wealth for overseas aid. Virtually nothing goes to countries which offer us no economic advantage. Will you and I be kinder tomorrow because of Diana?[43]

The service ended in pouring rain, and as those inside left, those outside filed past them to add to the mountain of floral tributes.[44]

## Dallas: preparing for Lambeth

In September 1997, Harry flew to Dallas, United States, for the 'Anglican Life and Witness Conference', which was a meeting of conservative bishops to reaffirm historic Anglican standards of Scriptural authority and sexual ethics. It focused on preparing bishops for the 1998 Lambeth Conference, to strengthen the Anglican Communion as a multicultural family, and to be updated in perspectives on international debt, interfaith issues, and homosexuality. In the letter of invitation to Harry, he was informed, 'When your name came up with the planning committee, we agreed your attendance is vitally important ... Please try to make it a priority to attend.'[45] It was sponsored jointly by the Oxford Centre for Mission Studies, headed by Canon Vinay Samuel, and the Ekklesia Society, headed by Canon Bill Atwood, which was based in Texas and had offices in the Bahamas, Nigeria, Uganda, Peru, Singapore and Australia. It was the forerunner of the much more substantial conservative Global Anglican Futures Conference (GAFCON) of the next decade. David Bussau, the revered founder of Opportunity International, headed the Australian office of the Ekklesia Society, and Harry wrote to him immediately to accept the invitation[46] and was sent a copy of the book *Gender Identity* in response. This issue was to take centre stage at both the Dallas conference and Lambeth, although the broader ambition was to develop and refine the theology of 'the Church of the South' so that it would help to shape the future of the Anglican Communion. Almost half of the 60 invitees were African bishops.

In the event, 45 bishops and four archbishops from 16 nations made it to the conference, of whom over half came from Africa. Only seven were invited from England, and the only three Australian bishops invited were Harry, Paul Barnett, and Peter Chiswell.[47] The only bishop invited from the United States was James Stanton, the conservative Bishop of Dallas. The Episcopalian churches in the United States had long been in dissolution. In 1989 Donald Robinson, then Archbishop of Sydney, had written to Alan Cole concerning a visit he had just made to the United States. 'There are now, by my count, 9 Anglican denominations operating in the USA, not to mention upwards of 30 independent congregations which have hived off from ECUSA. It is one great mess with some strange bright spots.'[48] In Sydney's eyes, Dallas was one of the few bright spots. Elected in 1993, the same year as Harry, Bp Stanton, who did not retire until 2014, was characterised as a 'strong advocate of biblical authority ... actively involved in reasserting traditional values of Christian faith, order, and morality at the national church level while strengthening mission and evangelism ministries throughout the diocese.'[49] The conference, it has been claimed, was largely paid for by his diocese.[50] The conference developed resolutions for presentation at Lambeth and forged teams to work on specific issues. Hence:

Record of Group Meeting at Dallas Ekklesia Conference
Decisions:

1. All would choose Lambeth Conference.
2. All would indicate preference for 'Sexuality' and 'Debt and Justice'.
3. The following people would research at least the past two Lambeth Conference Reports for information and past resolutions.
   a. Debt and Justice – Drexel Gomez
   b. Sexuality – Peter Chiswell
   c. Ethics Generally – Bill Wantland (bishop of the Diocese of Eau Claire[51])
4. R.H. Goodhew to be the clearing house.
5. We would begin formulating draft resolutions for circulation.
6. Bill Wantland to start a resolution on sexuality.
7. There was a need to raise the issue of Authority in the Communion –Peter Chiswell to dig out past statements on Authority.[52]

Peter Chiswell later wrote, 'It was great to go to America with Paul and yourself, even if we were all a bit 'ga! ga!' with jet-lag (or old age) for much of the time.'[53]

'The Dallas Statement'[54] of September 1997 affirmed that the bishops who attended chose to focus particularly on international debt and human sexuality. The statement argued a connection between the two.

> It is precisely unbridled economic individualism that has led both to the break up of families and the escalation of international debt. A concern for the social good of nations to be relieved of debt cannot be separated from a concern for the social good of nations through the promotion of strong healthy families through faithful monogamous heterosexual relationships …
>
> … we agree that the Church has no authority to set aside clear biblical teaching by ordaining non-celibate homosexuals or authorising the blessing of same sex relationships …

Harry never moved from this stance and became one of the Anglican Communion's leading defenders of 'traditional marriage' and of opposition to the ordination of practising homosexuals. Yet there was also caution in his response to the problem. A number of conservative Americans approached Harry to establish in the United States a 'missionary district of Sydney' so that orthodox Anglican congregations could come under his episcopal care. Harry consulted with his predecessor, Donald Robinson, who thought this particular proposal was 'both impractical and impolitic.'[55] He recommended consulting the Anglo-Catholic Association for the Apostolic Ministry, since they seemed to know all about episcopacy![56] He revealed that conservatives had been planning to break away from the Episcopal Church in the United States of America (ECUSA) for much longer than a decade, but he expressed the view that breakaway congregations in communion with Sydney instead of Canterbury would be an undesirable development. On the one hand it appealed to national pride that an Australian diocese could become the head of the Anglican Communion, but on the other hand this would surely only provoke 'other brands of Anglicans' to set up their conventicles within Sydney. What the situation called for was a ministry of encouragement to congregations out of sympathy with liberal bishops, rather than any formal episcopal oversight.

## 1997 synod, 13–15 and 23–24 October

Harry began his 1997 presidential address by 'celebrating the activity of God in our midst.' The sesquicentenary was an opportunity to reaffirm the diocesan heritage.

> We have ... inherited and continue a tradition of gospel preaching which offers all who hear a clear exposition of the Scriptural doctrine of salvation through faith only and an invitation to respond. This is our great treasure, it is a fidelity which God has blessed.

Harry reported on a 4.5% growth in attendance at Sydney Anglican churches between 1991 and 1996. The number of attendees in the 20–29 age group (15%) was almost double that of all Anglicans worldwide (8%), which Harry attributed to the long-term commitment to, and ongoing innovation in ministry to youth in the diocese. He covered the extensive cross-cultural work of the Anglican Church and reported that the 3rd generation of migrant families was more likely to be Anglican than the first, indicating that the Anglican Church was 'a conscious choice of many people.' He concluded a heartwarming litany of achievement and blessing with the comment, 'Like the writer to the Hebrews "what more shall I say? I do not have time to tell" of all the great and merciful things God is doing in our midst.'

He then moved into more troubled waters, under the heading 'Issues we face together.' First up was the ongoing discontent with the exclusion of women from ordination and the hardening of its opponents, who were increasingly restricting women to preach only to women and children. Just three days earlier, the first meeting of the Women's Advisory Council had been held.[57] Harry and Pam both served on the council, which progressively committed itself to review why so few women offered for theological training and to the practical task of finding employment for those who did.[58] Harry expressed his doubts that synod debate was the best way of finding the mind of God on the matter, thus laying the foundation for his idea of a special conference devoted exclusively to consideration of that matter. He then dealt with Indigenous matters in the light of the Wik decision (23 December 1996) that native title could coexist with pastoral leases. A 4–3 decision from the High Court, it unnerved pastoralists on the grounds of 'uncertainty.' Harry called for a generous response and spoke strongly on the damage done by racism. He also gave a nuanced treatment of church plants, both outside the diocese and in other parishes within the diocese, not denying that there was plenty of scope and need for them, but urging sensitivity. He set six goals that he hoped might be achieved before 2001, the year of his retirement, namely a 15 per cent increase in church attendance and of youth involvement in youth ministries, the raising of $10 million for the ministry of the cathedral, the development of theologically sound, 'eminently singable' music for public worship, a flow of suitable candidates for ordained ministry, and the strengthening of cross-cultural mission outside the diocese.

Now that the three-year moratorium (1993–5) on debating the matter of female ordination was over, it loomed large again in synod concerns. Harry dared to move on the issue because he did not think it was a matter to die for – the hardening division over the matter troubled him more – whereas most for and against female ordination were not for moving. Harry therefore proposed the holding of a special conference at which the matter could be discussed in a less combative manner than allowed by synod rules. To the surprise of many, Phillip Jensen successfully moved a motion, 'warmly' supporting Harry's proposal and calling for 'a conference that will encourage and strengthen the ministries of women in our churches.'[59] Those suspicious of Phillip's motives thought that this was a strategic move to ensure that the development of women's ministries would continue to be along lines different from those of men. It would effectively block the ordination of women to the presbyterate. Harry continued to hope for better things, but at least synod had conceded that the diocese needed a special conference on the women question. Shortly after the last day of synod, Alan Cole wrote to Harry. 'Well, the Lord answered our prayers, and brought you safely through what could have been a nasty Synod – praise His name.'[60] Cole acknowledged that some of 'the REPA mob' might call him a 'Barnabas'[61] because of his women's conference proposal, adding,

> Don't worry – I've often been called a 'Barnabas' too. At first I used to resent it: then I found I could accept it as a title of honour. … I'd rather be a Barnabas than a Paul (no reference to living agents!) I hope that is not <u>wicked</u> or cowardly of me, and I quite see the need of Pauls as well … But I know which of the two John Mark needed – and Paul, himself, just after his conversion.

## Transcendence: the only coin

It is unlikely that Harry was ever worried about being called 'Barnabas' or any other names. Admittedly, he may have been more distracted by his critics than he would have preferred and, certainly, he was much saddened by the treatment meted out to women in his diocese by the hardliners. But he understood that these struggles were only surface symptoms of a deeper human angst shared by all, to which he believed the gospel was the answer. Deep down, Australians feared they were losing their identity, their soul, and they were not going to find it by holding out against the aspirations of women, the Indigenous, the poor or any of the other disadvantaged in the community, all of whom, for their part, felt aggrieved that they had never been allowed to find their true identity in the first place.

In Harry's papers is a draft synod address dated 5 October 1997, just over a week before the Sydney synod began. It includes long extracts from the Constitution of the Anglican Church, which explains why he thought as he did about the regrettable loss of prayer book liturgy and the inadvisability of lay presidency. In the event he spared the synod from having to listen to these long extracts. More interestingly, however, the draft address includes even longer extracts from the prose writings of the Catholic poet, Les Murray. Harry agreed with both Murray's diagnosis of the Australian condition and of the cure for it; namely, reconnecting with the transcendent, to 'the true otherness to which we are as it were keyed in the depths of our being.' 'Without that transcendence,' wrote Murray, 'which is the only coin the soul recognises, you are left restless and unfulfilled.'[62] Murray believed that the 'desperate appeal' to Christians from their enemies is 'please prove us wrong, make us believe that there is more to it than this, show us your God and that Grace you talk about.' So Murray reminded his 'Co-religionists'

> We are more widely judged on our own best terms than we think, and more insistently expected to be the keepers of the dimension of depth than we find comfortable. We will be punished if we do try to live up to what we profess, but we will be punished much worse if we don't, because so many of our enemies are relying on us.[63]

Harry might have said, 'And this is precisely why we must be "Observably God's people".' But he did not give himself the opportunity because the large slabs of Murray's sharp diagnosis did not find their way into his presidential address either. Members of diocesan congregations, however, heard in more than one of Harry's sermons from the period that 'The absence of transcendence is the death of the soul.' Not for the first time did Harry put the insights of a poet at the service of evangelism. 'Ours is the knowledge of the transcendent Light which has come into the world,' proclaimed Harry. 'Ours is the task to bear witness to that Light.'[64] How appropriate then was his choice of C.S. Lewis's words for his 1997 Christmas sermon at St Andrew's Cathedral. 'The pure light walks the earth, the darkness, received into the heart of Deity, is there swallowed up. Where, except in uncreated light, can the darkness be drowned.'[65]

# 19

# Sixth Year (1998): Wimp, Women and Spong

Each calendar year, almost the first event organised by the Anglican Church to advance the gospel is the CMS Summer School. The timing is propitious. The Christmas afterglow still shines in the heart, replacing the year's accumulated vexation with goodwill. The Church is on its best behaviour, focusing on mission as its *raison d'être*. Wilting enthusiasm is redressed by stories of unconquerable courage, indomitable compassion, and hard-won progress on the frontline and at the fringes, those liminal spaces in which the seed of the gospel yields a surprising harvest. The world's best Bible teachers instruct the mind and galvanise the will of the 3,000 who attend daily. And members of the fellowship of believers, too often divided by politics, relax and communicate with each other, and remind themselves that their real opponents are outside the fellowship.

At the 1998 Summer School, held at Katoomba from 3 to 9 January, Harry preached at the communion service on the 4th and Phillip Jensen took the Bible studies. The leaders of the two major visions within the diocese – reform Anglicanism or separate from it – were thus together in the most promising of environments. Harry was challenged by Phillip's treatment of John 12:43, 'for they loved human praise more than praise from God', to pray that the love with which he loved others would be from God rather than human love. He also recorded finding Phillip's address on the cry of desolation of Christ on the Cross 'very helpful.' 'It made me think again of the grace and love of God and his Christ. My heart is so unresponsive. I felt the desire to be in his presence and be enveloped in that so great love.'[1]

The two visions – reform or separate – are radically incompatible, of course, and, while the grace of God bridged the divide occasionally, as here, the incompatibility remained. While at Summer School, Harry read Alister McGrath's biography of J.I. Packer.[2] He was struck by the contrast between Packer's thinking and that of Phillip who, during Summer School, spoke at St Hilda's, Katoomba, at a meeting of EFAC on 'Evangelicals and the Future'. 'Packer was set for the renewal and restoration of Anglicanism and along with Stott resisted Lloyd-Jones' call for evangelicals to leave and form evangelical congregations.'[3] That Harry aligned himself with Stott and Phillip with Martyn Lloyd-Jones demonstrates that the division between Harry and Phillip was far more than a personal one. The complexity of the matter, however, is shown by the irony that, whereas Phillip ended up happy to stay within the Anglican Church, J.I. Packer joined David Short and the congregation of St John's Shaughnessy in Vancouver in leaving the Anglican Church over the issue of the ordination of homosexuals. Providence disallows radical incompatibility from becoming a permanent state! On the one hand, 1998 was to witness the continuation of the grim struggle between Harry's and Phillip's visions for church schools, female ordination, and church planting. On the other hand, developments at the 1998 Lambeth Conference meant that, over time, the two visions converged, at least in the encouragement that both Harry and (in the end) Phillip's brother, Peter, gave to conservative dioceses within the Anglican Communion.

## Strategies for reforming the Anglican Church of Australia

When General Synod met in Adelaide from 14 to 21 February, the president, Archbishop Rayner, as we have seen, praised Harry's chairmanship of the 1997 National Anglican Conference, which he saw as the forerunner of a way, more creative than synods, of transacting the Church's business. Harry was thus able to secure the passage of a series of motions[4] committing the Anglican Church across Australia to the employment of NCLS data, to the holding of future conferences along the lines of the 1997 conference, and to the reorientation of the Anglican Church to mission and to post-ordination training of clergy and lay people in methods of church growth and church planting. Harry's priorities for Sydney were being duplicated throughout Australia.

Further, to the provincial bishops' meeting on 10 and 11 March 1998 at Bishopscourt, Harry submitted the report of the energetic John Lambert on the new schools being opened by the Sydney Anglican Schools Association. By the beginning of 1998, the acquisition of suitable sites and the opening of schools with over-subscribed student enrolments were encouraging. Although Lambert had hoped for more progress, he was assisted ably by the financial and managerial skills of Laurie Scandrett to open new schools, not only in Sydney, but in other dioceses. In New South Wales there were, by 1998, 75 Christian community or parent-controlled schools and 45 Anglican low-fee schools. The Anglican schools seemed to be very popular, and a National Anglican Schools Committee was a definite possibility.[5] By 2000 there were about 25 Anglican schools in the Diocese of Sydney alone, creating opportunities for contact with 50,000 children and parents, most of them non-churchgoing. A surprisingly effective instrument for expanding the Anglican Church's influence, both inside the diocese and beyond, had been developed at the very pinnacle of the impact of secularisation on the community.

## The church schools problem

One troubling effect of the new Christian schools was to show up the old church schools as less than 'Christian.' Phillip Jensen characterised the traditional church schools as 'semi-Christian.' Their high fees meant they were elitist, for a start. They needed and commanded money from among the more monied classes in a professedly egalitarian society. Academic excellence to gain entrance to the best university places and sporting prowess to command the respect of the physically powerful seemed to be valued more highly than Christlikeness in compassion, values or morality.

Unlike the new Christian schools, the older church schools had history that was not always exemplary. In the early 1970s, financial incompetence and fraud had led to the ruination of a group of Anglican schools under the SCEGGS (Sydney Church of England Girls' Grammar School) banner. As a result, the diocese devolved financial management to parents, while retaining representation on the school boards. A reprehensible solution, it freed the diocese from liability for debt while lumbering the boards with diocesan vigilantes who did little to promote the prosperity of the schools.[6] In 1995, a review committee had undertaken to streamline this arrangement without changing it radically. But, before its recommendations could be approved by synod, the board of Abbotsleigh School appointed a new head, Judith Wheeldon. She spoke with an American accent, was married to a former Labor Senator, and was not the 'right kind of Christian.' There was much distress among the Sydney faithful.

In the hysteria that ensued, it was rumoured that Wheeldon was Jewish and instructed her school captain to preach atheism. Both rumours were nonsense, but it became a cause célèbre. Phillip Jensen took full advantage of the outrage to propose far more drastic recommendations for the reform of the councils of church schools. They were to be made up only of those who were Christians, ratified by the ministers of the churches they attended. Principals and ideally all teachers would be confessing Christians. The outrage of the radicals was then matched by panic among the moderates. Would the best accountants, developers and architects now be ineligible to serve on Anglican Church school boards? Would parents withdraw their children from schools that had fallen into the hands of 'fundamentalists'?

The media fully exploited this row among the wealthy and powerful and sought Harry's response to it all. Harry thought excellence was a desirable aim, and he suspected that it was better for a school to have some teachers who could help pupils aspire to this even if they were not Christians. He was unimpressed by the Jensenite push for radical change and stricter regulations. He accepted that schools could drift from their Christian foundations, but he believed they were then overwhelmingly in good hands and that it was better to set broad expectations than to issue orders and enact restrictions. He considered expertise was a very important qualification in school council members and teachers, and was not persuaded that all of them had to be confessing Christians. However, he let it be known that he would let synod decide this matter and would not use his veto to stymie any requirements legislated by the synod.[7]

Harry was not alone in this stance. Bp Barnett spoke in SC against the Jensen push on private schools. He was of the opinion that it was necessary to accept their limitations. They were controlled by well-connected alumni who were very powerful, and to do a 'John Knox' on them could fail, losing them to the church.[8] Riley Warren, a good friend of the Jensens, sided with Paul and Bp Peter Watson in opposition to the Jensen move, which in the end was not approved by synod or SC.[9]

The final outcome, however, was far from a comprehensive defeat for Phillip. Henceforth, councils of church schools would be far more concerned with the Christian credentials of those who worked both in the classroom and in the board room. In truth, Harry suspected that Phillip had more right on his side in this matter than he had. He had been unsure about Judith Wheeldon's appointment. Based on his experience, he understood that the Head set the tone of the school, and if 'the Head is not a convinced and active Christian that lack of focus will impact over time on appointments, etc.' Harry came to see that he should have shared his concerns more forcefully with those responsible for the appointment. 'I think I looked a bit of a wimp,' he admitted.

## Special Trinity synod on female ordination

In the area of female ministry, Harry did share his concerns more forcefully. Sydney synod had never been to everyone's liking. It was an arena in which the politicians and the lawyers prevailed with tactics and dialectics in an atmosphere of hard-headed civility. It left the majority numb and chained to their seats, the distance from where they sat to the nearest microphone induced fear and trembling. Harry, more sensitive to process and less determined to win at all costs, had already changed the feel of synod. A number of the old traditions had gone. But the tradition of confrontation and disputation continued.

The traditional synod was a better forum for non-controversial matters than for such divisive issues as female ordination. Harry wanted that issue, the major contention of the decade, explored in a less confrontational climate. A better way had to be found, because the ongoing rejection of female ordination was too cruel to women who felt they had a calling to ministry. A reason why synod would keep rejecting it was that it kept losing women who supported it, and it constrained women (and men) through fear to say what they did not really believe.

Harry, as we have seen, had grown up under the significant ministry of women, including, when he was a catechist, the ministry of Deaconess Jean Standfield, who ran the Milperra branch church in the Parish of Panania. That such ministry was made more difficult in the late 1980s and 1990s was not a change that Harry welcomed. True, there had always been limitations placed on the ministry of women, but Harry was not conscious of them at the time. He recalls the dynamic ministry of Gladys Aylward, missionary to China. Archbishop Gough gave her permission to preach from the chancel rather than the pulpit. It was only in retrospect that Harry came to see the significance of that. He was formed spiritually, as we have seen, by women; by his Sunday school teachers, Merle Wright, Marjory Aspinall and Adelaide Millard, and by evangelist Monica Farrell and a Mrs Green who used 'to preach her heart out' in the open air in the city with the Pentecostals. Women had made significant contributions to the success of his own parish ministries, Angela Simmonds at Coorparoo and Sheila Stockdale at Wollongong.

He was also impressed by women missionaries who had done all sorts of marvellous things for their Lord. He instanced Sylvia Jeanes, who in 1967 went to Sabah with CMS, who founded missions and established schools and trained teachers and pastors, and would still be there long after Harry retired, over 40 years on the job.[11] For seven of those years in the 1970s, she had looked after 22 churches and two schools without any help. How she prayed, but no-one came. It sounded quite ridiculous to Harry when Trevor Middleton, Rector of Oak Flats in the Wollongong region, said to Harry that women should never have gone out as missionaries, that it was a great mistake on the part of the church to allow that. Harry began to see that a hardline on women's ministry was creating indefensible propositions about the actual form female ministry should take.

Interestingly, Pam did not influence his thinking on the matter. She was an analytical spectator of the debate, never seeking to sway Harry one way or the other. She professed to being puzzled as to why Donald Robinson had ordained women deacons in 1989. Did he do that because he was pressured, she wondered, and did he do it precipitately? And, while she wondered if those women who wanted to be ordained were always the best pioneers for the movement and was made uneasy by dioceses where so many women were being ordained that it was difficult to find a man, she did not want to see the ministry of women in any way curtailed. Women, she believed, 'had always kept the church afloat' and 'there have always been women who have stood head and shoulders over men.'

If Harry had changed his attitude to the ordination of women over time, it was very gradual, very considered. Bp Barnett, who never wavered in his opposition to female ordination, observed,

> I'll say this, if Harry made up his mind about something, you didn't push him easily. If he made up his mind about the ordination of women or matters like that, he wouldn't change in a hurry. He wasn't a flip-flop.'[12]

Paul, who had reached an opinion about it during Archbishop Robinson's time and has not changed since, cannot recall discussing the matter at any length with Harry, but he does recall that Harry once said in his hearing, about male headship, 'I just don't know what that means in terms of outward human relationships.'[13]

Precisely because the women's issue had damaged outward human relationships in the synod, Harry felt that a different way ahead had to be found. So, perhaps subconsciously encouraged to explore alternatives to synods by the happy experience of the national Anglican conference the year before, Harry, single-handed, devised the idea of the conference on female ordination, which was held on Saturday, 16 May 1998, at Trinity Grammar School in Sydney. Two papers, for and against, were prepared in advance. The paper in favour was by a team who had met regularly for discussion at the chambers of Keith Mason, then Solicitor General of NSW and President of the Court of Appeal. The paper against was prepared by a group led by Peter Jensen. It was expected that these position papers would be digested before the conference. The real architects of the case for ordination were Bill Lawton and John McIntyre, both of whom spoke passionately and effectively on that occasion, but the proceedings around the two papers were really a damp squib. Bp Barnett read his evaluation of the two papers, giving the honours to the negative side. The question, which is so obvious in retrospect, is why women were not the chief spokespersons in the opening scenes of the drama. When given the opportunity, women, ably led by Archdeacon Nicolios, did bring the conference alive in the afternoon. Some, especially Margaret Rodgers and Narelle Jarrett, sensed they were closer than ever to achieving approval for ordination to the priesthood and were encouraged on this rare occasion to voice their real hopes. Harry recorded in his diary, 'One of the most affecting parts was the final part of the women's presentation in the afternoon. In answer to a question about the difficulties of ministering in Sydney, the women spoke honestly and without rancour about their experiences.'[14]

The 330 present divided into 35 groups to discuss whether any 'generally acceptable approach' could be found to granting women the opportunity to fulfil the ministry of presbyter. The archbishop-in-council subsequently received 51 responses to the conference. Harry's own immediate response was not entirely negative. 'Comments afterwards varied from expressions of frustration to many favourable comments about the process. We may need to explore the virtues of the process for other important issues before the Synod.'[15] Again, this is evidence of Harry's interest in processes as well as outcomes. But the outcome here was not to his liking. SC's response to the conference was to endorse the Jensen line that lay and diaconal administration should be tried for five years as a 'principled' way of allowing women a way forward. This was a clever strategy to achieve at one stroke both the support of the majority in the SC and the implementation of lay presidency. But supporters of the ordination of women considered this tactic entirely unprincipled, designed to deny certain women what they most wanted by adopting a mechanism that the archbishop least wanted. Harry advised SC that he did not think this proposal would reduce tensions, and he came to think of the conference as a failure. '[T]he process of talking has not proceeded sufficiently for any real synthesis or greater corporate mind to develop.'[16] Phillip Jensen subsequently moved his proposal at synod, which endorsed it, but Harry vetoed it. No progress had been made.

Harry was increasingly prone to see his initiatives in terms of failure, inviting and receiving affirmations that he had not failed. That is not normally a good look, but, in his mercy, the Lord sometimes allows good things to come from things that don't look good. This time it came from Harry's most chronic epistolary adviser.

> It wasn't a failure – it kept people talking with each other face to face, and not flinging mud from a distance, or in the heated atmosphere in Synod. If God <u>wants</u> things changed in Sydney … He will first change people's hearts, and their understanding of the meaning and relevance of certain passages of Scripture for our day. Until that, argument is <u>useless</u> … I am inclined to think that, in a modern diocese, any such change should only take place when either the <u>totality</u>, or at least the vast majority, soberly believes, on good theological grounds, that it is right … That takes the load off you: your part is that of a loving Christian umpire, not a decision-maker (either way!) for the Diocese … you don't need to be a martyr for either side.[17]

The long-term effect of the Trinity conference was not to allow women to be ordained to the priesthood, but there was another long-term effect, this time unforeseen. The paper prepared in support of female ordination was entitled 'Not Compromise; Not Uniformity; But Liberty: A Case for the Ordination of Women to the Priesthood.' There the issue of the relevance of the subordination of the Son in the Trinity was first raised in the special synod debate with reference to female ordination. 'No passage of Paul's writings should be read to construe an order of subordination of females to males,' and there can be no analogy of that subordination in the Trinity. 'The Athanasian Creed specifies that there is no ordered subordination or hierarchy within the Godhead.'

The authors of this argument had the distinct impression that their opponents seem to have been genuinely surprised and disconcerted by it, not quite sure whether it was right or not. Very smartly, the diocesan Doctrine Commission got busy. They started like the Council of Trent, unsure if Luther's doctrine of justification by faith was right or not, but, for the most part, sure that they wanted to conclude that it was not right. The next year, 1999, they produced their report 'The Doctrine of the Trinity and Its Bearing on the Relationship of Men and Women.' Kevin Giles responded with his first magnum opus on this subject, *The Trinity and Subordinationism: The Doctrine of God and the Contemporary Gender Debate.*[18] Here, Kevin did not charge the Doctrine Commission's report with heretical subordinationism, but he did suggest that it was trending in that direction. The Anglican primate, Peter Carnley, however, did not hesitate to claim that it had indeed reached this destination. It was a novelty for the self-appointed defenders of orthodoxy, the Sydney conservatives, to be accused of heresy. But we are running ahead of our story.

## Assault on the Anglican Counselling Centre

It was also in May 1998 that another problem with long-term consequences surfaced in SC. John Woodhouse, Rector of Christ Church, St Ives, became chair of a SC inquiry into the operations of the Anglican Counselling Centre (ACC). Established two decades earlier, the ACC had built up a large clientele base, and its credibility as a recognisably Christian counselling centre was recognised both in Australia and overseas. Its director, Michael Corbett-Jones, was respected by his colleagues and revered by the many helped by the Centre. Over 25,000 persons had sought help through the ACC, including clergy, their families, CMS missionaries, church workers, members of local congregations and those in the general public referred to the centre by health professionals.

The ACC desired to follow best practice, and in 1998, on Harry's initiative, agreed to have its counselling procedures scrutinised by Dr Bill Andersen, Christian psychologist and academic. But, not waiting for Andersen's findings, SC established its own committee of inquiry. This was in response to a motion from one of its members, Colette Read, who was quoted in *Southern Cross* as having said, 'I am aware of allegations that the well-being of some people deteriorated through therapy at ACC.'[19] The committee of inquiry was established to deal with allegations that harm had been done through some techniques used by some ACC counsellors. In particular, it was alleged, whole families had been harmed by the doubtful practice of 'recovered memories', at least some of which were demonstrated by an impartial inquiry to have been totally false.

The inquiry may be seen as yet another manifestation of the fundamental culture clash within the diocese. Counselling can be done according to a cognitive, behavioural model. In Cognitive Behavioural Therapy (CBT) the client is taken through a process of rationally devising his or her own responses. This approach tended to be favoured by the conservative theologians of the diocese, since it can be aligned cognitively with Scripture. John Woodhouse was a gifted exponent of this approach. But counselling can also be done according to a psychodynamic, emotion-based approach. This approach was favoured by Michael Corbett-Jones. He was not himself doctrinaire in opposition to CBT and was quite capable of employing a comprehensive range of counselling models, and even undertook to do so when consulted by Bill Andersen.

Michael, however, was not given the opportunity to demonstrate his grasp of a wider approach. There were those in the diocese distressed by the results of ACC counsellors who were advocates of the possibility of 'recovered memories.' It is possible through the normal interaction between counsellor and client that, in seeking to stir up repressed memories, fabrication can result. Those who wanted the ACC 'fixed up' wanted to avoid situations where that could happen. SC's seven-member committee of enquiry, chaired by John Woodhouse, was made up of those who were highly qualified in their various fields, if not necessarily in matters in which they were now engaged. The days of the ACC were numbered, but it suffered a slow and painful death that we must chronicle below.

## Extended overseas trip prefatory to Lambeth

Increasingly mired in disputes that promised no easy resolution and bedevilled by ongoing inflammation of the lungs, Harry needed a change of pace. With some relief, he embarked on a two-month leave leading up to the 1998 Lambeth Conference. From 22 May to 13 June, Harry and Pam stayed with daughter Wendy Banister, husband Graham, and their three children, Nicholas, Chelsea and Jackson, in Raleigh NC, in the United States. Harry spent a lot of time in the gym and the pool, clearly intent on recouping his health, and bonding with his grandchildren. He did not find it easy to leave.

Then, from 13 June to 6 July, Harry and Pam stayed at Oak Hill Theological College in London, where Harry spent a lot of time in the library, the Elysium of all those who, like Harry, have introverted personalities and academic tastes. He set himself a daily routine of study, including Greek and Hebrew. He waded into the deep waters of N.T. Wright's *The New Testament and the People of God* (1992), clearly identifying with C.S. Lewis's sentiment, 'You can never get a cup of tea large enough or a book long enough to suit me.' The weekends he devoted to preparing for Lambeth. He noted, in anticipation of the battle to come with the principal gladiator for the homosexual cause, 'Dear Jack Spong is clearly a political animal in the procedure he is proposing.'[20] He caught up with Graham Cole, Principal of Ridley College, nearing the end of a six-month sabbatical leave. Harry confessed to envying the life of a theological teacher, but he explored the possibility of Graham becoming an assistant bishop, observing in his diary that he would make a great archbishop of Sydney.[21]

The rejuvenating power of leave evidently worked on Harry's psyche. A long-term chocoholic, he reports walking from the college to Southgate to get 'some chocolate for Pam (and myself).' He and Pam also consumed 'a whole 1/2 pound' of fudge in 'quite an abandoned manner.' They subsequently purchased '6 beautiful Belgian chocolates', all they felt they could afford, 'having one each for 3 nights.' At the Dillons bookshop, Harry indulged another of his addictions and bought a copy of Eliot's poetry. At Selfridge's he bought 'a beautiful lightweight sweater', evidence of that taste for fine clothing, admired and inherited by his son, David. Pam saw 'a most becoming hat', but they mulled (not prayed apparently) over that for four days before buying it. With Peter and Elizabeth Smart, they attended *Les Miserable*s at the Palace Theatre in 'various contorted postures' as the seating was not designed to take people with legs. They suffered a similar fate at the mecca of evangelicals, All Souls', Langham Place, where the service was so full they had to sit on a windowsill that was 'an awkward distance from the floor.' By contrast, the service was conducted 'with ease and dignity.'

From 6 to 16 July Harry and Pam explored Ireland, spending the first three days in the care of Chris and Jan Bellinger, Anglican evangelical stalwarts in both Dublin and Sydney. Chris was Professor of Veterinary Surgery at University College, Dublin, to which he was appointed from Sydney in 1995, having served on the SC during Harry's first two years in office and on General Synod. A steady stream of visitors from Australia had kept them abreast of church matters in

Australia. Harry and Pam returned to England in time for an EFAC retreat on 17 July at The King's School, Canterbury, the oldest continuously operating school in the world. The Lambeth Conference began that evening at the University of Kent, one of a number of British universities founded in the 1960s.

# 20

# Sixth Year (1998 Continued): 'The Winsome Face of Sydney'

Among the most onerous parts of the impossible job of Archbishop of Canterbury is preparing for Lambeth conferences, the decennial meetings of bishops of the Anglican Communion. Only 76 bishops had attended the first Lambeth Conference in 1867, but by 1990 there were 800 bishops in the Anglican Communion, and it was no longer dominated by English bishops. Bishops representing the largest number of Anglicans in the Communion – those in Africa – had found their voice. Archbishop Carey approached the conference apprehensive that it would be remembered as a stoush over homosexuality between North American liberals and conservatives from the developing nations.

## The 1998 Lambeth Conference

The reality was worse than he feared, a public relations disaster. The media fed a stunned public with images of an African bishop screaming that the book of Leviticus demanded the death penalty for homosexuals and seeking to exorcise the homosexuality out of gay activist, Richard Kirker.[1] Graham Leonard, the conservative Bishop of London, had refused to ordain Kirker to the priesthood as he was a gay man openly living with a partner. So Kirker helped to found and became the outspoken director of the Lesbian and Gay Christian Movement. He and radical liberal, John Shelby ('Jack') Spong, Bishop of Newark, United States, wrote a joint 'white paper on homosexuality' and released it just before the General Synod in England in November 1997. They intended to give the impression that there was massive support for this document, whereas there were actually so few supporters that Spong later claimed he foresaw a calamitous defeat if the matter were debated at Lambeth, and therefore he hoped it would not be.[2]

Lambeth conferences, however, were only held each decade, and those pressing for the liberalisation of the church's views on homosexual priests would not wait another 10 years for the church to again address the issue. So, they proceeded to push for the debate, which only provoked the conservatives who were much stronger and far better organised. Spong's actions were more courageous than wise. In the white paper he attacked a conservative manifesto, known as the Kuala Lumpur Statement on Human Sexuality,[3] as 'unworthy and highly prejudiced', and he did not spare the Archbishop of Canterbury, accusing him of 'weak and ineffective leadership' stemming from his 'rampant homophobia.'[4] Carey replied that Spong was 'hectoring and intemperate' and that his methods harmed those he sought to help. Spong's chances of success were further diminished by the publication in April 1998 of his book *Why Christianity Must Change or Die*. His belief that, because all humans bear God's image, they must all be respected, including those of a homosexual orientation – a claim of some force and validity – was compounded with his denials of the incarnation, resurrection and ascension. This was asking too much of bishops who are appointed to defend the faith.

Spong helped the conservative cause enormously by his immoderate assaults on African bishops ('Pentecostalists in mitres'), which the media reported just before the opening of the Conference. He disparaged their intellectual ability, asserting that they practised a 'very superstitious kind of Christianity' and had not faced the intellectual revolution wrought in the West by the likes of Copernicus and Einstein. New understandings of homosexuality, Spong suggested, were yet to reach them. These views were published under the banner headline 'Africans one step up from witchcraft.' In this Spong claims he was misrepresented by Carey's son, Andrew, in the *Church of England News*, which Spong asserted was 'the worst religious newspaper in the world.'[5] There was a storm of protest. Spong apologised for 'unintentionally alienating' the Africans, but they were in no mood to be patronised.[6] Archbishop Emmanuel Kolini of Rwanda was particularly offended and refused to accept Spong's apology.[7]

The minority conservative evangelical bishops of the Western World discovered that they had the backing of the huge majority of conservative bishops in the developing world, particularly in Africa, but also in parts of Asia and Latin America. The discovery was not self-evident from the start. It felt at first to Paul Barnett that in the Human Sexuality section, they were 'swimming against the tide.'

> The pre-circulated literature, the keynote opening address, the choice of the section head, and the sub-section head, and the theological facilitator attached to this Section were all coming strongly from the one quarter of pro-gay activism. The agenda for the liberation of homosexuals was prosecuted with missionary zeal. It was quite depressing.[8]

Those who disliked the surprising conclusion Lambeth eventually reached have asserted that the triumph of the conservatives was the outcome of a conspiracy of right-wing Americans, orchestrated no doubt at the 1997 Dallas Conference, which, as we have seen, had been attended by Harry, Paul Barnett, and Peter

Chiswell of Armidale. Muriel Porter writes:

> Certainly American conservatives had channelled enormous energy, finances and planning into wooing the Africans' vote at Lambeth 1998 ... At the Lambeth Conference ... they established a centre close to the Conference location, using it to provide the bishops from the developing world with every kind of assistance and encouragement. Food, mobile phones, free telephone links home, strategy talks, crib sheets, were all readily available to them. Some observers have likened the centre to a high-tech U.S. political campaign office.[9]

Of those chiefly aiding the right-wing Americans in their conspiracy, according to Muriel Porter, were Sydney evangelicals.

> One of the speakers at the centre's various events was ... Archbishop Harry Goodhew. And young Sydney graduates were to be found among the troops running the day-to-day operations of the centre. Not a great deal was written at the time about Sydney's involvement behind the scenes at Lambeth 1998, and not much is known outside Sydney to this day. Their involvement has assumed importance only in hindsight.[10]

Porter's source for this perspective was the gripping account of the conference by journalist Stephen Bates.

> The Franciscan Centre operation was in full gear. Over their free box lunches, the bishops would gather to hear the views of white Evangelical bishops, led by Bishop [sic] Harry Goodhew of Sydney, and to place their orders with the keen young stewards who could not do enough to help them.[11]

Lambeth's task force on human sexuality comprised 25 bishops, 'a widely varied group, including liberal bishop Jack Spong of Newark and his conservative counterpart, The Most Rev'd Harry Goodhew of Sydney Australia.' So reported Bp Martin Townsend of Easton, in Maryland, United States, in his diocesan newsletter.[12] Harry shared with Paul Barnett and three other bishops in a small discussion group within the task force. These included Jack Spong himself, Charles Bennison of Pennsylvania who considered that the church had written the Scriptures and it could re-write them, and a polished Englishman, Michael Scott-Joynt, Bishop of Winchester, influenced by Tom Wright towards a conservative position on sexuality. 'He was,' recalls Harry, 'a really delightful man with the mien and deportment of a Guardsman.'

At the conference, Harry became known as 'the winsome face of Sydney.'[13] Delegates were astonished that an archbishop as agreeable as Harry could be the archbishop of the Sydney diocese, renowned throughout the Anglican Communion for its habitual disagreeableness. Paul Barnett testified:

> At the Lambeth Conference in 1998 where he was on the conservative side of the debate on sexuality he won the respect of all, from both sides. It's safe to say that no Archbishop in the world is better known or more widely respected than our Archbishop.[14]

20.1 'The winsome face of Sydney'.

It may not have been only local pride that dictated this judgement. The *Church of England News* listed Harry as one of the 13 'outstanding figures' of the Lambeth Conference, and reported of him that he brought 'Sydney Anglicanism centre-stage' at the Lambeth Conference, and that 'trusted across the board, he emerged as a significant leader of the orthodox majority.'[15] Ray Smith also thought Harry was 'brilliant' at Lambeth. Harry respected the institution as worth preserving, seeking reform in a conservative direction from within, and sensitive to the reality that once you break away, you have little power.[16]

A presentation by lesbian and homosexual priests to the 60 bishops who had elected to study the issue of human sexuality at the conference was cancelled after two-thirds of the group voted against it. Among the objectors was Harry Goodhew. By contrast, a session addressed by novelist Susan Howatch on 'Harassed Heroines and Healing Centres' was attended by a great company of bishops who packed the marquee to hear her. Apparently not all bishops agreed with Harry that her novels were not suitable reading for clergy.

The responsibility of chairing the debate on this most contentious of all issues fell to Robin Eames, Primate of All Ireland, who condemned as lacking in Christian charity those who would not relieve him of the privilege. Peter Adebiyi, Bishop of Owo, in the Province of Nigeria with its 18 million Anglicans, took his stand on the authority of the Bible and said that 'homosexuality is a sin which could only be adopted by the Church if it wanted to commit evangelical suicide.' He was applauded, prompting Archbishop Eames to ask the bishops to refrain from applauding so as to allow for deeper reflection. Harry's contribution, assessed by Paul Barnett as 'excellent',[17] followed soon after and was reported thus in the press:

> 'We wish to be as compassionate as our Lord was to the woman taken in adultery when he said, "Go and sin no more", he said. 'I am glad this motion has produced strong feelings, because it is not an incidental matter, but a grave moral issue.' Everywhere in the Bible that homosexuality was mentioned it was always negative, he added. St Paul had selected a number of things from the Old Testament as the way of Christ, and one of them was that men and women should not lie with members of the same sex.[18]

Liberal bishops were stunned by the size of the defeat they suffered: 526 bishops voted for Lambeth Resolution 1.10, which rejected homosexual practice as incompatible with Scripture, while only 70 voted against it, and 45 abstained. The debate was held on a hot afternoon and tempers were as high as the temperature. Bishop of Worcester, Peter Selby, likened the debate to a Nuremberg Rally in the hate it generated. Michael Ingham, Bishop of New Westminster, Canada, walked out of the debate before the vote was taken. Spong, who left the conference early to write a pastoral letter to homosexual Christians to assure them that the decision would be reversed, adjudged the debate to be 'the bitterest and most unpleasant experience of my life.'[19] He saw there 'the death of the church visibly.'[20]

Richard Holloway, Primus of Scotland, characterised the part played in the debate by the Archbishop of Canterbury as 'pathetic.'[21] He reported feeling 'gutted, shafted and depressed.'[22] He later complained that 'Heterosexuals, especially Christian heterosexuals, are expert at calling on homosexuals to deny themselves consolations they themselves could not live without.'[23] His diagnosis of the African church was that it had been 'Islamified', making it more severe, Protestant [sic] and legalistic.[24] Disgusted, at the conclusion of the conference he flung his mitre into the Thames. In 2000 Holloway resigned as Primus. Three years later and retired, he was still bitter. 'I hated that conference. It was the worst experience of my life.'[25] Withdrawing into agnosticism, he says that it was the Lambeth Conference 'that would send me over the edge.'[26] It also, in his opinion, sent the Church of England over the edge: it began the unravelling of the Anglican Communion 'that has been gathering pace ever since.'[27]

Both those of a very liberal persuasion and the more extreme conservatives agreed that Lambeth was evidence that the worldwide Anglican Communion was indeed unravelling. More traditional evangelicals and Anglo-Catholics thought any report of the death of Anglicanism was exaggerated. Ray Smith, who accompanied Harry to Lambeth, for example, was left with the impression that the Lambeth Conference with the Archbishop of Canterbury was the closest body to an authoritative voice for the Anglican Communion at the time, that the majority of the bishops were of the opinion that resolutions of Lambeth should be respected and upheld, and that, though many bishops did not agree with the resolution on sexuality, they believed 'the Church' had spoken and they should accept that ruling.

The problem was not Lambeth, but choosing to ignore Lambeth. There were enough bishops who did not share Ray Smith's view to now devote themselves to 'unravelling' the Anglican Communion. There was much disagreement on what was really at stake, much indignant opposition to positions others held dear. There were those, like journalist Stephen Bates, who was motivated to write his account of the debate because he was so incensed at the treatment of gay clergy. But he appears to have been even more indignant at the behaviour of the liberal defenders of gay clergy.

> The liberals were sore, outplayed and out-voted in ways they had loftily never imagined, guilty of taking the developing world for granted and casually insulting and patronising them. They came across as rancorous and spiteful. It was game, set and match to the conservatives.[28]

There were those, such as Diarmaid MacCulloch, the self-confessed gay Professor of the History of the Church at Oxford University, who thought Lambeth exposed both 'the poverty of conservative evangelical thinking on sexuality' and a concerted attempt by conservatives 'to seize power in worldwide Anglicanism.'[29] There were those who thought the cultural differences were so vast as to render any unity impossible. Conservatives complained that the liberals, in their denunciation of African bishops, were too unaware of cultural differences, while liberals protested that African bishops were themselves guilty of cultural insensitivity in their refusal to countenance the possibility of new views on sexuality. After all, the liberals remonstrated, the 1988 Lambeth Conference had accepted the possibility of bigamy in certain African cultures. Why couldn't Africans now extend to them the same tolerance?

Richard Holloway concluded that bringing God into discussion of moral issues only made it impossible for people to judge those issues on their own merits, the only relevant argument being what the Bible said on the matter. 'The saddest aspect of a very depressing event was the way speaker after speaker quoted the Bible as though it was the final word on a complex subject, so that no further thinking needed to be done.'[30] Perhaps the majority of the bishops could be forgiven for bringing God and the Bible into the debate. Holloway accurately pointed to the main driver behind the conservatives when he said that it was a pity that the Conference had not focused on the 'key question' of how to interpret the Bible. The basic question was, should the Bible be treated as the literal word of God or should it be interpreted anew in every generation?[31]

For the conservatives, taking the Bible seriously and applying its truth to every generation was what had motivated them all along. Lambeth '98 was strong evidence, surprising to some, of the strength of evangelicalism within the Anglican Communion. It was a remarkable reflection of the work done by CMS in Africa and its insistence on the authority of the word of God. This historic dimension to the debate was acknowledged even in the press. One reporter became aware that the Anglo-Catholic SPG had concentrated on southern Africa, while the CMS had its main missions in Central Africa. Predictably, Desmond Tutu, Archbishop of Cape Town, had campaigned for the recognition of homosexual clergy, while the bishops of parts of Africa where the CMS worked campaigned against it.[32]

In the 'Third World' of the Global South, then, Sydney Anglicans, already well represented through missionary initiatives over a century in the making, found themselves with an unexpected opportunity. Reporting to SC back in Sydney, Harry observed:

> One can give thanks for the work of CMS both from UK and Australia, and of SAMS. There is now in evidence a group of African, Asian and Latin bishops who honour the Bible as the Word of God and who wish to allow it to guide the life of the Church.

As to the future, Harry prophesied that 'One of the ongoing results of Lambeth '98 will be a developing alliance between conservative bishops across the Communion.' Harry told SC that he had returned home with 'much more enthusiasm' for the Anglican Communion. He advised that the Diocese of Sydney should foster the growing biblical conservatism in the Anglican Communion. 'We need,' he said, 'to abandon an isolationist mindset and resolve to be an active participant in the life of the Communion.'[33]

Harry recorded that some in SC 'were not impressed.'[34] Clearly, there were now two options for Sydney; get more involved in the wider Communion influencing it for biblical faith, or get more involved only with the conservative parts of the Communion, leaving the rest to their own devices. Harry preferred the former option. He would have supported the spin doctors of Lambeth '98 who insisted on avoiding the 's' word: schism. He did, however, see and seize any opportunity to strengthen ties with the conservative African bishops and he suggested that

Sydney evangelicals not only needed to be humble in the relationship, but that developing closer links even with just the conservatives would mean being more open to charismatics, robe-wearers, and women in ministry. For they were thick on the ground among Bible-believing evangelical Anglicans worldwide!

Those who preferred the latter option of continuing in fellowship only with the conservatives received encouragement from the behaviour of the liberals subsequent to Lambeth. It is, after all, only an advisory body, and bishops do not have to take its advice. Most liberal bishops, apparently, had no intention of so doing. The Presiding Bishop of the Episcopal Church USA, Frank Griswold, refused to affirm that the resolution would rule out the ordination of practising homosexuals in some American dioceses. Within a year, Harry would be back in America to witness the determination of the Episcopal Church to ignore Lambeth.

Harry came out of Lambeth with increased stature internationally. His style of compassionate biblical orthodoxy won over many. The senior student of Oak Hill College in London, where Harry had stayed before the conference, wrote, 'Many of us are Anglican ordinands (including from overseas) and we are concerned about possible developments in our denomination: your loving firmness this summer has greatly reassured us.'[35] Prominent Melbourne businessperson and Anglican lay leader, Alan Kerr, wrote that he had been reading the excellent report on Lambeth that EFAC United Kingdom had put out.

> There were frequent references to your contribution at that great gathering, especially in one or two of the critical debates. So we are all indebted to you for your wider ministry as well as for your wise and temperate leadership in Sydney.[36]

For beleaguered American conservatives, the Diocese of Sydney as led by Harry was a beacon of hope. John Rodgers, Dean of Trinity Episcopal School for Ministry, thanked Harry for his 'strong leadership' at Lambeth. 'Most of us would never have dreamed that such a clear message might be sent to the Anglican communion at large and the Episcopal Church in particular.' He observed that the great majority of ECUSA bishops were determined to violate both Scripture and Lambeth, and he expressed the hope that Harry would join in the 'initiation and recognition of a distinct Episcopal Church' in the United States.[37]

## Resumption of the daily round

Following Lambeth, Harry and Pam spent five days in Belgium with Stuart Robinson, later Bishop of Canberra/Goulburn who was then serving with the Intercontinental Church Society in Brussels. Sydney welcomed back Harry's 'wise and temperate leadership' on 14 August. The pressure was turned on again like a tap. There were discussions with lawyers about the discipline ordinance and clergy accused of misdemeanours; he counselled clergy facing dire health outcomes, another whose marriage had broken down, and yet another whose son was on drugs; a fire broke out in the cathedral chapter house after Evening Prayer on Harry's first Sunday; a meeting of the council controlling the university colleges was 'its awful usual self', driving long-suffering Peter Smart to speak 'more directly and critically' than Harry had ever heard him; hospitality was extended to visiting bishops from Africa and South America; and he was moved at the National Police Remembrance Day at St Mary's Cathedral when young children of deceased officers placed wreaths.

On 18 September 1998, Harry opened Penrith Anglican College. On 29 September, he received Bill Andersen's report on his review of the ACC and met with David Tyndall to discuss preparations for the Sydney Olympics. On 2 October 1998, he reopened Elizabeth Lodge, a home for the elderly, and expressed his opposition to euthanasia, 'both ethically and pragmatically.'[38] On 3 October, he watched the federal election results with lawyer Bill Haffenden, then recuperating after surgery, and, reflecting that Howard's victory given his advocacy of a goods and services tax was 'remarkable', hoped he would remember 'the poor.'

Much to Harry's disappointment, Graham Cole, Principal of Ridley College, wrote to decline the offer of an assistant bishop's position.[39] At the end of October, he visited Hong Kong for the inauguration of the Province of Hong Kong and the installation of Peter Kwong as archbishop and primate. Harry observed that Margaret Rodgers, his press secretary, was greatly respected in Asia. He anticipated that arising from his visit, he would be invited to visit China, a hope that became a reality in January 2000.

Harry was alerted to the possibility that cross-cultural ministry might have been weakened by regionalisation. After Mersina Soulos, who had been the director of that ministry for HMS, spoke to him with 'great passion' about the importance of maintaining Anglicare's commitment to it, Harry pleaded her cause at a meeting of the HMS council, and a working party got off to a good start in addressing the deficiency.[40] From

20.2 In 2005, Margaret Fuller, Wollongong counsellor with Anglicare, received an Order of Australia medal for service to the community as a social worker and counsellor.

15 to 26 December he was miserable with a chest infection. Margaret Fuller shared with him how upset she was over the inquiry into the ACC, in response to which Harry prayed, 'Lord, what can I do to help the diocese have a more generous spirit?'[41]

## The 1998 Sydney synod

At synod Harry reported on Lambeth – having heard of so much suffering, he doubted if he would ever be the same again.[42] He was resolved to do more for the poor and for the preservation of the Anglican Communion.[43] He was enthusiastic about the fast-developing coalition of conservative Anglicans, all of whom thought lay presidency unnecessary and unAnglican. He would not be signing off on lay presidency because Sydney diocese did not need 'that extra bit of lead in our saddlebags when we try to be an influence beyond our borders.'[44] Harry called on Sydney to abandon its 'isolationist mindset' and become involved with the wider Anglican Communion. He explained that he was involved in the development of an international network of bishops who were committed to mission and evangelism.

Muriel Porter claims that the extent of Harry's involvement with this international network of conservative Anglicans 'took many by surprise.'[45] She perhaps means by this that she found it surprising. But it is not really so hard to understand. Harry was, as she observes, irenic, but this is far from amounting to accepting behaviour that he believed was contrary to Scripture. Like the majority of the conservative bishops, and unlike Sydney conservatives, he was encouraging of women's ministry and saw no point in lay presidency, but he drew the line at the ordination of practising homosexuals. He might have drawn it less offensively than some, but it was a clear line, nevertheless. Muriel Porter, however, is right in her interesting observation that Harry 'laid the groundwork for his successor's much more high-profile activity in the conservative world alliance. Ironically his rejection of lay presidency obviously helped immeasurably.'[46] Harry probably would not have agreed to playing a leading part in GAFCON, as Peter Jensen would do, because it was separatist, but he would not be displeased that his stand at Lambeth and his opposition to lay presidency helped the cause of Bible-based, mission-minded Anglicanism.

Women's ministry was the part of his address[47] over which he had 'laboured' most.[48] He said that he had been asked by some to make his own position plain. Indeed, Keith Mason had asked him to come out unequivocally in support of female ordination. He concluded a long section on the employability of women with the words,

> So where do I stand? In fact I don't. I pray ... I have prayed for a growing consensus that might indicate the mind of God. I have prayed for greater clarity in my own views. ... However I am persuaded that convictions about the role of women in ministry are not to be placed in the category of beliefs 'necessary for salvation'. In our Australian Church it is possible for women to be made priests. Should the Synod of this diocese ever decide to act in that way, it could. If you ask me whether I would withhold my consent if such a decision were made, my reply ... would be tentative but I would not withhold consent.[49]

The next morning Harry found himself reported in *SMH* as 'supporting the ordination of women!!' and he observed, 'My attempts to express my own mind appears to confuse people. What seems perfectly clear to me sounds confused to others – even Pam!'[50]

Such crises often elicit profound responses and always revealing ones. From Bangkok came a paroxysm of pain from the friend who had been so instrumental in his election. Stephen Gabbott wrote, 'I need to be honest and say that there have been times when I regretted my part in your election.' He confessed to feeling let down by 'several archbishops' and he wondered if the job was 'doable' anymore. He just could not understand 'why we have to have archbishops who seem unable to openly and with vigour support what we stand for in the face of all that seems so evil and querulous in the rest of the Anglican world.' He went on to ask:

> Is it really the job of the Archbishop to protect the weak/silly/erroneous from the rest of us? Are men like John Woodhouse, Phillip Jensen, Peter Jensen, Brian Telfer, Barry Newman and some others and those of us who want to follow their lead the evil, divisive, unloving men we are so often made to feel we are by those who do not appear to have made any meaningful contribution to the welfare of the Diocese, the spread of the gospel or the good reputation of our great God?

Wonderful questions, and even if they appear unnervingly self-righteous, he had a fascinating biblical justification for them. On the basis of 1 Corinthians 13, the famous chapter on love, he wondered:

> there are these two faces to love – a soft and gentle face and a hard and stern face. What struck me from 1 Corinthians is that the application of the faces is the opposite to what we might expect. Our natural response I think is to be soft and gentle with the weak and querulous and stern and hard with the aggressive and triumphalist. Is Paul suggesting a

reversal of these faces? To the triumphalist and aggressive, present the gentle and the kind face of love, but be stern and tough with those who are weak and vacillating? It could be, it seems to me.[51]

It's a revealing insight into the psyche of conservative Sydney Anglicans, who, it might be concluded, clearly want to be loved like everyone else. It must also have been hard for Harry when even his friends did not consider for a moment that his much prayed-over nuanced position on women's ministry might have been consistent with God's will or that he might have been right to have withstood the push for lay presidency. Stephen signed off 'With undimmed affection but residual bewilderment.'

Harry's critics, however, were neither confused like Pam nor bewildered like Stephen. They were shocked. Bruce Ballantine-Jones, an intrepid opponent of female ordination, wrote candidly to Harry. He felt duty bound to express his disappointment at the 'bombshell' of the archbishop's announcement that he was prepared to sign a bill authorising the priesting of women. Now they would have to oppose not only the ordination of women, but the archbishop as well. For fight on they must and 'never give up.' Upholding the Bible on this matter had to take precedence over concern for the feelings of those who 'lose.' Never before, contended Ballantine-Jones, had the diocese been put in a position where those who held the archbishop dear at a personal level had to oppose him because 'loyalty to God demands it.' Furthermore, other gospel causes would suffer as time and energy were expended 'on this terrible conflict.'[52]

Harry responded that the question 'what does obedience to Scripture involve on the question of women ministering in our congregations in Australia at the end of the 20th century?' was not as easy to answer as his critics maintained. He was concerned that the conservatives were becoming unreasonable and destructive in the practical outworking of their position. He could not see that there was any difference between a woman deacon or layperson presiding and preaching, which the conservatives were prepared to allow through lay or diaconal administration, and a woman priest not in charge of a parish doing the same thing, which the conservatives would not allow. If they amounted to the same thing, why dissent from the entire Anglican Communion by seeking to allow those not priests to administer the Lord's Supper?

Synod made sure that Harry was not given the opportunity to consent to female ordination. There was much discussion of his position, however, which disturbed the defenders of the faith once for all delivered to Sydney.

> The Archbishop shocked many with his announcement that he 'would not withhold his consent' ... More questions were raised than answers given by this declaration. Why 'yes' on this issue when there is a mass of Scripture on gender role and function, and 'no' on lay administration, when the Scriptures say not a word on who administers the Lord's supper?[53]

Synod had voted to 'rebuke' the primate, Keith Rayner, for his Melbourne synod sermon calling for a reconsideration of the received tradition of the church on homosexuality on the grounds that it put tradition on the same level of authority as Scripture. An amendment that sought to distance the synod from any suggestion that a common hermeneutic was employed to endorse female ordination and homosexuality was 'resoundingly defeated.' Clearly there were those in the synod who were keen to make such a suggestion.

The argument of the *Australian Church Record* (*ACR*) was that Melbourne was not the only diocese tempted to elevate tradition at the expense of the unique authority of the Scriptures. This heresy had now washed up on the shores of Sydney, thanks to Archbishop Goodhew. Harry had not distanced himself from a report of Australia's bishops that only a priest or bishop could celebrate the Lord's Supper, and because that was the product, not of biblical revelation, but of tradition, Harry had 'accepted a method of doing theology contrary to the evangelical faith.'

Further, when addressing the issue of female ordination, Harry was guilty of seeking a growing consensus within the Church on the matter. He had said that the demonstrable success of female ministers should be taken into account and that female ordination might be compatible with the 'reception' of Scriptural revelation. The *ACR* condemned reception as Catholic. It condemned consensus as a means to determine the truth of revelation. And it condemned experience as an indicator of truth. The archbishop was confused: he was mixing the 'Bible alone', which he professed, with 'Bible plus experience', which he practised. Harry's approach was thus linked to the theology of Tom Wright who had written that revelation was a play in five acts, with Old Testament revelation corresponding to the first four, and the New Testament corresponding with scene one of the final act. This fifth act was the last 2000 years of the Christian church, the age of the Spirit, which elevated the Spirit and pushed Scripture into the background, thus separating the word from the Spirit.

If it is a sign of good journalism that one side of a case only is put, then *ACR* is a good paper. But a different construction could be put on Harry's words. First, 'reception' was not only a technical Catholic term; it refers to the interpretations given over time to past data and is not the same as a revisionist or liberal construction. After all, the Catholics themselves had not so 'received' the Scriptures as to justify female ordination. Second, the biblical case for the ordination of women is not demonstrably more liberal than the biblical case against it. Third, Harry was not putting human consensus over against the Bible; he was talking about a consensus on the interpretation of the Bible. His opponents too often identified their interpretation of Scripture with what 'the Bible says.' It is always the job of an archbishop to seek diocesan consensus on biblical truth. Fourth, in seeking to understand and interpret Scripture aright, it is folly not to take experience into account. Fifth, it is ungenerous to take as evidence of 'confusion' Harry's humble words that he had 'prayed for greater clarity in [his] own views.' Sixth, Harry's approach joins the Spirit and the word; it was his critics' approach that separated them.

The *ACR* went close to libelling Harry with its insinuation that Harry was wading in what Thomas Cranmer, in a more brutal age, called 'the stinking puddles of the traditions of men', and not all conservative Bible-believers were happy with *ACR*'s assault on the archbishop.

> As I read it, I became increasingly angry at the grossly unfair and outright rude insinuations and direct put-downs ... I write for myself and my wife. After one of the dinners for ordination candidates at Bishopscourt ... I commented to Catriona that 'I would walk on hot calls for that guy.' She shot straight back, 'If you didn't, I would push you.'
>
> Be assured that as I have spoken to a number of other people, they share the same sense of outrage that our Bishop should be so poorly treated by those who ought to know better. My guess is that life as Archbishop brings plenty of pressures, but this must be particularly hurtful.[54]

Harry would not be the first or the last evangelical to be hurt by *ACR*'s editorial habit of shooting its own troops if they dared to call for deeper reflection on controverted truths. Harry, however, was good at dealing with hurt. He said his prayers and left it with the Lord to sort out and went to bed. But Harry may not have been so good at dealing with the political reality that the majority of synod seemed to be out of sympathy with his views, if not with him. And the danger in the Sydney culture always is that there is but a short distance between the condemnation of one's views and the condemnation of one's person. The mantra of Harry's opponents that there was 'nothing personal' in their attacks on him sounded hollow in the ears of his supporters, if not of the archbishop himself, who

*Sixth Year (1998 Continued): 'The Winsome Face of Sydney'*

20.3 Justice Keith Mason with Harry at the opening of Chesalon Beecroft nursing home, November 2000.

attributed it to testosterone!

So, divided over female ordination and lay presidency, synod degenerated into a battle of tactics. Phillip Jensen moved a motion representing SC's wish for a five-year experiment in lay and diaconal administration at the Lord's Supper. This motion purported to enact the one clear idea that emerged from the special May 1998 synod on female ordination. Lay and diaconal administration would preserve the notion of headship (1 Tim 2) by refusing to ordain women to the priesthood, while allowing women to administer the sacrament, thus increasing their employability. Harry declared the motion lost on the voices in what *ACR* labelled a 'Freudian slip', and when it was put again the voices were loudly in favour.

John Woodhouse then moved the third reading of the ordinance on lay and diaconal administration. Justice Keith Mason objected on the grounds that the ordinance would involve the variation of trusts, and that therefore synod was not competent to decide the matter. The archbishop ruled that Justice Mason's opinion was valid. A motion of dissent from the archbishop's ruling was then put and passed, a rarity and not a good look for Harry.[55] Richard Lambert, an experienced SC member, then made another point of order. He contended that the president could rule that this matter should not be debated because it was on the same subject matter as the previous motion, namely the five-year experiment. Harry accepted the point of order and disallowed further discussion. An attempt was then made to move dissent from Harry's ruling, but this was dismissed by Harry 'with a joke.'[56] Though he had Harry on the ropes, John Woodhouse then withdrew his motion – it could be on the agenda the following year.

From the Supreme Court in Sydney came a note to Harry from the President of the Court of Appeal, Keith Mason.

> I am sorry that my point of order exposed you to the dissent of Synod. I had hoped that it would be less painful than the consequences of withheld assent.
>
> I shall put in writing my reasons for doubting the validity of resort to our trust-varying power … I have for many years thought that the power was capable of abuse, and been aware of situations when it was (in my view) abused.
>
> Thanks for your most competent chairmanship of a difficult and largely arid session of Synod. And thank you for a sterling Presidential address. Quite apart from your remarks about women's ministry it was clear, informative and encouraging. Those of us who are hanging in by our bruised fingertips value this immensely.[57]

The last day of synod was Tuesday, 20 October 1998. The next day Philip Bradford, Rector of Hunter's Hill, wrote to Harry:

> Last night I felt ashamed to be a member of the Sydney Synod as I believe it acted in a most inappropriate manner. In particular, I was appalled by the disrespect shown to you as president of the Synod. Throughout the proceedings you remained outwardly calm and courteous and consistently showed remarkable Christian grace and I greatly admired you for that.

And from Anglicare, Parramatta, Howard Dillon wrote:

> This Synod Session will be characterised in my memory as the one when the hopefuls produced their wares. While I found some of the posturing a bit much, you maintained a Christ-like presence which I found both encouraging and a sense of blessing … The diocese has a great opportunity for leadership and to be the ultimate channel of God's blessing to the whole Australian Church. You have demonstrated that there are other ways of persuasion than a punch on the nose. I pray

that younger leaders will learn patience and generous acceptance and love from your godly example.[58]

Harry had his supporters, clearly, but the dissent from his rulings in synod was strong evidence that his desire to promote the unity of Sydney Anglicans by relieving the pain of female ordination advocates was having the opposite effect.

## More on Lambeth '98

On 5 August 1998, the same day on which Resolution 1.10 was passed at the Lambeth Conference, some bishops, led by Spong, had issued 'A Pastoral Statement to Lesbian and Gay Anglicans from Some Member Bishops of the Lambeth Conference.' Drafted by Bp Ronald Haines of Washington, DC, it said,

> it has not been possible to hear adequately your voices, and we apologise for any sense of rejection that has occurred because of this reality ... We pledge that we will continue to reflect, pray, and work for your full inclusion in the life of the Church.

As of 14 September 1998, 165 clergy, including eight primates and 10 Australian bishops,[59] had signed this statement.

On 10 November, Bp Barnett invited a small group of interested people, including BBJ and Robert Tong, to meet with Canon Bill Atwood, then in parish ministry in the Episcopal Church in America. He was a member of the American Anglican Council formed in 1996 to defend biblical Anglican orthodoxy against the increasingly rampant liberalism in the Episcopal Church. He was well known to conservative African bishops and reported on their inclination to depart, if necessary, from a church undermined by unfaithfulness to the Bible. The following day Atwood met with Harry, who feared losing the middle ground if the inclination to separate was not handled carefully. Harry agreed to explore with his friend, Bp Jim Stanton of Dallas, the wisdom of establishing an Australian equivalent of the American Anglican Council, but warned that it would only be too easy to precipitate the irreversible fragmentation of the Anglican Communion given the difference of opinion on so many issues. Afterwards Harry confided in his Day Book, 'I need to stay on top of this. I am not anxious to divide the Australian church prematurely.'[60] On the same day Boak Jobbins, Dean of Sydney, who had also been at the meeting with Atwood and who was of the opinion that the rapidly developing situation required wise oversight, asked Harry if he would be prepared to stay on as archbishop beyond the age of 70. Harry admitted that he would give the proposal serious consideration if the diocese asked him, but he would not be prepared to run this himself and risk the rejection that he believed the idea would probably receive.[61]

Four days later, Harry asked Paul Barnett to chair a small committee to capitalise on links forged at Lambeth with many like-minded bishops across the Anglican Communion by exploring the possibility of developing links with their dioceses. Was it the forerunner of GAFCON where, under Archbishop Peter Jensen, the Diocese of Sydney formed strong links with other conservative dioceses in the Anglican Communion? On asking Paul Barnett to chair a committee to develop the concept, Harry wrote, 'I do not wish us to lose the initiative to others in this area. We made the connections at Lambeth, the idea was ours, we have the credibility overseas, and I would like us to carry it forward.'[62]

The Committee on Companion Links Dioceses, made up of Paul Barnett, Margaret Rodgers, Evonne Paddison, Robert Tong, and Peter Tasker, then Rector of Dapto, reported on 25 February 1999. It recommended joining with 'a number of theologically like-minded dioceses' to contribute 'to the defence of the apostolic gospel', to allow the exchange of clergy, and to share theological resources in Bible teaching. It recommended establishing at least one 'companion' diocese in each continent, including Dallas in the United States, London in the United Kingdom, Nigeria in West Africa and Zaire in East Africa.

Meanwhile in late November 1998, in response to the 'Pastoral Statement to Lesbian and Gay Anglicans', Harry wrote a letter to all Australian bishops.[63] He challenged the view that none of the bishops at Lambeth had adequately heard the voices of those who wanted to change the Church's opposition to homosexual practice. There had been much listening. He also argued that he was not unaware of some of the arguments of those who wanted to interpret biblical prohibitions differently.

> I recognise ... that the Jewish and Christian requirement that sexual intercourse be contained within the circle of marriage between husband and wife may well be viewed as something of an aberration in the long history of human sexual practices. Such a containment to a marriage relationship could be understood, however, as an indication of Divine guidance rather than human predilection.

He feared that the 'Pastoral Statement' could confirm many people 'in practices that invite the judgement of God.' To this the bishops responded as follows:
- Ron Stone, Bishop of Rockhampton, agreed 100 per cent.
- Phillip Newell, Bishop of Tasmania, voted for the Lambeth Resolution, but was troubled by whether or not homosexual orientation was a 'given'

rather than chosen or acquired and on this the 'jury is still out.'
- George Browning, Canberra and Goulburn, agreed with Harry.
- Phillip Aspinall, assistant bishop, Brisbane, disagreed. He was one of the 'small minority' who signed the 'Pastoral Statement'.
- Roger Herft, Bishop of Newcastle, signed the 'Pastoral Statement' and abstained from voting for the Lambeth Resolution.
- Arthur Jones, Bishop of Gippsland, refused to sign the 'Pastoral Statement', but he too was troubled by the possibility that homosexuality might be from the Creator. 'The use of Scripture then to exclude homosexuals could be seen as a travesty.' He added, 'I found Bruce Ballantine-Jones' speech at the last General Synod to be full of emotional rage and quite scary. I admired his courage, but his reasoning escaped me because it was soaked in "outrage".' He also wrote,

> Despite your public assurances, I am not sure that you realise sufficiently the hurt experienced by those who are homosexual and members of the Church, especially in view of the unfortunate use of the word 'rejecting' in the amendment at Lambeth. We have a time-honoured phrase 'contrary to Scripture' which would have been so much better.

- Graham Waldron, Bishop of the Murray, agreed with Harry.
- Bp Richard Randerson, Assistant Bishop of Canberra and Goulburn, wondered if given shifting cultural understandings we should seek God's intent afresh.
- Philip Huggins, Grafton, voted for the Lambeth resolution and did not sign the 'Pastoral Statement', but he hoped that the matter could be dropped and that more important issues could be considered by church leaders.
- Brian Farran, Assistant Bishop of Perth, signed the 'Pastoral Statement' because he thought more listening was definitely called for and a very careful use of Scripture raised doubts about Harry's conservative interpretation of Scripture.
- Richard Appleby, Bishop of the Northern Territory, was one of 45 bishops who abstained from voting at Lambeth, regretting that the whole tone of the debate was harsh and condemnatory, and he happily signed the 'Pastoral Statement'.
- Tony Nichols, North West Australia, agreed with Harry 100 per cent
- David Silk, Ballarat, gave his full support 'in prayer and word.'

- David Murray, assistant bishop, Perth, did not say where he stood, but regretted the tone of the Lambeth debate.

On 9 December 1998, Harry posted his letter on the internet. Bruce Kaye, Secretary to the General Synod, wrote to say that Harry was quite correct. 'The idea of circulating a failed motion or push from Lambeth in the hope of suggesting the Lambeth decision was something other than what it was is quite mischievous. Well done – to make the point.'[64]

As the year progressed, Harry reported often on Lambeth. His emphasis, however, was decreasingly on human sexuality and increasingly on human suffering, on which the African bishops had reported in harrowing detail. For his 1998 Christmas Day sermon in St Andrew's Cathedral, Harry began by speaking of the manger scene as one 'full of delight', but moved on to speak of children in today's world suffering 'in ways almost too dreadful to detail': kidnapped, malnourished, starved, impoverished, deprived of health care or education, abused. Instead of being paralysed by such a reality, Harry insisted that 'this is definitely the place and the time' to make a difference, which we will if we remember that 'the largest task is doable' if God calls us to it. He reminded the congregation of the words of Jesus' mother, 'whatever he says to you, do it!'[65]

Harry's vision was increasingly international. He never thought of the world as his parish, as Wesley did. But he was convinced that the world was Jesus' parish, and, while archbishop, was intimately associated with three major instrumentalities to make it so. The first was EE, which was now each year reaching literally millions across the globe with the gospel; the second, his increasing opportunities to minister in international settings, such as Sri Lanka, Ethiopia and India, where he preached to tens of thousands; and third was the international network of conservative evangelical bishops across the Anglican Communion, especially those of 'the global South', who led dioceses with far more Anglicans and far greater populations with a much larger interface with the other great religions than the more liberal bishops of Western Christianity. There was a fourth that was to develop after he stepped down as archbishop. It involved visiting the vast slums in poor African countries. Harry and Pam were at first moved by the appalling conditions in the slums, but ever the evangelist, he saw the opportunity to take the gospel to mass populations, reminiscent of the mass conversions of outcaste Indians a century earlier.

# 21

# Seventh Year (1999): 'Faith Is Trusting God in Every Situation'

At the beginning of each year, routine commitments were entered into Harry's diary. The year 1999, however, was to be anything but routine. Division within the worldwide Anglican Communion evolved rapidly, and Harry found himself on a number of unexpected overseas trips to meet with bishops to deal with the fallout from the Lambeth Conference. His was, in any case, a role where business as usual was the exception rather than the rule, and whereas the new year began in the usual way with CMS Summer School, it soon diverged into new territory.

Harry again preached at the communion service at the CMS Summer School on 3 January. It continued to perform its God-given role of reducing friction among the clergy, as all present focused with heart and mind on mission. Harry spoke briefly with David Gilmour, and Phillip Jensen sought to speak with him about lay presidency. Following Summer School, Harry attended the Prayer and Spirituality Conference at St John's, the Catholic College, in the University of Sydney. It was attended by Rowan Williams, shortly to be elected Archbishop of Canterbury. In the college chapel, Harry read to conferees the Epiphany Sermon of St Gregory the Great, who, in 596 AD, had commissioned Augustine of Canterbury to take the gospel to England and is commonly taken to be the birth of *Ecclesia Anglicana*, the Church of England. Astrology was troubling the church then as now. Gregory refuted those who argued that, since a star led the three wise men to Jesus's manger, it was right to allow one's destiny to be shaped by the stars.

> We see that it is not the Child that hastens to the star, but the star that hastens to the Child, and so, if I may say this, it is not the star that is the Child's fate, but rather, it is the Child who is the destiny of the star.[1]

Fourteen centuries later, Harry had become a Church of England archbishop with a responsibility to that long tradition and to the wide Communion that *Ecclesia Anglicana* had become. In the richness and complexity of that context, Harry never forgot the simplicity of the truth that Jesus is the destiny of all things.

The Sunday following (10 January) the cathedral congregation worshipped in the chapter house, as refurbishment of the Cathedral had begun. Harry had a look inside the cathedral and observed that 'stripped of most of its interior [it] looks a grand building.'[2]

## Ministry overseas

On 16 January, Harry and Pam flew out on a round trip to Bangkok, Ethiopia, and Sabah. In Bangkok, old friends Stephen and Marion Gabbott, never ones to miss an opportunity, arranged for Harry on the morning after his arrival to preach and in the afternoon to meet up with a large number of expatriates, including workers with the Australian embassy, the Far East Broadcasting Company, and other Australian churches and missions, including a nurse who had worked at Ceduna, South Australia, where Harry had served with the BCA over three decades earlier. Harry was saddened to see the dozens of young prostitutes who lined the nearby streets, observing, 'Their life expectancy is limited.'[3]

On 19 January, Harry and Pam flew to Addis Ababa in Ethiopia, where they stayed with the Canadian Ambassador, John Schram, and his wife Alena. Harry opened extensions to the Addis Ababa Fistula Hospital, started in 1974 by Catherine Hamlin, who turned 75 during their visit. The extensions cost $A1.48 million, of which the Archbishop of Sydney's Overseas Relief and Aid Fund contributed $A1.3 million. It was then a dangerous time to be in Ethiopia, with war raging along the border with Eritrea. The dependants of the American ambassador were shortly to be ordered to leave. In the midst of this uncertainty, Harry spoke with Schram about faith, and the Schrams and Goodhews became good friends.[4]

21.1 Harry with Catherine Hamlin and staff at the opening of the Fistula Clinic extensions, 21 January 1999.

From 25 to 30 January, Harry and Pam attended a provincial conference in Sabah. Harry spent time with Bp Datuk Yong Ping Chung and the clergy and with the provincial SC, and thus sought to strengthen ties with a region that had previously received the highly effective ministry of Marcus Loane and Walter Newmarch. He asked especially to see the Sabah Theological Seminary, then being directed by CMS missionary, Sylvia Jeanes. She reported that Bp Yong's predecessor had held all full-time workers, male and female, to be equal, and thus succeeded in attracting women into full-time ministry. Bp Yong, however, was far more bound by Chinese culture, which made little room for single women. 'How the gospel needs to transform culture utterly,' she wrote to Harry later, 'but that doesn't happen overnight.'[5] On his retirement, she wrote again to Harry.

> I shall always be grateful the way you stepped down from your office to be with a simple person like me during your visit to Sabah. And you were able to listen, care and understand during a crisis period for me. Truly on that day God sent you to me.[6]

Of the whole period 19–31 January 1999, Harry recorded in his diary, 'Life too hectic to get any time to write.' He and Pam arrived home just in time for the Annual Law Service, which had become an important part of the annual routine. Less than a fortnight later, they were off again, this time to India, where Harry gave four addresses at the Maramon Convention (14–21 February) in Kerala for the Mar Thoma Evangelistic Association, the missionary wing of the ancient Mar Thoma Church. The Sydney diocese had a congregation of the Mar Thoma Church associated with Holy Trinity Anglican Church, Erskineville. Six years earlier, on 13 April 1993, less than two weeks after his election as archbishop, Harry had met Bp Zacharias Theophilus of the Mar Thoma Church of South India. He was, like Harry, warm-hearted and appealed to people of all ages. Harry had resolved at that meeting to visit India 'sometime.'[7] Harry took as his theme for the conference 'To live in my Father's world, to long for my Father's home and to do my Father's will is the calling of my life.' In preparation for these addresses, Harry had been himself deeply moved. 'The grace and mercy of God is so overwhelming. I am left dumbfounded. There is really no adequate response that can be made. He precedes us in everything. One can only surrender to it and give thanks.'[8]

Enormous crowds heard these addresses, gathered on the extensive sand-bed of the Pampa River at Pathanamthitta. It was not all smooth sailing for Harry, unused to handling such vast crowds. During one of his morning addresses, on 'God, the Holy Spirit', there was a disturbance. 'A child was frightened by a small snake or lizard on the floor where it was sitting. It's alarming to see how quickly a crowd could turn into a movement hard to control. Everything settled and we carried on.'⁹

Coming from a diocese famous for keeping women in their place, Harry and Pam were also surprised by the role of women in the conference. Admittedly, patriarchy was strongly in evidence. Harry took the women leaders' Bible study every morning at 7.30, on 1 Thessalonians, and the bishops who attended the conference sat at the top table, waited on literally hand and foot by a very attractive, beautifully dressed Indian woman. But there the patriarchy seemed to end. She was married to a member of parliament and he had relinquished to her his stockbroker business, which she ran; and, in her spare time, she drove racing cars. It was she who organised the morning devotions, and she, Pam and other women took the devotions. Pam was fascinated that the men were not troubled that the women had this role. She observed that to get to the convention, delegates drove over a bridge designed in 1925 by a woman who was an engineer. At the morning devotion taken by Pam she spoke on the theme of the Christian mind.

In a poll taken among the vast crowd to find the most appreciated speaker who was then invited to give the final address, Harry was chosen. One of the organisers, Mathew George Chunakara, congratulated Margaret Rodgers, head of Anglican Media, for assisting them to find such an impressive speaker. The metropolitan asked Harry for a copy of his addresses, as his own priests did not know how to preach like that. 'My brothers and sisters,' Harry told the crowd of upwards of 100,000 at the last meeting of the convention, 'faith is trusting God in every situation.' Preaching on Psalm 129 on 'persevering to prevail,' he said, 'The people in Psalms are singing the songs of tough faith.'¹⁰ The times required tough faith. In the month preceding the Convention, Graham Staines, an Australian missionary, and his two sons, Timothy, 6, and Phillip, 10, had been burned to death by a group of angry Hindus. There were numerous soldiers and police patrolling the town and the Convention site in the dry bed of the Pamba River. This was the first time the police had been in attendance at the convention. The national government of India, Harry noted, had been 'persuaded by its more determinedly Hindu elements to exercise greater efforts to support Hinduism.' This was a gracious way of reporting on the resurgence of Hindu fundamentalism and a new, dangerous wave of persecution of Muslims and Christians in India. Some years later Harry shared with Graham Staines' wife, Gladys, a session on forgiveness at the Christian Medical and Dental Conference held in Sydney. Her message then and later in India was that 'In forgiveness, there is no bitterness and when there is no bitterness, there is hope. This consolation comes from Jesus Christ.'¹¹ Harry was greatly impressed by her and was gratified to learn that, on

27 January 2005, she received the prestigious Padma Shri award from the Indian government for her work among the poor in Odisha.

After the last meeting of the Maramon Convention, Harry and Pam were collected by Bp Sam Matthew of the Church of South India and driven northwest to Kottayam. On the way they stopped at the Bethel Ashram, Thiruvalla, a mission exclusively to women, begun in 1924 by CMS missionary, Edith Neve, and Rachel Joseph, an Indian high school teacher. 'This was an impressive place,' records Harry, 'as were the staff and children.'[12] At Kottayam, Harry addressed over 100 of the clergy of the Church of South India, and he heard the amazing story of CMS missionary, Benjamin Bailey, one of the first English missionaries to work in India.

Harry was told that Bailey was a carpenter and built Holy Trinity Cathedral in Kottayam, that 'noble Gothic church,' observed Bp Daniel Wilson of Calcutta, 'the glory of Travancore.' It was possibly an even more remarkable achievement, however, because Bailey was not even a carpenter, but actually a clothier by trade! He was a personal friend of John Keats, the poet, and a gifted linguist. He translated the Scriptures into Malayalam, the language most spoken in Kerala, built a printing press, and was recognised as the leading lexicologist and typographer of Malayalam. A statue of this exemplary missionary was erected in his honour in the central municipal park in the city.

It was an inspiring culmination to an inspiring visit, perhaps equalled the following day, when he and Pam visited St Thomas's School, Trivandrum, which had over 5000 students. Established by the Mar Thoma Church as recently as 1990, Harry found it to be 'very impressive.' He and Pam arrived back at Bishopscourt at 9.15 pm the next day, ahead of another full day of commitments, at the end of which Harry wrote, 'Hard to shake off the effects of the last two weeks.'[13]

## The ongoing struggle for Lambeth '98 Resolution 1.10

Possibly he did not want to shake off its effects. His sermons on his return were full of encouraging stories of God at work by his Spirit in a variety of ways and places. The inspiring life of Benjamin Bailey, for example, made up part of Harry's 'President's Remarks' at a service for the bicentenary of CMS at the cathedral on 11 April 1999. India had been a welcome relief from the numerous very difficult problems Harry faced. On 24 February 1999 Harry had joined with seven other bishops[14] in writing an open letter to Frank Griswold, the Presiding Bishop and Primate of ECUSA, urging him to take whatever steps were necessary to uphold the moral teaching and Christian faith received by the Anglican Communion. In response to the open letter from Harry and others, on 10 March 1999, Griswold, with the approval of the nine episcopal members of his Council of Advice, invited the eight bishops resistant to the American rejection of Lambeth to visit America 'to see for themselves.' He pointed out that the Lambeth report on sexuality contained expressions of four different understandings of homosexuality, that discernment was now required to process them in the context of the faith of the church, that argument and controversy solves nothing and a new type of conversation was required, one appropriate to the church 'as a community of moral discourse.'[15] He was inviting them to visit America to see for themselves how members of ECUSA were responding to the Lambeth resolution on homosexuality.

Jim Stanton, Bishop of Dallas, suspected that Griswold did not believe his offer would be accepted, but he advised it should be. It would give the conservatives the authority to speak afterwards on what the American scene demanded.[16] Like Harry, however, Stanton was reluctant to go with those 'good souls' who believed ECUSA had already reached the point of no return. Disunity and the idea of a 'parallel jurisdiction' were not to his liking. 'We cannot be complacent about the situation here,' he admitted to Harry, 'but we do not need to launch a NATO-style attack either.'[17] Meanwhile, Harry noted, 'ECUSA presses on its way ... putting pressure on conservatives.' Bp Charles Bennison of Pennsylvania, who had been part of the small group Harry was in at Lambeth to deliberate on the issue, was in crusading overdrive, effectively removing the licences of eight conservative clergy in his diocese.[18]

Griswold's invitation was considered by six conservative bishops from around the Anglican Communion, including Harry. Meeting in Singapore on 13–15 April 1999, they heard the testimony of eight voluntary associations within ECUSA who believed that sections of their church had 'deviated significantly from orthodox faith and practice.'[19] In 18 dioceses, Lambeth Resolution 1.10 had been publicly refuted, and resolutions contrary to Resolution 1.10 were passed at four diocesan conventions. The Anglican Communion was bleeding. In the past 40 years, when the population of the United States had doubled, the membership of ECUSA had fallen from 3.4 million to 2.4 million. The situation was so dire and becoming so widely known that the bishops believed they must act urgently. They resolved to appeal to the Archbishop of Canterbury on the grounds that Lambeth had been ignored. They believed that pastoral support should be offered to those clergy whose licences were terminated, and ordination and bishops provided for beleaguered congregations.

For his part, Harry was not keen to have the orthodox bishops isolated and branded as secessionists, and he understood the Archbishop of Canterbury's reluctance to see the Anglican Communion torn apart 'however orthodox his own opinions [on] the matter of homosexual practice.'[20] So, the bishops at Singapore resolved to accept Griswold's invitation to visit a number of American dioceses, but they saw themselves as acting on behalf of the Archbishop of Canterbury, whom they would keep informed of their actions, and whom they believed might not rule out recognising a breakaway church from ECUSA should it come to that. Harry may even have hoped that his warm friendship with George Carey was paying dividends.

Carey, however, seems to have been alarmed by the pace of events and the multiplying pressure from conservative American congregations and ministers to move decisively against ECUSA. He appealed to the conservative bishops for a year-long moratorium on all correspondence proposing such drastic moves and that every opportunity for face-to-face encounters should be taken, including that proposed by Bp Griswold.[21] Moses Tay, Archbishop of the Province of South East Asia, who had already decided not to accept Griswold's invitation, replied to Carey hotly that 'It would be nice to be able to agree to the proposed moratorium on correspondence if you can also effect a similar moratorium on Bishops and Dioceses going against Lambeth's position on Biblical Authority and Morality.'[22] For his part, Harry assured Carey that they greatly valued face-to-face encounters, but he believed the plea for help from isolated faithful and traditional Anglicans could not be overlooked. He feared that if action were not taken soon, there would be 'significant defections from our ranks.'[23]

On the day after Harry sent this response, he received a message from Maurice Sinclair, Presiding Bishop of the Southern Cone of America, urging him to send it. 'He [Carey] knows that you are not a fire eater and he fully respects your leadership.' Sinclair concluded that they had Carey's 'guarded and cautious support', but Carey wanted the conservative bishops not to give the impression that they were representing a minority position – they were clearly in the majority.[24] They were undoubtedly in the majority in seeing homosexual practice as a bar to ordination, but it was not as simple as that. In condemning departures from Lambeth Resolution 1.10, they seemed to overlook the fact that no Lambeth resolutions were binding on individual dioceses – it looked as if they were trying to force on the Anglican Communion a new doctrine of provincial conformity, which the very independent Diocese of Sydney would be the last to support. If that is what Harry wanted to achieve, he was pressing for a procedure that was unconstitutional. As Griswold had already advised his American colleagues, 'the basic reality is that, for us in America, acts of General Convention take precedence over the opinions of the Lambeth Conference.'[25]

Harry returned from Singapore to find Bishopscourt had sustained considerable damage in a hailstorm, then rated as the third worst disaster in Australian history, not in loss of life, but in terms of the cost of damage to infrastructure.

## Harry's initiatives

In the maelstrom of activities that threatened to damage Harry's health more than the hailstorm damaged Bishopscourt, the majority were matters requiring his response rather than his initiative. As he was unusually interested in other people's passions, he always responded to their initiatives faithfully and usually with enthusiasm. For example, in August 1999, he warmly inaugurated new cross-cultural ministry arrangements at St Alban's, Belmore, in the Georges River region, building on the foundations of such resourceful advocates as Mersina Soulos, Alan Cole and Ray Smith, the regional bishop.

There were matters close to his heart, however, where he did take the initiative. One was ministry to youth. Harry had presided over a more than year-long process for the revamping of the Youth Department. It was amalgamated with children's and education divisions under one corporate body, with Lindsay Stoddart as CEO. Youthworks had two official launches, one on 22 April at Bishopscourt, followed by a more public launch in the auditorium of the Bishop Barry Centre in St Andrew's Cathedral School. At the latter, Harry spoke of his own experience as a young Christian and of his vision for more parishes with an active ministry to young people and children.[26] He also expended considerable energy in promoting low-fee Anglican schools with their great potential to ground young people in Christian values, a development enthusiastically taken up by prime minister, John Howard, who met with Harry on 7 May. It was again evident to Harry that here was another area where it was unwise for Sydney to go it alone: far better for Anglicans Australia-wide to adopt an Anglican systemic approach akin to the Catholics, Lutherans and Seventh-day Adventists.

On the international front, he continued to work to find a way to support African bishops, an impressive list of whom he compiled with the help of Margaret Rodgers, and with many of whom he forged strong links in the years ahead. At the end of April, Pie Ntukamazina, Bishop of Bujumbara in Burundi, stayed at Bishopscourt. He shared with Harry his feeling that African bishops needed 'theological stimulation'; and Harry reflected on joining hands with Jim Stanton, the conservative Bishop of Dallas, to give practical help to African bishops. It may have been the issue of opposition to the ordination of homosexuals that brought the likes of Ntukamazina, Stanton and Harry together in the first place, but it was a shared passion for mission that forged close friendships. Burundi, in the recent conflict, had suffered less than genocide-ravaged Rwanda, but its recovery was slower, and hunger and the chronic threat of violence had become normative. It was a situation that concerned Harry long past the time he stood down as archbishop. His admiration for Bp Stanton also grew with the years, for Stanton was a strategist after Harry's heart, giving priority in his own diocese to leadership development, youth work, church growth programs, and world mission, and aligning resources with this priority.

Another indicator of Harry's growing international reputation was his attendance at Billy Graham's Indianapolis crusade from 2 to 5 June 1999. Harry sat on the stage, and at one of the meetings, the spotlight fell on Harry as Billy reminisced about his crusades in Australia, especially his 1959 Crusade in Sydney. In his memoirs, Billy Graham himself never doubted that his time in Australia had been a 'God thing.' He had then received invitations to speak at more than a hundred crusades in different parts of the world. 'One invitation in particular captured my interest. For some reason I could not fully understand, although I believed it was the leading of the Holy Spirit, I had developed an overwhelming burden to visit the distant continent of Australia.'[27] With Harry present to prompt his recollection, he spoke of his time in Australia with such enthusiasm and at such length that he seemed to quite lose track of where he was. Billy Graham was then nearing the end of his international ministry, and Bill Conard, strategist for the Billy Graham Evangelistic Association (BGEA), was keen to discuss the future with Harry. Together with John Akers, ghost writer for Billy Graham, Conard prevailed on Harry to lead the group of clergy leaders at the Amsterdam conference the next year.

## Axing the Anglican Counselling Centre

Harry's international contacts and his own episcopal team were committed to a strategy of evangelism and growth, but the members of the diocesan SC, by contrast, were paralysed by politics. Harry found the meetings of SC where the 'fixers' dealt with the ACC the most depressing of all. If his episcopate had been mired almost from the start in the protracted Pymble matter, it was now bedevilled at its end by the excruciating execution of the ACC, an agony that continued for more than two years. The SC became as involved with the latter disaster as much as the former. It was a body ill-equipped to deal with either matter, but pursued both with the expenditure of an enormous amount of time. Harry warned SC to leave both matters to the diocesan machinery designed to deal with them and to avoid involvement in matters in which they had no expertise. Standing

Committee refused to heed this counsel, dragged synod into both matters, and then blamed Harry for failing to extricate SC from interminable inquiries. There were, however, unaligned members of SC who considered both issues were so big and stirred up so much emotion that it would have been unrealistic for SC to ignore these matters. They were motivated by a desire to help both situations be resolved fairly.[28] Harry probably felt this was help he could have done without.

SC's committee of enquiry into the ACC was chaired by John Woodhouse. He wanted it to be known that he was approached 'out of the blue' to chair the proposed committee and, when he protested that he had no expertise in counselling, was assured that the chair's job was to ensure due process.[29] The seven-member committee of enquiry interviewed only members of its executive and council. ACC staff were required to complete two questionnaires. No pilot exercise was conducted and the form of the second questionnaire was disputed by the ACC council. The committee itself admitted in its report that they 'chose to proceed with the questionnaire quickly while accepting that it might have been preferable to refine the questionnaire further and 'pilot' the questionnaire on a small group of counsellors to ensure consistency in their interpretation of the questions. These steps were foregone in the interests of time.'[30]

In his critique of the committee's research, sent to all members of SC, Dr Ian Cochrane, an expert in educational research, commented that this one decision was 'enough to make the whole of the research invalid.' He added, 'In all my analysis of research, and this extends to hundreds of studies, I have never come across any research that so obviously was prepared to sacrifice accuracy for time!'[31] He concluded that the committee's report was 'totally unreliable and invalid.'[32] Dr George Paul, a former academic with experience in management consultancy, noted, 'The Report is evidence that the enquiry was a thoroughly non-professional approach to an organisational review.' Members of the committee proceeded in haste, however, because they clearly believed that the ACC had to be dealt with quickly to prevent it from doing further damage.

The committee of enquiry adopted 22 recommendations. All but seven were supported by the ACC. However, at its meeting of 26 July, SC received the committee's report and resolved to adopt all 22 recommendations, recasting the seven disputed recommendations into four resolutions. In particular, recommendation 18 prohibited altogether the right of counsellors to employ any therapeutic practices (not clearly defined) that may lead to 'recovered' or 'enhanced memory'. In view of the dubious worth of such practices, this was probably a wise move. But, in order to repress those practices, SC effectively killed off the counselling centre, even though, as the report itself points out, and as synod was reminded by Revd David Crain in 1999, less than 5 per cent of ACC's counselling involved recovered memories of sexual abuse.[33] Working with recovered memories of abuse had never been a major feature of ACC practice. It should have been possible to excise this practice and leave the rest of the ACC intact, according to the findings of Bill Andersen's report, which Harry had received in September of the previous year.

Instead of working with the ACC executive and counsellors and mutually agreeing to tighter controls if and where they were needed (as recommended by Dr Andersen), the committee of enquiry and SC's decision destroyed the ACC. The committee of enquiry's recommendations effectively constrained how relationship counsellors might use their professional skills. Other constraints related to the demand for academic qualifications, not required by the government or other such agencies. Many counsellors resigned, disillusioned and unwilling to continue in an environment where they were unable to use their considerable experience and skills in a way they saw as being most beneficial to the client. Although SC reported that ACC was being integrated with Anglicare, 80 per cent of former counsellors did not transfer.

Among the many appalled counsellors was Margaret Lawton, who wrote directly to John Woodhouse.

> To blast off a nuclear device to obliterate such counselling in the ACC is an over-reaction of such an extreme nature, I can only conclude there is a strong sub-text to these recommendations, that is not being published… Your rationalism, John, provides no answer to, or substitute for, the deep emotional and spiritual healing in my soul, that I have experienced as I have been counselled within the ACC. It is like the truth Jesus speaks about, the pearl of great price, apart from which all else has been loss.[34]

Woodhouse replied that he had no doubt that the ACC had done 'enormous' good, but the counselling offered by the ACC had 'very significant potential for harm', and he found it 'difficult to understand [the] widespread unwillingness within the ACC' to contemplate that possibility. He spoke of 'grave (as yet untested) claims that harm has been done,' adding 'We really should take seriously the principle "first of all, do no harm".'[35]

By mid-2000, the number of counsellors had been reduced from 68 to 15. Not only had the majority left, but they had left in anger. The diocese no longer had a comprehensive counselling service. In its place, it had a lasting inheritance of anger and disillusionment to deal with. Scores of former clients (beneficiaries of

ACC) voiced their anger. The entire process had been carried on in an adversarial environment, resulting in conflict rather than reconciliation. At least 180 letters were written to SC, most of them critical of its actions. It stood to be sternly rebuked at the forthcoming synod.

## 'Come and see' visit to the United States, 27 September to 6 October, 1999

On 26 September, Harry flew out to New York. There he joined with Primate Maurice Sinclair and three other bishops[36] in fulfilment of the invitation of Frank Griswold, Presiding Bishop of ECUSA, to 'come and see' the American response to the Lambeth resolution declaring homosexuality to be incompatible with Scripture. The bishops visited not only those who wanted to see a radical departure from the Lambeth resolution, but also those who believed ECUSA had already departed from it so comprehensively that it was evidently sinking like the Titanic. Harry arrived back in Sydney on 8 October charged, together with Maurice Sinclair, with the responsibility of co-authoring a report on the visit. Dated 24 November 1999, the Report was sent off by Harry to the Archbishop of Canterbury and to Griswold. Carey wrote to Harry on 6 December 1999, 'I was struck by the generosity of so many of your comments, whilst also noting the clarity of your views on the central issues.' He thought it would be well received by Griswold, and added 'I believe your report sets the tone for future discussion and I hope and pray that we shall all work in the same spirit of respect and generosity to overcome the difficulties which we face.'[37] Not everyone would respond to the report so optimistically. The negatives in the report far outweighed any value the visitors found in the direction ECUSA was going.

The visiting bishops were aware that some on the conservative side, in the presence of diocesan officials, were unwilling to express themselves fully, admitting to feeling marginalised and unsupported by their bishops and the national church. They pressed the visitors to come to their aid. Those who held traditional views complained that they were treated with canonical strictness, while those who transgressed long-held moral standards went unchallenged. The House of Bishops seemed to find it difficult to exercise any discipline, and the General Convention seemed incapable of bringing wayward dioceses back into line. Those who sought to break with the homosexual lifestyle felt that their testimony to their struggle was not appreciated. There was 'hubris' in the liberals' dismissal of conservative biblical scholarship that 'strongly and competently' challenged more liberal interpretations. The visiting bishops found a church captive to culture, with a widespread acceptance of the view that homosexuality is innate and irreversible and therefore acceptable. ECUSA's capacity to proclaim divine revelation and the gospel was diminished and therefore in danger of leaving people in a lifestyle of unproven value and potentially everlasting detriment.

The visitors recommended that, since most in the Anglican Communion consider homosexual practice attracts God's condemnation, the American church should allow its universal responsibility to override local preference and implement a framework that would subject those departing from the church's norms to be effectively disciplined.[38] While the visiting bishops found many conservatives who, in spite of all, wanted to keep ECUSA together, many others confessed that they were close to following those who had already taken their leave of their near-to-apostate church. Harry was not surprised when, less than a month after his return, he received a detailed constitution and canons of a proposed new Anglican province in North America, together with elaborate arguments in justification of the split.

## The 1999 Sydney synod

The 1999 synod was the first ordinary session for the 45th synod, requiring another triennial election. Because the ACL already controlled SC, it was able to block the forwarding of my name to the synod, so that I was unable to stand for election to SC. Rod West, another of Harry's supporters, also lost his seat on SC. He was not voted off by synod; he just forgot to get his nomination in on time! The triumphant ACL even managed to get BBJ elected to SC for the first time in six years. Sensibly, Justice Peter Young made the cut. But Harry could now count on only about a dozen of the 59 votes in SC. His last two years, as his detractors waited impatiently for his successor, were to prove his most difficult.

Addressing some of the controverted matters in his presidential address in this highly politicised arena, Harry warned that 'The desire for power and influence, even in a good cause, is beguiling. It easily transgresses the boundaries of legitimacy.'[39] On the push for lay presidency, he said 'Unilateral action on a matter of concern to the Communion will not commend us.'[40] Of the intention of those who sought to dismantle the ACC, he observed, 'We must seek to ensure that this facility is available and well equipped to continue to offer help to all who come for assistance.'[41] To those who wished to separate the Diocese of Sydney from both the Australian Anglican Church and wider Anglican Communion, he appended his address with 'A challenge to Episcopalians' by John Stott, written in response to those determined to break with ECUSA. There are three options, advised Stott: separation, compromise, and refusing to give in (the way of witness). He commended the last, though 'it is the most painful of the three options, and it causes us considerable misery … But we are called to this.'[42]

The morning after the first day of synod, *SMH* had a photo of a contemplative Harry on the front page. Geoff Holt, CEO of Leonard Communications,[43] was deeply moved by the photo and wrote to Harry.

> I had all but forgotten the burden which you bear as the ecclesiastical guardian of Sydney's Anglican souls.
>
> And suddenly, there you are. Head bowed with the burden, alone in the darkness and the weight of Sydney on your mind …
>
> There are many of us (now pew sitting and in some senses on the outer limits of the church) who still long for it to be a fulfilling and meaningful place for all people. I'm sure that you are struggling with that and I want you to know that tonight my thoughts and prayers are with you.
>
> May what you seek for the church under God be realised and may you see your vision brought to fruition.[44]

On the same day Alan Cole also wrote to assure Harry of his prayers, adding 'With prayers for Pam, too – hard to stand by, and see her man continually gob-smacked.'[45]

The 1999 synod overwhelmingly endorsed lay presidency by a vote of 122 to 66 among the clergy, and 224 to 128 among the laity. Robert Doyle, lecturer in Church History at Moore College, said the vote was one of the most significant events since the Reformation. God works directly through his word and Spirit without a priestly mediator, he argued, but the Anglican Church had departed from that Reformation fundamental. 'This legislation is an "action statement". It says to the world that we want to get back to and maintain Reformation principles. I hope it encourages others around the world to do the same.'[46]

Harry vetoed it. While, on the one hand, he did not think it was the role of the bishop to thwart the will of the synod, especially when it was as strongly supported as this was, on the other, it was his role to guard the faith as determined in Anglican formularies, which has an order of ministry as part of it (bishops, priests and deacons), and to two of those orders are given the responsibility of administering the Lord's Supper. Harry thought lay presidency challenged that principle; it was contrary to the prayer book. If one is charged with a responsibility (as a bishop is at his consecration) then he has to fulfil it. He also thought, especially at this time when the Anglican Communion was so fragile thanks to ECUSA's reaction to Lambeth, that the diocese should not break out of communion with the Anglican church over an issue that, in his view, was not particularly vital and that no other diocese within the Anglican Communion supported. In fact, conservatives in America thanked Harry for not upsetting the rest of the Communion when far bigger issues were at stake.[47]

The primate, not surprisingly, wrote a personal note of appreciation.

> It is a courageous stand, because I know it will evoke strong opposition in your diocese with some. Yet it is, I am sure, the right decision. I believe it represents both the mind of the Catholic and Apostolic Church and of the authentic Anglican Evangelical tradition.[48]

Harry's refusal to assent to lay presidency was not universally condemned by Sydney Anglicans. Alan Cole, the advice-giving veteran, though he agreed with lay presidency, thought Harry had made the right call because, if introduced it might not only cause division between Sydney and other dioceses, but it might even provoke the secession within Sydney of parishes that could not agree with it. Not that Harry should allow the 'central church' people, counselled Cole, to hold him up as their champion.[49]

If John Woodhouse won the approval of synod for his advocacy of lay presidency, he lost it over his leading role in the dismantling of the ACC. It was an angry synod that now sought to undo the damage. A motion, receiving overwhelming support, requested SC to reconsider its adoption of the disputed resolutions resulting from the Committee of Enquiry into the ACC. But SC, at its meeting on 27 March 2000, resolved not to rescind the four resolutions, thereby effectively ignoring the spirit of synod's request. If the 1999 synod response to SC's destruction of the ACC was anger, the 2000 synod response was to be apoplectic.

Meanwhile, Harry was coming increasingly to the view that he must make a firm stand against the erosion of Anglican fundamentals by the ECUSA bishops. At a meeting in Kampala of conservative primates and archbishops, 16–18 November 1999, Harry reported on his 'come and see' visit to the United States and said,

> People asked us if homosexual practice was really a Church-breaking or Church-dividing issue. I believe that the New Testament would answer, yes. A life that does not conform to the moral pattern laid down by the Apostles is a contradiction of what it is to be in Christ and, as such, does damage to the body of Christ.[50]

An agreement was reached to take the whole matter to the next primates' meeting (Portugal, 23–28 March 2000) with the hope that the primates would make a strong response to the liberal ECUSA bishops and pull the Americans back into line with Lambeth. To Bp Maurice Sinclair he wrote after the Kampala meeting:

> Flying home, I once more felt strongly that we need some association of conservative bishops across the world. I am fearful of what is coming down the line. I do hope that the Primates' Meeting has a positive outcome, but I do have great concerns ... I think that unless conservatives stay together in a wide coalition that is active in sustaining Biblical religion within the life of the Communion, what is happening to conservatives in the United States is likely to happen to conservatives right across the Communion. They are my worst fears.[51]

On 30 November, Pamela's father, Kevin Coughlin, fell, his femur broken. Harry visited him on 12 December in Concord Hospital and prayed and read the Bible to him. Just a year earlier he had visited Pamela's brother, Rowley, in the same hospital – food poisoning. Kevin died on 15 December and his funeral was held five days later. His personality had not always been easy. His characteristic grouchiness had been controlled by his wife, but she had died 30 years earlier. That some discomfort within families can prove intractable this side of eternity echoed the year's unease in the wider church family. Harry, the mildest and most reasonable of men, was unable to calm either the conservatives in his own restless diocese who clamoured for lay presidency or the liberals in the wider church determined to adopt their culture's rejection of traditional Christian morality. It had been a tough year.

It was the more impressive, then, that Harry continued to find fresh ways of encouraging his clergy and people to act on the best international thinking on how to grow vital churches, having begun the year with his promotion of a BGEA plan entitled *Natural Church Development* and, towards the end of the year, commending to synod Patrick Johnstone's model for effective evangelisation. In spite of all, then, he did not lose focus on what he considered the main goal. It was a focus that enabled him both to report on the yield of fruitful work being done right across that energetic, if turbulent, diocese and, and at the same time, to show practical means of boosting the crop. It was a year in which he had given good, godly leadership.

# 22

# Eighth Year (2000–2001): 'A Small Victory'

The last year of an episcopate is usually a tough time for an archbishop as interest shifts, with a mixture of fear and hope, to the new broom and the new administration he sweeps into office. Harry's final year, ending on his 70th birthday, 19 March 2001, however, was tougher than most. He had lost control of SC and, with his ongoing opposition to lay presidency, frustrated the conservatives who never really supported him. Friction between Anglicans, chronic as it had been, broke new grounds of unrestrained antagonism. Peter Carnley, Archbishop of Perth, was elected primate. With the Sydney conservatives in mind, he let it be known that he would not submit to a bunch of 'bullying fundamentalists.' He stood for everything that Sydney stood against, and yet, in a revealing instance of realpolitik, Carnley was only elected through the connivance of Sydney conservatives, who calculated that it would better serve what they stood for if Carnley got the job rather than Harry. Within the diocese, the anguish over the abolition of the ACC proved as difficult to extinguish as a bushfire, culminating in the censuring of SC's handling of the matter by an enraged synod.

At a conference for all episcopal staff at Bowral on 30 and 31 March 2000, designed to maximise their effectiveness 'over the next 322 days', Harry reviewed his episcopate. He committed himself 'before God' to finish well, or, at least, since that would be hard, he told himself and his supporters 'you do what you can.' Peter Brain, inducted as Bishop of Armidale just a month earlier, led the thoughts of Harry's team with Bible studies on the apparently appropriate subject of depression.

22.1 Consecration of Peter Brain as Bishop of Armidale, February 2000.

Because adversity builds character and Christlikeness, observed Peter, depression need not be depressing! It was a call to re-dedication, and Harry wrote in his day book:

> Father, you have taught us to make yourself our hope in all circumstances. Help me to look at you, not at my circumstances, myself, or my difficulties, and to know that your grace is sufficient for me, that your strength is made perfect in, and because of, my weakness. Amen.

It was a prayer abundantly answered. In the face of much opposition and criticism, Harry was able to soldier on, just doing what he could. There was too much to do and his opportunities too great to be paralysed by his critics. In truth, he never seemed to be dispirited, discouraged, or depressed. Maybe the strange resolve to live for Christ, which he had made during that awful experience in his late adolescence when he felt that he must have committed the unpardonable sin, always protected him against despondency. If he could live for Christ when there was apparently no hope and no way back for him, then, in the face of mere human criticism, he could certainly live for Christ, in whom, he now believed, there was nothing but hope.

A story he told at the 2000 CMS Summer School spoke to him and of him – *to* him in its courage, and *of* him in its description of one who was not overwhelmed in spite of experiencing stress on a monumental scale. In *How the Irish Saved Civilisation*,[1] Thomas Cahill tells how Saint Patrick addressed the fear of death that constantly threatened in a 'warrior society'.

> It is possible to be brave – to expect 'every day … to be murdered, betrayed, enslaved – whatever may come my way' – and yet be a man of peace and at peace, a man without a sword or desire to harm, a man in whom the sharp fear of death has been smoothed away. … Patrick's peace … issued from his person like a fragrance. And in a damp land where people lived and slept in close proximity, everyone would have known sooner or later if Patrick's sleep was brought on by the goddess of intoxication or broken by the goddess of fear. Patrick slept soundly and soberly.[2]

And so did Harry, as Pam constantly witnessed to her astonishment.

## China, January 2000

Harry's appetite for the bold initiative was unabated, and early in 2000 he took on a new challenge, relishing the opportunity of visiting communist China.

Challenge it was: George Carey, as Archbishop of Canterbury, had visited China in 1994 and afterwards was ridiculed for swallowing state propaganda.[3] Since then, the Chinese government had become even more determined to distance itself from the mockery of religion in the Cultural Revolution and to claim that it upheld the legal protection of a citizen's right to freedom of religion. At the same time, it insisted that religious organisations had to be independent of overseas control, reflecting not only communism's affinity with atheism, but also China's humiliation during its colonial past.[4] There was much at stake.

The Anglican Church had been working among the Chinese of Sydney from at least 1879.[5] Before and during Harry's time, Revd Irene Mok had been working as an evangelist among them with singular success. By 1999 there were 10 active Chinese congregations in the diocese. On Alan Cole's peremptory counsel, Harry had formed the Chinese Ministry Task Force, with Ernest Chau as chair, for work among Chinese congregations and to facilitate post-ordination training for Chinese clergy. This, in turn, had led to the evolution of the Chinese Ministry Advisory Committee through the work of Archdeacon Geoff Huard. In August 1999, Harry had written to Ken Coleman, Manager of Cross-Cultural Ministries for Anglicare, to tell him he was keen to give Chinese ministry all the support he could.[6] He was therefore open to an initiative from the Bible Society to visit China.

From 10 to 21 January 2000, Tom and Merriel Treseder from the Bible Society and Roger Chilton, its chairperson, together with Harry and Pam, Peter and Elizabeth Smart, Margaret Rodgers and a film crew of three from Anglican Media, travelled to Hong Kong, Nanjing, Shanghai and Beijing on an official visit. Before they departed, Alan Cole wrote one of his letters to Harry, this time with 12 pieces of advice,[7] including:

> The wise way to deal with things is to smile and look pleasant and do not question openly anything said to you, though you may ask 'innocent' questions. Remember your contacts may get into trouble after you have gone, if you say too much.

In Nanjing they met the remarkable Bp K.H. Ting. He was a founder and president of both the Three-Self Patriotic Movement of the Protestant Churches in China, formed before the Cultural Revolution, and of the China Christian Council, formed after it. Bp Ting had studied in the Union Theological Seminary in New York and developed a theology of an indigenous Chinese Christianity that sought the welfare of the nation as well as the salvation of souls. Harry and the delegation visited the Nanjing Theological Seminary and the Amity Foundation,

22.2 Delegation to China, January 2000. Behind Pamela is Roger Chilton, chairperson of the Bible Society; on his left Margaret Rodgers, Anglican Media; Peter Smart (centre, crouching); Elizabeth Smart (back row, centre); on Harry's right, Tom Treseder, Director of the Bible Society, and his wife, Merriel.

both founded by Bp Ting. The Foundation, a Christian education, health, rural development and social welfare organisation, had entered into an agreement with the United Bible Society to establish the Amity Printing Press, which was to develop into the world's largest producer of Bibles.

In Shanghai, they visited the head office of the China Christian Council and the East China Seminary and, at the Shanghai Community Church, Harry preached through an interpreter for its pastor, Qi Gui Shi. In Beijing, Wang Zuo An, Deputy Director General, State Administration for Religious Affairs, hosted a banquet for Harry and Pam in the Great Hall of the People. It was not in the main dining hall, Harry observed, but even so, it was a memorable occasion. Alan Cole, always eager to help Harry get 'a more balanced view of the church in China' later advised Harry that the Chinese banquet in the Great Hall was 'a lot of political eyewash.'[8] On his return, Harry sought to have some Chinese students study at Moore College and some theologians teach in Chinese theological seminaries. In later years, much to Harry's satisfaction, Barry Webb from Moore College lectured in Old Testament at the Nanjing Seminary.

## The primacy

It was not long before the Anglican Church of Australia itself was to be subjected to its own dose of political eyewash. On 22 November 1999 Keith Rayner, Archbishop of Melbourne, retired from the primacy of the Anglican Church of Australia. The last Archbishop of Sydney to be elected primate was Marcus Loane. Bp Paul Barnett was one who regretted that. He thought that, as the oldest of Australia's dioceses and having had the primacy for most of the time, it was regrettable to lose the symbolism embodied in that office. 'We should have done everything we could to maintain that.'[9] While he concedes it is impossible to do justice to both roles as archbishop and primate, he nevertheless hoped that Harry would get the job. Paul considered Harry's relationship with Anglicans outside the diocese was 'outstanding' and he approved of what Harry achieved as a result of it. He doubts if he had been elected archbishop he could have achieved what Harry did in that area.

> Harry is a natural, of course. People felt within five minutes of knowing Harry that they knew him well. And he cared about them. He was good, generous, godly, pious. In my living memory, I think he had the best relationship of an Archbishop of Sydney with other bishops round the place, and with the media, I might add. He was excellent with the media. Someone in the ABC described him as 'the last Archbishop'. He always wore his clerical collar. He wasn't ashamed of it. He always conducted himself with a quiet dignity which people would have thought appropriate for an archbishop. He was pleasant, interested – yes, a nice man, Harry.[10]

One would have thought that the archbishop who had the best relationship with other bishops and the media would have been the most obvious candidate for the primacy. There were two problems: Harry's age and the lack of support from those who represented the Diocese of Sydney in the General Synod. On his election as archbishop, Harry had been advised that, though the ordinance required him to retire on reaching the age of 70, it could be extended to 71 by either synod or the SC.[11] He was about to turn 69 and would have only a little over a year as primate unless granted an extension. There were those who hoped for such an extension, including Harry himself. Synod would have been more likely than SC to approve an extension, but was never made aware of the issue, and, in any case, Harry was then out of favour with many on the synod owing to his refusal to support lay presidency. And it was hardly likely that SC, stacked with anti-Harry forces, would approve an extension. But, one would have thought, even a hostile SC would prefer Harry to the rampant liberal, Peter Carnley, who was the incarnation of all that the Sydney conservatives considered anathema.

Support for Harry from outside the diocese was strong. John Grindrod, who had retired as Archbishop of Brisbane a decade earlier and who had himself been primate before Rayner, had sounded Harry out. He could see that Harry's age was a problem, but he did not think it should be.

> Are you sure that your birth certificate has the right date on it?! You are such a young looking fellow! My point, though perhaps impossible, is serious. I would love you to be our next Primate. Important for Sydney and its 2000 events, 2001 and its Federation celebrations, the Anglican Church in this country and your unifying gifts. Your record of birth only needs to be about a 2 year clerk's error! Or even a biblical precedent that the sending out of 70 really meant 72. My final hope is that electors might realize that a 2 year Primacy is possible.[12]

On Thursday, 3 February 2000, the Primatial Electoral Board of the General Synod met for the election of the primate. The board was made up of all 20 of the diocesan bishops (in the event only 18 were present for the election), 12 clergy and 12 laity. Four ballots were conducted before a successful outcome was reached. In the first, eight of the 20 bishops received some support. Of these, four proceeded to the second ballot (Goodhew, Peter Carnley of Perth, Peter Hollingworth of Brisbane, and Roger Herft of Newcastle), from which three made it to the third ballot (Goodhew, Carnley, Hollingworth), before the final ballot between the two who made it through (Goodhew, Carnley).

In the first and second ballots, Harry received more votes than any of the other candidates. Then in the third ballot, Harry's lay supporters defected to Carnley or Hollingworth. Justice Peter Young's version of the event suggests that the Sydney voters indeed played politics, but their motivation is elusive. Justice Young wrote to Harry on the day of the election:

> I'm sorry that we could not get you elected as Primate. At lunch-time, it seemed OK as those outside Sydney thought there was a rock-hard Sydney lay block for you which would prevent anyone else succeeding.
>
> Unfortunately for the second last ballot, some of the block thought it would be clever to support Hollingworth and so eliminate Carnley. This rather stupid move not only couldn't succeed, but also shattered the perception that the Goodhew vote was solid. There was then sufficient leakage in the final ballot to get Carnley up.[13]

Justice Young probably got it half right: the leakage of votes from the laity did destroy the view that there was a solid block for Harry. But it seems unlikely that any leakage in the Sydney vote was due to the desire to eliminate Carnley because actually there was a greater leakage of the lay vote to Carnley than to Hollingworth. In the second ballot Harry received six of the 12 lay votes; Carnley, three and Hollingworth, three.

|  | VOTES BY HOUSE | | | AGGREGATE |
|---|---|---|---|---|
|  | Bishops | Clergy | Laity |  |
| Carnley | 6 | 5 | 3 | 14 |
| Goodhew | 5 | 5 | 6 | 16 |
| Herft | 1 | 2 | 0 | 3 |
| Hollingworth | 6 | 0 | 3 | 9 |

In the third ballot, Harry received only two of the lay votes; Carnley, six and Hollingworth, four. Since there were four Sydney lay electors, at least two must have voted for either Hollingworth or Carnley, and at least one must have voted for Carnley. Since one of the other non-Sydney lay members is known to have voted for Harry, it means that at least two of the Sydney lay representatives must have voted for Carnley. If they had not, Harry would have defeated Carnley in the third ballot, and – if Peter Young is correct – have prevailed in the fourth.

|  | VOTES BY HOUSE | | | AGGREGATE |
|---|---|---|---|---|
|  | Bishops | Clergy | Laity |  |
| Carnley | 6 | 7 | 6 | 19 |
| Goodhew | 6 | 5 | 2 | 13 |
| Hollingworth | 6 | 0 | 4 | 10 |

In the fourth and final ballot, between Carnley and Harry, three of Hollingworth's lay votes swung back to Harry and one to Carnley. In spite of the fact that some argued that it would be absurd to elect Harry for such a short time, a surprising number voted for that absurdity.

|  | VOTES BY HOUSE | | | AGGREGATE |
|---|---|---|---|---|
|  | Bishops | Clergy | Laity |  |
| Carnley | 10 | 7 | 7 | 24 |
| Goodhew | 7 | 5 | 5 | 17 |

Peter Young believed that the failure to elect Harry was due to 'a tactical blunder by some of the Sydney people', but Sydney Anglicans were not given to blunders in that arena! Margaret Rodgers would have been closer to the mark in her belief that the 'Sydney Reps did not try hard because they were opposed to [Harry] getting an extension. Such might cause Peter Jensen to miss out in the next Sydney elections by being that much older.'[14]

Harry was disappointed. God had opened the way for him through so much of his life. He must have wondered if God intended to find a way round the large obstacles of his age and the lukewarmness of the Sydney representatives. But after the election, he simply recorded in his diary, 'God is sovereign: my times are in his hands.' Harry's rusted-on supporters were not so accepting of the suggestion that the Sydney electors had supported Carnley over Harry. For them it was another bitter pill to swallow. Surely any self-respecting evangelical would have preferred an evangelical, even if an uncompliant one, to a rampant liberal. Instead, they elected Carnley, and their conservative friends then inveighed against Harry when he refused to boycott Carnley's installation in St Andrew's Cathedral.

The Bishop of Ballarat wrote to Harry reflecting on the politics of the election. He made no secret of the fact that Harry was his preferred candidate, the one best placed to present the faith 'as intellectually defensible, ethically responsible, and spiritually desirable' and who lacked 'neither courage nor gentleness.' He further reasoned 'that anything which could be done to strengthen the hand of the "Harry Goodhew school" in Sydney was likely best to serve the church.'[15] The Bishop of Grafton wrote 'I imagine dear Pam was relieved after yesterday's decisions in Sydney.'[16] But I imagine dear Pam's emotions lay elsewhere! Alan Cole, who had been offering frequent advice to Harry (and indeed others affected by the divisions in Sydney Anglicanism), reminded Harry that the Lord would 'overrule it all for good' and that the only answer to disappointment was 'to accept the decision wholeheartedly.'[17] To this Harry confessed:

> I was human enough to feel a little disappointed, Christian enough to know my times are in His hands, and political enough to know that Peter will provide quite a target for some of our brethren to shoot at.
>
> I have written to Peter expressing my commitment to pray for him, and to be as helpful to him as I possibly can within the bounds of traditional Christian understanding.[18]

As Harry anticipated, it was not long before Carnley would threaten those traditional bounds. Carnley stood for everything that the Sydney conservatives opposed. He participated in groups to promote both a new understanding of sexuality in the church and women bishops. He characterised as 'wicked' the consecration in Singapore of bishops for the American Church to give pastoral oversight to those who could not accept its departure from the Lambeth resolution on homosexuality (see below). Yet he condemned those who wanted to depart from Lambeth and establish alternative Anglican bodies. He warmed to the 'universal primacy' of the Roman Catholic Church.[19] Harry was soon to observe in his diary, 'Peter C is a very different primate from Keith Rayner.'[20] Carnley seemed to relish opposing the Diocese of Sydney and was more autarchic in style than Sydney, with its distaste for episcopal power, found congenial. Carnley was to address the Australian Bishops' Conference the following year on 'The Monarchical Episcopate.' Within the Trinity, the Father has a monarchical role with respect to the Son and the Spirit. He is first among equals – so the role of the bishop is 'ruling in respect to teaching, ordaining, liturgy.'[21] Sydney had a very different understanding of the bishop's role.

If it is true that Sydney's representatives in some way facilitated Carnley's election, it is a remarkable instance of how the struggle for internal control of the diocese was considered more importat than defending the faith beyond it. For those who regarded Sydney as the pure citadel and all outside it suspect, it was easy to imagine the rest of the Australian Church being led by a liberal. A robust external enemy would reinforce the validity of this perspective. A purer opposite as Primate would enhance this binary divide and make it easier for Sydney to break away if the occasion arose. In the history of Protestantism, purity is often attained through separation. It is addicted to the dynamics of fragmentation.

## American Episcopal Churches

Harry's disappointment at not being elected primate was not only personal. It meant that he would not be able to attend the primates' meeting (Oporto, Portugal, 22–29 March 2000) where the reining in of the liberal ECUSA bishops, critical to the future of the Anglican Communion, would be the main concern. Carnley was far less likely than Harry to confront the American liberals. Just a week before the Primatial election, an event had occurred that threw the problem into stark relief. On 29 January 2000, John Rodgers, who had been dean of the conservative Anglican seminary at Pittsburgh, and Chuck Murphy, a minister from South Carolina, were consecrated as 'missionary' bishops to the United States by two primates, Moses Tay, Archbishop of the Province of South East Asia, and Emmanuel Kolini, Archbishop of Rwanda. The new bishops would offer episcopal care for those American Episcopalians who felt betrayed by their own liberal bishops.

The consecrations took even conservatives by surprise and embarrassed Harry. Alan Cole advised Harry to have nothing to do with them as they will 'ruin any chance' of Sydney influencing other dioceses.[22] It was suggested that Tay acted precipitately because he was just about to step down, while Kolini is reported to have said, 'At the Genocide in 1994, the whole world stood back and no-one came to Rwanda's aid. We will never stand back when others are similarly threatened, physically or spiritually.'[23] John Rodgers had long been of the opinion that a province alternative to ECUSA should be established in the United States. Of 100 ECUSA dioceses, only four endorsed the 1998 Lambeth resolutions, and Rodgers believed that ECUSA had been irretrievably paganised and he was just waiting for other conservatives (such as Harry) to accept the inevitable and catch up with him.[24]

Harry had heard rumours that this unilateral action might be about to happen and did his best to contact Tay and Kolini to plead with them to desist.[25] He believed that the arrangement agreed to by conservative bishops was that no such action would be taken before the meeting of the 37 primates in Portugal. Further, it did not feel quite right to Harry that the consecrations had an element of secrecy about them. Yet he could see the point made to him by Roger Beckwith, Librarian of Latimer House, Oxford, that 'Presenting the Church with a "fait accompli" has been a favourite American tactic, and now the tables are turned on them.'[26]

There was no going back now, however, and Harry could only pray that the consecrations would 'indicate to the Church as a whole how desperate people feel about their inability to influence the decline in the spiritual life in their churches.'[27] Events were forcing him to choose between the competing factions, and there was never any doubt which side he would choose. He was unconvinced by the contention of Frank Griswold that the Episcopal Church in America was seeking to put the conservative's obsession with sexuality behind it so that it could get on with mission. He suspected that getting on with mission was not ECUSA's most conspicuous attribute and his interpretation of Scripture disallowed Griswold's reasoning.

> The greatest concern over this spiritual and moral drift is being expressed in those parts of the Communion where the gospel of Christ is most actively drawing people to the Saviour. I have no doubt that unless the Primates can reassure them with an appropriate response to the present crisis, they will act to support those whom they see as

faithful sisters and brothers marginalised for the sake of faithfulness to their Lord ... Fellowship and faithfulness must go hand in hand.[28]

Harry wrote to Carnley ahead of the primates' meeting in Portugal, enclosing a copy of the report he had written on his visit to ECUSA at Griswold's invitation. He invited Carnley to consider joining those asking ECUSA to refrain from ordaining practising homosexuals until a decision about the future was properly made by the whole Communion.[29] It appears that no response from the primate was forthcoming. One who attended the meeting wrote to Harry, 'I wish you were here. Carnley declared that they had an 80-page Bible study that the texts were not clear about homosexuality [sic]. He will have to pay for that one before the Great White Throne.'[30]

Predictably, the Portugal primates' conference failed to deliver the stout defence of the faith required by the conservatives. Bill Atwood reported to Harry, 'Sadly, the Singapore consecrations may have done in the whole process. Energy was diverted from the American situation, and they also muddied the water considerably.'[31] In their communiqué, the primates did urge the liberal American bishops 'to weigh the effects of their actions, and to listen to the expressions of pain, anger and perplexity from other parts of the Communion' and that the blessing of same sex unions and the ordination of 'declared non-celibate homosexuals' would 'threaten the unity of the Communion in a profound way.' Nevertheless, the communiqué called for the replacement of the 'demonising of opponents' and the use of 'overheated, politicised and polarised language' with 'listening' and 'holy communication.'[32] For Harry and his episcopal team, this failed to address the issue.

> We cannot identify in the communiqué any real pressure to reverse or at least halt practices believed by the Church to be spiritually destructive ... It is our intention to pursue this matter with colleagues around the world to determine what might be an appropriate response from those who uphold the 2000 year tradition of Christian moral teaching.[33]

Harry was now identified as a leader of the movement to strengthen the conservatives in their fight and, by the end of the year, he was prepared to affirm a new traditionalist network, the Anglican Mission in America, in its drive to establish alternative structures for disenchanted conservatives.[34] He sent Bp Ray Smith to Rosemont, Diocese of Pennsylvania, to represent him at a service on 26 November where about 90 people were confirmed by non-ECUSA bishops. Its ECUSA bishop, second in his liberalism only to Spong, was Charles Bennison, the one who had infamously said 'We wrote the Bible, we can re-write it again whenever we choose.'

Yet, typically, Harry's position remained more nuanced than that of the rampant separatists. He shared with the Archbishop of Canterbury a profound unwillingness to countenance the dismemberment of the Anglican Communion. 'The most desirable outcomes seem to be either some haven for orthodox people within ECUSA or, if not, an entity that is parallel with ECUSA that will have recognition by the primates and by the Archbishop of Canterbury.'[35]

## The Forsyth saga

Harry accepted his defeat at the election for primate with good grace as was his custom and devoted himself with unimpaired enthusiasm to the plethora of activities that crowded his diary in the coming months. Yet for all his faithful attention to his many duties, it did not feel like business as usual. His defeat for the primacy put him on his mettle as perhaps never before when responding to the usual challenges. They continued to come from the liberalism side now personified in Carnley and from the conservative side represented especially by the clergy in SC. It was the latter that now confronted him, resulting from an unexpected development.

On 26 February 2000 Peter Watson, bishop of the South Sydney region, was elected Archbishop of Melbourne. It was a surprise that Melbourne would elect a Sydney man, but Sydney bishop, John Reid, had gone close at a previous election, and Peter was not a stereotypical Sydney hardliner. He was suspected of supporting female ordination, although Margo, Peter's wife said, 'They call him a listening evangelical. He does not listen to me!'

Normally, SC would approve the appointment of Harry's nominee as an assistant bishop to replace Peter. But with the still raw memory of SC's refusal to support his nomination of Peter Kemp, Harry was right to suspect that it would not revert to normal practice this time round. An article in *SMH* on 17 March made Harry's predicament public news. 'Goodhew retires next March and could give a mate a good run at the top job. But the conservative group, with the numbers on the Sydney diocese's powerful standing committee will veto any Goodhew candidate. The likely result? No Bishop for South Sydney.'[36]

At a special meeting, SC gave Harry reason to believe that this was a real possibility. Clergy opposition to filling the vacancy before the next archbishop's election, still over a year away, meant SC would fall short of the percentage required by the ordinance for approval of the appointment.[37] Four days later, Robert Tong rang Harry to pledge that if he went back to SC about filling the vacancy, 'he could deliver a positive vote for a group of possible names.'[38] Harry doubted that the names would be to his liking, but if he presented another name, SC would probably not only reject his candidate, but also refuse to fill the vacancy at all.

A different way had to be found. Indeed, it had probably already been found. A little over a week after Peter Watson's election to Melbourne, Warwick Olson and Stephen Judd met with Harry. Consummate strategists, they will have helped Harry to devise the political masterstroke that gave his opponents a rare taste of defeat. Instead of putting the matter to SC, Harry announced to its members that he would convene a special meeting of synod to determine the matter. Complete shock! On cue, diocesan secretary, Mark Payne announced to the stunned SC that the synod papers had already been printed. It was one of Harry's great moments, observed an aficionado of the political arts, a demonstration that he could be political when he wanted to be. Alan Cole, however, considered it a risky strategy and did little to settle Harry's nerves with the observation that, if this didn't come off and Harry's nomination approved, 'both you and he will be "gob-smacked" ... and his chances for the future may be gone.'[39]

There is commonly a downside to the practice of politics, and this was no exception. Having alighted on a decisive mechanism by which to achieve his goal of filling the vacancy, Harry was torn over whom to recommend to synod. The most obvious candidate was Trevor Edwards, the Archdeacon of South Sydney who had been effectively running the region while his bishop, Peter Watson, was running the Glebe Board and other central ministries. Trevor was an able, efficient administrator, and three of Harry's bishops, including Peter Watson himself, recommended Trevor for the job. There were those, however, who advised Harry that Robert Forsyth would have a better chance of beating Peter Jensen in the election for his successor which was only about a year away. This advice was correct: Robert was to come second in that race and Trevor third.

Harry prevaricated. He told both Robert and Trevor that he was thinking about who to back and he had not made up his mind. They were both in the dark. There was a time when he said to both of them together, 'It will be one of you two.' Robert was jittery about becoming an assistant bishop. One night he could not sleep. He got up at 4 o'clock in the morning and had a glass of port, smoked a cigar, and then returned to bed. Harry went to the election synod on 4 May with two names in hand. He told Robert that he was the leading candidate, but if synod rejected Robert, he would then put forward Trevor's name. In the event, synod's support for Robert made that unnecessary, and he was consecrated on 13 June 2000, as an assistant bishop in the Diocese of Sydney for the South Sydney

Region. The significance of the overwhelming support Harry received in synod was that it showed how unrepresentative SC was – it would have been better for Harry and for the diocese had SC more truly reflected the will of the synod.

For Trevor's part, being overlooked by Harry in favour of Robert was a difficult experience. He found that, paradoxically, while Harry would give him all the time in the world and would focus without distraction on matters he brought to him, he could also be remote at times. But Trevor felt that Harry's opponents were a bigger problem than the frustrations he sometimes felt with Harry. Furthermore, he believed in the sort of evangelical Anglicanism that Harry espoused, and therefore he remained loyal to him. Trevor stayed on as Robert's archdeacon, and Robert thought he behaved superbly, the complete professional.

From the sidelines, venerable Stuart Barton Babbage observed that of the members of SC, on this occasion Harry had 'cunningly outmanoeuvred them.'[40] The retired Bishop of Armidale, Peter Chiswell, wrote to Harry that it was a 'real pleasure' to get the news that the synod had supported Harry 'against the blocking move of the Standing Committee … Well done.'[41] From the South Sydney Region, Liz Boyce wrote to thank the archbishop for 'going to so much trouble' to provide them with a new bishop and for making 'a wise choice.'[42]

In spite of the satisfaction felt by Harry's supporters, Robert's election was something of a pyrrhic victory. Robert was never identified as a Harry man as Trevor was. He had been a REPA colonel, admittedly in the moderate division. Phillip Jensen once thanked him that he had never used his position to attack St Matthias', and he never wavered in his opposition to the ordination of women. So, as the soft hardliner, he was more electable than Trevor anyway. He was also better known than Trevor through his popular 'Bah Humbug' column in SC.

Synod's approval, then, was rightly hailed as only 'a small victory.' Even so, Harry's opponents in SC did not care for the unaccustomed experience of being bested by their archbishop. Bruce Ballantine-Jones said that it was all unnecessary anyway as Harry would have had the support of ACL for Robert's appointment. But perhaps the point was that the archbishop of the day was not going to have his choice dependent on the approval of the few, when he knew that, in this matter, he had the support of the many.

## 23

# Eighth Year (2000–2001 Continued): 'No Other Name'

The newly elected primate, Peter Carnley, lost no time in fulfilling Harry's prophecy that he would provide 'quite a target' for some of the Sydney brethren 'to shoot at.'

## Carnley and the Easter faith

An article in *The Bulletin* magazine[1] by Archbishop Carnley and published on 25 April 2000, two days after Easter Sunday, led some Sydney churchmen to impugn his orthodoxy and to campaign for the boycotting of his installation the following Sunday as primate. In the weeks following the Primatial election, Harry had been petitioned not to permit the installation service at St Andrew's Cathedral or, if it did go ahead, to absent himself from it. The appearance of the *Bulletin* article only ramped up the indignation of Carnley's critics, and the furore was aired in the media. It was not the new primate's style to pour oil on troubled waters. On the ABC's *PM* program on 26 April, he claimed that his critics' complaints were 'entirely predictable', that they were the opinions of only a small group of Sydney fundamentalists, and that the rumpus was 'deliberately timed to coincide' with his installation as primate, and was mainly due to Sydney posturing over the election of a new bishop for South Sydney, then under way, and of a new archbishop for Sydney only a year away.

With the Sydney bear frothing at the mouth and Carnley's inclination to poke it with a stick, it was left to Harry to speak the calming voice of reason and orthodoxy into the latest explosive situation in the Anglican Church. Although in Singapore for the consecration of Bp John Chew Hiang Chea when the *Bulletin* article appeared, Harry drafted two long responses to the issues raised by the article. The first, released on Anglican media, was his refutation of Carnley's arguments on doctrinal and historical grounds; the second a letter to his clergy explaining why he would not boycott the service for the installation of the primate.

In the former, he felt bound to express his 'strong disagreement' with Carnley's treatment of the Bible which he considered 'unhelpful and misleading.' He also considered Carnley's comments appeared to contradict the Thirty-Nine Articles, the Good Friday Collects and the Nicene Creed. Carnley appeared to deny the universality and uniqueness of Christ's Lordship ('there is … one Lord, Jesus

Christ, through whom are all things and through whom we exist' – 1 Cor 8:6, ESV). In seeking to explain away the exclusivity of the Christian claim that there is 'no other name', Carnley was not only denying the essence of the gospel, but was also inferring that such exclusivity isolates Christians 'from any dealings with people of other faith communities.' On the basis of his own good relationship with people of other faiths, Harry was able to say, 'That is just not true.'

It was a comprehensive refutation of Carnley's position, yet Harry did not feel justified in boycotting the service of recognition for the primate. Because he was concerned to uphold 'the Catholic, Reformed, Protestant and Evangelical character of Anglicanism', he wanted to explain his decision. In a long and balanced letter to his clergy, Harry observed that the time and place of the service had been determined before the election of the primate and was not contingent on who would be chosen. Carnley had been properly elected as primate. Among the electors were representatives of the Diocese of Sydney, none of whom, to Harry's knowledge, 'made, at that time, any public and formal declaration of their unwillingness to accept his appointment.' In boycotting the service, to be consistent, he would also have to boycott the many meetings chaired by the primate and that would be 'tantamount to severing episcopal relationships with the Australian Church' and that was not something he wished to do at that point in time.

The letter was a catalogue of such arguments – very Harry! And widely appreciated. From Toowoomba in Queensland, Craig Berkman, who had been deeply influenced by Harry at Coorparoo, wrote concerning Harry's stated position on Carnley:

> I just wanted to say how your letter to the clergy in your diocese sounded so much like you! You have always taken the reasonable view on everything ... well considered, caring and reasonable. You will be remembered as such in years to come.[2]

## African interlude

With the Anglican Church of Australia widely tipped to be torn asunder between the new primate's rampaging liberalism and Sydney's intransigent conservatives, Harry found time to nurture his growing commitment to the church in Africa, combining it with his lifetime passion for evangelism. In Nairobi, Kenya, from 8 May, he attended the board meeting of the Network for Anglicans in Mission and Evangelism. He visited Bp Pie Ntukamazina, Bishop of Burundi, and preached in the cathedral on 14 May. Then he made a courtesy call on Archbishop Peter

Akinola, the powerful, newly elected Primate of Nigeria, before attending the synod of the Nigerian diocese of Kaduna, and preaching at its thanksgiving service. While Harry was speaking at the synod and Pam was addressing women in the cathedral, there was a riot. They were accompanied by an armed guard as they travelled south by car from Kaduna to Abuja, the capital of Nigeria. There were fires in the villages they passed through and the sound of gunfire, which the armed guard told them was to 'pacify' the people. Matthew Newhaus, the high commissioner (son of Theo, a Sydney Anglican clergyman), arranged for their safe exit. He delivered them to the airport in the high commissioner's car displaying the Australian flag. After Harry alighted, leaving Pam in the car, a policeman approached their driver and barked, 'You cannot stop here. Move on.' The taciturn driver said, 'I have the Prime Minister of Australia in this car. I have to stay here.' Neither Pam nor Harry ever expressed any anxiety about their own safety. 'You just take sensible precautions' was Harry's formula for safety on the African continent. They arrived back in Sydney on 26 May.

23.1 Pam and Harry with Comfort Fearon, wife of the Bishop of Kaduna, Nigeria, on a visit to Sydney in October 1999. Pam and Comfort are robed in celebration of the founding of the Mothers' Union in 1876.

## Anglican problems in the media

On 14 June, the ABC broadcast its expose of Anglican discord on its current affairs program, *Four Corners*, which boasted 'Investigative TV journalism at its best.' Entitled 'An Unholy Row', it interviewed the main actors in the current high drama: Peter Carnley, Harry Goodhew, Peter Jensen, BBJ, John Woodhouse, Julia Baird, Peter Hollingworth, Roger Herft and John McIntyre. It began ominously with Julia Baird, then convenor of MOW, declaring 'You see the politicking, the factionalism. You can see brutality,' followed by the words of compere Andrew Fowler (ABC journalist), 'behind the ceremonial pomp is a vicious struggle for power. The brawling rivals anything in party politics.' Peter Carnley, just a couple of weeks into his new job as primate, declared, 'I certainly am not going to be bullied by fundamentalist Christians, that's for sure.' Of the practice of Sydney

Anglicans planting churches in other dioceses, he thundered 'And if a parish in my diocese tried to do that, I would be jumping on them like a ton of bricks.' Jumping bricks did sound fearsome.

Carnley's robust confidence, understandable given his new status as primate, was in marked contrast to the despairing weariness of Julia Baird. For more than two decades the issue of the ordination of women had been considered and rejected by the Sydney synod. All the women who were pro-ordination had either gone into the priesthood in other dioceses or had left the church altogether. She claims that she personally was accused of destroying the church, of doing the devil's work, of being made to feel as if she was 'some kind of anvil' wanting to smash the church 'and, you know, make Germaine Greer pope.'

Between the jaunty ebullience of Peter Carnley and the terminal lassitude of Julia Baird was Harry's acceptance of reality. He was in a diocese where the authority of the bishop was not as respected as in some dioceses. He could not always persuade the synod to approve his policies because, he said simply, he was 'not persuasive enough a speaker.' He did not take it personally, acknowledging that SC had always been a robust body, 'quite vigorous at times. But it does its job.' Asked how often he got 'rolled', he replied, 'I win some, lose some.'

## Amsterdam Congress on world evangelism

From 29 July to 6 August, Harry, along with 10,000 evangelists, attended 'Amsterdam 2000'. The ambition of this congress was that all the unreached might be evangelised in 20 years. With representatives from 190 nations, its sessions, translated into 25 languages, were led by 300 of the world's most prominent Christian leaders, including Billy Kim of Suwon, Korea, President of the Baptist World Alliance; Bill Bright, President of Campus Crusade for Christ; Chuck Colson, President of Prison Fellowship; and theologians J.I. Packer and John Stott. Organised by the BGEA, it was understood that Billy Graham himself, then aged 81, was passing on the baton to the next generation of evangelists.

As arranged a year earlier by program director, Bill Conard, Harry was in charge of the 'track' for church leaders, one of three groups meeting behind the scenes. There was some doubt about whether Archbishop Carey would turn up, and Harry was asked to replace him if required. He prepared an address, should it be needed, to be given at a plenary session on 31 July. Entitled 'Preaching Christ in a Broken World', it amplified the point he had made in his dispute with Peter Carnley about proclaiming the uniqueness of Christ in an age when the Christian claim for exclusivity is galling for many.

> People of other faith communities have little respect for Christians who 'water down' the distance between their own faith's teachings and that of others. When we meet with those of other faiths they look to us to provide an apologia of our own theology and doctrine as they will do of theirs. If we do anything less we diminish Christ, we diminish ourselves, and we diminish those with whom we disagree.

In the event, Archbishop Carey did arrive. One of Harry's finest addresses was not delivered!

## South Africa

From 29 August to 6 September, Harry was in South Africa. He took the Bible studies for the synod of the Church of England in South Africa (CESA) in Johannesburg and preached in Cape Town at St James' Church. While in Cape Town he visited Njongonkulu Ndugane, Archbishop and Primate of the Church of the Province of South Africa (CPSA), which since 1938 had seen itself as a rival jurisdiction to CESA.

In reality, the Anglican Church in South Africa had become what some Sydney conservatives hoped for in Australia, with the evangelical wing separating from the rest of the Anglican Church. Harry, as we have seen, was not for separation, and worked for goodwill between the two churches. The third Bishop of CESA had been Dudley Foord, Harry's friend and classmate at Moore College, who had resigned in frustration at the intransigence of the two churches in 1989. Before him, Stephen Bradley, another Australian, had been the Bishop of CESA (1965-1984) and had regularly corresponded with Harry, as he had done with Archbishops Mowll, Gough, Loane and Robinson before him, and was to do with Archbishop Jensen after him. Stephen Bradley always hoped that Sydney (and possibly Melbourne) would separate from the rest of the Anglican Church in Australia so that it would be free to send missionaries to the needy areas in other parts of Australia, starved of the evangelical gospel.[3] Nelson Mandela was one of Harry's heroes, and he would have been interested in a little story that Bradley reported to him. Asked why he had never joined the Communist Party, Mandela is said to have replied, 'I could never do that, I am a Christian.'[4] That CPSA Archbishop Ndugane had been a prisoner on Robben Island with Mandela would only have strengthened Harry's preference for cordial relations between the two churches. Frank Retief, Bishop of CESA (2000-2010), spoke of Harry's one and only visit as 'an enormous blessing.'[5] Harry had the gift of encouragement in spades.

## The Olympic Games, Sydney 2000

Himself a keen sportsperson, Harry was always ready to capitalise on the evangelistic potential of the average Australian's passion for sport. Regularly, Harry and Pam were invited to test cricket matches and the opening of the NRL season and always accepted such invitations, not only because they believed it was in the interests of the church to be seen to be engaged in major events, but also because they really enjoyed meeting new people, and were alert to learning from those who had made their mark. Often such people shared with Harry and Pam their personal problems, an experience which Pam always felt was a privilege. That the Sydney Olympics should fall during his episcopate Harry saw as a remarkable opportunity for evangelism, pastoral care and hospitality.

On 26 September 1993, the same day as Juan Antonio Samaranch announced that Sydney had won the right to host the 2000 Olympics, Dr Mark Tronson, who had trained for the Baptist ministry and who had founded Sports and Leisure Ministries, had rung Bp Brian King to discuss how the Olympics might be used for the extension of God's kingdom.[6] Just a fortnight later, at his first synod, Harry had appealed to its members to 'see this as a unique moment ... an outstanding period in the life of Sydney.' Established in quick succession had been Quest Australia More Than Gold, the Sydney Churches Olympic Christian Network Committee under the leadership of Bruce Baird MLA, state Liberal deputy leader and a Sydney Anglican, and the archbishop's Olympic Games Task Force with Revd David Tyndall as director. Between them they organised possibly the most ecumenically comprehensive evangelistic effort ever supported by the Australian churches,[7] with Quest overseeing the distribution of 10,000 copies of the *Jesus* video to athletes during the Olympics and Paralympics.

From 14 to 18 September, Harry and Pam attended the Olympics as guests of Telstra. On the day before the opening ceremony on 15 September, they attended the International Olympic Family Welcome Reception at the Town Hall as guests of the Lord Mayor. Then, in the middle of the Olympics, from 19 to 26 September, Harry and Pam stayed at Norfolk Island, fellowshipping with Revd Ian Hadfield, his wife, Narelle, daughter, Bethany, and (Harry records) her doll, Emily. Harry had a run most days and swam in Slaughter Bay. After their Norfolk Island interlude, they returned to the Olympics as the guests of Peter Costello, the treasurer, on 27 September, of the premier on 29 September, and joined John and Sue Conde and their family for the closing session of the games on 1 October, when they were gratified to hear Samaranch declare 'I am proud and happy to proclaim that you have presented to the world the best Olympic Games ever.'

Never one to do only one thing per day, Harry had earlier attended the 10 am service at St Mark's, Darling Point. Over coffee afterwards he listened carefully to a visitor from Colorado who recounted that her mother, who had been married at St Mark's, had died when she was only 17. She was deeply touched that an archbishop had time for her and truly cared in listening to her pain.[8]

## 2000 synod

Synod began on 9 October. Harry said in his presidential address, in commenting on the perception of the diocese as one of conflict,

> When I was elected, the Synod spontaneously broke into singing 'A new commandment I give unto you that love one another as I have loved you' ... I think my greatest sadness in relinquishing this office will be my sense of failure in doing anything significant towards the realisation of that prayerful song. I am all too conscious of my own contributions to that failure.[9]

The next day, Alicia Watson, lay synod representative for Darling Point, wrote to Harry.

> Your influence has helped to give a face of compassion and care to our Diocese not evident previously. As a result of your quiet, gentle and loving persuasion, I believe much has been done to advance the evangelical cause throughout the world.[10]

From Mt Dandenong in Victoria, Henry Speagle, distinguished public servant and author, who had worked with Harry in 1995 on the matters raised by the prayer book debate, also wrote to Harry about 'the strictures' he had passed on himself at the 2000 synod.

> No one could have done more than you have to bring a spirit of charity and good sense into your very difficult position over the last eight years. You know all about the ugly face of evangelicalism and you have done all you can by precept and example, to show its kindlier and more sunny side ... How could anyone, set over as large a Diocese as Sydney, turn round a culture that goes back so many decades in its history? You have seen the great tragedy for what it is – a loveless Christianity – an oxymoron and an absurdity.[11]

Stuart Findlay, Rector of Gymea, wrote:

> To my horror and sadness I've learned much of the ways of power and manipulation as I've watched some parts of this Diocese at work ... As I reflect, I see how you have walked with deft balance, the narrow line between institutional conservatism and the sowing of new vision![12]

## Censure of Standing Committee

Having traced the sorry saga of the treatment of the ACC up to the end of 1999, we need now to report developments in the year leading up to the 2000 synod. On 4 April 2000 Chris Forbes, a lecturer in Ancient History at Macquarie University, greatly appreciated for his lectures on Jesus and the New Testament, attended a meeting to plan a response from those upset by SC's response to a 1999 synod resolution requesting it to review its handling of the ACC. The meeting was held in the home of Tom and Patricia Mayne. Tom, committee member of the Sydney Anglican Indigenous Peoples' Ministry, had worked alongside Harry at Ceduna over three decades earlier. He was a seasoned campaigner for justice for the abused, whether they be Indigenous people or the sexually abused or Anglicans unhappy with the exercise of power in the diocese. Patricia had been sexually abused as a child and had been helped by the ACC and was grateful for it, and was distressed that the help she had received would now be denied to others. Augmented by other disenchanted campaigners, the now-styled Anglican Counselling Centre Reference Group met with Harry on 14 April at St Andrew's House and received 'a very full hearing.' By 1 May, barrister Garth Blake, who had been very cautious, had come to the opinion that a motion censuring SC might be tried.

Chris rang the experts whose advice had been cited as justification for closing the ACC. Dr Bill Andersen considered the whole matter 'scurrilous' and was outraged particularly by the treatment of Michael Corbett-Jones. Then he spoke with Rob McMurdo of the Ellard practice, and found him 'distressed'. He still stood by most of the resolutions, but he said the committee never considered abolishing the ACC. He considered that outcome as purely political, and that the SC did not have the expertise to deal with the matter.

Meanwhile, in an open letter, dated Easter 2000, Michael Corbett-Jones announced his resignation from the end of the year, although it was effective immediately. At the SC meeting held on 26 June, the merger of the ACC with Anglicare was confirmed with the passing of the Anglican Counselling Centre (HMS) Integration Ordinance 2000, to take effect from 1 August 2000. The merger failed to cover the bases of the previous arrangement. There were now far fewer counsellors as so many had resigned, swearing never to work for the church again.

It was now necessary to go by referral to a private counsellor and be charged the going rate, which made receiving counselling beyond the means of many. The diocese no longer offered Christian training for counsellors.

During the synod debate on the censure motion, Chris Forbes argued that SC had acted, first, beyond the recommendations of its own inquiry; second, against the clearly expressed wishes of synod; and third, with disastrous consequences. For these actions SC members deserved to be censured. And they were, with two-thirds of the synod voting in support of the censure motion. This was accompanied with Forbes's warning that if SC didn't get it right this time, next time would be a motion of no confidence.

On 16 October 2000, John Woodhouse, who had led SC's inquiry into the ACC, made a personal statement to the synod.

> It is important for me to say to you that I have no doubt whatsoever in my own mind and heart that on this occasion the Synod has not understood, and that what the Standing Committee has done, and what I was involved in, was – as far as is humanly possible – utterly proper, completely open, and in fact absolutely necessary.

Because he believed that what he had done was right, he did not think it would be proper for him to resign. But, because so many in the synod had concluded that the advice he had given SC was wrong, he could not just do nothing. Therefore, he offered to stand down from SC if any member of synod thought that he should and said so in writing. At least one so wrote, and Woodhouse resigned.[13]

On 9 November 2000, a thanksgiving service was held in the cathedral for the ministry of Michael Corbett-Jones during his 20 years' service as ACC director. Harry recorded that Bp John Reid, who had a heart for the ministry of counselling, preached very well on that occasion. On his own retirement some months later, Harry would write to Michael, thanking him for his development of the ACC, and expressing his gratitude for the gracious response he had received from Michael on the many occasions in which he had sought assistance with cases that demanded counselling.[14] Michael responded with equal warmth. He had already established a counselling centre on the Central Coast, and his wife, Christine, was now teaching at a Christian school, where she had met Harry's 'most intelligent and friendly granddaughter Amy.'[15]

## The roller coaster ride to the finishing line

The ceaseless round continued till the end of Harry's episcopate on his 70th birthday, 19 March 2001. On 23 November 2000, he was interviewed at

23.2 David, Wendy, Harry and Robyn climb the Sydney Harbour Bridge, 25 February 2001.

Bishopscourt by Geraldine Doogue for an ABC *Compass* program entitled 'The Last Archbishop'. Pam was operated on for a ganglion on 14 December 2000, but continued to experience much pain, and was operated on again on 18 January 2001. On 15 December, David Short, Australian rector of an Anglican parish in Vancouver, Canada, discussed with Harry the situation over same-sex marriage. He wished to be assured that, if his congregation could no longer continue in the Anglican Church in his diocese, that they could have an association with the Sydney diocese. Harry advised him that anyone likely to be elected to replace him as archbishop would offer episcopal oversight if needed.

On both 18 November and 18 December, the cathedral chapter went on retreat to discuss the future of the cathedral. At the latter, Harry presided over a SWOT analysis, the sort of exercise he relished. That evening he had a 'delightful evening' with the staff, although some were anxious about the changes the new regime would bring. On Christmas Eve he preached at a 6.30 pm service of lessons and carols ('a great number present, well over 800') and again at 11.15 pm (Holy Communion) and yet again at 9 am on Christmas Day. From 6 to 11 January 2001, his last time as archbishop at CMS Summer School, he rejoiced that Joe and Sue Radkovic were preparing to go to Nairobi and was encouraged by the amazing work of Max and Hannah Collison in the slums of Nairobi, where Harry and Pam would assist after retirement. On 16 January, Harry began to pack his library: leaving Bishopscourt was to be a massive logistical operation. On 25 February 2001, with three of his children – Robyn, David and Wendy – he climbed the Sydney Harbour Bridge, and he noted in his diary the death of one of his heroes – Sir Donald Bradman.

## 24

# Stepping Down: 'God's Man in God's Time'

Rabbi Raymond Apple, Chief Minister of the Great Synagogue in Sydney, accorded Harry on his retirement the ultimate accolade in the Jewish vernacular, describing him as a 'Mensch'; that is, a true human being.[1] True human beings do not always like to retire, however, especially if they are male. As Harry's retirement approached, diocesan secretary, Warren Gotley, observed, 'I have watched a couple of Archbishops come to the end of their days and it's not a pretty sight.' He understood that it could be grim being an archbishop, but coming to a halt was grimmer still, especially for a fit activist like Harry. Retirement on 19 March 2001 (his 70th birthday) came too late for Harry's detractors, but too early for him. He was in the peak of health, thanks to his good genes, healthy lifestyle and exercise regime, and his capacity neither to internalise stress nor to project anger on to others, which usually exacts its revenge. It came too early, too, because he frankly enjoyed it all, though most could not understand why. Harry did not slow down in the least as the end loomed. The ceaseless round came to a screeching halt; the infrastructure was withdrawn; his staff were no longer his; his team now worked for another; the keys, both to Bishopscourt and to his silver-grey Ford Ghia, were surrendered.

As we have shown, major events in Harry's life normally attracted an avalanche of letters. On this occasion, he pre-empted them. Committed to ending well, Harry, before and after his last day in office, wrote letters of thanks to a vast number of people with whom he had served the Lord. Most were astonished that such a busy person had found the time to write such personal letters, but in a final surge at full throttle, he fitted it in around the plethora of farewells, evaluations, recognition and honours.

### Order of Australia

On Australia Day, 2001, Harry was appointed an Officer in the General Division of the Order of Australia. In a one-off manifestation of 'friendly deceit', Harry did not advise Pam of this impending honour in advance. He thought it might be a pleasant surprise for her to discover it for herself as a regular *SMH* reader.[2] She there read a positive account of her husband's 'achievements against the

24.1 Harry, appointed an Officer in the General Division of the Order of Australia, 2001, here with Pam and Christina, and Professor Marie Bashir, who on 1 March 2001, became the first female Governor of New South Wales.

odds.' The citation read, 'For service to the Anglican Church and to the community, particularly in the areas of education, reconciliation between white and indigenous communities, overseas aid and the value of maintaining strong family life.'

The award gave pleasure to many and not only for personal reasons. It was felt that here was rare recognition of the church by the community and government. The members of the diocesan Indigenous Peoples Ministry, including Ray Minniecon, were especially gratified that Harry's contribution to Aboriginal people was recognised.[3] The retired Bishop of Willochra, a high-church diocese, wrote generously that the award recognised the contribution of the Diocese of Sydney to the Anglican Church of Australia, to the worldwide Anglican Communion, and to Australian society in general.[4]

As for Harry's supporters within the diocese, the temptation to bask in his reflected glory was resisted, but it was impossible to resist the conviction that Harry, thus honoured in his own time, would be vindicated by history. Rod West, Moore College trustee and retired Headmaster of Trinity Grammar School, who never could contain his enthusiasm, did not even try to on this occasion.

> MARVELLOUS! MARVELLOUS! MARVELLOUS! The last seven or so years have been tumultuous ones in our larrikin diocese and you have led us through daunting times … Best of all – you have not allowed yourselves to be distracted from forging ahead with splendid initiatives, the last being to bring assistance to training programs for clergy in beleaguered countries. Your vision has been inexhaustible. You two have worked together as a team and your dedicated service will be seen to have been truly luminous when the history of the diocese is written.[5]

Nor did it go unnoticed that the ABC's news item reporting the award followed the story of a recipient who was recognised for the dangerous work of milking poison from 70,000 deadly red-back spiders. 'I thought the juxtaposition very neat,' observed one Harry partisan, 'but I shan't enlarge on the analogy.'

In spite of such justified sentiments, Harry was not embarrassed by the award. He was not only his usual grace under pressure, but, as one observed, also 'grace under applause.'[6] Wollongong friends wrote, 'We know you do not look to be in favour with man, but rather with God. However sometimes the two occur together – there is a precedent for that!'[7] A number of the letters of congratulation suggested that Pam should have received a similar honour. In view of their lifelong teamwork in ministry, Harry would not have dissented from that.

## Evaluation

The end of an episcopate is a time for evaluations, of course, and those who write to the retiree are in the habit of saying kind things. The kindest tributes, those most affirming of his godly leadership, came from those who served under him, his co-workers. Those who had made life difficult for Harry mostly said nothing, or, if they did write to him on his retirement, dwelt on the positive. Gerald Davis, the retired editor of *Church Scene* who had a nose for any whiff of hypocrisy from Sydney's power brokers, sensed that there was 'sincerity in many of the generous things' being said about Harry and kindness from people known to differ from him.[8]

From Alan Gill, *SMH*'s religion reporter for 20 years, and who had interviewed five Archbishops of Canterbury and four of Sydney, but had left *SMH* before Harry, came the following tribute, 'I think your ministry has been a blessing to Sydney. I have admired your quiet, courteous ways, unfailing good humour and common sense pastoral approach.'[9] In later life, Gill reflected that he had been pretty tough in his reporting on Sydney's archbishops, including Marcus Loane, in the rather unthinking way expected of secular reporters. He admitted that the joke about reporting on the Anglican church was that, in the absence of hard data, reporters should just write about 'the factions.' He would be much kinder about them if he had his time over again. He thought Harry was a 'wonderful, godly man' and 'always fair.'[10]

It was the genius of Harry that he was able to share in the chief interests of others, thus reinforcing their own passion. This, the mark of the servant leader, was much in evidence in the letters that poured in from diocesan clergy and laity. Patricia Judge, an international leader in the bioethical field and herself invested as a Member of the Order of Australia the previous year, wrote, 'I have particularly appreciated your support of and interest in some of the major bioethical debates. You have always been gracious and courteous, even when disagreeing.'[11] Peter Carroll, ex-CMS missionary at Oenpelli, wrote to thank Harry for his support for Aboriginal land rights and 'to acknowledge the important initiatives that Sydney

Diocese under your leadership has taken in support of Indigenous ministry.'[12] From The Evangelical Sisterhood of Mary, Sister Simone wrote, 'we feel privileged to have known you for nearly 20 [years] … We remember you and Pam in the love and fellowship of our Lord Jesus.'[13] Harry was partly responsible for getting them the land in rural Theresa Park, south-west of Sydney, on which they built their centre, 'Canaan of God's Comfort'. Ian Mears particularly thanked Harry for his encouragement to members of his diocese to support churches in third world countries,[14] as did Daniel Willis, who observed, 'The Christian community around the world will remember fondly the contribution you have both made.' David Mansfield, Director of the Department of Evangelism, thanked Harry for his 'enduring passion for evangelism.'[15] The 'brilliant' Debbie Gilhooly, whom Lindsay Stoddart credits with being one of the creators of Youthworks, wrote to Harry, 'Youthworks is a richer and better organisation due to your support and input.'

Clergy wives were prominent among the letter writers. Louise Bartlett wrote, 'Words cannot adequately express our gratitude for your gracious and godly statesmanship.' Wendy Hill, wife of the Dean of Students at Moore College, wrote, 'Thank you so much for your godly example. Michael and I have greatly appreciated your friendship and your wonderful hospitality. Thank you so much for making yourselves so available to people.' There were letters from old stalwarts

24.2 Harry and Pam visit the Evangelical Sisterhood of Mary, at 'Canaan', near Camden, a site that Harry helped them to procure.

of the diocese, uncertain of the future. 'It is with great regret that we think of your retirement. Short of a miracle the Diocese will never be the same again.'[16]

It was not surprising, given Harry's concern for their role in the church, that women were well represented among the letter writers. Ros Wicks spoke for many when she acknowledged Harry's 'gentle but firm leadership.'[17] Ann Kells wrote, 'We will miss you enormously. Thank you for being so caring and interested in us all.' Joan Young wrote, 'God has used you mightily as a sweet fragrance by which many of us have been refreshed and challenged.'

Perhaps the majority of letters testified to Harry's capacity to model what a true minister of the gospel should be like. For future archbishop, Glenn Davies, one of the outstanding aspects of Harry's leadership was the way he dealt with people. 'While maintaining the dignity of the office, you enhanced your role through your pastoral sensitivity to every situation.'[18] Andrew Glover, who had been influenced by Harry and his family at Wollongong, before he even began going to church, and was now curate-in-charge at Gerringong, wrote, 'I have especially valued those occasions when your personal counsel made the issues simpler and clearer for me.'[19] Simon Manchester, Rector of North Sydney, addressed Harry as both archbishop and archangel and thanked him for his 'normality in every day contacts' and for keeping 'out of the ungodly pattern of critical church life while staying bighearted for the lost.'[20]

It was widely appreciated that Harry had presided over the diocese in one of its most difficult decades, but he was different from his predecessors in ways that mattered. Revd Ralph Fraser, then living in retirement in Mowll Village, wrote, 'The Diocese will miss you as an Archbishop who has worked at the "coal face" in a variety of parishes in this diocese and another, and has a personal appreciation of the highs and lows of parochial ministry.'[21] Canon Holbeck, who, as we have seen, was relieved at Harry's appointment, was not relieved by his departure. 'We will all feel a great sense of loss upon your retirement. The Diocese was indeed blessed to have you as its Archbishop and your godliness and openness to all people provided a lot of hope and healing in the Diocese and beyond.' Holbeck's predecessor in the healing ministry, Jim Glennon, wrote an interesting assessment of Harry's episcopate.

> It has been relatively easy to have ministry during the time you have been Archbishop because one feels that there is a steady hand on the tiller and a wise course is being steered. One feels that our Anglican heritage has been drawn on and preserved as well as the needs of our time being addressed with sensitivity and courage.[22]

From the Supreme Court, Justice Peter Young thanked Harry for being 'such a friendly, yet strong Archbishop' and expressed his confidence that Harry's influence would 'endure for good in the Anglican Church for many years.'[23]

Harry may not have attained his stated aim of making the diocese dynamically Anglican, but he remained faithfully Anglican, and in his context that was achievement enough. A more traditional Anglican, Justice Michael Kirby, appreciated the point. From the High Court in Canberra, he wrote to Harry on his retirement. 'I could only agree with the nice comments about you in the *SMH*. It is impossible to be an Archbishop – or even a judge – and to please everybody. One shouldn't try. But you have made many achievements.'[24] Finally, it must be recorded that Alan Cole wrote asking forgiveness for all his 'little interfering notes,' which he said, were 'lovingly meant.'[25]

## Retirement farewells

24.3 Pam, Patron of the Mothers' Union, was presented with this quilt at the chapter house on 23 February 2001. It was stitched by 85 members of the Mothers' Union under the direction of Mary Coyne and Di Jobbins.

Retiring at about the same time as Harry were Edward Bede Clancy, Cardinal Archbishop of the Sydney Archdiocese, and Gordon Samuels, Governor of New South Wales. Clancy was in the job until the pope released him. 'I go out to the letter box every day,' he told Harry. He had tried to retire in 1998 and again in 1999, writing to Harry, 'When it will be formally accepted and a successor appointed, only God and the Pope know.'[26] His successor, George Pell, was not announced until 26 March 2001, by which time Harry had departed. All three were present at a function at Darling Harbour hosted by the premier. Ted, as Cardinal Edward Bede Clancy was known to Harry, asked Harry if he knew how to make a sponge. Gordon Samuels revealed that he had already become sufficiently competent in shopping and cooking to feed the family when his wife, Jackie, was on the stage.

At SC, meeting on 19 February, Ray Smith and Warwick Olson gave moving speeches. Standing Committee presented Harry with an electronic pen. Whoever chose it knew Harry well, as he loved gadgets like that. On Saturday

3 March Harry and Pam were farewelled at a service held by the Chinese churches. They were buoyed by the large attendance and the kindness and enthusiasm for the gospel so manifest on that occasion.[27] The day was overshadowed, however, by the death of Bruce Smith, beloved preacher and poet, whom Harry had visited two days earlier. On Sunday 4 March Harry and Pam worshipped in the Mar Thoma Church in Erskineville. The singing of the song 'Amen, Amen' brought back to them happy memories of the great time they had experienced at the Maramon Convention.[28]

Harry's successor, Peter Jensen, then Principal of Moore College, made a generous tribute at the college graduation on 12 March 2001 in recognition of Harry, who had been college president. They had not always agreed, and it must have been evident from Harry's elevation of Robert Forsyth to the episcopate that he hoped to prevent Peter's appointment as archbishop. Harry was determined to soften the diocesan culture and believed Peter was even more determined to toughen it. But Harry had left Peter in no doubt that Moore College was in his heart, and on two major difficulties where the two were at odds, Harry had encouraged Peter to express his views, which Peter considered both 'generous and gracious.'[29] At the graduation, Peter gave a litany of challenges faced by archbishops and then asked:

> How has our Archbishop coped with all this? The answer is plain to all who know him. He has continued to affirm others whenever he has had opportunity. He has been unbelievably patient, courteous and tactful. He never seems to panic, or even to think the worse of those who disappoint him. He has answered every physical and spiritual demand placed upon him. He has attempted to bring reconciliation and peace wherever it has been remotely possible. Most impressively, in an age when you cannot be certain of the orthodoxy of bishops he has held unswervingly to the faith and has been willing to stand for that faith in forums which have been hostile and uncomfortable. In the relatively short time in which he has been our Archbishop, his name has become known in world-wide Anglicanism for fidelity to the gospel and courage of opinion. And he has continued to reach out in mission.

Harry himself gave the graduation address on that occasion. Under the title 'The Gospel we preach', Harry spoke about ultimate reality – of Christ the Rescuer. College trustee, Rod West, felt that the message was soul-searing. 'Harry was at his best tonight,' he said to Pam afterwards, to which she replied, 'Harry is always at his best.'

Throughout February and March, removalists were busy packing up at Bishopscourt and unpacking under Pam's supervision at their retirement home in Figtree, a suburb of Wollongong. That exhausting operation was completed before their last four days, when the farewells reached a fitting crescendo.

On 16 March, the official diocesan farewell, a civic dinner, was held at the Westin Hotel in the presence of the state premier and the prime minister. Rod West declared it 'appropriate that a Civic Dinner should be accorded to our Archbishop, for Harry Goodhew has a passionate interest in the city and its welfare.' At a time when secularisation was hastening the separation of church and state, Harry took every opportunity to maintain their interdependence, in obedience to the biblical mandate, 'seek the welfare of the city ... and pray to the LORD on its behalf' (Jer 29:7). On Harry's self-assessment as a failure made at his last synod, West observed:

> The judgment that he has passed upon himself is shared by no one in the diocese, friend or doubter. (If there are any foes, they would have to be on the lunatic fringe!) ... His unruffled, courteous manner has hidden wells of strength. No force could deflect him from his purposeful direction of the diocese – a direction no doubt worked out initially on his knees.

## Harry lays up his pastoral staff

The next day, Saturday 17 March 2001, at 10.30 am, a service of thanksgiving and farewell was held in St Andrew's Cathedral to mark Harry's retirement. There were many poignant moments. When the Bible readings were read by sons David and Philip, it felt to outsiders symbolic of an imagined reality that the children were getting their father back after his years of unceasing toil. It was not like that in reality. He was never the absent father. In the first lesson from Isaiah 65:17–25, David read that, in the new Jerusalem, those who die at a

24.4 Justice Ken Handley, Chancellor of the Diocese of Sydney from 1980 to 2003, who spoke at Harry's retirement service, at his own retirement in January 2007.

hundred will be mere youths, and 'they will not labor in vain, nor will they bear children doomed to misfortune; for they will be a people blessed by the LORD, they and their descendants with them' (NIV). It almost seemed as if the new Jerusalem were in evidence. Harry was far from worn out by the trials of office; he was a very youthful 70, and his children had all arrived at a happy place. 'I love and admire my father greatly,' David says, 'and there are all sorts of ways in which I want to be like him.'[30]

Justice Ken Handley, chancellor of the diocese, gave a thank you address, a model of precision and brevity.

> We thank you for being among us as our friend and leader.
>
> Throughout your career, you have never allowed comfort and security to prevent you from launching out when you believed your Master was calling you.
>
> Your time with the Bush Church Aid at Ceduna demonstrated your godly spirit of adventure; your distinguished rectorship at Coorparoo demonstrated your capacity to minister courteously in an unfamiliar ecclesiastical environment.
>
> Your diocesan family has benefitted from your parish experience, in Beverly Hills, at Coorparoo, Carlingford and Wollongong. You understand what parish life is about.
>
> When you became our Archbishop you took up the task with statesmanlike dignity and discipline. Your tireless application to responsibility has been to our benefit. Your oversight of regionalisation has enriched and enhanced the life of our diocese.
>
> In the midst of a busy life, you have nevertheless graciously made time for individuals who have sought your counsel.
>
> The part you have played behind the diocese in the work of General Synod and your quiet contribution to the life of the Anglican Communion overseas has been a feature of your ministry that has been widely appreciated.
>
> We thank God for the wisdom and energy he has given you, and we are grateful that you have been willing to use those gifts for our benefit.
>
> And so it is, we say 'Thank you, Archbishop' (long applause).

24.5 Harry and his bishops at his retirement service, 17 March 2001. Left to right: Reg Piper, Brian King, Harry, Paul Barnett, Ray Smith, Robert Forsyth.

24.6 Retirement picnic for Harry and Pam at Bicentennial Park, Homebush.

On the Holy Table, the archbishop then laid up his pastoral staff, the visual reminder of his role as a shepherd of souls. It was to remain in the safe keeping of the dean until taken up by the next archbishop.

Harry then preached. 'I wish to finish,' he said, 'where I began: *coram Deo*.' Citing Revelation 22:17 (NRSV), 'Let everyone … come', he called on all to continue to live in the presence of God. He quoted Jacques Ellul, his favourite modern prophet, 'Action really receives its character from prayer,' and observed, 'I sometimes think God's people are at their best in prayer and at their worst in committees' (laughter). He spoke in conclusion of God, majestic in his magnanimity, reaching out that all might come and none perish.

He then invited Pam to join him in the pulpit to say a word of thanks. She quoted Psalm 16:5–6, 'LORD, you alone are my portion and my cup; you make my lot secure. The boundary lines have fallen for me in pleasant places; surely I have a delightful inheritance' (ESV). Pam was grateful for all the good and the bad that had happened and she believed that the best was yet to come. She talked about how prayer had become such an important part of the lives of the wives of Harry's team. For her part, not always knowing what to pray, she would just say, 'Lord – the diocese.' Moved, the congregation gave her words prolonged applause.

Nicky Chiswell then sang 'Jesus Loves Me', recalling the experience early in Harry's episcopate at St Barnabas, Broadway, when, gripped with chest pain, he had sung those words in dedication to his God. Finally, the congregation were invited to join other members of the diocesan family in a farewell picnic that afternoon. About 2,000 gathered at Bicentennial Park, Homebush, for that purpose.

## The last archbishop

The following day, Sunday 18 March 2001, the ABC *Compass* program, 'The Last Archbishop,' devoted to Harry's episcopate, went to air. It was exactly a week before the memorial service for Don Bradman. Broadcaster, Geraldine Doogue, opened the program with a series of observations about Harry and the diocese that would have been news to no Sydney Anglican.

> He is worried as he steps down that some have an impression of the diocese as 'arrogant' and 'aggressive' ... as Archbishop he has used his personal warmth and social skills to encourage more Christian compassion and humility ... The largest, richest and most influential Anglican diocese in the world ... The intense politics and lobbying that surrounds this top job, powerful forces that have been part of this diocese for over 150 years ... During his term he has won great respect and for admiration his friendly style and moderate leadership.

Julia Baird, convenor of MOW, then observed:

> I think Harry Goodhew is a gracious man and a good man and he is a caring person who has had a very difficult job at the top of a diocese that has been so intensely political. He has been undermined constantly, almost every way he turns, and it is a testament to him that he has managed to be gracious throughout that.

Invited to speak on the temperament of the diocese, Harry replied,

> It's vigorous, it's enthusiastic, it's sometimes a little self-righteous, very convinced that it is always right, but underneath very firmly committed to the fundamentals of the Christian faith as the Anglican Church has received it in terms of its doctrinal base.

Doogue then observed,

> You have said that one of your central regrets is that you weren't able to spread more effectively an ethic of love or generosity of spirit across the diocese, that you have heard three descriptions of Sydney Anglicans as arrogant, polarising and aggressive. This must really bother you.

'Well, it does, otherwise I wouldn't have said it,' replied Harry.

> Yes, it does, for while I think it appropriate to take firm stands on issues you believe are significant, I think there is a way of doing that which is appropriate to the humility which ought to go with Christian expression … In the Anglican church we have strong views which are different from others and we have to assert them, but I believe we should do it in a way which is gracious in accord with the Christian spirit.

Asked if he would be glad to leave the job, he said that he would be sorry to leave it. He thought of his position as father-in-God to a very large family, and he tried to move the family in the direction he thought it should go, which involved sometimes holding back the bolters and sometimes stirring up the recalcitrant.

Harry's devotees were thrilled. It was 'one of the most worthy shows ever broadcast', and Harry came across as 'so harmless, yet so wise.'[31] He gave a great example of how 'to communicate the human face of Christianity.'[32] 'We saw the *Compass* program last Sunday,' wrote two retired BCA workers, 'and thought you were great in enhancing the image of the church by your graciousness and gentleness.'[33] Harry was arguably as effective with the media as any clergyperson, bishop or otherwise, in the history of the diocese.

The next day, his birthday, his final day, was a last busy day at the office. Harry was interviewed on 2UE, giving model answers to controversial questions.[34] He wrote to the executive producer of *Compass* to express his appreciation for the way the program was presented. He said that he 'greatly appreciated the kindness of the ABC.'[35] He wrote to the state premier, the prime minister and the leader of the state opposition thanking them for their presence at the civic farewell, and, to the last, expressing the hope that her two children would enjoy their schooling at St Andrew's Cathedral School.[36] He wrote to Anglicare head, Howard Dillon, to express concern for his health. 'To Christ's People in the Church in this Diocese' he wrote to thank them for their expression of affection, and he wrote to the Rector of Figtree, Rod Irvine, whom he had nurtured at Coorparoo, and to the people of that church in the Illawarra, which he had done so much to bring to its fruitful heyday, to express his happiness at the prospect of spending more time in fellowship with them.

That evening, friends joined him for dinner at a seafood restaurant in Brighton-Le-Sands.

And it was all over.

# 25

# The Ministry of a Former Archbishop: 'The Inexhaustible Vision'

On 20 March 2001, the day after his formal retirement, Harry and Pam flew to the United States for six weeks to attend meetings and to visit their daughter Wendy and their grandchildren. Billy Graham staff members, Bill and Ruth Conard and John Coutts, arranged for Harry and Pam to have a week-long retreat in a log cabin at The Cove, the Billy Graham Training Center at Ashville in the Blue Ridge Mountains of North Carolina. There, they were treated like royalty and enjoyed a brief meeting with Billy Graham himself. In Pam's recollection 'the whole thing was magical.' They told Bill Conard how impressive it all was, and he said, 'It's Mr Graham,' – they never call him Billy – 'he sets the tone of how we do things.' There can hardly have been a more agreeable commencement to the ambiguous experience of retirement.

If Harry is any guide, then the retirement of a high-profile activist who long outlives his retirement date comes in two phases: transition, which can be psychologically challenging, followed by the discovery of a new rhythm of usefulness. Harry's diary during the early months of his retirement reveals that he was open to God's leading, but was not sure what it was. It is evident in his prayerful study of God's word at the time that his desire to know God's will for this stage of his life was a pressing need. On 6 May 2001 after studying passages of Scripture related to the life of King David, including David's own conviction that 'The LORD will fulfill his purpose for me; your steadfast love, O LORD, endures forever' (Ps 138:8, ESV), Harry noted 'God has his purpose – we play a part, a part determined by God – Lord show me my part now I pray.' His heartfelt search led him to restate fundamentals. On 15 May, he recorded:

> I have promised to study God's Word daily and to obey it and teach it
> to others. I have promised to pray daily. These are my first priorities.
> After that I should do whatever I can. Please show me where and how
> I should serve you.

He also prayed often in this period that he would be a better steward of his material resources and that he would live more frugally. That was a desire reinforced by a visit to the slums of Nairobi early in his retirement. He was also comforted by the renewal of close and constant contact with his old Wollongong friends and by

25.1 Harry and Rod Irvine, Rector of Figtree.

the opportunity to spend more time with his children and grandchildren. Rod Irvine, the Rector of Figtree, was delighted to have Harry back in his parish. He took advantage of Harry's presence to run by him the really difficult matters that confront church leaders, and welcomed him to staff meetings so that Figtree's large and growing staff could benefit from his wisdom. Rod would gladly have given him a permanent role in the parish, but Harry was far too busy attending to unfinished business without secretarial staff and fulfilling the many engagements which still filled his diary.

Uncertainty about his own situation was no barrier to Harry's usefulness. Because he had always been so interested in what others were doing apart from his own projects, he was able to encourage Christians in a very wide range of ministries. In answer to his prayers and consistent with his giftedness, he was enabled to give decisive assistance to two of those ministries in particular: to the poor in Africa and to the ministry of EE. But before he was in a position to offer such substantial help, he had to deal with two less agreeable matters, detritus from his previous struggles.

## The succession to Harry

Harry was worried by the succession and the future of the diocese. He did not want to see Peter Jensen become archbishop and he did not want John Woodhouse to be appointed as Principal of Moore College. They were two champions of the culture that he had done his best to change, and we have seen how determined he was to change it. But we have also seen that the hardliners were in no mood for such change. The culture had been set in concrete for so long that it would take sustained attention from a jackhammer to make any impact. It was, to use Cardinal Newman's more elegant simile, like attacking a granite mountain with a razor blade. No more victories would be allowed to the forces of moderation. Harry's wishes were again frustrated and both defeats were ugly.

As we saw in chapter 22, Harry had elevated Robert Forsyth to the position of Bishop of South Sydney in an attempt to give him a leg up in the election for archbishop. It went closer to succeeding than the hardliners expected. They had to resort to even stronger methods than usual to get their man, Peter Jensen, over the line. At the election synod, two of their number reflected, not on the faith, but on the good faith of Forsyth when it looked as if he would win the election.[1] It was an episode that continued to rankle with many, including media officer Margaret Rodgers. She later fulminated against 'The right end result but a hopeless, hopeless process. Badly managed from the front and fearfully managed from the forces … Very unchristian behaviour. I was just appalled. And I think a lot of people were.'[2]

The second matter, the appointment of Peter Jensen's successor as Principal of Moore College, caused equal angst in a smaller circle, this time mercifully invisible to the prying media. The appointment of the principal was the responsibility of the college trustees, although since 1984 an attempt had been made to invest the powers of the trustees in the college council. When the trustees refused to surrender their power, the usual battle ensued, with the members of the council condemning the trustees in a manner that one trustee characterised as 'horrifically insensate'. The trustees were then four in number: Rod West, retired Headmaster of Trinity Grammar School; Roger Chilton, Rector of Pymble; Peter Kell, Wollongong solicitor; and Harry Goodhew himself. One night, after Harry had retired and was living in Figtree, there came a knock at his door, and there was Doug Marr, the diocesan registrar, who presented Harry with a number of forms that he asked Harry to sign, relinquishing his position as trustee. Harry said, 'thank you very much' and Marr retreated without the signatures. Donald Robinson had remained as a trustee for a year after finishing as archbishop, and Harry did not have to step down as a trustee when his term as archbishop finished. He did not intend to stay on, but the urgency to dismiss him seemed inappropriate, so he delayed. But, as great indignation was expressed at his staying on, in the interests of peace, he eventually stood down, and was replaced by Peter Jensen. The new archbishop wanted to appoint John Woodhouse, while the trustees wanted to appoint a younger applicant, who interviewed astonishingly well, and, as a scholar of the writings of St John, was considered a desirable change from the college's traditional adulation of the writings of St Paul.

West recalls that one member of the council berated him at great length, accusing him of demeaning the archbishop and demanding his immediate resignation. West, Kell and Chilton were asked to leave the chamber to allow the council to decide their fate. Rather than cool his heels in an anteroom, Rod went home, but he understood the meeting went on for a long time, at the conclusion of which the trustees were invited to resign, as they had behaved so despicably. They said they would not resign. The council insisted that they must have total control. Chilton, a lawyer, argued that certain legal matters needed to be resolved before they could be shut down. The confrontation resulted in an expensive, but inconclusive, legal struggle, which dragged on for some months. Before its termination, so as to prevent further expense and fury, the three gave way to the archbishop. 'After all,' reflected Rod West later, 'we do have an episcopal system, which means that for better or worse, bishops should get their own way.' But, in that, West was not thinking like a Sydney Anglican, who often denied archbishops their way.

Harry's obduracy will seem strange to any not subject to diocesan politics, but the disquieted can be assured that Harry knew how to behave. Son Philip observed that, when Harry was archbishop, he did not breathe a word of criticism about anybody. He would say of those

> who were totally out to get him – 'so and so, he's just trying to serve the Lord the best way he can, so good on him. He's a good brother.' Mum was not quite hysterical, but she was more shrill.[3]

Following the election of Peter Jensen as his successor, Harry commended him to his correspondents as one 'deeply committed to the spread of the Gospel.' In turn, Peter never criticised Harry. All Sydney's archbishops have known how to behave, an essential requirement for the job.

## Africa

In the final years of his episcopate, as we have seen, Harry had developed a special interest in the challenges and opportunities facing African bishops. He was stirred by the claim that Christianity's centre of gravity was moving from the West to the two continents of Africa and Latin America, and that 8.4 million Christians were being added in Africa each year, or 23,000 per day. Harry enthused, 'Those who first preached in these places must be thrilled: having initially worked so hard for seemingly little response.'[4] Now, in retirement, he and Pam were able to make long visits to Africa, made possible by a gift from an anonymous source in Sydney. It was directed through Robert Tong, who told Harry that there was a concerned group that thought he should keep open his contact with the African bishops, and gave him $5,000 for the purpose.

From 27 July to 27 August 2001, Harry and Pam visited Nairobi, in support of the initiative of Dr Max Collison who was working in Kibera, the largest slum in all of Africa. The slums were a good base for evangelistic outreach, and Collison had there set up low-cost medical centres. Harry knew the Collison family from his time as a catechist at Revesby and, at a CMS Summer School, had asked Max if a retired bishop could help him with his work in Kenya. Max's first response was 'well, you could pray,' but later said to Harry, 'you could come over to Kenya.' On their first visit, they stayed for a month. Harry kept copious notes on the experience; he was there to listen and learn. 'The slums are like an onion,' he recorded. 'The greatest poverty is towards the centre.' The statistics were grim: the Nairobi slums occupy 1.5 per cent of the city's land, with 60–80 per cent of the population; 100 people to one tap; 5,000 to a toilet in one slum; average daily income $1 to $2 (Australian); clothes cheap, but water has to be paid for. Most of the slum dwellers are single mothers and children.

25.2 Pam at the Urban Mission Training Centre, Kibera Slum, Nairobi, August 2001.

25.3 Church in the Kibera Slum, Nairobi, August 2001.

When they first arrived at Kibera, Max asked Pam to complete a questionnaire before he would show her through the slum, to alert and forewarn her about the paucity of toilets and the plenitude of prostitutes. Her visit greatly moved her as she met up with women who, because they were believers, though they were dirt poor, wanted to keep out of prostitution. Max had already worked out a way to help them. Westerners, he knew, would be open to purchasing cards made in Africa, so they interviewed six women and established what was to become known as the Kibera Card Ministry. The Diocese of Sydney funded the card ministry in the first year out of its overseas aid budget. Pam presided over this program in Australia. She and Harry were pleased that it helped to raise practical social concern among Sydney Anglicans.

When later asked who had made the biggest impression on his Christian life, Harry nominated the wretched of the earth who had to live out the Christian faith in circumstances one could hardly imagine living in. To see it lived out in service with joy was very impressive. Once, commenting on the petition for our daily bread in the Lord's Prayer, Harry wrote:

> My wife and I were challenged many times when we were in the slums of Nairobi, Kenya. You would meet men and women; you would ask them how they were; and they would say, "We're rejoicing. The Lord is good. He's good every day." And you would look at the little hovels they lived in and the circumstances under which they lived, and you would feel very compromised.[5]

In their ministry in the Kibera slum, Harry and Pam became associated with the Centre for Urban Ministry, an extension of Carlisle College (a Church Army training college in Kenya and Sudan). Instead of training the students within the college precincts, they purchased an old building within the slum and did the training there. Harry taught there for a week, along with Revd Graham Crew from Gymea Anglican Church. An opportunity was thus initiated for Sydney to provide theological education through the Moore College program, which has gone into Kenya and other African nations.

25.4 Harry with students at Carlisle College, Nairobi, 2003.

Harry also made himself familiar with Christian ministry in another Nairobi slum, that of Korogocho in the north-east of the city. This work was led by Peter Mbotche, nurtured as a new Christian by Sydney rector, David O'Mara, who had worked in Nairobi with CMS. Mbotche welcomed people who arrived in Korogocho for work, and then would take a team and visit the villages from which they came. He had a youth worker by the name of John Ndegwa who was very poor, but spoke good English, learned by picking up novels in English – murder mysteries – that people had discarded in the streets. He was also an artist, and a Christian man had admired his work and taken him in and looked after him, even though he had dreadlocks! Under his influence, Ndegwa became a Christian and went to Carlisle College, where he was highly thought of as a student. He had a strong social conscience, and, in 2000, he wrote to the local paper observing that the church was more concerned to condemn homosexuality than to relieve the poor lost people in the slums. The newly appointed bishop told Ndegwa he did not like that article and therefore he would not ordain him. Ndegwa later wrote that it was Harry Goodhew who kept him going in his faith, and Harry baptised one of his children. Ndegwa was ordained in a Catholic Episcopal church and went back into the slums, where he opened schools, created employment programs for women, and founded religious orders for men and women to work in the slums. In November 2015, he was made Bishop of the Anglican Catholic Church in Kenya.

As the weeks in Nairobi passed, Harry's notes of their visit include his ideas for plans to address the need, lists of possible businesspeople and entrepreneurs whose help he might enlist, and details of individual Africans whom he might

25.5 Visit to Diocese of Mt Kenya West, 2003, with Bp Alfred Chipman.

help. Harry and Pam would later raise money to buy a plot of land and build a church at Korogocho and help a theology student and a male nurse with their studies until graduation. When Harry later spoke in Melbourne and mentioned the latter, a doctor afterwards said, 'I'll pay for him'; and after he spoke at Lavender Bay Anglican Church and mentioned the need for a new church and land, a parishioner gave him $8,000 for that purpose. The Goodhews' visit to Nairobi bore much fruit.

Between 2001 and 2006, Harry and Pam also paid two visits to the Diocese of Bujumbara in Burundi. Bujumbara is the capital of Burundi of which, thanks to the work of CMS, 10 per cent of the population of nine million is Anglican. CMS began work there in the 1930s and the number of Anglicans grew dramatically thanks to the East African Revival.[6] The visit was not without danger. The Burundian Civil War, arising from the ethnic divisions between the Hutu and the Tutsi, started in 1993 and was not ended until 2005. Pam spoke to a group of women who had just crossed over from the Congo and, a few months later, learned that many of them had been killed. Harry and Pam spoke in various churches and heard testimonies from church workers, lay preachers and catechists who had benefitted from the purchase of a number of bicycles, made possible by a gift from Christ Church, Lavender Bay. They distributed 100 Bibles and met with members of parliament and the president. A third visit had to be postponed because the bishop felt it was too unsafe. Harry and Pam also helped the bishop's wife complete a degree to equip her for social welfare work in the diocese.

Early in their married life, Harry and Pam had contemplated missionary work, but were denied that owing to Pam's health. Now they were enabled to work in the neediest of fields with greater leverage over a shorter period. Typical of all they did, this was a mission they pursued with all their strength while they had opportunity.

25.6 Bujumbura, January 2005, Bp and Mrs Ntukamazina.

## The One Sure Hope

Harry had spent a lifetime in pursing spiritual insight, which cascaded through his sermons. Retirement gave him the opportunity to express his findings in a more systematic format, and his devotional work, *The One Sure Hope* was published in 2005.[7] Replete with spiritual wisdom, it was designed as 'Studies in Isaiah for Lent and other times'. The studies, as first drafted, were too academic. Pam intervened decisively. 'You are writing this for me, you know.' So, he wrote them more simply and drew more deeply from the wells of evangelical piety to make them both more accessible and more devotional. A Queensland woman, who had lost her son, and in her poverty, had to move house five times, reported that the book seemed written just for her. She found 'great blessing' in being reminded of the promises of Isaiah.[8]

*The One Sure Hope* achieved what Harry (and Pam) hoped for. This book goes to Harry's deepest convictions about the relationship between humanity and God. On the experience of Hezekiah in 2 Chronicles 32:31, Harry observes, 'We must remember that God ... will do whatever it takes to make us true sons and daughters, not simply in status but in living truth. He will, in mighty grace, conform us to the likeness of his Son.'[9]

## Harry's role in reshaping Evangelism Explosion

Harry continued as a member of the International Board of Evangelism Explosion (EEI) on which he had served since the late 1970s, and now, in retirement, he made his greatest contribution to the development of this ministry. It has enjoyed astonishing, indeed explosive, growth that none could have foreseen, training millions to reach millions. EE might now just be the biggest missionary organisation in the world. There is another reason why Harry is gratified by EE's recent history. Its dramatic success has been built on a comprehensive change in the culture of the organisation, which has empowered a very good organisation to become great. Harry had longed to see such culture change in the Diocese of Sydney, but he had met with sustained opposition. Now he participated in a process that delivered dramatic culture change, and the measurable rewards surpassed all expectation.

Culture change is never easy. An organisation as brilliantly conceived and as effective as EE was bound to resist the necessity of change. Dr Kennedy put the brakes on change, being fairly certain that the initial EE prescription was fixed and final. It was not until 2005, four years after Harry retired as archbishop and just two years before Dr Kennedy's death, that the way was opened for a radical departure from the initial prescription. In that year, Revd Rick Bond (then Youth EE Director), together with Harry and Rod Story, sat in Dr Kennedy's office to talk about a report that Harry had been commissioned to produce to contemporise the material. Kennedy was a speed reader and he flipped through the document, digesting it all with admirable ease, and then he looked at Rod and said, 'I can see clearly what you are trying to do.' Rod said, 'That's very good.' Dr Kennedy continued, 'You want to kill EE.' Harry glanced at Rod and gave him a characteristic look: 'Now Rod, don't lose it.' But Rod responded also characteristically. He said, 'Jim, that is insulting. I have committed my life and my ministry to this organisation and I am committed to it for the future. The last thing I want to do is kill it.' This was Australian forthrightness with a vengeance: for a start, no American called Dr Kennedy 'Jim'. He looked across the table and said, 'Everything within my body screams "No – we cannot do this".' Then he added, 'But I trust you, and we'll think about it.' He and Harry talked a lot, and finally Dr Kennedy agreed, albeit reluctantly, that they could proceed to explore the proposal further.[10]

So, in 2006, Rod Story initiated, and Harry participated in a research and development program that resulted in the production of a revised version of the classic EE material. People were brought from all over the world to the Wollongong Golf Club, south of Sydney, to create a contemporary evangelistic tool. The new version was to become known as XEE. It is less prescriptive than the original EE; it is more concerned with the concept than with the particular; more concerned to discuss and less to lecture. 'You watch videos and discuss what you saw in the video and how you could use it,' observed Rod Story. 'There's not 92 points that you have to tick off and memorise.'

Dr Kennedy's health was seriously impaired from 2005 and he died in 2007. During that period, a process, in which Harry took a leading role, was initiated to thoroughly internationalise the ministry. Active in that process were Sterling Huston, newly appointed Board chairperson, who had at one time organised Billy Graham's North American crusades, and John Sorensen, who was to replace Dr Kennedy as EE President. Harry characterised Sterling Huston as 'a fine person, tall, intelligent, able, understated, and godly. He became a very able and good Chairman in place of Jim.'[11] Harry's influence on John Sorensen was as critical as his influence on Dr Kennedy. Sorensen testifies that what Harry has done for the ministry during his time as president has been 'world-changing.' EE, thanks to Harry, used to be akin to 'a local corner store and now it has become a huge department store.'[12]

Harry and Sterling Huston were clear that the ministry had to evolve both from being one based on the charismatic leader who personified the ministry to making the missional aspect dominant, and from its American base to an international one. Organisations were consulted that had gone through such a process after the death of a founding president, including Campus Crusade for Christ, Wycliffe Bible Translators, Summer Institute of Linguistics, Navigators, and World Vision. The critical thing was to work out how all these organisations addressed the question: How do you make work the fact that you are in the United States but have an international ministry? Do you have two organisations?

Equipped with all this feedback, Harry, John Sorensen and Sterling Huston consulted with many of the EE ministries throughout the world. Harry and John Sorensen visited South Korea, the Philippines and Hong Kong as well as Australia, while Sorensen and Huston visited South Africa and Britain. They experienced no push back; there was a genuine enthusiasm for working together and developing strong partnerships. To Sorensen, the wisdom that Harry had in talking to people of very diverse backgrounds on all these boards and to do it with such grace looked like a unique gift in the church universal. Huge respect was shown to him, not only because he was an archbishop – 'there are lots of archbishops in the world' – but because of his character.

Yet EE was too big a ship to be turned around quickly. Through the process of consulting both the major American missionary and evangelistic organisations and the many EE national ministries, the data compiled was mountainous. Huston realised that the task ahead was beyond them. He suggested engaging the services of Debra and David Brown, who ran a Canada-based business for consulting, advising and training in corporate governance. It was a master stroke, resulting in the development of a process for change that energised all parties and has grown the organisation exponentially. Debra, who joined the board, has since worked on a doctorate through Gordon-Conwell Theological Seminary on the EE restructuring process.[13]

In December 2007, the board of EEI debated and accepted a roadmap for radical reorganisation.[14] In March 2008, it voted itself out of existence, and was replaced by two new bodies: a Congress of Nations and a Board for EE International. The board is necessary to fulfil the requirements of corporation law in the United States and includes a number of members from outside the United States. In the Congress of Nations, there is a place for every EE 'Multiplying' Nation (that is, a national ministry that fulfilled a certain number of criteria including having an indigenous board of directors, about which Harry was particularly adamant). The congress was Harry's idea, as was the title itself. He always wanted it to be a parliament, not just a conference or yet another gathering of leaders. It had to be the parliament of the organisation where EE's policy is finally determined.

Debate was intense, and it took two years of discussion to finalise the new arrangements. Harry wanted real power to reside in the Congress of Nations, to stop the board becoming a law unto itself, and pestered the organisation with his view until it prevailed. He kept saying, 'Congress is the chief policy-making body, not the 12-person Board of EEI; so don't lapse back into allowing the Board to run the ministry.' The congress made recommendations to the board, which could only veto any recommendation if it was outside EE policies over which congress is the final authority in any case. The Congress of Nations meets every three years and sends recommendations to the EE board and executive team. The board meets three or four times a year. Harry shared in these quarterly meetings until in 2011; when he reached his 80th birthday, he decided not to seek re-election. It was a difficult decision, as he loved going to the board meetings and hearing about all the exciting things that are going on in the world.

Harry headed the committee responsible for organising the first Congress of Nations in Kuala Lumpur, Malaysia, in 2010 and he chaired the congress meetings without his hearing aid, which he had forgotten to bring with him from Australia. It was at this congress, with Harry in the chair and with all 30 nations represented around the table, that the idea came – it felt to John Sorensen to be of divine origin – that the 30 nations were each challenged to adopt a nation, so that when they came together three years later, 60 nations would be represented. Each of the multiplying nations was to be completely independent. Harry's solution to the potential problems this created was to have each of them sign a covenant, not with EEI, but with each other. Each non-multiplying nation partners with a multiplying one in order to be built up.

Harry assisted in the preparation for the second congress held in 2013 in Cape Town and shared in it. He also had an advisory role in preparation for the 2016 congress in Malang, Indonesia, which was attended by 86 nations. Congress has become a big event and getting bigger every time, with pomp and flags and ceremony, and lasts for about a week. John Sorensen likened it to the United Nations, with four representatives of every nation present.

Harry's interest in EE went far beyond his active involvement in its restructure. After his retirement as archbishop, he conducted week-long sessions for EE on 'Deepening One's Spiritual Life' and on 'The Mission of God' for either interns or field workers. He taught these courses each year in Fiji, twice in Indonesia, and in Malawi and Uganda. Over 600 staff participated. They were full-time fieldworkers who, on Sunday afternoons, would be out evangelising. 'They are so committed,' observed Pam. 'It makes us feel like slobs, somehow.' Harry wrote and recorded in the United States the series of lectures on these two topics for use in the online training program used by EE. These courses counted towards a bachelor's degree in a group of universities throughout the world.

The lectures on the spiritual life were published in 2011 in a book dedicated 'To my dear wife Pam: a woman who prays.' *Green: Growing Deep in a Shallow World* has been translated into Russian, Spanish, French, German and 11 other languages, and distributed to 6,000 people associated with EE. In *Green*, Harry insists that objectively there are things that, if done, you will grow, and if you don't, you won't. Read the Bible, pray, worship the Lord and witness, and fellowship with other Christians. What he says there, argues John Sorensen, is so basic and yet it is so profound. We are saved to be ambassadors.

By 2014, EE's culture of 'personality and policy power' had been replaced dramatically by one of 'people and proficiency power.' It was far more proficient because its policies were now developed by those – staff and trainees – who actually did the work of evangelism. It was an organisation with a culture far more consistent with Harry's understanding of good Christian governance and committed to problem-solving by mutuality and consensus, and it was a far more enjoyable movement to serve and work for.[15] It had achieved what Harry had longed in vain to see in the Sydney diocese: culture change in the interests of a Christian body proficient in its evangelism and warmly relational in its fellowship. It had developed in a way that the diocese had not, into a measurably more humane organisation: fairer, more altruistic, more generous, more caring, friendlier and kinder.[16] Dare one say: more Christian! EE's budget grew from $1.3 million in 1997 to $10 million in 2014.[17] In 2007, EE recorded 4.2 million professions of conversion worldwide; in 2014 it was 10 million.[18] Overall between 2007 and 2014, the ministry recorded 52 million professed conversions.[19] It was altogether more dynamic. Harry had every reason to be gratified: the dynamic Anglican was now sharing in the servant leadership of a dynamically evangelistic organisation.

## Retirement routines

Apart from the 'big ticket' items of Africa and EE, Harry and Pam continued in their customary ministry of hospitality to all and as seasoned advisers on how to make a parish hum. Pam thought they should put down roots in their local church at Figtree and not be away from home too much. She was involved in the leadership of the Mothers' Union at Figtree and also shared in the Manna House ministry, offering free home-cooked meals to people in the community. Harry functioned as something of a preaching coach for the staff at Figtree for a period.

His main advice was from Chappo, 'preach for about 20 minutes and about God.'

Harry did take locums at St Andrew's Cathedral, at Wollongong, and in Tasmania at Battery Point, Launceston and Sandy Bay. A decade after retirement he was still in demand as a conference speaker, especially on the health of churches. Over a three-year period to 2015, at the invitation of Kel Richards, he recorded programs for broadcast on 2CH on Sundays at 7.30 am.

Son Philip observed of his father, 'he does a great funeral and so people continue to ask him to take their funerals when they really should ask their own minister to do it.' While Acting Dean of St Andrew's Cathedral, he conducted the state funeral for Sir Roden Cutler on Thursday 28 February 2002. Sir Roden's son, David, later wrote to Harry: 'It was a beautiful service you arranged for Dad … Thank you … for your support and prayers during this difficult time; it was a great help to us all.' Harry preached at funerals for many local Illawarra clergy and lay people, and at the funerals of numerous prominent Anglican clergy, including John Emery (at whose funeral Chappo sat next to Pam and uttered throughout Harry's address, 'quite right, brother'), Boak Jobbins, Peter Chiswell, Robbie Douthwaite and Tony Lamb. Bp Cameron wrote to Harry after Boak's funeral (6 September 2012) in applause for the magnificent sermon he preached.

This 'most pastoral of Sydney's archbishops' found many opportunities in retirement to exercise pastoral care, not least to members of his own family. Son David's wife, Sandra, was very grateful to her father-in-law for his ministry to her own father. Ray Steele, a coalminer, in 2012, was diagnosed with stage 4 stomach cancer. He was not a churchgoer, but Sandra asked if it would be all right if Harry called on him and Ray agreed. After Harry talked with him, he gave his life to Christ and a few weeks later he died. Sandra had always loved Harry and now she had a sense of assurance that greatly comforted her on the death of her father. In many ways Ray sounds like Harry's own father, and Harry was always at ease ministering to working-class men.

25.7 Harry with Ray Steele, father of Sandra, Harry's daughter-in-law, in 1991.

Harry's interest in sport and physical activity continued undiminished until well into his retirement years. Cricket remained an absorbing interest. At Hunter's Hill Anglican Church, fellow cricket tragic, Russell Jackson, recalled how after a morning service, he and Harry sat on the stage in the church hall and swapped stories about the likes of cricketing greats Richie Benaud and Ray Flockton (both born in the year before Harry) with whom Harry had played. Russell's recollection that this conversation lasted until 2.30 pm sounds apocryphal.[20]

With Peter Chiswell, Harry bushwalked from Cradle Mountain to Lake St Clair in Tasmania (a week's walk) and went on other walks in New South Wales usually with groups. In September 2013, Harry and daughter, Robyn, walked the 192 miles Coast to Coast Walk in England from St Bee's, Cumbria on the west coast to Robin Hood's Bay on the east coast over 13 days. It was Robyn's idea, but Harry did not need much persuading. Robyn recalls that it was harder than either of them had anticipated, as the promotional material made it look like a comfortable stroll on even paths. In fact, a lot of it was stony and rough and precipitate. It was hard completing 14 miles of that every day. Walking through the Lake District, it was wet and very cold, with winds up to 60 miles an hour. Harry was the oldest walker by about 20 years. Yet he and another 60-year-old man, who had been training since undergoing a triple bypass nine months earlier, were the fittest on the walk. Of the 12 who enrolled to do the entire walk, only seven actually completed it.

Robyn was impressed not only by her father's perseverance, but also with his consideration for others and his care for those who lagged behind, including Robyn herself, who found the pace faster than comfortable. One day, they had to walk 26 miles and Robyn had blisters and she fell behind. Harry stayed with her and literally pushed her along for the last two miles, which were uphill through a forest. What did the two of them talk about over 13 days? 'Not a lot,' said Robyn. 'It was too difficult for deep conversations. It was mainly to encourage one another to keep going: one step in front of the other.' In one of the villages they passed through, Harry stood on a platform where John Wesley preached. 'He obviously needed a bit of elevation,' Harry mused. 'I had not realised that he was so short. Diets must have been different.'

Robyn noticed that, at the end of each day, Harry would unpack his bag and lay everything out carefully, and in the morning he would repack it with equal care, the action of a man who liked order, a tidy desk, clean shoes, and ironed clothing. Robyn observed occasional anxiety in Harry during the trip about being in the right place at the right time in airports and such places, and she concluded that these were matters Harry was used to Pam looking after, which helps to explain his keenness to have her go with him whenever he travelled.

## Health issues

Health dictated what Harry's mind resisted. With Pam increasingly burdened by macular degeneration, and him suffering a heart scare in 2016, it was, in the prescription of doctor son Philip, time 'to take things a little quieter now.' Harry protested 'I can't live that way.' Philip thought his dad had done well in retirement, but he understood that Harry found it hard not being as involved and that he lamented the fact that fewer people consulted him. Harry laughs when he says, 'I am not relevant anymore. Nobody knows who I am', but it is evident that such normal concomitants of old age trouble him. It is not that he seeks public acknowledgement, but he enjoys shaping things, particularly the intellectual challenge of getting his head around complex issues. Even late in life, his reading has been wide-ranging as he sought to keep his mind open to new ideas.

Retirement was also time to revive friendship with those who shared the experience of old age with them. Chappo, who had become identified with the REPA movement, and was grumpy with Harry over the Pymble matter and the prayer book, became very friendly again. Harry and Pam took him on long drives, after which he would thank them for the delightful conversation when he would do all the talking. He affirmed that 'old friends are the best friends.' Harry and Pam felt they had regained something of the warmth of friendship they had enjoyed with him in earlier years. In the kindness of God, retirement is far from one long frustration; it is also a time when the heat and din of the struggle subside and the Christian lives more deeply in the love Christ died to unleash on this needy world and especially on those who profess to be his servants and who obey his new commandment.

# Conclusion
# Legacy of Graciousness and Generosity

Noriko Dethlefs, academic and missionary, observed that there are two ways of making people change: by force (the wind) and by gentle warmth (the sun). 'My wanting to be like the sun,' she explains, 'is because that is the way I see Harry's ministry and he is my inspiration. When things are too hard for me to even work out "What Would Jesus Do?", I ask myself "What Would Harry Do?"'[1]

In the lives of countless Christians, Harry Goodhew has been the sunshine, the inspiration and guide on how to live for Jesus. He was so trusted, respected and loved for Jesus' sake that it gave his ministry a character that felt quite exceptional. It meant that he made an exceptional archbishop. The Diocese of Sydney in the Anglican Church of Australia has had outstanding bishops and archbishops. Harry's episcopate (1993–2001) was significantly shorter than most and more troubled. Yet, so exceptional were his distinctive gifts, that there were those who considered it appropriate to rank him above all the others.

Lloyd Waddy, a judge of the Family Court in Parramatta, who claimed to have known all of Sydney's archbishops from Howard Mowll on, assessed Harry's episcopate as equal to, 'if not outshining,' that of all his predecessors, and was convinced that 'the calm, wisdom, dedication and compassion [Harry] exemplified will last for decades and influence the Church well into the future.'[2] Wesley Girvan, who had been the Rector of Dapto in the Illawarra Region when Harry was appointed to Wollongong as rector, could remember all of Sydney's archbishops back to John Charles Wright (1909–33) who preceded Howard Mowll. All of them had known Girvan personally through his family construction company, which had built many churches in the diocese, including extensions to Bishopscourt. 'All those men had their particular strengths and gifts which were used by God,' wrote Girvan of the six archbishops he had known, 'but as a guide and true pastor of the flock, and teacher of the community at large, it is my opinion that [Harry] surpassed them all.'[3] Canon Jim Glennon, the founder of the healing service in St Andrew's Cathedral, was a third person who put Harry in the forefront of Sydney's archbishops. Ordained deacon in 1951, he had worked under all of Sydney's archbishops from Mowll on and had 'no hesitation' in expressing the view that Harry had 'equalled or excelled' his predecessors.[4]

As we have also seen, however, there were those in the diocese who had no hesitation in expressing a contrary view of Harry, as a failed leader, outmanoeuvred by the faction who considered themselves the natural and rightful leaders of the diocese. They felt he had let the side down on core issues, especially that of women's ordination, which was a slippery slope to the undermining of scriptural authority. It was not so much that Harry made strong statements against the conservative position. Indeed, he was not personally convinced of the validity of female ordination. But the problem was that he did not make strong, positive statements against some issues where the archconservatives wanted to hear sabre-rattling.

Four years into Harry's retirement came the first major assessment of his episcopate. Written by Chris McGillion, a Catholic journalist, it achieved a perspective and even-handedness not found in the accounts of committed insiders. It did, however, quote the unguarded opinions of committed insiders, some of which disturbed Harry and distressed Pam. The conservatives did not have it all their way. McGillion found ample evidence, for example, of 'the theological arrogance of the hardline conservatives.'[5] But, perhaps of necessity, the book's tone is dictated by the views of the then victors, those who considered themselves to be 'chosen', those who assumed that it was inevitable that the causes in which they had invested all their firepower, such as lay presidency, must become the doctrine and practice of the Church.[6] There is little awareness in the book of the possibility that a longer perspective might bring a different verdict, and that Harry's wisdom might be vindicated.

Which judgement is correct? Only time will truly tell, but already a re-evaluation of Harry's episcopate is taking place, one that is determined less by the political lens through which people and events are so often viewed in Sydney, and more by the character, style and breadth of vision Harry brought to his ministry. This book is a contribution to that re-evaluation.

We have suggested that Harry was, in some respects, the most radical of Sydney's archbishops – in terms not of political power, but of personal style. He brought to his leadership the combination of his Christian character, with its commitment to servant leadership, and his long experience in parish ministry, the latter certainly surpassing that of all his predecessors. It has been suggested that Harry may have been the only Sydney archbishop devoid of authoritarian instincts. He was never one to insist on tight control, and encouraged creative initiatives wherever he found them. He trusted and gave individual responsibility to his five bishops and encouraged parishes in their life and evangelistic endeavours. He had plans to change the culture of Sydney diocese, to challenge those who believed that a hard culture made the diocese stronger.

It was Harry's destiny to be elected archbishop effectively by the laity and given a mandate to foster the concerns of lay people for too long ignored in a highly clericalised diocese. He spoke of 'those who matter most – the people of God who form the congregations of the Diocese.' He felt called to be their pastor, often demonstrating greater interest in their initiatives than in his own, rare in any man, let alone an archbishop. This concern did not make sense to many, especially those of his own clergy, who did not share his theology of the laity. But for Harry, the role of the laity was not to support the church, but to be supported, encouraged and built up by the church. Harry shared the view of Bruce Kaye, who believed that for too long, 'Lay ministry has subjugated lay vocation ... But lay vocation in society is a million times more important than lay ministry in the Church.'[7]

Those who define Harry's episcopate as a failure give as a key reason his failure to include in his new team or in his plans some of the existing diocesan politicians, 'the influencers', to coin the current jargon. But Harry was elected to free the diocese from its politically controlled, fear-driven, club mentality. Could such a culture be changed with the same people continuing in the same positions? Unfortunately, some men are so powerful that, no matter the virtue of the cause, they have a need to be recognised and appeased; otherwise they will blow the ship out of the water. And this almost happened in Harry's time. It wasn't weakness or a failure that Harry chose this course of action. It was a result of his confidence and integrity. Robert Forsyth observed that Harry was fearless and that was why his critics found him so dangerous.[8] Tom Frame comments similarly:

> I think it is Harry's even temperament and fundamental decency that saw him rise above the small-minded vanity and petty competitiveness of those who also aspired to positions of seniority that distinguished him from others. Sadly, Anglicans don't tend to esteem those who have excelled in holiness, sanctity or humility. We tend to laud and magnify the noisy and the self-promoting, the managers and the organisers.[9]

Harry was uncomfortable with the popular perception that the Sydney diocese was stronger on truth than love,[10] that truth is primary, and that love has no opportunity unless it is based on truth. Harry preferred the opposite emphasis, that truth is not heard unless it arises from love, and he sought to change the culture accordingly. Precisely because that was not the belief of the most vocal of diocesan politicians, it needed to be heard. The diocesan instinct was always to defend itself, which is only logical if you always think you are right. But that conviction also weakens objectivity; it is a magnet forever pulling the mind in one direction. It weakens relationships: one can really only have fellowship with someone who has an open mind, for closed minds cannot mix. Harry was exceptionally open-minded, which may be the fundamental reason for his remarkable capacity to relate to and to encourage flagging spirits and doubting minds.

Even some of his supporters, however, were frustrated at Harry's humility. Peter Smart commented that he wished Harry had been more assertive in implementing his vision, an opinion even Pam agreed with at times. When Peter came to work for Harry, he found that he had goals that he had set for himself and a timetable for achieving them. He was so well organised and wasn't simply responding to events. He knew where he wanted to take the diocese. But Peter wishes that he hadn't been so quiet about it! As we have seen, Harry had a view about the importance of the role of the archbishop in the selection and training of its ordination candidates, a role that Moore College had taken over completely before his election and which it regained on his retirement. Harry's opponents believed that Moore College was the most important part of the diocese, that planting new churches had deservedly become the major and almost only strategy for future development, and that the diocese and its bishops serve those causes. Harry agreed that Moore College was of great importance and planting new churches a good strategy, but they were means, not ends. Their role is to be effective instruments in building the life of God's people in the diocese. Harry, the lifelong evangelist, never doubted that the corporate life of the diocese under the leadership of its archbishop needed to aim at making new disciples. But it must also be concerned with equipping and sustaining those individuals who follow Christ in their life and witness in their homes, in their callings, and in their local churches.

Some of his critics also admit that there is little doubt that Harry's strong support for conservative African bishops was foundational to the emergence of GAFCON, but Harry never wanted to break with Canterbury or to foster division within the Anglican Church. He wanted to hold the fort, while the archconservatives wanted either to leave it or evict the liberals from it. He also drew the line in a different place from the archconservatives. Harry, even at the end of his episcopate, as we have seen, still did not favour female ordination on balance,

Peter Smart, diocesan registrar and archbishop's personal assistant, 1997–2001, together with Harry in post-retirement relaxation.

but he did not believe it was a clear gospel issue, whereas for him opposition to the ordination of non-celibate homosexuals was. These considerations similarly guided his responses to the issues of lay presidency and the prayer book. He felt the synod's zealous advocacy of the former and opposition to the latter actually obscured the gospel.

It might be argued that, in comparison with the dramatic growth in all the churches he pastored and the spectacular gains of EE as a result of his work, Harry's achievements as archbishop were moderate. But we have seen that they were still substantial, and a summary of his achievements is lengthy.

- Church attendance in the diocese grew by 10 per cent, a healthy contrast with other Australian Anglican dioceses.[11]
- The number of regions in this large and heavily populated diocese was increased from four to five, each with its own regional bishop. Each region was given greater autonomy and responsibility. Paul Barnett, Bishop of the Northern Region, thought this a 'brilliant' development, making the diocese function more effectively than at any time since Archbishop Mowll.
- Sites for new churches were acquired in the developing parts of Sydney, where the population increased dramatically.
- Harry, an accountant before ordination, kept a watchful eye on diocesan finances. David Fairfull, merchant banker and CEO of the diocesan administration, helped to connect the diocese with businesspeople in the city. The finances of the diocese were kept in a healthy state, enabling the funding of a range of activities.
- The laity felt that the episcopal team, and therefore the diocese, was concerned about them and their work and ministry. The clergy felt cared for and appreciated the effort made to assist them in their local ministry.
- At a time when conservative forces firmly opposed allowing women to be ordained, Harry appointed an archdeacon for women (Di Nicolios), and encouraged rectors to allow women to teach and preach.
- Good personal relationships with governors, leaders and members of state and federal governments were established. Legislation made possible a dramatic expansion of new low-fee Anglican schools. Prime minister, John Howard, viewed this as one of his government's major achievements.
- Harry fostered good relationships with the leaders of various branches of the armed services.
- Positive relations were established with the major media outlets in print, radio and television. Harry was an effective media performer, typically well-liked and respected by journalists.

- The work of developing protocols for clergy conduct was initiated at a critical juncture when clerical abuse was beginning to be perceived as an international scandal. They were to stand the diocese in good stead, however, when it was inundated during his time in office with the tsunami of sexual abuse allegations in the wider church.
- Good relationships with other churches, Orthodox, Roman Catholic and Protestant, were established. Within the Anglican Church beyond his diocese, Harry had warm relations with bishops in the Province of New South Wales and in the wider Australian Church.
- At the international level, Harry established a significant relationship with the Archbishop of Canterbury, George Carey, and with the more conservative elements in the Anglican Communion. It was a good foundation on which his successor developed Sydney Anglicanism into a valuable export.

Harry did not spend all his time playing the political game. He had to keep a large number of initiatives in his purview, including many in which the politicians, focused on controlling the diocese, had no interest. Harry remained open to them all. He did not believe that only ideas generated in Sydney were worthy of implementation. He took a keen interest in everyone and in what they were doing, and delighted to see them exercise their gifts.

As archbishop, Harry was more mindful than other clergy of the needs of the church beyond their own diocese. Inclusive by temperament and conviction, he did not want to close the door on other dioceses. It was his burden 'to keep doors open in the household of faith.'[12] He was highly sensitised to the reality that, when Christians close doors in each other's faces, they also close to outsiders the door to the transcendent. There was always evangelistic method in Harry's ecumenical madness.

Even in secular Australia, as archbishop, Harry had important civic functions, requiring the occasional well thought-through challenge to, and cooperation with, the civic authorities. He took this part of his job seriously and was good at it. He never embarrassed the Church in public, but always acted in a way of which Sydney Anglicans could be proud and that raised the credibility of the faith. Stephen O'Doherty, Liberal member of parliament and NSW shadow treasurer, reflected at the time, 'The Archbishop has been a valued source of strength, advice, and wisdom to people in Sydney's tough business and political life.'[13] And in all these commitments, Bishopscourt played a central role.

And, as we have seen, Harry was never so busy that he neglected the spiritual life. True godliness, a passion for Jesus, is a requirement of the job, but one not always seen as clearly as in him. In Harry, Paul Barnett testified:

> God gave us a genuinely devout man of God. Genuinely human, with broad ranging interests, including a love of sport, Harry is authentically godly, with a deep desire to express Christ-likeness. At a time when people talk incessantly about an impersonal entity the 'gospel', it has been refreshing to know someone who speaks quietly of a person, his Master.[14]

It is an interesting exercise to compare Harry's achievements as Archbishop of Sydney with those of his time on the executive of EE, especially after he had left Sydney. As we have seen, Harry played a prominent role in the restructuring of EE, possibly the world's largest evangelistic organisation, and helping it adapt to changing conditions. He recognised the need and was central in orchestrating a remarkable change in its culture.

It was change of a type that he longed to see in the Sydney diocese. He had always tried to bring the many organisations that he served into line with true Christian values, believing that this would enhance their evangelistic effectiveness, his lifelong passion. As the direct result of his leadership of the diocese, however, he saw little change, much resistance and moderate achievement; whereas at EE, he saw little resistance, much change and huge achievement. In the years 2007 to 2014, reputedly EE was instrumental in an astonishing 52 million conversions. It is more than pious reflection to wonder if those eight years of culture change in EE were more important in the growth of the Lord's kingdom than his eight years as archbishop. But it certainly raises the question of what the culture of the Sydney diocese would now look like had Harry's plans for change been as welcomed by its politicians as by EE.

Harry's uniqueness, his dissimilarity to the diocesan culture, was, if only his opponents could have received it, a gift to that culture. It needed to be challenged, for while it was successful in defending the faith, it was increasingly defective in propagating it. Harry's contention that the diocese would be stronger if it were gentler was an experiment worth conducting. The inflexible defensiveness of the conservatives made the incarnate Word harder to find than the written word, and the Spirit harder to experience. The conservative evangelicalism of Archbishops Mowll and Loane had delivered well with its theology of the Lordship of Christ and its spirituality of disciplined holiness. But then the diocesan culture changed, hardening into a narrow biblicism. The project of defending a particular system of orthodoxy replaced the practice of submission to Christ's Lordship. Its appeal became more restrictive and its champions more assertive. They were known to

Bushwalking with Bp Peter Chiswell.

accuse those who disagreed with their interpretation of orthodoxy of being 'unconverted', thus sowing discord in the Lord's army.

Harry sought to recover the confident evangelicalism of Mowll and Loane. He wanted people to have a rich, transformative personal relationship with Jesus, and the gospel and the Word to be the instruments for that transformation. The prophetic role of challenging the dominant leadership has never been a popular one in the church and not a popular way of understanding history. History is made by the winners, the influencers, but, in the sovereign providence of God, salvation comes more often in spite of the winners than through them.

Perhaps, Paul Perini, archdeacon under Harry, asked the right question about Harry's legacy: does one remember him as a man or does one remember his episcopate? Perini has little doubt that it is the former.

> Harry allowed people to grow and to be healthy, to have a generosity with each other. He made a difference in people's lives, in the lives of individual clergy and their children whom he touched. There will be a lasting legacy as to what Christian leadership is. But it will be at that personal level. The strength of his leadership was its graciousness. You could say 'no' to Harry and he would not exclude you or victimise you as a result. He believed in leadership, Christ-like, empowering leadership. He believed passionately that churches could grow if the leadership was healthy. He saw that Anglicanism could be a dynamic, fantastic vehicle for this to take place.[15]

Harry was given the strength to do a prodigious volume of work for the Lord, but, astonishing as that has been, maybe who Harry is has been more important than what he has done. He has been able to participate in the Lord's work of bringing healing to the nation (Mal 4:2) because of his own spiritual health. Not as an institution, but as personified in Harry Goodhew, dynamic Anglicanism had the capacity to meet the hunger of the Australian soul for right thinking, right heartedness and right practice, that priceless fruit of the Spirit that comes from Christ alone. Yet the Bible does not allow a distinction between what one

Episcopal staff reunion, 2007. Left to right, front row: Dorothy Piper, Ray and Shirley Smith, Paul and Anita Barnett, Pamela King (Brian had died in 2006), Margo and Peter Watson, Harry. On the stairs, left to right: Pam, Reg Piper, Elizabeth and Peter Smart.

does and who one is. That on the last day, Harry would have to give an account for both, has been the rule of his life.

> For no one can lay any foundation other than the one already laid, which is Jesus Christ. If anyone builds on this foundation using gold, silver, costly stones, wood, hay or straw, their work will be shown for what it is, because the Day will bring it to light. It will be revealed with fire, and the fire will test the quality of each person's work. If what has been built survives, the builder will receive a reward. If it is burned up, the builder will suffer loss but yet will be saved – even though only as one escaping through the flames.[16]

# Notes

The following abbreviations for individuals are used in the endnotes

BBJ (Bruce Ballantine-Jones)
HG (Harry Goodhew)
ML (Marcus Loane)
SP (Stuart Piggin)

Primary sources for which no location is given are in the private possession of Archbishop Goodhew.

## Foreword
1. Cable 'M. L. LOANE', p. 123.
2. Reid, *Marcus L. Loane*.
3. Cable, 'M. L. LOANE', p. 123.
4. Now published as *Inside Sydney: An Insider's View of the Changes and Politics in the Anglican Diocese of Sydney, 1966–2013*, 2016.
5. Butterfield, *The Whig Interpretation of History*, p. 11.

## Prologue: 'God's Man for Sydney': Harry Goodhew's Election as Archbishop
1. Bruce's advice, here summarised, was consistent with the Appointment Ordinance 1982.
   1. Within 21 Days after the occurrence of the vacancy the administrator (in this case, Bishop John Reid) will summon an electing Synod.
      He shall announce the day on which nominations can be received. These nominations must be received by the administrator 21 days before the electing Synod meets.
      Action: Organise nomination.
   2. Not less than 10 days before the electing Synod, a list of all nominees, nominators and their seconders will be forwarded to each member of Synod.
      Action: Procure as many nominations and seconders as possible.
      This, explained Bruce, is designed to lock rectors and their parish synod representatives in together.
   3. Nominators and Seconders must decide who will nominate and second Harry Goodhew's nomination at each stage and notify the Secretaries of Synod.
      Action: Arrange a meeting of Harry's supporters to determine who will do this.
   4. On the first day of Synod, nominations shall be made and seconded. Apparently, it would be unwise to speak against any conservative candidate at this stage. The purpose of this first nomination will be to get Harry on to the select list.
   5. After the completion of the select list which shall be arranged by lot, the nominees will be proposed and seconded a second time and as many as possible should be encouraged to speak in support.
      When all speeches in respect of the nominee are made, the President will move that the name be included in the final list.
      Question: Is it best to go for secret ballot at this point?
      The purpose is to get three nominees on the final list.
   6. In moving from the final list to the final result, the best movers and seconders should be used.
2. The decision to reduce the Archbishop's retirement age from 70 to 65 was first proposed in 1992 in the lead up to the 1993 Archbishop's election. The Revd Lindsey Johnstone successfully sought to have the debate deferred on the grounds that 'candidates shouldn't be

knocked out at the last minute.' He argued that the bill was brought by supporters of Phillip Jensen's candidacy for Archbishop and had a political agenda behind it. 'It was intended to head off the election of John Reid, to make it harder to elect Harry Goodhew and easier to elect Phillip Jensen.' The bill was passed the next year, but later was successfully amended by Justice Ken Handley to allow the Archbishop of Sydney to stay on to 70. Justice Handley said he had been 'unimpressed' with the way the retirement debate had been handled over the past decade. 'Moving the goalposts on an individual basis is inappropriate in any organisation, but especially in a Christian organisation,' he said.

3. Dudley Foord to HG, 2 April 1993.
4. Shortt, *Rowan's Rule*, p. 2.
5. HG to S.B. Babbage, 17 February 2000.
6. Paul Perini, interviewed by SP, 21 October 2013.
7. Lindsay Stoddart interviewed by SP, 6 December 2012. Donald McGavran, author of *Understanding Church Growth* (1970), is revered as the father of Church Growth theory. Harry did not follow him slavishly.
8. Susan Rogers to HG, 21 February 1993.
9. Tom Frame to SP, 27 June 2018.
10. Riley Warren interviewed by SP, 28 August 2014.
11. Gerald Davis resigned from *Church Scene* at the end of 1995. He then worked for Anglicare, rejoicing that the tensions that afflicted so much of national Church life were not often seen there, owing, he thought, to the vision and integrity of its CEO, Howard Dillon, and its chairman, Martin Robinson. Gerald's daughter, Sarah, was a prominent member of the congregation at St Phillip's Caringbah, one of Sydney's flagship Bible-belt churches. She was advised by her Rector that there were feminist tendencies in her thought that needed to be crucified. Gerald anxiously prayed over what her response might be. He was relieved that she saw it as ridiculous and 'dined out' on it for a time. She was in a cell group at the church with editor, Jeremy Halcrow, whom Gerald valued. Gerald Davis to HG, 15 March 2001.
12. The official record of the election Synod is found at http://www.sds.asn.au/site/101816.asp?ph=sy#2.
13. Bruce Harris to HG, 5 April 1993.
14. On 10 August 1999 Paul Perini sent a copy of this speech to Harry with the covering note: 'Although the path has proved to be more difficult and unexpected I believe you have taken us forward in a very substantial way.'
15. John Chapman Interviewed by BBJ, 10 March 2010.
16. Orpwood, *Chappo*, p. 40.
17. SP, moving the motion for Harry's election as Archbishop, 31 March 1993.
18. Ibid.
19. Ibid.
20. Trevor Edwards, seconding the motion for Harry's election as Archbishop, 31 March 1993.
21. Trevor Edwards to SP, 24 June 2011.
22. Goodwin, *Team of Rivals*, p. 245.
23. Ibid., pp. 253, 665.
24. *SMH*, 2 April 1993.
25. Robert Grant, Headmaster, Sydney Church of England Grammar School to HG, 8 April 1993.
26. L. Vitnell to HG, 2 April 1993.
27. Presidential Address, 2000, p. 17.
28. R. Poulton to HG, 6 April 1993.
29. R. Warren to HG, 7 April 1993.

## 1. Parentage: All Families Have Mysteries

1. HG, Sermons, 45/1998, 2 December 1998 (at St Matthew's, West Pennant Hills).
2. Haygarth, *Scores & Biographies*. The Lillywhites were a famous English cricketing family in the 19th century.
3. *Queanbeyan Age*, 3 August 1889.
4. Much of the above is taken from Goodhew, 'Goodhews in Australia'.
5. Married 12 July 1924 in a Catholic Church.
6. Baden's first wife was a Catholic and may not have believed in divorce (see *SMH*, 10 August 1929; 5 April 1930, for reports on the divorce).
7. See, for example, the bizarre novel *Poor Things* (ed. Alasdair Gray).
8. Registration number 17273/1930 in the Registry of Births, Deaths, and Marriages.
9. HG, Day Book and Diary, 6 December 1998.
10. HG, Sermons, 10 September 1995 (150th anniversary of the opening of Christ Church St Laurence for public worship by Bp Broughton).

## 2. Early Days: Faith, Hope, Love and Cricket

1. Angus and Robertson, Sydney, 1948.
2. HG, Sermons, 31/1998, 8 November 1998.
3. 'Commercial schools (mainly for boys) offered a variety of courses such as business principles and economics, and were designed to assist boys entering into a business career after school' (https://education.nsw.gov.au/about-us/our-people-and-structure/history-of-government-schools/government-schools/reform-movement).
4. Paul Barnett, interviewed 22 March 2018.
5. 2 April 1993.
6. HG, Sermons, 8 May 1994.
7. On the church competition, see Ronald Cardwell's article: http://nswccu.nsw.cricket.com.au/content.aspx?print=1&file=42%7C40601j (Jack Russell to HG, undated but received 12 February 2001. Beryl Hollway [nee Walters] was the scorer for the Banksia Free Church cricket team and wrote to congratulate Harry when he was elected Archbishop).
8. Sydney Cricket Club, 15 March 2019, https://www.scgt.nsw.gov.au/sydney-cricket-club/whats-on/news/sydney-cricket-club-green-shield-trials/.
9. H. Heydon to HG, 28 December 1944.
10. Benaud, *Anything but ...*, pp. 22–4.
11. *SMH*, undated, but January 1945??
12. Rob Smith to SP, 24 September 2010.
13. Buzo, *Legends of the Baggy Green*, p. 81. Bradman was not knighted until three years later.
14. Cable, 'McCabe, Stanley Joseph', p. 208.
15. Stock, *Recollections*, pp. 252–4. In 1886 when A. E. Bellingham was studying at Cambridge, Stock 'much coveted' him, 'a splendid fellow', for CMS, and when told that he would have to return to Australia as his mother and sisters were in Sydney, exclaimed 'Oh, bother the Sydney relatives!'
16. Record of interview by D.W.B. Robinson and BBJ with Archdeacon John Bidwell, 7 August 1972, MTC Archives.
17. Goodhew, *The One Sure Hope*, pp. 41f.
18. These three concerns are identified in the centenary booklet, *St Andrew's Summer Hill, 1881–1981*, pp. 13–18.
19. 'Holy Trinity, Dulwich Hill 1886–1986', *Church of England Historical Society Journal*, vol. 33, no. 4, December 1988, p. 86.
20. Monica Farrell (b. Dublin, Ireland, 3 May 1898, d. 3 March 1982), founder of the 'The Light and Truth Crusade', conducted preaching campaigns in Great Britain, Ireland, France, Spain, Holland, Canada and Australia.

21. Bill Lawton interviewed by SP 17 July 2018.
22. Gwen Wade died in 1991, and Harry conducted the funeral service. Graham Wade produced a pamphlet on her.
23. HG, Sermon, Springwood, 21 April 1994.
24. Grubb, *C. T. Studd*.
25. Barry Newman to SP, 16 March 2019.
26. Tennant, 'Sermons of the Eighteenth-Century Evangelicals', p. 115.
27. Charles Finney, Lecture X.
28. HG to SP, 13 August 2019.
29. H. Edwards to HG, 2 July 1982.
30. Memorial Service for Revd John Eric Fowler, Holy Trinity Church, Dulwich Hill, 17 November 1963.
31. Ronald Ash gave this information to Jim Keith, a Sydney lay preacher, in early 2001.

## 3. Man of Promise and Pamela: 'A Balanced, Spiritually Minded Young Man'

1. *Pix*, 13 April 1946, p. 5.
2. 12 December 1946.
3. EFAC Australian Bulletin, 1993, no.1, p. 4.
4. 4 December 1946.
5. 28 March 2001. This Catholic view is based on Thomas Aquinas's approach to nature – 'grace perfects nature' not destroys it – it is against the divine to do so (Taylor, *A Secular Age*, pp. 90–91).
6. J. Driscoll reference, 13 January 1948.
7. J. R. Kinsman, 9 July 1948.
8. Reference from E. Wrighter, 3 December 1948.
9. Reference dated 15 May 1950.
10. Reference from P. M. Taylor, 15 October 1953.
11. Lukabyo, 'From a Ministry for Youth to a Ministry of Youth', p. 184.
12. Lawton, 'The Winter of our Days', pp. 13f.
13. He was to become the first Bishop in Wollongong in 1969 and was rather like Harry in personality and effectiveness: he was warm-hearted, generous with his time, and a very effective evangelist. Both remained strategic and practical supporters of youth ministry, and after he became Archbishop, Harry gave the inaugural Graham Delbridge Lecture (R. H. Goodhew, 'Graham Delbridge – His Contribution to Youth Ministry', 19 August 1996, in HG, Sermons, 1996).
14. A. Deane interviewed by SP, 5 May 2014.
15. Bob Glover to HG, 5 April 1993.
16. Tony Gray to HG, 7 July 1993.
17. Geoffrey Bingham, quoted in Bleby, *A Quiet Revival*, p. 124.
18. Heath, *Trinity, the Daring of your Name*, p. 84.
19. Howe, *A Century of Influence*, pp. 259f. See also Mansfield, 'Christian Social Order Movement', pp. 109–27.
20. Mansfield, *Summer is Almost Over*, p. 10. Joan Mansfield wrote a Master's thesis on the CSOM in the Anglican Church.
21. Pat Farrow to HG, 19 April 1993.
22. John Reimer to HG, 13 March 2001.
23. Goodhew, *The One Sure Hope*, p. 42.

## 4. Moore and Matrimony: One Ordination, Two Callings

1. HG, Sermon at Thanksgiving Service for Les Vitnell, 16 February, 1994.
2. Marcus Loane interviewed by Margaret Lamb, undated.

3. Bob Hill to HG, 14 November 1997.
4. Bill Lawton interviewed by Margaret Lamb, 10 September 1986.
5. Harry Bates to HG, 5 May 1982.
6. Chapter two, 'The Secret of Victory over Sin'.
7. Piggin and Linder, *Attending to the National Soul*, pp. 144–50.
8. Bill Lawton interviewed by SP, 17 July 2018.
9. Recollection of Jim Keith, 10 January 2011.
10. The biography of Nash, by Chambers, *Tempest Tost*, is dedicated to Mowll, 'Friend of C. H. N.'
11. HG, Marriage Renewal Service, St Augustine's, Neutral Bay, 13 October 1996, Sermons, 1996.

## 5. Early Parish Experience: A Lot of Visiting
1. Orpwood, *Chappo*, p. 213.
2. Chadwick, *Michael Ramsey*, p. 81.
3. Brooks, 'An Investigation into the Nature and Significance of the Early Parish Ministry of Harry Goodhew'.
4. A. Cole to HG, 24 February 2001.
5. An account of this is found in Goodhew, *Green*.
6. Ray Smith, interviewed 4 April 2018.
7. Eric Joseph to HG, 22 April 1982.
8. Jack Dain to HG, 10 March 2001.
9. Hugh Gough to HG, 6 May 1963, Personnel File, Goodhew, Richard Henry, P230206.
10. Trewartha, *Dedication and Determination*, p. 22.
11. Ibid, pp. 22, 78.
12. Ibid, p. 2.
13. Ibid, pp. 28, 39.
14. Ibid, p. 61.
15. Dulcie Wright, interviewed 13 October 2017.
16. Joy O'Neill to HG, 16 April 1993.
17. Robert Skinner to Lyn Davis, 1 May 2012.
18. HG and PG interviewed by SP, 26 March 2012.
19. Dulcie Wright, interviewed 13 October 2017.
20. Ibid.
21. Tom Mayne to SP, email 9 April 2012.
22. Ibid.
23. Patricia Mayne to SP, email 10 April 2012.
24. Tom Mayne to SP, email 9 April 2012.
25. Ray Smith, interviewed 4 April 2018.
26. Recollection of Ken Rogers, minister at Ceduna, 1976–1983 (22 September 2010).
27. Conversation with Ken Rogers, 22 September 2010.
28. Trewartha, *Dedication and Determination*, p. 78.

## 6. Parish Builder: 'Sunday at 7'
1. HG to ML, 30 May 1966, Personnel File, Goodhew, Richard Henry, P230206.
2. ML to HG, 31 May 1966, Personnel File, Goodhew, Richard Henry, P230206.
3. Sydney *Year Book*, 1971, p. 301.
4. Howard, *Preach or Perish*, p. 219.
5. Recollection of Peppi Whiteman, interviewed 10 January, 2020.
6. 15 April 1993.
7. Malcolm Babbage to SP, 3 June 2018.

8. ML to HG, 24 June 1970, Personnel File, Goodhew, Richard Henry, P230206.
9. HG to ML, 29 June 1970, Personnel File, Goodhew, Richard Henry, P230206.
10. ML to HG, 1 July 1970, Personnel File, Goodhew, Richard Henry, P230206.
11. HG to F.O. Hulme-Moir, 7 June 1971, Personnel File, Goodhew, Richard Henry, P230206.
12. HG to ML, 28 August 1971, Personnel File, Goodhew, Richard Henry, P230206.
13. ML to HG, 14 September 1971, Personnel File, Goodhew, Richard Henry, P230206.
14. Vic Smith, interviewed by Margaret Lamb, 10 August 1989.
15. Felix Arnott to ML, 23 August 1971, Personnel File, Goodhew, Richard Henry, P230206.
16. ML to Felix Arnott, 30 August 1971, Personnel File, Goodhew, Richard Henry, P230206.
17. HG, Day Book & Diary, 12 June 1993.
18. David Goodhew, interviewed by SP, 27 July 2018.
19. Keith Thompson to HG, 25 May 1982.
20. Rod Irvine to SP, 29 March 2019.
21. A. Cole to HG, 4 February 1988.
22. Stebbins, *D. James Kennedy's Explosion of Evangelism*, p. 20.
23. Ibid., p. 90.
24. Rod Story, interviewed by SP, 19 January 2017.

## 7. Rector and Archdeacon of Wollongong: 'For the Ministry That Lies Ahead'

1. Harry Goodhew's Presidential Address to the 2000 Synod, *2001 Year Book*, p. 386.
2. Orpwood, *Chappo*, pp. 38–42.
3. HG to ML, 11 June 1976.
4. ML to HG, 17 June 1976.
5. HG to ML, 24 June 1976.
6. ML to HG, 30 June 1976.
7. K. Short to HG, 29 June 1976.
8. HG to ML, 6 July 1976, Personnel File, Goodhew, Richard Henry, P230206.
9. 26 July 1976.
10. 8 November 1976.
11. Felix Arnott to ML, 7 July 1976, Personnel File, Goodhew, Richard Henry, P230206.
12. 24 June 1982.
13. Ken Short to ML, 2 June 1976, Personnel File, Goodhew, Richard Henry, P230206.
14. HG to ML, 14 December 1976, Personnel File, Goodhew, Richard Henry, P230206.
15. Lamb, Piggin and Radkovic, *Treasure in Earthen Vessels*, p. 64.
16. Frame, *Binding Ties*, pp. 21–2, 39–40.
17. T. Frame to SP, 27 June 2018.
18. T. Frame to SP, 28 June 2018.
19. David Goodhew, interviewed by SP, 27 July 2018.
20. Philip Goodhew, interviewed by SP, 26 July 2016.
21. 2 July 1988.
22. Recollection of Phyllis Younger, 16 April 2011.
23. Smith, *The Hospitable Leader*.
24. Peter Kell, interviewed by SP, 19 December 2012.
25. Harry was one of the contributors to *Agenda for a Biblical Church: Papers for the National Evangelical Anglican Congress, 1981*, Anglican Information Office, 2 volumes.
26. A reference to Timmy the dog, who seemed to enjoy attending services in the church.
27. HG to SP, 4 July 2018.
28. HG to Archie Parrish, 25 September 1981; Jack Dain to Archie Parrish, 2 October 1981; Archie Parrish to Jack Dain, 23 October 1981; Jack Dain to Archie Parrish, 3 November 1981.

## 8. Bishop of Wollongong: Episcopal Revival

1. Broughton Knox to HG, 1 May 1982.
2. Garrett, *Where Nets Were Cast*, p. 183.
3. David Hand to HG, 22 June 1982.
4. 13 May 1982. See also John Grindrod to DWB Robinson, 7 May 1982, Personnel File, Goodhew, Richard Henry, P230206.
5. 26 May 1982.
6. 28 April 1982. Harry and Pam were to attend his funeral in England.
7. 29 April 1982.
8. 2 May 1982?
9. Reid, *Marcus L. Loane*, p. 139; Blanch, *From Strength to Strength*, p. 379.
10. 4 May 1982.
11. D. B. Knox to HG, 21 May 1982.
12. D. B. Konx to DWB Robinson, 21 May 1982, Personnel File, Goodhew, Richard Henry, P230206.
13. 30 April 1982.
14. 2 May 1982.
15. 5 May 1982.
16. 3 May 1982.
17. God is able to make all grace abound toward you; that ye, always having all sufficiency in all things, may abound to every good work' (R. G. Fillingham to HG, 17 May 1982).
18. 30 April 1982.
19. 2 May 1982.
20. 3 May 1982.
21. Barry Newman was 'extremely delighted' (Barry Newman to HG, 18 May 1982).
22. David Peterson to HG, 18 May 1982.
23. 9 May 1982.
24. 19 May 1982.
25. 1 May 1982.
26. 29 April 1982.
27. Undated, but May 1982.
28. Barry and Robin Hall to Harry and Pam, 12 May 1982.
29. 4 May 1982.
30. 21 May 1982.
31. Rod and Helen Irvine to HG, 3 May 1982.
32. Lorna and Ray Lindsay to HG, 4 May 1982.
33. Undated, but May 1982.
34. 29 April 1982.
35. John Holle to HG, 14 May 1982. John Holle was a 'people person', too.
36. 3 May 1982.
37. 29 April 1982.
38. 23 June 1982.
39. Haydon, 'Consecration Sermons', p. 306.
40. Broughton dwelt on the conflict with Satan in spiritual ministry.
41. Alfred Holland, Bishop of Newcastle, was represented by his assistant, Bp Geoffrey Parker.
42. Jack Dain, another assistant bishop, was absent in England at the consecration of Michael Baughan as Bishop of Chester.
43. 15 July 1982.
44. HG to John Beiers, 24 August 1982.
45. HG to Alan Cole, 13 July 1982.
46. HG to David Hand, 1 July 1982.

47 Licence, 1 July 1982.
48 Roberts, 'Use of the Vatican II Lectionary'.
49 'The Role of the Leader: An Examination of the Influence of Ministerial Leadership on the Growth of Six Australian Churches from 1978 to 1989', MA (Hons), University of Wollongong, 1990.
50 Bp Don Cameron wrote to Harry congratulating him on his Wollongong MA: 'Formal qualifications may not be of consequence but in this case one is so glad to see your great intrinsic abilities formally recognised' (D. Cameron to R.H. Goodhew, 5 July 1990, 1994/73/10, SDA).
51 Goodhew, 'The Role of the Leader', p. 112.
52 Ibid., p. 174.
53 Goodhew, *The One Sure Hope*, p. 51.
54 Richard Donnelly, interviewed by SP, 10 August 2011.
55 The speech is reproduced in the school magazine.
56 Chadwick, *Michael Ramsey*, p. 104.
57 *Big League*, 9–15 June, 1993, vol. 74, no. 14, p. 28.
58 These words are not found in his book on the Diocese, *Inside Sydney* (self-published, 2016), but in drafts of the thesis on which the book is based, namely 29 July 2009 and 24 May 2012.

## 9. Bishop beyond Wollongong: 'Responding Obediently to God's Urgency'

1 Rod Story, interviewed by SP, 19 January 2017.
2 HG to R.W.B. Robinson, 11 June 1991, Personnel File, Goodhew, Richard Henry, P230206.
3 Report on our Recent Trip to Sri Lanka, 7 February 1986.
4 Frith, 'The Role of the Laity in Anglican Evangelicalism', pp. 41–43; Ballantine-Jones, *Inside Sydney*, pp. 17, 109, 227–228.
5 Report of the Archbishop's Commission of Inquiry, September 1992, p. 3.
6 Ibid.; The Report of the Committee on the Development of Parish Property and Ministry, June 1990, is found in *Report of the Standing Committee and other Reports and Papers, 1990*, pp. 103–121
7 Report of the Archbishop's Commission of Inquiry, September 1992, p. 12
8 David Fairfull, interviewed by SP, 29 February 2016.
9 This sentiment is found in the May 2012 draft of BBJ's doctoral thesis.
10 Paul, *The Deployment and Payment of the Clergy*.
11 Porter, *Frank Woods*, p. 106.
12 I am indebted to the research of BBJ, which is the basis for this account of the movement for new dioceses.
13 *Sydney Year Book*, 1984, pp. 203ff.
14 *Sydney Year Book*, 1985, pp. 421–432.
15 *The Australian*, 13 February 1989 – photo of Harry on the front page.
16 *Illawarra Mercury*, 29 January 1992, p. 2.
17 10/91 Ordination of Women to the Priesthood 1993: A Report to Synod.
18 A transcript of the proceedings has been published entitled *Women in Ministry Conference*.
19 10/91 Ordination of Women to the Priesthood 1993: A Report to Synod.
20 Patricia Hayward, interviewed by SP, 31 November 2011.
21 Record of Interview by D.W.B. Robinson and S. Ballantine-Jones with Archdeacon John Bidwell, 7 August 1972, Moore College Archives.
22 EFAC Australia Bulletin, 1993, No.1, p. 8.

## 10. Twin Crises: The Fraught Backdrop to Harry's Election

1 'One Almighty Row,' *SMH*, 18 April 1992.
2 'Unity in Diversity,' *Repaccusions*, vol. 2, December 1992, p. 9.

3. 'The Way ahead for Christian Liberty,' *Repaccusions*, vol. 2, December 1992, p. 8.
4. R.E.P. Association, Statement No.1, 6 March 1992, p. 3.
5. *The Bulletin*, 21 July 1992, p. 42.
6. R.E.P. Association, Statement No.1, 6 March 1992, pp. 1, 5.
7. *Repacussions*, vol. 1, September 1992, p. 3.
8. R.E.P. Association, Statement No.1, 6 March 1992, p. 8.
9. Letter to REPA members from Robert Forsyth et al., 22 April 1992.
10. Notes from REPA Think Tank, St Swithun's Pymble, 28 July 1992.
11. This claim is hotly denied in *Repacussions,* vol. 1, September 1992, p. 6, along with the claim that REPA was formed in response to the debate over the ordination of women.
12. John R. Reid, 'Partnership: a Better Way', *SC*, September, 1992.
13. Unsigned REPA circular dated 30 September 1992.
14. Questions/Answers, copy dated 5 August 1992.
15. B. Harris to HG, 5 April 1993.
16. Russell D. Clark, Open Letter to the Foundation Members of REPA, 14 March 1993.
17. Jensen, *Sydney Anglicanism*, pp. 166–7.
18. John Chapman, interviewed by SP, 4 March 2011.
19. *Repacussions*, vol. 3, May 1993.
20. Foye, 'Graving Another Testament, p. 53.

## 11. A New Archbishop for Sydney: 'A Blessing for the Whole Church'
1. Goodhew, *The One Sure Hope*, p. 46.
2. *Illawarra Mercury*, 3 April 1993.
3. 2 April 1993.
4. Rayner to HG, 2 April 1993.
5. 2 April 1993.
6. 5 April 1993.
7. 16 April 1993.
8. Rene Gregory to HG, 10 April 1993.
9. Susan Rogers to Harry and Pam, 1 June 1993.
10. Dean Eric Barker to HG, 3 April 1993.
11. Professor Brian Moloney to HG, 3 April 1993.
12. The Revd Douglas Crawford to HG, 2 April 1993.
13. 3 April 1993.
14. 6 April 1983.
15. 5 April 1993.
16. 2 April 1993.
17. 5 April 1993.
18. 14 February 2001.
19. G. Muston to HG, 2 April 1993.
20. 4 April 1993.
21. 6 April 1993.
22. 7 April 1993.
23. 5 April 1993.
24. 15 April 1993.
25. MOW papers, 5 April 1993.
26. MOW papers, Convenor's Report.
27. Undated, but April 1993.
28. 7 April 1993.
29. 4 April 1993.
30. John Fahey to HG, 14 April 1993.

31. Ken McKay to HG, 5 April 1993.
32. Phillip Heath to HG, 6 April 1993.
33. Walter Newmarch to HG, 2 April 1993.
34. 5 April 1993.
35. J. Emery to HG, 2 April 1993.
36. 10 April 1993.
37. 5 April 1993.
38. *Illawarra Mercury*, 3 April 1993.
39. 3 April 1993.
40. Brian Wilson to HG, 5 April 1993.
41. *Telegraph/Mirror*, 3 April 1993.
42. *SMH*, 14 June 1993.
43. Paul Barnett, interviewed 22 March 2018.
44. Jeremy Tonks to HG, 4 June 2001.
45. D.W.B. Robinson to HG, 1 May 1993.
46. 10 May 1993.
47. Raymond Heslehurst's recollection, 17 September 2013.
48. Canon J.E. Holbeck to HG, 4 May 1993.

## 12. Bishopscourt: Spectral Visions

1. Bp Cameron to the Secretary, Endowment of the See, 9 January 1992.
2. D. Robinson to Bp Cameron, 2 August 1991, Archbishop's Administration File, Bishopscourt, 1990–2000, Box 2015/004, SDA.
3. 24 October 1991, Archbishop's Administration File, Bishopscourt, 1990–2000, Box 2015/004, SDA.
4. 7 April 1993.
5. *SMH*, 12 January 1994.
6. David Mort in conversation with SP, 26 December 2013.
7. 23 January 1994.
8. David Mort has a copy of the sale catalogue.
9. Babbage, *Memoirs of a Loose Canon*, p. 207.
10. Jenny Macarthur-Onslow to Mrs R.H. Goodhew, 27 May 1994, Box 2015/004, SDA.
11. See http://about.nsw.gov.au/collections/doc/bishopscourt/# accessed 26 March 2012. - r00mjclergy.
12. Christine Jensen, interviewed 26 March 2012.
13. Pacey, *Bodalla and the Morts*, p. 11, says he drowned.
14. Stuart Barton Babbage to SP, 14 May 2012.
15. Presidential Address, 2000, pp. 1, 2.
16. Porter, *Sydney Anglicans and the Threat to World Anglicanism*, p. 153.
17. David Goodhew, interviewed by SP, 27 July 2018.
18. See https://sydneyanglicans.net/news/bishopscourt-decision-today.

## 13. Laying the Foundation: 'Dynamic Anglicanism'

1. Dorothy Steel to HG, 23 December 2000.
2. HG, Day Book & Diary, 13 April 1993.
3. HG, Day Book & Diary, 27 April 1993.
4. HG interviewed by Marcia Cameron, 15 February 2010, and cited in Cameron, *Phenomenal Sydney*, p. 180.
5. Listed as 'The Archbishop's Five Strategies' in every Year Book from 1996 to 2000.
6. HG, Memo to the Members of the SC, 25 October 1993.
7. Strategy document, 10 March 1994.

8. Paul Barnett, interviewed 22 March 2018.
9. Ray Smith, interviewed 4 April 2018.
10. Phillip Jensen, 'Church Planting', https://phillipjensen.com/church-planting/.
11. Phillip Jensen, 'Why Anglican?, https://phillipjensen.com/why-anglican/.
12. Chadwick, *Michael Ramsey*, p. 112.
13. 2001 *Year Book,* pp. 394ff.
14. Cameron, *Phenomenal Sydney,* p. 187.
15. David Fairfull, interviewed by SP, 29 February 2016.
16. *Anglicans Together,* no. 7, August 1994, p. 6.
17. HG, Diary, 28 January 1995.
18. Riley Warren to HG, 19 April, 1993, 2015/014/BOX 40, SDA.
19. Statement of Archbishop to Chapter, 26 May 1992, Archbishop's files, 2006/11, SDA.
20. Recollection of Paul and Sue Harrington, 1 March 2019.
21. HG to the SC, 23 August 1993, Archbishop's Files, 2006/11, SDA.
22. 7 April 1993.
23. 12 June 1993.
24. 28 June 1993.
25. HG, Day Book & Diary, 5 July 1993.
26. HG, Day Book & Diary, 22 July 1993.
27. Ray Smith, interviewed, 4 April 2018.
28. Ibid.
29. HG to the SC, 23 August 1993, Archbishop's Files, 2006/11, SDA.
30. Ray Smith, 'An Episcopal Ministry Model (From where I sit)', undated.
31. HG to BBJ, 26 July 2012.
32. Brian King to HG, 22 September 2000.
33. HG, Sermons, 1993, p. 20.

## 14. First Year (1993): 'Evangelistically Enterprising'
1. The Ordinal for The Consecrating of a Bishop, AAPB, p. 619.
2. Presidential Address, 1995, pp. 19–20.
3. HG, Diary, 29 December 1995.
4. Peter Kell, interviewed by SP, 19 December 2012.
5. Peter Young to HG, 27 July 1993.
6. HG, Day Book & Diary, 5 August 1993.
7. Riley Warren, interviewed by SP, 28 August 2014.
8. Peter Smart, interviewed by SP, 12 July 2016.
9. BBJ, this is a quotation from an early draft of his thesis; see also his book *Inside Sydney,* pp. 152, 162.
10. See, for example, Kaldor, *Who Goes Where?*
11. 8 October 1993, 2010/010/Box02, SDA.
12. Peter Kell interviewed by SP, 19 December 2012.
13. Presidential Address, 1993, p. 2.
14. Unlike the *AAPB,* Sydney Anglicans had not been extensively involved with the development of the *APBA.*
15. *Social Issues Update,* vol. 3, no. 2, October 1993.
16. Ballantine-Jones, *Inside Sydney,* p. 153.
17. Bronwyn Hughes, interviewed by SP, 5 November 2011.
18. 1 October 1993. Narelle Jarrett and Stan Skillicorn were co-signatories of this letter.
19. *Anglicans Together Newsletter,* No.5: 'An Open Letter to Members of Synod', September, 1993, p1, column 3.
20. *SC,* February 1994, p. 8.

21. D. Crain to SP, 27 October 1993.
22. Personal Statement to Sydney Synod, Wednesday 19 October 1994, David W. Gilmour.
23. Commission of Enquiry Incapacity and Inefficiency Ordinance 1906, The Reverend David W. Gilmour, 22 September 1994, p. 55.
24. SC, February 1994, p. 9.
25. Ibid., p. 7.
26. Telephone conversation with BBJ, 12 July 2010.
27. John R. Reid, 'Partnership: A Better Way', SC, September 1992.
28. See Piggin and Linder, Attending to the National Soul, p. 319.
29. 25 January 1994, 2010/010/Box02, SDA.
30. 17 February 1994, 2010/010/Box02, SDA.
31. SC, February 1994, p. 9.

## 15. Second Year (1994): 'Wild, Uncharted Waters'

1. SC, August 1994, p. 2.
2. SC, September 1994, In Touch insert, p. 2.
3. Bill Lawton to SP, 25 January 2019.
4. Harry spoke of 'the miserable truth of Rwanda – we are all sinners' (Sermons, 24 July 1994). In Rwanda, 93.5% of the population identified as Christians and 937,000 were slaughtered.
5. Hilliard, 'Sydney Anglicans and Homosexuality', p. 44.
6. Article by Clifford Longley in Daily Telegraph, 27 June 1994.
7. SC, August 1994, p. 14.
8. The Australian, 21 June 1994.
9. SC, July 1994, p. 4.
10. Naden et al. (eds), A Celebration of God's Faithfulness, pp. 39f.
11. SC, March 1994, p. 9.
12. Sermons, 22 May 1994.
13. SC, March 1994, p. 10.
14. SMH, 9 September 1994.
15. SC, October 1994, p. 9.
16. SC, June 1994, p. 29.
17. SC, July 1994, p. 13.
18. SC, September1994, p. 2.
19. SC, October 1994, p. 2.
20. SMH, 11 October 1994.
21. HG, Day Book & Diary, 14 September 1994.
22. Commission of Enquiry Incapacity and Inefficiency Ordinance 1906, The Reverend David W Gilmour, 22 September 1994, p. 16.
23. They wrote a paper entitled 'A Mild and Inoffensive Ordinance' and sent it to the Commission.
24. Commission of Enquiry Incapacity and Inefficiency Ordinance 1906, The Reverend David W Gilmour, 22 September 1994, p. 31.
25. Ibid., p. 20
26. HG, Day Book & Diary, 19 September 1994.
27. SMH, 10 October 1994.
28. To the secretary, SC, 23 August 1994.
29. HG, Confidential Diary 23 September 1994.
30. Ibid.
31. Riley Warren to HG, 19 April 1993, 2015/014/BOX 40, SDA.
32. HG, Sermon in Shore Chapel, 8 May 1994.
33. HG, Sermon at the dedication of the new centenary building at Shore Grammar School, 4 May 1994.

34 Address to Heads of Church Schools, Bishopscourt, 12 May 1994.
35 John Howard to HG, undated.
36 Howard, *Lazarus Rising*, p. 243.
37 Ibid., p. 487.
38 *SMH*, 11 October 1994.
39 *SC*, October 1994, p. 7.
40 *SC*, August 1994, p. 16.
41 Bill Lawton to SP, 25 January 2019.
42 Presidential Address, 1994, p. 26.
43 1995 *Year Book*, pp. 310–316.
44 Personal Statement to Sydney Synod, Wednesday 19 October 1994, David W. Gilmour.
45 *SC*, November 1994, p. 10.
46 *SMH*, 15 October 1994.
47 *SMH*, 13 October 1994.
48 *SMH*, 15 October 1994.
49 Ibid.
50 Ibid.
51 Ibid.
52 Conversation with BBJ, 26 July 2010.
53 24 October, 2010/010/Box02, SDA.
54 *Church Scene*, 21 October 1994.
55 *Church Scene*, 28 October 1994.
56 2010/010/Box02, SDA.
57 22 December 1994, 2010/010/Box02, SDA.
58 HG to All Members of Synod, 6 December 1994.
59 HG, Day Book & Diary, 1 December 1994.
60 HG, Day Book and Diary, 2 December 1994.
61 Commission of Enquiry Incapacity and Inefficiency Ordinance 1906, The Reverend David W Gilmour, 22 September 1994, p. 53.

## 16. Third Year (1995): 'Loyalty to Both Christ and the Church'

1 HG, Diary (undated).
2 Luke 10:42.
3 11 July 1995, Archbishop's Administration File, EE, 1995–2002, 2015/004/Box 27, SDA.
4 Day Book & Diary, 29 January 1995.
5 Day Book & Diary, 1 February 1995.
6 'Centralism: Real or Imagined, Which way for Sydney Diocese?' *ACL Newsletter*, March 1995, p. 1.
7 Ballantine-Jones, *Inside Sydney*, p. 160.
8 There are two accounts of this incident, both written by Bruce himself. One is in his *Inside Sydney*, pp. 160–162, and an earlier one in a draft of his doctoral thesis, which is rawer.
9 These quotations are from notes taken by Revd Jim Ramsay and given to BBJ the following day.
10 Churches where vestments are worn.
11 *Inside Sydney*, p. 162.
12 Ibid., p. 161.
13 Undated notes from David Crain.
14 These observations were in notes of the meeting taken immediately after by BBJ.
15 *SMH*, 8 July 1995.
16 As did the Diocese of The Murray.
17 *Inside Sydney*, p. 165.

18. See www.bettergatherings.com/index.php.
19. Jacques Ellul, *Prayer and Modern Man*, p. 174. This quotation was given to Harry on the occasion of his election as Archishop by his fellow Ellul admirer, Richard Donnelly.
20. Presidential Address, 1995, p. 15.
21. Ibid., p. 16.
22. Ibid., p. 22.
23. This was to be the single biggest difference between Harry's episcopate and that of his successor, Peter Jensen, who recruited the whole Diocese in the service of 'The Mission'.
24. David Crain to SP, 19 December 1995.
25. *ACL News*, February 1996.
26. Ibid.
27. ACL, 25 January 1996.
28. *SC*, March 2001.

## 17. Fourth Year (1996): 'I Smile No Longer'

1. 7 February 1996, Archbishop's Administration File, EE, 1995–2002, 2015/004/Box 27, SDA.
2. 16 January 1996, Archbishop's Administration File, EE, 1995–2002, 2015/004/Box 27, SDA.
3. 5 February 1996, Archbishop's Administration File, EE, 1995–2002, 2015/004/Box 27, SDA.
4. Ibid.
5. HG, Sermons, 5 March 1996.
6. John Sorensen, interviewed by SP, 26 July 2016.
7. Archbishop's Administration File, EE, 1995–2002, 2015/004/Box 27, SDA.
8. HG to Sterling Huston, 19 September 1996, Archbishop's Administration File, EE, 1995–2002, 2015/004/Box 27, SDA.
9. Sue Emeleus to SP, 19 August 2018.
10. Since the perpetrator hoped his name would, by his deed, be remembered forever, I have chosen not to name him.
11. HG, Sermons, 14/1996.
12. *SC*, April 1992.
13. Mayne, 'A History of Tamar', p. 211. Much of this account of Harry's handling of sexual abuse is based on this excellent thesis.
14. Mayne, 'A History of Tamar', p. 212.
15. Albatross Books Pty Ltd, Sutherland, 1990.
16. Mayne, 'A History of Tamar', pp. 218–20.
17. Millennium Books, 1995.
18. The names of AC1 and AC2 are now on the public record, but it is not relevant to this narrative to identify them here.
19. Report of The Wood Royal Commission: The Royal Commission into the New South Wales Police Service: Volume 5 The Paedophile Inquiry 1994–1997, p. 1002.
20. Mayne, 'A History of Tamar', pp. 85–87.
21. HG, Day Book.
22. Donald Robinson to HG, 25 May 1996.
23. *SC*, June 1996, p. 1.
24. Russell Powell at the Thanksgiving Service for Margaret Rodgers, St Andrew's Cathedral, 19 June 2014.
25. D. Cameron to HG, undated, but 16 December 1999.
26. *Church Discipline Ordinance 1996* in 'Acts, Ordinances & Regulations, 2002 Edition', Sydney Diocesan Secretariat, pp. 144–152.
27. Mayne, 'A History of Tamar', p. 91.
28. *Church of England Newspaper*, 15 March 1996, p. 8.
29. Paul Barnett, interviewed 22 March 2018.

30. Ray Smith, 'A Church for all Nations', sermon preached at St Clement's Anglican Church, Marrickville, 27 February 2000.
31. Ray Smith, interviewed 4 April 2018.
32. Ray Smith, 'An Episcopal Ministry Model (From where I sit)', undated paper.
33. Stephen Judd to SP et al., 19 June 1996.
34. *Synod Watch*, ACL, August 1996.
35. September 1996.
36. Notes of 'Blue Group' Meeting, 3 July 1996.
37. September 1996, pp. 8–10.
38. Quoted in Presidential Address, 1996, p. 22.
39. John Cornford to HG, 21 November 1996, Personnel File, Goodhew, Richard Henry, P230206.
40. 'Strong support for women preaching: survey', Media Release, 3 September 1996, Women's Ministry Reports, SDA, 201 6/024.
41. Presidential Address, 1996, p. 9.
42. Fletcher, *An English Church in Australian Soil*, pp. 207ff.
43. Presidential Address, 1996, pp. 12–13.
44. Ibid., p. 16.
45. Ibid., p. 18.
46. Ballantine-Jones, *Inside Sydney*, p. 182.
47. The Presentation Board meets with Parish Nominators to decide on names to fill vacant rectors' positions in local churches.
48. The Archdeacon's 51-page report to the Archbishop was released to the SC on 23 September 1996.
49. Lindsay Stoddart, interviewed by SP, 7 December 2012.
50. Fletcher, *An English Church in Australian Soil*, p. 197.
51. Mayne, 'A Brief History of Indigenous Ministry in Colonial Sydney', pp. 25–27. This section is based entirely on Tom Mayne's well-researched study.
52. Bill Bird, Alan Donohoo, Allan Cook, Geoff Huard, Tom Mayne, Ray Minniecon and Ray Welsh.
53. Harris, *One Blood*.
54. 11 December 1996, SDA, 2010/010/Box02.
55. HG, Sermons, 'Mr Thomas Smith', 2 December 1996.

## 18. Fifth Year (1997): The Coin of Transcendence

1. Peter Smart, interviewed by SP, 12 July 2016.
2. HG to John Lambert, 14 February 1997, Projects, NSW Provincial Bishops Conference, 1997–98, Archbishop's Files, 2010, SDA.
3. Bruce Kaye to HG, 21 March 1996, 2006/011/BOX 10, SDA.
4. Bruce Kaye to SP, 24 January 2019.
5. Kaye to HG, 21 March 1996, 2006/011/BOX 10, SDA.
6. Margaret Rodgers to Bruce Kaye, 29 July 1996, 2006/011/BOX 10, SDA.
7. Tim Foster to HG, 12 September, 1996, 2006/011/BOX 10, SDA.
8. HG to Tim Foster, 17 September 1996; 14 October 1996, 2006/011/BOX 10, SDA.
9. Margaret Rodgers to Bruce Kaye, 29 July 1996, 2006/011/BOX 10, SDA.
10. Brochure 'Exploring Our Future', 2006/011/BOX 10, SDA.
11. Steering Committee Members' Report, 3 July 1997, 2006/011/BOX 10, SDA.
12. 'Catch the Vision', 1997 National Anglican Conference Video.
13. HG to John Howard, 24 April 1996, 2006/011/BOX 10, SDA.
14. 'Catch the Vision', 1997 National Anglican Conference Video.
15. Conference addresses are reproduced in full in *National Anglican Conference Journal:*

'Exploring our Future', *Anglicans in Australia in the 3rd Millennium* Church Scene, Melbourne, 1997.
16. 'Spectacular Wall Hangings Mark Church's 150th Anniversary', press release, 4 February.
17. 'Catch the Vision', 1997 National Anglican Conference video.
18. Harry recounted this story in his Good Friday sermon at Figtree Anglican Church, 28 March 1997.
19. Recollection of Revd Bill Lawton, 25 January 2019.
20. J.L. Peterson to HG, 15 February 1997, 2006/011/BOX 10, SDA.
21. Kimberly Sawyer to SP, 6 December 2019.
22. Hybels preferred the descriptor of 'seeker sensitive'.
23. J. Chapman to HG, 4 April 1997.
24. John Chapman, 'Why Reform Will Never Take Place through Synod', January 1997.
25. Len Abbott to Margaret Lamb, 11 October 1990. Bp James Grant is of the opinion that this story is in the same genre as his reported prayer, 'Lord, don't let anything happen today.'
26. Elkin, *The Diocese of Newcastle*, p. 527.
27. HG, Sermons, 19/1997.
28. Ibid.
29. HG, Sermons, 44/1997, 18 September 1997.
30. Goodhew, *Green*.
31. Out of the Diocese of Australia, established 1836.
32. HG to all Bishops and Archdeacons, 7 July 1993, 2006/011, Box 13, SDA.
33. Stan Skillicorn to HG, 28 July 1993, 2006/011/BOX 13, SDA.
34. HG to Keith Rayner, 29 February 1996, Archbishop's Correspondence, 2010/010, Box 5, SDA.
35. *The Age*, 19 July 1997, Extra Features, 3.
36. Ibid.
37. Ivan Head to HG, 5 February 1997, Archbishop's Correspondence, 2010/010, Box 5.
38. Peter O'Brien to HG, 7 August 1997.
39. George Carey to HG, 14 August 1997.
40. Ibid.
41. HG, Sermons, 29/1997.
42. Media Release, 2 September 1997, 2006/011/Box 10, SDA.
43. Media Release, 6 September 1997, 2006/011/Box 10, SDA.
44. *Sun-Herald* and *Sunday Telegraph*, 7 September 1997.
45. Canon Bill Atwood to HG, 19 February 1997, Archbishop's files, 2015/004/BOX 40, SDA.
46. HG to David Bussau, 12 March 1997, Archbishop's files, 2015/004/BOX 40, SDA.
47. Bishop of Armidale.
48. 16 February 1989, 2010/010/Box02, SDA.
49. Dallas Diocese website, http://www.edod.org/index.php/diocese/house.html.
50. Bates, *A Church at War*, p. 130.
51. Wisconsin, USA.
52. Document of 8 October, Archbishop's files, 2015/004/BOX 40, SDA.
53. Peter Chiswell to HG, 8 October 1997, Archbishop's files, 2015/004/BOX 40, SDA.
54. 19 December 1997 in Archbishop's files, 2015/004/BOX 40, SDA.
55. D. Robinson to HG, 24 December 1997. ECUSA file Part I (1997–1998), HG papers.
56. D. Robinson to HG, 2 January 1998. ECUSA file Part I (1997–1998), HG papers.
57. This was a delayed development consistent with Recommendation 7.2 of Archdeacon D.D. Nicolios, *Report on Women's Ministry in the Diocese of Sydney*, April 1996, p. 30, copy in Women's Ministry Reports, 2016/024, SDA.
58. For the records of the Women's Advisory Council, see Women's Ministry Reports, 2016/024, SDA.

59 '1997 Synod Summary: Resolutions', 16/97, *Year Book 1998*, p. 325.
60 Alan Cole to HG on 27 October 1997 (2010/010/Box02, SDA).
61 Known in Scripture as an 'encourager'.
62 Murray, *A Working Forest*, p. 139.
63 Ibid., pp. 144ff.
64 HG, Sermons, 33/1997.
65 HG, Sermons, 48/1997.

## 19. Sixth Year (1998): Wimp, Women and Spong

1 HG, Day Book and Diary, 8 January 1998.
2 McGrath, *J.I. Packer*.
3 HG, Day Book and Diary, 7 January 1998.
4 15/98, 33/98, 53/98.
5 John Lambert to HG, 20 January 1998, Archbishop's Correspondence, 2010/010, Box 5.
6 Cameron, *Phenomenal Sydney*, p. 128.
7 Marr, 'Divine Intervention', p. 1.
8 Paul Barnett, interviewed 22 March 2018.
9 HG, Day Book and Diary, 7 December 1998.
10 HG, Day Book and Diary, 5 December 1998.
11 Hooker, Johnston and Gee, *Riding the Rapids*.
12 Paul Barnett, interviewed 22 March 2018.
13 Ibid.
14 HG, Day Book and Diary, 16 May 1997.
15 Ibid.
16 1999 *Year Book*, 475.
17 A. Cole to HG, 19 May 1998.
18 IVP, 2002.
19 May 2000.
20 HG, Day Book and Diary, 20 June 1998.
21 HG, Day Book and Diary, 21 June 1998.

## 20. Sixth Year (1998 Continued): 'The Winsome Face of Sydney'

1 Bates, *A Church at War*, p. 137.
2 Spong, *Here I Here I Stand*, p. 439.
3 15 February 1997, http://www.globalsouthanglican.org/index.php/blog/comments/the_kuala_lumpur_statement_on_human_sexuality_2nd_encounter_in_the_south_10.
4 Spong, *Here I Here I Stand*, p. 440.
5 Ibid., p. 444.
6 Bates, *A Church at War*, p. 132f.
7 Ibid., p. 133.
8 Paul Barnett, 'One Bishop's Reflections on Lambeth 1998', ACL Synod Dinner 15 October 1998, http://acl.asn.au/old/pwb_dinner98.html.
9 Porter, *Sydney Anglicans and the Threat to World Anglicanism*, p. 55.
10 Ibid., p. 55.
11 Bates, *A Church at War*, pp. 134ff.
12 *Crosswinds*, ECUSA file Part I (1997–1998), HG papers.
13 Judith Nichols to the author, 24 September 2010.
14 *SC*, March 2001.
15 14 August 1998, p. 8.
16 Ray Smith, interviewed 4 April 2018.

17 Barnett, 'One Bishop's Reflections on Lambeth 1998'.
18 *Church of England News*, 14 August 1998, p. 11.
19 Spong, *Here I Here I Stand*, p. 427.
20 Ibid., p. 455.
21 *Guardian*, 6 August 1998.
22 *Times*, 6 August 1998.
23 Holloway, *Godless Morality*, p. 80.
24 *Independent*, 7 August 1998, 9.
25 Bates, *A Church at War*, p. 140.
26 Holloway, *Leaving Alexandria*, p. 310.
27 Ibid., p. 323.
28 Bates, *A Church at War*, p. 140.
29 See https://www.stephenbateswriter.com/non-fiction.
30 Holloway, *Godless Morality*, pp. 79f.
31 *Independent*, 7 August 1998, p. 9.
32 *Daily Telegraph*, 7 August 1998.
33 HG, A Report to the SC on the 1998 Lambeth Conference, 24 August 1998.
34 HG, Day Book and Diary, 24 August 1998.
35 Carl M. Chambers to HG, 17 November 1998.
36 9 April 2001.
37 John H. Rodgers to HG, 25 August 1998. ECUSA file Part I (1997–1998), HG papers.
38 HG, Sermons, 26/1998, 2 October 1998; For Harry's opposition to euthanasia, see Chapman and Leeder, *The Last Right?*, pp. 62f.
39 14 October 1998.
40 HG, Day Book and Diary, 8 and 18 December 1998.
41 HG, Day Book and Diary, 21 December 1998.
42 Presidential Address, 1998, p. 3.
43 Presidential Address, 1998, pp. 6, 7.
44 For this same reason, in 2004 when Peter Jensen was Archbishop, the Synod refrained from pressing for lay presidency.
45 Porter, *Sydney Anglicans and the Threat to World Anglicanism*, p. 99.
46 Ibid., p. 99.
47 Presidential Address, 1998, pp. 10–14.
48 HG, Day Book and Diary, 24 September 1998.
49 1998 Presidential Address, see *1999 Yearbook*, 350, also Sydney Diocesan Secretariat, http://www.sds.asn.au/site/101341.asp?ph=sy.
50 HG, Day Book and Diary, 13 October 1998.
51 Stephen Gabbott to HG, 26 October 1998.
52 BBJ to HG, 23 October 1998.
53 *ACR*, 1 February 1999, p. 8.
54 Andrew Katay to HG, undated but received 8 February 1999.
55 BBJ, *Inside Sydney*, pp. 172–4.
56 *ACR*, 1 February 1999, p. 9.
57 Undated, but received 22 October 1998.
58 21 October 1998.
59 Phillip Aspinall, Adelaide; Gerald Beaumont, Perth; Brian Farran, Perth; Ian George, Adelaide; Roger Herft, Newcastle; Peter Hollingworth, Brisbane; David Murray, Perth; Richard Randerson, Canberra & Goulburn; Andrew St John, Melbourne; Ronald Williams, Brisbane.
60 HG, Day Book and Diary, 11 November 1998.
61 Ibid.

[62] HG to Paul Barnett, undated notes, but 15 November 1998, Archbishop's files, 2015/004/Box 43, SDA.
[63] Dated 1 December 1998, but sent on 30 November, Archbishop's files, 2015/004/box 43, SDA.
[64] Bruce Kaye to HG, 10 December 1998.
[65] HG, Sermons, 42/1998, 25 December 1998.

## 21. Seventh Year (1999): 'Faith is Trusting God in Every Situation'

[1] HG, Sermons, 2/1999.
[2] HG, Day Book, 2–10 January.
[3] HG, Day Book, 17 January 1999.
[4] J. Schram to HG, 24 February 1999
[5] Sylvia Jeanes to HG, 20 February 1999.
[6] Sylvia Jeanes to HG, 7 March 2001.
[7] HG, Diary, 13 April 1993.
[8] Day Book, 27 December 1998.
[9] Day Book, 19 February 1999.
[10] 'Archbishop preaches to 100,000 in India', SC, April 1999.
[11] See http://staines.qld.edu.au/about-staines/a-history-of-service/.
[12] HG, Day Book, 21 February 1999.
[13] HG, Day Book, 26 February 1999.
[14] David Gitari (Archbishop of Kenya), Emmanuel Kolini (Archbishop of Rwanda), Donald Mtetemela (Archbishop of Tanzania), Maurice Sinclair (Presiding Bishop of the Southern Cone of America), Moses Tay (Archbishop of South East Asia), Ghais Malik (President Bishop, Jerusalem), and Colin Bazley (an earlier Presiding Bishop of the Southern Cone). Harry was the only one of the eight not a Primate – so it was known as the Primate's Letter.
[15] Archbishop's Administration File, ECUSA, 1999, 2015/004/Box 45, SDA.
[16] Jim Stanton to HG, 23 March 1999, ECUSA file Part 2 (January–July 1999), HG papers.
[17] Jim Stanton to HG, 2 April 1999, ECUSA file Part 2 (January–July 1999), HG papers.
[18] Day Book, 6 April 1999.
[19] 'A letter from Singapore', Harry and five others, 15 April 1999, Archbishop's Administration File, ECUSA, 1999, 2015/004/Box 45, SDA.
[20] HG to Alistair Macdonald-Radcliff, 25 February 1999, ECUSA file Part 2 (January–July 1999), HG papers.
[21] Archbishop Carey to HG et al., 5 May 1999, ECUSA file Part 2 (January–July 1999), HG papers.
[22] Moses Tay to George Carey, 4 August 1999, ECUSA file Part 3 (August–December 1999), HG papers.
[23] HG to Archbishop Carey, 1 June 1999, ECUSA file Part 2 (January–July 1999), HG papers.
[24] M. Sinclair to HG, 2 June 1999, ECUSA file Part 2 (January–July 1999), HG papers.
[25] 'And What Did the Presiding Bishop Recently Say?', Now Online, posted 21 March 1999.
[26] HG, Sermons, 30 April 1999.
[27] Graham, Just As I Am, p. 325.
[28] Chris Bellinger in discussion with SP, 4 May 2019.
[29] John Woodhouse to Margaret Lawton, 30 August 1999. He did not reveal to her who proposed to set up the committee or who assured him that his lack of expertise in counselling was not a problem.
[30] John Woodhouse, et al., Report on the Anglican Counselling Service by the Committee appointed by the SC of the Anglican Synod of the Diocese of Sydney (March, 1999), pp. 101f.

[31] Ian D. Cochrane, A Shortened Analysis of the Results and Research Methodology of the Woodhouse Committee Investigation of the Anglican Counselling Centre, May 1999, pp. 4, 5.
[32] Ibid., p. 11.
[33] Woodhouse, Report on the Anglican Counselling Service, p. 68.
[34] Margaret Lawton to John Woodhouse, 19 August 1999.
[35] John Woodhouse to Margaret Lawton, 30 August 1999 and 27 September 1999.
[36] Bp Simon Makundi of Mount Kilimanjaro, representing Archbishop Donald Mtetemeia, Province of Tanzania; Bp Peter Njenga Karioki of Mount Kenya South, representing Archbishop David Gitari, Province of Kenya; Bp John Rucyahana-Kabango of Shyira, representing Archbihop of Emmanuel Kolini, Province of the Episcopal Church of Rwanda.
[37] Archbishop's Administration File, ECUSA, 1999, 2015/004/Box 45, SDA.
[38] 'Way of Faithfulness', ECUSA file Part 3 (August–December 1999), HG papers.
[39] Presidential Address, 1999, p. 20.
[40] Ibid., p. 16.
[41] Ibid., p. 17.
[42] Ibid., p. 24.
[43] Geoffrey Holt, an occasional Anglican preacher, with an interest in church growth, ministry and his profession of advertising copywriting. In 2009 Holt published *Goodbye Old God: New Refreshment for Tired and Thirsty Spirits*. Its title page has a commendation from Harry: 'Whole-hearted, imaginative, vigorous, and prepared to push boundaries.'
[44] Geoff Holt to HG, 12 October 1999.
[45] Alan Cole to HG, 12 October 1999.
[46] *SC*, November 1999, 21.
[47] Peter Toon to HG, Advent 1999, ECUSA file Part 3 (August–December 1999), HG papers.
[48] Keith Rayner to HG, 10 November 1999
[49] A. Cole to HG, undated but 10 November 1999
[50] Harry Goodhew, 'My personal report on a recent visit to the Episcopal Church of the United States of America made at Kampala in November 1999', ECUSA, Singapore and Kampala Meetings ECUSA, HG papers.
[51] HG to Maurice Sinclair, 26 November 1999.

## 22. Eighth Year (2000–2001): 'A Small Victory'
[1] Hodder and Stoughton, London, 1995.
[2] HG, Sermons, 2 January 2000.
[3] *Independent*, 14 September 1994.
[4] *Freedom of Religious Belief in China*, Information Office of the State Council of the People's Republic of China, Beijing, 1997.
[5] Piggin and Linder, *The Fountain of Public Prosperity*, p. 420.
[6] HG to Ken Coleman, 16 August 1999, Archbishops' files, 2016/001/box 12, SDA.
[7] Alan Cole to HG, 17 December, Archbishops' files, 2016/001/box 16, SDA.
[8] Alan Cole to HG, 10 March 2000, 2010/010/Box02, SDA.
[9] Paul Barnett, interviewed 22 March 2018.
[10] Ibid.
[11] E. D. Cameron, President of the Synod to HG, 1 April 1993, Personnel File, Goodhew, Richard Henry, P230206.
[12] 5 June 1999.
[13] Peter Young to HG, 4 February 2000.
[14] HG, Day Book, 3 February 2000.
[15] David Silk to HG, 24 February 2000.
[16] Philip Huggins to HG, 5 February 2000.

17. Alan Cole to HG, 10 February 2000.
18. HG to Alan Cole, 14 February 2000.
19. See http://archive.wfn.org/2000/02/msg00049.html.
20. HG, Day Book, 9 November 2000.
21. HG, Day Book, notes on Carnley's address, 13 March 2001.
22. Alan Cole to HG, 3 February 2000, ECUSA file, Part 4, HG papers.
23. Quoted by Robert Duncan, Bishop of Pittsburgh, in a circular to his clergy and lay leaders, 1 February 2000, ECUSA file, Singapore Consecrations, HG papers.
24. John Rodgers, 'Petition to the Primates' Meeting and the Primates of the Anglican Communion for Emergency Intervention in the Province of the Episcopal Church of the United States of America', Northfield, Illinois, 1998, pp. 43–54.
25. HG to Emmanuel Kolini, 23 December 1999, ECUSA file, Singapore Consecrations, HG papers.
26. Roger Beckwith to HG, 2 February 2000, ECUSA file, Part 4, HG papers.
27. HG to Peter Toon, 31 January 2000.
28. *Church Times*, 11 February 2000.
29. HG to Peter Carnley, 14 February 2000, ECUSA file, Singapore Consecrations, HG papers.
30. Bill Atwood to HG, 27 March 2000.
31. Bill Atwood to HG, 31 March 2000.
32. 'Final communiqué from the Primates of the Anglican Communion in Oporto', 28 March 2000.
33. 'An Initial Response to the Communiqué of the Primates' Meeting from the Archbishop of Sydney and the Regional Bishops of the Diocese of Sydney', 31 March 2000, ECUSA file, Singapore Consecrations, HG papers.
34. *Christianity Today*, 14 December 2000; see also Hassett, *Anglican Communion in Crisis*, p. 2.
35. HG to Bp Bob Duncan, 16 August 2000, ECUSA file, Part 4, HG papers.
36. *SMH*, 17 March 2000. Harry quoted these words in addressing the special synod on 4 May 2000.
37. HG, Day Book, 3 April 2000.
38. HG, Day Book, 8 April 2000.
39. Alan Cole to HG, 9 April 2000, 2010/010/Box02, SDA.
40. Babbage, *Memoirs of a Loose Canon*, p. 208.
41. Peter Chiswell to HG, 14 May 2000.
42. Liz Boyce to HG, 17 October 2000.

## 23. Eighth Year (2000–2001 Continued): 'No Other Name'

1. Carnley, 'The Rising of the Son', pp. 40–43.
2. Craig Berkman to HG, 2 May 2000.
3. Piggin and Linder, *Attending to the National Soul*, pp. 420–2.
4. Stephen Bradley to HG, 19 December 1994, 2007/001/BOX 09, SDA.
5. Frank Retief to HG, 20 March 2001.
6. David Tyndall, 'Evangelicalism, Sport and the Australian Olympics', PhD, Macquarie University, 2004, pp. 204, 5.
7. Ibid., p. 365.
8. Alicia Watson to HG, 10 October 2000.
9. 2001 *Year Book*, p. 401.
10. Alicia Watson to HG, 10 October 2000.
11. Henry Speagle to HG, 27 November 2000.
12. Stuart Findlay to HG, 19 January 2001.
13. Letter dated 19 October 2000 to John Woodhouse in the author's possession.

[14] HG to M Corbett-Jones 23 February 2001.
[15] 17 March 2001.

## 24. Stepping Down: 'God's Man in God's Time'
[1] *Christian-Jewish Scene*, no. 48, September/October 2001.
[2] HG to Peter Sinclair, 24 January 2001.
[3] Alan Donohoo et al. to HG, 1 February 2001.
[4] Bruce Rosier to HG, 26 January 2001.
[5] 29 January 2001.
[6] Bruce Kaye to HG, undated.
[7] Jeff and Margaret Fuller to HG, 27 January 2001.
[8] Gerald Davis to HG, 15 March 2001.
[9] 7 February 2001.
[10] Alan Gill, interviewed by SP, 22 February 2016.
[11] 7 February 2001.
[12] 20 February 2001.
[13] 19 March 2001.
[14] To the Archbishop … from your friends … in St Andrew's House, undated [March 2001].
[15] Ibid.
[16] Helen Kerle to Goodhew, 6 February 2001.
[17] To the Archbishop … from your friends … in St Andrew's House, undated [March 2001].
[18] 15 March 2001.
[19] 19 February 2001.
[20] Simon Manchester to HG, 27 February 2001.
[21] The Revd Ralph Fraser to HG, 8 February 2001.
[22] 16 March 2001.
[23] Peter Young to HG, 16 March 2001.
[24] 20 March 2001.
[25] 24 February 2001.
[26] E. Clancy to HG, 5 January 1999, Box 2015/004, SDA.
[27] HG to Ernest Chau, 7 March 2001.
[28] HG to Abraham Athyal, 5 March 2001.
[29] Peter Jensen to HG, 27 February 2001.
[30] David Goodhew, interviewed by SP, 27 July 2018.
[31] Adele Smith to HG, 20 March 2001
[32] John Kidson, chaplain, Southern Cross University, 3 April 2001.
[33] Bob and Phyllis Collie, 22 March 2001.
[34] Adele Smith to HG, 20 March 2001.
[35] HG to Mark Edmonson, 19 March 2001.
[36] HG to Kerry Chikarovski, 19 March 2001.

## 25. The Ministry of a Former Archbishop: 'The Inexhaustible Vision'.
[1] McGillion, *The Chosen Ones*, pp. 78–83.
[2] Margaret Rodgers, interviewed by Marcia Cameron, 9 May 2011.
[3] Philip Goodhew, interviewed by SP, 26 July 2016.
[4] HG, *The One Sure Hope*, p. 52, citing Jenkins, *The Next Christendom*.
[5] From *Green*, pp. 101f.
[6] Reed, *Walking in the Light*.
[7] Goodhew, *The One Sure Hope*.
[8] Ena Mays to HG, 11 November 2007.
[9] Goodhew, *The One Sure Hope*, p. 45.

10. Rod Story, interviewed by SP, 19 January 2017.
11. Email from HG to the author, 28 January 2017.
12. John Sorensen, interviewed by SP, 26 July 2016.
13. Brown, 'Using Governance as a Tool for Transforming Organizational Culture', pp. 370–372.
14. Ibid, p. 387.
15. Ibid, pp. 409–413.
16. Ibid, p. 415.
17. Ibid, p. 423.
18. Ibid, p. 426.
19. Ibid, p. 458.
20. As told to SP by Russell Jackson, 26 July 2015.

## Conclusion: Legacy of Graciousness and Generosity

1. Email to SP, 19 April 2011.
2. From Lloyd Waddy, Judges' Chambers, Parramatta, to HG, 29 July 2001.
3. 26 March 2001.
4. Glennon to HG, 16 March 2001.
5. McGillion, *The Chosen Ones*, p. 69.
6. Ibid., p. 53.
7. Bruce Kaye, 'The Trouble with the Laity: The Challenge of Lay Vocation in Australia,' The 1994 Felix Arnott Lecture, 2 September 1994, pp. 3, 4.
8. Robert Forsyth, interviewed by SP, 24 October 2012.
9. Tom Frame to SP, 27 June 2018.
10. Presidential Address, 2000, pp. 17, 18.
11. 'A decline of just 2% in Anglican attendance [between 1991 and 2001] masks different experiences in each diocese. Significant falls in attendance in most rural dioceses have been counterbalanced by a significant increase in attendance in the Sydney diocese. Other metropolitan dioceses tended to be static in attendance' (John Bellamy & Keith Castle, *2001 Church Attendance Estimates*, NCLS Occasional Paper 3, February 2004, p. 7).
12. Shortt, *Rowan's Rule*, p. 2.
13. SC, March 2001.
14. Ibid.
15. Paul Perini, interviewed by SP, 21 October 2013.
16. 1 Corinthians 3:11–15.

# Bibliography

## Primary sources: Harry Goodhew

### A. In Harry Goodhew's private collection

Correspondence, 1944–2012.
Day book and diary, 1993–2001.
Sermons and addresses, 1982–2007.
ECUSA files.
'Graham Delbridge – His contribution to Youth Ministry', inaugural Graham Delbridge Lecture, 19 August 1996, in HG, Sermons, 1996.
'My Personal Report on a Recent Visit to the Episcopal Church of the United States of America made at Kampala in November 1999', ECUSA, Singapore and Kampala Meetings.
'The Role of the Leader: An Examination of the Influence of Ministerial Leadership on the Growth of Six Australian Churches from 1978 to 1989', MA (Hons), University of Wollongong, 1990.
'Report on our Recent Trip to Sri Lanka', 7 February 1986.
Rodgers, John, 'Petition to the Primates' Meeting and the Primates of the Anglican Communion for Emergency Intervention in the Province of the Episcopal Church of the United States of America', Northfield IL, 1998.

### B. In Sydney Diocesan Archives (identified by SDA in endnotes)

Archbishop's Administration File, Bishopscourt, 1990–2000, Box 2015/004, SDA.
Archbishop's Administration File, ECUSA, 1999, 2015/004/Box 45, SDA.
Archbishop's Administration File, EE, 1995–2002, 2015/004/Box 27, SDA.
Archdeacon D.D. Nicolios, 'Report on Women's Ministry in the Diocese of Sydney', April 1996, Women's Ministry Reports, 2016/024, SDA.
Correspondence, Archbishop's Files, 1994/73/10; 2006/11; 2006/011; 2010/010/Box02 and Box5; 2015/014/BOX 40, SDA.
Evangelism Explosion, 1995–2002, Archbishop's Administration File, SDA 2015/004/Box 27.
'Exploring Our Future', 2006/011/BOX 10 SDA.
Personnel file, Goodhew, Richard Henry, P230206.
'Strong Support for Women Preaching: Survey', Media Release, 3 September 1996, Women's Ministry Reports, 2016/024, SDA.

### Sydney Diocesan Reports and Synod papers

10/91 Ordination of Women to the Priesthood 1993: A Report to Synod, https://www.sds.asn.au/1091-ordination-women-priesthood-1993.
Gilmour, David W., 'Personal Statement to Sydney Synod', Wednesday 19 October 1994.
Presidential addresses, 1993–2000.
Report of the Archbishop's Commission of Inquiry, September 1992.
The Report of the Committee on the Development of Parish Property and Ministry, June 1990, is found in *Report of the Standing Committee and other Reports and Papers, 1990*, pp. 103–121.
*Social Issues Update.*
Sydney *Year Book*, 1971–2016.
Woodhouse, John, et al., Report on the Anglican Counselling Service by the Committee

appointed by the Standing Committee of the Anglican Synod of the Diocese of Sydney (March 1999).

**Published primary sources**

Report of The Wood Royal Commission: The Royal Commission into the New South Wales Police Service: Volume 5 The Paedophile Inquiry, 1994–1997.

**Talks, addresses and unofficial papers**

Barnett, Paul, 'One Bishop's Reflections on Lambeth 1998', ACL Synod Dinner 15 October 1998, http://acl.asn.au/old/pwb_dinner98.html.
Clark, Russell D., Open Letter to the Foundation Members of REPA, 14 March 1993.
Jensen, Phillip, 'Church Planting', https://phillipjensen.com/church-planting/.
Jensen, Phillip, 'Why Anglican?', https://phillipjensen.com/why-anglican/.
*National Anglican Conference Journal: 'Exploring our Future', Anglicans in Australia in the 3rd Millennium*, Church Scene, Melbourne, 1997.
Smith, Ray, 'A Church for all Nations', sermon preached at St Clement's Anglican Church, Marrickville, 27 February 2000.
*Synod Watch*, ACL, August 1996.

**Interviews (by SP unless otherwise indicated)**

Babbage, Malcolm, 3 June 2018.
Babbage, Stuart Barton, 19 April 2012.
Ballantine-Jones, Bruce, 10 June 2010.
Banister, Wendy, 19 December 2012.
Barnett, Paul, 22 March 2018.
Bidwell, Archdeacon John, Record of interview by D.W.B. Robinson and B. Ballantine-Jones with 7 August 1972, Moore Theological College Archives.
Chapman, John, interviewed by BBJ, 10 March 2010.
Chapman, John, 4 March 2011.
Crain, David, 3 March 2016.
Deane, Arthur, 5 May 2014.
Donnelly, Richard, 10 August 2011.
Edwards, Trevor, 14 June 2011.
Emeleus, Sue, 19 August 2018.
Fairfull, David, 29 February 2016.
Forsyth, Robert, 24 October 2012.
Fuller, Margaret, 12 July 2016.
Gabbott, Marion and Stephen, 19 May 2014.
Goodhew, David, 27 July 2018.
Goodhew, Harry and Pam, 28 July 2010; 17, 20 January 2011; 28 May 2011; 1 July 2011; 26 March 2012; 27 October 2015; 19 October 2016; 19 January 2017; 5 August 2019.
Goodhew, Philip, 26 July 2016.
Goodhew, Robyn, 23 October 2013.
Hughes, Bronwyn and Graeme, 5 November 2011.
Irvine, Rod and Helen, 17 February 2011.
Jensen, Christine, 26 March 2012.
Keith, Jim, 10 January 2011.
Kell, Peter, 19 December 2012.
Lawton, Bill, interviewed by Margaret Lamb, 10 September 1986.

Lawton, Bill, 17 July 2018.
Loane, Marcus, interviewed by Margaret Lamb, undated.
Perini, Paul, 21 October 2013.
Rodgers, Margaret, interviewed by Marcia Cameron, 9 & 23 May 2011.
Smart, Peter, 12 July 2016.
Soulos, Mersina, 13 July 2010.
Sorensen, John, 26 July 2016.
Smith, Ray, 4 April 2018.
Smith, Vic, interviewed by Margaret Lamb, 10 August 1989.
Stoddart, Lindsay, 6 December 2012.
Story, Rod, 19 January 2017.
Warren, Riley, 28 August 2014.
West, Rod, 16 March 2011.
Whiteman, Peppi, 10 January 2020.
Wright, Dulcie, 13 October 2017.

**Theses, lectures and unpublished typescripts**

Brooks, James, 'An Investigation into the Nature and Significance of the Early Parish Ministry of Harry Goodhew with a Particular Focus on the Impact He Had and the Changes He Brought to St. Bede's Beverly Hills Anglican Church', Church History IV, Moore College final essay, 2011.

Brown, Debra L., 'Using Governance as a Tool for Transforming Organizational Culture', Gordon-Conwell Theological Seminary, D.Min, 2016.

Cochrane, Ian D., A Shortened Analysis of the Results and Research Methodology of the Woodhouse Committee Investigation of the Anglican Counselling Centre, May 1999.

Foye, Jonathan, 'Graving Another Testament: A Critical Discourse Analysis of the Sydney Anglicans', PhD, University of Western Sydney, 2016.

Frith, Eric William, 'The Role of the Laity in Anglican Evangelicalism with Particular Reference to the Diocese of Sydney, 1960-1982', MA Thesis, Charles Sturt University, 2017.

Goodhew, John, 'Goodhews in Australia,' typescript, 29 March 1995.

Goodhew, Richard Henry, 'The Role of the Leader: An Examination of the Influence of Ministerial Leadership on the Growth of Six Australian Churches from 1978 to 1989', MA (Hons), University of Wollongong, 1990.

Kaye, Bruce, 'The Trouble with the Laity: The Challenge of Lay Vocation in Australia,' The 1994 Felix Arnott Lecture, 2 September 1994.

Lukabyo, Ruth, 'From a Ministry for Youth to a Ministry of Youth: Aspects of Protestant Youth Ministry in Sydney 1930-1959', PhD, University of Wollongong, 2018.

Mayne, Patricia Anne, 'A History of Tamar (1996-2008) in Relation to the Anglican Church of Australia in General and the Diocese of Sydney in Particular', PhD, ACU, 2016.

Mayne, Tom, 'A Brief History of Indigenous Ministry in Colonial Sydney, in the Sydney Anglican Diocese and beyond and of the Sydney Anglican Indigenous Peoples' Ministry Committee', January 2016, typescript.

Roberts, V., 'The Use of the Vatican II Lectionary in Australian Anglican Churches', D. Min., San Francisco Theological Seminary, 1987.

Tyndall, David, 'Evangelicalism, Sport and the Australian Olympics', PhD, Macquarie University, 2004.

**Newspapers and newsletters**

*Anglicans Together*
*The Australian*
*The Bulletin*
'Centralism: Real or Imagined, Which way for Sydney Diocese?' *ACL Newsletter*, March 1995.
*Christianity Today*
*Church of England Newspaper*
*Church Scene*
*Crosswinds*
*EFAC Australian Bulletin*
*Guardian*
*Illawarra Mercury*
*Independent*
R.E.P. Association, Statement No.1, 6 March 1992, p. 3.
'The Way ahead for Christian Liberty', *Repaccusions*, 2, December 1992, p. 8.
'Unity in Diversity', *Repaccusions*, 2, December 1992, p. 9.
*Southern Cross (SC)*
*The Sydney Morning Herald (SMH)*
*Telegraph/Mirror*
*Times*

**Published secondary sources**

*Agenda for a Biblical Church: Papers for the National Evangelical Anglican Congress, 1981*, Anglican Information Office, Sydney, 1981, 2 vols.
Babbage, Stuart Barton, *Memoirs of a Loose Canon*, Acorn Press, Melbourne, 2004.
Ballantine-Jones, Bruce, *Inside Sydney: An Insider's View of the Changes and Politics in the Anglican Diocese of Sydney, 1966-2013*, BBJ, Sydney, 2016.
Bates, Stephen, *A Church at War: Anglicans and Homosexuality*, I.B. Tauris, London, 2004.
Bellamy, John and Castle, Keith, *2001 Church Attendance Estimates*, NCLS Occasional Paper 3, February 2004.
Benaud, Richie, *Anything But ... An Autobiography*, Hodder & Stoughton, London, 1998.
Blanch, Allan M., *From Strength to Strength: A Life of Marcus Loane*, Australian Scholarly Publishing, North Melbourne, 2015.
Bleby, Martin, *A Quiet Revival: Geoffrey Bingham in Life and Ministry*, New Creation Publications, Blackwood, 2012.
Butterfield, Herbert, *The Whig Interpretation of History*, 1931 [Pelican Books, 1971].
Buzo, Alexander, *Legends of the Baggy Green*, Allen & Unwin, St Leonards NSW, 2004.
Cable, K.J., 'M.L. LOANE: Archbishop Mowll', *JRH*, 1.2, December 1960, pp. 123-4.
———, 'McCabe, Stanley Joseph (1910-1968)', *Australian Dictionary of Biography*, Volume 10, Melbourne University Press, Carlton,, 1986, p. 208.
Cahill, Thomas, *How the Irish Saved Civilisation*, Hodder and Stoughton, London, 1995.
Cameron, Marcia, *Phenomenal Sydney: Anglicans in a Time of Change 1945-2013*, Wipf & Stock, Eugene OR, 2016.
Carnley, Peter, 'The Rising of the Son', *The Bulletin*, 25 April 2000, pp. 40-43.
'Catch the Vision', 1997 National Anglican Conference Video.
Chadwick, Owen, *Michael Ramsey, a Life*, Clarendon Press, Oxford, 1990.
Chambers, David H., *'Tempest Tost': The Life and Teaching of the Rev. C.H. Nash*, Church Press Publications, Melbourne, 1959.
Chapman, Simon and Leeder, Stephen (eds), *The Last Right? Australians take sides on the right to die*, Mandarin, Port Melbourne, 1995.
Elkin, A.P., *The Diocese of Newcastle: A History of the Diocese of Newcastle, N.S.W*, Australasian

Medical Pub. Co., Sydney, 1955.
Ellul, Jacques, *Prayer and Modern Man*, Seabury Press, New York, 1973.
Fletcher, Brian H., *An English Church in Australian Soil*, Barton Books, Canberra, 2015.
Frame, Tom, *Binding Ties: An Experience of Adoption and Reunion in Australia*, Hale & Iremonger, Alexandria, 1999.
*Freedom of Religious Belief in China*, Information Office of the State Council of the People's Republic of China, Beijing, 1997.
Garrett, John, *Where Nets Were Cast: Christianity in Oceania since World War II*, Institute of Pacific Studies, University of the South Pacific in association with World Council of Churches, Suva, Fiji & Geneva, Switzerland, 1997.
Giles, Kevin, *The Trinity and Subordinationism: The Doctrine of God and the Contemporary Gender Debate*, IVP, Downers Grove, 2002.
Goodhew, Harry, *Green: Growing Deep in a Shallow World*, Green Tree Press, Fort Lauderdale, 2011.
———, *The One Sure Hope: Reflections from the Book of Isaiah*, Aquila Press, Sydney South, 2005.
Goodwin, Doris Kearns, *Team of Rivals: the Political Genius of Abraham Lincoln*, Simon & Schuster, New York, 2005.
Graham, Billy, *Just As I Am: The Autobiography*, HarperCollins, Sydney, 1997.
Gray, Alasdair (ed.), *Poor Things: Episodes for the Early Life of Archibald McCandless, M.D., Scottish Public Health Officer*, Dalkey Archive Press, Chicago, 2001.
Grubb, Norman P., *C.T. Studd: Cricketer and Pioneer*, The Religious Tract, London, 1933.
Harris, John, *One Blood: 200 Years of Aboriginal Encounter with Christianity: A Story of Hope*, Albatross, Sutherland NSW, 1990.
Hassett, Miranda, *Anglican Communion in Crisis*, Princeton University Press, Princeton, 2007.
Haydon, Colin, 'Consecration Sermons,' in Francis, Keith A., and William Gibson, (eds), *The Oxford Handbook of the British Sermon 1689–1901*, 1st edn, Oxford Handbooks in Religion and Theology, Oxford University Press, Oxford, 2012.
Haygarth, Arthur, *Scores & Biographies*, vol. 1, 1744–1826, Lillywhite, London, 1862.
Heath, Phillip, *Trinity, the Daring of Your Name: A History of Trinity Grammar School, Sydney*, Allen & Unwin, Sydney, 1990.
Hilliard, David, 'Sydney Anglicans and Homosexuality', *Journal of Homosexuality*, vol. 33, no. 2, 1997, pp. 101–123.
Holloway, Richard, *Godless Morality: Keeping Religion out of Ethics*, Canongate, Edinburgh, 1999, p. 80.
———, *Leaving Alexandria: A Memoir of Faith and Doubt*, Canongate, Edinburgh, 2012, p. 310.
Holt, Geoffrey, *Goodbye Old God: New Refreshment for Tired and Thirsty Spirits*, Leonard Publishing, Strawberry Hills NSW, 2009.
Hooker, Ashleigh; Johnston, Jack; and Gee, Diane, *Riding the Rapids: The Story of Sylvia Jeanes*, SPCK Australia, Adelaide SA, 2007.
Howard, Donald, *Preach or Perish: Reaching the Hearts and Minds of the World Today*, Donald & Nan Howard, Camden NSW, 2008.
Howard, John, *Lazarus Rising: A Personal and Political Autobiography*, HarperCollins Publishers, Pymble NSW, 2010.
Howe, Renate, *A Century of Influence: The Australian Student Christian Movement 1896–1996*, UNSW Press, Sydney, 2009.
Jenkins, Philip, *The Next Christendom*, Oxford University Press, Oxford, 2004.
Jensen, Michael, *Sydney Anglicanism: An Apology*, Wipf & Stock, Eugene OR, 2012.
Kaldor, Peter, *Who Goes Where? Who Doesn't Care?*, Lancer, Homebush West NSW, 1987.
Lamb, Margaret; Piggin, Stuart; and Radkovic, Susan, *Treasure in Earthen Vessels: A History of St. Michael's Anglican Cathedral, Wollongong*, St Michael's Cathedral, Wollongong NSW, 1984.

Lawton, Bill, 'The Winter of Our Days: The Anglican Diocese of Sydney 1950–1960', *Lucas*, vol. 9, July 1990, pp. 11–32.
Mansfield, Bruce, *Summer is Almost Over – A Memoir*, Barton Books, Canberra, 2012.
Mansfield, Joan, 'The Christian Social Order Movement 1943–51', *JRH*, vol. 15, June 1988, pp. 109–27.
Marr, David, 'Divine Intervention: Radical Evangelists Are Fighting for Control of Sydney's Anglican Schools', *SMH*, Spectrum, 12 May 1998, p. 1.
Matthews, Cathy Ann, *Breaking Through: No Longer a Victim of Child Abuse*, Albatross Books Pty Ltd, Sutherland NSW, 1990.
McGavran, Donald, *Understanding Church Growth*, Wm. B. Eerdmans, Grand Rapids MI, 1970.
McGillion, Chris, *The Chosen Ones: The Politics of Salvation in the Anglican Church*, Allen & Unwin, Crow's Nest, 2005.
McGrath, Alister, *J.I. Packer: A Biography*, Baker, Ada MI, 1997.
Murray, Les, *A Working Forest*, Duffy and Snellgrove, Potts Point NSW, 1997 [1982].
Naden, Kathryn; Wighton, Michelle; Riches, Francine; and Short, Monica (Eds), *A Celebration of God's Faithfulness: AEF History, Testimonials, Indigenous Theology, Sermons and Bible Studies*, AEF, Highpoint City Vic., 2017.
Orpwood, Michael, *Chappo: For the Sake of the Gospel – John Chapman and the Department of Evangelism*, Eagleswift Press, Russell Lea NSW, 1995.
Pacey, Laurelle, *Bodalla and the Morts*, Laurelle Pacey, Narooma NSW, 2010.
Park, Ruth, *The Harp in the South*, Angus and Robertson, Sydney, 1948.
Paul, Leslie, *The Deployment and Payment of the Clergy*, Church Information Office, London, 1964.
Piggin, Stuart and Linder, Robert D., *Attending to the National Soul: Evangelical Christians in Australian History, 1914–2014*, Monash University Publishing, Clayton, 2020.
———, *The Fountain of Public Prosperity: Evangelical Christians in Australian History*, Monash University Press, Clayton, 2018.
Porter, Brian, *Frank Woods: Archbishop of Melbourne, 1957–77*, Trinity College, Melbourne, 2007.
Porter, Muriel, *Sydney Anglicans and the Threat to World Anglicanism: The Sydney Experiment*, Ashgate Pub., Farnham, Surrey, 2011.
Reed, Colin, *Walking in the Light: Reflections on the East African Revival and its Link to Australia*, Acorn Press, Brunswick East Vic., 2007.
Reid, J.R., *Marcus L. Loane: A Biography*, Acorn Press, Brunswick East Vic., 2004.
———, 'Partnership: a Better Way', *SC*, September, 1992.
Shortt, Rupert, *Rowan's Rule: The Biography of the Archbishop*, Hodder & Stoughton, London, 2008.
Smith, Terry A., *The Hospitable Leader: Create Environments Where People and Dreams Flourish*, Baker Books, Grand Rapids MI, 2018.
Spong, John Shelby, *Here I Here I Stand: My Struggle for a Christianity of Integrity, Love, and Equality*, HarperCollins, San Francisco, 2000.
Stebbins, Thomas H., *D. James Kennedy's Explosion of Evangelism*, Evangelism Explosion Publishing, Fort Lauderdale, 2002.
Stock, Eugene, *My Recollections*, James Nisbet & Co., London, 1909.
Taylor, Charles, *A Secular Age*, Harvard University Press, Cambridge, 2007.
Tennant, Bob, 'The Sermons of the Eighteenth-Century Evangelicals' in Francis, Keith A., and William Gibson (eds), *The Oxford Handbook of the British Sermon 1689–1901*, Oxford University Press, Oxford, 2012, p. 115.
Trewartha, Sue (compiler), *Dedication and Determination: 100 Years St Michael and All Angels Anglican Church Ceduna*, St Michael and All Angels Anglican Church, Ceduna, 2009.

# Sources

The author wishes to thank the following individuals and organisations for permission to reproduce their material in this book:

DAVID GOODHEW: Figs 2.3, 25.7; Plates 1a, 8c.
HARRY GOODHEW: Figs 1.1, 2.1 (Leicagraph Co. photo), 2.2, 3.1 (photo: Ossie Emery, 1953), 3.2, 4.1, 5.1, 5.2, 5.3, 5.4, 5.5, 6.1, 6.2, 7.1, 8.5, 9.1, 9.2, 12.1, 14.1, 18.1, 20.1, 21.1, 22.1, 23.1, 24.1, 24.3, 24.4, 25.2, 25.3, 25.4, 25.5, 25.6, Conclusion; Plates 1b, 4a, 4c, 5c (photo a gift to HG from the BGEA).
ROD AND HELEN IRVINE: Fig. 25.1.
JIM LONGLEY: Fig. 14.2 (1994).
RAMON WILLIAMS: Figs 11.1, 11.2, 11.3, 24.5, 24.6; Plates 1c, 2b, 2c, 3a, 5b, 6a, 6b, 7a, 7b, 8a, 8b.
ANGLICAN MEDIA: Figs. 20.2, 22.2; Plates 2a, 3b, 3c, 4b.
ANGLICARE ARCHIVES: Figs 8.6, 20.3; Plate 6c.
BRIDGECLIMB: Fig. 23.2.
EVANGELICAL SISTERHOOD OF MARY: Fig. 24.2.
*SOUTHERN CROSS* ARCHIVES: Figs 8.3, 15.1.

Sources and details for figures not listed above or supplied in main text are as follows:

CHAPTER 8: Fig. 8.1: Cartoon by Vince O'Farrell, *Illawarra Mercury*, April 1982. Used with permission; Fig. 8.4: *Illawarra Mercury*, 2 April 1993. Used with permission.
COLOUR PLATE 5A: Photo by Steven Siewert, *SMH*, 13 October 1998. Used with permission.

# Index

Abbotsleigh School 272
Aboriginal Evangelical Fellowship 199
Aboriginal people 67, 189, 199, 207, 239, 248–50, 252–5, 267–8, 338, 342–4
Aboriginal Task Force 249–50
Abrahams, Stuart 4, 6, 11
Adam, Darrel 6
Adebiyi, Peter 284
Adelaide diocese 41, 45, 65, 73, 76, 133, 261, 271
Africa 250, 333, 363–5
    bishops 35, 265, 281–9, 297, 300, 308, 332–3, 356, 372
    dioceses 298, 308, 332–3, 335
    missionaries to 35, 55, 144, 287
    slums 300, 340, 353–60
Akers, John 309
Akinola, Peter 332–3
All Souls' Langham Place 124, 279
Allen, Don 55
Amsterdam Congress on world evangelism 309, 334–5
Andersen, Bill 278, 289, 311, 338
Anderson, Don 6
Andrews, Mary 242
Anglican Church League (ACL) 134, 140, 185–93, 218–22, 226, 239–44, 258, 313, 330
Anglican Church of Australia viii, 52, 131, 135, 143, 149, 198, 201, 221, 239–40, 252, 271, 321, 332, 342, 369 (see also the 'national church')
Anglican Communion 82, 192, 211, 213, 247, 252, 259, 262–6, 271, 281, 284–8, 290, 292, 297–301, 305–7, 313–6, 326–8, 342, 349, 374
Anglican Counselling Centre 70, 179, 277–8, 289–90, 309–15, 317, 338–9
Anglican Education Commission 247
Anglican Media 163, 190, 197, 202, 253, 289, 304, 319–20, 414
Anglican Retirement Villages 33, 137, 163, 201, 345
Anglican schools 113, 137, 161, 198, 205–6, 240, 251–2, 271–3, 308, 373
Anglicans Together 147, 190
Anglicare 95, 119, 161, 163, 182, 195, 200, 235, 242, 250, 289, 296, 311, 319, 338, 352, 379n11
Anglo-Catholicism 25, 56, 102, 146, 187, 221, 266, 285, 287
Apple, Raymond 341
Appleby, Richard 299
Archbishop's Commission of Inquiry 2, 126–8, 168
Archbishop's Vision for Growth 4
area deaneries 111, 127, 163, 170, 173, 181–2, 241
Arkell, Frank 118
Armidale 12, 63–4, 86–9, 103, 106, 108, 114, 139, 197, 201, 222, 283, 317, 330
Arn, Win 84
Arnott, Felix 77, 81–82, 88, 91, 102
Ash, Ronald and Joan 35, 41
Aspinall, Marj 33–4, 274
Aspinall, Phillip 299
Atwood, Bill 264, 297, 327

Australian College of Theology 7, 57
Aylwood, Gladys 274

Babbage, Malcolm 75
Babbage, Stuart Barton 2, 75, 103, 157, 161, 330
Bailey, Benjamin 305
Baird, Bruce 336
Baird, Julia 245, 333–4, 351
Baker, Ken 55
Ballantine-Jones, Bruce ix, 1, 2, 9, 10, 16, 119, 125–8, 132, 134–6, 138, 145, 185, 189–92, 194–5, 210–11, 217–8, 221–2, 243, 246, 252, 292, 297, 299, 313, 330, 333
Ballantine-Jones, Raema 136, 145
Banister, Graham, Nicholas, Chelsea and Jackson 159, 278–9
Bangkok 302
Barker, Frederic 142
Barnett, Anita 151, 227, 377
Barnett, Paul 167, 170–1, 174, 179, 184, 273, 321, 350, 377
    and 1993 archbishop's election 8, 11–12, 15–17, 140, 192, 257
    his assessment of Goodhew 30, 151–2, 175, 227, 275, 285, 375
    his Anglicanism 164
    on Sydney's clericalism 168
    his regional strategy 180
    and the Blue Ticket 190
    and the 'Pymble matter' 194, 202–3
    and the prayer book 207
    on the value of regionalism 241, 244, 373
    on Lambeth 1998 265, 282–5, 297–8
Barrie, Robert 6
Bartlett, Lawrie 190, 207
Bartlett, Louise 344
Bashir, Marie 342
Bates, Harry 53
Bathurst diocese 108, 146, 201
Beal, Rob 55
Beazley, Kim 253–4
Beckwith, Roger 326
Begbie, Alan and Effie 73
Begbie, Gordon 128–9
Belita 67
Bell, Mavis 66–7
Bellinger, Chris and Jan 279
Bellingham, Arthur 33
Benaud, Richie 31–32, 124, 367
Bendigo diocese 102
Bennett, Ernest Joseph 6
Bennison, Charles 283, 306, 327–8
Berkman, Craig 332
Bethel Bible reading program 84, 97–8
Beverly Hills (St Bede's) 9, 62–6, 77, 105, 111, 349, 403
Bible
    authority of 34, 124, 132, 138, 140, 239, 284–5, 287, 293, 307, 370

classes and studies 34, 37, 123–4, 187, 253, 259–60, 270, 317, 335
interpretation of 132, 185, 287, 292, 294, 298–9, 326
Bible Society x, 319–20
Billy Graham 25, 42, 63, 92, 103, 161, 230–31, 309, 316, 334, 353, 362
Bingham, Geoff 46, 124
Bird, Bill 199, 392n52
Bishopscourt 70, 99, 142, 155–62, 171, 176–7, 179–80, 205, 220, 227, 236, 271, 294, 305, 308, 340–1, 348, 369, 374
Blake, Garth 338
Blanch, Reg 202
Blue Ticket, the 184–92, 217, 219–20, 225–6, 243
Bobin, Warren 6
Bomford, Ray 185
Bond, Rick 362
Bonner, Max 13
Bowles, Ralph 252–3
Boyce, Liz 330
Boys, Max 3
Bradford, Philip 296
Bradley, Stephen 335
Bradman, Donald 32, 340, 351
Brain, Neil 6, 118
Brain, Peter 317
Brennan, Patricia and Rob 154
Brennan, Ted and Judy 106
Bright, Bill 334
Brisbane diocese 53, 55–6, 76–9, 81–4, 91, 93–5, 102, 105, 111, 114, 239, 299, 322
Broadway (St Barnabas') 10, 24–5, 135, 161, 176–7, 350
Brook, John 202
Brooking, Stuart 94
Brown, Debra and David 363
Browning, George 256, 299
Bunyan, John 40
Burge, Lorraine 49
Bush Church Aid Society 36–8, 62, 65–9, 126, 163, 302, 349, 352
Bussau, David 264
Butchard, Graham 30

Cable, Ken viii, 2, 32, 203
Caldwell, Stanley John 6
Cameron, Donald 10, 55, 76, 108, 129, 148–9, 163, 169–70, 174, 187, 236–9, 242, 244, 366, 385n50
Cameron, Neil 194
Campaigners for Christ 44
Camperdown Children's Hospital 48, 51
Canberra and Goulburn diocese 102, 108, 131, 173, 201, 250, 252–6, 263, 288, 299
Carey, Andrew 282
Carey, Eileen 261
Carey, George 198–9, 250, 260–3, 281–2, 285–6, 307, 312, 319, 328, 334–5, 374
Carlingford (St Paul's) 18, 20, 56, 73–6, 78, 105–6, 109, 143, 349
Carmichael, Amy 66

Carmichael, Ian 244
Carnley, Peter 102, 277, 317, 322–8, 331–4
Carpentaria diocese 102
Carr, Bob 200, 262, 348, 352
Carroll, Peter 343–4
Cash, Frank 57
Cass, Bettina 254
Catholics (Roman) 30, 35–6, 43, 56, 102, 122, 128, 158, 212, 235–6, 246, 262, 269, 293–4, 301, 308, 325, 370, 374, 380n6, 381n5
Ceduna, SA 4, 36, 65–73, 237, 248, 302, 338, 349
Chadwick, Owen 168
Chadwick, Virginia 206
Chambers, George 35
Chambers, Oswald 37
Chapman, John 12, 15–16, 50, 55, 60, 63–4, 74, 80, 83, 86, 103, 138–9, 153, 230, 257–9, 366, 368
Charismatic movement 56, 69, 138, 180–1, 185, 261
Charles, Prince 198–9
Chau, Ernest 249, 319
Chea, John Chew Hiang 331
Chikarovski, Kerry 352
Chilton, Roger 319–20, 355–6
Chinese ministry 42, 58, 241–2, 249, 274, 289, 303, 347
    visit to China 318–20
Chiswell, Nicky 177, 350
Chiswell, Peter 51, 86, 108, 114, 222, 265–6, 282–3, 330, 366–7, 376
Christ Church St Laurence 24–5, 146, 158
Christian Social Order Movement 49
Christmas, Gerald 109
Chunakara, Mathew George 304
Church Army 64, 104, 108, 126, 358–9
church growth vii, 4, 8, 14, 55, 71–72, 75, 77, 80, 83–4, 96–9, 105, 112–3, 120–21, 182, 189, 219, 241, 271, 316
Church Missionary Society (CMS) 35, 41, 43, 65, 74, 76, 103, 114, 122–4, 126, 138, 163, 216, 259, 270, 274, 277, 287, 301, 303, 305, 318, 340, 343, 356, 359–60, 380n15
Church of England in South Africa (CESA) 335
Church of the Province of South Africa (CPSA) 335
church planting 125, 167–8, 180, 182, 197, 201, 228, 240–1, 246, 267, 271, 334, 372
Churchward, Ken 124
Clancy, Edward Bede 36, 346
Clark, Russell 138
Clarke, Geoff 55
Cochrane, Ian 310, 397n31
Cohen, David 104
Cole, Alan 64, 83, 84, 103, 144, 161, 187, 196, 212–13, 236, 241, 249, 265, 268, 276, 308, 314–5, 319–20, 324, 326, 329, 346
Cole, Graham 255, 279, 289
Cole, Vic 190
Coleman, Ken 319
College of Preachers 74
Collins, John 55
Collison, Margaret 207

Collison, Max and Hannah 340, 356–7
Colson, Chuck 334
Conard, Bill and Ruth 309, 334, 353
Conde, Susan and John 262, 336
Conomy, Vicki 254–5
Continuing Education for Ministers (CEFM) 125–6, 179
Cook, David and Sheila 156
Coorparoo (St Stephen's) 53, 55, 76–85, 87–92, 96, 104, 106, 114, 120, 154, 165, 252, 257, 274, 332, 349, 352
Coral Ridge Presbyterian Church, Fort Lauderdale, USA 84–5, 216
Corbett, Max and Val 35
Corbett-Jones, Christine 339
Corbett-Jones, Michael 277–8, 338–9
Corney, Peter 171, 222
Cornford, John 245
Costello, Peter 336
Coughlan, Kevin 46, 48, 50, 63, 316
Coughlan, Marjorie 49, 63, 79, 316
Coughlan, Rowley 49
Coughlan, William George 48–9
Coutts, John 353
Coyne, Mary 346
Crabb, Larry 121
Crain, David 192, 220, 225–6, 311
Cranmer, Thomas 57, 294
Crawford, David 60, 108
Crew, Graham 358
cricket 20, 31–32, 37, 50, 64, 71, 77, 123–4, 227, 336, 367
cross-cultural ministry see multiculturalism
Cursillo 197–8
Cutler, Roden and David 366

Dain, Jack 65, 100–2, 169, 174, 244, 385n42
Dallas, USA 263–6, 282, 297–8, 306, 308
Darling Point 158, 171, 337
Davies, Glenn 131, 171, 218–20, 245, 345
Davies, John 157–8
Davies, Laurie 4, 186
Davies, Linda 157–8
Davis, Gerald 9, 213, 343
Davis, Steven John 6
Day, Austin 146
Deane, Arthur 45
Deasey, Michael 202
Decade of Evangelism 126
Defty, Grahame 6
Dein, Terry 139
Delbridge, Graham 45, 128, 381n13
Dempster, Quentin 149–50, 236–7
Denman, Stephen 33
Department of Evangelism 8, 74, 103, 126, 230, 344

*Index*

Dethlefs, Noriko 115, 369
Diana, Princess of Wales 263–4
Dicker, Hazel 35
Dillon, Howard 250, 296, 352, 379n11
Diocesan Executive Board (DEB) 127–8, 164, 167–8, 184, 217
disaster response 195, 198, 233–4, 263–4, 308
Disney, Julian 254
divorce 21, 23, 126, 129–30
Dixon, Chris 110
Doctrine Commission 125, 222, 224, 277
Doncaster, Ted 153
Donne, John 110, 216,
Donnelly, Richard vi, 115, 391 first n19
Donohoo, Alan 249, 392n52
Doogue, Geraldine 262, 340, 351
Douthwaite, Robert 55, 366
Dowling, Florence 66, 67
Dowling, Owen 102, 131–32, 135
Downes, Graham 'Basher' 94
Doyle, Robert 262, 314
Duffecy, Jim 38
Dulwich Hill 27, 29, 38–9
Dulwich Hill Central School 29–30, 34–5, 38
Dulwich Hill (Holy Trinity) 27–8, 31, 33–5, 40–1, 45, 48–9, 105, 146
Dulwich Hill South (St Aidan's) 46–7, 50
'dynamic Anglicanism' 163–6, 179, 182, 189, 197, 240, 246, 365, 376

Eagle, Michael 55–6
Eames, Robin 284–5
ECUSA 265–6, 288, 305–7, 312–6, 325–8
Edwards, Fred 55
Edwards, Harry 41, 49–50
Edwards, Jonathan 37, 113
Edwards, Ruth 183
Edwards, Trevor 3, 6, 12, 14–16, 181, 183, 329–30
Ellul, Jacques 114, 223, 350, 391 first n19
Emanuel, R.B. 41, 43
Emeleus, Sue 231
Emery, John 55–6, 150, 366
episcopal team see leadership team
Ethiopia 300, 302
euthanasia 289, 395n38
Evangelical Fellowship in the Anglican Communion (EFAC) 82, 163, 174, 239–40, 270, 280, 288
Evangelical Sisterhood of Mary 344, 414
Evangelical Union 49, 55, 57
evangelism 34, 39, 44–5, 64, 82, 84–5, 120, 204, 241–42, 249, 261, 334–5
    see also Department of Evangelism; Evangelism Explosion
Evangelism Explosion (EE) 80, 84–5, 94, 97–8, 100, 102, 120–21, 161, 175, 214, 216, 229–32, 250, 260, 300, 354, 361–5, 373, 375

413

Fahey, John 147
Fairfax, Vincent and Nancy 115
Fairfull, David 128, 155–6, 163–4, 167, 169, 235–6, 373
families, ministry to 20, 119, 179, 198–201, 235, 254, 257, 266–7, 342
Farran, Brian 299
Farrell, Michael 28
Farrell, Monica 33, 35, 274, 380n20
Fearnley, Terry 28
Fearon, Comfort 333
female ordination (see ordination of women)
feminism 117, 166, 239, 379n11
Fewtrall, Roslyn 62
Figtree (All Saints') 9, 16, 62, 94, 105, 111, 113, 202, 348, 352, 354–5, 365–6, 393n18
Fiji 260, 364
Fillingham, Robert Gordon 103–4, 143
Findlay, Stuart 337–8
Finney, Charles 39–40
Fletcher, Brian 245, 247–8
Flockton, Ray 367
Flower, Neil 217
Foley, Sue 235
Foord, Dudley 1, 2, 5, 54–5, 74, 103, 109, 214, 335
Forbes, Chris 11, 15, 131, 190, 338–9
Forsyth, Robert 10, 12, 14–5, 17, 135–6, 139, 148, 166, 168, 191, 201–2, 247, 252–3, 328–30, 347, 350, 354–5, 371
Foster, Tim 253
Fowler, Andrew 333
Fowler, Dorothy 36, 105
Fowler, John Eric 36–7, 39, 41, 43, 105, 381n30
Fowler, Margaret 36, 105
Frame, Tom 5, 93–4, 371
Francis, Mark 156
Fraser, Joyce 38
Fraser, Ralph 345
French, Betty 105
Frith, Peter 6
Fuller, Jeff 115, 167, 197
Fuller, Margaret 50, 115, 167, 179, 197, 289–90
Fundamentalism 54, 134–6, 272, 304, 317, 331, 333

Gabbott, Marion 9, 17, 50, 192, 242, 302
Gabbott, Stephen 1, 5–7, 9–11, 50, 138, 228, 291–2, 302
GAFCON 264, 290, 298, 372
Gail, Sally 251
Gair, Graeme 147
Galea, Ray 230
Gatenby, Narelle 15
Geerkans, Kevin and Dorothy 35
Gelding, Amy 35
General Synod viii, 49, 126, 132–3, 153, 168, 172, 190, 192, 198, 207, 218–22, 245, 252, 256, 271, 279, 281, 299–300, 321–2, 349

*Index*

Georges River region 30, 162, 174, 182-3, 241, 308
Gerber, Philip 239
Gibson, Fay and John 75
Gilbulla Conference Centre 8, 107, 199
Gilchrist, Alex 44
Giles, Kevin 131, 277
Gilhooly, Debbie 344
Gill, Alan 343
Gilmour, David 193-6, 202-4, 208-10, 213-5, 217, 239, 301
Gippsland diocese 146, 248, 299
Girls' Friendly Society 35
Girvan, Wesley 369
Glebe Board 163, 329
Glennon, Jim 345, 369
Glover, Andrew 94, 345
Glover, Bob 46
Goldsworthy, Graham 55, 56
Goodhew, Amy 339
Goodhew, Baden Powell Richard 20-21, 23-5, 27-8, 36, 41-42
Goodhew, Christina Dalgarno 20-28, 33, 94, 106, 143, 167, 227, 257, 261, 263, 342
Goodhew, David 25, 36, 63-4, 67-69, 74, 79, 82-3, 95-6, 159, 162, 188, 279, 340, 348-9, 366, 414
Goodhew, Harry
    his sense of accountability vi-vii, 9, 130, 215, 217, 230, 377
    importance of Anglicanism 52-3, 82, 84, 110, 112, 164, 166, 168, 207, 225, 228, 284, 290, 301, 328, 345-6, 376
    Archdeacon viii, 34, 60, 72, 98-100, 104
    use of the Bible 34, 38-40, 54, 79, 260, 290, 293-4, 299, 326, 353
    birth and early years 1-20, 42
    Bishop of Wollongong viii, 5, 53, 64-5, 93, 98, 101-133, 172, 179, 188, 257
    calling to the ministry 41-3, 303
    ability to communicate with children and teenagers 34, 45, 74-5, 84, 93-4, 115, 205, 249
    consecration as Bishop 36, 41, 53, 65, 101-4, 106-111, 116
    conversion 33-4, 37
    desire to change diocesan culture vii, 11-12, 106, 128, 149, 169, 178, 223, 278, 290, 294, 303, 337, 347, 354, 361, 365, 370-1, 375-6
    election as Archbishop of Sydney 1-19, 53, 56, 75, 116, 120, 125-6, 133-48, 151, 154-5, 157, 164, 170-3, 184-5, 187-8, 190, 192, 205, 257-8, 291, 303, 321, 372, 378n2, 379n12, 391n19
    employment pre-ordination 43-46
    evangelism, passion for 44, 64, 69, 77, 80-82, 84, 97, 99, 110, 112-13, 121, 126, 153, 165, 176, 204, 216-7, 229-30, 269, 290, 309, 316, 332, 336, 344-5, 364-5, 372
    funerals 36, 61, 110, 177, 240, 242, 316, 366, 381 first n22
    guidance 73, 76, 86-92, 143, 149, 253, 298
    health 27, 28, 176, 203, 227, 241, 260, 278-9, 290, 308, 341, 349-50, 268
    on how to grow churches (see church growth)
    installation as Archbishop of Sydney 152-4
    international perspective and ministry vii, 83-5, 100, 120-1, 213, 230-2, 250, 263-6, 290, 300, 308-9, 316, 347, 361, 363, 374

leadership style and effectiveness vii–ix, 7-9, 11, 14, 32, 62, 71, 80, 97, 100-1, 104-7, 111-2, 125-6, 149, 154, 173, 180, 185, 208, 215, 245, 251, 256, 258-9, 263, 288-9, 296, 307, 309, 316, 343-5, 351, 365, 369-70, 372, 375-6
importance of the laity viii, 3, 11, 16, 60, 68, 75, 80, 93, 97, 104-5, 113, 194, 196, 207, 370-1, 373
importance of the local parish church 98-9, 119, 168-9, 173, 225, 372
managerial skill and experience 14, 52, 95, 112, 117, 120, 126, 128, 372
missionary-mindedness 34-5
at Moore College 52-7
openness to new ideas from home and abroad 9, 56, 83-4, 120, 371-2, 374
his ordination 56-8, 62-4
relationship with his parents 25-29
parish appointments
    Bondi 60-63
    Beverly Hills 63-65
    Ceduna 65-72
    Carlingford 73-76
    Coorparoo 76-85, 87-92, 96, 257
    Wollongong 86-98
pastoral skill 40-41, 62, 70-71, 96, 111, 117, 119, 121, 142, 146, 231, 239, 345, 366
personality and giftedness ix, 8, 14, 22, 36, 50, 53, 59, 62, 71, 74, 79, 82, 90-91, 96, 103-4, 106, 109, 114, 119, 321, 335, 363, 369, 371-2
and prayer 38, 39, 54, 61, 71, 76, 78, 109, 111, 115, 141, 151, 163, 223-4, 238, 291, 294, 318, 324, 353
preaching 8, 34, 38-9, 57, 64, 74, 79-80, 94, 97, 108, 113, 123, 150, 152-3, 176, 223, 263-4, 300, 304, 350, 365-6
presidency of synod 187-90, 205-6, 208-9, 211, 244-8, 266-9, 295-6, 313, 337
and the primacy viii, 102, 317, 321-5, 328, 331, 396n14
radicalism vii, viii, 96, 127-8, 149, 178, 223, 271, 361-3, 370
respect for the life of the mind 49, 53-4
schooling 29-32, 38, 41-2
resists separation 225, 270, 290, 297, 313-4, 325, 328, 335, 348, 372
spirituality ix, 4, 8, 13, 32-41, 51, 53-4, 56, 58, 88-9, 115, 141, 153, 166-7, 176, 188, 227, 239, 260, 270, 274, 301, 303, 318, 361, 364, 374-5
sporting prowess 20, 24, 28-32, 37, 50, 56, 71, 74, 94, 119, 226-7, 336, 341, 366-7, 375
storytelling ability 46, 74
theological orientation 34, 231, 288
tolerance and inclusiveness 35-6, 39, 46, 49, 53, 56, 69, 80-82, 142, 146, 188, 199, 221, 238, 240, 374
vision and mission statements for the diocese 127, 163-8, 180, 189, 197, 267, 270, 314, 317, 342, 348, 370
wide reading and love of poetry 8, 37, 75, 83, 94-5, 106, 115, 216, 238, 260, 269, 279, 368
welfare and poor relief 117-9, 150, 188-9, 195, 200, 207-8, 239, 290, 300, 353, 356-60
affirms women's ministry 24, 59, 107, 126, 130-2, 140, 147, 161, 183, 187-8, 191-2, 197, 206, 232, 245-7, 267-8, 274-7, 290-6, 345, 373 see also women's ordination
sympathy for the working class 24, 27, 33, 117, 173, 188-9, 366
on worship 80, 84, 110, 127, 160, 166, 222-4, 245-8, 257, 267, 279
Goodhew, Henry 20-21
Goodhew, Jane 20
Goodhew, Joyce 20, 26

*Index*

Goodhew, Lena 21, 23, 24, 27, 32
Goodhew, Marjorie 21
Goodhew, Pam
    conversion 47
    early years 42, 46-8
    her good memory ix,
    health issues 35, 62-3, 73, 142, 227, 340, 360, 368
    her hospitality 78, 97, 160, 365, 368
    marriage 46, 50, 58-9
    musical competence 49-50, 160
    personality 50, 59, 88, 96, 324
    relationship with Harry ix, 17-18, 46, 50, 57-8, 73, 86, 122, 167, 184, 291-2, 347, 367-8, 372
    her role in Harry's ministry 4, 51, 58-9, 73, 76-8, 87-8, 91, 97, 99, 106, 111, 116-9, 123-4, 154, 183, 208, 300, 336, 340, 343, 350, 356
    presides over refurbishment and management of Bishopscourt 156-61
    arranges funeral for Harry's mother 26
    and women's ministry 69, 72, 78, 116, 124, 267, 274-5, 304, 333, 346, 357-60, 365
Goodhew, Peter 20, 26-7, 31
Goodhew, Philip 25-6, 64, 67-9, 74, 76, 78-9, 83, 94, 98, 111, 142, 188, 348, 356, 366, 368
Goodhew, Robert 20-21
Goodhew, Robyn 59, 61-4, 67-9, 73-4, 78-80, 83, 90, 95, 340, 367
Goodhew, Sandra 96, 366
Goodhew, Sue 20, 26
Goodhew, Wendy 23-6, 49, 59, 63-4, 67-9, 74, 79-80, 83, 90, 93, 95, 141-2, 150-2, 278, 340, 353
Goswell, Arthur 75
Gotley, Warren 5, 6, 341
Gott, Wayne 3, 6
Gough, Hugh 63, 65, 101, 162, 274, 335
Grafton diocese 102, 109, 201, 299, 324
Graham, Merle Joan 6
Great Depression 30, 48
Green, Mrs 274
Greenwood, John 77
Greer, Germaine 334
Gregory, Ian 20
Gregory, Rene 106, 143
Gregory, Ron 143
Grindrod, John 102, 108, 322
Griswold, Frank 288, 305-7, 312, 326-7
Guilford, Wallace 34
Guthrie, Roy and Rita 143

Hadfield, Ian, Narelle and Bethany 336
Haffenden, Bill 289
Haines, Ronald 297
Hamlin, Catherine 302
Hammond, Greg 105
Hammond, T.C. 52, 57, 178
Hand, David 102

Handley, Ken 195, 202, 209–10, 213–4, 348–9, 379n2
Hanlon, Reg 107
Harrington, Paul 172
Harris, Bruce 10, 138
Harris, John 249
Harris, Len 104
Harris, Tim 6, 9, 131
Harvey, Darren 216–7
Harvey, Richard Kenneth 6, 216
Harvey, R. 6
Hatton, Neville 6
Hawtrey, Gwen 37, 41
Hayward, Patricia 147
Head, Ivan 262
Healing Ministry 106, 154, 284, 311, 345, 369
Heaps, John 30
Heath, Phillip 161, 214, 247
Herbert, Ron 55–6, 87
Herft, Roger 124, 299, 322–3, 333, 395n59
Heslehurst, Raymond 6, 15, 115, 153
Hewetson, David 74
Heyward, Oliver 102
Hibberd, John 5
Hicks, Lesley 9
Hill, Michael 7–8, 344
Hill, Wendy 344
Hilliard, W.G. 62–3
Hinduism 122, 255, 304
Holbeck, Jim 106, 154, 345
Holland, Alfred 102, 384n41
Holle, John 55–6, 384n35
Holle, Vera 66–7
Holley, Carol 243
Hollingworth, Peter 234, 322–3, 333
Holloway, Richard 285–7
Holt, Geoff 314
Holy Trinity Adelaide 45, 172, 182
Home Mission Society (HMS) see Anglicare
homosexuality 198, 261, 264, 271, 279–87, 293, 298–9, 306–8, 312–3, 315, 325–7, 359, 373
Hong Kong 289, 319, 363
Hope, Marion 67
Hope, Robert Marsden 115
Horsburgh, Michael 170
Horton, Silas 191
Hosking, Richard 55
Howard, John 27, 38, 205–6, 234, 253–4, 262, 289, 308, 348, 352, 373
Howes, Phil 94
Huard, Geoff 319
Huggins, Philip 299, 324
Hughes, Bronwyn 190
Hummerston, Stan 71

Huston, Sterling 231–2, 362–3
Hybels, Bill 4, 84, 120, 257–8, 393n22

Illawarra Grammar School (TIGS) 113–5, 249, 251
Illawarra Steelers 118–9
Imisides, John 55–6
Incapacity and Inefficiency Ordinance 1906 195, 202–3, 208–10, 213
India 66, 123, 241, 300, 303–5
Indonesia 121, 232, 364
Ingham, Michael 285
Ingham, Peter 36, 43
InterVarsity Fellowship 11, 55
Irvine, Helen 82
Irvine, Rod 82, 105, 111, 113, 183, 236, 352, 354

Jacups, Kevin and Anne 104
James, Richard 94
James, Ron 4, 9, 146
Jamieson, Hamish 102
Jarrett, Narelle 130–1, 275
Jeanes, Sylvia 274, 303
Jensen, Christine 158, 160
Jensen, Peter 12, 17, 145, 149–50, 159–61, 166, 203, 213, 222, 239, 250–1, 275, 290–1, 298, 324, 329, 333, 335, 347, 354–6, 391 first n23, 395n44
Jensen, Phillip 1, 3, 5–13, 16–17, 135–9, 145, 167, 181, 203–4, 210, 214, 230, 262, 268, 270, 272–3, 276, 291, 295, 301, 330, 379n2
Jews (ministry to) 61–62, 204
Jobbins, Boak 151, 184, 187, 214, 297, 366
Jobbins, Di 346
Joel, Asher 147
John, J. 121
Johnson, Frank 56
Johnstone, Lindsay see 378n2
Johnstone, Patrick 316
Jones, Arthur 299
Jones, Beth 235
Jones, Eric 241
Jones, John 55, 56
Jones, William Wynn 35
Joseph, Rachel 305
Judd, Stephen 2–3, 6–7, 10–11, 16, 161, 183, 185–6, 190, 218, 225, 237, 243, 329
Judge, Edwin 54, 101, 222
Judge, Patricia 343

Kampala Primates' meeting (1999) 315–6, 397n50
Katoomba Christian Convention 44
Kaye, Bruce 153, 198, 252–3, 256, 300, 371
Keating, John 153
Keating, Paul 7, 139, 205
Keble, John 168
Keith, Jim 57

Kell, Faye 115, 167
Kell, Peter 4, 6–7, 9–10, 15, 92–3, 98, 107, 115, 167, 171, 183–4, 187, 250, 355
Kells, Ann 345
Kells, Geoff 127–8, 164, 173
Kelley, Cecil 55–6
Kemp, Peter 11, 171–2, 184–5, 328
Kennedy, Jim 84–5, 100, 121, 230–31, 361–2
Kerle, Clive 64, 86, 103, 139
Kerle, Helen 103
Kerr, Alan 288
Keswick piety 36–7, 45, 53–4, 56, 88
Kim, Billy 334
King, Brian 31, 160–1, 172, 175–6, 181–2, 336, 350, 377
King, Pamela 175–6, 182, 377
King George Hospital 51, 62
King's School, Parramatta 114, 262
Kirby, Michael 346
Kirker, Richard 281
Kitchen, Philip 150
Knapp, Jack 109
Knight, Harold 129
Knox, Broughton 53–4, 101, 103, 108, 133, 140, 144–5, 178, 384n40
Knox, David 133
Kolini, Emmanuel 282, 325–6, 396n14, 397n36
Korea 334, 363
Kwong, Lo Shui 42
Kwong, Peter 289
Kyme, Brian 146

Labor Party 7, 29, 117, 200, 222, 272
Lakshman, Peiris 124
Lamb, Margaret 104–5
Lamb, Tony 56, 108, 129, 243, 366
Lambert, John 206, 271
Lambert, Richard 213, 295–6
Lambeth Conference 126, 250, 263–5, 271, 278–90, 297–301, 305–7, 312–6, 325–6
land rights see native title
Lang, Allan 55
Langtree, Campbell 159
Lausanne Congress on World Evangelisation 83
Lawton, Bill 36, 53, 55–6, 190, 198, 207–208, 255, 275
Lawton, Margaret 311, 396n29
lay presidency (lay and diaconal administration) 57, 126, 179, 183, 187–8, 197, 201–2, 210–13, 222, 225, 237, 245, 254, 258, 269, 276, 290, 292–3, 295, 301, 313–17, 321, 370, 373
lay readers 41, 57, 68, 93, 110, 111, 202
Leask, Ken 59
leadership team 30, 160, 163–6, 168–76, 178–84, 191, 217–8, 241, 244, 251, 261, 309, 317, 327, 341, 350, 371, 373
Lee, Dorothy (Wollongong) 96
Lee, Professor Dorothy 253

Leghorn, Robert M. 39
Leonard, Graham 281
Lewis (Scotland) 22, 26
Lewis, C.S. 96, 152, 269, 279
Lewis, John 102, 146–7
Liberal Party 77
liberalism 3, 15, 53, 134, 138, 185, 191, 214, 238, 244, 253, 266, 281–8, 294, 297, 300, 312, 315–6, 322, 324–8, 332, 372
Lin, Peter 162
Lincoln, Gordon 6
Lindsay, Ray 105
Liturgical Commission (General Synod) 198, 207–8, 255
Liturgical Panel (Sydney diocese) 222, 224, 250
Llewellyn, Kevin 6
Lloyd-Jones, Martin 270
Loane, Joan 114
Loane, Marcus viii, ix, 52–5, 59, 65, 73, 76–7, 86–9, 91–92, 103, 108, 128, 142, 155, 178, 187, 227, 237, 239, 303, 321, 335, 343, 375–6
Longley, Jim 195, 200–1, 414
Love, Larry 54
Lucas, Brian 235–6
Luke, Kevin 6, 9
Luscombe, Robert 6

Macarthur Anglican School 6, 18, 113, 205
McCabe, Stan 32
Macarthur-Onslow, Jenny 158
McCarthy, Tony 6, 11, 186, 190, 243
MacCulloch, Diarmaid 286
McDonald, Garry 61
McDonald, Moyra 61
McDonald, Reuben 61
McGavran, Donald 4, 84
McGillion, Chris 212, 221–2, 370
McGrath, Alister 239–40, 270
McIntyre, John 248, 275, 333
McKay, Hugh 254
Macken, Neil 217
McKerrow, Phil 202
McMurdo, Rob 338
Macquarie University 3, 11, 126, 131, 338
Mabo and Wik decisions see native title
Malcolm, Arthur 253
Malone, Neville 104
Manchester, Simon 94, 345
Mandela, Nelson 335
Mansfield, David 344
Maple, Grant 247
Mar Thoma Church 303, 305, 347
Maramon Convention 303–5, 347
Marchoni, Eric and Joy 65, 105

Mardi Gras 198, 200
Marr, Doug 355
Marrett, Charley 41
Marrickville 24, 27, 31, 33, 36, 48, 50–51
Marryatville, SA 73, 76
Marsh, Barry 6, 55–6, 107
Marshall, Sylvia 104
Martin, Kara 150
Martin, William 33
Mary Andrews College 161
Mason, John 222
Mason, Keith 161, 245, 275, 290, 295–6
Matters, Paul 118
Matthew, Sam 305
Maurice, Frederick Denison 168
Maxwell, L.E. 54
Mayne, Patricia 70, 235, 237, 338, 391n13
Mayne, Tom 69, 70, 248–9, 338
Mbotche, Peter 359
Mears, Ian 344
media 91, 164
    ABC 10, 198, 232, 234, 331, 333, 340, 351–2
    Goodhew's effectiveness in 118–9, 149–50, 214, 236–8, 250, 262, 264, 272, 285, 321, 341–2, 352, 366, 373
    sensationalises church conflicts 7, 13, 131, 134–5, 154, 193, 202, 204, 211–2, 221, 261, 263, 281–2, 331, 333, 355
Media Council (Anglican) see Anglican Media
Melbourne Bible Institute 57, 124
Melbourne diocese 129, 132, 135, 142, 168, 171–2, 199, 222, 250, 259–61, 293, 328–9, 335
Middleton, Trevor 274
Millard, Adelaide 36–7, 39, 41, 274
Millard, Ernest 35–6, 41–3,
Miller, Richard Anthony 6
Minn, Herbert 52
Minniecon, Ray 342
Mission to Seamen 66
missionaries and missionary movement 15, 34–5, 37, 41–42, 56, 66, 122–4, 138, 183, 242, 274, 287, 303–5, 343, 360, 369
missions 40, 64
Moir, Gladys 33
Mok, Irene 319
Monaghan, Les 82
Moore, Charles 21
Moore College
    academic staff 5, 7–8, 17, 32, 35, 52–4, 56, 64, 74, 76–7, 131, 145, 171, 180, 203, 207, 253, 262, 314, 320, 344
    students 32, 36, 50–7, 64, 82, 86, 105, 150, 160, 257, 262, 335
    entry requirements for 41, 52, 179
    focus on the Bible, the gospel and mission 108, 121
    Goodhew's relationship with and ministry to 178–80, 197, 260, 320, 347, 354–5, 358, 372

Morpeth 192
Morris, Leon 62
Mort, Charles 157
Mort, Charles Sutcliffe 158
Mort, David 157
Mort, Marianne 158
Mort, Thomas Sutcliffe 157–9
Mort, Theresa 158
Mostyn, Frank 6, 142
Mothers' Union 116, 200, 254, 333, 346, 365
Movement for the Ordination of Women (MOW) 147, 154, 206, 333, 351
Mowll, Howard viii, ix, 35, 45, 52, 54, 57–8, 62–3, 86, 142, 151, 156–7, 160, 227, 335, 369, 373, 375–6
Mowll Retirement Village 33, 345
Muir, Tom 6, 9, 65
Muir, Val 65
Mulready, David 248
multiculturalism 150, 162, 173, 182–3, 240–1, 239, 241, 249–50, 254, 264, 267, 289, 319
Murphy, Chuck 325
Murray, Andrew 37
Murray, Bill 36, 118
Murray, David 146, 300, 395n59
Murray diocese 153, 299, 390n16
Murray, J.K. 102
Murray, Les 269
Muston, Ged 146

Nash, C.H. 57
national church, the 135, 146, 165, 207, 220, 240, 247–8, 256, 265, 312–3, 332, 374, 379n11
National Anglican Conference (1997) 250, 252–6, 271
National Church Life Survey (NCLS) 126, 185, 189, 230, 259, 271, 400n11
native title 189, 199, 249, 267, 343
Ndegwa, John 359
Ndugane, Njongonkulu 335
Nee, Watchman 37
Neve, Edith 305
New College 103, 289
Newcastle diocese 102, 108, 124, 192, 201, 228, 261–2, 299, 322
Newell, Phillip 102, 298–9
Newhaus, Matthew 333
Newman, Barry 202, 243, 291, 384n21
Newman, Charlie 6, 9, 16
Newman, Ernie 35, 38
Newman, John Henry 354
Newmarch, Walter 303
Newtown, 23, 27, 33, 43
Nichols, Tony 299
Nicholson, Gary 13
Nicholson, W.P. 40
Nicolios, Di 183, 186, 192, 206, 232, 245, 247, 275, 373
Nixon, Merv 118

Noble, Jim 60
Norfolk Island 336
North Queensland diocese 102, 146
North Sydney region 170, 180–2, 217, 373
North West Australia diocese 146, 299
Northern Territory diocese 299
Ntukamazina, Pie 308, 332, 360

O'Brien, Peter 5, 56, 171, 227–8, 262
O'Doherty, Stephen 374
O'Farrell, Vince 107
O'Mara, David 359
O'Mara, Terry 195
O'Neill, Joy 66
O'Reilly, Bill 32
O'Reilly, Colleen 147
Oak Hill Theological College, London 279, 288
Oakley, William 123
Olson, Warwick 164, 183, 185–6, 190, 225, 236, 329, 346
Olympic Games (Sydney 2000) 182, 189, 262, 289, 336–7
Open Air Campaigners 38, 50, 77
Opportunity International 264
ordination of women see women's ordination
Ormerod, Neil and Thea 235
Owen, John 56
Oxford University 17, 259, 264, 286, 326

Packer, J.I. 270–1, 334
Paddison, Evonne 298
Page, Gilbert 104, 108
Papua New Guinea 30, 102
Park, Ruth 27
Parker, Lenore 207
Parramatta 25, 27–8, 31, 262, 296, 369
Parramatta Conference (1992) 131–2
Parramatta region (Western Sydney) 101, 103, 128–9, 170, 172–6, 181–2, 217
Parramatta (St John's) 11, 128, 131, 171, 185
Parrish, Archie 100, 121
Patrick, Alan 104
Patrick, Lewis 6
Paul, the Apostle x, 24, 92, 141, 215, 260, 268, 277, 285, 291, 355
Paul, George 310
Paxson, Ruth 37
Payne, Mark 329
Payne, Jim 77
Pell, George 346
Penong, SA 66, 69
Penrith Anglican College 289
Pentecostals 211, 274, 282
Perini, Paul 2–3, 6–7, 11, 179–81, 376, 379n14
Perth diocese 102, 124, 146, 172, 299–300, 317, 322

Peterson, David 5–6, 104, 107, 131, 207, 222
Peterson, John 255–6
Pickering, Matthew 94–5
Pierce, Duncan 55
Piggin, Stuart 1–19, 107, 183, 185–6, 190, 218, 237, 243, 247, 313
Pilgrim Press 38
Piper, Dorothy 172, 377
Piper, Elizabeth 172
Piper, George 105
Piper, Lucille 206
Piper, Reg 172, 182, 184, 350, 377
politics (diocesan) 1, 17, 131, 137–40, 144, 169–70, 176, 184–91, 195, 218–23, 225, 244, 247, 251–2, 270, 273, 294, 309, 313, 317, 321–4, 329, 333, 338, 351, 354–6, 370–71, 374–5
Port Arthur massacre 233–4
Port Lincoln, SA 72
Porter, Muriel 132, 283, 290
Portugal Primates' meeting (2000) 315, 325–7
postmodernism 239, 252, 260
Poulton, Ross 6, 18
Powers, Ward 55–6
Prayer Book 34, 57, 65, 96, 110, 162, 166, 188, 193, 197, 207, 221–5, 240, 245, 247, 257, 259, 269, 314, 337, 368, 373
preaching 74, 75, 107–8, 124, 274
    see also Goodhew, Harry – preaching
Premadasa, Ranasinghe 123
Presbyterians 84, 109, 180, 236, 246
Property Trust 13, 155–6, 163
Prott, Neil 214, 217, 230
Province of New South Wales viii, 108, 146, 198–9, 201, 207, 247, 251–2, 271, 374
Puckeridge, Val 68, 69
Pulsford, Heather 147
'Pymble matter' 103, 154, 193–7, 202–5, 208–10, 213–5, 217, 309, 368

Quee, Allen 111

Radcliffe, Henry 55
Radkovic, Joe and Sue 340
Ramachandra, Vinodh 123
Ramsay, Jim 136, 218, 230, 390n9
Ramsey, Michael 62
Randerson, Richard 299
Rayner, Audrey 221
Rayner, Keith 135–6, 142–3, 199, 221, 254, 256, 261, 271, 293, 315, 321–2, 325
Reed, Bruce 120
Reformation, the 134, 142, 153, 183, 314
Reformed Evangelical Protestant Association (REPA) 6, 9, 11, 135–40, 142–3, 148, 166, 178, 181, 186–7, 190–1, 193, 196, 212–4, 218, 268, 330, 368
regional councils 111, 129, 182, 241, 247
regionalisation 111, 126, 128–9, 151, 163, 174, 180, 183, 186, 188, 197, 225–6, 240–42, 244, 289, 349, 373
Read, Colette 278

Reid, John ix, 8, 10-12, 16, 90, 103, 107-8, 130, 137, 139, 169-70, 328, 339, 379
Reimer, John 50
Reilly, Isabel 83
Religious Instruction (in schools) 68-9, 93, 110, 205
REPA see Reformed Evangelical Protestant Association
revival 22, 38-9, 45, 110, 113, 134, 168, 183, 360
Retief, Frank 335
Rich, Bill 65
Richards, Kel 366
Richard Johnson Anglican College 115
Richardson, Kath 33
Ridley College, Melbourne 62, 255, 279, 289
Riverina diocese 108, 201
Robert Menzies College 3, 15, 179
Roberts, Delle 111-2
Roberts, Vic 111-2, 119, 171, 192
Robinson, Donald William Bradley 38, 53, 56-7, 76, 101, 103, 105-9, 111, 119, 120, 125, 127-33, 138, 147, 153, 155, 166, 169, 171, 179, 187, 222, 234, 237, 265-6, 274, 335, 355
Robinson, Dorothy 92
Robinson, Martin 379n11
Robinson, Peter 6, 9
Robinson, Stuart 288
Rockhampton diocese 298
Rode, Betty 124
Rodgers, Bruce 33
Rodgers, John 288, 325-6
Rodgers, Margaret 170, 190, 202, 237-8, 253, 275, 289, 298, 304, 308, 319-20, 324, 355
Rogers, Andrew 131
Rogers, Ken 4, 66, 77, 382n26&27.
Rogers, Susan 4, 5, 143
Rosier, Bruce 102, 342
Royal Prince Alfred Hospital 63
Royal, Snowy 38
Runcie, Robert 123, 261
Rwanda 198, 255, 282, 309, 325-6, 389n4
Ryan, Bob 71, 72

St Andrew's Cathedral 2, 10, 33, 107, 152-4, 199-201, 214, 229, 232-3, 250, 256, 261-3, 267, 269, 289, 300-1, 305, 324, 331, 339-40, 348, 366, 369
St Andrew's Cathedral School 161, 247, 308, 352
St Andrew's House 11, 198, 242, 338
St George's Girls High School 47
St Matthias', Centennial Park 7, 161, 181, 330
St Paul's Cathedral, London 259
St Paul's College, University of Sydney 56, 77, 262
St Peter's Campbelltown School 113
Sabah 274, 302-3
Salmon, Bryant 72
Salvation Army 28, 30
Samuel, Vinay 264
Samuels, Gordon and Jackie 346

Samways, Miss 46
Sandilands, Maurice 30
Sawyer, Kimberly 256
Scandrett, Laurie 131–2, 135, 184–5, 190–1, 243, 271
Schramm, John and Alena 302
Schuller, Robert 84
Scott-Joynt, Michael 283
Scripture teaching – see Religious Instruction
Scripture Union 38, 44, 82
sectarianism 35, 36
secularisation viii, 7, 134, 136, 149, 154, 191, 239, 272, 348, 374
Sefton, Ruth 163, 251
Selby, Peter 285
sexual abuse vii, 70, 198, 200, 234–9, 252, 296, 300, 311, 338, 374
Shatford, Ruth 255
Shearer, Rosalind 6
Shearman, Donald 102, 109
Sheumack, David 146
Short, David 94, 271, 340
Short, Gloria 98–9, 111
Short, Ken 64, 86–7, 89, 92, 98–9, 101, 108, 111, 118, 129, 142, 171, 202
Sidebottom, Dianne 66
Silk, David 221–2, 299, 324
Simmonds, Angela 274
Simpson, Graham 123
Sinclair, Maurice 307, 312, 316, 396n14
Sindell family 21, 22
Singapore 122, 144, 264, 306–8, 325, 327, 331
Skillicorn, Stan 250
Skinner, Ernest 66–7
Skinner, Robert 66–7
Slamon, Barry 55
Smart, Elizabeth 114–5, 167, 179, 249–51, 279, 319–20, 377
Smart, Peter 113–16, 167, 183–4, 249–51, 279, 289, 319–20, 372, 377
Smith, Bronwyn 77
Smith, Bruce 32, 74, 146, 347, 350
Smith, Dave 146
Smith, Nola 77, 82
Smith, Ray 30, 45, 64, 86, 88, 166–7, 173–5, 182, 192, 202, 215, 229, 241, 284–6, 308, 327, 346, 350, 377
Smith, Rob 32
Smith, Shirley 377
Smith, Tom R. 6, 229, 249
Smith, Vic 77, 80, 90
Smith, William Saumarez 107
Sorensen, John 362–5
South American Missionary Society (SAMS) 126, 287
Soulos, Mersina 182, 241–2, 289, 308
South Coast Labour Council 118
South Sydney region 148, 170, 173, 181–3, 217, 228, 242, 247, 328–31
Speagle, Henry 337

Spong, Jack 279, 281–5, 297, 327
Sri Lanka 122–4, 300
Staines, Graham, Timothy, Phillip and Gladys 304–5
Standfield, Jean 274
Standing Committee viii, 15, 101, 220, 235, 346
    opposes DEB 127, 164, 167–8, 217
    members of 138, 155, 170, 194, 213, 279, 295
    and sale of Bishopscourt 161–2
    challenge to archbishop's authority 169–70, 172–4, 184–5, 190, 251, 321, 334
    unrepresentative 186–7, 190, 226, 287, 330
    and the 'Pymble matter' 202–4, 211, 213–4,
    elections to 184, 189–92, 218, 225–6, 242–4, 313
    synod's authority over 248
    on private schools 273
    on women's ministry 276
    on the Anglican Counselling Centre 277–8, 309–12, 315, 321–2
    and the appointment of Robert Forsyth as bishop 328–30, 338–9
Stanton, James 265, 297, 306–9
Stanway, Alf 122
Stebbins, Tom 229, 231
Stedman, Ray 84
Steel, Dorothy 163
Steele, Ray 366
Stockdale, Sheila 274
Stoddart, Jan 25
Stoddart, Lindsay 2–4, 6, 25, 183, 185, 192, 220, 237, 247, 249, 308, 344
Stone, Harry 28
Stone, Ron 298
Story, Rod 80–82, 85, 90, 94, 120–121, 214, 231, 362
Stott, John 82–3, 117, 124, 239, 270, 313–4, 334
Studd, C.T. 37
Student Christian Movement 49
Sunday School 33, 42, 46, 50, 60–61, 69–70, 252, 274
Swift, Ted 24
Sydney Anglican Schools Corporation 205–6, 271
Sydney Church Ordinance 92, 112
Sydney Grammar School 32, 262
Sydney Missionary and Bible College 45, 156, 179
Sydney University 2, 21, 54–5, 57, 163, 176, 254, 262, 301
Symonds, N. 6

Tait, Archibald Campbell 238
Tamworth 114, 179
Tasmania 20, 36, 56, 102, 233, 298, 366–7
Tasker, Peter 247, 298
Tay, Moses 307, 325–6, 396n14
Taylor, Jim 55–56
Taylor, Robert 33
Telfer, Brian 291
Templeton, Elizabeth 253, 255
Theophilus, Zacharias 303

Thomas, Mesac 20
Thompson, Mark 8, 15
Thorburn, Trevor 55
Tierney, Betty 66
Ting, Kuang-hsun 319–20
Tong, Robert 139, 243, 297–8, 328–9, 356
Tonks, Jeremy 151
Townsend, Martin 283
training
    of clergy 17, 52, 64, 82, 111–2, 126, 129, 160, 178–9, 197, 208, 229, 240, 249–50, 271, 319, 342, 357–8, 372
    of laity 7, 58, 82, 85, 97, 111–2, 116, 175, 260, 271, 361, 365
Treseder, Tom and Merriel 319–20
Tribunal Ordinance 1962, 194, 202, 210
Trinity Conference on female ordination 267–8, 275–7
Trinity Episcopal Seminary, Pittsburgh 122, 173, 288, 325
Trinity Grammar School 29, 35, 48, 243, 273–7, 342, 355
Tronson, Mark 336
Trott, Louise vi
Tutu, Desmond 253, 287
Tyndall, David 289, 336

Union Bible Seminary, India 123
University of New South Wales 1, 135, 204
University of Queensland 83

Vaughan, John 33
Vickery, P.C. 90
Vision for Growth 4, 125
Vitnell, Les 6, 18, 55–56
Voss, Hugh 55

Waddy, Lloyd 369
Wade, Graham 38, 183, 237, 381 first n22
Waldron, Graham 299
Wantland, Bill 265
Warren, Riley 6, 7, 18–19, 171, 184, 205, 273
Watson, Alicia 337
Watson, Margo 151, 328, 377
Watson, Peter 74, 151, 164, 170–171, 173–4, 181, 183, 190, 250, 273, 328–9, 377
Weaver, Owen 55
Webb, Barry 320
Webb, Ida Joyce 6
Webb, Ronald 6
Weir, George 29
Wesley Centre 10, 187
Wesley, Charles 107
Wesley, John 37, 113, 168, 300, 367
West, Rod 190, 243, 313, 342, 347–8, 355
Western Sydney region see Parramatta region

Westminster Abbey 250, 261
Wheeldon, Judith 272–3
Wheeler, Ray 55–6
White, Paul 37
Whitefield, George 38
Whiteman, Peppi and Peter 105
Wicks, Ralph 102
Wicks, Ros 345
Wilkinson, Shirley 49
Williams, Basil 86, 104
Williams, Ramon x, 407
Williams, Rowan 301
Willis, Daniel 344
Willochra diocese 102, 171, 342
Wilson, Bruce 146
Wilson, Daniel 305
Winnall, George Alexander 6
Wishart, Rod 119
Wolfe, Digby 83
Wollongong High School 5, 92–3
Wollongong (Illawarra) region 104, 109, 111–2, 153, 170, 182, 274, 352, 369
Wollongong (St Michael's) 4, 51, 84, 86–98, 104, 109, 116, 128, 274, 349, 366
Wollongong University 12, 112, 115, 187–8
Women's Commission 254–5
women's ordination 24, 107, 126, 130–2, 135, 138, 147–8, 150, 153–4, 161, 185–92, 197, 199, 206, 232, 242, 245–7, 261, 267–8, 271, 273–7, 288–297, 328, 330, 334, 370, 372–3
Wood Royal Commission 234–8
Woodbridge, David 6
Woodhouse, John 1, 3, 9, 139, 211–14, 217, 221, 230, 253, 277–8, 291, 295–6, 310–11, 315, 333, 339, 354–5, 396n29&30
Woods, Frank 129, 172
Woolley, Thomas 158
World Vision 122, 363
World War II 31, 35, 45, 49
Wright, Dulcie 68–9
Wright, John Charles 159, 369
Wright, Ken 68
Wright, Merle 33, 274
Wright, N.T. (Tom) 227–8, 279, 283, 293

Yaeger, Bill 84
Yong, Datuk Ping Chung 303
Young, Ann 6, 12
Young Evangelical Churchmen's League 36
Young, Joan 345
Young, Peter 184, 194, 243, 313, 322–4, 346
Youth Department (Church of England/Anglican) 41, 44–6, 163, 229, 249, 308
youth and university ministry 48–9, 51, 64, 74–5, 77, 81, 84–5, 90, 123, 125, 192, 205, 216, 241, 252, 257, 267, 308–9, 359, 362, 381n13
Youthworks 249, 308, 344

Stuart Piggin has been designated 'the historian of the Australian soul'. He co-authored the prize-winning two-volume history of Australian Evangelical Christians, *The Fountain of Public Prosperity* and *Attending to the National Soul*, which has been acclaimed as 'monumental' and a 'masterwork'. Stuart was the Director of the Centre for the History of Christian Thought and Experience at Macquarie University from 2005 to 2016, and the founding President of the Evangelical History Association of Australia. He has known Harry and Pam Goodhew for forty-five years and has served alongside Harry in parish ministries and in the Diocese of Sydney Synod and Standing Committee.

Front cover photo: Harry Goodhew in the jersey of the Illawarra Steelers, Wollongong's Rugby League club until its amalgamation with St George club in 1998. In the economic recession of 1991, the Steelers helped with a food appeal for the Home Mission Society and Harry encouraged the Steelers by his understanding of football's role in maintaining morale, an example of his skill in fostering synergy in local communities.

www.ingramcontent.com/pod-product-compliance
Lightning Source LLC
Chambersburg PA
CBHW071732150426
43191CB00010B/1548